Naming and Thinking God in Europe Today

CURRENTS OF ENCOUNTER

STUDIES ON THE CONTACT BETWEEN CHRISTIANITY AND OTHER RELIGIONS, BELIEFS, AND CULTURES

VOL. 32

Naming and Thinking God in Europe Today
Theology in Global Dialogue

Edited by

Norbert Hintersteiner

Amsterdam - New York, NY 2007

This publication is sponsored by Österreichisches Bundesministerium für Bildung, Wissenschaft und Kultur, and by the European Commission (Erasmus Socrates Programme)

The article by Robert Cummings Neville "The Role of Concepts of God in Crosscultural Comparative Theology" is reprinted with kind permission from J. Hackett and J. Wallulis (eds.), Philosophy of Religion for a New Century: Essays in Honour of Eugene Thomas Lang, Dordrecht: Kluwer Academic Publishers 2004, 243-59.

Manuscript Editor: Anne Malcolm
Copy Editor: Henry Jansen

Cover illustration and design:
Rita Dick & Thomas Stadler
A-5011 Oberndorf
Austria

The paper on which this book is printed meets the requirements of "ISO 9706:1994, Information and documentation - Paper for documents - Requirements for permanence".

ISBN set volume 1-3: 978-90-420-2204-1
ISBN: 978-90-420-2205-8

Printed in the Netherlands

Contents

Acknowledgments

The idea for the book *Naming and Thinking God in Europe Today: Theology in Global Dialogue* and its foundational European project grew out of conversations with the coordinators of an earlier, similar, but smaller endeavor on this topic at Lund University, and was inspired by the initial advice of Robert Schreiter. Cf. *The Concept of God in Global Dialogue*, edited by W. Jeanrond and A. Lande, Maryknoll: Orbis 2005. Pursuing the project on a European scale was made possible only by the enthusiasm of François Bousquet (Paris), Jacques Haers and Georges De Schrijver (Leuven), and the enduring commitment of the many partners to the project throughout Europe with whom I was privileged to collaborate. Further, the EU Socrates project, from which this book stems, owes its success to sponsorship by the European Commission as well as to the administrative support of the theological faculties in Vienna, Mainz, Leuven, and Paris, who hosted the project over the years. While my thanks go to the many people involved at the mentioned institutions, I am especially grateful to Josef Weismayer (Vienna) and Leonhard Hell (Mainz) who provided the initial springboard and administrative home base.

This work further bears the traces of those who have contributed their translation, editorial, and research skills to it. My thanks go here especially to Michael Parker (Frankfurt) and Robert Gascoigne (Sydney) for their translations of various contributions. For her editorial work on the manuscript I am deeply grateful to Anne Malcolm (New York). For their help as project or research assistants, I thank Markus Ebenhoch and Linda Kreutzer (Vienna), George Bratusca (Cluj), as well as Greg Finley and Aaron Massey (Washington). I also want to express my sincere thanks to the publisher, Rodopi, and especially Fred van der Zee, Henk Vroom, and Jerald Gort for including the volumes of this project in the *Currents of Encounter* series. Finally, for her enduring love and support, I thank my most truthful friend Bernadette Moch.

Finally, the endeavor of three European Socrates Intensive programs from 2003 to 2005, of which this volume is a first published result, owes its vitality and perduring influence to the many students from across Europe who participated so earnestly, who demonstrated great insight and creativity, and who made the seminars overall a superb and unforgettable experience. This volume is dedicated to them.

Norbert Hintersteiner
March 2007

Norbert Hintersteiner

Introduction

This volume is the first publication of a three-year long European Socrates Intensive program entitled "The Concept of God in Europe's Global Religious Dialogue," during which three groups of between eighty and one hundred graduate students and Ph.D. candidates from theology and religious studies departments from universities in twenty European countries met for three ten-day conference seminars from 2003 to 2005. Joined by their professors and other experts in their respective fields, who presented papers during these seminars to stimulate discussion and enrich prospects for further research, participants explored major challenges in the matter of *naming and thinking God in Europe today* vis-a-vis and through *global dialogue*. Most papers presented in May 2003 in Vienna have been reworked to include material generated by the rich discussions at the seminar and are now compiled as essays here. The volume at hand not only reveals the broad spectrum of its topic, in addition to the plurality of approaches to exploring it, but it also documents the vivid seeking undertaken by a new generation of European theologians and scholars of religion who openly engage the question of how to live and believe in Europe today in the face of increasingly complex global relations and challenges. By presenting this collection to a broader audience, the organizers of the seminar, together with the authors of these essays, invite their readers to participate in further dialogue and reflection on the topics at hand, in an effort to better address central theological questions for the sake of Europe's and the world's future.

In Europe, different traditions of enquiry into thinking of and about God draw on varying theoretical and philosophical foundations that in many ways compete with one another. Due to socio-cultural and political divides, along with the complex histories and intellectual rivalries between Eastern and Western Europe, these theological traditions often suffer from isolation and from mutual misunderstanding. Can these tensions be better addressed and can these conflicts be better understood? Can they be regarded as an opportunity rather than an obstacle to refashioning and advancing Europe's theological role in a global world?

Especially since 1989, specialists in theology and the religious sciences have recognized a second challenge: Europe, in searching for its identity and role on a global stage, bears the emerging signs of novel cultural, socio-economic, religious and political dynamisms. And an overall paradigm shift is occurring that reflects the conflicting dynamics of global modernity and its attending de-/re-traditionalizations, post-traditionalities, and returns of religion(s), fundamentalisms, hybrid cultures, crosscultural formations and inter-religious interactions, etc. Thus, in Europe, the acts of thinking and naming God are continually set within new contexts that must be studied and understood.

Further, we must take seriously our questions of interreligious and cross-cultural dialogue, particularly as immigration increases and peoples of non-Christian faith traditions name and think God in ways that differ from and sometimes conflict with Europe's dominant religion(s) and secular culture. Is there a place for God-talk at all? How can God be named and thought in Europe as it finds itself in midst of crosscultural and interreligious process of global nature? What function and impact will God-talk have in such processes and for a globalizing Europe that continues to redefine itself and its spiritual heritage as religions such as Islam, Hinduism, and Buddhism come into the Western foreground? How, if at all, can or will Europe be able to search for and envsion a new religious role in a globalized world?

The essays in the present volume are organized and grouped around four broad themes. In Part I, *Europe's God in a Globalizing World*, Peter Beyer's opening essay addresses the difficulties of religious specification in relation to the increasing globalization of society with particular emphasis on the European context. Drawing on the sociological theory of Niklas Luhmann, Beyer sees a global religious system in which a limited set of religions define themselves with reference to one another, thus favouring a tendency toward monotheistic abstraction. Within Europe, such abstraction has been respecified in largely non-religious methodologies, yet Christianity remains a shadowy, though culturally important, presence in European self-conceptions. Finally, Beyer argues that the challenge of Islam in Europe is that certain groups deliberately refute the European modes of respecification and seek a superior position for Islam in relation to economics, politics, law, education, health, art, sport, media , and science.

Anne Kull's essay examines the effects of globalization, technology, and postmodernism on the conceptualization of God. She develops her reflection on globalized God concepts in critical dialogue with economics, communications, and biotechnologies. Drawing on Donna Harraway's cyborg figure, Kull argues that the traditional idea of "nature" is being challenged by our "cyborg" lived reality which offers new metaphors to both academic and popular theorizing for comprehending our embodied selves and even our inherited religious dualisms. In what Edward Cousins calls the "Second Axial Period", technocultural and technobiological globalization is moving religion to indeterminate, relational truths. Kull concludes that the concept of the cyborg makes it possible to affirm our createdness in the *imago dei* with a new specificity, along with the creativeness of the rest of nature.

In his essay, John D'Arcy May proposes to show that God as understood in Europe will be grasped more precisely if the mediation of transcendence becomes culturally multifaceted and ethically self-conscious. In his search for ways of transforming European images of God in order to make them more receptive to this multiplicity of mediations, he first examines the postcolonial situation and its effects upon theology. May then tries to discern the echoes of transcendence mediated for us by other voices using different languages for the divine and modulated by experiences of dominance. In conclusion, he formulates several lacunae that arise for European theology from the confrontation of postmodernism with postcolonialism; namely, loss of praxis, loss of transcendence, and loss of nature.

In the succeeding essay, Jacques Haers emphasizes globalization not only as an obvious challenge, but also as an opportunity for European theologians who are called upon to review their thought, concepts, and methods from the perspective of encounter and community. He then attempts to define globalization in such a way to allow a liberating praxis in the service of the poor and marginalized via a strong eschatological vision. Strongly maintaining that Europe's context is the whole world, Haers advocates a theology of encounter and conversation. Drawing on liberation theologians of the Two Thirds World, he argues for the building of a holistic, global community and the preferential option for the poor. Haers finally seeks to demonstrate that the problems raised are highly relevant to our ways of talking about and constructing images of God.

In the final piece of this part, Hans-Joachim Sander holds that the God question can be approached from questions about power. The "metaphysical God" has had a determinant impact on European God-talk since the age of classical Greece. The Enlightenment gave rise to a disjunct in the metaphysical God and the personal God of Judeo-Christian religious history, thus stripping God-talk of its power beyond religious communities. Sander then discusses the "local God" of contextual theology which has eschewed metaphysical concerns for empowerment of the poor and confrontation of the global mission of the First World. He sees another differentiation of the same problem in the Religious God in the New World where sentiments such as "God Bless America" herald a new religious power in the battle of Good versus Evil. Finally, Sander concludes that the Pastoral God, or "God as a Verb," is the most Christian and effective means for recapturing public power in which God-talk becomes the means for naming the power of local peoples struggling for general acceptance of their human needs and human dignity.

In Part II, *Geographies of God in Europe*, François Bousquet's essay seeks to survey and classify the major theological books and articles focusing on access to God through concepts published in France between 1970 and 2000. He first examines the hermeneutical approach to God from the angles of gift, communication, the human body, and aesthetics. He follows this with the scholarship surrounding language mechanics such as the names of God and the appropriateness of theological language. Bousquet then demarcates studies according to the rift he sees between phenomenology and ontology within fundamental theology. He then includes a section on simultaneous exchanges between natural and philosophical theology, biotechnology and faith, and the social sciences and theology. Bousquet next proceeds with authors who have confronted the scandal of evil in the 20th Century, particularly the Shoah and carves out the impact of social sciences and a wide mystical current. Finally, he notes the acute importance of theology encountering other religions and wisdom traditions. With all the above literature in hand, Bousquet detects a converging line of thought in which God is paradoxically absent and confirmed in theological self-effacement.

In the succeeding paper, András Máté-Tóth proposes the main themes of a successful Central Eastern European theology of the Second World. First, he argues that one can observe that there is a theoretical distinction between a reflected and an unreflected, latent contextuality. In the theological publications of Eastern Europe, there is rarely a thoroughgoing consideration of how specific contexts intersect with theological perspectives, thus leaving theology from this region properly characterized as latently contextual. Máté-Tóth then proceeds to a description of the violence of ideological-political suppression by the Communist party states meant for the Church, reducing most theological thinking to the level of sheer survival and the training of priests. To properly address the challenges emerging within the growing culture of modernity in these societies, a critical evaluation of theology is necessary to avoid a kind of hermeneutical naiveté. Máté-Tóth holds that this can only be done by ensuring academic quality through the refurbishing of theological schools and faculties along with stressing intellectual rigor over facile ecclesiastical approval. He concludes that such "re-reading" will ensure that new, original insights can arise anew out of the context of Eastern European theology.

In his essay, Karel Skalický argues that along with the fall of communism and Marxist-Leninist ideology, "strong" atheism collapsed as well, resulting in the philosophies that had been repressed and exiled in the "underground" of the collective consciousness being given back their freedom. The question of God's existence, which had been off-bounds for forty years, was suddenly allowed, and free thinking was once again possible. Skalický holds that this rebirth leads to the reexamination of the philosophical question of God-talk largely influenced today by the following five great philosophical achievements: 1) the analysis of language of Ludwig Wittgenstein; 2) the phenomenological method of Edmund Husserl; 3) the hermeneutical phenomenology of Martin Heidegger; 4) the transcendental philosophy of Joseph Maréchal; and 5) the dialogical personalism of Martin Buber. Skalický argues that all of these philosophical insights have brought forth positive progeny in Western European theology and can thus provide a rediscovered vantage point for Eastern European God-talk as well.

In the following paper, László Holló seeks to address the role that images of God play in Romania as a country at the crossroads of East and West and at the intersection of Catholic, Protestant, and Orthodox religious cultures, which he says can be cast in terms of the discussion about the the "clash of civilizations" following Samuel Huntington. He argues that while differing religious images of God have an important influence on culture, the roots of cultural conflict are rarely explicitly religious. After a brief socio-cultural history of the region of Transylvania, and a statistical analysis of the national / religious affiliation of Romanians in general, Holló argues that conflicts result from a chain of historical, political, economic, and demographic causes with religion, playing, at best, a secondary role. In the cases where religious language is used in conflict, it is not so much a question of its verity in representing the sacred as it is an act of coopting religion as a vehicle for nationalistic egoism and self-aggrandizement.

Peter Stilwell's essay surveys a selection of twentieth century Portuguese poets to demonstrate the variety of trends in religious experience expressed in their work. He identifies certain recurring themes in the way religious ideas are dealt with in contemporary Portuguese literature. Stilwell examines the work of major Portuguese poets including Teixeira de Pascoaes, Fernando Pessoa, José Régio, Ruy Cinatti, Sophia de Mello Breyner Andresen, Rui Belo, and José Saramago. Stillwell demonstrates that even in the work of authors who are professedly atheist or agnostic, religious indifference is rare. Respect for Christ and the Virgin and a genuine affection for their humanity are universal while a purely dogmatic understanding of God identified with Church teaching is met with doubt or unbelief. Stilwell notes a concerted movement toward the horizon of relations with others and the world in the work of these artists, without their renouncing the value, freedom and dignity of the subjective dimension.

Opening Part III, *Musing on God in Europe*, Siegfried Wiedenhofer argues that the fundamentalist and liberal understandings of religious faith, though misguided, are inseparably connected, such that neither error can be seen in isolation from the other. Because either viewpoint is based upon complex religious experiences, the resulting categorization of "fundamentalist" and "liberal" must be regarded as equally multifarious and nuanced phenomena. Wiedenhofer demonstrates that rather than denoting clear black and white divisions, it is easier to understand both models as existing on a continuum, with one pole being pure misunderstanding of faith and pure disbelief. He shows that the opposite pole will be a unitive tension of positive insights from both fundamentalism and liberalism. Finally, Wiedenhofer asserts that it is in the healthy tension between the two where the freedom that sustains true faith in God and true thinking about God resides.

In the succeeding essay, Maureen Junker-Kenny asks what the concept of God can contribute to a future that must grapple with the violent history of Europe in the twentieth century having endured the trauma of the Shoa and bitterness of two world wars, which continue to haunt the offspring of the victims, survivors, perpetrators, and contemporary witnesses. Junker-Kenny begins by comparing Paul Ricoeur and Avishai Margalit on the link between memory and ethics and finds that the faculty to remember is not necessarily matched by a corresponding ability to forgive. She then delineates Ricoeur's counter-thesis to Hannah Arendt who views promising and forgiving as two properties of human agency at the same level, while Ricoeur holds that forgiveness has to be opened up from elsewhere. Next, Junker-Kenny considers some of the philosophical reasons why the question of forgiveness cannot be resolved at a secular level and must be examined before the step to theology is made. Finally, she draws conclusions on forgiveness as the "eschatology of memory" for the concept of God and for the interplay of religious convictions in debates in the public realm.

In the following piece, Amador Vega Esquerra argues that the erosion of representative language in the modern world and the resulting loss of fields of meaning have led to an urgent need to establish a new relationship with the holy. He contends that there has been an ascension of transcendent themes in contemporary art which were once the exclusive province of traditional religion. Employing examples of Rothko, Caro and Pollack, Esquerra claims that modern art, and especially abstractionism, has taken hold of the creative and destructive power proper to myths and the kind of attitudes one finds in the iconoclastic movements in periods of spiritual reformation. He asks to what extent the artist in an environment without cultic consciousness is worthy of mediating what traditionally is understood only as the activity of divine grace. For Esquerra, contemplative observation, readiness for sacrifice, and proclamation are the three requisite elements of the grammar of the holy in modern art. He asserts that it is not the content within a work of art that speaks to the observer, but rather that by sanctifying the eye external reality links with the internal reality.

In the ensuing study, Georgios D. Martzelos examines two interdependent gnoseological trends in the theology of the Church Fathers: kataphatic theology, which accentuates the approachable, understood, and known aspects of God; and apophatic theology, which denotes the unapproachable, incomprehensible, and unknown facets. Even though modern society is so imbued with information and knowledge that appears to place no limits on humanity's ability to gain absolute knowledge of the universal reality, Martzelos avers that the Fathers demonstrate that the ontological gap between the created and the uncreated does not allow gnoseological access to the uncreated on behalf of the created. The only way to bridge the gap and keep the biblical sense of God intact is by using kataphatic and apophatic theology in their indissoluble unity. Finally, Martzelos concludes that the theology of the Eastern Fathers provides a challenge to our globalized, interrelgious social reality, since many other religious traditions presuppose the projection of anthropomorphic representations and properties to the sphere of the divine.

Vincent Holzer's essay examines the "theological turn" in phenomenology wherein philosophers are talking about God and are drawing upon traditionally theological categories such as revelation and faith. Following Dominique Janicaud, Holzer details the fundamental dissociation of being and appearance which allows this theological "turn" to happen. Holzer contends that the shift to theology is completed when identifying how things, values, people, and any reality appear in relation with an eventual absolute reality. He concludes by arguing that such movement leads to a misdiagnosis in the contemporary relation between philosophy and theology and also results in an unwarranted defensive posture on the part of the philosopher in his effort to preserve the integrity of the phenomenological method from the encroachments of theology.

In the following study, Georg Essen argues that even though monotheism has been seemingly triumphant in the Judeo-Christian West, monotheistic religion and culture are not without their dark sides of hate, fear and violence. Therefore, an apologia for monotheism is now necessary which connects the defense of monotheism with human freedom and the humanity of our social existence. Unlike Jan Assman who argues for abolishing the distinction between God and the world, Essen contends that such an identification actually prevents one from rescuing any notion of freedom at all. He suggests an ethical monotheism which guarantees the distinctions between justice and injustice, oppression and liberation, along with an individuating awareness that calls people to a freedom that means responsibility for themselves and for their neighbors. Finally, Essen argues that within an intercultural and interreligious context, ethical monotheism provides a framework for the equality of all people, makes their freedom possible and protects them in spite of their differences.

For Ioannis Kourembeles, the globalization and variety of our civilizations confronts us with a God that can be found in many places and in many forms, and therefore the exclusion of others based on the stressing of social difference is not in agreement with the Christian spirit. Through a thick engagement with Jürgen Moltmann, Kourembeles contends that a thoroughgoing Christian trinitarian monotheism must first be clarified among Christians themselves, so that their dialogue with other religions might be based firmly on dogmatic theology. He asserts that fundamentalist groups within Judaism, Islam, and Christianity attempting a restoration of what they see as "original" values and practices limit critical thought and open dialogue, and thus perpetuate the kinds of religious violence that has recurred in Europe for centuries. Kourembeles shows that exclusion and anathema, exile and violence, do not belong to the kingdom of God, because God is Love. Finally, Kourembeles avers that ecumenical and interreligious dialogues are natural expressions of Christianity, and can be an effective force in civil confrontation with agnostic culture in stressing the soteriological power of the Christian message for all of humankind, not only for Christians.

Georges De Schrijver's article discusses Gianni Vattimo's religious vision which approaches faith from the inner workings of spirituality. Vattimo tends to avoid the pitfall of an external approach (which is only able to establish a classification of analogous truth), which De Schrijver sees as a serious step forward. De Schrijver claims that in order to access this inner side of spirituality, Vattimo deemed it necessary to plunge into his own tradition, and thus God's *kenosis* in Christ has heavily influenced the way in which Vattimo tries to get at the mystical core of non-Christian religions. Following Vattimo, De Schrijver holds that a deep understanding of one's own Christian tradition of *kenosis* is indispensable for awakening to a sensitivity that spontaneously appreciates other religions' approaches to emptiness. Finally, though Vattimo sees the world's religions moving toward a period of secularization in order to "incarnate" their basic values and virtues in the every day life of today's complex world, Schrijver concludes that secularization is not necessarily the logical outcome of a kenotic religion.

In the subsequent article, Armin Kreiner examines the different models that have been developed to conceptualize God's action in the world. These models can be arranged along a continuum: on the one end of the continuum is the maximalist or "determinist" thesis of God's sole and universal efficacy in which everything is caused by God alone; on the opposite end of the continuum is the minimalist or "deistic" thesis that God, after having created the world, does not act in the world at all. Kreiner then reviews the strengths and weaknesses of the various alternatives which have been proposed including the model of secondary causality, the interventionalist model, and the process model. Finally, after delineating the weaknesses of these models, he advocates the compromise of the recent "Open View" model proposed by evangelical theologians which holds that God acts in the world by the power of persuasion even though s/he could act through coercion.

In the succeeding piece, Tomasz Węcławski analyzes the problem of why the actual world is often so disparate from our expectations of what it should be or, conversely, why our ideas of what should be are so out of step with what is. He asserts that the paschal event of Jesus' death and resurrection is the nexus through which we experience our world, including ourselves, and through which we simultaneously discover the word "God" as Love and full of meaning. Węcławski then examines the question of Love for death and life which is revealed in Christ's death and resurrection. He subsequently details the crisis of freedom that results from the refusal of the call of this Love.

Finally, Węcławski describes the idea of God in Jesus as dead and risen and how this corresponds to Love and freedom.

In the final essay of this part, Leonhard Hell considers various contemporary Trinitarian theologies and especially the theological appropriateness of *communio* in addressing particular questions in systematic theology. He sees the common element amongst all such theologies as the premise that plurality is not a secondary, merely derived character in the being and life of God, but rather God is from all eternity one in the differentiation of three persons. Hell sets out a series of criteria by which one might critique the legitimacy and usefulness of this approach to the theology of the Trinity. He then assesses several modern psychological and sociological theories that have provided some terminology for the communal doctrines of the Trinity. Lastly, Hell criticizes any formulation of Trinitarian communio which misunderstands the Trinity as an interpersonal interaction of three equally originating subjects.

Opening Part IV, *Europe's God in Global Dialogue*, Keith Ward's essay asserts that the idea of "God" is not one, but many ideas, with diverse histories and cultural influences, existing within a range of views of the spiritual and the material. He contends that different religions are not simply closed by nature to one another, but rather share common ideas of the divine as supreme reality and also portray the spiritual journey as the overcoming of egoism in the quest of a fulfilled relationship with such a reality. Ward also maintains that diversity can be celebrated as a natural condition of the manifestation of human creative imagination in the interpretation of religious experience, and not as a regrettable fall into heresy. For Ward, it follows that religions are epistemically on par with one another and thus epistemic humility is warranted since global theology becomes an obligation of faith.

In the subsequent article, Josef Wohlmuth concentrates on the problem of transcendence in Jewish thought, the related question of the God-world-man relation, and the resulting problems for religious language. He focuses specifically on the thought of Franz Rosenzweig, Emmanuel Levinas, and Jacques Derrida through briefly presenting each position and its respective challenge to Christian theology. In Derrida, Wolmuth sees a close-meshed network of relationships between God and the world, so that one can speak of a mystical, and even incarnational, dimension as when Derrida discusses transcendence in the subject. Wohlmuth then argues that Rosenzweig understands liturgy as a source of mysticism which inspired the early Church and can take on new meaning if it is linked with the Jewish mysticism of the name. Conversely, Wolmuth asserts that Jewish thinkers can ask Christianity whether its understanding of incarnation preserves the absolute mysterium tremendum of the mysticism of the name, or whether it confines the idea of God to the immanence of our thought. Finally, Wolmuth suggests Franz Rosenzweig's thesis of complementarity as a healthy basis for coexistence around the theology of incarnation.

In the succeeding essay, Ghasem Kakaie provides a brief account of the traditional God of theism or Religion's God followed by a concise discussion of the God of pantheism and panentheism, and then a more extensive comparative account of God in Meister Eckhart and Ibn 'Arabī's theory of the Unity of Being (*Waḥdat al-Wujūd*). Contrary to those who would portray Eckhart and Ibn 'Arabī as pantheists, Kakaie asserts that great gaps remain between the doctrine of the Unity of Being and pantheism. He demonstrates that if one were to compare these thinkers' understanding of God and contemporary Western philosophical views, their views would be closer to panentheism rather than pantheism. For Kakaie, both Ibn 'Arabī and Eckhart managed to think from the point view of the Unity of Being, while maintaining important aspects of the God of ordinary religious believers. He concludes by noting that both mystics were countering the dominant theological exaggerations of their times and cultures with Ibn Arabi countering the Muslims' exaggeration of God's transcendence and Eckhart countering the anthropomorphism of medieval Christian theology.

For Bettina Bäumer, it has become apparent that the monolithic and absolutistic European concept of God has been largely drained of living content and of a corresponding spiritual experience in that it no longer incites reactions of atheism and has become boring and ineffective for the majority. She argues that Hinduism provides testimony to a still-living experience of God in a variety of ways that provide a unique chance to revive the European experience of God. Bäumer focuses on three aspects of the experience of God in Hinduism: 1) Hindu polytheism, which Bäumer argues is an insight into the manifold nature of the divine rather than heresy, the unfair designation it has been assigned by many theologians and missionaries; 2) the feminine aspect of the divine which can counterbalance the overly patriarchal Judeo-Christian concept of God; and 3) the apophatism of Advaita Vedanta in which God (Brahman) never becomes an object of knowing or sense experience.

In the following essay, Marcus Schmücker examines the theistic Vedānta of the Viśiṣṭādvaita school of Indian philosophy through one of its most influential adherents, Veṅkaṭanātha. According to Schmücker, Veṅkaṭanātha holds that everything that can be thought as different from God is related to him in such a way that no single thing can be said to exist separately, yet God can remain in His absoluteness without being affected by anything different from Him. Schmücker demonstrates that Veṅkaṭanātha claims that on the basis of authoritative scripture, there is no equivalent or more highly valued second other than God (*īśvara*) because everything different from God qualifies again only God. This paradigm is described by Veṅkaṭanātha as the relation of the supporter to the supported, of the ruler to the ruled, of the principal to the subordinate, of that which is characterized by a body to the body itself, and as the relation of cause and effect. God is not limited by all that stands in necessary relation to God, because everything different belongs only to God.

In the succeeding essay, Aasulv Lande analyzes how the Buddhist tradition has gone about naming and thinking the "beyond" through the prism of what he calls Buddhist incarnation. He avers that this "beyond" is implied within Buddhism by the interaction and coexistence of both the immanent reality, including aspects of sangha, and ultimate reality as illustrated by terms such as Buddha, dharma, and, indirectly, by sangha. Lande approaches this dichotomy by examining particular concepts of Buddhist ultimacy integral to Japanese Buddhism such as "Buddha nature" (*bussho*) or "original Buddhism" (*honga-ku shiso*). Lande then addresses the century long debate within the Kyoto school of Buddhist philosophy surrounding terms such as "absolute nothingness" (*zettaimu*). He concludes with a discussion of Buddhist philosophies that actually oppose ideas of "Buddha nature" or even the term "nothingness" found in critical Buddhism as well as in the new Buddhist trend of engaged Buddhism.

Given the rise of comparative theology, Norbert Hintersteiner assesses some of the questions and theses as put forward in the newly evolving discipline. First he proposes the subject of intercultural translatability or untranslatability of traditions as heuristic lenses and epistemological entry points to the discourse and practice of comparative theology. He follows with examples suggesting that theology in many ways (foremost in its crosscultural religious translation processes) has always been an inherently comparative discipline. He then examines the practice of comparative theology through some of its contemporary definitions, followed by an analysis of the comparative work of Francis Clooney, one of the pioneers of contemporary comparative theology. He concludes by summarizing various dimensions and systematic points that emerge as essential to the contemporary fabric of a comparative theology.

Given the challenge to the theology of religions voiced by comparative theology in the past decade, in the following essay, Perry Schmidt-Leukel assesses the benefits and limits of comparative theology for the future and its relationship to the theology of religions. He sets out by briefly explaining how he understands the theology of religions and its three basic options of exclusivism, inclusivism, and pluralism. Schmidt-Leukel then argues that there is neither a way out of the theology of religions nor any real theological alternative to these three basic options. He asserts that if "comparative theology" is really taken as genuine theology while remaining at the same time seriously comparative, it cannot avoid these questions, but in fact will lead straight into them. For Schmidt-Leukel, the theology of religions is still vital and essential. Indeed, he avers, the pluralist option lights a promising path into the theological future to which comparative theology can and should make an essential contribution.

In what follows, Klaus von Stosch offers a critical response to Perry Schmidt-Leukel's paper "Limits and Prospects of Comparative Theology" in which Schmidt-Leukel attempts to reveal the mistaken efforts of comparative theologians to find a way beyond the current impasse in the theology of religions. Stosch asserts that, contrary to Schmidt-Leukel, the pluralist answer to the problem of a theology of religions is not valid because one cannot insist on the truth of one's beliefs while accepting that the opposite of one's beliefs is equally true. Stosch then argues against Schmidt-Leukel's claim that comparative theology does not lead out of the impasse of theology of religions because comparative theology has a philosophical framework that excludes the possibility of a merely theoretical comparison of religions altogether.

In the final essay, Robert Neville examines the role of concepts of ultimacy in crosscultural comparative theology. He first briefly recalls the historical problems with comparison of the concept of God as concern for ultimacy in Western monotheisms and Eastern religions. Following Charles Peirce, Neville then details a semiotics of interpretation which allows that religions or theologies can only be compared where they are found to have concepts interpreting the same object in the same respect. He next proposes the hypothesis that "ultimate significance" is a concept which is vulnerable enough to allow correction for bias in theological comparison. Neville concludes by concisely demonstrating how the vague concept of "ultimate significance" would function in crosscultural comparisons of ultimacy between Buddhism, Confucianism, Daoism, Judaism, Christianity and Islam.

By concluding this introduction, it is hoped that, taken as a whole, this volume's scholarly contributions become heuristic in at least two ways: first, that they provide a useful theological account imidst of Europe's ongoing changes, including its search for a new spiritual identity which in many ways is accompanied by ideological, socio-economic and religious tensions. Second, that this volume's account serves as a platform upon which European studies of ways of naming and thinking God can become more context-sensitive and effective. Within such heuristic objectives, at least two theological issues may prove salient to any thoroughgoing endeavor – consideration of the experience of God and the attending academic methodologies applied in study of this experience within specific European milieus, and the manner in which concepts of God, though varying from one cultural context to another, may be robustly brought to bear within discourse in ways that are fair and mutually beneficial.

The overall project not only brings contemporary traditions of enquiry on God from Eastern and Western Europe into mutual presentation, discussion, and reconsideration, it also seeks to stimulate scholars to rethink and test these traditions, while engaging with and respecting Europe's cultural, religious, and socio-economic diversity vis-a-vis the global. In this regard, the overall project, especially in its two subsequent works to this volume,[1] includes studying crucial areas of conflict (conflicts of worldview and ideology, geopolitics, and global religious dialogue) through a process of critical and dialogical hermeneutical interaction with ways of naming and thinking God. In this way the project hopes to discover and generate opportunities for a multivalenced as well as relevant reflection on God that achieves mutual intelligibility without surrendering to a dogmatic untranslatability at one extreme or a crude relativism at the other.

---

[1] J. Haers, N. Hintersteiner and G. De Schrijver (eds.), *Postcolonial Europe in the Crucibles of Cultures: Reckoning with God in a World of Conflicts* (Amsterdam / New York, 2007); F. Bousquet and N. Hintersteiner (eds.), *Thinking the Divine in Interreligious Encounters* (Amsterdam / New York, 2008).

PART I

EUROPE'S GOD IN A GLOBALIZING WORLD

Peter Beyer

"God's in His Heaven ... Where He Belongs": Religions, Europe, and Monopolar Transcendence in Global Society

Introduction: God and Indeterminacy in Global Society

I make my observations in the context of a globalized social system. Arising thus, they not only emerge from within global society, but they also reflect some of its most important features. Among these is an effective (and in that sense, real) distinction between scientific and religious perspectives, which includes a distinction between theoretical and theological observation. That difference is particularly consequential when we come to speak of "God." For most religious and theological thinking, God (or various equivalent concepts) is a foundational reality that profoundly affects what happens in our world. Religious perspectives start from this reality; they concern themselves with communication by and with this reality; and without that root assumption, they cease to be religious. Scientific understanding, on the other hand, assumes that it is possible to arrive at relatively true and consequential statements about reality on the basis of empirically generated data; it does not formally recognize the conditions legitimizing religious claims and data, except in so far as these claims are susceptible to empirical investigation. For science, God as reality is inaccessible and therefore irrelevant. People's behavior in light of their religious standpoints, however, is neither inaccessible nor irrelevant.

This distinction between religion and science is fairly commonplace, and, in the context of this conference, probably not all that controversial. It is nonetheless a distinction I make at the outset in order to make my position clear: my analytic stance in this endeavor is entirely scientific and therefore treats the "God concept" as something contingent, something that depends on particular conditions for its effectiveness and which, in that light, is not requisite in the way it is for a religious perspective. Whether we lead our lives as if God exists, and what we mean by that if we do; these are, scientifically speaking, variable qualities. Accordingly, in this presentation, I take a sociological look at how the God-concept operates generally in contemporary global society, more specifically how it operates in the European region of that society, and why.

In summarizing the general direction and conclusion of my observations, I wish to suggest (1) that contemporary global society structurally favors the differentiation of a particular, instrumental, function system for religion; (2) that this system manifests itself principally in the form of a limited set of religions that identify themselves (and are identified by others) with reference to one another; (3) that this mutual identification favors monotheistic (re-)structuring of these religions, or, at minimum, a tendency toward religious self-observation that attributes multiple divine manifestations to a single transcendent principle (Roland Robertson's "superior being"); (4) that the high degree of abstraction in such a "monotheism" makes structural respecification especially important if religions are to be and remain effective, direct forces in the life of global society; (5) that, within Europe, such respecification involves resorting, implicitly, to non-religious methodologies; (6) that Christian religion and the Christian God nonetheless remain a somewhat shadowy – if culturally and symbolically still important – presence in European self-conceptions; and finally, (7) that the particular challenge of Islam in Europe today is that various movements within it deliberately refute this trend toward respecification, claiming an equal yet incommensurate status between Allah and the Christian God while asserting that Allah / God must remain (or become) a *religiously* effective super ordinate force, directly conditioning the operation of other domains such as politics, economy, law, education, health, art, sport, mass media, and science.

In the remainder of this presentation, I address these seven assertions sequentially. My expectation is that, if the reader finds my find theoretical framework somewhat unusual, my conclusions themselves will be unsurprising. It is in the balance of the two where I foresee making a contribution to the debate on the concept of God in Europe.

The Religion System of Global Society

One of the more striking features of contemporary debates about world religion is the persistence of assumptions that derive from a distinct and quite small subset of religions. Whether we are looking at official government policies around the world, scientific debate, legal decisions, religious discourse (especially, but by no means exclusively, *interreligious* dialogue), educational curricula, media presentations, or simply day-to-day interaction, there is strong evidence for the globally spread agreement on the nearly self-evident existence of at least five religions, namely Christianity, Islam, Buddhism, Hinduism, and Judaism; as well as a variable but still limited set of others, depending on region or circumstances. These latter include, most consistently, Sikhism, Daoism, Zoroastrianism, and Jainism; and less consistently, a variety of others, for instance Shinto, Baha'i, African Traditional (ATR), new world African religions like Candomblé, Vaudou, or Rastafari, Wicca, Scientology, and so forth.[1] What counts as religion is only occasionally limited to this core and/or penumbral set of religions. Usually the range of religion as such is agreed to be broader, while it is nonetheless vague in its precise boundaries.

In this context, the "core" religions form the implicit or explicit terms of reference for understanding, deciding, and discussing what religion is. The situation is reminiscent of how we understand global political realities: there are a limited number of clearly defined and legitimated (i.e. sovereign) states. These set the terms for the understanding of a global political system; and as with religion, there is always the possibility of more or different states, and what counts as politics or political action is certainly not limited to the activity of the recognized states. Although the comparison between states and religions cannot be carried too far, it is more than accidental or metaphorical. What we are dealing with are in fact parallel phenomena whose social structures are to a large degree mutually conditioning, thus giving rise to developments that are temporally modern and both socially and spatially global.

My argument, in brief, is that this shared recognition of core religions is symptomatic of the historical and modern development of a particular and peculiar religious social system, one that has arisen in parallel with a number of other such systems, the political system of states just mentioned; and others focused on economy, science, health, education, the arts, sports, and mass media. As will quickly become evident, I draw many of my key concepts for understanding this global situation from the sociological theories of Niklas

1 For a more detailed treatment of different aspects of this argument, see P. Beyer, "What Counts as Religion in Global Society? From Practice to Theory," in *idem* (ed.), *Religion in the Process of Globalization* (Würzburg, 2001), 125-50; *idem*, "Defining Religion in Cross-National Perspective: Identity and Difference in Official Conceptions," in A.L. Greil and D. Bromley (eds.), *Defining Religion: Investigating the Boundaries between Sacred and Secular* (London, 2003), 163-88.

Luhmann.[2] Two main features of my perspective are as follows. First, the aforesaid religious system has arisen with a structure that is parallel to these other systems and is marked in its characteristics by the simultaneous development of these other systems. Second, this religious system is therefore highly selective and contingent in the sense that it favors the construction of religions in certain ways and not others; and in that it cannot be said to incorporate the entire domain of social activities that might conceivably count as religious. In consequence, the characteristics of this religious system cannot be understood simply in terms of their religious qualities. The system is not just the natural expression, as it were, of something *sui generis* called religion. It is just as importantly a system on its own terms, equal in status to other, non-religious ones.

I cannot, in the time available to me, embark on a detailed description of how this peculiar religious system arose, nor treat even in cursory fashion all of what I see as its main features.[3] I therefore limit myself to those aspects of the history and those characteristics of the system that are germane to the issue at hand, namely the role of the God concept in contemporary global and European society.

Any historical narrative of the origins of contemporary social structures must to some degree adopt an arbitrary beginning in an arbitrary place. For my purposes, that beginning and that place is European society of the late medieval and Reformation periods. It is here that we can observe the solid beginnings of an increasingly accelerated shift in social structures toward a reliance on what Luhmann calls "function systems" as the dominant infrastructure of society. These instrumentally oriented institutional domains – above all for capitalist economy, sovereign state-centered politics, positive law, empirical science, and orthodox[4] religion – not only became the key features of

---

2 See especially N. Luhmann, *Funktion der Religion* (Frankfurt a. M., 1977); *idem*, *Soziale Systeme. Grundriß einer allgemeinen Theorie* (Frankfurt a. M., 1984); *idem*, *Die Gesellschaft der Gesellschaft* (Frankfurt a. M., 1997); *idem*, *Die Religion der Gesellschaft* (Frankfurt a. M., 2000); cf. P. Beyer, "Religion as Communication in Niklas Luhmann's Die Religion der Gesellschaft," in *Soziale Systeme* 7 (2001): 46-55.

3 See P. Beyer, "The Modern Emergence of Religions and a Global Social System for Religion," in *International Sociology* 13: 151-72; *idem*, "The Religious System of Global Society: A Sociological Analysis of an Emerging Reality," in *Numen* 45: 1-29.

4 "Orthodoxy" may be somewhat inadequate as the parallel adjectival qualifier for the religious system; it should at a minimum include the idea of "orthopraxy." It is probably most parallel to the idea of sovereignty in the political system. Another possibility would be to say "faith-based." This term indicates modern religions' typical way of

modern European society, but also in the course of their development they have become the structural basis of contemporary global society. Thus, although this foundational shift began historically in Europe, the more complete construction of these systems took place only in the course of their globalization. To use Roberston's formulation,[5] these function systems became global universals, not simply through their expansion and universalization as European particulars, but just as (if not more) critically through their particularization by, and in, other regions of the world. Ironically, given that this religious system is not nearly as powerful or as clearly structured as the other systems, it nonetheless bears this dialogical characteristic in an especially clear manner.

The differentiation of a religious system that was institutionally distinct from the rest of European society began with the late Roman imperial development of the Christian church, especially its episcopal and monastic organization. This emerging system received an important additional dimension with the late medieval rise of a plurality of European states that structured themselves in rivalry with the ecclesiastical institutions, thereby contributing to their mutual differentiation. The Protestant Reformation and the Catholic counter-reformation of the sixteenth century mark a further critical moment, especially in so far as they sought to "purify" Christian religion, to rid it of its worldly accretions. What all the reformers demanded was that religious orientations and activity be structured and judged purely on religious terms, whether through the idea of justification by faith alone – by insisting on the complete sovereignty of God – or by asserting the church as a *societas perfectas* distinct from secular society. That the reform movements resulted in the irrevocable pluralization of the religious domain was due less to differences in theological agendas than to the rising of political states. Nonetheless, the Reformation period spawned a revision of religion by Europeans as something both distinct and fundamentally plural: religion was asserted as its own separate sphere expressing itself in a diversity of religious forms. Initially, during the seventeenth and eighteenth centuries, the latter were conceived along what one might call traditional lines. There were four religions: Chris-

styling their "knowledge" and is therefore more parallel to the concept of "empirical" in modern science. The point of qualifying religion with an adjective here is to underscore its modern singularity and to thereby avoid the misunderstanding that I am talking about religion anywhere at any time.

5 R. Robertson, *Globalization: Social Theory and Global Culture* (London, 1992).

tianity, Islam, Judaism, and Paganism, the latter with special reference to Greco-Roman religion.

As critical as the intra-European developments were, they represent only one phase or dimension of the overall historical construction and transformation. The other, and at least as important, dimension was that the Europeans were simultaneously embarking on their worldwide expansion, a process that confronted them with even more religious plurality – which they either condemned or imagined as additional, distinct religions – and that enjoined responses from those other regions over which the Europeans exercised an increasing influence up to the twentieth century. In a nutshell, the necessity of facing up to the Europeans posed the question in the imagination of indigenous religious heritages of whether or not to collaborate with their classification as one or more of a plurality of religions. In some regions, such as those dominated by Islam, the prevailing answer was a more or less a straightforward "yes," since its carriers already had a long tradition of differentiated self-conception: Islam, if it was not just one religion among others, was definitely systematic, and in that sense, a differentiated religion. Something similar could be said for Buddhism, with its long history of institutional differentiation in the form of organized monasteries. Somewhat more ambiguous responses were forthcoming from the South Asian region, but today the distinctions of Hinduism, Sikhism, and probably Jainism are pretty much self-evident, at least for their more elite practitioners and outside observers. In East Asia, by contrast, the situation is far more uncertain: institutionally speaking, Shinto and Daoism have only haltingly been reconstructed as religions; and so-called Confucianism, for all intents and purposes, hardly at all. These last cases especially illustrate the degree to which the religion-formation process has been optional, somewhat arbitrary, and contingent on the peculiar circumstances in the different regions. The net result is a relatively clear global religious system that, for adherents and outsiders alike, consists of a limited, but variable, set of religions. These religions differentiate themselves from each other, and from other institutional domains, both through internal structuring and theological reflection as well as through outside observation: their identities consist of movements toward convergence or orthodoxy/orthopraxy along with external recognition, and both these with reference to other social systems and in mutual contrast with other religions.

If, for the sake of argument, we can accept this historical narrative, there remains the critical question of the systemicity of this phenomena, of what makes the religious system a system and what specifically is religious about it. It is here that the Luhmannian conceptual apparatus is particularly useful. It allows a controlled comparison of the systemic with the non-systemic and of the religious with the non-religious. In this regard, five concepts are particularly germane: the ideas of *binary code, contingency formula, communicative elements, communications medium,* and *systemic programs*. The first four identify the system as a system religious in its nature; the last concerns the system's differentiation into several religions.

The notion of *binary code* asks: What basic, dual-termed distinction, both of whose terms are understood to be religious, lends structure to what operates as religion in contemporary global society, such that we can differentiate between religion and non-religion? The answer to this question is not straightforward, largely because the global religious system relies so heavily on different religions for its concrete structure. Relatively different binary codes operate in different religions. To illustrate: salvation/damnation, *nirvana / samsara*, *moksha / samsara*, *halal / haram*; and very often, there are other, second-level codes, such as pure/polluted and auspicious/inauspicious, and most especially, the common moral distinction between good and bad or moral and immoral. Overall, however, I would contend that all of theses codes constitute variations on what, in English, can be expressed as the difference between "blessed" and "cursed." The first of these terms denotes a religiously positive state, the second a religiously negative state. Although this suggestion may sound controversial, this is not the place to defend it properly. Suffice it to say that this distinction seeks to approximate the manner in which modern religions translate the world into specific, religiously relevant terms. It contrasts with corresponding codes in other systems, such as the difference between scientific truth and falsity, economic ownership and non-ownership, political government and opposition, medical illness and health, or sports victory and defeat.

In terms of identifying religion, it is perhaps what Luhmann calls the "contingency formula" that interests us most in the present context. This, roughly speaking, refers to the core notions that "make religion necessary." In the domain of economy, the idea of "scarcity" would play this role: exchange and ownership are necessary because goods and services are understood to be, by definition, scarce. Similarly, in the political domain, the idea of "collective good" or "order" would occupy this position. For religion, it is the God-concept, including its non-anthropomorphic renderings. Religion, from its own perspective, is necessary because God or Brahman – or any other ultimate reality – exists and constitutes the condition of the possibility of anything. The religions, as constructed in modern global society, give primary and identifying reference to that assumption in a way that other institutional domains definitely do not. One of the most critical assumptions underlying the modern differentiation of instrumental systems is that God (or an equivalent), while religiously conceived as the foundation of all reality, in *social reality* refers primarily to the domain of religion, and only secondarily, or through the broader influence of religion, to the rest of society, to its other systems in particular. I shall return to this notion in the next section.

If religious binary codes and contingency formulae refer us to what religion is fundamentally all about, the next question is how these foundational ideas are put into social practice. What communicative actions express religion? This is where religious practice, especially but not exclusively ritual, enters the picture. That said, it is important in this regard to distinguish between core religious communication and a wide variety of more peripheral communicative acts that may be religiously relevant (or the subject of religious signification), but which correspondingly contribute less directly to the reproduction of the religious system. Core religious practices, such as prayer, sacrifice, meditation, pilgrimage, devotional exercise, sermons, and in the case of some religions, religio-legal rulings, are those which establish the fundamental communication *with* the gods or their equivalents. They reproduce the core power and social reality of religion. One key consequence of this observation is that religion in today's world cannot simply be "belief." The mental convictions and understandings of people must receive real social expression in communication, or, if one prefers, in social action. It is communication and action that socially constitute religion. Beliefs are only components, which, by themselves, are fairly irrelevant. I insist on this aspect because the critical question for religion in today's global society is not whether people believe what religions teach, but rather how their convictions bear significant social effects, regarding what constitutes religion as such and, equally critically, regarding their influence upon the operation of other systems in the non-religious domains.

Asking what the most important religious elements are in a system calls into question the nature of a system's religious communications medium – another way of asking about the form that religious power takes. In this case again, we run into a fair amount of diversity among religions, but terms like the Abrahamic notions of "faith" or "grace," the Hindu notion of *shakti*, or the Buddhist idea of "merit" come to mind. The difficulty with respect to religious power is that religions generally also express their sense of power in terms that are largely claimed by other systems, and by these, often more effectively. One thinks, for instance, of religion as the source of "knowledge" or "truth" (science); of religion as source of healing (health); of religion as law (law); of religion as enlightenment (education), as generalized strength (sport), as beauty (art), sometimes even as spiritual wealth (economy). All these metaphoric expressions point to a difficulty with regard to what medium is specifically and uncontestedly religious and only religious; and thereby to the equivocal differentiation of religion as one of the instrumental systems.

Finally, it is through specific programs that religions lend meaning and coherence or self-reference to their elements, codes, media, and formulae. Systems constitute themselves in that their elements refer to one another. If the elements of a system are its building blocks (here the religions), then programs are the recursively structured ways by which these elements, together, create a boundary between that which belongs to the system and that which does not. It is through programmatic convergence of this sort that, for instance, prayer is related to the possibility of salvation, salvation to the nature and will of God, and God in turn becomes the understanding partner in the religious communication that is prayer. It is by means of programs that the identified religions constitute themselves as socially recognized and operative entities. And far from excluding contestation and conflict over which religions are to be recognized – what belongs to a given religion and what does not – the notion of program explicitly includes these possibilities. Religious programs generally include ways of determining what is authentic and authoritative; and thereby what is superstition, heresy, charlatanry, apostasy, or just another legitimate religion.

As I have already noted, the possibility of generalizing about contemporary religions in terms of the categories just outlined is a reflection of the selective way in which the religious system, like the other, parallel systems, has been constructed. I make no claim that "religion" is inherently like this, that it must construct itself in terms of codes, formulae, media, elements, and programs. My contention, however, is that historically this is what has happened and that therefore, among the panoply of social action systems that might abstractly count as religious from an analytical perspective, there is also this particular system. This development has involved a generous amount of reimagination of received religious traditions and practices, their transformation, or even, if one wishes, their distortion from the forms in which they may previously have been embedded. It has also called forth the religiously new, as exemplified by quite a number of modern religious movements around the world. If this perspective can be accepted as a useful one, then my next task is to examine some of the consequences it has had, especially, but not exclusively, in contemporary Europe.

The God-Concept: Monotheism as Symptom of Convergence

The many disputes, rivalries, and contestations in the contemporary religious domain generally follow two fault lines, namely that between religion and non-religion and that between one religion and another. Thus, for instance, questions of orthopraxy or orthodoxy dispute what belongs to a particular religion and what does not belong, whether the excluded element is deemed to be non-religious or part of another religion. Frequently the range of religious influence is also at issue. The religious domain, like the other instrumental systems, because of their recursive structure, has a tendency to be totalizing, claiming relevance to absolutely anything and everything in human life. Corresponding to the economic tendency to turn everything into a commodity, and the political tendency to regulate everything, one can also detect a religious tendency to sacralize (both positively and negatively) everything. This characteristic leads to disputed claims, in the case of religion to issues having to do with privatization and the range and degree of public religious influence. These issues concern the boundaries between religion and non-religion. In addition, given the absence of anything resembling a global religion – and this in spite of occasional claims by some religious representatives that all religions essentially say the same thing – the identification of religions almost always includes a sometimes contested distinction between one religion and another. Put a bit differently, religions identify themselves in terms of their own programmatic criteria, by contrasting themselves with other instrumental systems, and with benign or dismissive reference to other religions. Thus, to take but one example, whatever one decides Hinduism to be, it cannot be the same thing as the Indian state, and especially not the same thing as Islam or Christianity. To be sure, these boundaries are contested areas, but that is precisely the issue. It is in the crucible of contestation that the critical boundaries attain concrete social reality.

Such comparative identification exerts, among its other consequences, a certain contextual pressure on religions, at least through their elite and theologically inclined representatives, compelling them to be clear about their identities, about what it is that fundamentally makes them what they are in contrast to other religions and other systems. In return, this results in a corresponding contextual pressure toward a clearer convergence around central and unifying ideas and practices. Given the structural importance of contingency formulae for distinguishing what religion as such is all about, we can therefore expect the "God-concept" to become a prime identifier and unifier, meaning, among other things, that the sense of transcendent reality in each religion will have a tendency to be thought and presented as a self-referential unity. The situation favors explicitly monotheistic religions like Judaism, Christianity, and Islam, leading perhaps to the success of movements in these religions that lay particular stress on divine singularity and unity; and thus the relative decline of more popular forms which are more inclined to emphasize the importance of divine multiplicity for the sake of the everyday relevance of the divine. The situation also favors a sort of monotheistic observation within and of the other religions, notably Buddhism and Hinduism, even if these have a practical history of structuring themselves much more around the multiplicity of divine personages, even at the level of elite belief and practice. In this way, the "God-concept" acquires a key role in the mutual identification of religions, whether this is now the Christian Trinitarian God, the Jewish Yahweh, the Allah of Islam, the Hindu Brahman (or probably more likely Vishnu or Siva), the Buddhist Buddha, the Sikh Sat Guru, the Jain Mahavira, or even the Candomblé Odolumare.

Thus the "God-concept," or its equivalent, bears significance for identifying religions in the current context of global society; and identification is important for clarity about what it is that is supposed to have an influence in society. For religion to be effective, it must be able to assert its specificity vis-à-vis other spheres of influence, especially the other instrumental systems. For a particular religion to be effective, its difference with respect to other religions must also be clear. The utility of the "God-concept" for this purpose does, however, have a converse side, and this concerns its respecification. Because a monotheistic or henotheistic concept is highly effective in identifying a religion, it thus faces, by its much generalized nature, the additional challenge of bringing itself to bear in concrete and highly variable situations. If the monotheistic religions, as currently reconstructed, have had an advantage in terms of identification, one could say that the operatively polytheistic or polycentric religions may have an advantage when it comes to respecification. Different divinities with different characteristics may be more suitable for addressing the wide range of human needs. Whether we are speaking of different practical needs, ranging from providing an overall meaning to life, to healing a particular affliction, or whether we are addressing the differences in individual religious tastes; a multiplicity of spiritual beings by itself already accomplishes a large portion of the respecification task. This may explain why, historically, theological monotheism so often gives way to practical polytheism, the former more often than not being the province of elites who have other levers at hand for exercising influence in their world than do the less privileged masses. Thus, for instance, popular Catholicism and popular Sufi Islam, like popular Hindu religion, popular Chinese religion, as well as most traditional African religions, have historically been more prevalent in the various regions of the world where the masses dominate than the stricter monotheistic versions have been. The fact that polytheistic reconstructions of religion do not seem to be gaining significant ground in today's world (even though they are by no means in danger of disappearing) indicates that the question of respecification is not simply a matter of pluralizing a contingency formula; the nub of the problem, and of its varied solutions, is mostly located elsewhere. Put in somewhat different terms, respecifying God has proceeded mostly by other means; and in any case concerns the rivalry and difference among instrumental systems, between religion and non-religion, at least as much as that between one religion and another; and even here there is more at stake than differences among God-concepts.

Instrumental Religion and Instrumental Systems

If the prevailing response to the challenge of respecification is not in the God-concept itself, in the contingency formula of religion, then, following a Luhmannian scheme, we must look elsewhere among the typical structures of the modern religious system. For other systems, such as economy, polity, or science, it would be useful to look at the communications or power media in this regard. It is through money, political power, and the generation of data (i.e. "factually true" statements) that these systems mesh concretely in everyday life. For religion, this is far less the case because of the already mentioned difficulty in constructing a univocal and effective religious power medium. Far more fruitful in this case is examination of developments in the binary codes of religion. Above I suggested that something like the blessed / cursed distinction operates at the core of contemporary religions. One may or may not find this convincing, but in any case the fact that religion in today's world makes its presence felt predominantly through religions rather than a general religion renders the question of an overall religious code somewhat moot. More significant is what has been happening at the level of individual religions; and here it is not only particular translations of the general code that are of interest, but just as compelling, and in certain cases more, a number of what Luhmann calls second or supplementary codings.

The most general codes of the major religions focus on particular versions of what in European languages is called "salvation." Religious communication of the Abrahamic religions refers both directly and indirectly to the distinction between salvation and damnation; and in Hinduism and Buddhism this place is held by *moksha / nirvana* and the cycle of *samsara*. This does not mean, however, that all religions must be salvation religions, or that salvation is the only important structuring code in the most globally recognized religions. Indeed, one could argue that each of the major religions actually relies, at least as much, on other, supplementary codes or respecified versions of the general codes that have real effects in the wider social world. Thus, although salvation/damnation is still important in most versions of contemporary Christianity, one also witnesses a rather heavy reliance on the moral coding of good/bad or moral/immoral. And indeed, among those versions of Christianity that seem to have let the possibility of damnation recede into the background, the role of the moral code may be even more critical. Similarly, and this is a point to which I shall return in the next section, the currently most powerful versions of Islam supplement and specify the salvation/damnation code, not only with the moral code, but more significantly with the religio-legal codes of *halal / haram*, "that which is enjoined" and "that which is forbidden." Additionally, one could go so far as to say that relatively few Hindus are immediately concerned with *moksha / samsara,* and that they are more directly concerned with *dharma / adharma*, pure / polluted, or auspicious / inauspicious. One can make parallel arguments for most other religions as well. In each case, the most general code receives respecification into other codes that translate or supplement the former for the sake of the greater immediacy of religious communication. Although this has probably always been the case within the religious domain of societies, in the modern and now global context, the fact that these codes structure a particular instrumental system, among other such systems, gives this feature a peculiar relevance.

A difficulty with most of the supplementary codes is that, in the context of the other systems, they cannot be claimed very easily by religions as their exclusive domain. This is especially the case with the difference between moral and immoral, a distinction with a long history of association with religious specification, but one which today as in the past also largely escapes such determinations: morality can and does receive religious grounding, but it is not distinctly religious the way salvation/damnation or *nirvana / samsara* are. One symptom of this situation in the contemporary world is the frequent application of moral judgments to religious action, as in questions of gender equality or the lack of it. Religion and morality are not simply identical; they are, in many ways, also different. Similarly, the possibilities for supplemental and respecified religious codings are limited by the positive incorporation of some of the most important of them in one or another of the other parallel systems. I have already had occasion to mention the ways in which religious truth must distinguish itself from scientific truth, religious law from secular positive law, religious healing from medical healing, and religious power from political power. Some of these competitions are of much older provenance than others, but all are pertinent in today's global societal situation, where the instrumental systems built around them dominate the constructions and distributions of social power, status, and influence. In this context, the question is not whether religious truth, law, healing, or power are valid – within the religious systems they are clearly so – but rather which of the systems will prevail in the determination of the codes associated with them. One of the historical advantages of most of the non-religious systems is that they have managed to instrumentalize and even technicize these distinctions to a high degree, meaning that the structuring of codes like true / false, legal / illegal, ill / healthy, in-power / out-of-power, and especially owning / not-owning, has shown itself to be highly effective in augmenting the presence and influence of their typical ways of structuring the world. The tremendous expansion in this regard in the areas of scientifically-based technology, medical healing, legal proceedings, government regulation, and monetary identification of items is the most obvious evidence. In so far as the religious system attempts to appropriate one or more of these codes for itself – perhaps precisely because the codes have shown themselves to be so effective – the question then becomes whether typically religious or secular logics will prevail in their determination; and what will be the result. If I may generalize from the little evidence we have, although the secular logics do not always carry the day, they do seem to have a way of asserting themselves at the end of the day, probably because they bear more concrete and immediate effects. Even where religious determinations have been highly visible, such as in Christian democracy or Islamic economics, these have shown themselves either to be relatively ineffective as politics or economics or, more frequently, the secular logics have transformed these efforts into little more than a secular version with a religious veneer. Concretely this means that one has had to find ways of religiously justifying what the secular logic seems to require, or at least ways of not letting the religious logic extend too far.

The one significant prevailing exception to this tendency of secular logics may be the case of Islamic law. Applying Shari'a to the construction of legal systems has been done extensively and effectively in various countries such as Iran, Pakistan, and Nigeria. Even here, however, as the Iranian case currently illustrates, the jury is still out, as it were, on the consequences of the positive codification of Islamic law, and above all, on the effect of political regulation on legal procedures. Given the close relation in the contemporary world between law-making states and law-interpreting courts, it may not be surprising that the difficulties in a religious legal system will be revealed in the challenges of constructing a religious political system.

Instrumental Systems and the God-Concept in Europe

As this last speculation illustrates, the general considerations of the role and importance of the religious system and of religious determinations varies from region to region in today's global society. Although it is tempting to address such variation strictly in terms of differences among the various states in the world, treating the latter in effect as separate societies, it is at least as effective to look at broader regions such as Europe, North America, Latin America, the North African-Middle Eastern belt, South Asia, sub-Saharan Africa, and so on. This must be done, however, without reifying such differences into speculation about "civilizational" differences à la Huntington.[6] Such a restrictive categorization may be part of a typical strategy of asserting difference in global society, but scientifically it can no more be taken as an evident point of departure than can supposedly inherent differences between nations, cultures, religions, and other group identifiers. With those caveats in place, we can now look at the particular region which is Europe (in its entirety).

Europe is an area where all the major instrumental systems have been solidly institutionalized for quite some time. That includes Europe's religious system, which is here clearly differentiated and structured as different relig-

6 S. P. Huntington, *The Clash of Civilizations and the Remaking of World Order* (New Delhi, 1996).

ions along with a penumbral domain of various religious movements and observed spiritualities. Among the religions, Christianity in its three main subdivisions of Roman Catholicism, Protestantism, and Eastern Orthodoxy has for centuries been and is still the dominant religion, even though all the other major religions and quite a number of the more minor ones have, in the twentieth century (and in the case of Judaism, well before), achieved a significant minority status. That said, the particular structure of the religious system in Europe, its place, importance, power, and internal character are in many ways particular to this region; and in saying this, I definitely do not wish to imply that Europe is exceptional, since in this respect all regions of the world have their unique particularities.[7]

Concerning religion, among these European particularities, three of them seem to be especially important for understanding the role and significance of the God-concept. These are religion's historical ties with the European political system (the states); the relatively low level of religious authority or, what is simply the other side of this coin, the high degree of privatization; and the corresponding way in which religion thereby becomes respecified – or not. Here I deliberately avoid the term "secularization," not because this would be inappropriate for describing contemporary Europe, but rather because its use would focus the discussion too immediately upon the non-religious domains and would thereby confuse the central issue, which is the particularity of the religious system in Europe. The three aspects are of course interrelated, but they also do not simply flow from one another. This justifies their separate treatment.

Historically, and especially in the post-Reformation period, the dominant Christian religion in Europe came to be highly organized, with most of the main church organizations arising or being closely identified with the various states, whether Catholic, Protestant, or Orthodox. Moreover, as the structure and primary legitimation of these states after the latter part of the eighteenth century became more and more centered around the idea of nation and nationalism, the religious identities of states became, to a greater or lesser degree, integral to national cultural identities. If nation and religion were not identical, then, at least in most countries, the particular church or churches that dominated came from early on to be seen as a key characteristic of the nation.

7 P. Berger, "Reflections on the Sociology of Religion Today," in *Sociology of Religion* 62 (2001): 443-54; G. Davie, *Europe: The Exceptional Case. Parameters of Faith in the Modern World* (London, 2003).

In this regard, France with its strong tradition of *laïcité* is only a partial exception. The Roman Catholic character of this nation constituted an important background feature somewhat analogous to the status of Protestantism in the United States. This European prevalence of established churches and the association of religious and cultural identity is still of importance today, in spite of the almost universal decline in the power of the churches and in the level of involvement in them. Although one might be tempted to view this association simply as a kind of cultural inertia or nostalgic habit that is eventually destined to disappear, the equivocal history of the secularization thesis should warn us against this option. As recent scholarly contributions point out,[8] the established churches and Christian identifications still operate in Europe as, in Martin's terms, "shadow" establishments (subtle and seemingly weak, but nonetheless real and even comforting presences), or as effective public memories or heritages. Politically parallel to this continuing positive position of the churches, and of Christian religious heritages in European countries is the still preponderant position of the individual states (more in number now than ever before, almost as many as the vast remainder in the Eurasian land mass), both as territorially and culturally defined units and institutions. The state in Europe is meant to guide and to provide in a way and to a degree that prevails in few other regions of the world, especially since the fall of most state socialist regimes at the end of the twentieth century. The churches, I would contend, by association if not in terms of their actual ability to exercise signify-cant influence, are also still part of this European pattern of expectation when it comes to large overarching institutions.[9]

If we can for the moment accept this contention, then the question that poses itself is how one accords the continuing importance of religion and the churches with the low levels of religious involvement and weak religious authority in Europe, so low and weak that even a repentant secularization theorist like Peter Berger maintains that this is the one region of the world where the theory is valid.[10] And in fact, many countries of Europe show very low levels of religious practice, felt religious importance, and even traditional reli-

---

8 G. Davie, *Religion in Modern Europe: A Memory Mutates* (Oxford, 2000); D. Hervieu-Léger, *La religion pour mémoire* (Paris, 1993); D. Martin, *Pentecostalism: The World Their Parish* (Oxford, 2002).

9 P. Beyer, "Modern Forms of the Religious Life: Denomination, Church, and Invisible Religion in Canada, the United States, and Europe," in D. Lyon / M. Van Die, *Rethinking Church, State, and Modernity* (Toronto, 2000), 189-210.

10 Berger, "Reflections."

gious belief. Moreover, although religious leaders, especially the pope, receive a fair amount of attention, and a significant minority of the population still looks to them for guidance, there is precious little evidence in most countries (there are important exceptions to this) that their words and directives meaningfully condition the outlook and behavior of the vast majority of their supposed flocks. It is of course possible that there is an underlying "religious demand" in European populations that is only waiting for the right conditions (supply) to manifest themselves concretely;[11] but even if this were to be the case – and there is little evidence for this prognosis – we would still have to explain how religion can have the importance that I am claiming for it under the present circumstances of weak religious authority and high level religious privatization. An attempt to answer this question can avail itself of the systemic structural categories that I have introduced, especially the idea of religious respecification.

Looking first at the contingency formula of European Christianity, the God-concept that has prevailed here for quite some time is, as is usual with expressly monotheistic religions, a much generalized one. This is the case even in Roman Catholicism and Eastern Orthodoxy with the relative decline in their popular forms that allow for focus on numerous minor deities such as saints and other lesser spiritual beings. Moreover, what we have also witnessed in most of European Christianity is a decline in the effective religious presence of the main counter-deity, the Devil. The net result is that most if not all religious communication funnels much more directly through a single concept of the divine. This is not necessarily an ineffective strategy if religion is to have concrete influence in societal life, but it does require greater emphasis on other structures of respecification. As indicated above, main candidates in this regard are the binary codings of a given religion. Yet here as well, European Christianity has long taken a path that prevents this trend from, as it were, picking up the slack. Along with the decline in the effective communicative presence of the Devil, European Christianity, like much, if by no means all, of Western Christianity, has accepted a corresponding decline in the real possibility of damnation, thereby rendering its historically central binary coding monopolar in effect. Even in Evangelical forms of Christianity in regions like North America, damnation, while a real possibility, is applicable mostly to those outside the "communion of saints," a vaguely defined group,

---

11 R. Stark and L. Iannaccone, "A Supply-Side Reinterpretation of the 'Secularization' of Europe," in *Journal for the Scientific Study of Religion* 33 (1994): 230-52.

which almost by definition does not operate within the same religious meaning structures. What this means more broadly is that European Christianity cannot use the salvation/damnation code to great effect because half the code is inoperable, limiting its ability to translate events in the world into religiously meaningful terms. Under such circumstances, as indicated above, second or supplementary codings can fill the gap, and here the primary candidate for European Christianity has been and still is the binary code of moral / immoral. Religiously based communications regarding morality are among the mainstays of contemporary religious leaders, ranging from the more conservative censure of illicit sexual behavior to the more liberal condemnation of social injustice. As noted, however, moral interpretations in contemporary society are not the undisputed domain of the religious system; they are possible and happen regularly without any overt reference to religious meaning. One need only think of the distrust that so many Europeans have of genetic engineering, a distrust that appears to be only partially based on the fear of possible health and environmental damage. An additional example might be the current prevailing sentiment against American foreign policy, which also has a moral component that can be (but need not be) religiously grounded. The upshot here is that the use of the moral code to respecify the God-concept is a privatized (not dependent on religious authority) option.

In the absence of other coding possibilities, the European Christian religious system is left to operate at a very high level of generalization: God is in his heaven, which is where it seems the majority of Europeans think he belongs. This does not mean that religion is irrelevant in Europe, nor does it indicate its restriction to the private proclivities of a minority of individuals and voluntary groups. Instead, in the light of the history of their association with state, nation, and even, if one wishes, civilization, God and religion together become a kind of generalized background guarantor of meaning, order, and value, the respecification of which is not accomplished in the religious system itself, but rather in the relation of that system to others. Put somewhat differently, the highly generalized and privatized nature of the religious system is a symptom of a failure to instrumentalize religion to anything matching the degree managed in other systems. Accordingly, that instrumentalization is left, almost by default, precisely to the other, more successfully instrumental systems. In Europe, as in most other rich and powerful regions of global society, the instrumentalization of religion, or the respecification of the God-concept, is accomplished through the other systems, especially the state, the law, education, science, and the health systems; but also systems for the arts and the mass information media. The difference between this situation and one where religion is simply irrelevant (or at least in which it fails to take the form of a differentiated societal system beside the others) can be seen when events conspire to treat the religious system precisely as if it were totally irrelevant. It is in this context that we can understand the specific challenge that contemporary Islam, especially contemporary European Islam, presents.

Christian Europe and the Challenge of Islam

Islam is not the only religion that can be viewed as a challenge to the prevailing lack of respecification and instrumentalization in the broad European Christian religious system. Even within European Christianity, there are minority movements, such as among certain neo-Pentecostals and some conservative Catholics, that promote a publicly and instrumentally effective form of this religion. Nonetheless, for historical, demographic, and geopolitical reasons, but also for reasons particular to strong movements within contemporary Islam, Islam has been the one religion to attract the most attention in this regard, including among European scholars. The historical reasons for this have to do with the fact that Europe to some degree has defined itself over against the adjacent African and Asian territories dominated by Islam. Without Islam, it is difficult to understand how the idea that Europe is a separate continent could ever have attained self-evidence. Demographically, the prevalence of Muslims in recent waves of immigration to Europe has lent a certain ambiguous visibility to Islam as a religious and cultural identity. These, along with questions of citizenship, socio-economic status, and national identity, have all become part of the same problematic related to the challenge of global migration. Geopolitically, militant Islamic movements around the world have contributed their share in keeping this religion and its adherents saddled with a highly politicized image that emphasizes a kind of anti-Western, anti-secular, and highly exclusivist stance. Mixed in with all these factors, however, are characteristic features or resources within Islam itself, elements that relate directly to the structural factors I have already discussed.

In terms of the God-concept, Islam has been, and is still, one of the most clearly monotheistic religions in the world today. Under those modern conditions that pressure religions to reconstruct and define themselves more clearly with respect to other systems and other religions, this monotheism has been emphasized all the more, explaining in part the success and spread of movements such as Wahhabism, Salafism, and neo-Sufism, which emphasize the oneness of God and the centrality of Qur'an and Sunna. Yet such monotheistic and scripturalist emphases are not unique to Islam, they are parallel to, for instance, similar monotheist and scripturalist (or its ultramontanist equivalent) movements in Christianity. Overall, in a great many senses, modern developments in Islam are structurally similar to those in other religions, something that is not surprising given that both have reformed themselves as modern religions, subsystems of a global system of such religions. Where Islam – or at least certain important movements within it – has been different, however, is in the area of binary codings as elements in the structuring, respecification, and instrumentalizing of religions. Here the distinction between salvation and damnation, as found in all three Abrahamic religions, is central; and the moral / immoral polarity has also operated as a significant second coding. In addition, however, the *halal / haram* binary has come to have a peculiar prominence and visibility, especially but not exclusively in so far as it is expressed in terms of Islamic law or Shari'a. To be sure, the idea of processing the world in terms of things that are permitted and things that are forbidden is not at all unique to Islam. Even the strategy of translating this impulse into religio-legal terms is shared by movements in Orthodox Judaism, and it has weaker resonance in the Hindu *dharmasastras* or the Sikh *rahit*. Yet in various contemporary Islamic movements, ranging from the Iranian revolutionary government and movements to institutionalize Shar'ia in various countries, to directions such as the Tablighi Jamaat and the Jamaat i-Islam, to efforts toward "Islamic" everything (state, economics, science, education, sport, arts, entertainment, media, and so forth), the tactic of judging all aspects of life in terms of whether they are enjoined, neutral (i.e. in the final analysis, permitted), or forbidden has gained considerable momentum in Islam, and efforts to carry this out have gone into far greater detail and level of development. These sometimes aggressive, but almost always sincere, endeavors lend a comparatively unique quality to Islam as concerns structures of respecification and instrumentalization. They represent almost the opposite of the prevailing European Christian tendency – whether accepted by the religious leadership or not – to operate as almost a background guarantor for the secularized world of the other instrumental systems. It is, I believe, in this sense that Islam presents a challenge to European sensibilities at the moment. Added to its historical role in representing the European "other," to its association with poor and marginalized immigrants, and to its stereotypical identification with political militancy, Islam's currently greater efforts to instrumentalize itself make it seem to many, peculiarly "un-European."

It is within this context, therefore, that I think we can understand current calls, somewhat unique to Europe, for the formation of a European Islam,[12] or at least for posing the question as to the extent that this is possible.[13] Evidently, for such a European Islam to arise, it is not enough that the number of Europeans practicing Islam increase, nor that Muslims in Europe identify themselves as Europeans. A European Islam means essentially a "tamed" Islam, one that, in the terms that I am using here, accepts a high degree of privatization along with public recognition and a generalized guarantor status that currently characterizes European Christianity. Respecification and instrumentalization should be left, first and in privatized fashion, up to the individual, then publicly to the other systems.

Conclusion

As a way of concluding, it might be instructive to compare the European situation concerning both Christianity and Islam to the situation in North America, another region that is both rich and powerful in current global society. Here Christianity has also historically been the dominant religion, and this is only the first of many similarities that include privatization of the religious system and a high degree of secularization in the other instrumental systems. What is missing, or what is at least far weaker in North America is an effecttive Christian church establishment and the corresponding notion of Christianity as a critical feature of public institutions and of the public chain of memory. (Quebec presents an interesting and partial exception to this pattern and is correspondingly, in terms of the question I am discussing here, the most "European" portion of North America.) In that context, the sense of nation in both the United States and Canada is not or is no longer tied directly or explicitly to Christian identity, even though culturally they still exhibit a whole range of Christian derived orientations ranging from eating habits and family patterns to public holidays and the status of the individual. On the other hand, the level of immigration to these countries from non-Western por-

[12] J. Nielsen, *Towards a European Islam* (Basingstoke, 1999); O. Roy, *Vers un islam européen* (Paris, 1999).

[13] F.J. Buijs / J. Rath, *Muslims in Europe: The State of Research* (Amsterdam, 2003).

tions of the world is significantly higher, although the proportion of those immigrants who are Muslims is also much lower, North American immigration still being dominated by Christians. Additionally, the Muslim populations in North America are more diverse in terms of socio-economic status and, in the United States, include a high percentage of indigenous, mainly African-American Muslims. The high percentage of Christians among the immigrants to North America accentuates the already high level of internal Christian pluralism there, again undermining the possibilities for this religion to act as the sort of "shadow" establishment that it does in most parts of Europe. There are other differences besides, one of the most important of which is the denominational organization of religion, which makes it virtually impossible for any religious group, movement, organization, or orientation to even claim to "speak for" a specific religion, let alone the nation. The net result is that Christianity in North America does not have the overarching status that it has in Europe – and this is in spite of much higher levels of belief and practice in both North American countries, but especially the United States – and neither Christianity nor Islam can claim or hope for the sort of public and official unity and centralized recognition that still seems possible in Europe. What this means is that the level of respecification of the God-concept, or the degree of instrumentalization of religion, makes less of a difference in these countries and in this region. North Americans, by and large, share the popular suspicion of a stereotyped Islam that is common in European countries; after 9/11, Americans especially are probably more paranoid about militant Islam. Yet symptomatically, while there is certainly discussion about the Americanization of Islam,[14] the idea of an American Islam (as opposed to a merely "liberal" or "moderate" or an African-American Islam) has thus far gained no purchase whatsoever. Correspondingly, while the literature on Islam in Europe is dominated by the question of the public status of Islam – the relation of Muslims to the wider society – in North America these questions receive comparatively little attention, while ethnographic, local, and detailed work on Muslim communities, movements, and organizations is multiplying almost beyond the capacity of a single scholar to keep up with it.[15]

In summary then, the God-concept in Europe has a rather different and peculiar importance in Europe, for which it is difficult to find parallels in

---

14 Y.Y. Haddad and J.L. Esposito (eds), *Muslims on the Americanization Path?* (Atlanta, 1998).

15 K. Leonard, *Muslims in the United States: The State of Research* (New York, 2003).

other regions of global society. I have tried here to analyze some of the reasons for this situation by looking at several of the features and the functions of the global religious and other global instrumental systems, which provide the basic structures of global society and therefore also of the European region. I do not claim that what I have offered here is the only way to understand this situation, nor that my conclusions are necessarily all that surprising. What I hope is that these reflections by a partial outsider may contribute in some small way to a better appreciation of how religion can be and remain significant and consequential, even in the otherwise highly secularized context that is the European subcontinent.

Anne Kull

Speaking of God in the New World Order, Inc.

Introduction

The "world scene," referred to as "globalization," is often experienced as a paradox: the world is growing both more global and more divided, more thoroughly interconnected and more intricately partitioned. Cosmopolitanism and parochialism, globalization and provincialism are no longer opposed; they are linked and mutually reinforcing. As one increases, so does the other. Sociologists have referred to this phenomenon with the neologism "glocalization," an abbreviated analytical term that characterizes the complex process of the simultaneous reassertion and increasing relevance of the local and global over the national. But the route to globalization and localization is often not open to choice: what manifests as globalization for some manifests as localization for others; what signals a new freedom for some descends upon untold others as an uninvited and cruel fate. Zygmunt Bauman has described the result as being "willy-nilly on the move." Immobility is not a realistic option in a world of permanent change. And yet the effects of that new condition are radically unequal. Being local in a globalized world is a sign of social deprivation and degradation. When public spaces are removed beyond the reaches of localized life, localities lose their meaning-generating and meaning-negotiating capacities and are increasingly dependent on sense-giving and interprêting actions which they do not control.[1]

Depending on one's sources, globalization can be more about the economy, trade, or technology, especially information technology. Accordingly, the agents of globalization also vary: multinational corporations, the United States, the United Nations, the World Bank, the International Monetary Fund, the World Trade Organization, CNN, Disney, and Hollywood. Some commentators also cite international crime networks. Now we may have to include al-Qaeda. Historically, globalization is a process continuous with modernity, with the capitalist world system, and with the world system of (nation) states. Globalization in its present phase frees capitalism from its territorial-

[1] Z. Bauman, *Globalization: The Human Consequences* (New York, 1998).

juridical embeddedness in state and national economies. Its exact origins, however, cannot be dated.

This vast connectedness and intricate interdependence is also sometimes referred to as the "global village," or by the World Bank as "borderless capitalism." But as it has neither solidarity nor tradition, neither limits nor one center, and because it lacks an integrated wholeness, it is a poor sort of village. And as it is accompanied less by the loosening and reduction of cultural demarcations than by their reworking and multiplication, and, often enough, their intensification, the village is hardly borderless. Where the borders are, and who draws them, who benefits and who falls into misery, is a puzzle of utmost importance. In the process of globalization, the erosion and the undermining of locally entrenched social and cultural "totalities" was triggered by the availability of vehicles of fast travel for bodies and for information. The transport of information, which does not involve movement of physical bodies, or involves moving them only secondarily and marginally, gathered speed faster than the travel of bodies, until the appearance of the computer-served World Wide Web rendered information, in theory as well as in practice, instantaneously available throughout the globe. If the once constitutive idea of a universalized modernity (the intention to broadly equalize life conditions and opportunities) bears some similarity to the condition of globalization, the resemblance is rather superficial. Globalization is less an idea, plan, or blueprint than it is the effect of something that happens everywhere, yet is guided and controlled by nobody. It is the indeterminate, unruly, and self-propelled character of world affairs; it does not have a board of directors or a managerial office; and this centerless event is unintended and unanticipated. Globalization says, "Yes, your actions may have global effects," and "No – we don't know how to plan globally."

For most social scientists, the debate over the meaning of globalization focuses on whether it is centrally and fundamentally a form of economic progress. The new speed in spreading the news globally is part and parcel of economic transformation. In this view, globalization is the liberalization of markets that enable free trade. This also entails the assumption that democratic reforms go hand in hand with "free market" ideology.

Sociologists of religion have rightly insisted that globalization has an important religious dimension. One has only to take note of the ecumenical movements, particularly those after the Second World War, and interfaith movements and dialogues, particularly since the 1970's. A missionary faith such as Christianity cannot afford to reject all aspects of globalization – it must accept and affirm some of them. But the most important aspects of globalization are not those of technology, economics, politics, or of the fact of rapid social change in the abstract. The important aspects are the more than six billion people who are affected and positioned unequally in the process of globalization. The participation of those many faces of globalization within the conversation about globalization is variously situated. Yet those faces are created equally in the image of God, regardless of their politically, economically, or educationally enhanced power. This is a traditional claim, well-known to Christians. But who is paying attention to this claim in Europe? Sociologists have long shown that the institutional churches of Europe play a considerably reduced role now compared to their counterparts of almost any point in European history. The churches are no longer able to command the active allegiance of anything but a small minority of European people (though passive allegiance remains high). No public sanctions exist to prevent the European citizen from opting out of the churches' teachings, either partially or completely.

Yet the churches remain significant players on a different level of social reality. As voluntary organizations, they are both influential and effective, and they compete successfully with comparable institutions. They are, for example, considerably more successful at recruitment than most political parties or trade unions. Often, they are relatively wealthy (especially the churches of Northern Europe). It is also noteworthy that there seems to be no connection between financial strength and the most obvious indicators of religious vitality (in terms of participation). And if one is to inquire as to who goes to church anyway, then according to the European Values Study, for those under thirty-five years of age, the churches appear to have lost their credibility altogether. Of course, Europe's population is aging, and if not for the recent trend toward increased life expectancy, the decline in church attendance would have been even more rapid. If one looks more closely, one will see that in the pews there are predominantly women, and in the leadership positions, mainly men. Also the interrelationships between religion and social class are complicated. In Western Europe, there are churchgoers among the educated and the professional classes; in Central Europe, this pattern is largely reversed, as the less-educated, rural residents are the more frequent churchgoers. In Eastern Europe, the church offered space in which ideologies other than communist could find their place; thus churches were the favored venues for the gatherings of the artistic and intellectual elite. And there are many other variations of this interrelationship, all open to research and reflection. Theology, to its own detriment, has not always picked up where the sociologists, anthropologists, and/or natural scientists have left off.

The New World Order, Inc.

Donna Haraway, a culture critic, historian of science, and biologist from the University of California, Santa Cruz, has used an ironic term to describe this situation, the "New World Order, Inc."[2] The growth of technology, most particularly of communications[3] and the biotechnologies, has knit the world into a single web of information and causality. In this New World Order, Inc., the technical, textual, organic, historical, mythic, economic, and political dimensions of entities, actions, and worlds collapse into one another.[4] This is a matter of fundamental theory and practice, not at the level of "good guys" and "bad guys." It is an imaginary configuration, yet it reflects an actual political situation that brings about fundamental changes in the nature of class, race, and gender in the emerging world order. This new world order is a transition from the comfortable hierarchical dominations of old to frightening new networks. Through transnational enterprise, new cultural and natural forms (human and non-human) are literally brought into being by technological, multi-billion-dollar, interdisciplinary, long-term projects. The New World Order, Inc. affects the home, market, paid work place, state, school, clinic-hospital, and church; and within its structure, the private sector and the military are closely integrated. Among the main features of The New World Order, Inc.,

---

2 One of the first to talk of a New World Order was George Bush, whatever he implied by this. But the context was the end of the cold war and the collapse of the Soviet Union, and the fall of the Berlin Wall in November, 1989. The change was so cataclysmic that even knowledgeable analysts were unable to make basic predictions for a six-month period. Cf. Donna Haraway's *New World Order, Inc.* (New York / London, 1997).

3 Time magazine named Ted Turner, founder of Cable News Network (CNN) as its 1991 "Man of the Year." The award was made in recognition of the political impact of CNN in various international crises, from Tiananmen to the Gulf War to the Soviet coup. The electronic media also succeeded in replacing the print media as the principal source of political news within the United States. Electronic media like the BBC, the CNN and others have had a significant impact on the direction of international political change for decades. Not only direction, but also the speed of change.

4 Advances in weaponry are also of enormous importance. The destructive capability of contemporary weaponry has also internationalized what had been considered the individual defense policies of (imaginarily) sovereign national states.

one must include "a massive intensification of insecurity and cultural impoverishment, with common failure of subsistence networks for the most vulnerable."[5] From the search for security come new forms of insecurity: the modern state and corporate world gather massive amounts of data on citizens, their incomes, their health, their consumption preferences, school and tax records, etc. Computers have made coding, viewing, storing, and recalling information on persons and events faster and more efficient. Almost everything we do creates trails of records. This control system – determining, defining, information-providing, reassuring and frightening – also known as the Information Age (or the transition from modernity to postmodernity) is a home, the natural habitat of technoscientific culture. It is a place where nature and culture are border terms, diffracted constructions.

The Reverse Side of the New World Order, Inc.

The reverse side of the New World Order, Inc. is the "world in pieces" phenomenon, which encourages circumscribed, intensely specific, intensely felt public identities, while at the same time such identities fracture the received forms of political order that attempt to contain them, most notably these days the nation-state. Instead of a few, analogous blocks (East vs. West), we observe many smaller, more diversified, and more irregular ones. Instead of *cuius regio, eius religio,* the globally broadcasted media defines for many what is their proper hope and source of security. Especially in Europe, the fragmentation and crumbling of religious memory and tradition began with the emergence and historical development of modernity. A religious memory that is a unified, integrated, unconscious of itself, and powerful chain of experience has become an illusion of the nostalgic gaze. This is not a matter of lack of information – information is more freely available now than ever before; rather, there is a lack of ability to organize the mass of historical-religious information by relating it to specific lineages with which people authentically and sincerely identify. There is increased mobility (voluntary, and even more, involuntary – the number of refugees is steadily growing); we have great difficulty these days in staying out of one another's way. Differences of belief, sometimes quite radical ones, are, more and more often, di-

5 D.J. Haraway, *Simians, Cyborgs, and Women: The Reinvention of Nature* (New York, 1991), 172.

rectly visible, directly encountered, and ready at hand for suspicion, worry, repugnance, and dispute – or perhaps for tolerance and reconciliation, even for attraction and conversion, although the latter outcomes are, right now, not exactly common. Togetherness comes in many varieties. Dialogue between persons or groups with differing beliefs (if at all permitted) is fragmentary, episodic, or both. Fragmentation means also that consensus, regarding the fundamentals of what should constitute a culture or a religion, seems unlikely to be found in the face of so much discord. Collective selfhood in such a milieu is characterized by the recurrence of familiar divisions and motifs, persisting arguments, standing threats, and memories.

One ordinary and greatly misunderstood exception to the trend toward fragmentation relates to our technologically mediated encounter with our own bodies – technology is no longer external to human life and nature, but internal to its very constitution. The findings of those who call themselves "Cyborg Anthropologists" tell us that there has been a huge, one is tempted to say, ontological shift, not only in the nature of human society, but in that of our very bodies. This mutation has been brought about, on the one hand, by exposure to simulated images in the most traditional media, and, on the other, by the slow penetration into our daily lives of almost invisible technological gadgets, from contact lenses to personal computers. This change can be welcomed, or viewed as threatening. In either case, it raises the question of God. We live in the narratives spaces of our culture, and this can be liberating or oppressive. Theologians must choose how to present the Christian message so that the cyborgs (the real us in Europe – vaccinated, medicated in all ways, trustful of all kinds of medical technologies) find a wholesome course in our rapidly changing world. The social fact of the cyborg also raises the question of human creativity and evil. None of these questions is new, but the stakes are now much higher.

Looking Out From the Inside

In the New World Order, Inc., who are the natives? Those we may be quick to identify as "natives" have not throughout time had a stable viewpoint, but have themselves engaged in questioning their allegiances and their dispositions in private and public networks. Culture is always in the making. In this materials-oriented world, boundary creation and maintenance are testing our imagination. Charting demarcations, locating them, and characterizing the populations they isolate, or at least set off, is at best an arbitrary business, imprecisely accomplished. The discernment of cultural breaks and cultural continuities, the drawing of lines around sets of individuals following more or less different forms of life – other voices in other rooms – is a good deal easier in theory than it is in practice.

Most of us are not very certain who we actually are, what our possibilities and limits are, what our status in nature/culture is, and perhaps more importantly, whether or not we have a future and what it looks like. The loss of presumably rigid boundaries within and between cultures is accompanied by anxiety that we may be losing culture(s) and cultural identities, on the one hand, and nature(s) and natural identities on the other. Yet, there is an important difference between respect for a tradition and nostalgia. Graham Ward writes:

> It is a difference Christian theologians must seek to maintain on theological grounds, for belief in the operations of a Trinitarian God in and through time and creation requires Christian theologians to recognize when a new move is taking place in the history of the world, transforming its cultures. Although God never changes, the acceptance of the Pauline insight that "our salvation is nearer than when we first believed" assumes a divine economy in which the Christ event is continually unfolding in the world, manifesting God's relationship to creation. Eschatology cannot be disassociated from providence. There is a messianic working in time, change, and history that brings about redemption.[6]

Nostalgia has no future, and the backward glance is petrifying.

> It petrifies by fetishizing. The nostalgic gaze sacralizes concepts, objects, forms, and states from the past and reproduces them in a present that simulates and commodifies their pastness. Nostalgia recovers falsely, because, in participating in a sense of bereavement, it recovers only substitutes for a loss of origin or end.[7]

Nostalgia is a dangerous theological temptation; it has pervaded modernity since the nineteenth century, appearing in many guises, from existential estrangement and the sense of historical decline, to an awareness of inauthenticity and the absence of the simple and spontaneous. Nostalgia makes us blind both to the nature and the culture we actually live in.

Nostalgia is timid and panic-struck. And in a state of panic those immersed in nostalgia may turn violent. This is often the case both in international relationships and personal relationships. Fear of change and transformation, theologically speaking, is idolatrous, and psychologically speaking, re-

---

6 G. Ward, "Between Virtue and Virtuality," in *Theology Today* 59 (2002): 55-70.

7 Ward, "Between Virtue and Virtuality," 70.

gressive. Nostalgia and accompanying panic is detectable also in our relationships to nature and culture: a sort of panic about the breach of the borders between nature and culture, the organism and the machine, the physical and nonphysical. Somehow, with the disappearance of borders, reality itself seems to be disppearing.

The last foothold seemed to be the body itself, although the importance of embodiment entered theological discussion relatively recently. But real life is full of surprises, even here. In the 1980s, Donna Haraway suggested that we are all cyborgs, hybrids of (cybernetic) machine and organism. The cyborg is a metaphor, a phenomenological description, a trope, a figuration. There are other analogies or metaphors available in our culture; that is, machine-based analogies – Susan Blackmore's "We are the meme-machines," and Stephen Jay Gould's "The Human is a machine" (regarding the genes, those famous replicators). We also have organism analogies (the human is a rational animal, e.g.). If at first sight, organism metaphors seem nature-friendly, in reality they translate into maintenance of the status quo. They suggest that one must remain at one's place within the hierarchical order. A cyborg is a self-regulating organism that combines the natural and artificial together in one system. Cyborgs do not have to be part human, for any organism/system that mixes the evolved and the made, the living and the inanimate, is technically a cyborg. This would include biocomputers based on organic processes, along with roaches with implants and bioengineered microbes. The cyborg can be seen both as a phenomenological description and as a symbol of cultural (post-) modernity. The cyborg resists any form of categorical symbolization.

Thus, who are our kin in the fully artifactual technonatural world, our natural habitat? What kind of livable world are we trying to build? There is specificity to how we operate with and in the world, and it takes a high degree of sophistication to understand the nuances of our engagement in the New World Order, Inc.

The conjunction of technology and discourse is crucial. Were the cyborg only a product of discourse, it could perhaps be relegated to science fiction, of interest to science fiction lovers, but not of vital concern to the broad culture. Were it only a technological practice, it could be confined to such technical fields as bionics, medical prostheses, and virtual reality. Manifesting itself as both technological object and discursive formation, it partakes of the power of the imagination as well as of the actuality of technology. Imagining the possibilities for transformation is a spiritual matter. The spiritual is of interest to theologians, but spirituality must speak of the real sky and earth, not the zodiac sky or nostalgic nature. Spirituality is the focus on stories and myths of something more that goes beyond the here and now and tells us what the here and now can become.

Cyborg suggests that contemporary practices are unfinished, ongoing, continuously maintained, and something in which one's own practices can potentially intervene. Donna Haraway writes, speaking of feminists, that "'We' do not want any more natural matrix of unity and . . .no construction is whole. Innocence, and the corollary insistence on victimhood as the only ground for insight, has done enough damage."[8]

The advent and probability of (posthuman) cyborgs horrifies some people and excites others. The cyborg will bring out new and old divisions: we see the beginnings of these divisions in the debates on cloning. The Catholic Church and many other institutions and governments call for a ban on human cloning experiments, while scientists sign petitions calling for more research. But cloning is one issue that got political, drawing public attention. Everyday cyborgization happens without dispute or discussion, and without much attention from theologians. One thing is certain; there are many different types of cyborgs and many different ways to categorize them. Cyborgs can be restorative, normalizing, enhancing, and so on. The social implications of extremely intense and intimate relationships between biological and mechanic elements are largely not acknowledged by the broader public. A striking attempt to confront these issues is Steven Spielberg's movie *A.I.: Artificial Intelligence* (2001). Perhaps there are more important distinctions to make than measuring where the biological ends and the machines begin. One might start with justice and injustice, sustenance and destruction, wholesomeness and deficiency, wisdom and stupidity, etc.

Yet one can and should ask: Does the cyborg fit in with our myths and stories? If we look at the Old Testament, it is now widely agreed that the predominant understanding of the human being in the Hebrew Scriptures is holistic and nonreductive physicalist. Many Jewish and Old Testament scholars have argued that biblical anthropology knows nothing of this dualistic picture of a person, which claims that a human being is a composite of two entities, a material body and a spiritual or non-material soul. There is somewhat less agreement on New Testament conceptions of human nature. Some argue that the New Testament presupposes dualism, others ask whether such passages (e.g., Mt 27:50 "He (Jesus) gave up his spirit", also Mt 10:28; Luke 16:19-31;

---

8 Haraway, *Simians, Cyborgs and Women*, 157.

John 12:25; Rev 6:9-11, and a few others) are to be taken literally or metaphorically? Is such talk merely accommodation to the thought of the times, or is it The Biblical Teaching, the core item of our faith? The present theological, philosophical, and scientific considerations tend to reject the sorts of dualisms separating body, mind, and/or soul. Theological reasons include: (1) the claim that dualism is not biblical and that theology ought to reject Greek conceptions in favor of the original Hebraic conceptions of the Bible; (2) the related claim that resurrection of the body (rather than immortality of the soul) was the original Christian account of life after death; and (3) the claim that dualism has led to an un-Christian depreciation of the physical creation. A variety of consequences would follow from the nonreductive physicalist view of the person, not only for theology but also in the fields of ethics, spiritual development, medicine, and psychotherapy.

Yet, we may still ask, doesn't the cyborg figuration introduce another kind of dualism, organic vs. artificial? A short answer is: No. When the culture / nature distinction is radically destabilized (along with its distinctive cohorts – artificial/human, sex/gender, life/death), nature, culture, gender, etc. become boundary concepts. The cyborg needs its organic and artificial components equally; it is not a finished product, but always in the making. The cyborg destabilizes knowledge to make space for faith that "human being" is indefinable, fictional, factual, and fantastic because it is capable of putting one's own mode of being into question. The cyborg has many forms, and none of them is "necessary." Haraway claims that all entities take shape in encounters, in practices; and they are not necessarily natural, or original. The construction of the human is historically specific, and every generation has to make its own decisions. N. Katherine Hayles writes:

> If my nightmare is a culture inhabited by posthumans [another term for the cyborg] who regard their bodies as fashion accessories rather than the ground of being, my dream is a version of the posthuman that embraces the possibilities of information technologies without being seduced by fantasies of unlimited power and disembodied immortality, that recognizes and celebrates finitude as a condition of human being, and that understands human life is embedded in a material world of great complexity, one on which we depend for our continual survival.[9]

[9] N. K. Hayles, *How We Became Posthuman: Virtual Bodies in Cybernetics*, Literature and Informatics (Chicago / London, 1999), 5.

Our most obvious choice is between a military macho-cyborg, a Savior-figure with ever-loaded gun, and a feminist figuration of extended kinship with our human and non-human artificial partners.

The New World Order, Inc. – Intensification

Globalization is a facet of human culture and history undergoing transformation in our time and giving rise to new realities. Terrorism is one of these realities but perhaps not the only significant one. This transformation is expressed in quintessential ways in the phenomenon of globalization, but it is larger than globalization. Ewert Cousins is one of those thinkers who has spoken of this vast set of transforming events in terms of a First and Second Axial Period.[10]

The Axial Period concepts are said to provide a deeper understanding of our times than the terms "modern" and "postmodern." The Axial Period concepts build upon the work of Karl Jaspers, who suggested that in "the period between 800 and 200 B.C.E., peaking at about 500 B.C.E., a striking transformation of consciousness occurred in three geographic regions, apparently without the influence of one on the other."[11] In this period, the great schools of Chinese philosophy (Confucius and Lao-tze) came into existence, and the Upanishads emerged in Hinduism, as well as the new religious traditions of Buddha and Mahavira, the Jewish prophets (Elijah, Isaiah, and Jeremiah) who called forth a new moral awareness, and the Western philosophy of the Greeks – the pre-Socratics, Socrates, Plato, and Aristotle.

The First Axial Period ushered in a radically new form of consciousness. Whereas primal consciousness was tribal, Axial consciousness was individual. This sense of individual identity as distinct from the tribe and from nature is the most characteristic mark of Axial consciousness. From this flowed other characteristics: consciousness that is self-reflective and analytic and that can be applied to nature in the form of scientific theories, to society in the form of social critique, to knowledge in the form of philosophy, and to religion in the form of mapping an individual spiritual journey. This self

10 E. Cousins, "The Convergence of Culture and Religions in Light of the Evolution of Consciousness," in *Zygon: Journal of Religion & Science* 34 (1999): 209-19.

11 Cousins, "The Convergence of Culture and Religions," 211.

reflective, analytic, critical consciousness stood in sharp contrast to primal mythic and ritualistic consciousness.[12]

There was also a loss in this Axial consciousness, namely, the alienation from nature, the tribe, and the organic relationships of community. However, the great religions of the world as we know them today grew out of this period, including Christianity and Islam, the two religions that emerged from the roots of Judaism. "The common structures of consciousness found in these religions are characteristic of the general transformation of consciousness effected in the Axial Period."[13]

If we note the monumental significance of the First Axial Period and its restructuring of human consciousness, we can appreciate the depth and breadth of the assertion that we are now in a Second Axial Period. Cousins writes, "Like the first, it is happening simultaneously around the earth, and like the first, it will shape the horizon of consciousness for future centuries. Not surprisingly, too, it will have great significance for world religions, which were constituted in the First Axial Period. Then it was individual consciousness; now it is global consciousness."[14]

The transformation of consciousness that is engendered by the Second Axial Period is defined over against the First Axial Period, but goes in different directions. The forces of divergence were the critical motor of the earlier transformation, whereas convergence drives the current axial movement. This convergence does not obliterate the identities of the particular persons and groups and identities that inhabit the globe, but in "center-to-center" union, the convergence includes the dynamics of individuation within itself. Teilhard called this double rhythm "complexification." Cousins claims that now "the religions must meet each other in center-to-center unions, discovering what is most authentic in each other, releasing creative energy toward a more complexified form of religious consciousness."[15] Yet we come to know God not only through scriptures and traditions; we come to know God also through our natural-artificial bodies, our (technology enhanced and mediated) senses, our brains, and perhaps through artificial intelligence. We know how faulty and fragile our sense of God can be, and how perverted our ideas of God often

12 Cousins, "The Convergence of Culture and Religions," 213.

13 Cousins, "The Convergence of Culture and Religions," 213.

14 Cousins, "The Convergence of Culture and Religions," 215.

15 Cousins, "The Convergence of Culture and Religions," 216.

are. We also know that our idea of God does not encompass all that can be said about God.

Christianity constituted one of the earliest forms of globalization, and its own standardizations of the ideas such as what constitutes the self, embodiment, and God have deeply influenced global ideas of what constitutes humanity and humanity's destiny.

I said previously said that the present, postmodern condition is a technoscientific one. What is technoscience? While science and technology are clearly different things, they are also mixed together in ways that are impossible to untangle. Their symbiosis is much greater than their respective parts and symbiosis is profoundly changing human culture. For one thing, a majority of all scientists and engineers who have ever lived are alive right now and they are busy! What is this doing to us? The hardest thing about understanding this explosion of new knowledge and new things – surrounding us, inside us, beside, above and below us – is mentally stepping back from it to ask what its key features are. How is the world changing? How to take measure of this intensification by and through technology and science? If we look at scientific activity, it is obvious that the life expectancy of any scientific truth can be expected to drop, thanks to the number of hypotheses offered to replace it. This decline is not caused by ill fate or by chance but by scientific method itself. The more you look, the more you see. Instead of selecting one truth from a multitude, the multitude increases. Instead of moving toward a single truth, historically science leads to multiple, indeterminate, relative, or perhaps better, relational truths. The social consequence of this is the indeterminacy of thought and values that rational knowledge was supposed to eliminate. It has been noticed by many analysts that our current modes of rationality that have served humankind well for centuries are not moving societies forward into a better or more understandable world. Humans are compelled to question their modes of knowing and rationality, not because these are not efficient, but because these are not sufficient –whole realms of the aesthetic, of ethics and religion have been left out.

God and the *imago dei*

Nobody denies that Christians should explain what they mean by saying "God." David Tracy has recently discussed this issue in his article "The Post-

Modern Re-Naming of God as Incomprehensible and Hidden."[16] Many theologians have spoken of the kenotic God, in the attempt to understand how God relates to the world. The term "postmodern" is like a red flag to many a traditional scholar. I must admit I resisted it at first myself. It seemed trendy and quite empty of real meaning. However, gradually it began to seem obvious that certain modern assumptions weren't working any more, and that in modern theologies there are important gaps. Tracy writes that "Post-modern movements of thought, precisely as postmodern, have attempted to think the unthought of modernity. By calling into question the forms of modernity's central self-understanding, including the ontotheological form of modernity's naming of God, postmodern thinkers have initiated new ways, at once radically new and curiously ancient, for naming and thinking God." Tracy points particularly to the aspect in naming and thinking God by the postmoderns who retrieve two radicalized and largely marginalized figures of the tradition: prophets and mystics. The postmodern thinker is far more likely to affirm the positive reality of the notion of the radical incomprehensibility of God and/or the Void, more in the tradition of Pseudo-Dionysios, Scotus Eriugena, Marguerite Porete, Meister Eckhart, and Cusanus. The postmodern understanding of incomprehensibility refers not only to our human finitude and lack of understanding of God, but rather to incomprehensibility as a positive affirmation of God's very reality (Karl Rahner). Is it because of the lesson of Apostle Paul, Augustine, and many others, namely that we are finite and capable only of looking at a confused reflection in a mirror, not yet face to face? Or because humility and timidity have been confused? Our contemporary theologians, attempting to avoid arrogance and idolatry, have placed constraints on what we can say about God.

Suspicion is a theological theme in relation to the doctrine of the fall. It traces how thinking can go wrong as an after-effect of the fall. Finitude is also a theological theme, perhaps more in relation to the doctrine of creation. Both themes are intimately connected with theological anthropology. Theological anthropology attempts to determine the proper niche of humanity, regarding nature from one angle, and regarding God from another. What is the image of God in humans, and what is our relationship with God about? Is it a competition (generally a disapproved option), submission (approved by Islam, ambivalent to approval by Christianity), or co-creation? Are we copying God's

16 D. Tracy, "The Post-Modern Re-Naming of God as Incomprehensible and Hidden," in *Cross Currents* 50 (2000): 240-47.

deeds in our activities, or translating God's creativity into human creativity in a context dependent way? Are we determined by God or interpreting, according to our best understanding, the unfolding of our destiny in God's creation? Are we, as theologians, de-contextualized brains in the vat, or are we deeply embedded, coherent with, or congruous with our world?

At the intersection of the global and the local, of theology and technonature, of church and academy, the concrete question we face is whether or not Christian theology should give up the notion of humanity as created in the "image of God" in light of discoveries in and challenges from biology, cosmology, and the computer sciences. The answer is maybe, yes, and maybe, no. In what sense "maybe?" In the afterlife of modernity, we have become aware of the need for theology to move beyond facile confessionalism and accept the responsibilities and challenges of public discourse, discourse that is not *a priori* immunized from transcommunal critique. A post-foundationalist understanding of rationality suggests that we can no longer hide behind a simple fideism that begins with the assumption that "our" tradition has the final interpretation and absolute truth about what God is like and how God is imagined. Like all human endeavors, theology is fallible, and like most human endeavors, it is corrigible and correctable. More and more often it can be found that God is described as the ground of being, of becoming, or of new possibilities. Abstract and non-personal (although often communal) terms are used to describe our relationship to God. The mythical and the most primitive idea of God as a supernatural being who interferes with natural events, or is an independent cause of natural events, does not ring true to most contemporaries. Yet, for doxological purposes, personalist language is quite appropriate.

Perhaps the most important contribution of the early Reformers was their radical and revolutionary focus on justification by faith alone. This opened space for speaking of "human being" not in abstract metaphysical terms, but in historical terms as created and addressed by the Word. Calvin made it clear that we should interpret the image primarily in light of Jesus Christ; the reparation of the image will shed light on the original nature of the image (I.15.4). For Luther, to be Christian is to be in the making (*Christianus est in fieri*), which is suggestive for our theme of the emergence of meaningful talk about God and the human being in the context of the technoscientific New World Order, Inc. Clear articulation of these intuitions was inhibited, however, by the fact that neither they nor their followers challenged the classical way of asking the question: namely, what happened to the substance of the human soul after the image was lost? Although Genesis does not say that the image was lost, this question continued to dominate the discussion.[17] The reformers also opened the door to the idea that links the *imago dei* to our human destiny, although the groundwork for this idea lay in Irenaeus's Christological proposal that Jesus is the "recapitulation" of the human story. It is the idea that the *imago dei* is ultimately God's intention and goal for humans; it is a movement with a goal. To be recognizably in the tradition of Christian thought, we cannot abandon the notion of *imago dei* but we may have to reconsider what it means. The concept of destiny seems more adequate to express the dynamics of nature-culture.

Preliminary Conclusions

The first and most general proposal is that we should abandon the persistent thought model that God's glory is magnified when nature is conceived as purely passive, and that God's power, correspondingly, is diminished if God's creatures are empowered. Even if it is advisable to let God be The God, to accept that God is free to reveal God-self in ways left up to God-self, it does not necessitate the understanding that God forbids active searching and creativity on the part of humans and the rest of nature. The concept of omnipotence has actually always meant that there are things God could not do (e.g., to lie) and that God, de facto, has chosen to cooperate with the powers of the creatures that were given by God in the first place.[18] Gregersen has pointed out that the term "the almighty God" should be understood "within the grammar of Christian practice – that is, as an invocation of God by believers who already understand themselves as participating in a two-way communication with God."[19] And as all priests and ministers have learned in their pastoral ministry, ordinary believers are seldom guided and informed by systematic doc-

---

17 F. LeRon Shults, "Imago Dei and the Emergence of Sapiential Life," in N. H. Gregersen / Chr. Hjollund (eds), *Coping with Evil: Perspectives from Science & Theology* (Aarhus, 2003), 104.

18 E.g., Thomas Aquinas, *Summa Theologiae* I:25 (on the meaning of divine omnipotence) and the doctrine of the divine-human cooperation in the concursus of divine providence that was held in common by Catholics, Lutherans, and Reformed.

19 N. H. Gregersen, "The Creation of Creativity and the Flourishing of Creation," in *Currents in Theology and Mission* (Festschrift for Philip Hefner: Created Co-Creator) 28 (2001): 404.

trines, not simply because they have seldom studied theology, but because ordinary life does not work in that way. What could this mean for the destiny of systematic theology? For one thing, it is easy to see why theologians' descriptions of faith are often resisted, because many traditional believers do not recognize their own way of living and understanding in what the theologians write. From the other side, systematic expositions of faith and doctrines may be necessary, or at least conducive, to growth in sensitivity to God's nature and presence in all contexts.

Perhaps it is crucial for humans not to focus on the question of existence of God as such (*Ding an sich*), but rather on the how question: How we can speak of God without arrogant and imperialist inflection and yet dare to make knowledge claims about God? Are our concepts of "culture" and "nature" and the other terms available to us reliable? Philip Hefner has a helpful designation, the "created co-creator." "Homo sapiens are God's created co-creator," he says, "whose purpose is the 'stretching/enabling' of the systems of nature so that they can participate in God's purposes in the mode of freedom."[20]

The created co-creator is an abstraction of Christian beliefs about God and the human-God relationship; however, it receives its specific content from the cyborg at the present historical moment. Yet the created co-creator also contributes to the cyborg: it gives the cyborg an ever-needed narrative of hope and ambiguity, of transformation that is connected with the Christian mythos of reliability and renewable character of our world. The cyborg does not know how to talk about itself religiously. Yet the emergence of cyborgs does not mean that the Christian narrative, or other narratives available to us, cease to exist. In fact, these narratives will configure, to a great extent, the kinds of cyborgs we will become.

To use punctuation as a metaphor, God apparently created by inaugurating a colon rather that a period. The world is given, and yet it is in the process of unfolding. Thus being a creature means enjoying the gifts of life and actively participating in God's creative works. God's creativity not only sets the scene of creation, but also supports and stimulates the productivity of the creatures. Humanity is not in the center of creation by being separated from other creatures, but by being placed in the midst of nature *as* nature. Humanity stands in kinship relationship with the rest of nature, yet how we are to conceptualize and live this understanding is a highly debated issue.

---

[20] P. Hefner, "Biocultural Evolution and the Created Co-Creator," in Ted Peters (ed.), *Science and Theology: The New Consonance* (Boulder, 1998), 185 and *passim*.

It is ironic – and God seems to love irony – that just now, when theologians have barely accommodated the so-called Epic of Evolution with their worldview (despite the fact that it has functioned in one form or another as a contemporary creation myth that is taught to children in the schools), they must factor the human technological creation into all of this. It seems that for theologians it has been easier to accept creativity and change in the rest of nature than in the realm of human technological creativity.

How to relate both globalizing and localizing tendencies to the belief in One Trinitarian God in the age of technoscience? One should insist that both of these tendencies must be intensified, that neither can be collapsed in favor of the other. And doubtlessly, for the established churches it is not the most comfortable situation: for many it may simply appear to be a sign of capitulation to the secular spirit. Intellectually, the challenge is in conceptualizing the belief that God is intrinsic within the process of nature-culture and that Christ is at the very core of the movement of the world process toward its final destiny. Practically, it means that while the churches are still overwhelmingly prescientific and nostalgic in their attitudes, the theologians must do the work of elaborating the concept of God that would be the sufficiently reasonable response to account for the trustworthiness of the process of culture-nature, both in its intense globalization and fragmentation. We must put our knowledge (and that includes technoscientific knowledge) and experience (and that includes, but is not limited to, religious experience) of the world together in a coherent way that supports values, sustainable ways of living, and moral behavior. The spiritual does not contradict the material. The spiritual refers to the way in which our consciousness is organized. And it is a challenge to our religious communities to provide meaningful understandings of what the evolving world can become.

John D'Arcy May

Europe's God: Liberator or Oppressor? The Postcolonial Mediation of Transcendence

Europe's God is Israel's God, and therein lie both the historical dynamism that has propelled Europe to world dominance and the historical dilemmas of European Christianity's compromises with power: its justification of war, its religious intolerance, its complicity in colonialism, its responsibility for the Holocaust, and its assertions of superiority.

It makes a considerable difference whether one believes in a universal principle (*Tao, Brahman*) or in a personal being (*Yahweh, Allah*) who can demand loyalty and intervene in history.[1] Europe's history with this God who lays claim to absolute truth and boundless love has made Europe – and the broader world influenced by five centuries of European domination – what it is today. At the same time, this history has also brought forth a God in Europe's image. Here we can see the God of Israel transformed into God as defined by Church dogma; the God of Abraham, Isaac, and Jacob, the God and Father of our Lord Jesus Christ, becomes assimilated to the God of the philosophers and theologians, and the consequent influences on the interpretation of scripture are subtle but clear.[2] To the precise extent to which the evangelization of peoples by European missionaries has been successful, the God of Israel has been mediated for other cultures by specifically European conceptions of the divine. Many have become Christians who know nothing of Europe and who seek their own religious identity, and some of these people are beginning to resist European models of Christianity. In what follows, it is my purpose to show that God as understood in Europe will be understood much better if the mediation of transcendence becomes culturally multifaceted and ethically self-conscious.

---

1 Cf. R. Stark, *One True God. Historical Consequences of Monotheism*, Princeton / Oxford, 2001), ch. 1. Looking at monotheism as a sociologist, Stark maintains that the historically significant religions are based on some sort of supernatural exchange with the divine, and that as societies develop they have "fewer gods of greater scope" (23).

2 See R.S. Sugirtharajah (ed.), *The Postcolonial Bible* (Sheffield, 1998), especially the editor's own contribution, "A Postcolonial Exploration of Collusion and Construction in Biblical Interpretation," 91-116.

To speak as if there could be *alternative* Gods to "Europe's God" is of course to make a mockery of divine transcendence. In proclaiming God as either Liberator or Oppressor, we are indulging in projections, imaginings, and conceptualizations, which, strictly speaking, state nothing about God in Godself. In this sense, talk about God is impossible in any language, and by rights we should reject any attempt to name God or fashion an image of God, just as Jews and Muslims do. Yet Christians who believe they have received the gift of faith by the grace of revelation have no choice, for when we take our lead from the Jesus of the Gospels and speak to God with the easy familiarity of childhood it is "the Spirit herself bearing witness with our spirit that we are children of God" (Rom 8:16), because "the Spirit herself intercedes for us with sighs too deep for words" (Rom 8:26). Ours is the "Christlike God" revealed in the life, death, and resurrection of Jesus.[3]

But when we turn, as we must, to give an account of this God in the manifold conceptualities of theology, we find that "we" – Europeans or Christians who share European traditions – no longer speak with undisputed authority. Our understandings of God, although sanctioned by councils and hallowed by tradition, are contested by new voices that are in fact echoes from our missionary and colonial past. Liberation theologies have questioned whether the God projected by Europe was not in fact the distorted symbol of oppression; the dialogue of religions has disclosed wholly different ways of conceptualizing transcendence; feminist and ecological theologies have laid bare the patriarchal and individualistic bias encoded in traditional God language. We are beginning to realize that the crises being experienced in Christology, ecclesiology, and spirituality have deeper roots in an uncertainty about who God is or may be,[4] and what it means to "know" or "see" God. The absolute transcendence of God as *totaliter aliter*, God's immutability, omniscience, and omnipotence, are called into question by attempts to have God participate in the cosmic process and the history of suffering. In our search for ways of transforming European images of God in order to make them more receptive to this multiplicity of mediations, we shall first take a closer look at the postcolonial situation as it affects theology. We shall then try to discern the echoes of transcendence mediated to us by other voices using different languages for the divine and modulated by experiences of dominance. In conclusion, we

3 See J.V. Taylor, *The Christlike God* (London, 1992).

4 See R. Kearney, *The God Who May Be: A Hermeneutics of Religion* (Bloomington / Indianapolis, 2001).

shall formulate some questions that arise for European theology from the confrontation of postmodernism with postcolonialism.

Postcolonialism and Postmodernity: Europe as Creator and Creature of Globalization

It is no longer possible to speak of "Europe" without at the same time speaking of Western Europe's colonial past. Europe *is* what it has *become* as a result of this history of exploration and conquest. By the same token, however, one cannot speak of the "modern world" – which is no longer identical to the "West" – without referring to Europe's internal religious struggles, revolutions, and wars. Europe's colonial expansion has created the global disorder out of which a "world order" is slowly and painfully emerging. The "West" originally meant the preeminence of the Latin Christianity of Western Europe over the Greek Orthodoxy of the East. Much later, after reason and science had wrested intellectual hegemony from theology, the concept of "modernity" arose to characterize the West. These developments crystallized around the Renaissance, the Reformation, and the Enlightenment, reaching a symbolic turning point in 1648, when the Peace of Westphalia marked not only the end of the religious wars that had devastated Europe but also a quest for intellectual certainty which superseded Medieval pluralism and the skepticism of Renaissance humanism.[5] The resulting rationalism assisted at the birth of the modern "subject," for which the rest of reality becomes "object" and periphery (Descartes' *cogito ergo sum* with its spirit / matter dualism, Nietzsche's *Wille zur Macht*, Hegel's *geschichtslose Völker*). But a less Eurocentric historiography locates the key developments that led to modernity much earlier, in 1492, the date that marks the "discovery" of a New World from Europe's point of view. This event became constitutive of Europe's self-awareness as the Christian and therefore civilized "West," in contradistinction to the schismatic East, the Islamic heresy, and the alien paganism of America, Asia, and Africa. Before 1492, the "West" meant the Hellenistic, the Roman,

---

5 This theme is developed persuasively by S. Toulmin, *Cosmopolis: The Hidden Agenda of Modernity* (Chicago, 1990), and by D. Loy, *A Buddhist History of the West: Studies in Lack* (Albany, 2002), especially ch. 4, "The Lack of Modernity." For its ecumenical relevance, see J.D. May, "European Union, Christian Division? Christianity's Responsibility for Europe's Past and Future," in *Studies* 89 (2000): 118-29.

the Christian; after 1492, "modernity" means the European, Western, and capitalistic.[6]

Modernity as a concept, but also as the myth of unlimited power and the right to use violence in the name of "progress" and "development," takes its rise at exactly this point. Europe *invents* a world it imagines it has "discovered." Each *conquistador* found the New World he wanted to find. Europe defined itself by defining the conquered peoples as polar opposites, as fundamentally "other" and for that very reason as destined to become the "same" as Europeans, wherever necessary by force. Terrible as the physical violence was that was unleashed on the conquered peoples, its full destructive potential can only be measured by the *cognitive* violence that wiped out cultures and religions simply because they were not Christian, which was as much as to say "not European." "European" meant not only superior but universally valid: "our" values are *general* values, to which others are morally obliged to conform. Europe's failed attempt to subdue Islam in this way is now having fateful consequences.

The necessary counterpart of this Eurocentrism was Orientalism, the attitude of mind that lent literary and scientific respectability to the disqualification of everything in the cultures, morals, and politics of the "others" that was not European.[7] As Europeans systematically plundered the precious metals of South America using slaves from Africa – thus laying the foundations of the capitalist economy that financed later industrial and military expansion – indigenous medicines, agriculture, technology, and science, in many cases supe-

6 Here and in what follows I base myself on the idiosyncratic but illuminating interpretation of the "transmodern" by E. Dussel, *Von der Erfindung Amerikas zur Entdeckung des Anderen: Ein Projekt der Transmoderne* (Düsseldorf, 1993), who in addition to detailed first-hand research makes extensive use of T. Todorov, *The Conquest of America: The Question of the Other* (New York, 1989). I am also grateful for discussion with my former student Søren Asmus, whose M.Phil. dissertation (*I is an Other: Dialogue as First Theology – Emmanuel Levinas and Henning Luther as Sources for Ecumenical Theology*, Irish School of Ecumenics, Trinity College, [Dublin, 1996]) brilliantly analyzed modernity from this perspective and who pointed out to me the parallels between the treatment of the proletariat in Europe and the subject peoples in the colonies (personal communication, 25 January 2003). Britain's treatment of the Irish over many generations can stand as a paradigm of both styles of domination.

7 Since E. Said's *Orientalism: Western Conceptions of the Orient* (London, 1991 [1978]) and *Culture and Imperialism* (London, 1994) the term has entered into the debate about "postcolonial theory," see B. Moore-Gilbert, *Postcolonial Theory: Contexts, Practices, Politics* (London, 1997).

rior to those of Europe, were deliberately destroyed to make way for European markets and manufactures.[8] In this context and in this sense Europe became the "center," the rest of the world, its "periphery." The *conquista* was justified because the "others," who were lazy, stupid, and childish by nature, were to blame for their own subjugation: they had not been able or willing to grasp that civilization, education, and development are historical necessities. This general attitude transferred easily to religion: to be Christianized, which was the equivalent of being civilized, meant to accept the indubitable truths of the Christian faith and the moral and intellectual values it inspired as the sole path to salvation. This faith, however, was presented exclusively in terms that had found acceptance in Europe. Any other possible way of expressing it was dismissed as inconceivable.

This sketch of the European colonial heritage is admittedly rough to the point of caricature, but it could be verified either explicitly or between the lines of many a missionary diary, letter, or report. To the extent that it constitutes a theology, it represents the heritage of five centuries of European world domination, but it also hints at the challenge now facing European Christianity. The entrenched certainty that European values are universally valid and superior to all others is collapsing (indeed, in my view "postmodern" thinking is a symptom of the resulting collective nervous breakdown, as the "clear and distinct ideas" to which thinkers such as Descartes and Leibniz aspired are found to be neither certain nor universal). Europeans are beginning to realize that they can no longer *be* Europeans without acknowledging these rejected, exploited, and oppressed "others" as part of a human community that is wider and more diverse than Europe's own ethnic and religious plurality, but is only grudgingly being acknowledged in the integrity of its difference.[9] As a result, an "ethic of otherness" is emerging.

Another reason why it is impossible to speak of Europe without being aware of these five centuries of domination is that Europe is not only the

---

8 See C. Alvares, *Decolonizing History: Technology and Culture in India, China and the West 1492 to the Present Day* (New York: / Goa, 1991).

9 See J.D. May, *Transcendence and Violence: The Encounter of Buddhist, Christian and Primal Traditions*, New York / London, 2003), ch. 1, where I call this "internalizing the primal other" with respect to the Australian Aborigines. Theo Sundermeier, *Den Fremden verstehen: Eine praktische Hermeneutik* (Göttingen, 1996) rightly points out that the European human sciences, including theology, have so far failed to face the "strangeness" of the other; they can see the European in the others and the others in their difference from Europe, but not yet the others in and as themselves.

creator of the resulting "modern" world, but also its *creature*. The reaction of the rest of the world to Europe's provocation has affected modern Europe and made it what it now is. To its surprise, Europe is learning that it *can* be defined – by others.[10] What Europe once defined as its periphery is now – to the extent that neocolonial dependency allows – politically independent and culturally autonomous, and imploding upon Europe in the form of immigrants, refugees, and asylum seekers. Although they bring with them economic stimulus, cultural enrichment, and religious diversity, as the histories of immigrant countries such as Canada and Australia show, they nevertheless confront the Europe of nation states with a formidable challenge at the very time it is preoccupied with integrating its own considerable ethnic diversity. The role of Christianity in all this is far from clear, but there is no point in harking back nostalgically to Medieval Christendom as an overarching, religiously sanctioned social order. The Basel Ecumenical Assembly of European Churches (1989) explicitly rejected any such proposal.

The ghosts of past imperialisms are thus the uninvited guests at the banquet of European prosperity: for the French, the Algerians, Vietnamese, and West Africans; for the English, the Irish, Indians, Pakistanis, Singhalese, West Indians, Nigerians, and East Africans; for the Germans, the Jews, Slavs, and Turks. When the transparent foil of the United States of Europe is taken away, a tapestry of ethnic, cultural, linguistic, and religious groups is laid bare: Basques, Catalans, Bretons, Celts, Slavs, the few remaining Jews, and many more, often with deep cultural roots in particular *places* (Ireland, Wales, Serbia, Kosovo, the Basque country). As if on a palimpsest, the handwriting of Europe's indigenes becomes legible, mingled with that of Hindus, Sikhs, Buddhists, Muslims, and neo-pagans. The political and legal frameworks that could contain such diversity do not yet exist.

Many of those who are seriously concerned about urgent problems of cultural autonomy and intercultural understanding in schools and workplaces, in civil and criminal law, and in social policy instinctively want to make the "others" (who present problems precisely because of their otherness) *like us*, to Europeanize them, so that we can then apply *our* rights, laws, and values to them. Today's liberals thus resemble the well-intentioned missionaries of yes-

---

[10] "Es mag Europa überraschen, dass Europa heute interpretierbar geworden ist", R. A. Mall, "Interkulturelle Philosophie und die Historiographie," in M. Brocker / H. Nau (eds.), *Ethnozentrismus: Möglichkeiten und Grenzen des interkulturellen Dialogs*, (Darmstadt, 1997), 69-89, 71; *idem*, *Philosophie im Vergleich der Kulturen: Interkulturelle Philosophie – Eine neue Orientierung* (Darmstadt, 1995).

teryear. While it must be acknowledged that decisive developments in areas such as individual freedom, democracy, the rule of law, human rights, and the unhindered pursuit of knowledge did occur in Europe, the impression still lingers that Europe, because it was Christian, was the *only* source of these values for the whole of humanity. Europe, which once inflicted its internal wars and ideological conflicts on the entire world, has nevertheless become an experiment in peacemaking on a hitherto unparalleled scale and has taken important initiatives in non-violent conflict resolution, the implementation of human rights, the seeking of debt reduction for the least developed countries, and the enforcement of ecological standards. A comparison with current US policies makes clear how stark the contrast is between European postcolonialism and American neo-imperialism.

The result of this reciprocal development – Europe as both creator and creature of modernity and globalization – is an extremely complex process of communication at many levels, in many media, and in many cultural idioms. This amounts to the emergence of a global public sphere in which symbolic exchanges of various kinds are continually being negotiated.[11] The body of writing known as "postcolonial theory" is an attempt to formulate the paradoxes and contradictions implicit in this process. It was inspired by what used to be called "Commonwealth literature," the realization in metropolitan Britain that settler societies such as Australia, New Zealand, and Canada as well as the former colonies of Asia and Africa were producing serious literature in English which drew on sources other than British culture and experience (the French reception of writers such as Aimé Césaire and Léopold Senghor followed a different pattern, for they were regarded as representatives of French culture *outre-mer*, but the challenge of Fanon, Foucault, and Derrida was all the more radical when it came). Another powerful impulse was given by Edward Said's *Orientalism* and *Culture and Imperialism*, which demonstrated, through examples from their own classical literary and historical works, that the high cultures of Britain and France were themselves dependent on the colonial exploitation that provided the economic basis for higher education, humanistic scholarship, and literary activity (Jane Austen's *Mansfield Park*,

11 See J.D. May, "Contested Space: Alternative Models of the Public Sphere in the Asia-Pacific," in N. Brown / R. Gascoigne (eds.), *Faith in the Public Forum*, Adelaide: Australian Theological Forum 1999, 78-108; id., "God in Public: The Religions in Pluralist Societies," in *Bijdragen* 64/3 (2003): 1-16.

whose heroine lives with relatives in a stately home financed by slave plantations in the West Indies, is a good example).[12]

As Said demonstrated and Homi Bhabha confirms, the European construction of the colonial "other" arose out of a mixture of awe and contempt, fascination and terror, and took the shape of colonial fantasies that owed more to Europe's denial and repression of the human realities with which it was confronted than to scientific objectivity.[13] Christian missionary education, according to Bhabha, played a key part in this. It produced what he calls "colonial mimicry," designed to be "the same" as European culture, but "not quite," so that the rationale for domination remained intact. The Bible as the Word of God in the language of the colonizers evoked a "sly civility" which hid the indigenes' refusal to accept it under a cloak of acquiescence.[14] The Europeans' "essentialism of difference" led to the formation of hybrid cultures. The "denied knowledges" that remained nevertheless reasserted themselves, first as "traces" in the dominant metropolitan discourse, and later as statements of "colonial contra-modernity" in the metropolitan languages.[15] With the displacement brought about by mass migration to the metropolitan centers, the problems of the "transnational" became problems of the "translational." The resulting tensions and misunderstandings suggest "cultural difference and incommensurability," which "unsettles the liberal ethic of tolerance and the pluralist framework of multiculturalism."[16]

Postcolonial theory has shown a tendency toward becoming increasingly abstruse and abstract.[17] Its themes are foreshadowed vividly by novelists such

---

12 See Said, *Culture and Imperialism*, ch. 2/II, also 3/III on Yeats.

13 See H. Bhabha, *The Location of Culture*, London / New York, 1994), 77, with reference to fetishism as the "masking" of difference in narcissistic fantasy; 82-83 on the ambivalence of colonial fantasy; 132 on the difference between *Verleugnung* and *Verdrängung* in Freud.

14 See Bhabha, *Location of Culture*, 85-92 on mimicry; 98-99 on the source of the expression "sly civility."

15 See Bhabha, *Location of Culture*, 110-15 on hybridism and difference, 173-75 on "reading against the grain" of the metropolitan world in order to contest its assumptions.

16 See Bhabha, *Location of Culture*, 172-74, 177.

17 See Ph. Darby's introductory chapter to P. Darby (ed.), *At the Edge of International Relations: Postcolonialism, Gender and Dependency*, London and New York, 1997), 12-32, where he criticizes the postcolonialists, including Bhabha, for moving away from their Third World moorings to essentialize, universalize and de-historicize their topic – exactly what they accuse Eurocentric thinkers of doing.

as E.M. Forster (*A Passage to India*), Joseph Conrad (*Heart of Darkness, Lord Jim*) and V.S. Naipaul *(A Bend in the River, In a Free State, Half a Life*), and it is difficult to say what outcomes it envisages in concrete terms, but it does capture the communicational dilemmas of those whose displacement forces them to live within multiple identities. It also drops European theology a large hint: if European theologians were re-read in full awareness of *their* postcolonial context, could their grandiose theologies too be "deconstructed" to reveal layers of interest – of which they are scarcely aware – underlying their apparently pure doctrinal content? This exercise in *Ideologiekritik* with its suspicion of *mauvaise foi* now becomes our agenda.

Traces of Dominance and Mediations of Difference

I first became aware of what European theology might look like when refracted through the prism of extra-European culture and experience upon reading Thomas Ohm's book on Asian critiques of Western Christianity in the 1960s.[18] It is easy to accuse Ohm of essentialism for speaking of "Asia in general" yet drawing typical examples from widely different contexts, but his experience was generally first hand, and he was ready to admit that there was more than a "grain of truth" in many of the criticisms he heard. Again and again, he reports Asian readings of Western Christian doctrines and attitudes that disturb the complacency of doctrinal orthodoxy, whether Catholic or Protestant, and show that missionary preaching and piety had quite unintended effects.

I had another such experience while attending consultations at the Ecumenical Institute in Bossey in 1976 at which Asian and African theologians were emphatic in their rejection of European models ("we want love, not logic," "we've had enough of your Karls'" – although it struck me that the terms of the debate were basically those of dialectical theology in pre-war Germany: Barth vs. Bultmann!).[19] The African contributors and the African American theologian James Cone argued that the assertion of culturally specific alternatives to Western formulations and practices forces the Western churches to become aware of their hidden agenda of domination; the Asians,

18 T. Ohm, *Asiens Kritik am abendländischen Christentum* (Munich, 1948). The book is based on talks given in the early 1940s in various parts of Germany.

19 J.D. May, "Kulturelle Identität und wirtschaftliche Abhängigkeit als Probleme ökumenischer Kommunikation," in *Una Sancta* 32 (1977): 70-83.

among them Christopher Duraisingh and Wesley Ariarajah, insisted on the theological acknowledgement of religions that owe nothing to Christianity. The paper presented by Ludwig Rütti systematized this situation of ecumenical non-communication in a way that only needs some updating to retain its validity for today.[20] Rütti broadens the scope of what is widely taken to be "ecumenism" – i.e, the effort to overcome the separation of the European churches in the Great Schism and the Reformation – in the light of the Edinburgh missionary conference in 1910 (which is usually regarded as the birthplace of the modern ecumenical movement) and links the ensuing crisis of the missionary movement with a crisis of Western identity. The specifically ecumenical questions raised by the "success" of Western missions – the tensions and misunderstandings caused by attempts to "adapt" and "inculturate" European Christianity in Latin America, Asia, Africa and the Pacific – were not squarely faced in the context of Western dominance and Third World dependence. More specifically, the "primal" religions of indigenous cultures raised the question of ethnic identity; the "universal" religions of Asia questioned the exclusiveness of Christian claims; and the economic "dependency" institutionalized by the neocolonial order stimulated theologies of liberation, which in turn inspired black and feminist theologians. In this context, Christian theology was unmasked as the ideology of Christian superiority, the so-called absoluteness of Christianity, which placed it beyond criticism, comparison, or alternatives and linked it indissolubly with the project of Western domination.[21] Though there is a sense in which every religious belief system has an irreducible core of conviction unique to itself, the acknowledgement and expression of which is an intrinsic part of its theology or equivalent mode

---

20 L. Rütti, "Westliche Identität und weltweite Ökumene," in P. Lengsfeld (ed.), *Ökumenische Theologie: Ein Arbeitsbuch* (Stuttgart, 1980), 285-96. I made sure that this rigorous analysis was included in this otherwise rather Europe-centered project carried out by the Catholic Ecumenical Institute, University of Münster; see also my *Sprache der Einheit*, 251-84.

21 On this, see J.D. May, "Vom innerchristlichen zum interreligiösen Dialog," in Lengsfeld, *Ökumenische Theologie*, 426-32; see also the hard-hitting analysis of the problems caused for the Christian ecumenical movement by interreligious dialogue in S. Wesley Ariarajah, *Hindus and Christians: A Century of Protestant Ecumenical Thought* (Amsterdam / Grand Rapids: Eerdmans, 1991); *idem*, "The Impact of Interreligious Dialogue on the Ecumenical Movement," in J.D. May (ed.), *Pluralism and the Religions: The Theological and Political Dimensions* (London, 1998), 7-21; and J.D. May, "Is Interfaith Dialogue Undermining Interchurch Dialogue? Ecumenics as the Framework for an Integral Ecumenism," in O. Rafferty SJ (ed.), *Reconciliation: Essays in Honour of Michael Hurley* (Dublin, 1993), 159-75.

of self-understanding, in the age of European colonial expansion it did not seem to occur to European theologians that Europe too is a context and European theology a succession of local theologies, nor that acknowledgement of core religious visions can be mutual.[22] Only now is it being realized that relations between religions must be *two-way* and *twin-track*: if the autonomous center of the tradition can neither be deduced from historical and cultural factors nor compromised by comparisons, it is equally true that it would never come to full self-realization if it were not communicated to "religious others" through social media such as scriptures, rituals, and institutions.

It thus becomes necessary to relativize Christian claims without abandoning the specificity of Christian faith. Though much progress has been made in the dialogue between Christian Europe and its New World and Third World "peripheries," and though Europe is no longer the only "center" in a polycentric world, the danger still exists in the establishments of Western learning that liberation theology will be domesticated, the interreligious dialogue neutralized, and feminist and ecological theologies marginalized. Russian, later Greek Orthodoxy, despite the enormous dialogical potential of Trinitarian theology and the lead given by outstanding individuals such as V.N. Lossky (1903-58), G.V. Florovsky (1893-1979), and John Zizioulas, has been fully preoccupied with mediating the Greek patristic tradition to the Latin West, whose theologies it sees as being modernist and abstract (one great exception – in the non-Chalcedonian context of Oriental Orthodoxy – being Paulos Mar Gregorios of India, who pursued the dialogue with both the sciences and the religions).[23] As a result, Orthodoxy still seems profoundly suspicious of all other "inculturations" of apostolic Christianity and hostile to the relativizing tendencies of interreligious dialogue. Protestant theology appears increasingly polarized between liberal pluralism and fundamentalist evangelicalism, unless one finds the attempts by thinkers such as Wolfhart Pannenberg and Jürgen Moltmann to mediate between history and eschatology convincing; and the Roman Catholic Church, after having been persuaded to accept the study of doctrines in their historical contexts by pioneering historians of theology such as Yves Congar and Henri de Lubac, is reasserting

---

22 Cf. R. Schreiter, *Constructing Local Theologies* (London, 1985).

23 See P. Gregorios, *The Human Presence: An Orthodox View of Nature* (Geneva,1978). For a helpful survey see R. Williams, "Eastern Orthodox Theology," in D. Ford, (ed.), *The Modern Theologians: An Introduction to Christian Theology in the Twentieth Century*, 2nd ed. (Oxford, 1997), 499-513.

absolutist positions which we imagined were overcome at the Second Vatican Council.[24]

It is my contention that the development of alternative Christianities outside the European sphere of influence – and the crisis of communication between these and their Western opposite numbers – has to do with Europe's God: with the ways in which God has been conceived in Europe and perceived outside Europe in contexts of colonial dominance and emancipation. In order to argue this case, I would like to use the cipher "transcendence" to stand for what *may* be intended by the term "God" but in such a way as to leave the content of this symbol as open as possible.[25] This move, of course, immediately involves me in the problematic we are discussing. Even a purely formal concept such as transcendence is not without context, and the very notion of employing such a concept to point beyond all specific determinations, and of defining what it means to be human in terms of it, is a profoundly European one.[26] Given this proviso, in European theology's own language we can nevertheless say that European Christians have at times identified "God" as the *object* of the finite mind's capacity for transcendence, e.g. in Medieval scholasticism and its modernizing neo-Thomist counterparts (*mens capax infiniti; intellectus quodammodo omnia*), whereas in other cases God has been understood as transcending even the *intentionality* that orientates the human towards transcendence, e.g., in some mystical theologies and the "dialectical theology" of Karl Barth. A powerful mainstream tradition, however – not just

24 Again, the survey by F. Kerr in Ford, *Modern Theologians*, 105-17, reminds us of the significance of the *nouvelle théologie*. On recent developments see J.D. May, "Catholic Fundamentalism? Some Implications of Dominus Iesus for Dialogue and Peacemaking," in M.J. Rainer, (ed.), *Dominus Iesus: Anstössige Wahrheit oder anstössige Kirche?* (Münster / Hamburg / London, 2001), 112-33.

25 By this I do not mean to suggest that the term is equivalent to "Reality" as used by John Hick for the unknowable noumenon beyond the "phenomena" of religion, see his *An Interpretation of Religion: Human Responses to the Transcendent* (Yale, 1989). Transcendence as used here, though it may be determined in many ways – in terms of knowledge and love, being, and emptiness – is itself empty of content yet has a practical orientation: it signifies in the first instance a perspective from within experience – and which is therefore contextual – which extends beyond experience, thus making possible specifically human activity; it does not connote the pre-experiential Kantian "transcendental."

26 I owe clarification of this point to my Jamaican former student Rev. Livingstone Thompson. For a mature statement of this orientation in Catholic theology see K. Rahner, *Grundkurs des Glaubens: Einführung in den Begriff des Christentums* (Freiburg / Basel / Vienna, 1976), 42-46: "Der Mensch als Wesen der Transzendenz."

what later came to be known as "apophatic" or "negative" theology – always clearly asserted the unknowability of God in Godself.[27]

In practice, many forms of piety and preaching have fallen short of a truly transcendent conception of God, and upon encountering apparent equivalents of transcendence in cultural traditions outside Europe, all too often the response of missionaries was either to deny the very existence of anything resembling "religion" and "morality" in these cultures, or to say that "God" – *our* God – "was there before we came." One of the most powerful paradigms for these relationships was the European rejection of the Islamic "heresy" as a willful distortion of divine revelation. Another was the shock of discovering millions of creatures on the South American continent who were only reluctantly acknowledged to be human at all. These encounters disturbed the certainties in which European conceptions of revelation and salvation had been cast, but it was to be many centuries before the profound reorientation that was called for began. The theological principle *extra ecclesiam nulla salus,* formulated during the early persecutions as a response to the first apostasies, was reasserted by St Augustine in the course of the Donatist and Pelagian controversies over the efficacy of baptism and the gratuitousness of grace. The subsequent history of this adage shows how European theologians were forced into ever more ingenious rationalizations to account for the possibility of truth and salvation *outside* the sphere of Christianity (which in the counter-Reformation period came to mean Roman Catholic orthodoxy, although Protestant theology too was eventually compelled to address the salvation of the unbeliever). The discovery of the New World was a turning point in this development, when the Spanish Dominican theologians Francisco de Vitoria (1493-1546), Melchior Cano (1505-60) and Domingo Soto (1524-60) laid the foundations for a more inclusive solution. The theology of Karl Rahner shows a remarkable continuity with the refinements introduced by his Jesuit forebears, especially Francisco Suarez (1548-1619).[28]

---

27 See the careful analysis of numerous texts from the patristic and scholastic traditions by Jean Luc Marion, "In the Name: How to Avoid Speaking of 'Negative Theology'," in J.D. Caputo / M.J. Scanlon (eds.), *God, the Gift, and Postmodernity* (Bloomington / Indianapolis, 1999), 20-53.

28 The story of the Church's attempts to reconcile divine grace and human freedom in the context of those who cannot have heard of the gospel has been told by F. Sullivan, *Salvation Outside the Church? Tracing the History of the Catholic Response* (Mahwah, 1992), especially chapters 5 and 6 on the Dominican and Jesuit responses.

In the great Catholic and Protestant missionary eras that coincided with European colonialism and imperialism, the theological challenges came thick and fast. In India, once the implications of Vedânta and Neo-Hinduism began to be grasped, it could be said that the impersonal Absolute, *Brahman*, and still more, the personal forms of the supreme deity, such as Shiva and Vishnu, could be construed as in some sense equivalent to Europe's God as revealed in the incarnation.[29] In China, the Great Lord (*shang-ti*) or "heaven" (*t'ien*) could plausibly be interpreted as symbols of transcendence, though lacking the characteristics of a personal God to whom love and obedience were due.[30] In Africa, John Mbiti and others have discovered many apparent examples of Supreme Beings which were rapidly assimilated to the God of Christian revelation.[31] At the same time, however, there are others – including African theologians – who vigorously contest any continuity between indigenous deities, spirits, or conceptions of transcendence and the Christian God.[32] Similar rejoinders have come from Buddhists, notably Gunapala Dharmasiri and K.N. Jayatilleke of Sri Lanka for Theravâda Buddhism,[33] and Nishida Kitarô and Nishitani Keiji of the Kyôto School for Zen-inspired Japanese Buddhist philosophy.[34] Though in all these cases it may be possible to speak of "transcendence" in some sense as the depth dimension of religious experience, in none

29 Indian equivalents of "incarnation," the avatâras" or "descents" of deities into human, animal, plant, or even inanimate forms, are more "cosmic" in scope, whereas Christ, the unique incarnation of the one God, is the "head" and "recapitulation" of the whole creation; see N. Sheth SJ, "Hindu Avatâra and Christian Incarnation: A Comparison," in *Philosophy East and West* 52 (2002): 98-125. I would like to thank Fr. Sheth for helping me to clarify this point and for sending me his article. The Indian theologian who has gone furthest in this direction is undoubtedly Raimundo Panikkar, though there is a rich tradition of attempts at correlation by both Hindu and Christian theologians; see R. Boyd, *An Introduction to Indian Christian Theology*, rev. ed. (Madras, 1975).

30 See H. Küng / J. Ching (eds.), *Christianity and Chinese Religions* (New York, 1989).

31 J.S. Mbiti, *Concepts of God in Africa* (London,1970).

32 Notably O. P'Bitek, *African Religion in Western Scholarship* (Kampala / Nairobi / Dar es Salaam, 1976). The debate goes back to the attempt by Placide Tempels to formulate a "Bantu philosophy" See also the controversy bet-ween Ennio Mantovani and Theodor Ahrens on equivalents of "sacrifice" in Melanesian cultures in *International Review of Mission* 89 (2000): 515-28; 90 (2001): 462-66.

33 G. Dharmasiri, *A Buddhist Critique of the Christian Concept of God* (Colombo, 1974); K.N. Jayatilleke, *The Message of the Buddha* (London, 1975), ch. 8.

34 On these, see J. Heisig, *Philosophers of Nothingness: An Essay on the Kyoto School* (Honolulu, 2001).

of them is it considered legitimate to equate the object of this experience with the Christian God. In some cases – particularly the critiques stemming from Hinduism and Buddhism but also increasingly those of African philosophy[35] – the critics of Europe's God find plenty of support in Europe itself: German idealism seems to move in the same direction as Neo-Hindu *advaita* (non-dualism); the intellectual rejection of Christianity by Theravâda Buddhism has a lot in common with British logical empiricism; the Japanese Buddhist philosophers find much that is congenial in phenomenology and existentialism. The God whom Nietzsche pronounced dead and whom Heidegger refused to identify with Being stands exposed as the great *obstacle* to enlightenment and emancipation – in the various senses these words can have – in both Eastern and Western traditions.

It is astonishing how little account theologies regarded as postmodern actually take of extra-European mediations of transcendence.[36] Though George Lindbeck included a chapter on the dialogue of religions in his "postliberal" study of doctrine,[37] ambitious essays such as those by Jean-Luc Marion,[38] John Milbank,[39] and Oliver Davies[40] are so preoccupied with theology's transition through Western modernity – especially in relation to continental phe-

---

35 See the perceptive critiques of the racism latent in the mainstream European philosophical tradition by E.C. Eze, *Postcolonial African Philosophy: A Critical Reader* (Oxford, 1997); *idem*, *Race and the Enlightenment* (Oxford, 1997); and V.Y. Mudimbe, *The Invention of Africa: Gnosis, Philosophy and the Order of Knowledge* (London / Bloomington / Indianapolis, 1988).

36 In the survey by G. Ward in J. Ford, *Postmodern Theologians*, 585-601, only Thomas J.J. Altizer's investigations of Buddhism and Michel de Certeau's awareness of the colonization of the other and the "policing of this Other throughout the development of modernity" (597) engage seriously with the implications of the "strangeness" of the Other for theology, though J. Byrne, *God: Thoughts in an Age of Uncertainty* (New York / London, 2001), makes integral use of the Buddhist *anâtman* (no-self) teaching; see T. Sundermeier, *Den Fremden verstehen*, where the criticism is generalized to apply to the human sciences as well as theology.

37 G. Lindbeck, *The Nature of Doctrine: Religion and Theology in a Postliberal Age* (London, 1984).

38 J.-L. Marion, *God Without Being: Hors-Texts* (Chicago / London, 1991).

39 J. Milbank, *Theology and Social Theory: Beyond Secular Reason* (Oxford, 1990); Milbank makes a somewhat arbitrary and impatient attempt to dismiss religious pluralism as an offshoot of global capitalism, *idem*, "The End of Dialogue," in G. D'Costa (ed.), *Christian Uniqueness Reconsidered: The Myth of a Pluralistic Theology of Religions* (Maryknoll, 1990), 174-91.

40 O. Davies, *A Theology of Compassion: Metaphysics of Difference and the Renewal of Tradition* (London, 2000).

nomenology and deconstruction – that they scarcely mention the implications of specific religious Others for Christian conceptions of God. Joseph O'Leary's engagement with Derrida and Michael Barnes's with Levinas go some way towards making good this deficit,[41] while Roger Haight's Christology is the first to have been conceived with the situation of global religious pluralism in mind.[42] The evolving "theology of religions" has been the site of renewed interest in the challenge of religious otherness by both Catholic and Protestant theologians,[43] though by no means all of them make the alienation between European Christians and the "others" produced by colonial and neo-colonial exploitation a central or even peripheral part of their thematic.[44]

It is perhaps no exaggeration to say that the classical statements of Christology, such as "Jesus is God" and "God became human," have become functionally unintelligible in the transition to modernity. Karl Rahner diagnosed the problem as the loss of Trinitarian theology: not only have ordinary Christians become devotionally monotheist, but theology itself effectively disregards the Trinity after having confirmed its status as a special revelation. Taking for granted that "God" has been revealed in Christ as three-personed, "since St Augustine, contrary to the tradition preceding him, it has been more

41 J. O'Leary, *Religious Pluralism and Christian Truth* (Edinburgh, 1996); M. Barnes, *Theology and the Dialogue of Religions* (Cambridge, 2002); and see my review article, "The Elusive Other: Recent Theological Writing on Religious Pluralism," in *Studies in Interreligious Dialogue* 13 (2003): 114-24.

42 R. Haight, *Jesus Symbol of God* (Maryknoll, 1999).

43 Again, the brief survey of the field by G. D'Costa in J. Ford, *Modern Theologians*, 626-44, is incisive and informative; a much fuller account, with a bold new proposal to supersede the somewhat shop-worn tripartite division into "exclusivist," "inclusivist" and "pluralist" theologies – which D'Costa would also wish to deconstruct – has been presented by P. Knitter, *Introducing Theologies of Religions* (Maryknoll, 2002), while D'Costa has taken a quite different and more conservative tack in his *The Meeting of Religions and the Trinity* (Edinburgh, 2000).

44 The contrast becomes apparent when the philosophically and theologically sophisticated evangelical approach of S.M. Heim, *Salvations: Truth and Difference in Religion* (Maryknoll, 1995) and *The Depth of the Riches: A Trinitarian Theology of Religious Ends* (Grand Rapids, 2001), is compared with the withering criticism of the whole project of interreligious dialogue by K. Surin, "A Politics of Speech: Religious Pluralism in the Age of the McDonald's Hamburger," in: G. D'Costa, (ed.), *Christian Uniqueness Reconsidered*, 192-212, and Paul Knitter's sustained attempt to correlate the "suffering other" produced by colonial exploitation with the "religious other" encountered by Christian mission, see especially *One Earth, Many Religions: Multifaith Dialogue and Global Responsibility* (Maryknoll, 1995); and see my review article on Heim and Knitter, in *Mid-Stream* 37 (1998): 108-13.

or less agreed that each of the divine persons could become [hu]man" in order to reveal this "information" to Christians.[45] It is no wonder that we are witnessing a revival of Trinitarian theology and a rediscovery of the pneumatological as well as the Trinitarian emphases in Rahner's own work.[46]

The question then becomes: will this renewed Trinitarianism solve the problems of modern theology, as a number of contemporary writers seem to assume? Rewarding as it is to be reminded by the theologians cited above of the riches of scripture and tradition beyond the rather narrow scope of much of classical theology, in my view the problem lies much deeper. Despite attempts to show that Trinitarianism unlocks the full potential of theology and enables a fresh approach to a host of issues ranging from the understanding of nature to the encounter with other religions, the terms of the discussion are such that attempts to "include" religious traditions that owe nothing to Christianity within the plan of salvation revealed in Christ have generally failed, while the rational construction of meta-languages with which to express the elements of salvation common to all traditions turns out to *exclude* those that cannot be reduced to Western (particularly modern rationalist) understandings of rationality. But it is precisely this "otherness" that makes particular historical traditions distinctive as religions, just as it is precisely what distinguishes believing Hindus or Muslims from Christians that cannot be stated in a meta-language. As a result, the most influential quasi-official theologies in both Catholic and Protestant ecumenical circles are still constructed in such a way as to preserve the superiority and incomparability of the Christian revelation.

The curious situation thus arises that postmodern theologies such as those advanced by John Milbank or Oliver Davies declare that theology produces its own rationality from within the resources of revelation and is thus immune to the criticism of "secular reason" and to the implications of radically different religious rationalities, hence the necessity of confronting these postmod-

---

45 See the excerpts from K. Rahner, "Remarks on the Treatise 'De Trinitate'" and "On the Theology of the Incarnation", *Theological Investigations*, vol. IV, in: G.A. McCool (ed.), *A Rahner Reader* (London, 1975), especially 137.

46 See, for instance, J. H. Wong, "Anonymous Christians: Karl Rahner's Pneuma Christocentrism and an East-West Dialogue", in *Theological Studies* 55 (1994): 609-37; Jacques Dupuis, "The Christological Debate in the Context of Religious Plurality," in *Current Dialogue* 19 (1991): 18-24. It has even been suggested that there are affinities between Rahner's developed theology and the "deconstructionist" thinking inspired by Jacques Derrida and practiced by Jean-Luc Marion; see M. Scanlon, "A Deconstruction of Religion: On Derrida and Rahner," in J. Caputo / M. Scanlon (eds.), *God, the Gift, and Postmodernism*, 223-28.

ern theologies with postcolonial mediations of transcendence. The recall to liturgical prayer and apophatic mysticism has enormous potential for renewing European theology, but there is also something introverted and introspective about it, whereas the God invoked by many Third World theologies is embarrassingly concrete and disturbingly transcendent at one and the same time. Europe's God is being transposed from the ideologically constructed Oppressor of colonial theology into the Liberator called upon by Christians in the situations of oppression created by Western dominance.[47] Europe's God, in effect, is being decolonized.

Our focus of attention is thus the discontinuity between "God" and "transcendence" in postcolonial situations. It is undeniable that what we are calling "transcendence" has been a factor in postcolonial contexts. Though Christian missionaries often offered significant resistance to colonial exploitation, the violence perpetrated by colonizers and the counter-violence unleashed by independence movements and revolutionaries has equally often been inspired and sustained, not only by secular ideologies, but by various forms of religion as symbolizations of transcendence (even Marxism and Nazism have been interpreted as quasi-religious eschatologies, while Zionism might be termed a quasi-secular messianism). The paradox for theologians is that it is precisely the element of religious ultimacy in such movements that is at least partly responsible for the violence they generate and for the fanaticism with which it is pursued. At the moment, Islam bears the brunt of such accusations, but examples from all other world religions are not far to seek.[48] It is not always

---

[47] To offer just a few examples, this is the theme developed by J. L. Segundo, *The Liberation of Theology* (Maryknoll, 1976), with his call to "close the hermeneutic circle" which begins and ends with praxis ("Faith without works is dead. Faith without ideologies is equally dead," 181); by L. Boff, *Christentum mit dunklem Antlitz: Wege in die Zukunft aus der Erfahrung Lateinamerikas* (Freiburg / Basel / Vienna, 1993), who seeks to uncouple evangelization and power; and A. Pieris, *An Asian Theology of Liberation* (Maryknoll, 1988), who confronts the Latin Americans with the transcendent dimensions of "practice" evident in Asian traditions. The mature theology of G. Gutiérrez, as it appears in *On Job: God-Talk and the Suffering of the Innocent* Maryknoll, 1987) or *We Drink from Our Own Wells: The Spiritual Journey of a People* (Maryknoll, 1984), seems entirely open to this perspective; for an analysis of the crisis faced by liberation theology in the 1990s, see D. Tombs, *Latin American Liberation Theology* (Boston / Leiden, 2002); see also J.D. May, "What Do Socially Engaged Buddhists and Christian Liberation Theologians Have to Say to One Another?" in *Dialogue* 21 (1994): 1-18.

[48] See R. Scott Appleby, *The Ambivalence of the Sacred: Religion, Violence, and Reconciliation* (Lanham *et al.*, 2000); R. M. Schwartz, *The Curse of Cain: The Violent Legacy of Monotheism* (Chicago and London, 1997); R. Stark, *One True God: Historical*

realized, for example, that the prototypical colonial situation in modern Europe is that of Ireland, where Britain held its dress rehearsal for imperialism (under Elizabeth I, Virginia was being colonized by the same noblemen who were also being granted expropriated lands in Ireland).[49] The Reformation reached Ireland in the form of British colonialism: though Presbyterians were regarded as Dissenters and played their part in movements for Irish emancipation (e.g. the United Irishmen of 1798), it was Irish Catholics who were regarded as a recalcitrant and barbaric religious minority, and what was done to them was done under the auspices of the Church of England. The repression of Irish Catholics by the Penal Laws (1695) and in the aftermath of the 1916 Easter Rising reached levels of violence comparable to those employed in India and Africa. This was not religious violence except in the broadest of senses – with the possible exception of Cromwell (1649), the colonizers were too cynical to deserve that label – but the resistance to it was often religiously inspired: by Catholicism in Ireland (violently, after political leaders such as the Catholic O'Connell and the Anglican Parnell failed to achieve emancipation), by a renascent Hinduism in India (largely non-violently, thanks to Gandhi, though the communalism inspired by the new ideology of *Hindutva* is extremely violent), and by resilient indigenous traditions such as those of the Kikuyu and the Zulu in Africa.

Similar observations could be made about the conflict in the Middle East: though Jews supported Muslims in repelling the Christian crusaders, and though the Zionists who emigrated to Palestine to escape European anti-Semitism were initially secular, by now the religiously orthodox Jews have come to terms with the secular state of Israel and oppose the Palestinians on biblical grounds, while among the Palestinians the fundamentalist Muslims have more and more influence. As in Northern Ireland, the conflict could not be said to be *about* the religious faiths involved; but it cannot be denied that they provide a context of legitimacy: the most hardened Loyalist, who may not have seen the inside of a church for many a long year, is still vaguely

---

Conse-quences of Monotheism (Princeton / Oxford, 2001), G. Kepel, *La revanche de Dieu: Chrétiens, juifs et musulmans à la reconquêt du monde* (Paris, 1991); K. Armstrong, *The Battle for God: Fundamentalism in Judaism, Christianity and Islam* (London, 2001).

49 For more detail and additional literature, see J.D. May, "Instrumentalisierung des Christentums durch die Politik? Das Beispiel Nordirland," in *Una Sancta* 50 (1995): 141-50.

aware that he fights to preserve a Protestant heritage, and his Republican counterpart, who may have abstained from the sacraments for the duration of the armed struggle, is nevertheless aware that to be truly Irish is to be Catholic. The suicide bombers from Gaza are regarded as Muslim martyrs, and the Jewish settlers on the West Bank, even if they come from the Bronx, see their occupation of the land in Biblical terms.

The violence in the former Yugoslavia during the 1990s reveals a similar pattern: deeply engrained Catholic (Croatia), Orthodox (Serbia), and Muslim (Bosnia, Kosovo) traditions lend symbolic legitimacy to a conflict that is about ethnic identities and territorial entitlements rather than religious faith as such. The deliberate destruction of the library in Sarajevo by the Bosnian Serb nationalists in 1992, precisely because it was the repository of that multicultural city's priceless cultural treasures and the symbol of its identity, is a vivid illustration of this. Here, too, the parameters of the conflict are set by the legacies of colonialism: its fault lines retrace the borders of the Austro-Hungarian and Ottoman Empires. In some of these cases the Christian "God" has once again appeared as Israel's God, the God of Battles and the Lord of Hosts, invoked by conquering invaders but also by subject peoples when they rise up in the name of their own cultural values and religious convictions. The God of mercy and compassion, the equally Jewish God to whom Jesus prayed and who was proclaimed in his name by Christian missionaries, turns out to be discontinuous with the misappropriated God of Jews, Muslims, and Christians in contexts of bitter postcolonial conflict (we have seen shocking examples of this in the Middle East conflict and the first and second Gulf wars). I have referred to such cases as "failures of transcendence" on the understanding that transcendence is at bottom a *practical* affair, the horizon within which the flourishing of fully human life becomes possible, but which can also be so determined by narrow and hostile interests as to make both physical and cognitive violence seem legitimate.[50]

The Christian God – as *Europe's* "God" – has thus been continually mediated back to Europe through situations of violent conflict and the prism of other peoples' traditional symbol systems. This God, whom European Christians know – and in whom many non-Europeans have found faith – as the benevolent Creator of all that is, the One whose truth is fidelity to his covenant with Israel and through Israel with all peoples, whose justice and compassion are proclaimed by the prophets and made known in Jesus, has nevertheless

50 See, at greater length, May, "Introduction," in *Transcendence and Violence*,.

been perceived by peoples subjected to European colonization in his name as their ultimate oppressor, the one who defines and inspires the injustices perpetrated on them. How could this be? The answer must lie, not only in the manifest oppression practiced by the colonialists, but also in the way they seemed able to justify it by invoking this God and his decrees. This in turn takes us back to the way this God was understood, conceptualized and made known by Europeans. The Christ-like God revealed in the humanity of Jesus was not always mediated successfully for Europe's subject peoples; instead, either consciously or unconsciously, either deliberately or inadvertently, the Europeans brought a God who sought to displace and destroy all that pointed to transcendence in ways that were not (European) Christian.

Now that the postcolonial situation has developed as outlined in section one above, this God – Europe's God – is being projected back to Europe through the lens of religious symbols that owe nothing to Europe's traditions, echoed by an *oikoumene* in which Christians succeed in communicating with Christians and religious Others across all barriers of culture, prejudice, and dependency. The image and echo that come back can make "God" all but unrecognizable to Europeans, but perhaps they also show up the shortcomings and limitations of Europe's ways of conceiving God. These ways, of course, have been extremely varied, and the outbreaks of violence in colonial history have by no means always been motivated by specifically European or specifically religious ideas. Nevertheless, the many and varied experiences with God in colonial contexts created by Europe are also producing new theologies that challenge Europe to think again about God. These new ways of understanding God, hitherto inconceivable in Europe, may, in the context of ecumenical communication, lay the foundation for a deeper and stronger *koinônia* among Christians of all traditions, a truly "realized" catholicity.[51] The resulting agenda is far too vast to be adequately treated here, but it may prompt some very brief concluding reflections on the multiplex mediations of the transcendent that the postcolonial situation has initiated.

[51] See J.D. May, "Realised Catholicity: The Incarnational Dimension of Multiculturalism," in *The Australasian Catholic Record* 76 (1999): 419-29.

Conclusion: Liberator or Oppressor?

It lies in the logic of what we have been discussing to conclude that it no longer makes sense to distinguish and oppose "Western" and "non-Western" theologies, because increasingly all theology is being done in the complex multimedia of global space with its virtual simultaneity and real virtuality. Yet this virtual space, with its enormous potential for delusion and manipulation, urgently needs to be criticized and unmasked as yet another medium of domination, this time by integrated global market forces rather than the competing nationalisms of colonial times. The God who can inhabit this new global public space is similarly no longer any one tradition's God as the winner of a contest of truth, uniqueness, or authenticity, but the God who is *en jeu,* present yet continually deferred in the interplay of meanings, represented *in absentia* by a process of communication between the "narrators of transcendence," the human and historical bearers of God-knowledge, the religions themselves. We have seen that Europe's traditional God, already a culturally specific and multi-contextual mediation of the tribal God of Israel, has all too often appeared in Europe's colonial history as the Oppressor of peoples unjustly subjected to the hegemony of European imperial powers. This God, who is primordially the Liberator of Israel and whose covenant with the people of Israel for the sake of all the nations is extended to all the world's suffering in Jesus as the renewed covenant of God with humanity, can once again offer the hope of liberation to all who are oppressed.[52] This, however, presupposes the recovery of key elements in the understanding of God that have faded from European Christian consciousness but that can be restored in the ecumenical dialogue with newly-emerging Christianities inspired by European evangelization. These lacunae in European tradition may be summarized as follows:

Loss of praxis (*Praxisvergessenheit*): Christianity, in all its forms, has always been a faith stressing good works and moral living, practical charity and the *imitatio Christi.* Yet at the same time, dogmatic theology has been intellectualized to the point where it could detach itself from ethics and continue as a self-contained discourse about divine things, to the degree where it was capable of betraying the orientation of transcendence towards *praxis,* even to the lengths of genocide, legitimating the destruction of peoples, their cultures,

[52] See the recent bold development of this theme by A. Pieris, "Christ Beyond Dogma: Doing Christology in the Context of the Religions and the Poor," in *Louvain Studies* 25 (2000): 187-231.

and their environments in the name of evangelizing and civilizing them. While there were always those who recalled theology to its responsibility by acknowledging the humanity of subject peoples and learning to respect their cultures and religions, the disjunction between principle and practice was mercilessly exposed: Theology that does not spring from the *praxis* of liberation is inauthentic and may very well be collaborating with the oppressor; "practical atheism" can go hand in hand with doctrinal orthodoxy. Despite Jürgen Moltmann's justified protest that this owed little to indigenous Latin American traditions but simply repeated European theorizations of *praxis* in the admittedly urgent situation of economic exploitation and political dictatorship, this corrective was necessary and has still not been fully assimilated into European theology. The "hermeneutical privilege" of the poor, of women, of the colored is a necessary provocation.

Loss of transcendence (*Transzendenzvergessenheit*): In the light of what has already been said about the thematization of transcendence in European theology, both traditional and modern, it may seem surprising to accuse it of less-than-transcendence in its language about God, but it could be argued that Europe has all too often objectified and reified God for its own ends – often enough immediately bound up with domination and oppression (forced conversions, Inquisition, Crusades, *conquista*, Holocaust). The correctives offered by the negative theology of the mystics (Eckhart's *Deitas*, "God beyond God"; Rahner's *Geheimnis*, the pre-conceptual experience of transcendence) have not easily translated into the social and ecological ethics demanded by modernity, nor have they sufficed to open theology up to the profound otherness of alternative accounts of transcendence. The Buddha's radical critique of all varieties of substantialism on all levels of reality, including language and ideas, has not been easy to assimilate, but its critical appropriation promises a way of deconstructing the absolutism that still distorts the Christian conceptualizations of God as articulated in evangelical theology and Catholic ecclesiology alike.

Loss of nature (*Naturvergessenheit*): There is something disturbingly symptomatic in the Christian missionaries' haste to supplant and even destroy the cultures of the "primitive" peoples among whom they found themselves. One way of theorizing this is to suggest that the transcendence of the Christian God was conceptualized in such a way that God became an idealized entity beyond the parameters of space and time and therefore beyond the possibility of contamination by anything "earthy," except at the one, unique, miraculous point of contact in the incarnation. The rhythms of the cosmos, the cycles of regeneration and rebirth were abhorrent as mediations of God's presence, even symbolically; the thought of pagan rituals having any part in divine worship was inadmissible, and patently immoral customs were to be stamped out. This was not the whole story, of course, but what it amounts to is a tendency to repress the chthonic, the rootedness of the human in the natural. As a result, the repressed realization that the human is animal and material, that indigenous peoples are not so much "primitive" as more fully integrated with their natural environments, returned to conscious awareness in the form of animosity and aggression. European theology has scarcely begun to realize this dualism encoded in its most cherished formulations. If it is to be worked through and overcome, precisely in the ways we speak of God, and if Western Christianity is to integrate the natural, an intensive dialogue with "primal" traditions is inescapable. A significant Western contribution to this task is the de-masculinization of patriarchal traditions by feminist theologians.

The mediations of transcendence to the sciences, politics, and the arts now required of European theology in the global space of postmodernity will be more plausible, I believe, and the currency of "God" will be enhanced, to the extent that Europe's God, while remaining unambiguously Israel's God, Jesus' God, and Muhammad's God, is once again mediated by liberative *praxis*, radical transcendence, and oneness with nature. The postcolonial context offers Europe an historic opportunity to complete itself by relearning to mediate transcendence in these ways.

Jacques Haers

Thinking about God from the Perspectives of Encounter and Community: A Challenge for European Theology in a Globalized World

This paper emphasizes the challenging reality of globalization as an opportunity for theologians, in particular, for European theologians, who are called upon to review their thought, concepts, and methods from the perspective of encounter and community,[1] while taking into account the preferential option for the poor and an eschatological vision. My introduction and conclusion will articulate the European perspective in its worldwide context.[2] This paper further consists of two main parts: a reflection on globalization, and suggestions for a theology of encounter and conversation, having as its key features the building of a holistic or global community and the preferential option for the poor. These two parts are linked by an attempt at defining globalization in a way that allows a liberating praxis at the service of the poor and the excluded. Although my goal is to underscore the role and responsibilities of European theologians, I will use worldwide theological references with a predilection for liberation theologians of the Two Thirds World, so as to better highlight a global viewpoint. Indeed, I am convinced that the vocation of European theology is highly relevant to global interests: Europe's context is the whole world. I also want to stress at the outset that within this paper I will be "doing theology"; that is, I intend to demonstrate that the problems raised here are germane to our ways of talking about God and our ways of constructing images of God.

---

1 This paper relates to my forthcoming article: "Defensor Vinculi et Conversationis: Connectedness and Conversation as a Challenge to Theology."

2 While rereading my paper, and taking into account other papers offered at the Vienna gathering, I have become aware that my understanding of "European" may be focused too one-sidedly on Western Europe. When, therefore, I use the word "Europe," it is safer to assume that it refers mainly to "Western Europe." My first impression, however, is that the existing tensions between Western and Eastern Europe will strengthen some of the theological points I want to make.

Introduction: A Thought Provoking Situation Analysis

In my own country, Flanders as a part of Belgium, recent research done by a group of sociologists under the direction of Mark Elchardus at the Vrije Universiteit Brussel shows that the experiences of "uneasiness" (onbehagen) and "mistrust" (wantrouwen) shared by many Flemish people reflect profound cultural undercurrents, probably at work since the 1960s. This shows, among other things, people's difficulty in living their lives from the perspective of a fundamental social togetherness.[3] Indeed, growing individualism, with its stress on autonomy and detraditionalization, has provoked a breach in the sense of social connectedness. As the latter is critically necessary for successfully coping with and confronting one's limitations creatively, uneasiness and mistrust arise naturally when it is lacking. As a healing remedy for this crisis in Flemish society, Elchardus, following Charles Taylor, stresses the key importance of both authenticity and the sense of collective connectedness.

As worldviews,[4] these attitudes reflect the context rendered by modern and postmodern tendencies toward stressing the autonomous and creative subject, as well as the individual's needs and desires. Authors who reflect on the meaning of such worldviews for the Christian understanding of who God

3 See: M. Elchardus / W. Smits, *Anatomie en oorzaken van het wantrouwen* (Brussels, 2002); M. Elchardus / J. Siongers, "Het onbehagen van de grenzeloosheid. Een empirisch onderzoek naar het verband tussen detraditionalisering, zingeving en onbehagen," in H. De Witte, *Openheid of leegte? Over zingeving by jongeren*, DIROO Cahiers 7, Leuven / Leusden, 2001), 35-73. For the Brussels research team TOR (Tempus Omnia Revelat), see: < http://www.vub.ac.be/TOR/ >. Over the last years, these feelings of mistrust and uneasiness appear to have diminished in strength. Elchardus points to the existence of a new fault line or social divide in Flemish society, measured in terms of individualism, authoritarianism, ethnocentrism, and opposition to representative democracy. He also highlights the role of the media in this process of growing uneasiness. See also, for parallel analyses: B. Pattyn / L. Van Liedekerke, "Angst en onzekerheid in de moderne samenleving," in: *Ethische Per-spectieven* 11 (2001): 1-2, 29-45; A. Depuydt, J. Deklerck and G. Deboutte (eds.), *"Verbondenheid" als antwoord op "de-link-wentie"? Preventie op een nieuw spoor*, DIROO Cahiers 6 (Leuven / Leusden, 2001).

4 See e.g. J. Van der Veken / Leo Apostel, *Wereldbeelden: Van fragmentering naar integratie* (Kapellen, 1992). Worldviews are multifaceted intellectual constructs with which people attempt to describe their world, to situate themselves in it, to devise practical ways of acting, and to provide visions of the future. I will emphasize that, after modernity and postmodernity, globalization constitutes a new worldview, which it will be important to articulate and to define precisely.

is, such as Godfried Danneels and Leo Moulin,[5] Michael J. Buckley,[6] and Guido Van Heeswijck,[7] point out that Christianity has not remained faithful to its central focus on relationship with God in Christ, substituting it instead with a theological science that attempts to inculturate itself to a society that is increasingly influenced by modern science's modes of thinking – thought frameworks that do not readily allow for a metaphysics capable of dealing with relations between God and the world. Consequently, Christianity itself may have unwittingly contributed to the atheism and individualism at work in societies characterized by competition based economics.[8] To complicate matters, in the European context, words such as "subject" and "individual" must be understood as they are used by national(istic) and ethnic groups that strongly emphasize their own identity, their own cultural and economic needs, and their own autonomous rights over against other peoples. Bart Pattyn, relying on ideas developed by Mary Douglas, analyzes the individualism of such "enclaves," i.e., communities with strong group feelings and strong group control, but with less clearly defined norms and distinctions. "We-enclaves," or virtual enclaves, are characterized by a solid we-feeling (belonging and togetherness), but they exclude people who are not accepted as members of the group. This means that strong feelings of connectedness may coincide with a genuine, powerful, and aggressive egocentrism.[9] Such an enclave mentality can only be countered by an awareness that the building of communities always calls for a universal scope. This awareness emerges when one considers the victims of one's community building, the excluded peoples who receive no share in the we-feeling that defines the enclave.

The analysis of this particular Flemish reality in Western Europe seems to contradict the very aims and premises of the European Union, which was born

---

5 G. Danneels / L. Moulin, "Het 'geseculariseerde' Europa evangeliseren," in *Collationes* 15 (1985): 387-418.

6 M.J. Buckley, *At the Origins of Modern Atheism* (New Haven / London, 1987).

7 G. Van Heeswijck, *Voorbij het onbehagen. Ressentiment en het Christendom* (Leuven, 2002).

8 The issue is very complex and it is not possible here to provide an in-depth analysis of the role played by the developments in theology with regard to secularization and atheism. The important remark to be made is that Christian faith is profoundly related to the relationship with God and to community and life together. Both of these oppose egoistically lived individualism.

9 B. Pattyn, "Virtuele en politieke enclaves," in *Ethische Perspectieven* 12 (2002): 78-92.

out of the divisions that had brought about the Second World War. The EU vision concerns the attempt to build a closely knit community in which otherwise potential enemies are made dependent upon one another for stability, as a measure to obviate the eventuality of wars between them. This aims at a community that respects diversity and alternatives as its very foundation. Indeed, Europe knows what it means to not be able to rely on a community wherein people take responsibility for one another. Europe's history of conflict and war provides a long and still growing list of infamous killing fields, and it reminds Europeans of the potentially horrific pitfalls of identity creation.[10] Suffering has led Europe to the insight that the building of a European community is not a dispensable luxury; it is, on the contrary, an absolute necessity. Therefore, we can see why Europe attempts to weave, pro-actively, networks of mutual interdependence – economically, socially, culturally, and politically. Europe's ill-advised temptation, however, is to build a comfortable enclave, a safe European haven, with its strong feelings of togetherness *ad intra.* This would reflect a subtle form of egocentrism, mirroring the feelings of uneasiness and mistrust underscored by the sociologists. The fight against and the struggle with nightmares of insecurity and fear that produce egocentric individualism on personal, ethnic, and European levels, are ongoing. Research by the team of Mark Elchardus demonstrates the all too real implications of this struggle for people's mental health. The true battle for Europe lies in maintaining a creative tension between the empowerment of identities and mutual responsibility: how to build a community that is based on diversity? This can ultimately be achieved only if the building of the European community is not perverted by the enclave mentality of fortress Europe.[11]

At this stage, I should mention that in Europe issues of worldview and (egocentric) identity have always been closely linked to an understanding of God and its theological articulations, appearing, for example, in such expressions as "our God" or "God is with us" or "we are God's people." The real

10 A. Maalouf, *Les Identités meurtrières*, Le Livre de Poche, 15005 (Paris, 1998), 11: "... ces habitudes de pensée et d'expression si ancrées en nous tous ... cette conception étroite, exclusive, bigote, simpliste qui réduit l'identité entière à une seule appartenance, proclamée avec rage."

11 Related to this issue is the question of whether the movement toward togetherness is born out of a mere defensive reflex (one wants to preserve one's own identity against others), or also embodies the awareness of an original togetherness that ultimately has to be understood worldwide.

danger concomitant with the use of specific worldviews always also reflects the potential risk in conceiving of God as a concrete idea or image. This is true, for example, in the case of colonization as it is linked to a particular image of mission. Accordingly, then, it is imperative that we further examine the link between our understanding of God and globalization.

The Challenges of Globalization

Currently, Europe is moving toward an integration that is respectful of internal diversity. In our globalizing world, this constitutes a clear and courageous statement. European theologians are conditioned by a context in which the tension between efforts to build community and egocentrism remains a powerful challenge linked to a holistic view of community and to a sensibility mindful of the suffering of the excluded. It follows, therefore, that European theologies will attempt to be sensitive to issues of identity, solidarity, and exclusion, in addition to the importance of community and connectedness. With regard to globalization, theologians are challenged to address these tensions and to incorporate them into their thinking.

The process of globalization is an undeniable fact in our contemporary world. It challenges us, not only as we may want to promote its opportunities of closer worldwide networking, but also as we become more aware that it produces suffering, injustices, and poverty on a scale never seen before. Two Thirds World theologians are particularly sensitive to this double faced reality. Tissa Balasuriya begins his article on globalization in the *Dictionary of Third World Theologies* as follows:[12]

> Globalization can be understood as uniting the world for the common good of all. In this sense it is desirable and can lead to the greater happiness and fuller hu-

[12] T. Balasuriya, "Globalization," in V. Fabella / R.S. Sugirtharajah (eds.), *Dictionary of Third World Theologies* (Maryknoll, 2000), 91-94. Literature on globalization is plentiful. As background for this paper I used the following: P. Beyer, *Religion and Globalization*, Theory, Culture & Society (London, 1994); D. Held / A. McGrew (eds.), *The Global Transformations Reader: An Introduction to the Globalization Debate* (Cambridge 2000); R. Petrella, *Écueils de la mondialisation: Urgence d'un nouveau contrat social,* Les grandes conférences (Montreal, 1997); R.J. Schreiter, *The New Catholicity: Theology between the Global and the Local* (Maryknoll: Orbis, 1997); T.H. Sanks, "Globalization and the Church's Social Mission," in *Theological Studies* 60 (1999): 625-51; J. Sobrino / F. Wilfred (eds.), "Globalization and its Victims," in *Concilium* 2001/5.

> manity of all peoples. But globalization as commonly known in the Third World refers to a new development model of a globally integrated market economy. It has different strands, impacting one another toward exponential growth of global interdependence, but their overall effect is to incorporate all peoples into a single world unit for production, consumption, trade and investment, information flow, and culture. This global system imposes itself as the only viable alternative available to economic and social life. While the system benefits the rich and powerful, it has adverse consequences on the majority poor of the Third World.

Globalization is undoubtedly an ambiguous phenomenon, requiring much interpretation and clarification. It is also a "worldview": in defining and shaping globalization we must attempt to situate ourselves in the world while paving viable opportunities for the future and assuming our responsibilities with regard to people who suffer the consequences of heightened oppression and injustice. In what follows, I sketch a few of the important features that must be taken into account in working toward this endeavor, and I propose a metaphor for globalization that will allow us to indicate some of the crucial theological issues that are at stake.

One must first of all admit that globalization is real. It is a fact of life:[13] our world is characterized by a growing complexity due to its interconnectedness, which is heightened dramatically by rapidly increasing means of communication due to impressive technological innovations. I consciously use superlatives here, as the changes that have taken place over the past twenty years have profoundly altered perceptions of the world in which we live as well as ways of life. Today we must take into account worldwide events when we discuss economy, ecology, and politics. An economic crisis in Argentina ripples out across the entire world; climatic changes and energy scarcity have local origins but worldwide consequences; terrorism is a new form of worldwide war, and conflicts that appear to be local have in fact profound international ramifications. We have become more aware, with AIDS and SARS, that health issues are global. We live in a risky world, precisely because of its global complexities.[14]

---

13 Of course, globalization is also a word we use to interpret the reality in which we live. Reality is interpreted reality and the issue of hermeneutics is unavoidable. The facts are always interpreted facts that come to be understood through the interpretations given and that, by way of these interpretations, assert their reality. How we speak about globalization, therefore, cannot be indifferent to interpretation: our way of speaking shapes the very fact of globalization.

14 U. Beck, *The Risk Society: Toward a New Modernity* (London, 1992).

As an undeniable fact, globalization has profoundly changed our ways of thinking as well as the political and economic outlook of our world. We have learned to take complexities into account and our sciences have become sensitive to this reality. Moreover, the idea of networks and interconnectedness, with its tensions between the local and the global, and with its nodes, hubs, and relations, begins to condition our ways of thinking and acquiring information as we come to depend upon, more and more, the resources of the Internet.[15] Some international organizations, therefore, have gained an importance and an autonomy that they still find difficult to assume. The World Bank, UNHCR, and the United Nations acquire and voice their own viewpoints, as is evident on their websites. They increasingly represent a global perspective with particular attention on the poor and those who suffer the consequences of violent conflict. There is a struggle going on regarding the control of such organizations, especially as they emerge as independent political actors. One can only hope that they will be able to strengthen and sustain their independence.

On a cultural level, we perceive, in a globalized world, the tensions between local identities and the pressures of a global, worldwide culture, against which local resistances build. Is it possible to combine these global and local forces? Referring to Roland Robertson,[16] Robert J. Schreiter describes the

> encounter of the global and the local as "glocalization" ... some of the most salient features in religion and theology today can best be described from the vantage point of the glocal. Neither the global, homogenizing forces nor the local forms of accommodation and resistance can of themselves provide an adequate explanation of these phenomena. It is precisely in their interaction that one comes to understand what is happening.[17]

This approach is further developed in the idea of "global theological flows," of interaction and communication between theologies that arise in various places and under various circumstances or contexts. According to Schreiter, global theological flows are

---

15 See D. Cohen, "All the World's a Net," in *New Scientist* (April 13, 2002): 24-29, on the network theories of Albert-László Barabási.

16 R. Robertson, "Glocalization: Time-Space and Homogeneity-Heterogeneity," in S. Lash / R. Robertson (eds.), *Global Modernities* (London, 1995).

17 Schreiter, *The New Catholicity*, 12.

> defined as an interlocking set of mutually intelligible discourses that together make up an antisystemic global movement. It was suggested that they may be the form of "universal" theology in a globalized world, for they address global systems (in the case of liberation theology, the global economic system) and interlink responses to it. They may not be universal in the transcendental sense, but they achieve a certain universality on the basis of their sheer pervasiveness."[18]

This approach toward globalization allows us to use the interactive processes and communicative networks to develop resistances against the injustices and oppression brought about or heightened by globalization. It favors a creative approach to globalization from below, from the perspective of those who suffer and are in need of a different approach to globalization: "people can indeed exercise power over globalization, but only by means of a solidarity that crosses the boundaries of nations, identities, and narrow interests. A corporate-driven, top-down globalization can only be effectively countered by globalization from below".[19] The aim here is to construct global communities of resistance and change, precisely from the perspective of and in solidarity with those who suffer the consequences of globalization. We are very close here to theological ideas of preferential options for the poor and communities of solidarity, as they will be explored further on.

The important thing here is that globalization generates conflict because of the inevitable sufferings in a world where some know how to use the opportunities of globalization to their own advantage, and have the power to do so, and where others become pawns in a game of interests over which they have but little influence. In many ways this is an old game. The conflict that surfaces within the context of globalization is not new. It has always been with us without ever, even in the history of colonization, having assumed the worldwide proportions of today. This conflict between the oppressed and the oppressor is often veiled behind other conflicts of nationality, ethnicity, cultures, etc. Some reflection is necessary to uncover its deep roots and to arrive at defining its real battlefield. At this stage, the study of globalization and the praxis in service of the downtrodden and excluded will have to rely on the skills taught in the conflict sciences, most particularly with regard to the mat-

---

18 Schreiter, *The New Catholicity*, 114.

19 J. Brecher, T. Costello and B. Smith, *Globalization from Below: The Power of Solidarity* (Cambridge MA, 2000). Research on local resistance, from a theological point of view, is also being done in Leuven by Daniel Franklin Pilario, Lope Florente Lesigues, Victorino Cueto and Lawrence Nwankwo, from the perspectives of Pierre Bourdieu, Mikhaïl Bakhtin, Michel de Certeau, and the concept of empowerment respectively.

ter of conflict resolution.[20] In what follows, I will stress the importance of Third Party Mediation and field diplomacy[21] in the effort toward community reconciliation.[22]

Reinterpreting Globalization

Globalization is a worldview not only in the sense that it reflects a fact about the real world in which one lives, but also in its role as a framework of interpretation and reference that one uses to understand this world and to situate oneself within it. If globalization is such a framework, then one cannot remain indifferent to its interpretive influence in guiding one's praxis, one's actions, and one's commitments. We must consider, then, whether it is possible to develop an interpretative framework that allows one to take into account the potentialities of globalization – its emphasis on communication and networking, the idea of a worldwide community, etc. – as well as its dangers that become tangible and visible to its victims. Is it possible to think the potentialities of globalization from the perspective of its victims, so that these may generate creative "tactics"[23] that induce contextualized praxes of liberation?

---

20 For an introduction to conflict studies, see L. Reychler / T. Paffenholz (eds.), *Peace-Building: A Field Guide* (Boulder / London, 2001). See also the unpublished licentiate thesis in theology: E. López Pérez, *Incarnate Forgiveness: Gift and Task of Field Diplomats from a Christian Perspective* (Catholic University, Leuven, Faculty of Theology 1999).

21 R. Moreels / L. Reychler, *De agressie voorbij: Terreindiplomatie* (Zellik, 1995).

22 See: J. Haers, "Close Encounters of the Third 'Week': Enkele voorzichtige theologische overwegingen naar aanleiding van een gesprek over herstel en strafbemiddeling" in *Metanoia* (1997): 58-80; J. Haers, *Wrede Weefsels, Vrede Weefsels* (Averbode, 2001).

23 The word "tactics" is used here in the sense given by Michel de Certeau, as opposed to the idea of a "strategy": "J'appelle 'stratégie' le calcul des rapports de forces qui devient possible à partir du moment où un sujet de vouloir et de pouvoir est isolable d'un 'environnement'. Elle postule un lieu susceptible d'être circonscrit comme un propre et donc de servir de base à une gestion de ses relations avec une extériorité distincte. La rationalité politique, économique ou scientifique est construite sur ce modèle stratégique. J'appelle au contraire 'tactique' un calcul qui ne peut pas compter sur un propre, ni donc sur une frontière qui distingue l'autre comme une totalité visible. La tactique n'a pour lieu que celui de l'autre. Elle s'y insinue, fragmentairement, sans le saisir en son entier, sans pouvoir le tenir à distance." (Michel de Certeau, *L'invention du quotidien.* 1. Arts de faire. Nouvelle édition, établie et présentée par Luce Giard, Folio / Essais, 146 [Paris, 1990], xlvi). Tactics move in what we

Our framework for understanding globalization, as well as our metaphors, intentionally attempts to express, in a difficult move of solidarity, the situation of the victims. To succeed, we will have to become aware of the victims' cry[24] for a sustainable life that is possible only in a worldwide community where everyone take responsibility for others.

The situation of Burundese refugees on the Burundian-Tanzanian border suggested to me a reflection on borders and frontiers. Refugees live on a borderline; they are no-persons in a no-zone. All the characteristics and features that would normally, in the context of a life-giving community or society, give refugees their status, their respect, and their self-esteem, have been taken from them on the borderline. Refugees no longer belong to the societies and communities from which they received stability, peace, and recognition. They have been stripped of what solidified their identity and purpose.

Globalization is often seen as the disappearance or removal of borders: communication and exchange can flow freely in all directions; opportunities abound for everyone to move about and improve their living conditions. Markets become worldwide, offering tempting goods to all consumers. From this perspective, in fact, globalization appears to be a happy series of events, at least at first glance. Indeed, rigid borderlines have always excluded people from the opportunities given to others. Globalization seems to promote a free world for everyone. But things don't really work out like that, as Two Thirds World people never tire of emphasizing. Market dynamics favor the rich and the wealthy who impose their power and their lifestyle on the poor and the powerless. Most assuredly, one needs money and power to profit from market opportunities. Greed and the hunger for power, once kept at bay by borderlines, now flood the world and provoke unforeseen levels of distress. Local

---

will call the frontier space of encounter, as opposed to the borderline of clear separations.

24 The awareness of the cry of the victims as a cry of suffering and of hope derives from a central theme of liberation theology. It reflects the concept of "lugar" or place, as analyzed by Ignacio Ellacuría, and corresponds to an attitude of compassion as it is also expressed in the new testament use of the verb *splangnitzômai*. See L. Pérez Aguirre, *La opción entrañable ante los despojados de sus derechos*, Alcance 44, (Santander, 1992); J. Comblin, *Cry of the Oppressed, Cry of Jesus: Meditations on Scripture and Contemporary Struggle* (Maryknoll, 1988); I. Ellacuría, "Hacia una fundamentación filosófica del método teológico latino-americano," in *Encuentro Latinoamericano de Teología* (Mexico D.F.,1975), 609-35; J. Sobrino, *El prinicipio-misericordia. Bajar de la cruz a los pueblos crucificados*, Presencia teológica 67 (Santander, 1992).

cultures are at pains to survive, and people are deprived of the empowerment and strength they once received from them. Local political forces lose their capacity of resistance as they become powerless in the face of global power games. Borderlines may have been a way to exclude, yet it appears that they were also a protection. Should those borderlines, therefore, be reclaimed and reasserted?

If borders are to be reasserted, however, the specter of the refugees, those no-persons in a no-zone, looms renewed. What refugees ask for, torn between competing communities at war, is peace: war and conflict should cease, so that new communities may arise in place of conflict. The refugee's suffering is the blood that flows when communities are ruptured, when connectedness and cohesion disappear, when mutual responsibilities erode. This is the case for political refugees as well as for economic refugees and immigrants: they call for a home that will exist only when reconciliation, in the form of a more just distribution of wealth and resources, is established. From the perspective of refugees, it is necessary for the murderous antagonists to become protagonists of a shared life-giving history and community. Refugees point to the importance of community building encounters, with the antagonists and between the conflicting parties that have caused their suffering. Refugees represent a suffering third party that attempts to reconcile all those involved in a conflict. In that sense, they call for spaces of encounter, wherein people meet face to face and converse with one another. They call for "frontiers,"[25] fields for dis-

---

25 The word "frontier" is related to the Latin "frons," meaning "face." A frontier is a place where people meet face to face. The idea of frontier, therefore, relates both identity (the frontier delineates one's identity) and relations. The idea I wish to defend here is very well put by Amin Maalouf, on p. 11 of his *Les Identités meurtrières*: "… des êtres portant en eux des appartenances qui, aujourd'hui, s'affrontent violemment; des êtres frontaliers, en quelque sorte, traversés par des lignes de fracture ethniques, religieuses ou autres. En raison même de cette situation, que je n'ose appelé 'privilégiée', ils ont un rôle à jouer pour tisser des liens, dissiper des malentendus, raisonner les uns, tempérer les autres, aplanir, raccomoder …. Ils ont pour vocation d'être des traits d'union, des passerelles, des médiateurs entre les diverses communautés, les diverses cultures. Et c'est justement pour cela que leur dilemme est lourd de signification: si ces personnes elles mêmes ne peuvent assumer leurs appartenances multiples, si elles sont constamment mises en demeure de choisir leur camp, sommées de réintégrer les rangs de elur tribu, alors nous sommes en droit de nous inquiéter sur le fonctionnement du monde." Whereas Maalouf stresses the multiple identities of frontier people, I prefer – so as to emphasize the suffering of people – to highlight the fact that they are stripped of their identities and left on their own, in an in-between that is a no-persons-land. For the concept of "frontier," see also "The Art of Negotiating Frontiers," in *Concilium* 2 (1999).

covery, wherein both their personhood as well as the need for a life-giving community are emphasized.[26]

From the perspective of refugees calling for frontier spaces of encounter and reconciliation, wherein new types of community are able to come into existence and grow, the question of understanding globalization as the universalization of frontier spaces of encounter arises (as opposed to dividing borderlines and as a necessary alternative to the disappearance of borders). This approach to globalization calls for a praxis that creates and enables such frontier spaces as new types of community, a praxis that is undertaken together with the victims of community conflict and originating in their reality. The concrete issue here will always be how to shape globalization processes in such a way that they institute and promote frontier spaces of encounter and create viable, sustainable communities.[27]

Theological Reflection: Features of God

From the preceding it becomes clear that a theology adapted to the challenges posed by and from within a globalized world will necessarily emphasize three crucial perspectives: (1) encounter, conversation, connectedness, holistic belonging; (2) the preferential option for the poor; and (3) the vision of a reconciled world as a community of peace. When looking at these issues from a purely *theo*-logical viewpoint, the stress shifts to (1) God as Creator of a connected world, (2) God as the one who commits himself to the poor in solidarity with them, and 3) God as the one who empowers from the perspective of a vision. This is a truly Trinitarian perspective,[28] in which the Trinity itself is

[26] It is not sufficient to call for "respect for others," as these "others" may still be defined from the perspective of the "I"; the I decides who is an acceptable other and who is not. It is, therefore, important to introduce a concept such as "frontier of encounter," where at the limits of the "I" the other irrupts in the reality of the "I" or interrupts its history as a stranger from "beyond" the border.

[27] This links up with the plea for a new social contract as voiced by Ricardo Petrella in his Écueils de la mondialisation. From a theological point of view, one should refer to the so-called mestizo theologies, as pioneered by Virgilio Elizondo. See his: *The Future is Mestizo: Life Where Cultures Meet*, rev. ed. (Boulder, 2000). See also D.G. Groody, *Border of Death, Valley of Life: An Immigrant Journey of Heart and Spirit*, Celebrating Faith (Lanham *et al.*, 2002).

[28] An overview of these ideas as well as a background to them can be found in P. Álvarez de los Mozos, *Comunidades de solidaridad* (Bilbao, 2002), particularly in his conclusions (241-46). The author emphasizes solidarity and concentrates on the net-

seen as the core dynamism of reality: both God and reality – also human existence – are revealed together.[29] Before approaching these theological aspects, however, some fundamental theological ground must be covered.

Issues of Fundamental Theology

There is a double concern in the sphere of fundamental theology that needs to be addressed. First, one must clarify the concepts of encounter, conversation, and connectedness, as these will constitute the core of our theology. Then, concerning the theological logic appropriate to our approach, it must link the local and the global, as well as respect the tension between the historical event and the universal relation between the Creator and creation.

To clarify the concepts of encounter, conversation, and connectedness, I rely on the ideas of Guy Lafon, as expressed in his *Le Dieu commun*.[30] Here he emphasizes the fundamental priority of conversation over isolated, au-

---

work of communities of solidarity, which he approaches from a personal, politico-economic, and cultural perspective. In doing so, he wants to criticize a too one-sided approach to the idea of the preferential option for the poor. Like Patxi Álvarez, and also Aloysius Pieris in his *God's Reign for God's Poor: A Return to the Jesus Formula* (Gonawila, 1999), he refers to the 34th General Congregation of the Society of Jesus. Pieris emphasizes the ideas of "the poor as our friends in the Lord" (54) and of the covenant community of the "victims of Mammon, who serve as the vicars of Christ" and the "renouncers of Mammon, who witness to God's Reign on earth as the true followers of Jesus" (58). Another reference that is crucial for the following pages is: J. Sobrino, Bearing with One Another in Faith, in: *idem* / J. Hernández Pico, *Theology of Christian Solidarity* (Maryknoll, 1985), 1-42. For further information on issues of liberation theologies that form the backbone of the following pages see also V. Fabella / R.S. Sugirtharajah (eds.), *Dictionary of Third World Theologies* (Maryknoll, 2000); I. Ellacuría / J. Sobrino (eds.), *Mysterium Liberationis: Conceptos fundamentales de la teología de la liberación*, 2 vols. (Madrid, 1990).

29 One should refer here to the thought of both Karl Rahner and Catherine Mowry LaCugna. For an introduction, see: E. T. Groppe, Catherine Mowry LaCugna's "Contribution to Trinitarian Theology," in *Theological Studies* 63 (2002): 730-63. The Trinitarian perspective should also reflect the narrative requirements which will be set out: the Triune God is revealed precisely in history, and this in a double form. Our discourses about the Trinity take their origin in the concrete life of Jesus of Nazareth, in whom God reveals Himself, and they are deepened in the praxis of Christian life in the Spirit of Jesus, the Christ. Human history and the discovery of God are narratively connected.

30 (Paris, 1982).

tonomous, and creative subjectivity, which at best defines itself through its relations with the world outside of itself, and, at worst, defines the outside world as a mere part of itself. In the perspective of Lafon, conversation is a transcendental condition of human life, one that may easily pass unnoticed, even if it is always present within concrete human history and structured by real encounters.[31] Religion, according to Lafon, consists in the free assent to be part of the conversation, and thus to be a part of the game of life and death that binds human beings together. So, the core of religion lies in the welding together of a community within the space of conversation as an (absent) in-between that may be called "God."[32] Following Lafon, I want to emphasize the ontological priority of the idea of connectedness over the idea of an autonomous and creative subject as it is present within modernity and postmodernity. Globalization, as a worldview in the sense we described earlier, reinforces an emphasis on connectedness and togetherness as the solid ground of subjectivity. It is not sufficient to think of relations and encounters as some kinds of attributes of solid subjects through which these attributes relate to one another; rather, subjectivity, individuality, and identity cannot be considered apart from the relations, encounters, and conversations that constitute them. Moreover, as was argued above regarding the concept of virtual enclave, subjectivity is not really overcome as an egocentric power if the web of relations, encounters, and conversations is not taken in its holistic meaning; i.e., as referring to the whole of creation.

The theological logic involved in an approach that stresses encounter and conversation and that claims as the core of Christian faith the encounter with God in Jesus Christ,[33] as transmitted through the myriad concrete encounters

31 For people to find themselves involved in such conversation means that they share history and belong together with all their differences even in the midst of violent conflict between them. The temptation of European philosophy is to consider the togetherness as built upon the coming together of several I's. Theologically, this means forgetting about creation as a whole and considering the Trinity as the coming together of three separate I's.

32 "Dieu désigne ce au nom de quoi les hommes s'allient dans une alliance sure, imbrisable, et … l'on vise, en employant ce nom, une absence tenue pour irrémédiable, indépassable, indéfiniment poussée à bout" (79).

33 This kind of theology, in which the relation with God in Christ is seen as the central core of the Christian faith, can be found in the work of Karl Rahner, with his stress on the transcendental experience and the self-revelation of God, as well as in the Vatican II Constitution on Revelation, Dei Verbum. For Karl Rahner, who never really developed a narrative approach to theology, see his *Grundkurs des Glaubens: Einführung in den Begriff des Christentums* (Freiburg / Basel / Vienna, 1977), as well as his writings

that constitute the history of the church and the church itself, is narrative. The narrative, here, is more than a mere literary technique or device that may be used, for example, to analyze and study biblical texts. Narrativity refers to a structure of human existence: human beings are constituted by the stories they tell, the stories they ascribe to, and the stories they pass on to others in the plot structure of their own lives, as an invitation for others to share in and identify with the experiences that have empowered them.[34] Johann Baptist Metz and Paul Ricoeur have stressed the existential, contextual, and time features of human narrative existence and their importance for Christian faith and theology.[35] Narrativity produces an open logic; i.e., the stories human beings are involved in are open in the sense that they await the decisions and responses of those human beings to further the stories and pass them on to others. Faithfulness to a given tradition and creativity in its understanding and transmission are inseparably linked. Narrativity links the local histories of people to global concerns, by viewing the latter as always articulated through the lens of the former. This is a form of the so-called hermeneutical circle, where the reciprocal clarifications of the whole and the parts are claimed.

In what follows, both theological logic and method of argumentation are assumed to be connected to the profound narrative structures of human existence: through narratives, human beings are welded into one community that is constituted precisely by the individual stories of those human beings within it. This understanding allows us to give proper attention both to the historical and to that which transcends historical concreteness. It allows for historical diversity, while nevertheless claiming to refer to *the* Christian faith as such. A narrative approach to theological concepts underscores the importance of the

---

on sacramental theology, particularly his conception of *Realsymbol* as presented in "Zur Theologie des Symbols," in K. Rahner, *Schriften zur Theologie*, vol. IV (Einsiedeln / Zürich / Cologne) 275-311.

34 A very good example of this narrative logic is provided by Roland Barthes' analysis of Ignatius Loyola's Spiritual Exercises, interpreted as Ignatius' way to offer his own experience of the encounter with God so as to invite others to enter into a similar encounter. See: R. Barthes, *Sade, Fourier, Loyola*, Tel Quel (Paris, 1970.) M. Ende's *The Neverending Story* (London, 1991) offers a tale illustrating the narrative process and inducing the reader to enter into its dynamism.

35 For more information, see: S. Hauerwas / L. G. Jones (eds.), *Why Narrative? Readings in Narrative Theology* (Grand Rapids, 1989); W.J.T. Mitchell (ed.), *On Narrative* (Chicago / London, 1981); T. Peter Kemp / D. Rasmussen (eds.), *The Narrative Path: The Later Works of Paul Ricoeur*, Cambridge MA / London, 1989).

contextualization of concepts, especially as they emerge ever new in the current ever changing dynamism of human communities and cultures. At its most basic, narrativity implies a time structure capable of rendering one sensitive to the empowering and critical features of both history and social vision. Moreover, within narrative, it is not possible to dislocate past, present, and future from one another, even if it pays to distinguish among them.

God as the Creator of a Connected World

Antonin Dalmace Sertillanges has shown how in the thought of Thomas Aquinas, creation is a relational concept.[36] Of course, caveats must be introduced to ensure that the relation between God, the Creator, and his creatures is not misunderstood as placement of Creator and creature on the same level. A similar remark can be made regarding patristic authors such as Origen of Alexandria and their understanding of creation. Origen's cosmological schemes are misunderstood when they are not viewed as description and articulation of the multifaceted experience of the encounter with God.[37] The advantage of such an understanding of creation as relation is that it links up with a concept of revelation in which the self-revelation of God and the relation between God and his creatures are at the center of Christian faith, a view that is also found in the documents of the Second Vatican Council, more specifically, in its constitution about divine revelation.

It is important, however, to realize that the "idea of creation as relation" should not be over-spiritualized or over-individualized. The relation of creation concerns not only the relation between God and an individual human being alone. This individual relation is always situated in and mediated through the relation between God and the whole of reality and the relation between the individual human being and the rest of creation. Creation is, in that sense, a "material" and "historical" reality. Therefore, it is reasonable to speak about the whole of reality as "creation" and to develop over and over again cosmologies as a part of protology, as they stress creational togetherness and wholeness.

---

36 *L'idée de création et ses retentissements en philosophie* (Paris, 1945).

37 A particularly interesting book is: M. Rutten, *Om mijn oorsprong vechtend: Origenes ofwel het optimisme van een mysticus*, Mystieke teksten en thema's 5 (Kampen / Averbode, 1991). See also, of course, H. Crouzel, *Origen* (Edinburgh, 1989).

Changes in our scientific understanding of the world, particularly the theory of evolution and the growing awareness of our universe's complexity, also suggest an understanding of creation that indicates an interconnected and evolving world in its relationship to God. This means that the relationships between creatures and Creator are always mediated by the relationship to the whole of creation and by connectedness with the whole of reality.[38]

Liberation theologians working on the notion of creation,[39] however, always emphasize that one should not hide the fact that creation as it is now dwells a far cry away from perfection and the ideal of connectedness we usually attribute to the concept: creation is a broken creation, in which great suffering takes place. This fact calls for a nuanced vision of creation, one that takes into account commitment to those who suffer and one that stimulates a praxis at their side working against the causes of their suffering. We recognize herein structural parallels between the notion of creation and the globalization of our world. The concept of creation must be deepened both as the idea of fundamental and holistic togetherness, and as the attempt to safeguard that holistic view through preferential attention to those who suffer. For liberation theology, an awareness of holistic creation translates into a praxis of the preferential option for the poor.

God as the One Who Commits Himself in Solidarity with the Poor

God, as He reveals Himself in the life of Jesus of Nazareth, is the God who sides with the poor.[40] Plenty of stories about Jesus' life illustrate this fact, and so does the life of Jesus itself, ending as it does on a cross: a death befitting a rejected and excluded human being, a no-person. In times of globalization, if

---

38 Such views of creation as a connected whole in relation to God are found in S. McFague, *The Body of God: An Ecological Theology* (Minneapolis, 1993) and in L. Boff, *Cry of the Earth, Cry of the Poor* (Maryknoll, 1997). The latter emphasizes also very strongly the preferential option for the poor. Ecological theologies or ecotheologies stress the belonging to the cosmos as a whole.

39 A well-known example is P. Trigo, *Creation and History*, Liberation and Theology Series (Tunbridge Wells, 1992).

40 The word "solidarity" jumps to mind and it is often used, particularly in the official Church documents. One should take into account, however, that solidarity should not be understood as specifically a gesture of the rich person to the poor person. Rather it indicates reciprocity and mutual presence to one another, constitutive of community building. This is also true for the relationship of solidarity between God and the poor.

we intend to take seriously the opportunity inherent in the coming to be of a worldwide, global, community – as presented and promised to us in Jesus' predication and praxis of the Kingdom of God – it is necessary to understand that the holistic, worldwide dimension of this community requires careful attention, and in particular, preferential attention for the poor, the victims, the excluded, the no-persons, the frontier-people who cry for spaces of encounter that will bring about communities of solidarity. They constitute the focus from whence to view reality.

God, in sharing our humanity, focuses on the poor and excluded. The preferential option for the poor[41] is, then, a truly *theo*-logical option, in which people, following in the footsteps of Jesus of Nazareth, are willing to become poor, so as to share the plight and the struggle of the poor. In this praxis they also discover intimately, in their very experiences of solidarity and poverty, who God Himself is. Therefore, a real kenotic attitude is required of us all, as we attempt to open up to the desires, the longings, and the sufferings of the poor, in order to side with them and in order to build a community with them.[42] The preferential option for the poor, however, does not merely indicate an attitude of compassion and listening; it also trusts the creativity of the poor and the victims in fighting the causes of their suffering and their ability to bring about a renewed community.[43] The issue of solidarity and compan-

---

41 Some introductory material on the issue: G. Gutiérrez, *The Power of the Poor in History* (Maryknoll, 1984): G. Gutiérrez, "Option pour les pauvres: bilan et enjeux," in *Alternatives Sud* 7 (2000): 27-37; J. O'Brien, *Theology and the Option for the Poor*, Theology and Life Series 22 (Collegeville, 1992); D. Dorr, *Option for the Poor: A Hundred Years of Catholic Social Teaching* (Maryknoll, 1992); N.F. Lohfink, *Option for the Poor: The Basic Principle of Liberation Theology in the Light of the Bible*, Berkeley Lecture Series 1 (1987); J. M. Castillo, *Los pobres y la teología. ¿Qué queda de la teologiía de la liberación?* Cristianisme y sociedad 49, 3rd ed. (Bilbao, 1998); J. Sobrino, "Theology from amidst the Victims," in M. Volf, C. Krieg and T. Kucharz (eds.), *The Future of Theology: Essays in Honor of Jürgen Moltmann* (Grand Rapids / Cambridge, 1996), 164-75; G. V. Pixley / C. Boff, *Opción por los pobres* (Madrid, 1988).

42 This implies a movement for the poor and the crucified, suffering people. Very often, this movement is unsettling as it forces us to change our perception of reality and our language and views on God. Indeed, the poor and suffering people are not necessarily the ones we would define as being poor or suffering, but those who impose themselves on us as such, in that they reflect God's transcendence over against all our attempts to immanentize God from the perspective of the I.

43 Ignacio Ellacuría stresses this as he claims the crucified people to be the place where Jesus is present.

ionship is crucial, particularly if one wants to avoid a paternalistic approach to the fate of the poor and excluded.

The dynamisms of field diplomacy and third party interventions in conflict resolution processes offer interesting perspectives for understanding this kenotic attitude.[44] Indeed, the third party can be viewed as the friend of two enemies, one who attempts to represent each antagonist to the other, allowing both parties to play out their conflict in the secure environment of a friendship, thereby permitting an optimally creative search for solutions to the real conflict at hand.[45] Field diplomacy requires a long term presence with people, leading to intimate acquaintance with their situations and with their experiences, needs, and hopes. Poverty and exclusion, understood as conflicts, are solved not primarily "from above," with the strategies of those who are in control and have theories about how to resolve conflicts, but foremost "from aside" those who suffer. Here, on the scene of suffering, the need for healing is most acute and the patient work of solidarity – reflecting the thirty "hidden" years of Jesus' youth – provides for tactics of resistance to injustice and of reconciliation amidst suffering.

God as the One Who Empowers From the Perspective of a Vision

Patxi Álvarez de los Mozos[46] points to the fact that the preferential option for the poor, because of a renewed emphasis on the cultural dimensions of our reality,[47] requires the notion of solidarity towards the building of communities of solidarity, which, in contact with one another, will form a worldwide net-

---

44 I have attempted to develop these themes in my *Wrede Weefsels, Vrede Weefsels*. Field diplomats and third parties are those who care for the reconciled community, those who attempt to build and sustain the bridges that build communities. They represent the parties to one another and, in that sense, are real ambassadors.

45 K. Raiser in his *For a Culture of Life: Transforming Globalization and Violence* (Geneva, 2002), emphasizes the link between the issues of globalization and violence, and their transformation, concentrating on the notion of "life."

46 See the conclusions of Comunidades de Solidaridad.

47 See also G. De Schrijver (ed.), *Liberation Theologies on Shifting Grounds: A Clash of Socio-Economic and Cultural Paradigms*, BETL 135 (Leuven, 1998). The emphasis on the cultural dimensions allow for clarifying the tactics of resistance and the empowerment provided to people in their cultural contexts. It also poses anew the issue of the relations between culture and Christian faith, particularly as it surfaces in the construction of worldviews.

work embodying global solidarity. One finds similar reflections in Aloysius Pieris' *God's Reign for God's Poor*, and in Jon Sobrino's *Bearing with One Another in Faith*. The preferential option for the poor constitutes a community, and a community can only be constituted seriously if it shows a preferential sensitivity for those who suffer, particularly for those who suffer from the very mechanisms by which the community is being built. It is in the special care for the poor that the Kingdom of God comes about.

This means that the preferential option for the poor is profoundly linked to the central vision of the Christian faith, i.e., the Kingdom of God. Such vision is already at work in our broken world, here and now, precisely through those who suffer from the fact that it is not yet realized. The vision is not a mere future event:[48] its realization in the life of Jesus as God's presence amidst creation is the empowering force towards praxis of the fulfillment of what has been promised by God in Jesus. It is expressed in sacramental and liturgical life, as well as in religious vows, which represent the rules for the strategies of building community: poor with the poor against poverty, obedient with the oppressed against oppression, celibate with the lonely against solitude and exclusion.[49] By celebrating this vision and by attempting to put it into practice, against all odds and against our own powerlessness in the matter, the preferential option for the poor takes on the form of shared community. Maybe the greatest challenge in the midst of such community building is the invitation to forgiveness and reconciliation. Here even a violent conflict is interpreted as a conversation, be it an undesired and painful one, which holds a key to mutual belonging and "reciprocal anonymity."[50]

---

48 From this perspective, one can understand Karl Rahner's objections to apocalyptic eschatological language.

49 Cf. my *Geloften aan de grens* (Averbode, 2000).

50 This last expression I derive from Karl Rahner's concept of "anonymous Christians," by emphasizing not what are usually considered to be its inclusivistic overtones, but by focusing on the idea the other is considered as an anonymous "same," i.e. receives the same rights and respect as I would be giving to those who are close to me. The reciprocal indicates that this attitude also hopes for reciprocity and mutuality, i.e., that the other would consider me as an anonymous "same." I would be given the same rights and respect as the other would grant to those who are close to him or her. "Anonymous reciprocity" expresses the priority of the creational togetherness over the antagonism between the "same" and the "other."

Conclusion

What has been presented here represents a Trinitarian theology, but one that arises within the economy of salvation – taken in the life of Jesus and in the praxis of today – and, therefore, in the historical praxis of people who, in line with the God who reveals Himself as a committed God in the life of Jesus of Nazareth, Christ, are empowered to take on the challenge of God in Jesus, and in this Spirit, commit themselves to the creation of a reconciled creation wide community amidst a broken world in which the poor and the excluded reveal God's presence as the crucified Jesus, as Christ.

The challenges described do not seem to be particularly or specifically "European." Nonetheless, in the global task at hand, European theologians will play an important role, precisely because of the opportunities offered by their European context in which the issues of community building and exclusion are discussed and debated as key issues. First, they will enter into a listening attitude, sensitive to the voices that in the classical schemes of theology and in its classical approaches do not receive sufficient attention. This reflects the faith they articulate in their theologies about a God who commits himself to suffering and excluded people from the perspective of the Kingdom of God, and so also compels us to change our very understanding of God. Second, Europe's greatest asset consists in its experience in community building, in its social heritage, and in the much diversified perspectives it has to offer, even amidst the worst conflicts and tensions. Europe's major temptation in the coming years will be its tendency toward isolation and enclavism, its attempts to build a fortress Europe, which therein betrays its own inclination toward self-destruction. Therefore, the major task for European theologians will be how to combine, in thought and commitment, the perspectives of a preferential option for the poor and the construction of a worldwide community that reflects God's own dream and promise of the coming Kingdom. Their challenge, ultimately, is ecclesiological.

Hans-Joachim Sander

From a European Subject to a Global Verb: God in Terms of Pastoral Relativity

God is power,[1] and that is reason enough to talk about God. Regarding the origin of this talk, it is fair to surmise that the very concept of "God" was invented to deal with religious problems.[2] Beyond religious problems, God's power is fragile. Indeed, one may quite seriously question if this power has

---

1 Throughout this article, God is examined through a semiotic lens, i.e., the focus is on what the sign "God" represents in discourse about God. To deal with God or to talk about God one has to invent, produce, and discuss signs for God. This is not to deny that other approaches are possible for dealing with what the sign of God actually stands for. But it means that within each perspective regarding God, the sign "God" is a major factor. For semiotics, cf. C.S. Peirce, *Semiotische Schriften*, 3 vol., Frankfurt, 1986-1993; *Writings of Charles S. Peirce: A Chronological Edition*, vol 1ff., edited by M.H. Fisch / E.C. Moore / C.J.W. Kloesel (Bloomington, 1982ff; *Religionsphilosophische Schriften*, übers. u. Mitarb. v. Helmut Maaßen, edited by Hermann Deuser (Hamburg, 1995). In the collection "Gott: Erfahrung und Geheimnis", in *Concilium* 37/1 (2001) the impact of semiotic grammar regarding God-talk is ignored. The term "power" is used here following Michel Foucault's analysis of power, cf. M. Foucault, *Von der Subversion des Wissens* (Frankfurt, 1987); In *Verteidigung der Gesellschaft: Vorlesungen am Collège de France (1975-76)* (Frankfurt, 1999); *Die Anormalen: Vorlesungen am Collège de France (1974-1975)* (Frankfurt, 2003). For theology, Foucault's term pastoral power has a special impact, cf. Michel Foucault, "Warum ich die Macht untersuche: die Frage des Subjekts," in H. L. Dreyfus / P. Rabinow, *Michel Foucault: Jenseits von Strukturalismus und Hermeneutik* (Frankfurt, 1987), 243-50. See also the readers by J. Engelmann (ed.) / M. Foucault, *Botschaften der Macht* (Stuttgart, 1999) and by J.R. Carrette (ed.), *Religion and Culture by Michel Foucault* (Manchester, 1999). For the theological discourse about Foucault just beginning in German theology, cf. H. Steinkamp, *Die sanfte Macht der Hirten: Die Bedeutung Michel Foucaults für die praktische Theologie* (Mainz, 1999); J. Hoff, *Spiritualität und Sprachverlust: Theologie nach Foucault und Derrida* (Paderborn,1999); M. Pfannkuchen, *Archäologie der Moral: Zur Relevanz von Michel Foucault für die theologische Ethik*, Münster: Lit 2000; C. Bauer / M. Hölzl (eds.), *Gottes und des Menschen Tod? Die Theologie vor der Herausforderung Michel Foucaults* (Mainz, 2003).

2 "Religious" is taken here in the broad sense of the term meaning not only religious communities or religious traditions, but cultural, social, political, and intellectual mentalities dealing with a special sort of power once called "the holy." Cf. M. Eliade, *Das Heilige und das Profane: Vom Wesen des Religiösen* (Frankfurt, 1987); R. Caillois, *Der Mensch und das Heilige: Durch drei Anhänge über den Sexus, das Spiel und den Krieg in ihren Beziehungen zum Heiligen*, expanded edition (Munich, 1988).

real importance outside a religious context in the broadest sense of the word. In some circumstances, however, the concept of "God" is invented in deference to religious power structures outside the religion that is inventing it, while it achieves a dual purpose that finds it strengthening the interior workings of the "subservient" religious group. Depending on how it is used, such a concept can be wielded variously in order to increase or to decrease religious power.

One early European invention of a God concept outside of religion had a major impact on God-talk in general. It took place in early and classical Greece while people calling themselves "philosophers" attempted to abandon discourse that was centered mainly on mythology.[3] Philosophers used the concept of "God" to provide an alternative intellectual landscape in an effort to challenge the overweening power of religious ritual. In their attempts, they shaped a world of ideas, wrought a sea change in religious practice, and thereby forged the keystone of European God-talk: the metaphysical God.

The Metaphysical God: Power of and Confrontation with Old Europe

From Socrates to Descartes, from Plato to Whitehead, from Aristotle to Anselm, from Plotinus to Leibniz, from Thomas Aquinas to Kant, from Cusanus to Heidegger, God-talk has proceeded from either a metaphysical or an anti-metaphysical perspective. The God-concept treated, broadly, the nature of beings of the world and the nature of "being" itself. This discourse about

---

3 This does not mean that they could bring to an end or even avoid mythological discourse. There is no such thing as the famous change "from mythos to logos." This once-favored perspective underestimates the representational abilities in mythological approaches to natural and historical realities and overestimates the discursive abilities in rational approaches to social and personal realities. On the contrary, the new type of intellectual in old Greece had to invent new subjects of mythological discourses for presenting their own views. But by doing so, they were able to transform mythology into the linguistic sort of mythologizing present in philosophy today. Cf. L. Brisson, *Einführung in die Philosophie des Mythos*, vol. 1 (Darmstadt, 1996): "Platons Versuch, mit der Tradition reinen Tisch zu machen, zwingt ihn, angesichts unlösbarer Fragen seinerseits Mythen zu produzieren. Ebenfalls scheitert, wer, wie die Vertreter des allegorischen Verfahrens, die mythischen Elemente systematisch in philosophische Begriffe zu übersetzen sucht. Nur ein Denken, das seine Grenzen kennt, entgeht dem Irrationalismus. Paradoxerweise beruht die Macht der Vernunft in dieser Einsicht in ihre Beschränkung." (3)

God accepted or rejected the metaphysical God, agreed with or denied its meaning, and sought to construct or deconstruct it as an idea.

The universal applicability of this God-talk is a convincing argument in favor of a metaphysical God. This God can easily become the subject in any branch of intellectual discourse. The most pressing challenge to the viability of the metaphysical God concept comes from the plurality of alternate frameworks for reality. The systems of life, nature, and history do not function in compliance with metaphysical ideas. Although they have only relative meaning, the hard science's seeming incompatibility with metaphysics also raises the question of metaphysics' relativity. Relativity becomes an argument as soon as intellectual discourse stops to focus on universality through the frameworks of particular realities. At first this discourse found its subject in the question of the true relations between Sun, Earth, and planets. After Copernicus, Kepler, and Galileo, metaphysical universality broke down in relation to the nature of the universe. God's relation to human beings could not be based on the central astronomical position of the Earth.

The final break with the power of the metaphysical God happened during the Enlightenment with its focus on the particular reality of the subject. Before the Enlightenment, the metaphysical God existed in compliance with particular realities. Although the relative meanings of life, nature, and history were never a major subject for metaphysics, these realities do matter for religion. Religious perspectives come out of particular realities and their discourses empower particularities to be the locus for confronting the universality of the world. In this sense, the God of the philosophers and the God of Abraham, Isaac, and Jacob could easily be combined – together they produce a powerful form of God-talk – from this God-talk emerges the concept of the personal God which is at the same time the almighty Creator of all reality, all beings, and any being at all. This type of God gives birth to the dogmatic God of Christian religion. The dogmatic God is a particular reality characterized by utmost universality. It has a life form constituted by a combination of beliveing and being, subjectivity and objectivity, wisdom and reason, Holy Scripture and classical scriptures, Jerusalem, and Athens.

Before the Enlightenment, the bipolarity of a metaphysical God and a personal God empowered Europe to become a civilization that believed in having a global mission. Processing this belief into social, political, scientific, cultural habits, Europe enabled itself to transform its local issues of religious self-understanding into a global right to power. Thus, the European discovery of the world functioned as a sign from God. God was a kind of resource for the early modern European globalization of the world. But at the same time, this sign opened up the door to the importance of particular realities not to be subdued by universal outlooks. As soon as the power of different particular realities functioning with their own and special systems shattered the old metaphysical framework of the world, the dogmatic combination of a metaphysical and religious God lost its convincing force and its energizing disposition. The God of the philosophers and the biblical God separated. This meant a de-powering process. God's bipolar existence came to an end and in religious terms only a personal God remained.

Of course, the personal God brings with it a serious form of God-talk, but it faces a problem in terms of power: In compliance with enlightened modernity, the God of Abraham, Isaac, Jacob, and Jesus lost its universal meaning. In order to present this God in universal terms, at least a right to believe or, more consequently, a will to believe becomes strictly necessary.[4] After this separation, God's power depends on the personal will of those who believe in its universality. In consequence, religion has become a personal act, and in the end God-talk is a private matter. The dogmatic God of religion still has power

[4] Cf. W. James, "The Will to Believe," in *idem*, *The Will to Believe and Other Essays in Popular Philosophy* (New York, 1956), 1-31 (first published 1897; German: "Der Wille zum Glauben," in *idem*, *Essays über Glaube und Ethik* [Gütersloh: Verlagshaus 1948], 40-67). James himself interpreted this will, not as a strictly personal decision of individuals, but as a social chance for persons acting as individuals in relation to others. This will stands for a right to belief: "my 'Will to Believe' – luckless title, which should have been the 'Right to Believe…'" (taken from a letter to F.H. Bradley in 1904, cf. Hans Joas, *Die Entstehung der Werte* [Frankfurt, 1999], 68). The logic of this will to belief is not taken from individualistic voluntarism or set by fundamentalism; the logic follows pragmatism. Whoever wants to realize what believing in God means has to pay attention what kind of action is made possible by this belief. Somebody willing to believe in God can set actions which give a clue of what this God could be all about: "In truths dependent on our personal action, then, faith based on desire is certainly a lawful and possibly an indispensable thing." ("The Will to Believe," 25). See the forceful dissent by Bertrand Russell representing *ex negativo* the significance of James' description for the modern development in terms of religion and God: "James' Doktrin ist ein Versuch, einen Oberbau von Glauben auf einer Basis von Skeptizismus zu errichten, und wie alle derartigen Versuche beruht er auf Trugschlüssen. In seinem Falle entstehen die Trugschlüsse durch das Bemühen, alle außermenschlichen Tatsachen zu übersehen. Berkeleyscher Idealismus gepaart mit Skeptizismus veranlaßt ihn, Gott durch den Glauben an Gott zu ersetzen und zu behaupten, das sei ebenso gut. Wir haben darin aber nur eine Abart des subjektivistischen Wahnsinns zu sehen, der charakteristisch ist für die ganze moderne Philosophie." (B. Russell, *Philosophie des Abendlandes: Ihr Zusammenhang mit der politischen und der sozialen Entwicklung*, 6th ed. [Vienna, 1992], 825)

to stabilize religious communities but this God does not have sufficient power for a global mission.[5]

The enlightened separation was the graveyard for the power structure of the metaphysically and personally shaped God. Nietzsche, of course, wrote the famous advertisement of this God's death. This death did not mean the end of God-talk, but power had become a bad habit for God. While there is still much public talk about God, while there are still socially influential Churches, old traditional religions, and meanwhile a bunch of new religious movements that continuously talk about God, preach God, advertise for the life of God,[6] still, nobody can gain real public power with arguments referring to a God whose power depends on the belief of subjects.[7]

The God of the European community is a recent example of this, especially the current political struggle to introduce God into the forthcoming constitution of the European Union. There is no reason not to lobby for this God,

---

5 For such a stabilizing function cf. Ingolf Dalferth, "'Was Gott ist, bestimme ich!' Reden von Gott im Zeitalter der 'Cafeteria-Religion'," in J. Beutler / E. Kunz (eds.), *Heute von Gott reden* (Würzburg, 1998), 57-78: "[Die Theologie ...] spricht stets aus der Perspektive der Beteiligten, weil sie den christlichen Glauben und nicht ein philosophisch reformuliertes Substitut in (religiöser) Beobachterperspektive neutral zu beschreiben sucht, ob das nun in Gestalt einer monistischen oder pluralistischen Metaphysik geschieht. Theologie hat über eine bestimmte Einstellung zur Wirklichkeit Rechenschaft abzulegen, die im Bekenntnis des Glaubens zum Ausdruck kommt. Diese Einstellung fügt wissenschaftlichen Detail- und metaphysischen Totalbeschrei-bungen unserer Welt keine religiöse Beschreibung hinzu, sondern wirkt wirklichkeitserschließend, indem sie unsere Welt in allen ihren Details unter jeder Beschreibung coram Deo beurteilt" (69). With such ideas, theologies and churches may resist attempts to put together one's own, self-evident religious beliefs ("Cafeteria-Religion"), but then they will have no place in the many cafeterias of this world. It is diminished to a highly cultivated place where people drop in because they don't want anything else than the one and only dish served at this place under the name of God. It looks like such restaurants will have a hard time staying in the market.

6 Cf. R. Hempelmann *et.al.* (eds.), *Panorama der neuen Religiösität: Sinnsuche und Heilsversprechen zu Beginn des 21. Jahrhunderts* (Gütersloh, 2001).

7 Cf. Peter Strasser's longing for a religious universalism strictly separated from any religious will to power: "Die Frage des religiösen Universalismus ist also auf keinen Fall mit der Frage identisch, welche Religion sich letztendlich durchgesetzt haben wird." ("Die Menschheit vor dem Absoluten. Religiöser Universalismus und religiöses Empfinden," in F. Uhl / A. Boelderl (eds.), *Zwischen Verzückung und Verzweiflung: Dimensionen religiöser Erfahrung* [Düsseldorf, 2001], 129-49, 132). For a theological dispute with Strasser's will to religious believing beyond religious communities, cf. A. Halbmayr / J. Mautner, *Gott im Dunkeln - Religion in den Lebenswelten der späten Moderne: Gespräche mit Evelyn Schlag, Bettina Bäumer und Peter Strasser* (Innsbruck, 2003).

but whoever takes the field at the end of the day, it will not matter a great deal. Nobody can claim power by referring to this legalistic God-talk or by making claims based on the absence of such legal representation. The constitutional God will not change societies for the better or for the worse. A European Union that supports a constitutional God will not thereby overcome the private status of religious communities and this God will not give public glory to the strivings of premodern social and political habits. A European Constitution is no habitat for such a thing as a truly blossoming, thriving life form of God.[8]

There is an urgent problem that post-metaphysical European God-talk has impressed upon theology. It motivates the search for some sort of final subjectivity in God. This searching remains after the universal meaning of God has faded away. The idea goes somehow like this: If one can only reasonably talk about a personal God without a metaphysical universality, there must be some sort of personal identity behind that concept, the identity of a somewhat almighty subject or at least the identity of a superhuman person nevertheless faced with the same urgent necessity to live in freedom and to undergo breath-taking empathic suffering at the same time.[9] Guardini put it well in his famous question: "Why, God, all those terrible deviations on the road to salvation, all this suffering of the innocent, all this guilt?"[10] It is only such a familiar, fragile kind of identity that could be accepted so willingly, so immediately, and so unquestioningly and still be taken seriously enough to be embraced so personally.

The now urgent subject of European God-talk is theodicy. After the Shoa, it has become even more pressing. But theodicy is a leftover from the time when the metaphysical God still had a good grip on the personal God. The subject of theodicy is an unsolvable question for the metaphysical God and at the same time a never-ending story for the personal God. It is the signpost on top of the eroded power structures of European God-talk.

---

[8] For alternatives in Christian European Lobbying, see the issue on "Christliches Europa?" in *Wort und Antwort* 4 (2003): 145-92, especially Ignace Bertgen's report (147-51).

[9] "Wenn Gott wirklich das Risiko einer Freiheitsgeschichte einging, dann wird umso unentbehrlicher auch das Zeugnis, daß Gott sich nicht unbeteiligt heraushielt, sondern sich von ihr und ihrem Leiden betreffen läßt, ja sich selber ihm aussetzt." (T. Pröpper, *Evangelium und freie Vernunft. Konturen einer theologischen Hermeneutik* [Freiburg, 2001], 273).

[10] Ernst Tewes, "Romano Guardini," in *Liturgisches Jahrbuch* 19 (1969): 140.

In relation to this European approach to God and its confrontation with the doubt of God's existence challenged by theodicy, one is tempted to use the already famous words of Donald Rumsfeld, acting US Secretary of Defense, "That's old Europe." There is no doubt that one can shape rationally convincing God-talk in terms of such an "Old Europe,"[11] But it remains quite doubtful if such intellectual enterprises will bring back God's former power. This Old European God is a subject "making sense but having no meaning" – not enough to make a difference today. Such a theology will probably suffer the fate of civil religion. It belongs somehow to the traditional European world, but its subjects and discourses don't matter very much. Of course, one cannot argue against the truth claims of such a theology by questioning whether it matters. But there are alternatives for God-talk. An important alternative was invented in the non-European regions of the World.

The Local God: The Power of Others' Worlds and Confrontation with the First World

The universality of the European God became the premise for a global mission. It meant power for the First World and its economic offspring. But it meant, at the same time, powerlessness for those who could not live at the center of this mission. Their powerlessness did not end after the death of Old Europe's God, and it still remains as a pressing problem quite different from theodicy. The question for those whose fate is to experience powerlessness is not, "why this suffering," but "how to live in this suffering." This shift from the metaphysical remains of the personal God led to an important discovery for God-talk: God is a power that is especially important in situations of powerlessness. For the use of this power it is not necessary that God be metaphysically convincing or personally accepted. It is only necessary that this God maintain importance within the local situation of this powerless suffering. After the death of the metaphysical God the local God was born.

This local God is not affected by the problems the metaphysical God cannot solve in relation to particular realities. On the contrary, the local God lives out of minutely particular realities. Particularity is its strength. Realities that are bound to special situations, unprecedented sufferings, non-ideal relations,

11 Mentioned as one example of a whole series of highly elaborated theodicy theologies: Armin Kreiner, *Gott im Leid. Zur Stichhaltigkeit der Theodizee-Argumente* (Freiburg, 1997).

are valuable contexts for the text this local God-talk produces. These contexts confront the global mission of the First World from the obverse side of the mission: the silent failures, the forgotten violence, the ignored suffering, the not-yet confessed oppression such a global mission has produced in its era. Therefore, this local God is not a purely local power. It starts out as a local power, but it is eager to step outside its particular locality. The local God has the power of confrontation toward the global mission of the European and any other First World entity. It is empowered through preferential options for those who have to live locally on the dark side of the First Worlds' global missions.

The leading contextual theology to date has been liberation theology. It deals with the particularity of the poor as a *locus theologicus*. It does not ask what the being of poorness is all about, but how this poorness may mark the beginning of global change in the power structures of the world. Similarly, feminist theology and theologies of Christian minorities within an overwhelming religious pluralism focus on special particular contexts in the effort toward global change to a better world.

With this strategy, the metaphysical problems of God-talk can be overcome. By the global logic of local experience, liberation theologians can transform the personal God missing its other pole, the metaphysical God. They appropriate the power of this personal God, not through metaphysical universality, but through a much needed plurality. With such a perspective, suffering changes its meaning. It is hardly an argument against God's universal power, but a locus to demonstrate what God's power is all about. The local God is focused on martyrdom, not on theodicy.[12] This is its strong side. It has overcome the God of Old Europe.

But one task remains: To find a local alternative for the old strength of the bipolar metaphysical and personal God – the universality of God's power. The local God urges confrontation with significant human or inhuman situations. But if people do not share the same contexts, it is difficult to import significance into other contexts. As long as the contexts are different, discourse about the meaning of local Gods remains an intellectual enterprise. It is something for theologians in the First World, not for a political transformation of this World. The local God cannot gain the power to transform other

[12] Cf. *Concilium* 1/2003: "Martyrium in neuem Licht," especially P. Casaldáliga, "Offener Brief an unsere Märtyrer," 132f. and the somewhat classical example of liberation theology: J. Sobrino, *Sterben muß, wer an Götzen rührt: Das Zeugnis der ermordeten Jesuiten in San Salvador. Fakten und Überlegungen* (Fribourg / Brig, 1990).

contexts than its own. For this reason, there is no significant European locus for a theology of liberation – such a transfer hasn't happened yet. And after the end of a global political bipolarity, the chances for such a transformation have become even weaker. The local God has contextual power, but its God-talk has no trans-contextual power. It remains of local interest.

There exists another solution for this problem that doesn't act in compliance with the local grammars of diverse contextual Gods. A local God denying its local context solves the problem of missing universality. This local God is not a matter of locality and contextuality. It is a matter of pure power to be experienced within a special context. This local God has a will to power, not only a will to locality. It has just recently emerged and shown its force. It is a power that strikes deeply by the ambiguity of its force. And it has discovered a way to bring religion back into the public power game.

The Religious God: Power of the New World and Confrontation in the New World

The most efficient way to acknowledge and work with local Gods while advancing one's own mission agenda is to become religious. Such mission agendas may be furthered by "statements" that include the force of violence. Through violence and through claims about the universal nature of a local God (a claim that shifts the center of power away from the local and into the hands of those specialist arbiters of the universal), the pure locality of a God can be denied. This is a trans-modern strategy. In Old Europe the religious God was bound to the idealism of the metaphysical God. The religious God had to be the God of the philosophers. It had to be a God of social and theological virtues, a God of universal moral standards. As soon as the religious God became independent of the God of philosophers and revealed its violent nature, Old Europe answered with the Enlightenment and broke away from the public meanings of religious communities. The modern world emerged, an arduous habitat for the religious God. This breaking with the religious importance of God was empowered by reason. As long as reason remained the only valid universal perspective, this secular approach to the problems of life could control religious powers. But reason alone is a pretty weak power strategy. It has to produce lasting progress in order to be generally accepted. As soon as progress becomes fragile, reasonable power strategies fall apart.

The religious renewal of the recent decades has taken place within such a fragile situation. European modernity has come to an end without finding a successor for its global mission. For this reason, Old Europe is driven by the new public meaning of religion, and it doesn't know what to do with it. Religion is no longer a power dealing with the enlightened modern state. It deals with a major problem the modern state has not been able to solve: the difference between public good and public evil. There is power in this difference. Old Europe has been focused on public legality and policies of righteousness. The difference between good and evil arose as a concern for religion within personal rather than public borders.

But in the New World, people have invented another way of religious life. It combines revolution *and* religion and it uses the political force arising from the difference between good and evil. In North America, a coalition force backed the fight for freedom, which was fashioned by believers in the Enlightenment. The goal of complete religious freedom was highly ranked on the American Revolution's agenda. The New World embraced the separation of Church and State from Old Europe advanced by the Enlightenment, while it nonetheless continued to use religious strategies in realms of political power. The struggle for the abolition of slavery is one prominent example.[13] In keeping with this combination of religion and revolution, the New World found a new source to back its global mission – democracy and the belief in its superiority over other forms of political power. "God Bless America" is not simply a sign for civil religion; it is a statement by a public power backed by religion.

It is within the semiotic range of this statement, "God Bless America," for one to take public action toward the separation of good and evil. Empowered by religious freedom and by religious commitments at the same time, this kind of democracy not only provides a political context for human rights, but stands up for policies that are against evil and in favor of good. The religious God of this democracy is a public life form looking for global representation. It gets public power by backing secular global missions, which exist to fight evil political structures. It is no contradiction to say that the USA is one of the most religious and at the same time one of the most secular countries.[14] This

---

13 Cf. M.E. Marty, *Modern American Religion*, 3 vol. (Chicago, 1986-1996).

14 In 2000, only 9% (= 23 million people) were estimated to be non-religious, whereas 235 million people are Christians (84 %, about 69 % or 191 millions of them are affiliated Christians), 5.6 million Jews, 4 million Muslims, 2.5 million Buddhists (cf. D. Barrett / G. Kurian / T. Johnson (eds.), *World Christian Encyclopedia*, 2nd ed.,

context of secularity actually supports religious power. Its locality denies its local importance while it follows a cultural, economic, and political mission with decisive global perspectives. This is the real alternative to Old Europe – a New World full of religious opportunities for its people and full of power for their religious communities.

Such a new religious power structure attracts attention from other religious powers. Its power incites other powers toward the reactionary viewpoint that their perspectives are the only true religious ones. This results in religious power struggles. There is a luring attraction to demonstrate one's alternative religious power, i.e., the almighty power of a religious God not backing a New World. It is not by chance that the terrorists of 9-11-2001 attacked New York. This city is the citadel of a secular global mission backed by religious believers. In attacking this City, a religious God can demonstrate its overwhelming force. This religious God has a trans-modern nature and a will to a premodern power. It used the weaknesses of secular society – uncontrolled mobility, instant publicity, fragile economy. This attack opened the door for a second-wave globalization following the economic globalization in the post-1989 era. This second wave is a globalization that religiously backs and religiously attacks the global secular mission the New World has as its political agenda. This globalization plays off the difference between public good and public evil as democracy and anti-democracy, respectively.

In such a global world that is politically and religiously confronted with good and evil, it is impossible for only one religious God to demonstrate its existence. There will always be a plurality of global missions backed by diverse religious Gods. In such a plurality, the will to global violence is included. These religious Gods have no problem with theodicy or with the local settings of their own contextuality. But they are confronted with the powers of other religious Gods. They need to overpower them, no matter what the costs will be. One may well ask whether there is an alternative to a God-talk that bases itself in the wielding and machinations of power. Yet there is an alternative vision, and it has a nearly forgotten European origin.

[Oxford, 2001], 772). See also S. Mead, *Das Christentum in Nordamerika: Glaube und Religionsfreiheit in vier Jahrhunderten* (Göttingen, 1987).

The Pastoral God: Power of the Relativistic World and Confrontation with the Global World

On the one hand, "God" can be used as a sign by a will to absolute power. This is the dark side of monotheism's history and the reason for a renewed dispute about its dangers.[15] On the other hand, as the dramas of the local God have proven, God's power can be used to resist, politically and culturally, any habit of absolute power. But the local God itself needs power to adhere to that resistance. The religious God has power, but its global option of God-talk is full of dangers beyond any chance for a reasonable calculation. The terrorist attack of 9-11 and the recent War in Iraq have shown that God's power can still be used in "monocultural" ways to shape a political landscape of unbounded power. Here, God-talk is confronted with the problem of God's power in its own language.

One can use this problem to demonstrate an alternative God-talk: God is a power that manifests in part within language that uses the God-concept for the production of power in worldly terms. As a powerful sign, God is a Verb to be experienced within worldly actions; he is not a subject active in demonstrations of religious power. The kinds of worldly actions I'm referring to here are those that are dependent on God's power for the creation of a dignified, fully human life. Vatican II highlighted this doctrinal solution in its last text, the Pastoral Constitution *Gaudium et spes*. It urges God-talk to take place within a special context, that of the pastoral agenda of the language used for naming God. There are two topics at the top of this agenda: first, the vocation of every human, by God, to live a human life and not to be forced to live an inhuman life, and second, the "world-loyalty"[16] of the Church to mankind in all its pressing problems. *Gaudium et spes* put this in confessional terms: "this holy synod, in proclaiming humanity's noble destiny and affirming that there exists in it a divine seed, offers the human race the sincere co-

---

15 For the "marketing power" of the idea in monotheism cf: R. Stark, *One True God: Historical Consequences of Monotheism* (Princeton, 2001). Regarding the crux of the dispute, cf. J. Assmann, *Die Mosaische Unter-scheidung: Oder der Preis des Monotheismus* (Munich, 2003). For the defending side of the monotheistic castle, cf. J. Manemann (ed.), *Monotheismus*, Jahrbuch Politische Theologie 4 (Münster, 2003).

16 Regarding this concept, cf. Alfred North Whitehead, *Religion in the Making* (New York, 1974), 59.

operation of the church in fostering a sense of sisterhood and brotherhood to correspond to their destiny" (Gaudium et spes No. 3).[17]

This agenda means a specific combination of dogma and history. This combination itself was an invention of the French *Novel Theologie*, being a European theology departing from the grammar of Old Europe.[18] It leads to a God-talk paying attention and tribute to the signs of the times: "In every age, the church carries the responsibility of reading the signs of the times, and interpreting them in the light of the Gospel is to carry out its task" (*Gaudium et spes* 4). With this pastoral God, theology is able to present dogma on the basis of an actual historical situation. This solves the problem of universality left over from the era of the metaphysical God. Such signs of the times are not all kinds of events in history, but a representation of special human needs within time. God-talk depends on this representational act. Yet it is not the local context here that is essential for the presentation of a meaningful God. On a basic level, local context defines what is essential for meaningful God-talk. Dialect here provides the bridge in speaking with others about the universal God. In global reality, the significance of any event, however, goes beyond the way it is defined on a local level. Powerful God-talk in this context becomes an act of naming a very special power: the power of local peoples struggling for general acceptance of their human needs and human dignity. To talk about God means to name the universal human meaning of such a struggle. This act of naming is not simply to give words to a reality. It is a process of overcoming the not-naming of such struggles, a dangerous state that, when left unarticulated, becomes a potential premise for perpetuating abuses of power.

To overcome such not-naming, one needs power, and this power arises from the confrontation between events widely focused with events widely forgotten. This confrontation disrupts any appearance of self-evidence for power structures. And power structures themselves are here confronted by a sudden loss of language. This loss is also essential for speaking about God universally. Local contexts are not necessarily universal, but the human situation of lacking language to deal with experiences of powerlessness has a universal importance. The pastoral God does not change the world as much as it removes the inherent danger in discovering an absence of such a language. The pastoral God can only be named on the basis of powerlessness. It urges

[17] A. Flannery (ed.), *The Basic Sixteen Documents of Vatican Council II: Constitutions, Decrees, Declarations* (Northport, 1996), 164f.

[18] G. Alberigo *et al.* (ed.), *Une école de théologie - le Saulchoir* (Paris, 1985).

respect for powerlessness by naming its relation with God. It affirms its solidarity with people living in powerlessness. This act creates a locus for God within the anonymity of powerlessness. Herein we may find a renewed global mission statement for a God-talk that stands in contrast to the religious power of a God that operates by not naming its powerlessness. Pastoral God-talk becomes a strong and just counter-power in its resistance to global-local ambitions that use the concept of God as a basis for the wielding of worldly power.

PART II

GEOGRAPHIES OF GOD IN EUROPE

François Bousquet

Thirty-Years' Worth of Studies and Publications on the Subject of God

The aim of this lecture is to classify and analyze the bibliography of major theological books and articles published in France between 1970 and 2000 with the subject of "God" as their focus. This is an ambitious program because the bibliography accumulated over the years is enormous. As it would be impossible to be exhaustive, the reasonable approach is to propose a synthesis – however impossible this may seem – that traces the evolution of the various questions and concerns involved in such an endeavor.

While studying the available corpus of documents, it quickly became evident that the bibliographical timescale would have to be expanded; ten years is an insufficient period to reflect the unfolding and the impact of lasting thought by long-standing authors and it does not permit adequate scope to examine the seminal influences of dialogue and exchange among authors. Tracing these various influences requires a generation's worth of material – at least thirty years' worth.

I will begin by mentioning several types of works that will *not* demand our attention. Translations, first of all, will be excluded from our list, (no small loss!), as is the immense contribution that German giants like Barth, Bultmann, Bonhoeffer, Rahner, Balthasar, and Moltmann have brought to French theology (the latter from *Le Dieu crucifié* [Cerf, 1974], to *Dieu dans la création* [Cerf, 1988]),[1] followed by Jüngel (*Dieu mystère du monde*, 2 vol. [Cerf, 1984]), Hans Küng (*Dieu existe-t-il?* [Seuil, 1981]), the works of Tillich, and the Dutch theologian Schillebeeckx (beginning with *Dieu en révision*, culled from *Dieu et l'homme* [CEP, 1970]); and notwithstanding the more specifically Trinitarian approach of Walter Kasper, *Le Dieu des chrétiens* (Cerf, 1985), and finally the translation of noteworthy books by several liberation theologians such as Gustavo Gutiérrez (*Le Dieu de la vie* [Cerf 1986] or *Dieu ou l'or des Indes occidentales* [Cerf, 1992]).

---

[1] We will only mention the name of the editor and the year of the book's first printing, after the title and the author. The place of publication will be cited only if it is not Paris.

Also excluded, regrettably, are non-French authors writing in French, such as the Swiss Pierre Gisel, or Bernard Morel, (*Dieu n'existe pas, il l'a toujours dit* [Lausanne, 1993]), the Canadian (Jean-Claude Breton, *Dieu de nos paroles* [Médiaspaul, 1995]), or the Belgian Adolphe Gesché with his *Dieu pour penser. III. Dieu* (Cerf, 1994).

Three other categories of works that encompass an impressive number of titles also fall outside the limits of our project, because their primary aim is not to construct the concept of God – the object of our present examination. These include biblical studies, publications intended for the general public, and books of spirituality.

Whereas there is much to admire in the exegetical work of biblical scholars, without whose groundwork any theological reflection would be impossible, only three examples of Old and New Testament studies will be included in this study: Henri Cazelles, *La Bible et son Dieu* (Desclée, 1998), Jacques Briend, *Dieu dans l'Ecriture* (Cerf, 1992), and Etienne Babut, *Le Dieu puissamment faible de la Bible* (Cerf, 1999).

There is an abundant variety of books on our topic for the general public, some of which have been extremely useful: *Dieu selon les chrétiens* by Henri Bourgeois (Centurion, 1974), *Aujourd'hui Dieu* by Marcel Neusch (DDB, 1987), *Dieu* by André Dupleix (Centurion, 1988). Others have an original approach: *Dieu a des problèmes*, by René Boureau (Cerf, 1990) and *La plus belle histoire de Dieu*, by Jean Bottéro, Marc-Alain Ouaknin and Joseph Moingt (Seuil, 1997). Their place, however, is elsewhere.

Not cited here are any of the innumerable books on spirituality, all with varying degrees of value, produced by diverse movements and individuals, not to mention the great classical texts of the Church, issued from various schools and undergoing the constant process of reediting and revision. Worthy of salute is the appearance of a new type of "witness" literature, emanating from notable figures who describe their spiritual journey quite apart from any church affiliation, in contrast to the old-style books on "conversion." In a single generation, we have gone from the *Dieu est Dieu, nom de Dieu*, of Maurice Clavel to *Dieu, un itinéraire* by Régis Debray (Odile Jacob, 2002). Close observation of this phenomenon, even if it is sometimes disappointing (there is much more smoke here than fire), reveals a significant displacement of emphasis, which is due to the difficulty of identifying God's presence in our culture, even when one refers to a spiritual tradition as a framework for one's experience (cf. "L'expérience mystique: Dieu ou le divin?" *Christus*, no. 162, 1994; or "Le temps des religions sans Dieu," in the June 1997 issue of *Esprit*).

Also worth mentioning is the fact that the years preceding the Jubilee year 2000 saw the flowering of Trinitarian studies (for example *Croire en Dieu notre Père*, by Joseph Caillot (DDB, 1999), and *Dieu le Père tout-puissant* by Jean-Pierre Batut (CERP, 1998)). Other older titles had already recovered a Christological or Trinitarian approach (for instance, *L'inouï de Dieu*, by Michel Corbin (DDB, 1980)). A series of studies along these lines by François-Xavier Durwell, all securely grounded in Scripture, had previously broken new ground; we will simply cite the most ambitious: *Le Père, Dieu en son mystère* (Cerf, 1987).

Despite all this pruning, the remaining body of publications still makes selection a daunting prospect: What criteria should guide our search for new directions? One solid criterion would have us identify and compare emerging themes based on the question of *access* to God through concepts. And a corresponding question thus arises: What are the different *approaches* to the question of God, among theologians or philosopher-theologians, that have really contributed to debate over the last thirty years?

With this question as a guideline, we can risk evaluating the different types of approach to God – their different "styles" of thought that determine their angles of access. The particular style of each author not only expresses a specific mindset but also determines the kind of reception he (or she) will garner from the scholarly community and the general public.

The Hermeneutical Approach

No doubt the oldest current in our tradition is the hermeneutical one, wherein the interpreter is aware of the "wounded cogito" (in the European conscience) but continues nonetheless, thanks to Revelation, to think the Absolute from the other side of this rift.

Claude Geffré is the most significant witness to this tendency, with numerous articles and a whole series of works to his credit: *Un nouvel âge de la théologie* (Cerf, 1972); *Un espace pour Dieu* (Cerf, 1980); *Le christianisme au risque de l'interprétation* (Cerf, 1983), particularly pp. 149-187: "Du Dieu du théisme au Dieu crucifié"; *Passion de l'homme, passion de Dieu* (Cerf, 1991); *Profession théologien* (Albin Michel, 1999); *Croire et interpréter* (Cerf, 2001). His editorial work, his patient insistence on giving the hermeneutical approach its place within university theology, his personal/scholarly journey, which has changed over the these thirty years from a more fundamental approach to theology into a theology of religions, make him an eminent representative of a common progression. Regarding the concept of God, one of Geffré's articles ("L'approche de Dieu par l'homme d'aujourd'hui," *Revue des Sciences Religieuses* 68 [1994]: 489-508) furnishes a brilliant résumé of the hermeneutical approach. If the spiritual situation of contemporary man could be characterized as nihilism together with the reemergence of the search for meaning, secularization and the appearance of new religiosities, technical breakthroughs and the primacy of experience, then the vantage point from which to question the notion of God – a God who is no longer *necessary* – can only be a sense of the gratuitous, as Geffré maintains. The hidden roots from which a search for God might spring are those familiar to all within the category of human existence: the quest for Another, the epic narratives of human tragedy and the archetypal figures of human transcendence.

Others subscribing to this approach deserve mention. The works of Ghislain Lafont have significant breadth. After beginning with *Peut-on connaître Dieu en Jésus-Christ* (Cerf, 1970), which clearly announced his point of departure, Lafont, in a second book, *Dieu, le temps et l'être* (Cerf, 1986), retraces his steps from Christology to fundamental theology, interpreting the "wounded cogito," (to use Paul Ricoeur's expression), by progressing from " le temps perdu" (lost time) to "l'être introuvable" (undiscoverable Being), to a recovering of memory ("le temps retrouvé"), along with new and ancient revelations of Being ("anciennes et nouvelles révélations de l'être") – thus leaning toward ethics and eschatology ("une ouverture vers l'éthique et l'eschatologie"). And Alexandre Ganoczy, who taught in Würzburg after a brief sojourn in Paris, is the author of a very fine book, *Dieu grâce pour le monde* in the *Manuel de Théologie*, under the supervision of Joseph Doré, (Desclée, 1986), which espouses a hermeneutical perspective.

Four other interesting and original approaches find their place within the framework of hermeneutics. First, there is a somewhat controversial current that reflects on the topic of God from the angle of *communication*. Three names can be situated within this framework; and for each name, I will cite a single title: Guy Lafon, *Le Dieu commun* (Seuil, 1982); Antoine Delzant, *La communication de Dieu* (Cerf, 1978); Joseph Caillot, *L'évangile de la communication* (Cerf, 1989).

Next, less numerous and unfortunately less visible, there have been a few tentative efforts to renew an approach to God via the human body. Notable in this category are Yves Ledure, with two books: *Si Dieu s'efface, La corporéité comme lieu d'une affirmation de Dieu* (Desclée, 1975), *Transcendances, essai sur Dieu et le corps* (DDB, 1989), and then François-Bernard Michel, a doctor, with *La chair de Dieu* (Flammarion, 1990).

A third approach might be called the "aesthetic" one, with its focus on the concept of Beauty. A book by Jean-Dominique Robert, *Essai d'approches contemporaines de Dieu en fonction des implications philosophiques du beau* (Beauchesne, 1982), is not very conclusive, with its overly metaphysical view of beauty as transcendental. The aesthetic theology of Hans Urs von Balthasar has not as yet inspired others to come on board – it requires some degree of engaged interpersonal meditation as a support to its claims. There are, however, two notable approaches within this category. The first devotes its attention to what used to be defined as "the spiritual in art," of which we can find an example in a special number of the journal *Christus* (no. 105, 1980), "Le Beau Dieu", or again in a book by Jean-Pierre Jossua, *La beauté et la bonté* (Cerf, 1987). The second engages our reflection with a very precise study of iconography – the best representative of this school being François Boespflug, *Dieu dans l'art* (Cerf, 1984); *La Trinité dans l'art d'Occident* (Strasbourg, Presses universitaires, 2000). One of his most impressive articles is *"Dieu* dans l'art contemporain: notations et interrogations" (in *Trajets, Cahiers Universitaires Catholiques*, 2001, pp. 52-61). Therein he demonstrates convincingly that the disappearance of figurative representations of the Godhead, (once past the great period of Western art that stretches from the twelfth to the eighteenth centuries), denotes the incapacity of contemporary man to "figure " *himself* – from the time of his narcissistic wound received in the course of the past century.

Finally, thanks mainly to the groundwork of Jean-Pierre Jossua, *Pour une histoire religieuse de l'expérience littéraire* (4 vol., Beauchesne, 1984-1998), we now have a new field of investigation regarding the possible interrelation between the works of major writers – novelists, poets, playwrights, (mostly contemporary) – and the question of God. This field, which has only just been cleared, deserves the attention of theologians who might well find it surprisingly fertile if cultivated in depth.

The Question of the Naming of God, and the Pertinence of the Language of Theology

The mention of hermeneutics leads immediately to an awareness of the mediating power of language, whether with reference to God or to revelation.

A book like that by André Dumas, *Nommer Dieu* (Cerf, 1980) is confined by the hermeneutical approach and by linguistics. The chain progressively linking its questions is revealing: those questions concerning the names for God (God under Scrutiny, the Objective Godhead, the Hidden God, the Disappointing God, God named), refer us to a double *problématique*, one concerning the Word of God in language and Scripture, the other concerning the "places" where God can be named, with the proposal that "suspicion" be replaced by "protest" against the death of man.

The question of the pertinence of theological language is more specific than that of God's names. Books by our Belgian neighbors, Antoine Vergote (*Interprétation du langage religieux* [Seuil, 1974] and Jean Ladrière (*L'articulation du sens*, 2 vol. [Cerf, 1984]) have had considerable influence. Both of these directions developed in France in the course of these last thirty years. On the one hand the question of theological language was explored in the study by Michel Combès, *Le langage sur Dieu peut-il avoir un sens?* (Toulouse, 1975), and more recently by Dominique Bourg, *Transcendance et discours* (Cerf, 1985), along with number six of the journal *Les quatre fleuves*: "Peut-on parler de Dieu?" (Seuil, 1976). On the other hand, there is the question of the word, of how to speak about God. This last point is the theme of a traditional meeting of French theologians every two years at Chantilly. In 1979 the subject under discussion was "Dire ou taire Dieu: Le procès de Dieu entre paroles et silences," in *Recherches de Science Religieuse* (1979), nos. 3 and 4, with, as principal speakers: J. Moingt, R. Marlé, S. Breton, G. Lafon, P. Beauchamp, M. de Certeau, J. Greisch, etc. The same problem regularly mobilizes the catechetical journal *Catéchèse,* as the titles of the two following numbers testify: "Dire Dieu" (July 1976) and "Dire Dieu en France aujourd'hui" (nos. 110-11, 1988). This problem has profoundly revived by the works of Francis Jacques since his first masterful study *Dialogiques: Recherches logiques sur le dialogue* (P.U.F., 1979).

A Double Perspective in Fundamental Theology

Within the typology of possible ways to consider access to God, we could say that the role played by fundamental theology has been gradually reinforced, but with an emerging cleavage becoming apparent over the course of time, which now makes it necessary for the tenants of both streams of thought to clarify their basic presuppositions. Without running the risk of amalgamating too hastily, we can already distinguish two very distinct approaches.

A first approach entails a return to phenomenology. With a view toward rapprochement with negative theology, which the manifestation of Christ subjects to critical tension, this approach requires a somewhat descriptive treatment of the question of God. Its weak point is its treatment of history.

The principal protagonist of this method is without a doubt Jean-Luc Marion; his work is well known and commands respect. Here we will simply mention a few of his most important books: *L'idole et la distance* (Grasset, 1977); *Dieu sans l'être* (Communio-Fayard, 1982); *Prolégomènes à la charité* (Editions de la Différence, 1988); *Etant donné* (P.U.F., 1997); *De surcroît: études sur les phénomènes saturés* (P.U.F., 2001). The philosopher Michel Henry has invested in comparable research with his most recent texts (cf. *C'est moi la vérité* [Seuil, 1996]; *Incarnation. Une philosophie de la chair* [Seuil, 2000]). Another phenomenologist whose writing has as much literary quality as his thought has depth, Jean-Louis Chrétien, has published a series of compact little books that are developed along the same lines: *L'effroi du beau* (Cerf, 1987); *La voix nue: phénoménologie de la promesse* (Editions de Minuit, 1990); *L'inoubliable et l'inespéré* (DDB, 1991); *L'appel et la réponse* (Editions de Minuit, 1992); *L'arche de la parole* (P.U.F., 1998); *Le regard de l'amour* (DDB, 2000).

Two interconnecting debates were born from this approach. The first debate centered around the problem of Being, and Jean-Luc Marion's book, *Dieu sans l'être*, sparked a number of reactions. Philosophers and theologians intervened: two volumes of collected articles emerged, one directed by Dominique Dubarle for the Philosophy Faculty of the Institut Catholique de Paris, entitled *Dieu avec l'être* (Beauchesne, 1986), the other for the CERIT of Strasbourg, *L'être et Dieu* (Cerf, 1986); both were concerned with exposing the danger of allowing a phenomenological approach to play the part of what Father Dubarle called a "theological ontology." Esteemed professors from the institute of the Hautes Etudes, H.Cazelles, P. Vignaux, P. Hadot, G. Vajda, J. Jolivet, F. Ruello, E. Zum Brunn, etc., subsequently published a book, *Dieu et l'être* (Ecole Pratique des Hautes Etudes, 1978), which was an exegesis of Exodus 3:14 and the Koran 20:11-24, resurrecting the old quarrel about the interpretation of God's manifestation in an ontological or non-ontological light.

The second debate originated with a book by Dominique Janicaud, which was no mere superficial reaction, *Le tournant théologique de la phénoménologie française* (Eclat, 2001). I leave it to Vincent Holzer to comment on this work, as this is precisely his subject at our convention. Suffice it to say that what was at stake for Janicaud was the validity – or the scandal – of drifting from an ontological to a phenomenological stance, along with the theological implications of this drift, particularly for those whose reaction was outrage.

A second approach does not give up on locating the foundation of knowledge about God, while it nonetheless refers to experience. This school, however, considers the "noetic" to be the end product of an approach whose area of concern is, in any case, the "Christian fact" or the incarnated church. To view this in a phenomenological light, if there *is* a "phenomenon" here the accent will have to be on the explicitly formulated communication it gives rise to, a recognition of the practice of faith involved, while taking care not to neglect the interiority of the practitioner. It is within this framework that the critical process will have to look, as rigorously as possible, for new directions, with constant reference to its initial place of emergence. Shuttling back and forth between liturgical celebration and its ethical expression in Christian life, a living experience of God takes form gradually along the lines that Scripture and Tradition have determined from the origins in the light of the judgment and the promise contained in the Word of God. Here the question of God is, visibly, a practical question. A book like that by Henri-Jérôme Gagey and André Lalier, *Dieu* (L'Atelier, 1997) exploits this particular aspect, just as do other adherents of the school of Joseph Doré, and in his wake: Henri-Jérôme Gagey, Vincent Holzer, François Bousquet, and Jean-Louis Souletie; all of them, who are members of the Institut Catholique de Paris, expect to formalize and publish a synthesis of this second approach in the near future.

In a middle area between the two approaches is possibly Jean-Yves Lacoste, with his seminal work *Expérience et Absolu* (P.U.F., 1994), who might be an inspired mediator because his phenomenology is rooted in the liturgy, which he considers to be an anticipation of the *eschaton*.

Between Philosophy and Theology

Five subgroups can be ranged within this somewhat vague heading. First we have the erudite study of the relationship that philosophers, both modern and contemporary, entertain with the concept of God – a subject of some volume. We can cite three encyclopedic works, to begin with, which are both precise and attractive: *Le Dieu des philosophes* (Editions universitaires-Mame, 1992) by Pierre Magnard, *La question philosophique de l'existence de Dieu* (P.U.F., 1994) by Bernard Sève, and *Dieu dans la philosophie contemporaine* (Bayard 2003) by Gérard Bailhache. And there are still other definitive works by authors of whom we can regrettably cite only a few titles: *Dieu selon Hegel* by Francis Guibal (Aubier-Montaigne, 1975); *Heidegger et la question de Dieu* (Grasset, 1980) by Richard Kerney and Joseph Stephan O'Leary; *Philosophie et théologie dans la pensée de Martin Heidegger* by Philippe Capelle (Cerf, 1998); and finally, *Nietzsche et l'ombre de Dieu* by Didier Franck (P.U.F., 1998).

Next we have those philosophers who are personally implicated in a search for fundamentals and who propose their own itinerary to their readers. Claude Bruaire, at the Sorbonne, has been an excellent guide, beginning with *L'affirmation de Dieu* (Seuil, 1964) and proceeding with *Le droit de Dieu* (Aubier-Montaigne, 1980), and *Pour la métaphysique* (Fayard, 1980). Pierre-Jean Labarrière, a long-term student of Hegel's with the breadth and breathing capacity of a long-distance racer, has produced a very thought-provoking corpus of works (we will mention only a few landmarks), whereas his major area of interest is now with the Flemish and Rhineland mystics: *Dieu aujourd'hui* (Desclée, 1977), *Le discours de l'altérité* (1983), *Les visages de Dieu* (DDB-Bellarmin, 1986). Recently, Henri Laux published a short and cogent text: *Le Dieu excentré* (Beauchesne, 2001).

We should also mention those who might be called "Prophetic Watchmen," who survey currents of thought and their reorientation, whether collectively – as with the faculty members of the Institut Catholique de Paris, with their volume *Dieu* (Beauchesne, 1985) – or individually, as with Philippe Capelle (for example, in his study on "la question philosophique de Dieu en théologie chrétienne" in *Le statut contemporain de la philosophie première*, [Beauchesne, 1996], 121-46) or with Yves Labbé, in his articles on fundamentals ("La question de Dieu parmi les philosophies contemporaines," in *Revue des Sciences Religieuses* 69 (1995): 497-516; "La connaissance naturelle de Dieu en théologie [1950-2000]," in *Revue des Sciences Religieuses* 77 [2003]: 43-74). But we might also consider, as concerns the latter who was a professor at Rennes and then at Strasbourg, that his personal trajectory has taken him from *Humanisme et théologie* (Cerf, 1975), *Le sens et le mal* (Beauchesne, 1980), *Essai sur le monothéisme trinitaire* (Cerf, 1987), *Le nœud symbolique* (DDB, 1997), *La foi et la raison* (Salvator, 2000), *Dieu contre le mal* (Cerf, 2003) on an journey that is entirely his own.

Thus this domain is the site of continual exchange, with attention accorded particularly to the mutations to be found within "natural theology," (understood according to its meaning in Catholic terminology), along with the significance that one continues to find in "philosophical theology." The latter concept may seem unstable, but it expresses the necessity of keeping both eyes open, the one of reason and the other of faith, as soon as one views the concept of God through Christian eyes. Both eyes must come together in focus, while taking care to keep reason and faith quite distinct, united but without any confusion according to a principle we might qualify as "Chalcedonian."

The Persistence of Traditional Approaches

The "traditional" may not be the liveliest of sectors, but it remains vital in at least certain circles. One can find a little of everything here. At the Sorbonne, before his death, Claude Tresmontant held to an Aristotelian line of thought while attempting to modernize it (cf. *Comment se pose aujourd'hui le problème de l'existence de Dieu* [Seuil, 1966]). Others, acting sometimes as philosophers, sometimes as theologians, subscribe to a neo-Thomist inspireation: Jean Javaux, *Une affirmation raisonnée de Dieu* (Beauchesne, 1974), Marie-Dominique Philippe, *De l'être à Dieu* (Téqui, 1977), Bertrand de Margerie, *Les perfections du Dieu de Jésus-Christ* (Cerf, 1981), Marie-Joseph Nicolas, *Court traité de théologie* (Desclée, 1990), etc. This stream of thought has not run dry, as a recent publication by Stéphane-Marie Barbellion quite honorably testifies: *Les "preuves" de l'existence de Dieu, Pour une relecture des cinq voies de saint Thomas d'Aquin* (Cerf, 1999).

An Interest in the Rapport Between Science and Faith

This well-documented sector is full of dissimilar works. Its main concern is the question of "science and faith," not the question of God in His own right.

One hesitates to mention Maurice Corvez as a leading proponent, with his *De la science à Dieu* (Téqui, 1986); one would also prefer to forget the collective volume bearing the names of Jean Guitton, Grichka, and Igor Bogdanov, *Dieu et la science* (Grasset, 1991) which the critics quite fairly condemned; one can note the public's interest in the productions of Jacques Arnould, for example, *Dieu, le singe et le big-bang* (Cerf, 2000). In fact, the issue of ecology is what garners the most fascination for this camp, and for believers, the relationship between Nature and Creation (or Salvation). One can reasonably commend the work of Jean-Michel Maldamé, a Professor at the Faculté de Théologie of l'Institut Catholique de Toulouse and a member of the Pontifical Academy of Science: *Le Christ pour l'univers* (Desclée, 1998) over the work of a non-theologian like Jean-Marie Pelt, whose *Dieu de l'univers* (Fayard, 1995) was a great favorite of the general public.

A Preoccupation With the Scandal of Evil

One cannot deny the impact that the various horrific events of the twentieth century have had on mankind's conscience during the past three decades. Our various theodicies find their Waterloo at this point, precisely where a theology of the cross can become a touchstone. Our French awareness of the phenomenon is of course no exception: the influence of Jewish reflection on the Shoah comes to mind at once (with Hans Jonas' *Le concept de Dieu après Auschwitz* [Rivages, 1994]), and Moltmann's interpretation of the problem (*Le Dieu crucifié*, translated in 1974), followed by the insistence by liberation theologies to combat violence and injustice in the name of God; all of these have contributed to keeping meditation on this everlasting problem on the front burner. There has scarcely been a year when the question did not come to the forefront. François Varillon's book *La souffrance de Dieu* (Centurion, 1975) has had a great impact. So many others have followed that we will limit the list to these: Jean-Pierre Jossua with *Discours chrétiens et scandale du mal* (Chalet, 1979); François Varone, *Ce Dieu absent qui fait problème* (Cerf, 1981); and *Ce Dieu censé aimer la souffrance* (Cerf, 1986); Juan Miguel Garrigues, *Dieu sans idée du mal* (Criterion, 1982); and Dominique Gonnet, *Dieu connaît aussi la souffrance* (Cerf, 1990). Meanwhile, certain philosophers have contributed firmer foundations upon which to ground the different problematics. Paul Ricoeur himself has contributed a small opus with a wide audience, *Le mal, un défi à la philosophie et à la théologie* (Geneva:

Labor et Fides, 1986); but Yves Labbé, whom we have already cited, has devoted time and energy to building on this foundation as well, starting with his *Le sens et le mal, Théodicée du Samedi-Saint* (Beauchesne, 1980) and continuing through his most recent work, *Dieu contre le mal: Un chemin de théologie philosophique* (Cerf, 2003). Jean-Luc Blaquart, the dean of the Faculté de Théologie of the Institut Catholique of Lille is perhaps at present the innovator who is opening up the newest vistas, with two books following close upon each other: *Dieu bouleversé* (Cerf, 2001) and *Le mal injuste* (Cerf, 2002). Meanwhile, the yearly meeting of French theologians was dedicated to this theme in 2002 (cf. "Résister au mal: Cultures et théologie face au problème du mal," *Recherches de Science religieuse* 90 [2002]).

Critical Works Sparked by the Impact of the Social Sciences

During the '70s and '80s books of a quite radical sort appeared; or at least they made a powerful impression, whether on the frontiers of psychoanalysis (for instance, to cite only one author at a time, Jacques Pohier: *Au nom du Père* [Cerf, 1972] and *Quand je dis Dieu* [Seuil, 1977]), or whether from a sociological point of view, (the best example of which would be Yves Lambert's book *Dieu change en Bretagne* [Cerf, 1985]).

The decisive author in this category is certainly Maurice Bellet who, with his particular genius, offers a book annually, ridding us, without fear or concessions, of all the accumulated dross of the years, thereby freeing the well-spring of spiritual energy of all the obstructions one could name: commonplace certainties unexamined at their base, engrained habits never criticized, ideological binds and mixed motives hastily erected to combat panic, etc. A sampling of this prolific production, that clears up so much of what would otherwise become stagnant in religious thinking, can give us an idea of the sweep of his preoccupations: *Le point critique (*DDB, 1970), *Foi et psychanalyse* (DDB, 1973) *Naissance de Dieu* (DDB, 1975), *Le Dieu pervers* (DDB, 1979), *Théologie express* (DDB, 1980), *La Voie* (Seuil, 1982), *L'issue* (DDB, 1984), *L'immense* (Nouvelle Cité, 1984), *Critique de la raison sourde* (DDB, 1992), etc.

Two remarks are warranted as an outcome of weeding through the religious field for works that concern God specifically, and not merely the on question of faith. The first concerns the difficulty of calling God "Father" at a time when problems of filiation and masculine identity agitate our society.

The foremost work to wrestle with this subject is *Dieu le Père* by Dominique Bourdin and Jean-Louis Souletie (L'Atelier, 1999). The second remark would underline the positive impact of certain works with a pedagogical bent. We will mention simply the delightful booklet by Nicole Fabre (*Le Dieu des enfants* (Epi-DDB, 1991)) with its chapter headings in the shape of children's questions: ("Does God wear glasses?") "Dieu porte-t-il des lunettes?" ("Is God a teddy bear?") "Serait-il un nounours?" etc.

A Mystical Current

The term applies to two top-ranking authors, Stanislas Breton and Michel de Certeau. They resist all classification, each with a very strong intellectual and spiritual personality. They have nourished the reflections of a good number of seekers of God, at least among the intellectual community.

Stanislas Breton, a religious thinker of the passionist order, develops something different from a purely phenomenological theology. One could qualify his product as a radical theology of the cross, which becomes a "mè-ontologie," not exactly an ontology without being an anti-ontology, a constant quest forever under tension, where the nihilist fascination is never awarded the field but is confined to what one might call the super-essential Nothing – to pastiche the Cappadocian fathers. A Nothing Who is also Principle, the source of all that He is precisely not, an idea inviting us on a mystical and critical path at whose end the world of the senses is not abolished but restored to us in its pristine beauty and simplicity. We will mention just a few titles which belong to his mental landscape, one that strikes us as a bushy undergrowth, whereas in fact there is a very powerful and constant factor at work there: *Du Principe* (Aubier-Montaigne/Cerf/Delachaux et Niestlé, 1971); *Vers une théologie de la croix* (Clamart, 1979); *Unicité et monothéisme* (Cerf, 1981); *Deux mystiques de l'excès: J.J. Surin et Maître Eckhart* (Cerf, 1985); *Poétique du sensible* (Cerf, 1988); *La pensée du rien* (Kampen, Kok Pharos, 1992); *Vers l'originel* (L'Harmattan,1995); *Philosophie et mystique, existence et surexistence* (Grenoble, Jérôme Millon,1996); *L'avenir du Christianisme*, (DDB, 2000), etc.

Michel de Certeau, on the other hand, is a very innovative historian of spirituality both in his methodology and in his fundamental intuitions; we can name here his historical work *La fable mystique* (Gallimard, 1982), as well as a truly theological work *La faiblesse de croire* (Seuil, 1987). He is someone who was able, at the crossroads of a multiplicity of disciplines – history, psychoanalysis, social studies, spirituality, theology – to characterize the quest for God as the quest for the great Absent One in our history, who invites each one of us in particular to knit up the threads of his life with the life of others, to embrace an existence that is "not without" these others, an intellectual search that is "not without" these multiple criss-crossing currents, for a mystical life that cannot ignore the many wounds and traces revealing God's absence for those who can read them as an unending Advent.

At the close of this rich panorama, what are the emerging lines of thought capable of recalibrating our problematics? What are the promising building-sites for new constructions? The first great transformation is that which extracts the question of God from an extremely limited area of debate – a context still confined to Western Europe and theoretical atheism well afoot until 1989 – and transplants it to our present-day field, where it encounters a double front: that of practical indifference wedded to increasing secularization, and that of the discovery of the other religions and Wisdom traditions of the world, within a context where globalization and the multiplicity of cultures is favored by our new recently developed means of mass communication.

Our thinking on the subject of secularization has taken on a new look. There have been two new waves, one represented by the "death of god" theologians, and one by the "theologians of secularization" that were persuasive for some time but have not endured. They came to us from the Anglo-Saxon countries, through the translations of the works of Gabriel Vahanian: *La condition de Dieu* (Seuil, 1970); *Dieu et l'utopie* (Cerf, 1977); of John A.T. Robinson (*Dieu sans Dieu*, a poor title in comparison with the original English one, *Honest to God* [Nouvelles Editions Latines, 1964]); of Paul van Buren, William Hamilton, J.J. Altizer, and Harvey Cox. The collection *Christianisme en mouvement* (Casterman), directed by René Marlé, was an in-depth examination of their work, as was Christian Duquoc's book, *L'ambiguité des théologies de la sécularisation* (Duculot, Gembloux, 1972). Now that we have been able to identify better the characteristics fostering secularization (namely, the progress of technology and the globalizing of our liberal economy), the field of research in France is oriented more toward the positive evaluation of faith in God as a pertinent social factor, with the Christian God, incarnate and Trinitarian, as the source of our will to live together (cf. for example *Dieu au XXIe siècle*, by Bruno Chenu and Marcel Neusch [Bayard, 2002] or one sociologist's book that made a great impression: *Dieu change en Bretagne*, d'Yves Lambert, [Cerf, 1985], and no. 160 of the journal *Christus*, in 1993,

"Présence et absence de Dieu : l'épreuve de l'indifférence"). The place of access to faith is then designated as the totality of places where human beings can ally themselves with one another, where they can engage their freedom in an ever-growing solidarity (cf. André Lalier, *Dieu est intéressant* [L'Atelier, 1998]). We can rest assured that a major shift in the years to come will involve a fresh paradigm allowing us to articulate the particular historical versions of Christianity with the universality of faith in Christ.

Will the encounter with other religious and wisdom traditions lead to dialogue, with all the mutuality and open-hearted listening this implies, or will this encounter turn into the traumatic culture shock that Huntington foresaw – reinforced today by the recent events that have taken us from Manhattan on September 11, 2001 to Baghdad in April 2003? This convention and the two others that will follow are dedicated to shedding light on this question. What emerges is the fact that for Christian theology, dialogue is no longer to be considered a local but a fundamental thing, that it is no longer solely a speculative concept, but a practical attitude that is both reasoned and responsible. In any case, an enormous distance has been covered enlarging the scope of French theology. Just to concentrate on a few emblematic works within this massive literature, from *L'homme et ses religions* by Henri Desroche (Cerf, 1992) to Joseph Maïla and Dominique Wolton's book *De Manhattan à Bagdad* (DDB, 2003), and not to neglect these mainstream successes: l'*Encyclopédie des religions* (2 vol., Bayard, 1999) under the direction of Frédéric Lenoir and Ysé Tardan-Masquelier, and *Le livre des Sagesses* (Bayard, 2002). The focus on spirituality has had more success, finally, than the primary one of ethnological, or more broadly, of anthropological import. Somewhere between the two, theology with its specialized discipline is called upon to demonstrate its validity within a context that still bears traces of the once traumatic separation between Church and State, that still suspects Christian thinkers of lacking independence, and so denies theology its place on a par with other sciences or university disciplines.

The renewal of studies on the philosophy of religions should be noted, a renewal magnificently illustrated by the three powerful volumes by Jean Greisch entitled *Le Buisson ardent et les Lumières de la raison: L'invention de la philosophie de la religion* (3 vol., Cerf, 2002-2003). True enough, the debate initiated here takes place inside the university community, rather than in resonance with the immediate churchly concerns of this particular period, but without these preliminary investigations we might be deprived of the necessary tools for the patient and minute observation that will be needed to avoid ambiguous conclusions in future rounds of interreligious dialogue. Yet this new field is already upon us, as the following studies on Christian monotheism prove. To note just this first aspect; we can cite already: Pierre Gibert, Maurice Jourjon, Henri Bourgeois, and their *Sens chrétien du monothéisme* (Lyon, Profac, 1982); *Colloque sur le Dieu unique* (Buchet-Chastel, 1985); André Manaranche, *Le monothéisme chrétien* (Cerf, 1985); Yves Labbé, *Essai sur le monothéisme trinitaire* (Cerf, 1987); not to forget this recent important Swiss contribution with a collection under the direction of Pierre Gisel and Gilles Emery: *Le christianisme est-il un monothéism?* (Geneva: Labor et Fides, 2001). More basically, however, the reflection on God is beginning to migrate within theology toward what Stanislas Breton calls in philosophical terms *L'autre et l'Ailleurs* (Descartes et Compagnie, 1995). In any case, there is a new awareness of other cultural and religious traditions opening up the theological spectrum.

Self-Effacement of God, Affirmation of God's Presence

To wind up this overly lengthy inquiry we might state the following paradox: we are on the threshold of a period where God appears simultaneously absent and His presence certified. There is a surprising convergence of studies in different fields, year after year, that can give us pause: in spirituality (François Varillon, *L'humilité de Dieu* [Centurion, 1974]), in Christology (Christian Duquoc, *Messianisme de Jésus et discrétion de Dieu*, Labor et Fides [Genève 1984]), in fundamental theology (Michel de Certeau, *La faiblesse de croire* [Seuil, 1987]), in dogmatics (Bernard Rey, *La discrétion de Dieu* [Cerf, 1997]), in exegesis (Etienne Babut, *Le Dieu puissamment faible de la Bible* [Cerf, 1999]), all of which underline the self-effacement of God – not his disappearance from our culture, but his manner of being present incognito, in the crucified Christ, which opens a space for our free response to the ever renewed and ever reiterated invitation to faith.

At the same time, there is the return in our time to an impressive attesting of faith, when questions *about* God give place to questions *by* God: Who do you say I Am? And how do you treat your brother?

András Máté-Tóth

Thinking About God in Central Eastern Europe: Social Experiences and Theological Challenges

Contextuality

The last decades have seen the drafting of many contextual theologies.[1] The most significant of these is probably liberation theology with its innumerable books and projects. Experiences of a poverty that cried out to heaven led many who had received their theological training in Western Europe (Munich, Mainz, Tübingen, or Strasbourg, Louvain, Nijmegen, Paris) to the insight that the theological positions of a Eurocentric theology had to be reflected upon anew.[2] Theological positions and biblical texts had to be read and commented upon in a new manner through the lens of the experience of poverty, or more precisely, the experience of God in the context of poverty. As modern hermeneutics says, texts come alive only when they are read – or, to put the point more radically still, unread texts do not "exist." Texts are created through the act of reading. Liberation theology, for example, is a deconstruction of Latin American reality, which was construed by an alternative type of reading. Previous statements, debates, and opinions are criticized, dismissed, and even partly destroyed, in order to create space for a new way of reading. This deconstruction then leads to a theologically based reconstruction. When one examines the methodology of liberation theology more closely, one realizes it is a matter more of who writes it and less of what is actually said.[3] Contextuality begins with people.

The same observation can be made with respect to feminist theology or ecological theology. Women have reflected on their own culturally determined social and ecclesial situations. They have discovered an uneasiness and have asked themselves if they are going to conform to this male-dominated world and Church, and if whether other options are open to them. Since they have not felt at home in situations of domination, since their female experi-

[1] S. Bergmann, *God in Context: A Survey of Contextual Theology* (Hants, 2003), 32ff.

[2] R.J. Schreiter, *Abschied von Gott der Europäer: Zur Entwicklung regionaler Theologien.* With a foreword by Edward Schillebeeckx (Salzburg, 1991).

[3] C. Boff / L. Boff, *Wie treibt man Theologie der Befreiung?* (Düsseldorf, 1986).

ences call attention to discrepancies with regard to God, to biblical texts, and to the structures of this world, they have been obliged (so to speak) to develop a new theology because the old one had become intolerable for them. Indeed, without a sense of foreignness or intolerableness, no one changes his standpoint in society or academic life – and the same applies to theology. A third condition of contextuality, in addition to self-discovery and the experience of foreignness is the instrument of reading. While it is often said that every one has spectacles through which s/he sees the world, it is often forgotten that these "spectacles" are not completely identical with the location and conditions under which one lives. In the same situation, people often make different decisions. One stays, the other goes. One stays and is loyal; the other stays and starts a revolution. Poverty in the Third World, or more precisely, in two-thirds of the world, affects many people, but they all respond to it differently. The instruments play a decisive role.

For liberation theology, the primary instrument was the post-conciliar (European) theology, which made possible a freer reading of the Bible and an increased recognition of the historically and socially conditioned nature of the deposit of the faith. Another instrument was the wave of revolutions in Latin American, which showed these committed Christians that there were other options available than a suffering loyalty. These rebels and the people who followed them posed a question that required an urgent answer on the part of the priests, catechists, bishops, and theologians: Where do I stand? Do I remain in this wave of revolution on the side of the (Christian) people who revolt, or do I stand on the sidelines and attempt to check the wave? The revolutionaries were an "instrument" that compelled them to make a decision that excluded every possibility of remaining aloof.

This situation is precarious and difficult, because it dirties political "clean hands." Neutrality no longer exists: one gets dirty, one way or another. Political virginity is irretrievably lost. The refusal to decide is itself a decision, since the inherent drama of the situation forces all to take part. In feminist theology, this "instrument" was less western European post-conciliar theology than American feminist literature in the form of large-scale novels, poems, and meditations. Without the feminist revolutionary wave in America, there would be no feminist theology. Feminist theology would not have been able to develop had the media not persistently communicated that many women were in fact willing to fight for a just society and Church at the cost of their own position and reputation. The dialectical interplay between social trends and intellectual commentary cannot be denied. But it is unnecessary to discuss which came first, the chicken or the egg.

The following three movements in the post-war period were determinative of the contextuality of theology: self-discovery, foreignness, and the scandalous trends of society. Whether a contextual theology will (and can) be generated from the experiences of Central Eastern Europe depends upon the conditions established by liberation and feminist theologies.

"Second World"

A social analysis aiming to facilitate an appropriate theological discourse within the context of new political and social developments raises the fundamental question of whether it is at all correct to define the post-Communist reformed countries in Central Eastern Europe as one single region. If not, then we must abandon the dream of a theology "after Gulag."[4] The relevant scholarly works on this subject and a large measure of collaborative theological work, as well as contacts with colleagues in this region, lead us to propose treating Central Eastern Europe as *one cultural region with manifold diversity.*[5]

It is a characteristic of cultural regions that they have produced relatively homogeneous populations, cultures, or qualities. A region cannot be tied down to its special geographical location. In general terms, where a region was developed as a practical instrument of trade, planning, or research, we have what Howard Odum calls a "composite societal region" with a relatively high degree of homogeneity, as attested to by numerous historical and statistical indices. This homogeneity is not a result of uniformity, but is rather the result of the integration of many heterogeneous particulars that thereby generate a *unity based on plurality,* and a number of characteristic traits are formed which distinguish such regions from other regions. In terms of cultural identification, "region" means "a sense of place," including everything connected with the symbolic construction of a place.

When we speak of the reformed countries of Central Eastern Europe, we can speak of a cultural region which is marked above all by its shared fate over the last fifty years, by the societal activities and technologies developed

4 A. Máté-Tóth, "Eine Theologie der Zweiten Welt?" in *Concilium* 36 (2000): 278-85.

5 A. Máté-Tóth, *Theologie in Ost(Mittel)Europa* (Ostfildern, 2002), 92ff.

there, and by the characteristic mode in which its national and ethnic traditions have been further developed.

These countries, states, and societies have a very long common history, in which the last fifty years certainly stand out. A fundamental element of this shared history is the common memory of a uniform totalitarianism. This experience is naturally one that other countries in Europe and other continents share, but one important difference is that the reformed countries attained (or were forced to implement) an excessively rapid democratization. These countries have not had fifty or one hundred years (even if we include their respective pre-War histories) to learn how to cope with modern societal conditions. In the space of a few years, they have had to learn how to cope with all the problems entailed by a multiparty system, the market economy, free media, etc. The structural reforms were introduced overnight, and still require reforms in people's self and social understandings that cannot take place instantly.

In addition to the experience of persecution, there are other aspects of the current milieu that have been reflected upon by the social sciences, but that have been insufficiently addressed by theology. Otto Luchterhandt helps us see the wider historical background when he writes:

> After the schism of 1054, the influence of the Eastern Church extended to the areas settled by the East Slavs (Greater Russians, Ukrainians, White Russians), by most of the South Slavs (Bulgarians, Macedonians, Serbs) and by the Romanians. Papal jurisdiction covered the peoples to the west and the north, in the Baltic regions (Estonians, Latvians, Lithuanians), the western and northern groups of South Slavs (Poles, Slovaks, Czechs, Slovenians, Croatians), and the Hungarians. The jurisdictional and confessional boundary between the churches became, in the course of the centuries, a cultural border between "Western" and "Eastern" Europe affecting all areas of life; in the Balkans, this border cuts through Romania (in Transylvania) and Bosnia-Herzegovina. During the period of communist rule a strong unifying regime was superimposed on this boundary, but it re-emerged clearly after the fall of communism in the Eastern European Revolution (1989-1991) with its characteristic differences, not only in the ecclesiastical sphere, but also in political and legal culture .... The basic element common to the churches of Eastern Europe is that they are particularly close to the dominant ethnic group in the state and hence "national churches," and they are, in a specific sense, churches of the people (*Volkskirchen*).[6]

---

[6] O. Luchterhandt, "Kirchen – Osteuropa," in D. Nohlen *et al.* (eds.), *Die östlichen und südlichen Länder* (Munich,1997), 284-91.

The particular role played by linguistic nationalism in this process distinguishes these regions from others in Europe. This has meant that the historical emotional ties of these nations generally embraced other, larger regions than those in which the populations speaking their language had lived. These emotions ran especially high where linguistic minorities lived in well-isolated areas. These feelings gradually caused border tensions and an ever greater uncertainty regarding national status. Another dimension of the role played by nationalism was these societies' existential fear of genuine annihilation.[7]

The framework of the nation in this region had to be continually secured, stabilized, fought for, and defended, not only against the means of power of existing dynastic state borders, but also against the apathy of the native population. The national-existential fear of annihilation persists as a tangible reality in these societies.[8]

The topic of regionality is important in that it helps us identify more precisely the historical and cultural context that a "Theology of the Second World" must hold in view.

Theological Inheritance

The theological inheritance of Central Eastern Europe is damaged for two reasons. Theological works and perspective in this region from the pre-War era could not be organically developed in the period of the Communist dictatorship. In the "free states" of the West this development took place *inter alia* through the theological events connected with the Second Vatican Council, but the conciliar period in these free churches was a time of silence in the captive churches of the red dictatorship. In this epoch of oppression and persecution, normal theological work could not be carried out – apart from a few original attempts. The context of this epoch of repression could not be the object of theological reflection, nor could it be the object of public academic debate. Some structural and thematic aspects of this inheritance will be outlined as follows.

7 I. Bibó, *Die Misere der osteuropäischen Kleinstaaterei* (Frankfurt a.M., 1992).

8 G. Schöpflin, *Nations, Identity, Power* (New York, 2000).

Structural Aspects

From a structural perspective, theological work in Central Eastern Europe was done by the clergy. The social status of the clergy was, in most of these countries, close to the ruling powers; the term "kyrial" has been used here. Virtually the only task of theology was the training of priests. After the 1950's, the new rulers detached the theological faculties from the state universities, and many professors were forced to emigrate. Many Jesuits, who had often played a leading role in the theological faculties, settled in the West. In most countries, the new professors were theologians loyal to the state; in the state appointments to university chairs, academic quality was less important than political loyalty. In some countries public theological activity was completely banned, so that the theologians had to teach in the underground, often at great personal risk, and in situations of great poverty – i.e. without libraries, public discussion, or the usual structures of academic life.

As a result, forced compromises often created an atmosphere of mistrust. Since no publicly debatable political strategies were available, all decisions were somehow suspect. Even among theologians, no one could be entirely certain how far one's colleagues had collaborated with the Communists. The archives of the state security police in former East Germany contain very sad stories of this comic communication in the constant presence of third party informants.

Substantial Contents

These structures partly explain the substantial contents of the theological inheritance of the region. One can observe a direct line running from nineteenth-century anti-Modernism until the present day. This tradition is characterized by a basic apologetic stance: against the Reformation, Modernism, national interests, atheistic materialists, and today against democratic liberalism and the pluralism of opinions. This line bears the clear imprint of ultramontanism. The contextual problems of the region were "resolved" by looking devotedly toward Rome (beyond the Alps) and the structural and material influence of Rome in this period was greatly intensified.

Nevertheless, one ought not to forget that many bishops from this region voted with the minority at Vatican I against the dogma of infallibility, perhaps not for theological, but for monarchical political reasons, and later were sufficient masters of their own house to delay the public promulgation of this dogma in their dioceses. The consistent ultramontanist line became completely unambiguous and unbroken in the years between the Wars. Theology served the fortification and restoration of the cultural and political position of the Church in a period that saw the inexorable and progressive marginalization of the Catholic Church in modern society.

The Communist takeover meant that this marginalization was carried out so brutally that the Church was almost totally destroyed. The only instrument available to the theology of this region to help the Church survive and to demonstrate the apodictic incompatibility of the Communist ideology with the faith of the Church was this ultramontane apologetics. This theology had to provide strong support to the unity of a Church under siege, and this brought with it a strong overemphasis on the unquestionable and indisputable nature of Church teachings. Theology remained a completely priestly activity and served to train future clergy. These priests were to exercise their office with an unshakable certainty of faith, backed up by a theology that provided unambiguous answers. This intellectual concept saw questions about official doctrines or readiness for dialogue with the enemy's ideology as dangerous, indeed treasonable. New theological impulses, research, or original proposals could not emerge in the "church of (academic) silence," or at least not on the official level.

The assessment of the theological achievements of the underground church, which in some countries was the pillar of Christian faith, is a highly complex question. Only in a few cases was genuine theological work carried out in this underground church. Often the theologians who were active there tried to hand on in the underground what they taught publicly in the period before Communism. In some few cases there were original ideas, which, given the much harried situation, were naturally condemned to remain at the stage of preliminary sketches. One can perhaps name two examples, without discussing these in detail. On the question of Church ministry, there was the work of Felix Davidek, who also ordained women to the priesthood; another example from Czechoslovakia was Oto Madr, who developed an ecclesiology profoundly marked by moral theology, and believed that the survival of the Church would be ensured through personal holiness. We also have the new interpretation of the figure of Jesus in the Gospels as a model for a Church of discipleship by György Bulányi, the Hungarian Piarist priest.

The Theological Task: Evaluation

The Church has changed in the last fifty years, not only in free Europe, but also behind the Iron Curtain. The changes took place in both political regions of Europe under different external conditions. In Central Eastern Europe, there was a temptation to believe that after the fall of Communism, the Church would automatically revitalize itself: with the pressure gone, life would blossom in full vigor again. Such expectations, which were also found outside this region immediately after 1990, proved deceptive. Theology in Central Eastern Europe must carefully evaluate its new situation with intellectual honesty. It must analyze anew its relation to the sciences, to the tradition and to the Church as it really exists. As in social life generally, so also in theology – it is completely impossible to think that the only task today consists in teaching Church doctrine. The Church itself has become problematic, and the self-evident truth of this understanding of revelation is gone. Academic theology is no longer able to maintain that multiple paradigm shifts in philosophy and the radically new social and political context in our countries can be ignored because revelation is unaffected by them. The "theology of the Second World" cannot permit itself a hermeneutical nativité.

Ensuring Academic Quality

Theology is a science like all other sciences in terms of its intellectual procedures. In this sense, the Churches in the region of Central Eastern Europe have a great deal of work to do in considerably improving the structural conditions for the practice of theology. This task is very comprehensive, and I do not intend to list the individual items here; but some priorities can be indicated. It is urgent to improve the functioning of the theological libraries and replenish their stocks. Theological colleges and faculties must again have genuine professorial chairs and institutes that can afford to employ teaching assistants. Professors should be appointed according to standard academic criteria, and only afterward should the necessary ecclesiastical permissions be sought. To reverse this order would recall the typical way appointments are made under the ideological systems, where loyalty can quickly become more important than quality.

Improving academic standards includes not only a willingness to dialogue with other sciences, but also a readiness for continual conversation within theology itself. Without academic discussion there is no scholarship – this applies to theology as well. In the theological publications of Central Eastern Europe, the lack of genuine academic debate is evident. One explanation is that internal discussions were taken by outsiders as a sign of weakness during the period of oppression, and it was easy for outsiders to play off the discussion partners against one another for political purposes; examples abound. Many theologians in our countries believe even today that the Church is still under siege, primarily from liberalism. But a deeper look reveals this to be a particular view of theology as the intellectual presentation of the unambiguous and indisputable doctrine of the Church. A renewal of the practice of theological disputation will have to include the task of reflection on the theory of what theology is.

Reflection on Experiences and Themes

In theology, experience informed by personal testimony within its social context is increasingly recognized as important. Indeed, one of the most necessary tasks of a "theology of the Second World" is to reflect theologically on the experiences of peoples and societies in a manner that acknowledges the reconstructions and decipherings of those who were forced to live through the tribulations that shape their social and self-understandings.

Experiences themselves, however, are always very personal mysteries. They are accessible only through the multiple interpretations of those involved, which are always mediated by social mores and the perspectives of others. Theology has always had a very strong interpretative function, which obliges it to lend a certain credence to the mysteries of experience in order to preserve their originality as much as possible. Interpretations that are too hastily theoretical make it impossible for this originality to emerge, and this is why the "theology of the Second World" must be a patient, slow enterprise that accepts a multiplicity of interpretations. Otherwise, we are in danger of suppressing original experiences by means of traditional cliché.

These cultural experiences suggest what the main themes of a Central Eastern European theology of the Second World might be. And while it is impossible here to explore even one of these themes in detail, it is important to speak generally about the methodology entailed in their development. First, we must observe that there is a theoretical distinction between a reflected and an unreflected, latent contextuality. In principle, every human communication is embedded within a particular context; but there is a strong qualitative difference between communications that are formulated under the auspices of contextual self-reflection and those that are not. In the theological publications of our region, social and political reflection typically make their way into introductions and into "background" descriptions of authors' topics, yet rarely is there a thoroughgoing consideration of how specific contexts *intersect* with theological perspectives. Hence, the theology from this region is properly characterized as latently contextual. Nevertheless, some original attempts have been made.[9] What is needed now is a careful analysis not only of what the ideological-political suppression by the Communist party states meant for the Church, but also how people's thinking became infiltrated with a specific logic as a result of this situation.

To properly address the challenges emerging within the growing culture of modernity in these societies, a critical *relecture* of the Second Vatican Council is necessary. Here the fear of equating the Council itself with post-conciliar developments in Western Europe must be overcome. The "re-reading" of the Council should be critical by way of acknowledging that new, original insights can still arise from specific historical contexts. In a region plagued with ethnic conflicts, the concept of "catholicity" needs to be newly interpreted. Only in the wake of such theological reflections can ecclesiological themes such as the role of the laity, the distribution of power in the Church, and the role of the sacraments in pastoral care be given their place in a wider context. Until now, we can only hope that at least one step in this direction is taken each year, so that the new contexts forged by practical challenges within the Church will compel theologians to produce an original, aptly reflective theology.

Translated by Michael Parker

---

9 C.S. Bartnik, *Formen der politischen Theologie in Polen* (Regensburg: Pustet 1986); A. Máté-Tóth, "The 'Second World' as Context for Theology," in: J. Nieuwenhove / J. van Goldewijk (eds.), *Popular Religion, Liberation and Contextual Theology* (Kampen, 1991), 183-91; *idem*, *Eine Theologie der Zweiten Welt?*; *idem*, "Ost-Erfahrung - Ost-Theologie: Die Zeichen der Zeit als theologische Herausforderung," in: I. Baum-Gartner, *Den Himmel offen halten: Ein Plädoyer für Kirchenentwicklung in Europa* (Innsbruck, 2000), 237-54; A. Máté-Tóth / P. Mikluscak, *Nicht wie Milch und Honig: Unterwegs zu einer Pastoraltheologie der postkommunistischen Länder Ost (Mittel) Europas* (Ostfildern, 2000); *idem*, *Kirche im Aufbruch: Zur pastoralen Entwicklung in Ost(Mittel)Europa. Eine qualitative Studie* (Ostfildern, 2001); A. Nossol, *Brücken bauen: Wege zu einem christlichen Europa von Morgen* (Freiburg, 2002).

Karel Skalický

Thinking About God Philosophically in Europe Today: A Czech Perspective

Introduction

With the fall of communism in Eastern Europe, Marxist-Leninist ideology collapsed as well, along with its militant atheism, which I call "strong" atheism in contrast with the "weak" atheism of certain postmodern philosophies, for example that of O. Marquard. This "strong" atheism was especially supported in former Czechoslovakia by those thinkers who were confessed Marxist-Leninists and who received their formation in Marxist-Leninism between 1945 and 1955. This is the same generation of Czechoslovakian communist intellectuals who divided along two opposing lines of thought in the 1960's: the scientific line was inspired by the neo-positivists, and was led by Ladislav Tondl; the anthropological line was influenced by various currents of existentialism, and was represented by thinkers such as Milan Machovec, Vítěslav Gardavský, Zbyněk Fischer and many others. In this second group, Machovec was later to plead vigorously in favor of a Marxist-Christian dialogue.

The dissolution of Marxism-Leninism as a monolithic ideology helped contribute finally to the collapse of the authoritarian communist regime in 1989. As a result, the philosophies that had been repressed and exiled in the "underground" of the collective consciousness were given back their freedom. The question of God's existence, which had been off-bounds for forty years, was suddenly allowed, and free thinking was once again possible. The philosophical question of God's existence (and hence also "weak" atheism) is largely determined today by the following five great philosophical achievements: 1) The analysis of language of Ludwig Wittgenstein; 2) The phenomenological method of Edmund Husserl; 3) The hermeneutical phenomenology of Martin Heidegger; 4) The transcendental philosophy of Joseph Maréchal; 5) The dialogical personalism of Martin Buber. These five autonomous intellectual achievements undermined "strong atheism" and thus led to a new context for thinking about the existence of God.

The Analysis of Language and Semantic Atheism

Ludwig Wittgenstein points the way to the possibility of a "newer atheism" with his linguistic philosophy in which he attempts to overcome certain philosophical pseudo-problems that arise through the inauthentic and incorrect use of language. Wittgenstein summarizes his chief concern in the *Tractatus logico-philosophicus* in the following words: "What can be said at all can be said clearly; and whereof one cannot speak, thereof one must be silent."[1]

Wittgenstein does not intend here to set limits to thought, as Kant once sought to do, but he only wants to limit the linguistic expression of thought. He is aware that in order to set a limit to thought, it would be necessary to think both sides of this limit, i.e., not only the conceivable, but also the inconceivable, which is an evident contradiction, since the inconceivable cannot be thought. Hence Wittgenstein only wants to limit the *linguistic expression* of thought; that is, not the border between what can be thought and what cannot, but between what can be said and what cannot.

But what does inexpressible or unspeakable mean? The answers to this question take separate directions. For Carnap, Russell, and Ayer, what cannot be stated clearly is meaningless, and only meaningful propositions can be thought. A proposition is meaningful, however, only if it is verifiable. And it is verifiable only if it is based on sensible experience. As a result, metaphysical assertions are meaningless because they cannot be verified. Metaphysics is untenable not because it is an enterprise that exceeds the power of human reason, as Kant thought, but for the simple reason that it is a muddle of false problems without any real consistency. Consequently the proposition "God exists" is neither true nor false, but meaningless. Obviously, the same holds true of the negation "God does not exist." This proposition is likewise neither true nor false, but meaningless. Hence the affirmative and the negative propositions are both meaningless. If metaphysics is entirely meaningless, however, how does one explain its strong impact throughout human history? Carnap explains this influence solely in virtue of its capacity to convey strong subjective feelings, and goes so far as to formulate the following proposition about metaphysicians: "Metaphysicians are poets who do not know how to write poems." But is Carnap's proposition itself empirically verifiable?

---

[1] L. Wittgenstein, *Tractatus logico-pilosophicus: Tagebücher 1914-1916* (Frankfurt, 1963), 1.

This is, briefly, the meaning of semantic atheism. But is this type of atheism the only possible logical result of Wittgenstein's "linguistic turn"? Absolutely not. It suffices to examine two of Wittgenstein's assertions, in order to show that he did not equate the inexpressible with the meaningless.

The first assertion, that the inexpressible is not simply meaningless, is found in the following three propositions of the Tractatus: "not *how* the world is, is mystical, but *that* it is" (6.44). "The contemplation of the world *sub specie aeterni* is its contemplation as a limited whole. The feeling of the world as a limited whole is the mystical feeling" (6.45). "There is however the inexpressible; this *shows itself*; it is the mystical" (6.552).[2]

The second statement is in Wittgenstein's *Diaries*. Under the entry June 11, 1916, he writes: "The meaning of life, i.e., the sense of the world, we could call God and associate this with the parable of God as father. Prayer is thinking about the meaning of life."[3] Here, Wittgenstein also admits that we have in us a genuinely existing inclination which we cannot suppress, "to dare to put up resistance to the limitations of language and to attempt to say that which cannot be said." He wrote in 1929/1930: "This beating on the walls of our cage is indeed absolutely hopeless," and yet "it is proof of the human spirit's inclination which I personally cannot respect deeply enough. I would never wish to ridicule it at the cost of life itself."[4]

In his *Philosophical Investigations*, Wittgenstein works out the concept of "language game" in order to do justice to the complexity of language. This concept was further developed by the Oxford linguistic analysts, who formulated the so-called principle of use, according to which the meaning of a word was a reflection of its use within a language. Gilbert Ryle writes that this principle is meant to prevent human language from putting on "deforming shoes" like those once worn by Chinese women.[5]

The excessively narrow criterion of verificationism is finally overcome here. In addition to the languages of the empirical sciences, other languages are admitted, such as ethical, legal, historical, lyrical, narrative, metaphysical and religious languages. D. Antiseri writes that the principle of verification was thereby exposed as *self-contradictory, crypto-metaphysical,* and *incapa-*

[2] Wittgenstein, *Tractatus*, 6.44-45, 6.522.

[3] Wittgenstein, *Tractatus*, 6.522.

[4] E. Baccarini, "Ludwig Wittgenstein: Linguaggio-logica-Dio," in *Il problema di Dio: Lezioni di filosofia* (Rome, 1987), 271.

[5] G. Ryle, "Ludwig Wittgenstein," in *Rivista di Filosofia* 2 (1952): 191.

ble of justifying universal claims of scientific theories, since it was based on induction.[6]

This "linguistic revolution" led on the one hand to semantic atheism; on the other, it made possible a new formulation of the unchanging truths of faith in the modern language of our contemporary culture by virtue of a deeper understanding of religious and theological language. Evidently, the new logical analysis of language proved a two-edged sword. For this, we must thank Wittgenstein.

Phenomenology and Methodological Atheism.

The second great revolution in this course of events was led by Edmund Husserl in his phenomenology, which we shall call a *phenomenology of essences.* Further developments were the *atheism of epoché* and methodological *atheism.*

The "phenomenological revolution" was described by Husserl himself as a *religious conversion.* His *Cartesian Meditations* are characteristically close to the words of St. Augustine: *Noli foras ire, in te redi, in interiore homine habitat veritas* (Do not go outside yourself, go within yourself; truth dwells in the interior person). The main idea of Husserl's philosophy is the *epoché* or *bracketing-off* of the naive, spontaneous, and natural conviction on the part of human beings that the surrounding world *exists* and does so independent of our consciousness. This critical reduction was undertaken by Husserl in at least three versions: 1) the Cartesian, 2) the intersubjective, and 3) the ontological (i.e. ontological in Husserl's sense of this term).

We cannot here go into the details of these three ways, but let us turn our attention at once to the outcome, which is the most relevant matter in view of our question: *How does Husserl think about God?* In Husserl's entire work, one can find neither a clear affirmation nor a clear denial of God's existence. The problem of the truth of theism or atheism is never broached by him. The reason for his silence is that Husserl's phenomenology *radically brackets off the question of every existence*; but this does not mean Husserl does not speak of God – he does so! But since he wants to remain true to the principle of the primacy of consciousness, he does not ask whether God exists, but only what

[6] D. Antiseri, "Idee metafisiche e sviluppo della scienza nel razionalismo critico di Karl Popper e nell' epistemologia post-popperiana," in *Metafisica oggi: Nuovi interventi in un dibattito sempre attuale* (Brescia, 1983), 41-42.

form God takes in human consciousness. Husserl is not interested in God as such, but rather the idea of God in us, which in Husserl's thinking takes different forms.

In Husserl's *Ideas Pertaining to a Pure Phenomenology*, the idea of God is a gnoseological *limit-concept,* an idea that has to be attained with gnoseological necessity, so that even the atheist who genuinely philosophizes can never avoid it.[7] In other writings, Husserl describes the idea of God as: 1) an *absolute pole idea* which unites all the forces in the human person; 2) the justification of human attempts at self-realization; 3) the ideal of the perfect life, the synthesis of all ideals; and 4) the immanent goal or end in the individual persons or in the community, which functions like an infinite *evolutionary telos.* The idea of God as a *pole idea* is therefore the "teleological foundation of being."[8] The idea of God, originally conceived as the limit of individual perfection, later becomes the final goal, i.e., the *absolute telos,* toward which humanity moves by realizing reason (viz. the truly human community) in history.

Husserl's philosophical enterprise was extraordinarily fruitful for Marxism, psychoanalysis, analytical philosophy, structuralism, the humanities, and hermeneutics. Many philosophers took up Husserl's phenomenology and developed new branches. His most important followers include Martin Heidegger, Merleau-Ponty, Hedwig Conrad Martius, Edith Stein, Roman Ingarden, Eugen Fink, Ludwig Landgrebe, and in the Czech Republic, Jan Patočka, Radim Palouš, and Erazim Kohák.

In view of Husserl's fundamental ambivalence about the question of God's existence, his phenomenology can be interpreted from two different angles: 1. To the extent Husserl remained bound to the immanent principle of the Cartesian *cogito*, he created a philosophically radical atheistic methodology, which made him the father of what we wish to call *methodological atheism.* 2. Because of the strongly utopian aspect of his philosophy, which was meant to prepare the way for God's kingdom of reason in the desert of the twentieth century, the Jewish philosophers from Prostějov found it considerably more important to clarify the function of *the idea of God in our consciousness* than to develop the *speculation* about a Being of God that would be independent of our consciousness.

7 E. Husserl, *Ideen zu einer Phänomenologie*, I, par. 79, 1.

8 A. Diemer, "La phénomenologie de Husserl comme métaphysique," in *Les études philosophiques I* (1954), 21.

Hermeneutical Phenomenology

Martin Heidegger's philosophy was certainly the most influential extension of Husserl's phenomenology. While Husserl's phenomenology is only concerned with essences, Heidegger's hermeneutical phenomenology takes up the question he bracketed off, viz. *Being*. In doing so, Heidegger posed anew, in its full power and depth, the metaphysical question: "Why does something exist, rather than nothing?" In this section I assume that the outlines of Heidegger's philosophy are sufficiently well known, and turn at once to the question that is of primary interest to our topic: *What does Heidegger think about God?*

It is well known that Heidegger's *Being and Time* (1927) and *What is Metaphysics?* (1929) led to accusations of "nihilism" and "atheism." Sartre himself, who presented his own atheistic existentialism as the fulfillment of ontological phenomenology, confirmed this view. Yet Heidegger's answer to Sartre was not long in coming. In his *Letter on Humanism,* Heidegger categorically denied these accusations by defending his positive interpretation of Being, and radically distanced his thinking from an atheistic existentialism.

If Heidegger cannot be accused of atheism, then we have to ask again: *How – and what – does Heidegger think about God?* In order to answer this question satisfactorily, we must divide it into three separate issues: 1.What does Heidegger think about the *biblical God,* i.e., the God of Abraham, Isaac, and Jacob, the God of Israel and of Jesus, and why does he not also consider, for example, the God of Mohammad? 2. What does Heidegger think about the *God of Western metaphysics* and so-called *onto-theological logic*? More precisely, what does he think about God as the *summum bonum, actus purus, ens supremum, causa sui?* 3. What does Heidegger think about the *"divine God"* for whose coming and return his own thinking seeks to prepare the way?

In answer to the first question, there is no clear and express denial of the biblical God in Heidegger. However, Heidegger maintains that authentic philosophical questioning is incompatible with primordial Christian faith. In his *Introduction to Metaphysics,* he writes:

> One for whom the Bible is divine revelation and truth already has the answer to the question: "Why does something exist, rather than nothing?" even before he puts that question: that which exists, to the degree that it is not God himself, is created by him. God himself "is" as the uncreated Creator. Whoever occupies the ground of such faith, can comprehend and understand why we pose our question,

> but he cannot really question without ceasing to be a believer – with all the consequences of such a step.[9]

But can we really draw the conclusion from these words of Heidegger that it is completely impossible for one who poses an authentic philosophical question to remain rooted in the footing of biblical faith, since (as the philosopher from Meßkirch asserts) "a Christian philosophy is an impossibility and a misunderstanding"? If so, then Heidegger is certainly an atheist with respect to the biblical God.

As for the second question, we can say that Heidegger's well-known critique of metaphysics as "forgetfulness of being" *(Seinsvergessenheit)* means that metaphysics, defined by Aristotle as the *scientia entis in quantum ens* ("the science of the existent *qua* existent), was so blinded by an interest in the existent that it defined Being itself only as the highest existent, and hence as "the most existent of all existents"[10] – thus turning metaphysics into onto-theo-logic and making God, as the ground of that which exists, "the cause as *causa sui.*"

So for Heidegger the most fitting name for the God of philosophy is *causa sui,* and this philosophy is so enchanted with the existent that it forgot Being. Such a philosophy is, however, a nihilistic metaphysics that has led to the modern age. Heidegger calls this age the "time of the conception of the world," i.e., the time of the objectifying reduction of the world to the *conception of the world* and to the triumph of the will to seize power in and through technology. Because of this fateful involution of western metaphysics, "thought came to question the ontological character of metaphysics." It is precisely this that inspired Heidegger to make the following statement, which is extremely interesting in the context of our investigations:

> Anyone who has come to know theology – both that of the Christian faith and that of philosophy – as it has grown from its origins, will prefer to be silent about God today in the sphere of thinking .... Accordingly, the god-less thinking, which is compelled to abandon the God of philosophy, God as *causa sui,* is perhaps closer to the divine God.[11]

Can we conclude then that these two atheisms, i.e., the atheism that denies the God of the Christian faith and the atheism that denies the God of onto-theo-

9 M. Heidegger, *Einführung in die Metaphysik* (Tübingen 1957), 5.

10 M. Heidegger, *Identität und Differenz* (Pfullingen, 1957), 67.

11 Heidegger, *Identität,* 51.71.

logic, are somehow necessary if a new theism is possible? Can we conclude that the double negation of God can lead to the affirmation of a "divine God"?

In response to the third question, "How does Heidegger think of this 'divine God'?", in his essay on Rilke, Heidegger characterizes our modern age with Hölderlin as "the needy time," which through the absence of God, through the "deficit of God," spreads its darkness in the night of the world.[12] This needy time is "deeply marked by a double deficit, a double 'no': from the *no longer* of the gods who have fled and from the *not yet* of the God who is to come." Within this context, Heidegger warns us not to strive to construct a God by ourselves, nor to invoke the traditional God. Rather, we must prepare ourselves with the essential thinking about Being for the future reappearance of God. For, as Heidegger writes, "It is only on the basis of the truth of Being that we can think of the essence of the holy. Only on the basis of the essence of the holy can one think of the essence of divinity. Only in the light of the essence of divinity can one think of what the word GOD is meant to specify."[13]

Heidegger developed here a clear upward movement from Being to the holy, from the holy to the divinity, and from divinity to God; and for our purposes, the intensification from Being to holiness is the most important transition. The connection between Being and the holy is a close one, since the latter reveals itself only in the opening up of Being, and hence beyond any conceptual or intuitive thinking. The realm wherein Being is unveiled is thus not on the level of objectifying thought, but rather on the level of feeling.

In the writings of his second phase, Heidegger speaks of a kind of ontological *quadrilateral*, which encompasses heaven, Earth, mortals, and divine beings. But who are the "divine ones"? Are they messengers of divinity, whose hidden leadership allows the "divine God" to manifest?

I hope that what I have written here suffices to convince the reader that Heidegger did not teach a radical atheism. The opposite is true, since his critique aims to lead directly to the roots of atheism and nihilism, in which (for Heidegger) the epilogue of western thought is played out. Heidegger wanted to prepare the path in our "needy time" for a divine God, and some have said that we can acknowledge Heidegger as one who indeed has done so, while others (e.g. Martin Buber) simply do not accept his claim that Being is *think-*

12 M. Heidegger, *Holzwege* (1950), 248.

13 M. Heidegger, *Platons Lehre von der Wahrheit: Mit einem Brief über den "Humanismus"* (Bern, 1954), 102.

able – a quality that is intended as a condition for the appearance or reappearance of this "divine God." "It is not we who make God come," Buber maintains energetically, "rather, the one who is to come will come as he himself wishes." For Buber, this has always been the difference between magic and religion. He repeats that "God does not let himself be conjured up," and continues:

> Obviously, the one whose appearance is conceived as fully or partially achieved through such modern-magical influence, has nothing in common with the God that we human beings (despite our different faiths) ultimately agree upon, except the name, and it is unacceptable to speak of a re-appearance.[14]

Here we must note that Heidegger emphatically denied this charge of magic in his interview with the news magazine *Spiegel.* When asked: "Do you think that we can bring God here by our thinking?" Heidegger answered: "We cannot bring him here by our thinking; we have at most the capacity to make ready the willingness to wait for him."[15]

Transcendental Philosophy

The fourth philosophical enterprise that has noticeably influenced philosophical thought, and hence the philosophical question of God, is the transcendental philosophy of Joseph Maréchal and his followers, Karl Rahner, Johann B. Lotz, Bernard Lonergan, Emerich Coreth, and in the Czech Republic, Karel Říha and Josef P. Ondok.

This philosophical movement interprets Thomas Aquinas' teaching on the *obiectum formale quod* and *obiectum formale quo* of our knowing faculty in the light of the Kantian transcendental *a priori,* in such a way that in positing an affirmative judgment (e.g., "this tree is tall") God is co-affirmed. This clearly audacious thesis is, however, not easy to prove. By means of a precise analysis of the transcendental conditions of possibility of our conceptual knowledge, these thinkers attempt to show that we cannot not make judgments; that is, that the "is" of judgment cannot be affirmed, without implicitly co-affirming the *esse entis* and the *esse subsistens* as the ultimate condition of the possibility of human judgment.

[14] M. Buber, *Gottesfinsternis* (Zürich, 1953), 91-92.

[15] M. Heidegger, *Antwort: Martin Heidegger im Gespräch* (Pfullingen, 1988), 100.

Transcendental philosophy thus becomes the *metaphysica operationis humanae,* the object of judgment behind the linking verb *est* becomes the *esse entis*, and the *esse*, as the light of the *intellectus agens*, becomes the immediate condition, while the *esse subsistens* becomes the ultimate condition of human cognition. It must be said, however, that this does nothing at all to resolve the question of whether the *esse subsistens* can be identified as the biblical *Ego sum qui sum*, or more precisely as the *Ehjeh asher Ehjeh.*

Dialogical and Personalist Thinking

The fifth philosophical enterprise we must examine is founded upon the discovery of dialogical and personalist thinking. It started with Martin Buber, and was further developed by Franz Rosenzweig, Ferdinand Ebner, Emmanuel Levinas, and in the Czech Republic, by Karel Vrána, Jan Sokol, and Jolana Poláková. Buber's assertion, *In the beginning is the relationship,* offers the most immediate and surest access to a renewed philosophy of Being. In fact, "to be" is a verb that is conjugated according to "persons." The "person" that best allows us to grasp the deepest meaning of the verb "to be" is not the third person, upon which both classical and medieval philosophy concentrated; nor is it the first person, with which modern philosophy is concerned. Rather, it is the second person, i.e., "you are," to which dialogical personalism turns. In "you" the difference between being and thinking is made clear. In fact, each of us discovers our own "I" through the "you" of the other who addresses us. Neither the "I" nor the "you" in this relation can be arbitrarily reduced to an "it," or to our own hypostasizing projection. This relative consistency of the various "you" to whom our "I" relates, is undergirded by the unconditional consistency of the *absolute "You."* If we extend the trajectories of all our relationships, they intersect in the eternal You. The personal relationships of our "I" with the various human "yous" possess their ethical guarantee and ultimately their ontological ground in the relationship between our "I" and the absolute and personal *"YOU OF GOD."*

This means that all discourse about God in the third person is secondary and derivative, and often distorted and misleading. The call of the divine YOU is original and essential. As Walter Kaufman has asserted, no better expression has yet been found for God than the *"absolute YOU."*

Conclusion: Consequences for Theology

In order to give a complete overview of the present-day philosophical forms given shape by godlessness, it would be necessary to include treatment of Karl Jaspers and his interpretation of philosophical faith. No less important would be an account of heterodox Marxism, which prepared the way for the ideological dissolution of systematic Marxist-Leninist atheism thanks to the philosophical achievements of Vítěslav Gardavský, Milan Machovec, Zbyněk Fischer (pseudonym: Egon Bondy), Leszek Kolakowski, and Ernst Bloch. A more thorough treatment of Jaspers' philosophical faith would be especially useful, since he addresses the problem of the relation between philosophical belief and faith in revelation, a key consideration. Heterodox Marxism, which maintains, with Gardavský, that "God is not entirely dead", is particularly compelling in the work of Milan Machovec, who wrote *Jesus for Atheists*; and of Leszek Kolakowski, who certainly considers himself an inconsistent atheist. I think especially here of Ernst Bloch, who worked out his own form of atheism, which I would like to call "eschatological atheism." But I will not speak about these contemporary thinkers here.

For reasons of space, I shall conclude with a short overview of the theological consequences of these various forms of atheism: 1) Semantic atheism has proved most fruitful for theology by deepening our understanding of language in general and the language of theology in particular, where it made possible a hermeneutically precise theological task and also a theology of language. 2) Methodological atheism has proved highly useful in the methodology of religious studies, especially in the phenomenology of religion, but also in the sociology of religion, as is clearly apparent in Peter L. Berger's sociological theory of religion. 3) Heidegger's philosophy, although it has been accused of atheism and nihilism, had a very positive effect on theological thinking, since it contributed to the emergence of the existentialist theologies of Bultmann and Rahner. 4) The eschatological atheism of Ernst Bloch can boast of numerous theological progeny, especially in the theology of hope of Jürgen Moltmann, Wolfhart Pannenberg, and others, as well as in the political theology of J.B. Metz and the theologies of revolution and liberation. 5) The inconsistent atheism of Kolakowski is ultimately, according to Gerhard M. Martin, a theological provocation. Martin writes, "Christians who have gone in for the stimulant of a humane and theological atheism must allow themselves to be asked about their *proprium*, their own essence, and search for an answer. The evidence of the banal is the judge over every form of authoritarian theological doctrinal assertions. Kolakowski's patient, inconsistent atheism cuts deeper under the skin of the Body of Christ than any consistent and vulgar type."[16]

Hence while the atheism of the nineteenth century proclaimed in the name of Nietzsche: "God is dead," the atheism of the twentieth century, in the name of Gardavský, has admitted humbly in a low voice: "God is not completely dead." As a final remark on our topic, "Thinking about God philosophically in Europe today," allow me to paraphrase St. Augustine: "We know that for those who love God, even atheism leads to the Good."

Translated by Michael Parker

[16] L. Kolakowski, *Geist und Ungeist christlicher Traditionen* (Stuttgart / Berlin / Cologne / Mainz, 1971), 9.

László Holló

Thinking God in National and Religious Conflicts: The Case of Romania

In Eastern Europe Romania is at the crossroads of East and West. Here the Orthodox culture, which is Eastern, meets the Catholic and Protestant cultures, which are Western. This unique situation is a challenge for the churches, since religion also forms a part of national identity. The primary aim of this study is to show that while differing religious images of God have an important influence on culture, the roots of cultural conflict are not religious. Religious images of God are rather influenced by historical, political, economic, and demographic factors.

Posing the Question

During the Cold War, the attention of the Free World was turned to the East-West conflict, and few could have imagined the degree of pent-up national and religious frustration in the Eastern Block, which was believed to be a monolithic power. Now that the system of Communism has collapsed, Eastern Europe is threatened by new national and religious conflicts, resulting in repression, flight, and expulsion, with all their accompanying misery and suffering.

The contemporary discussion about the threat to world peace is shaped by the famous prognosis of Samuel P. Huntington about a "clash of civilizations" – the phrase originally appearing in the form of a question. Since its publication (in German under the title *Kampf der Kulturen*) Huntington's book has gone through several editions, unleashing an interdisciplinary debate that could have scarcely been anticipated.[1]

In his book, Huntington looks at developments in global politics in the twentieth-century. The basic thesis of his paradigm is that divisions among peoples are no longer ideological, political, or economic. He says, "The great division of humanity and the leading source of conflict in the future will be

1 Cf. S.P. Huntington, *Kampf der Kulturen: Die Neugestaltung der Weltpolitik im 21. Jahrhundert* (Munich / Vienna, 1996).

cultural. Nation states will remain the most powerful global political actors, but the main conflicts in global politics will be between nations, groups, and different civilizations. The clash of civilizations will dominate global politics. The fractures among civilizations will be the battle lines of the future."[2]

Huntington divides the contemporary world into eight great civilizations: Chinese, Japanese, Hindu, Islamic, Western, Latin American, African, and Eastern-Christian. The boundaries within this new world do not run along the lines of states or alliances, but cultures. In addition to origins, language, history, values, morality, customs, and institutions, religion is an especially important distinguishing characteristic of people in a culture, and it is the most important source of identity and a motivating power for conflicts.[3] Especially since the conflicts surrounding the war in Iraq, talk of "civilizations" has become suspect for many, as it had for others before this development.

The topic of my paper, "Thinking God in National and Religious Conflicts: The Case of Romania" may be cast in terms of the discussion about the "clash of civilizations," since Romania is composed of peoples of many different nationalities and religions and is thus a microcosm of a world in which different nations and religions, and thus different cultures, live together.

After the major upheavals of 1989, the global economy was supposed to bring prosperity and democracy and also happiness to Romania. If this has not yet been the case, the search for causes should not be restricted to culture, but must address the fundamental economic and political history of the country. I realize that such an approach might be accused of being "backward looking" – a charge often made of southeastern European society as a whole, but I am willing to take such a risk.

In the following section, I examine the early political history of Transylvania, since the national and religions conflicts in Romania mainly revolve around events taking place there.

The Background of the Conflicts

All present-day countries of southern Europe were created as independent nation states in the nineteenth and early twentieth centuries. The creation of the nation state was the crowning achievement of a glorious struggle. National

---

2 Huntington, *Kampf*, 19-20.

3 Huntington, *Kampf*, 414.

histories stand entirely in the service of this idea, and derive from past historical legitimacy for their current national borders. Hence for Romanian national consciousness, there is an unbroken continuity extending from the Dacian kingdom (or the heritage of the Romans) to the present-day state of Romania.[4]

Romanians consider themselves to be the indigenous population of the area around the Carpathian Mountain range – a population that looks back on a history of over two thousand years – and they view all others in this region as foreigners. Relying on the postulate of a Dacian-Roman-Romanian origin, and proffering an ensuing historical continuity, a direct line of descent is drawn from the Dacian kingdom to Burebista and Dezebal and the greater Romanian State established in 1918. According to Popescu, continuity "is the cardinal question and a national issue or national duty in the view of official Romanian history, since Hungarian, philo-Slavic, or German historians from the Habsburg Empire maintained that the land of the Romanians was emptied by autochthones and the ethnic vacuum filled by Slavs, Huns, Avars and other peoples, and later by Hungarians and Germans."[5]

In addition, it is maintained that "when the Romanian people emerged as an autonomous Latin people, it was already Christian, so that it is one of the few nations that emerged as Christian without the need to provide an exact dating of its Christianization, and this has remained so until the present."[6] The Romanian people are the only Latin nation with an Orthodox faith, and at the same time, the oldest Christian nation in Europe.

The bordering provinces are problematic since they have a strong mix of ethnic groups. Transylvania represents such a place, where Hungarians and Romanians have lived together for centuries. The issue is complicated by the fact that the Hungarian kings began to settle in this area with German colonists beginning in the twelfth century.

---

4 Cf. C.C. Giurescu / D.C. Giurescu, *Istoria Românilor din cele mai vechi timpuri până astăz* (The History of Romania from the Most Ancient Times Until Today) (Bucureşti, 1975).

5 E. Popescu, "Creştinismul pe teritoriul României până în secolul al VII-lea, in lumina noilor cercetări" (Christianity in the Territorium Romania until the Seventh Century in Light of Recent Research) in *Orthodoxia Românească* (Rumänische Orthodoxie) (Bucureşti, 1992), 85-99, here 85.

6 *"Viaţa religioasă din România". Studiu documentar al Secretariatului de Stat pentru Culte* (Religious Life in Romania: Documentation of the State Cultic Ministry) (Bucureşti, 1999), 17-18.

The Concept "Transylvania"

The old Hungarian name for this region is "Erdély" oder "Erdőelve," from which the Romanian term "Ardeal" is derived.[7] The Latin translation "Transsilvania" is derived from Hungarian and means "the land beyond the forest." According to an Egyptian interpretation, the German name "Siebenbürgen," is derived from "Cibinburg," the region of the Hermann dwellers.[8]

The demarcation of Transylvania is not without problems. In the Treaty of Trianon (June 4, 1920) Romania was promised the historical region of Transylvania (56,883 to 61,622 km^2), wide parts of the eastern regions of Hungary, i.e., Marmarosch and Sathmar; the Kreischgebiet; and the eastern part of Banat. Since 1945, "Transylvania" is understood by the Romanians to include all these regions promised to Romania and formerly belonging to the Hungarian half of the Austrian-Hungarian Empire.

A Short History of Transylvania

Transylvania, separated by the Carpathian Mountains from the territory of Old Romania, is not only a geographical unity, but differs from other regions of Romania in terms of its cultural history, its Western influence, its historical development, and its strong confessional traditions.

The present-day region of Transylvania was populated by Indo-European peoples and then by Agathyrsen, Skyten, Thracians, Getians, and Dacians. After the Roman occupation (105-271), it was ruled successively by the Goths (271-380), the Huns (375-455), the Gepidae (455-567) and later the Avars (567-827) and the Slavs (600-895). Prior to the Hungarian settlement, southern Transylvania was shortly subject to Bulgarian rule (827-895). The Magyarian settlement in 896 ended the migration of the peoples in the Carpathian basin. [9] The Magyars were the first people who built cities.

---

7 Cf. E. Wagner, *Historisch-Statistisches Ortsnamenbuch für Siebenbürgen* (Cologne / Vienna, 1977), 23.

8 Cf. E. Illyés, *Nationale Minderheiten in Rumänien. Siebenbürgen im Wandel* (Vienna, 1981), 12.

9 Cf. K. Horedt, *Das frühmittelalterliche Siebenbürgen* (Thaur / Innsbruck, 1988), 17; L. Makkai, "Herausbildung der ständischen Gesellschaft (1172-1241)," in B. Köpeczi (ed.), *Kurze Geschichte Siebenbürgens* (Budapest, 1990), 175-240.

In the course of the eleventh and thirteen centuries, Transylvania was part of the Hungarian Empire, but formed a special unit. The first non-Magyarian peoples were the Transylvania Saxons[10] who settled at the behest of Geysa II (Géza, 1141–61) and who, in addition of the Hungarian "comitia nobles"[11] and the Szekler,[12] formed the third order "nation" of Transylvania. [13]

After the battle near Mohács (1526) the Turks conquered a great part of Hungary in a short time. The old kingdom was divided into three parts: one part settled by the Turks, another Western kingdom ruled by the Habsburgs, and finally the East Hungarian regions; Transylvania was not controlled by the Turks and its Prince raised repeated claims to the Hungarian throne. After the death of the anti-King Ferdinand of Habsburg, Johann Zapolya, in 1542, the government of Transylvania recognized Turkish rule. But the bloody disputes between the Habsburgs and the princes of Transylvania, recognized by

[10] The Transylvania Saxons originate largely from regions on the left bank of the Rhein, from Lothringen, Burgund, Flanders, present-day Luxemburg, from the Mosel and from Wallonian territory in what is today Belgium. As they were called into the country in the middle of the twelfth century the scribe in the king's court chancellery called them "theutonici,""saxones"and "flandrenses." Andreas II bestowed on them the "Golden Charter" (1224) privileges on the territory of the "king's land" with full territorial autonomy. Cf. E. Wagner, *Quellen zur Geschichte der siebenbürger Sachsen 1191-1975*, (Cologne / Vienna, 1976), 12-15.

[11] The administrative and territorial division of Transylvania in the middle Ages consisted of three districts, seats, and comitia. While the peoples in the districts and seats (Szeklers und Saxons) were free and possessed autonomous rights, the comitia was based on the feudal system and consisted of nobles and serfs. Cf. Illyés, *Nationale Minderheiten*, 9.

[12] A substantial number of the Magyars in Transylvania today, approximately one third, are Szeklers (Hungarian: Székely), who are ethnically and linguistically inseparable from Hungary. The Szeklers belong to the Hungarian tribes that were the first to settle in the Carpathian basin. They have maintained the area in which they settled from the Middle Ages and have asserted themselves as an independent ethnic group. At the time of the incorporation of Transylvania into Romania, they numbered circa 590,000 to 600,000. Cf. Illyés, *Nationale Minderheiten*, 4.

[13] Nations formed in or prior to the fifteenth century, those that form the political unity of Transylvania, have little in common with the modern idea of nationhood formulated in the French Revolution. These national groups do not make claims to separate nationhood or national independence. Neither do they constitute a nation based on language, as the example of the Hungarians and Szeklers, who have Hungarian as their common language, makes clear. Nevertheless these two groups differ considerably in terms of their existing social structures. Cf. A. Priberski (ed.), *Europa und Mitteleuropa?* (Vienna, 1991), 176.

the Turks, continued, even when the Habsburgs were simultaneously the princes of Transylvania as a result of the treaty of 1691. [14]

The insurrection of the Hungarians, led by Franz Rákóczi II, led to his declaration as prince in 1704 in Weißenburg, and ended with the Sathmar Peace of May 1, 1711; from that time the parliament of Transylvania was not ruled by an elected Prince, but by the ruler of a great power, who lived far away in Vienna and who let himself be represented locally by the commanding General and his governor. The narrowing of religious tolerance at the beginning of the Catholic Reformation brought many difficulties in its wake. The Orthodox Romanians proceeded more skillfully. They were offered a new, Greek-Catholic confession, and already by 1698, a Greek Orthodox bishop had concluded a formal Union with Rome. The attempt by Emperor Joseph II to introduce German as an official language (1784) created the conditions for later Hungarian nationalism. Although he withdrew this ordinance in 1790, it had already given Hungarian nationalism a strong impetus.

In the Revolution of 1848-1849 the nationalities in Transylvania first came into conflict through the Civil War. The Hungarian Revolutionary government concluded an agreement between Transylvania with Hungary. The parliament of Transylvania affirmed the union in the first legal article of 1848, also with the support of the Saxons. In the subsequent civil war, Romania and Saxony stood on the side of the Emperor's troops. In 1849, with Russian help, the Revolution was crushed. The failure of the Habsburg wars against Prussia from 1859-1860 and 1866 finally led to the historic compromise of 1867, namely to the formation of the Austrian-Hungarian Monarchy.

In the Hungarian half of the Empire, the problem of nationality was regulated by Article 44 of 1868. The laws ruled that all nationalities had equal rights, but this liberal position was nevertheless interpreted by a part of the civil administration to the detriment of the non-Magyars.[15] With the collapse of the Austrian-Hungarian Monarchy at the end of the First World War, the Romanian National Assembly proclaimed, despite Magyarian protest, the annexation of Transylvania by Romania, a move endorsed by the Allies and

14 Emperor Leopold I, Emperor of Austria and King of Hungary, occupied Transylvania in the course of his great military campaign against the Turks in 1687 and took the title Prince of Transylvania.

15 Cf. Z. Szász, "Politik und Nationalitätenfrage in der Zeit des Dualismus (1867-1918)," in Köpeczi, *Kurze Geschichte Siebenbürgens*, 597-624.

their partners in the Treaty of Tiranon (June 4, 1920).[16] Transylvania was divided for the first time on August 30, 1940 by the Second Vienna Arbitration Agreement. Northern Transylvania and the Szeklerzipfel became Hungarian; central and southern Transylvania remained Romanian.[17]

On August 31, 1944 Romania capitulated to Russia and declared war on Germany. Transylvania was occupied by Russian troops. In the Allied Peace Treaty with Romania, Transylvania was finally promised to Romania.

The Development of the Population of Transylvania

As said previously, the first city-dwelling people in the Carpathian basin were the Hungarians. The Hungarian possession ended the migration of peoples that had taken place in this area. At the beginning of the possession, Transylvania was not desolate, but scarcely populated.[18] Until the general conscription in the eighteenth century, census taking was the responsibility of the Transylvanians. A general census was first taken in 1850, since the census of 1786 failed to count military families on military borders. Research into the settlement history shows that from the Magyarian possession of the land, the Magyars were in the majority in the regions of historic Hungary. In the regions of Transylvania, until the eighteenth century, the Magyars were ten times as large as other groups. [19]

The first non-Magyarian peoples who settled after the Hungarian possession of the Transylvania were the Transylvania Saxons. In a Charter, Andreanum (1224), bestowed by the Hungarian King Andreas II, the Transylvania Saxons received extensive legal privileges as well as political and ecclesial autonomy.[20] According to historical documents, the first immigration of no-

16 Cf. L. Révész, *Minderheitenschicksal in den Nachfolgestaaten der Donaumonarchie* (Vienna, 1990), 108.

17 Bilateral negotiations between Hungary and Romania collapsed; therefore both governments agreed to subject themselves to the arbitration of the German Empire and Italy. On August 30, 1940, a decision was handed down which did not completely satisfy Hungary, and Romania found it to be a dictate

18 Cf. Wagner, *Quellen*, 3.

19 Cf. Illyés, *Nationale Minderheiten*, 13, with reference to several sources.

20 It is the most important medieval charter of the Transylvania Saxons.

madic peoples, the Walachia, later called Romanians, began in the early thirteenth century north of the Danube in the region of Transylvania.[21]

The maintenance and development of the Romanian population in Transylvania was guaranteed by their way of life. As a nomadic people, the outlying Carpathian Mountains and valleys provided them protection from devastation from Turkish-Tartar attacks. The increase in the Romanian population in Transylvania was as much due to the mass exodus out of Romanian principalities through lengthy Ottoman rule as it was to the fact that a great part of the Romanians who immigrated to Transylvania belonged to the mass of outcast peasants who did not contribute to defending the land.[22] Therefore they were not included in the alliance of the three Transylvanian nations (Hungarians, Szeklers, and Saxons) founded in 1437. It was the Hungarians, together with the Transylvania Saxons, who defended Transylvania from enemy attacks and paid a high price in blood, while the Romanians contributed practically nothing to military defense for a century.[23]

It was Greek Catholic priests who in the second half of the eighteenth century worked out the Dacian-Roman theory of the origins of the Romanian people and language. The theory maintains that the Hungarians conquered an old Romanian country. This theory can be summarized as follows: the strong, centralized Dacian kingdom emerged in 70 B.C. in present-day Transylvania. The Roman Emperor Trajan conquered it from 101-106 A.D. The Dacians withdrew to the mountains and continued to live there. As Emperor Aurelius in 271 A.D. settled Roman Legions south of the Danube in the Balkans, some of the Romans withdrew into the mountains. The confluence of the Dacians and the Romans led in time to the creation of the Romanian people and language.[24] This theory fails to answer a number of questions. In particular, the

21 Cf. Makkai, *Herausbildung der ständischen Gesellschaft*, 180-95.

22 The Romanian principates of Walachia and Moldau received their independence in the fourteenth century, but they came under Turkish rule at the beginning of the fifteenth century.

23 Cf. Wagner, *Quellen*, 68f.

24 Cf. dazu C. Daicoviciu, *Le probleme de la continuite en Dacie: Observations et precisions d'ordre historique et archeologique*, Bucarest 1940; *idem*, "Au sujet dese monuments chretiens de la Dacie Trajane," in *Melanges Marouzeau* (1948), 119-24; Gh. Ştefan, "Le probleme de la continuite sur le territoire de la Dacie," in *Dacia N. S.* 12 (1968), 347-354; E. Popescu, "Das Problem der Kontinuität in Rumänien im Lichte der epigraphischen Entdeckungen," in *Dacoromania, Jahrbuch für östliche Latinität* I (Freiburg / Munich,1973), 66-69; S. Stoicescu, *Continuitatea Românilor* (Bucureşti, 1980); E. Popescu, "Continuitatea daco-româna. Formarea poporului român si a limbii

lack of source material constitutes a problem, since the first mention of the "Walchia" in Transylvania dates from the second half of the twelfth century.[25] – The goal of this theory was the recognition of the Romanians in Transylvania as the "fourth nation" alongside Hungarians, Szeklers, and Saxons. This theory has been elaborated in the last decades, and in 1980 the Socialist state of Romania even celebrated the 2050th anniversary of the founding of the Romanian state by the Dacians.[26]

Against this hypothesis, one must hold that in their language, customs, religion, and dress, the Romanian people borrowed many Greek, Slavic, and Albanian elements, which rather point to an origin in the Balkans. More likely, the original homeland of the Romanians is not Transylvania-Dacian, but Aurelian-Dacian.[27] Later settlers in the territory of Transylvania are the Steiermark, Tirolese, Saxons, and the Banta Schwabians from Bohemia. The first settlers arrived between 1718 and 1739. The bulk of the settlers came to Transylvanian as a consequence of the colonization of 1763 during the rule of the Austrian Empress Maria Theresia (1740–1780).[28]

The first Armenian settlers had already arrived in Transylvania by the Middle Ages. Additional groups suffering religious persecution followed. In 1850 they numbered around 7,000, the largest portion settling in Magyrian regions. The settlement of the Jews began at the end of the eighteenth and the beginning of the nineteenth centuries. In 1920, statistics show the Jewish minority in Transylvania numbered 171,443. A strong wave of settlement resulted from the division of Poland. The greatest part of the Jewish population spoke Magyarian. The Slavs settled in Transylvania in the course of the nineteenth and twentieth centuries. A large number of them became assimilated Romanians. Migratory Gypsies appear in greater numbers for the first time as a consequence of the Turkish wars. According to official figures they numbered 409,723 in 1992 and 535,250 in 2002. However, the number of Gypsies

---

române. Rolul crestinismului," in: *Glasul Bisericii* 6-9 (1980), 573-87; S. Brezeanu, *La continuite daco-roumanie. Science et politique* (Bucarest, 1984).

25 Cf. W. Öschlies, *Die Deutschen in Rumänien. Teil I. Nachbarn seit Jahrhunderten. Berichte des Bundesinstituts für ostwissenschaftliche und internationale Studien* (Cologne,1980), 8.

26 The proof of this continuity, which is based largely but not exclusively on Hungarian historiography, is disputed. Cf. Priberski, *Europa*, 179.

27 Cf. Priberski, *Europa*, 179.

28 Cf. Wagner, *Quellen*, 36.

living in Romania is estimated to be around three million. In the long run, the Gypsy minority, not the Hungarian or German minorities, constitutes the most challenging ethnic problem.

The Ethnic Structure of Romania

In January 1992 and March 2002 a census was taken in Romania, the first since 1977. The new numbers make clear that the minorities constitute a shrinking portion of the total population. In 1977 they constituted about 12%, in 1992 10.6%, and in 2002, only 10.5% of the population.

In 1992, the census showed a population for Romania of 22,810,035 inhabitants. If one analyzes the numbers from the 1992 census with respect to nationalities, one must conclude that the Romanian census follows (again) the Soviet example: every local dialect is made into a nation. In 1992, as in 1977, in order to reduce the strong numbers of nationalities, Romanian officials divided the German minority for statistical purposes into three nations: Germans, Saxons, and Schwabians, and they divided the Hungarian minority into two nations: Hungarians and Szeklers. These political machinations nevertheless failed, since almost all Saxons and Schwabians declared themselves "German." This strategy was even less successful with respect to the Hungarians. The statistics are also conspicuous for how they separate the Lipovanen from the Russians, to whom they belong in terms of origin and language, and from whom they are separated occasionally by religious membership. This new development in the history of Romanian census taking appears to reflect the present politics of nationality, whose goal is the reduction of ethnic minorities.[29]

In 1992, the Romanian census showed a population of 22, 810,035, whereas in 2002 it was only 21,698,181.[30] The official figures on nationalities show the following numbers: Romanians, 19,409,400 (89.5%); Hungarians,

---

[29] In this connection it is interesting to note the percentage of Romanians in the total population. In 1920, it was 71.9%; in 1977, 88.1% increasing to 89.3 % in 1992. Correspondingly, the percentage of minorities dropped from 28.1% to10.7% during the same period.

[30] Cf. *Recensământul populației și locuințelor 18-27 martie 2002* (Population and Residence Statistics from March 18-27, 2002). The preliminary data cited on April 10, 2003 according to Institutul Național de Statistică-România (The National Administration for Statistics - Romania).

1,434,377 (6.6%); Roma/Gypsies, 535,250 (2.5%); Germans, 60088 (0.3%); Ukranians, 61091 (0.3%); Russians/Lipovans, 36,397 (0.2%); Turks, 32596 (0.2%); Serbs, Tartens, Slovakians circa 20,000 (0.1%); and those under 10,000 are Bulgarians, Croats, Greeks, Jews, and Tschehen.

Ethnic or National Churches in Romania

As has been suggested, the cultural history of the nationalities in Transylvania cannot be separated from the historical role of their churches. In the course of history the churches or church officials were on the forefront of those fighting for their national interests.

According to official numbers, the majority of the Romanian population (86.7%) are members of the Romanian-Orthodox Church.[31] This Church has accompanied and served the Romanian people through its history and often made essential contributions to the maintenance of their ethnic and national identity.

The Hungarian and German minorities are, by contrast, overwhelmingly Roman Catholic or Protestant. The Catholic Romanians (5.6%) belong to three different rites: the Latin, Byzantine, and the Armenian. There are six Roman Catholic dioceses. Of this number, four (Alba Iulia, Satu-Mare, Oradea and Timisoara) are Hungarian-speaking with approximately 700,000-750,000 Christians (a number of which are of German origin, and a smaller number are Tschechischen, Polish, and Croatian) and two dioceses are Romanian speaking in the Old Romanian Empire (Bucharest and Iasi) with approximately 300,000-350,000 Christians. The diocese with the largest number of Roman Catholics is the Archdiocese of Alba Iulia (Hungarian: Gyulafehérvár; German: Karlsburg), which was founded in 1010.

Since the readmission of the United Greek-Catholic Church, which was created in September 1790 through a manifesto of 54 Orthodox proto-popes, then outlawed in 1948 and readmitted in 1990, its members constitute approximately one percent of the Romanian population. The Greek-Roman Catholic Christians are divided into five dioceses (Alba Iulia and Făgăras, Cluj-Gherla, Maramureş, Oradea Mare, and Lugoj) and are all Romanian-

[31] In this connection it should be mentioned that official estimates of religious communities are doubtful. On the basis of these estimates the Greek-Catholics are placed at circa 750,00 members, and the Baptists circa 300,000. The neo-Protestant communities are unhappy with the official numbers.

speaking. The number of Catholic Christians belonging to the Armenian rite includes only a few hundred Hungarian speaking adherents.

The Reformed Church (Calvinists), originating in the sixteenth century, has approximately 700,000 largely Magyarian adherents and represents an important minority. The Lutheran tradition in Transylvania reaches back to the sixteenth century, when the resident Catholic Saxons converted to Protestantism between 1542-1547, and presently numbers about 25,000. A smaller number of believers in Transylvania are Baptist (circa 130,000 members), Unitarian (approximately 65,000), or Jewish (6,000 members).

After the annexation of Transylvania by Romania, the Karlsburg resolutions from 1 December 1918 guaranteed, in chapter II, 2, the "equality and complete autonomous religious freedom for all confessions in the state."[32] Article 137 of the Romanian constitution of 1923 guarantees "all religious cults (churches) the same freedom and support as long as their exercise does not encroach upon the public order, good morals, and legal organization of the state."[33]

The relation between the Romanian state and the Roman Catholic Church is regulated in the Concordat between the Holy Office and Romania, which was agreed to on May 10, 1927 and published on May 29, 1929. This limited on the one hand, the nearly thousand year old autonomy of the Catholic Church in Transylvania, in that it subjected the regions around Romania and Catholic bishoprics founded forty-three years earlier, in 1883, to its control – a total of twenty-six parishes and countless bishoprics in Bucharest – but on the other hand, it gave them the status of juridical persons and the freedom to act autonomously.

During the course of the negotiations leading to the Concordat, the ruling government managed to achieve their demand that all six Roman Catholic dioceses be consolidated into a single Church province in Bucureşti. The Archdiocese Bucureşti and the diocese Diözese Iaşi are in Old Romania, and the people are almost entirely Romanian, the other four Catholic dioceses being in Transylvania. These four dioceses previously belonged to Hungary, and

---

32 *Marea Adunare Naţională întrunită la Alba-Iulia în ziua de 1 Decemvrie 1918. Acte şi documente* (The Karlsburg Resolutions at the Romanian National Assembly from November 18, 1918, Records and Documents) "Egală îndreptăţire şi deplină libertate sutonomă confesională pentru toate confesiunile din stat."

33 From the Romanian Constitution from March 28, 1923, cited in Wagner, *Quellen*, 284.

before the shifting of the Romanian-Hungarian border, the faithful shared the same Hungarian traditions and enjoyed a similar level of culture.

This new Church structure corresponded to the interests of the ruling government at the time, but did not meet the Church's pastoral needs. For the four Roman Catholic dioceses of Transylvania, this compromise had catastrophic consequences, since it fixed the disadvantages of national minorities by institutionalizing them in ecclesial structures.

After World War II, the nationality statutes of February 6, 1945, as well as the provisions of the Paris Peace Treaty of February 10, 1947, regulated the situation of the national churches. Both called for complete religious freedom for all inhabitants of Romania.[34] Similar affirmations of religious freedom can be found in the first Communist Constitution of the People's Republic of Romania from April 13, 1948 and the Constitution of the Soviet Socialist Republic of Romania from August 21, 1965.

In the churches, especially the Catholic Church, the socialist state saw a genuine threat to the consolidation of the Communist regime. In order to do away with this threat, they began a campaign of intimidation. Many priests were arrested, the Catholic press was banned, and in order to legitimate these actions, on July 17, 1948, the People's Republic of Romania unilaterally declared with immediate effect as null and void the Concordat that had been agreed to by the Holy Office and Romania on May 10, 1927. The annulment of the Concordat robbed the Roman Catholic Church of its legal status.

The basis for the new Church politics in Romania until 1989 was the culture law (*Legea cultelor*) laid down on August 4, 1948. The new law subjects the Church to the power of the State. In practice, this means that the State controls the highest administrative, financial, and economic institutions of the Church and limits its function exclusively to liturgical and pastoral matters. A further law determines that community Church leaders can only hold office with the approval of the highest State authorities. Members of the clergy are obliged to swear a loyalty oath upon taking office. The provisions of the school reform law, which provided an economic basis for century-old traditional confessional schools of the national minorities of Transylvania, were done away with.

The school reform law was published one day before the cultural law on August 3, 1948 and so all confessions and private schools were converted into state schools. At the same time the State expropriated the remaining wealth of

34 Cf. Wagner, *Quellen*, 353.

the Church without any compensation. The Church's increasing resistance was met by the government with an arbitrary limitation of the number of dioceses with bishops. Thereby, three Greek Catholic and two Roman Catholic Bishops were removed from office. This event led to the dissolution of the Romanian United Church (Greek-Catholic) and the arrest of the remaining bishops.

Since the fall of the Ceausescu regime, the 1948 ban on the Greek-Catholic Church in Romania has been rescinded and the Roman Catholic Church, which was "tolerated" outside the law, has likewise regained its legal status. The Catholic Church hierarchy is also now complete since the consecration of Bishops on March 14, 1990. After the seat of the Archbishopric of Bucureşti was filled, the problem of canonical representation of the Catholic faithful in Transylvania received renewed attention.

With this came the opportunity to learn from the mistakes of the past and to create a situation that, with the help of a new organization, both met the requirements of the pastorate, as well as the diocese, in which national minorities lived, by guaranteeing them a certain independence. With this goal in mind, the Bishops of the four dioceses of Transylvania delivered a memorandum on the Holy Office, in which they requested the creation of a new Church province under the leadership of the diocese of Alba Julia. Unfortunately, the Roman diplomats appeared unable to understand the problems of the minorities. The diocese Alba Julia received its independence upon achieving the status of an Archbishopric, but the other three dioceses are still subjected to the Archdiocese of Bucureşti.

The Catholic pastoral leadership of Transylvania is convinced it is necessary that the Holy office guarantee it that minimum of independence that it is entitled to by canon law by virtue of its status as a Church province. They "cannot imagine their future under a leadership whose goals and means are so fundamentally different from their own, unless their common relationship of belonging to the Church of Christ could be organized from a starting point of independence."[35] The reference to differing goals and means is to be understood as the de-nationalization of the Old Romanian dioceses practiced over the past decades. They have undertaken to hinder or eliminate everything connected with pastoral care for national minorities in the areas of their jurisdiction. For the Churches of the national minorities, every statement of church

[35] "Memorandum der Diözesanbischöfe Siebenbürgens vom 26. Februar 1990 an den Heiligen Stuhl." Cited in *UKI-Pressedienst* (1990), 6.

politics from the leader of the Old Romanian Church diocese that compromised its position, but was made in the name of the entire Catholic Church, was unacceptable.

The expectations of the minorities for the concession of their rights to autonomy, and the lack of understanding or mistrust of the population of the resulting resistance, has led to a continuous division that appears not to have been resolved, even until the present day.

Thinking God in National and Religious Conflicts

In Romania, two religious worlds overlap: the Eastern Christian Orthodoxy and Catholic and Protestant Western Church Christianity. This situation represents a challenge for the churches, especially since confessional identity and nationality often coincide. The examples represented will make clear that conflicts result from a chain of historical, political, economic, and demographic causes. Religious reasons played a secondary role, since although religions have been essential in forming cultures, cultural conflicts have not resulted directly from religious views, but rather from behavioral patterns that have developed over many years.

I have not for that reason treated the question of fundamental differences between Eastern and Western Christianity – for instance the clear differences in their images of God. Despite various differences between the Eastern and Western Church, one can say that at the early stages of conflict, religious elements played a marginal role, or no role at all, but when conflicts escalate, religion provides a clear and precise language for protecting and articulating threats to cultural identity.

On a purely theological level, as well as in terms of Church polity, Protestantism differs more from Eastern Orthodoxy or Roman Catholicism than the latter two differ from each other. Nevertheless, church-dividing elements are strongly emphasized from a Western perspective, whereas those between Protestantism and Catholicism are neglected. The largely peaceful coexistence of Catholics and Protestants as a result of secularization, as well as the less frequent contact with members of the Orthodox communion, may be causes for such undervaluations of differences.

Ruptures at the micro level are realities, but they do not result in cultural breaks just because Orthodox, Catholics, and Protestants have different rites. Ruptures are marked by socio-economic problems that result from structurally conditioned systematic oppression, discrimination, and the privileging of some at the expense of others.

In experiences of extreme hardship, when people have already lost everything, religion is often the only thing that cannot be taken away from them. For that reason, it is not surprising when in such situations that the separating, apocalyptical elements of religion are activated and emphasized. Poverty and oppression, marginalization and isolation, are the breeding grounds for enlisting religion as an ally in the struggle for identity and recognition.

Christianity has a paradoxical relationship to nationality. As a monotheistic religion it is universal and transcends nationality; at the same time however, precisely because of its universalism, it must look for a special relation to culture and the particularity of every people with whom it wishes to communicate. The Church recognizes national identity as an objective given and as a value.[36]

The Catholic magisterium has accorded great importance to nationality as a foundation for the transcendent "more" of human being, and it rejects the assimilation of one culture into another, but rather desires that every people be given its own space for cultural identity and that every nation should respect and encourage this. Papal documents correspondingly call people not to give up their cultural and national identity and singularity.[37]

According to Vatican II, human persons "can succeed in realizing their essence only through culture."[38] Here culture means primarily the native tongue, the nation, and often, the religion of a people. Such a concept of culture is shared by countries in separate cultural spheres. Since man is by nature mistrusting of what is foreign, this can lead to the delimitation and depreciation of other nations. Then national pride can turn into nationalism, which represents a danger. Nevertheless, it would be an unacceptable reduction to treat the problems of minorities simply as the expression of a romantic partic-

36 Cf. "Libertatis consciencia and Mater et magistra," in: *Texte zur katholischen Soziallehre: Die sozialen Rundschreiben der Päpste und andere kirchliche Dokumente*, edited by Bundesverband der Katholischen Arbeitnehmer-Bewegung Deutschlands – KAB (Einführung von O. v. Nell-Breuning SJ und J. Schasching SJ), 7th edition (Cologne, 1989).

37 "Every country, rich or poor, has a culture that is received from its predecessors: institutions for material life, works of the intellectual life, artistic, and intellectual works, and religious art. To the extent they represent true human values, it would be a great error to give them up." *Populorum progressio* 40, also *Mater et magistra* 181.

38 *Gaudium et spes* 53.

ularism standing in contrast to universalism. The central question here is one of human rights, namely the right to cultivate group traditions and collective forms of life.

An analysis of national and religious conflicts must concern itself with the relation between religion and nationalism. Wolfgang Palaver has pursued this question in an article about the religious dimension of nationalism.[39] He assumes that the deepest seeds of nationalism and those of archaic religion are identical. The Bible of Jews and the Christians presents a universal religiosity, and to this extent does not allow any nationalism, but "historical Christianity itself has lapsed from the demands of the biblical texts."[40]

For this reason, it can be said that the evident dangers of nationalism are also present in the churches. In general, religions can be useful means for influencing the masses, especially under the influence of spirituality. In addition, today as a result of an increasing de-Christianization or simply the emergence of an unbelieving world, the combination of nationalism and religion has become clearly visible. Even where religion is not lived out or different religious teachings are not known, traditional religious confessional communities simplify the building of political groups. In these cases the confessional influence of Christianity is not as much a question of its truth or image of God, but more an opportunity for using religion as a vehicle for nationalistic egoism and self-aggrandizement.

There is an extreme position in which Church and nation are identified; here religion and nationality are one. All those who question this identity are drummed out of the community. The Diaspora situation or existence on the borderline of religions intensifies this position. The identification of church and nation is a means of excluding all foreign cultures and ideological influences in order to defend a national self-consciousness that protects one's own culture, language, and identity. This national self-consciousness can in certain circumstances take the form of an emotionally hardened nationalistic character.

Clearly, a complete identification of nationality and confession cannot be justified from a Christian standpoint. The attempt to put Christianity in the service of national purposes, and even national arrogance and injustice, is an essential contradiction and an unworthy amalgamation of religion and poli-

39 W. Palaver, "Die religiöse Dimension des Nationalismus," in *Theologisch-praktische Quartalschrift* 3 (1994): 225-33.

40 Palaver, Die religiöse Dimension, 231.

tics. Such mistakes, especially coming from churchmen, are to be strictly rejected.[41] Against the human wretchedness and aloofness of so many Christians, the Church should represent the transnational character of true Christianity, without however abandoning believers in minority positions who face threatening situations.

The churches of Transylvania, like the universal Church, are challenged today to actively join with others in taking a position on the question of nationality, to thereby give people a secure orientation. This does not exclude resisting dangerous nationalistic trends where they arise. Every form of nationalism and chauvinism, every distain or contempt for another people, whether it be the majority or minority, is to be vigorously rejected from a biblical perspective. Nationalism and chauvinism are always un-Christian and contradict the truth that every person is, without exception, created in the image of God.

Translated by Michael Parker

41 Cf. on this Pius XII., Christmas Message 1951. "Politicians, yes even men of the Church, want to at times, to make the Bride of Christ into their ally or into an instrument of their national or international designs. But thereby they would touch on the inner essence of the Church, and damage it in its own most life. With a single word they would reduce it to the same level upon which conflicts about earthly matters are settled." Cited in A-F. Utz / J.-F. Groner (eds.), *Aufbau und Entfaltung des gesellschaftlichen Lebens: Soziale Summe Pius XII*, vol.2 (Freiburg / Schwitzerland, 1955), 4183a.

Peter Stilwell

God in Twentieth-Century Portuguese Literature

In this brief study I will be dealing almost entirely, though not exclusively, with poetry. An overview of a small number of authors aims to give the reader some idea of the variety of trends to be found in twentieth century Portuguese literature, with respect to religious experience.[1]

There are certain constants in the way religious themes are dealt with in contemporary Portuguese literature. Christ and the Virgin have pride of place, but the religious dimension is constant as are explicit references to God – even in the work of authors who are professedly atheist or agnostic, such as José Saramago[2] or the poet António Mega Ferreira[3]. Indifference is rare.

The question is not, therefore, whether "God," as a word or a concept, is present, but the theological implications of the sometimes very different approaches to what is ultimately – at least from the Judaic, Christian, and Islamic perspective – beyond all human conception. How do questions relating to religious experience impact on the worldview of individual writers and on Portuguese culture as a whole?

The religious expressions we find in literature should not be looked at in isolation, nor should they be considered merely an outcrop of an author's underlying theological system. They should rather be seen as an integral part of

---

1 For overviews on some aspects of the topic see: M. De Lurdes Belchior, "Cristo e a poesia portuguesa contemporânea," in *Reflexão Cristão* 24 (1980): 12-22; S. Dimas, *A Intuição de Deus em Fernando Pessoa*, Col. Épheta, Edições Didaskalia (Lisbon, 1998); F.J.B. Martinho, "Deus na Poesia Portuguesa Contemporânea: um Pai ausente?," in *Paternidade Divina e Dignidade Humana*, Semana de Estudos Teológicos 1999, Faculdade de Teologia (Lisbon, 1999), 219-34; J.C.S. Pereira, "Fé e experiência cristãs na Literatura Portuguesa," in *A Igreja e a Cultura Contemporânea em Portugal*, coord. M. Braga da Cruz and N. Correia Guedes, Universidade Católica Editora (Lisbon, 2000), 73-131; J. Serrão, "O Anticlericalismo na Literatura Portuguesa," in *idem*, *Portugueses Somos*, Livros Horizonte, [Lisbon] n.d.; 167-210.

2 A member of the Portuguese Communist Party, Saramago's returns repeatedly to religious themes, though always in a deeply critical fashion as though to justify the violence generated by Marxist ideology in the twentieth century by caricaturing violence associated with religion.

3 In an interview, the writer professed to be an agnostic, but when asked to explain the repeated use of the word "God" in his poems he confessed it emerged spontaneously when writing.

the world opened up to us in the literary text,[4] or of the form we are given to contemplate.[5] They are set within a work that does not necessarily seek to imitate "objective reality" but is a fiction, a *poésis*, a creation that must hang together as a coherent whole if it is to have aesthetic value and involve the reader. The Christian theologian is called on to enter that world and appreciate that form, as he entered and appreciated those of the founding texts of his tradition. He must then determine where the horizons of these worlds touch, collide, fuse, or diverge; what is common, what is unique, and what, as in any developing organism, has acquired new form to remain the same. Unlike literary critics, Christian theologians bring with them certain overriding criteria embedded in the questions they raise. What opens up new vistas of human freedom and dignity? What contributes to a deeper understanding of Christ? This is much as it was when the early Church reentered the world of Biblical tradition, from which it looked back on the words, gestures, and Paschal Mystery of Jesus and saw in them more fully the "new creation".

We should perhaps start by addressing the question of the tense relationship between literature and institutional religion in Portugal. Joel Serrão[6] considers an anticlerical streak to be characteristic of most Portuguese literature. He follows its roots back to long before the French Revolution and relates it to the monopoly held for centuries by the Church in the field of education and the controlling hand of the Inquisition over all cultural activities until Pombal imposed reforms at the end of the eighteenth century. Although often aggressive, this anti-clericalism by no means signified a break with Christianity or its fundamental doctrines and values, much less a rejection of belief in God. Even when, here or there, the Christian faith was questioned, it remained the

4 Cfr. P. Ricoeur, "Le monde du texte," in *Du texte à l'action: Essais de'herméneutique*, II (Paris, 1986), 112-15 "Ce qui est en effet à interpreter dans un texte, c'est une proposition de monde, d'un monde tel que je puisse l'habiter pour y projeter un de mes possibles les plus propres. C'est ce que j'appelle le monde du texte, le monde propre à ce texte unique" (115).

5 See H.U. von Balthasar, *The Glory of the Lord: A Theological Aesthetics, I: Seeing the Form* (Edinburgh, 1982). "The form as it appears to us is founded on the fact that, in it, the truth and goodness of the depths of reality itself are manifested and bestowed, and this manifestations and bestowal reveal themselves to us as being something infinitely and inexhaustibly valuable and fascinating. The appearance of the form, as revelation of the depths, is an indissoluble union of two things. It is the real presence of the depths, of the whole of reality, and it is a real pointing beyond itself to those depths" (118).

6 "O Anticlericalismo na Literatura Portuguesa", in *Portugueses Somos*, Livros Horizonte, [no date], 167-210. The following quotes are taken from this article.

ultimate religious horizon against which the ebb and flow of conflicting emotions and political ideologies were set.

Almeida Garrett (1799-1854), after applauding the expulsion of the religious orders, laments, "When I see the convents in ruins, the ex-friars begging, and the barons [who acquired their properties] in coaches, I remember the friars with emotion [*tenho saudade dos frades*] – not the friars that were, but the friars that might have been." Garrett dreamed of a union between the Gospel spirit and contemporary liberal ideals, in a way similar to Alexandre Herculano (1810-1877), alternately anticlerical and favorable to the Church, who offers this concise summation: "I believe that God is God and men are free."

Even the poet Gomes Leal (1849-1921), who at an early stage was virulently anticlerical and a militant atheist, condemning "Satan, or Christ, or the Eternal Father," while calling on science to "go punish their great crimes! / Tear out the cancer God and lock up Hell,"[7] showed a latent ambiguity in his feelings when he underwent a spectacular conversion at the death of his mother and ended his life a devout Catholic.

A quote from Eça de Queiroz (1845-1900) underlines the conflict felt by many of his contemporaries in choosing between a faith based on divine revelation and the liberal ideal of a life guided by the light conscience alone:

> If you believe in a God in Heaven [explains Doctor Goofier] who guides us from above, and in original sin and in a future life, you need a class of priests who will explain the doctrine and moral teachings revealed by God, who will help you purify yourself from the original stain and prepare you for your place in Paradise! You need priests. And it appears to me an appalling lack of logic that you undermine their credibility in the press ....
> Astonished, João Eduardo exclaimed ...: But Your Excellency surely has no need of priests in this world ....
> Nor even in the next. I don't need priests in this world, since I have no need of a God in Heaven. Which is to say, my boy, I have my God within me, or the principle that guides my actions and my judgments. In other words, conscience .... You may not find this easy to understand .... What I am proposing is in fact subversive doctrine ....[8]

And yet, Eça's work shows clearly that this liberal ideal, though attractive, did not entirely convince him. He is deeply critical of venal, ambitious, and lecherous clergy and will have no truck with the empty piety he finds in for-

7 *O Anti-Cristo* (Lisbon, 1988), 259.

8 Eça de Queiroz (1845-1900), *O Crime do Padre Amaro*, 1880.

mal religious practice. Christian revelation, however, in the person of Christ himself or as mediated through the lives of saints or the poverty of mendicant friars, is something he accepts and respects.

It is only at the turn of the century that we begin to notice a drift away from Christianity in its traditional form to alternative belief systems of a Gnostic tendency. Outstanding examples are Pascoaes and Pessoa.

Teixeira de Pascoaes (1877-1952)

Jorge de Sena calls Pascoaes' religious outlook a "primitive syncretism," and sees in it an attempt to turn Catholic Christianity into an "audacious paganism."[9]

Much as his contemporary D. H. Lawrence (1885-1930), Pascoaes considers the emotional intensity at the center of his poetic experience to be akin to religious emotion. "In religious emotion there is poetry; in poetic emotion there is God."[10] By God, however, he does not appear to mean the transcendent Creator and Redeemer of the Bible; rather he seems to have in mind a supposedly pre-Christian religious experience with a slef inclined to nature.

Well before D. H. Lawrence set out to find the "spirit of the place" and experience the primitive vitality of Native American traditions in New Mexico, Pascoaes was developing, on similar lines, his idea of "Saudade."[11] Commenting on Unamuno's *Por Tierras de Portugal y de España*, he writes:

> The *Lusitanian sadness* is the mist of a religion, of a philosophy and therefore of a State. Our *sadness* is a Woman, and that Woman is of divine origin and is called *Saudade*; but *Saudade*, in its highest and most divine sense .... *Saudade* is carnal love spiritualized by pain, or by spiritual love materialized in Desire: it is a marriage of the Kiss and the tear: it is *Venus and Mary in one*: it is the synthesis of Heaven and Earth: the point at which all cosmic forces cross: it is the center of the Universe: the soul of Nature within the human soul and the human soul within the soul of Nature: *Saudade* is the eternal idiosyncrasy of our Race: a characteristic physiognomy, the original body with which it appears amongst other Peoples; by it God will distinguish us, at the Last Judgment, from all other Peoples ....

[9] Cf. *A Poesia de Teixeira Pascoaes*, Brasília Editora (1982), 24.

[10] Teixeira de Pascoaes, *A Saudade e o Saudosismo* (Dispersos e Opúsculos) (Lisbon, 1988), 88.

[11] A feeling which is typically Portuguese: a mixture of homesickness and nostalgia, fruit perhaps of a long seafaring tradition.

> *Saudade* is the *Misty Morning*[12]: the perpetual spring: it is a latent state of mind which tomorrow will become conscious and [give rise to] the Lusitanian Civilization. Such is our sadness: its spirit, wholesome and divine."[13]

Naturally, Pascoaes distances himself from Christianity. To his mind, its form is incompatible with the native religion he sees rising:

> Yes: in the Lusitanian soul there is the mist of a new religion; and that is why Catholicism, imported from Rome, never became Portuguese, as for example it became Spanish. The insistence with which it has been cultivated in Portugal, however, has contributed to corrupt our character; therefore, we must fight it, as one combats all inimical invaders, be they of the educational, artistic, literary, religious or philosophical kind.[14]

Fernando Pessoa (1888-1935)

In a very different key are the writings of Fernando Pessoa. As with Pascoaes, he feels particularly attuned to the religious dimension. "You understand me," he comments in a letter to Armando Cortes-Rodrigues, in 1915, "because you, as I myself, are fundamentally a religious spirit."

One of the outstanding writers, he feels isolated in his generation, as though he had moved ahead of his fellow travelers on a "journey ... among souls and stars, through the Forest of Terrors ... with God, the final destiny of this infinite road, waiting in the silence of His greatness ...."[15]

Unlike Pascoaes, the divine is to Pessoa the unknown and all emphasis is on the quest for Him, the "infinite path." Twenty years later, shortly before his death, he tells Casais Monteiro he no longer considers "direct communication with God" to be possible. In an unpublished verse he sums up this belief as: "I see God's shadow ...." Avoiding the alternative but treacherous

12 A reference to the popular belief that King D. Sebastião will return on a misty morning to save Portugal. The king disappeared in battle in North Africa, leading to a dynastic crisis at home and the loss of independence to Spain; during the ensuing fifty years the dream of the king's return and a messianic future gave rise to what is known as "Sebastianismo."

13 Pascoaes, *A Saudade*, 25.

14 Pascoaes, *A Saudade*, 33. To carry on the comparison with Lawrence, perhaps Pascoaes would share his criticism of Christianity for proposing an abstract universal love, as opposed to a concrete bodily relationship with actual people.

15 "Letter of the 19th of January 1915," in *Escritos Íntimos, Cartas e Páginas Autobiográficas, Europa-América* (Lisbon, 1986), 95-99.

path of magic, he tells us, and bypassing the search for mystical experience, he chooses alchemy instead: "the most perfect path of all, for it involves the transmutation of those who follow it."

The alchemy he is considering is, however, the alchemy of words – as when he speaks of "stars of unknowing" that "teach us the idea of light." His spiritual struggle is carried forward in the very act of writing. Which is why he is so strongly against "insincere literature" with no "a fundamental metaphysical idea, or through which does not pass, be it only as a breath of wind, any notion of the gravity and mystery of Life."

The multiple heteronyms under which he writes very probably have their origin, as some have suggested, in his fragile psychological makeup, but as an art form they in fact reflect the manifold outlook and fragmented personal identity common in contemporary plural Western societies.

Of particular interest to our present line of enquiry, if it were to be further developed, would be the heteronym Alberto Caeiro and Pessoa himself. Caeiro reflects the influence of Walt Whitman and at times a worldview not unlike that of some mystical traditions: "The only intimate meaning of things / Is that they have no intimate meaning at all" (Poem V); "To think of God is to disobey God, / Because God did not want us to know him, / Which is why he has not shown himself to us." (Poem VI).

In the poems he writes under his own name, the voyage of self-discovery and the search for ultimate meaning are more notable. "Everything has another meaning, O soul, / Even having a meaning ..." (*Tudo tem outro sentido, ó alma, / Mesmo o ter um sentido ...*).[16] And that "other meaning" is of course the unnamable: beyond reality, beyond God himself. For the word "God" veils an underlying ambiguity: in common usage, its more often than not a concept that refers to one more person or thing in the general order of things, though greater than all others; and yet it functions also as a cipher for the ultimately unknowable, for "God is the great Interval / But between what and what?" (*Deus é o grande Intervalo / Mas entre quê e quê?*).[17]

But at the heart of Pessoa's work lies the paradox of the modernist movement. Taking to its limit the Cartesian rift, modernists seek to experience, poetically, a secure basis for knowledge, even knowledge of God, at the very source of self-consciousness. The paradox this represents was evoked by Pessoa and his fellow modernists when they chose *Orpheo* as the title for their

[16] From a poem first published in Samuel Dimas, 131

[17] *Obras de Fernando Pessoa – I*, 1093.

literary review. Set on bringing their inmost soul to the light of consciousness from the netherworld of the unconscious, they realized their task was condemned from the start. "Damned be the day I prayed for knowledge!" Pessoa exclaims. "Where has my unconscious gone / That consciousness as clothing wears?" (*Maldito o dia em que pedi a ciência! / .... / Que é feito dessa minha inconsciência / Que a consciência, como um traje veste?*[18])

José Régio (1901-1969)

A glance at José Régio, considered a representative of Portugal's second modernism also known by the name of its literary review, *Presença*, helps to bridge the gap between Pessoa and the poets of the *Cadernos de Poesia*.

Resigned to being always on the brink of unbelief in God – probably the rationalized and distant God of doctrine – but well rooted in the Biblical and Christian traditions, Régio sees the best in himself, God's image, as no more than remorse or illusion. Depressed, feeling abandoned by God, he identifies with Jesus in his passion and death.[19] With Him he questions the Father:

Pai!, mas porquê tal cruz? por que me abandonaste Logo que à tua imagem me criaste	Father! Why such a cross? Why did you abandon me As soon as in your image you had created me
Deixando-me ser tal que em mim a tua imagem Não é senão remorso, ou, muito além, miragem?[20]	Letting me be such that in me your image Is nothing but remorse, or, far beyond, illusion?

Then, as with Christ, Régio feels God's power. From the depths of his oppression he is stirred to rise above his pain, for "in the extremity of breathless agony, / God shows himself a father, extends to me his hand, / Casts me far up beyond my condition."[21] This is not the self-analysis of Pessoa, nor is Régio trying to see God face to face. Rather, as in the psalms, he is giving voice to what moves his spirit before Another he cannot envisage.

---

18 *Obras de Fernando Pessoa*, 1116.

19 Regio's fascination with Christ on the Cross, almost to the point of obsession, can be captured at his home which still houses his impressive collection of crucifixes.

20 J. Régio, "Levitação," in *Mas Deus é Grande*, 2nd ed. (1961).

21 Régio, "Levitação."

Ruy Cinatti (1915-1986)

Ruy Cinatti represents a new generation of writers with a structured theological background. When Cinatti entered university in 1934, the Catholic Church in Portugal was gathering the pieces scattered by the Republican Revolution in 1910. Separation of Church and State, imposed in 1911, had proved to be no more than a form of Jacobin regalism. Church property was nationalized, the clergy was encouraged to retire and marry on a State pension, parishes were handed over to lay sodalities, papal documents were censored, bishops were exiled. It was the second time in a century the Church had seen its relationship to the State so deeply shaken. And in this case it reacted in the best possible way. A Plenary Council was called, and, breaking with a tradition going back to Portugal's independence from Castile in the twelfth century, a framework was hammered out whereby the Church chose to organize itself free from State support. The option was prudent. Salazar's regime was taking its first steps and showing a marked tendency to control all sections of society. Neighboring Spain was plunging into a violent civil war with religious undertones. In Russia, religion was being crushed by the communist State.

Following Pius XI, the Portuguese bishops set up Catholic Action. In many respects it was an answer to the Salazar's National Union youth movement (the Mocidade Portuguesa), and, not surprisingly, one of its first branches was for university students (the Juventude Universitária Católica, or JUC). To many of the young, introduced to the best of contemporary European Catholic thought, we owe the first direct influence in nearly two centuries of enlightened Catholic thought on Portuguese literary culture.

Ruy Cinatti joined the JUC in 1935, shortly after entering Agricultural College. On finishing his studies, he left in 1946 for East Timor as secretary to the new Portuguese Governor. The Japanese had devastated the territory in 1945 upon abandoning it to the Allied forces. Cinatti's poetry was, at first, introspective: struggling with personal doubts and insecurities. Extensive experience in the field lead, however, to moments of poetry in which feeling, intellect, and will coalesced with the ever changing landscape and the Timorese people in moments of vibrant intensity. Successive personal crises then altered his spiritual quest and in the late sixties God is no longer a central figure in his poetry, but is viewed as if from the corner of his eye, subtly reflected in his relations with others.

CONDIÇÃO HUMANA
Uma grave e miserável incidência.
Perco-me na vida
a ver vidros partidos na calçada.
Há, no entanto, um momento
Em que o sol reflecte vidros
estilhaçados no espírito ....
Há caminhos abertos. Sigo-os
iluminado. Procuro
chegar.[22]

HUMAN CONDITION
A grave and miserable incidence.
I get carried away in life
on seeing broken glass on the cobbles.
There's a moment, however,
when the sun reflects splintered
glass in the mind ....
Paths are opened. I follow them
in the light. I try
to reach their goal ....

There is a particular occasion on which Cinatti recalls becoming conscious of where his search is heading. It is on Christmas Day 1966. His life is unraveling. An unfinished PhD weighs on his mind, and he has been unable to persuade the Government to reform in its policy for East Timor. Suddenly, standing before the crèche, Cinatti realizes the answer lies not in justice decreed, nor in the endless struggle for moral virtue, nor even in the spiritual search for mystical union, but in realizing the simple truth that he is loved and wanted.

NaCl – NATAL – 1966 [23]
Les chérubins sont des boeufs ailés
APOLLINAIRE
Senhor, tu nascestes neste dia
e eu aqui estou,
nascido no mesmo dia.
Apetece-me brincar com as palhinhas.
Pousar o dedo no boi, digo, no beiço,
no focinho do boi, senti-lo húmido
da língua que o lambe.
Depois levá-lo à boca para saber
a que sabe.
Lembrando o que há tanto tempo
sucedeu,
quando um boi, um dia,
me lambeu a face,
de relance a boca.

NaCl –CHRISTMAS – 1966
Les chérubins sont des boeufs ailés
APOLLINAIRE
Lord, you were born on this day
and here I am,
born on the same day.
I feel like playing with the straw.
Rest a finger on the ox, I mean, the lips,
on the nuzzle of the ox, feel it damp
from the tongue that licks it.
Then raise it to one's mouth
to know the taste ....[24]
Remembering what happened so long ago
when an ox, one day,
licked my face,
briefly my mouth.

---

[22] R. Cinatti, "O tédio recompensado," in *Obra Poética* (1968).

[23] "NaCl" is the chemical symbol for Sodium Chloride, the common salt mentioned in the poem. For someone with Cinatti's education in science the title would simply read "Salt – Christmas – 1966".

[24] "Saber" can be simultaneously the verb "to know", the noun "knowledge" and the intransitive verb "to taste (of)."

Sal, apenas sal, queríamos nós.	Salt, only salt, did we want
O boi e eu.	The ox and I
Cloreto de sódio, símbolo	Sodium chloride, symbol
como aprendi no liceu.	as I learnt at school.
Senhor estamos tão sós	Lord we are so alone
que até um boi nos valia.	that even an ox would comfort us
Senhor, tu nasceste neste dia	Lord, you were born on this day
e eu aqui estou	and here I am
à espera que me dês o sal	waiting for you to give me the salt
da tua boca.	from your mouth.
O boi lambeu-me.	The ox licked me.
Obrigado, Senhor![25]	Thank you, Lord!

Sophia de Mello Breyner Andresen (1919-)

Much as Cinatti, Andresen breaks with the romantic tradition of Pessoa's first modernism. She is skeptical of finding truth and God's presence in the depths within.

DA TRANSPARÊNCIA	OF TRANSPARENCY
Senhor libertai-nos	Lord free us from
do jogo perigoso da transparência	the dangerous game of transparency
No fundo do mar da nossa alma	In the deep sea of our soul
não há corais nem búzios	there are no corals or shells
Mas sufocado sonho	But suffocated dream
E não sabemos bem que coisa são os sonhos	And we don't quite know what dreams are made of
Condutores silenciosos canto surdo	Silent conductors deaf singing
Que um dia subitamente emergem	Which suddenly emerge one day
No grande patio liso dos desastres[26]	On the great smooth courtyard of disasters

Generally considered one of the greatest twentieth century Portuguese poets, she was a close friend, from the start of her literary career, of Ruy Cinatti and Jorge de Sena. Equally at ease with classical mythology and the Catholic faith, she draws a careful line, even in her early poetry, between the gods of ancient Greece – whose religious value and continuing symbolic relevance she recognizes – and He to whom she prays but whose name, out of reverence, she almost always refrains from mentioning.

---

25 Cinatti, *O tédio recompensado*, 208.

26 "Geografia" in *Obra Poética III*, 2nd ed. (Lisbon,1991), 88 (Ant. 217).

Tu não nasceste nunca das paisagens,	You were never born from landscapes,
Nenhuma coisa traz o Teu sinal,	Nothing bears Your sign,
É Dionysos quem passa nas estradas	It is Dionysus who passes on the roads
E Apolo quem floresce nas manhãs	And Apollo who flourishes in the mornings ....
A presença dos céus não é a Tua,	The presence of the skies is not Yours,
Embora o vento venha não sei donde.	Though the wind comes I know not from where.
Os oceanos não dizem que os criaste,	The oceans do not tell us You created them,
Nem deixas o Teu rasto nos caminhos.	Nor do You leave your footprints on the paths.
Só o olhar daqueles que escolheste	Only the look of those whom You have chosen
Nos dá o Teu sinal entre os fantasmas.[27]	Gives us Your sign amongst the phantoms.

The search for God centers, as in the later Cinatti, on relations with ones fellow human beings:

Ali não vi as coisas que eu amava	There I saw not what I loved
Nem o brilho do sol nem o da água	The shining sun or water
Ao lado do hospital e da prisão	Beside the hospital and the prison
Entre o agiota e o templo profanado	Between the pawn-broker and the profaned temple
Onde a rua é mais triste e mais sozinha	Where the road is sadder and more solitary
E onde tudo parece abandonado	And where all seems so abandoned
Um lugar pela estrela foi marcado	A place by the star was marked
Nesse lugar pensei: "quanto deserto	In that place I thought: "how much desert
Atravessei para encontrar aquilo	Have I crossed to find that
Que morava entre os homens e tão perto.[28]	Which resided amongst us and so near

An "attention outward turned" is how she defines her poetic attitude to life, and she identifies it closely with her faith:

A minha vida, o mar o Abril a rua	My life: the sea, April, the street
O meu interior, uma atenção voltada para fora	My inward side, an attention outward turned ....
Não trago Deus em mim mas no mundo o procuro	I do not bring God within me but in the world I seek him
Sabendo que o real o mostrará	Knowing that reality will show him
Não tenho explicações	I have no explanations
Olho e confronto	I look and question
E por método é nu meu pensamento[29]	And by way of method my mind is naked

---

27 "Sinal de Ti", in: *Obra Poética*, 71-72.

28 *Obra Poética II* (Lisboa), 115.

29 *Antologia* (Porto,1985), 218.

Rui Belo (1933-1978)

Belo started writing as a member of *Opus Dei*, at the end of the fifties. He studied Canon Law in Rome, but broke with the movement with an understanding of his faith that left little room for doubt. Vatican II was in full swing by then, and in Portugal, many Catholic intellectuals were challenging Salazar's regime, posing questions of human rights, social solidarity, and colonial policy.

The hierarchy, however, tried to restrain political protest and social unrest amongst its members. Those involved in Catholic Action had learned to live according to the motto *sentire cum ecclesia.* They had understood it to mean living the Gospel as a living tradition in the Church, but now they found they were being called on to stifle their consciences and support the social and political interests of an institution fearful of facing up, as they saw it, to flagrant violations of the Gospel spirit by the regime[30]. Many young Catholics then broke with the Church, though not with their deeper commitment to Christian values. In today's world, it is not easy to understand, but at the time the break left them feeling orphaned and defeated, as in Belo's poem:

Nós os vencidos do Catolicismo

Nós os vencidos do catolicismo
que não sabemos já donde a luz mana
haurimos o perdido misticismo
nos acordes dos carmina burana
  Nós que perdemos na luta da fé
não é que no mais fundo não creiamos
mas não lutamos já firmes e a pé
nem nada impomos do que duvidamos
  Já nenhum garizim nos chega agora
depois de ouvir como a samaritana
que em espírito e verdade é que se adora
Deixem-me ouvir os carmina burana
  Nesta vida é que nós acreditamos
e no homem que dizem que criaste
se temos o que temos o jogamos
"Meu deus meu deus porque me abandonaste?"[31]

We the vanquished of Catholicism

We the vanquished of Catholicism
who no longer know wherefrom the light flows
draw the lost mysticism
from the sounds of the *carmina burana*
  We who have lost the struggle of faith
it is not that in our depths we do not believe
but that we no longer fight firmly and on foot
nor impose nothing of what we doubt
  No longer is any Garizim enough for us
after hearing with the woman of Samaria
that in spirit and in truth one should adore
Let me hear the *carmina burana*
  It is in this life that we believe
and in man they say you created
if we have what we have we stake it all
"My god my god why have you abandoned me?"

---

30 An excellent description of the climate of the time is given in João Bénard da Costa's recent book, *Nós, os vencidos do catolicismo* (Tenacitas, 2003). The title is a direct quotation of Belo's poem.

31 "Todos os Poemas," in *Círculo de Leitores* (Lisbom), 369. Belo chose not to start any word with a capital letter. No word should be made to stand out from any other for

Belo, as many of his contemporaries, now draws "the lost mysticism" from the joys and sorrows of the people, evoked in the reference to the medieval "accords of the *carmina burana.*" Influenced by Marxist and Socialist thought in intellectual circles, a new respect for popular culture emerges. Belief shifts from the security of doctrine to "this life" and to "man they say you created". It no longer implies merely intellectual agreement and liturgical participation, but calls for full personal commitment, with its social and political consequences: "we stake it all." Here lies the poet's sense of defeat. Belo was brought up identifying the "struggle of faith" with that of the Church against strong political and cultural opposition. Now he has ceased to be loyal to the Church and to the institutional interests of Catholicism. He has, so to speak, changed sides. Although vanquished, a more radical fidelity nonetheless emerges.

José Saramago (1922-)

Mention must be made of José Saramago, Nobel Prize winner, as his books have been widely translated. Born before Ruy Belo, his better-known writings were published from the eighties onward. But, although much of his work draws on religious themes, Saramago's feelings for things spiritual lie closer to those of his own generation of Marxists writers. At times it is in fact difficult to tell whether there is genuine interest in the themes he chooses, or whether we are being treated to a literary presentation of a traditional Marxist critique of religion.

Saramago ill-treats the God of Israel, but shows a deep affection for a neurotic Christ, and in a tortuous way seems to be trying to underline Christ's humanity. My personal displeasure as a reader comes not so much from Saramago's apparent lack of feeling for things theological, as from the lack of any spiritual depth in his outlook on humanity. There is little or no creative tension in the characters, who seem entirely conditioned by the social and psychological circumstances in which they are set.

A good example of the God Saramago rejects is given in a scene of his *Evangelho Segundo Jesus Cristo:* Jesus rows out into the Sea of Galilee with the Devil onboard and suddenly a mist blows up and surrounds him. God's

---

merely physical reasons. So the fact that "god" is not written with a capital letter should not be taken to imply he had ceased to believe in God.

voice is heard through the mist and the Devil challenges Him. Eventually, God foretells the future of Christianity for Jesus to hear: the martyrs, the Crusades, the Inquisition. Then the Devil says, "You have to be God to like so much blood." Here the Devil proposes that God forgive him, much as in centuries to come He will forgive so many. So much evil might thus be avoided. But God replies, "I will not forgive you, I want you as you are, and, if possible, even worse than you are now, Why, Because the Good which I am would not exist without the Evil you are, a Good which might exist without you would be inconceivable, to such an extent that not even I could imagine it, so, if you end, I end, For me to be Good you need to continue to be Evil, if the Devil does not live as the Devil, God does not live as God, the death of one would be the death of the other."[32]

Conclusion

In concluding this very limited and selective overview of Portuguese literature in the twentieth century, a number of provisional points can be made. Indifference to religion is rare. Respect for Christ and a genuine affection for his humanity is universal. A cold, dogmatic understanding of God, often identified with Church teaching, meets with doubt or unbelief at an existential level. An inner quest for some form of religious experience is found in almost all the authors mentioned, except, perhaps, for Saramago.

The most interesting point for me, however, is the movement outward, toward lived relationships with others and the world, as an informed Catholic laity emerges on the cultural scene. The inward movement of the first and second modernism is reversed, but without renouncing the value, freedom and dignity of the subjective dimension, as tended to occur in neo-realist literature. Here, God is not sought in the depths of the soul, nor reduced to one more object "out there," but is found as it were on the horizon of relations with others that in some way evoke an identification with Christ.

---

[32] *O Evangelho Segundo Jesus Christo*, 2.ª ed. (Lisbon, 1991), 391-93.

PART III

MUSING ON GOD IN EUROPE

Siegfried Wiedenhofer

Thinking God Between Fundamentalism and Liberalism

Today there are two worldwide movements that stand in a deep tension, both struggling against and provoking one another. In the face of the collapse of the East-West conflict, neo-liberalism in politics, economics, and religion has gained an enormous impetus. Fundamentalism in culture, politics, and religion has also increased in intensity and breadth. In modern European history, this double movement has been widely seen in many variations. And now with globalization, it is becoming generalized. For this very reason, it is important to consider contemporary theological questions about God in the context of both fundamentalism and liberalism.

European Modernity Between Liberalism and Fundamentalism

Liberalism has existed as a political concept since the nineteenth century and as an economic concept since the twentieth century. From a broader sociological perspective, however, it is fair to say that liberalism has functioned as a fundamental characteristic of modernity since the Enlightenment; namely, as modernity's emphasis on individual freedom, which has an unquestioned status in the modern self-understanding.[1]

The liberal conception of freedom[2] postulates individual responsibility and the rationality of the entire world order, particularly the rationality of human desires within a society organized to satisfy these desires. This liberal conception of freedom originally had a universal, emancipatory intention. Its goal, in the face of feudalistic restrictions and inequalities, was a new legal, social, and political freedom for all. In this conception, individuals are equals before the law, are equal as citizens of the state, and are equal participants in the free market. This concept of reason and freedom proved, however, to be

---

1 Cf. R. Vierhaus, "Liberalismus," in *Geschichtliche Grundbegriffe: Historisches Lexikon zur politisch-sozialen Sprache in Deutschland*, vol. 3. (Stuttgart, 1982), 741-85; R. Walther, "Exkurs: Wirtschaftlicher Liberalismus," in *Geschichtliche Grundbegriffe*, 787-815.

2 Cf. Summary of D. Langewiesche / H. Vorländer, "Liberalismus," in *Theologische Realenzyklopädie*, vol. 21 (Berlin / New York, 1991), 73-83.

abstract and unhistorical inasmuch as it failed to reflect upon its own historical and social conditioning. Ironically, now that the liberal concept of reason has come to prevail globally, its potential for irrationality has become increasingly evident. Social and political lack of freedom reproduces itself in Capitalism under the auspices of capital and labor. The rational legitimation of this situation is found in such phrases as the "free play of forces'' and in the claim that social inequality results from the inequality of individual needs. This is one reason why the universal welfare promised by Communism was so attractive for so long. Liberalism as a fundamental worldview and as an economic program was able to attain its newfound plausibility only after the breakdown of Communism and in reaction to its totalitarian character.

We find an analogy to this development in politics.[3] The political and social upheavals resulting from the inability to resolve questions of religious truth following the Religious Wars of the seventeenth century led to a situation in which absolutist attempts to establish peace were tempting: the result was the establishment of peace through the power of an absolute sovereign to whom all were subject, the creation of a political and civil realm above and removed from traditional religion and morality, and the confinement of morality and religion to the private sphere of the individual. At the end of this development, and in the face of the current massive pluralism within societies, and their pluralism in values, present-day liberalism is only able to offer formal solutions to the resulting conflicts.[4]

Fundamentalism is the counterpart to liberalism. Originally, "fundamentalism" referred to a movement among particular groups within American Protestantism at the beginning of the twentieth century. Since the 1970s, however, the term has been increasingly used to characterize many other, similar phenomena: first its reference was extended to influences within Islam, but later it also applied to movements in Hinduism and Catholicism; finally it came to refer to all sorts of ideologies, and political, cultural and religious programs.[5] All these different "fundamentalisms" are similar inasmuch

---

3 Cf. R. Koselleck, *Kritik und Krise: Eine Studie zur Pathogenese der bürgerlichen Welt*, 2nd ed. (Frankfurt a. M., 1976 (1959); (*Critique and Crisis: Enlightenment and the Pathogenesis of Modern Society* [Cambridge, 1988]).

4 Cf. U. Rödel / G. Frankenberg / H. Dubiel, *Die demokratische Frage* (Frankfurt a. M., 1989).

5 Cf. T. Meyer (ed.), *Fundamentalismus in der modernen Welt: Die Internationale der Unvernunft* (Frankfurt a. M., 1989); M. Marty / S. Appleby (eds.), *The Fundamentalism Project*, vol. 1-5 (Chicago, 1991-1995).

as they all contest important elements of the Enlightenment and the process of modernization – for example, secularization, pluralism, individualism, and relativism. Hence fundamentalism is often understood as a global counter-movement to modernity, a form of anti-modernism.

Yet this view fails to consider that fundamentalism is also a central aspect of European modernity itself, of its Jacobian element, as it were.[6] This has to do with the fact that European modernity arose under the influence of the "developed religions" and against the background of the differentiation of cultures in the Axial Age of the first thousand years B.C.E. In the ensuing cultural and religious revolution, a profane "this worldliness" and a sacred "other worldliness" developed into separate spheres. For the first time, the question of the mediation of the two worlds, and the ordering of the earthly realm according to the truth of the divine world, became important. Now it became essential to ask how the transcendental absolute truth can be given form and be made present in the earthly sphere.

In the age of European Enlightenment, conditions were manifest for the first time that made it appear that autonomous reason could realize its aims. The institutions and traditions that previously formed the critical standard for society; for example, the state, the legal system, and organized religion, proved themselves to be in need of criticism.[7]

On the one hand, the transhistorical authority of these institutions was exposed by reference to their historical origins, and they were measured against the eternal truths of reason, which identified and established reasonable relations among society's institutions and traditions. On the other hand, it was recognized that social relations had kept reason imprisoned and that only a revolutionary change of these social relations could free reason from its enslavement.

The clearest example of this Enlightenment concept of reason, which both expressed its ideals most boldly and made its weaknesses most apparent, is the French Revolution. The theory and practice of the Jacobin Republic is no more than an attempt to reconstitute the connection between these social rela-

---

6 Cf. on this point and the following: S.N. Eisenstadt, *Die Antinomien der Moderne: Die jakobinischen Grundzüge der Moderne und des Fundamentalismus. Heterodoxien, Utopismus und Jakobinismus in der Konstitution fundamentalistischer Bewegungen.* Transl. by Georg Stauth (Frankfurt a. M., 1998) (*Fundamentalism, Sectarianism, and Revolution: The Jacobin Dimension of Modernity* [Cambridge/ New York, 1999]).

7 Cf. R. Schaeffler, *Religion und kritisches Bewusstsein* (Freiburg /Munich, 1973), 45-71.

tions in the name of reason. The disestablishment of traditional religious authority, however, did not lead to the expected unity of human reason in matters of the truth and justice; on the contrary, it led to new conflicts. The resulting Reign of Terror was a logical consequence of the revolutionaries' identification of eternal reason with their own theory.

The nineteenth century dialectical theoreticians of history (especially Hegel and Marx) drew their own conclusions from this. There was a new seriousness about the mutually conditioning relationship between historical social relations and critical reason. Criticism could no longer appeal to a suprahistorical reason, but only to an historical reason, i.e., a reason that develops in and through its relations. Criticism in this view is dialectical. It achieves its legitimacy by overcoming factual contradictions through a process of consciousness that leads to a resolution and the overcoming (*Aufhebung*) of these contradictions.

This dialectic of reason, however, is difficult to maintain. Correspondingly, within European modernity, totalitarian, absolutist, and (in this sense) fundamentalist concepts of rationality – for example, scienticism, scientific communism, nationalism, as well as liberal, postmodern conceptions – question the existence of a universal reason and end in an inevitable pluralism of rationalities. Accordingly, we see that whether the polemic is fueled by "fundamentalist" or by "postmodern" conceptions, communication, dialogue, and reasonable discussion in search of common truth in modern Europe fails to take place.

Thinking God in Modern Europe: Between Liberalism and Fundamentalism

By analogy, a dual movement also exists in the modern history of European Christianity: there are fundamentalist, exclusivist absolutist claims, on the one hand, and liberal, or postmodern, currents and theologians, on the other.

Modern European liberal theologies are (to somewhat oversimplify) theologies that attempt to reconcile Christianity with modernity; they are therefore essentially liberal or postmodern theologies. In the seventeenth and eighteenth centuries, the Church in France was already confronted with a new type of individual: the self-confident layman and citizen whose status was derived from his education or economic success.[8]

In the lives of such educated citizens, faith had ceased to be an all-encompassing and integrating factor; rather, it required decision or conscious assent. The educated citizen began to inquire into the grounds of faith and to ask for rational justification. This questioning extended from anti-clerical elements and a large number of the undecided to respectable believers who wanted to still their nagging consciences. As the educated now inquired into the legitimacy of Church teachings and proclamation, their faith became less symbolic and more theoretical. Inasmuch as faith was only partially identified with the Church, it became increasingly privatized and spiritualized. Civil life no longer required faith in the Church's in order to be meaningful.

The economically successful middle class also lost its privileged place within the Christian narrative. Wealth was no longer understood as a result of Divine Providence, but was achieved through ones own work. Church teaching still derived the necessity of work from the universality of sin and saw it as primarily a consequence of the Fall. Work itself was understood as punishment or atonement for sin. The middle class Burgher, by contrast, saw not only enjoyment and satisfaction in work as a result of its visible success (that is, in riches, prominence, and power) but also understood work as a natural and fundamental activity of life and therefore as a source of meaning and fulfillment. This made religion appear, to some extent, irrelevant to modern life. The individual appeared to be adequately self-sufficient. He understood himself as autonomous, as a strong subject with needs and wants, who strives for and finds happiness in the comprehensive and reasonable satisfaction of those physical and spiritual needs. Secularization of the public sphere in European modernity and the varied attempts of Christian theologians (in particular, in liberal theology, and in modernist and pluralistic theologies of religion) to reconcile this liberal modern spirit with Christian faith, are extensions of this development.[9]

---

8 Cf. B. Groethuysen, *Die Entstehung der bürgerlichen Welt- und Lebensanschauung in Frankreich* (Frankfurt a. M., 1978 [1927]) (*Origines de l'esprit bourgeois en France. I. L'Église et la bourgeoisie*, 4th ed. [Paris, 1956]).

9 Cf. M. Jacobs, "Liberale Theologie," in *Theologische Realenzyklopädie*, vol. 21, Berlin / New York, 1991), 47-68.; V. Conzemius, "Liberaler Katholizismus," in: *Theologische Realenzyklopädie*, vol. 21, 68-73 (1991); S. Wiedenhofer, "Bürgerliche Gesellschaft und Zivilreligion," in R. Burkholz / C. Gärtner / F. Zehentreiter (eds.), *Materialität des Geistes. Zur Sache Kultur - im Diskurs mit Ulrich Oevermann* (Weilerswist, 2001), 207-31.

On the other hand, there were fundamentalist tendencies within the Christian Church that were opposed to Enlightenment and Modernity, especially in the Catholic Church from the middle of the nineteenth century on.[10] In the second half of the twentieth century, the leader of the Catholic traditionalists, Archbishop Marcel Lefebvre, expresses this position clearly: "No one, whether Muslim, Protestant, or animist can achieve salvation without the grace of the Catholic Church, that is, without the grace of the cross of our Lord Jesus Christ. There is only one cross, through which man is saved, and this cross is entrusted to the Catholic Church, and to no one else."[11]

Evidently, extreme fundamentalist and liberalist interpretations of Christian faith in God are a continual possibility and danger. Why this is so will become evident when we consider the dialectical form of religious faith in God.

The Dialectic of Religious Faith in God

A minimal condition for considering a phenomenon to be "religious" in character consists in the tension of a dual relation. Religion is based in the fundamental conviction and experience that God (or the Divine, the Holy, the Salvific, the True Being and Life) encounters us in the World and in History by means of the World and History. Hence a certain commonality between "God" and "World" is presupposed. On the other hand, religion also consists in the fundamental conviction and experience that God (or the Divine, the Holy and the Salvific, the True Being and Life) is not identical with the World, that there is a strict distinction between "God" and "World."[12]

In religious faith, these two contradictory poles are inseparably connected: without the earthly, without worldly signs and witnesses, there is no appearance of the Divine in this transitory world. God's action can only be perceived in a worldly, human context; that is, by means of worldly or human signs of

10 Cf. H. Kochanek (ed.), *Die verdrängte Freiheit: Fundamentalismus in den Kirchen*, Freiburg / Basel / Vienna, 1991).

11 Citation according to A. Schifferle, *Marcel Lefebvre - Ärgernis und Besinnung: Fragen an das Traditionsverständnis der Kirche* (Kevelaer, 1983), 167.

12 Cf. R. Schaeffler, *Religion und kritisches Bewusstsein*, 135-253; S. Wiedenhofer, "Identität und Kommunikabilität kultureller und religiöser Traditionen im Verständnis christlicher Theologie," in B. Schoppelreich / S. Wiedenhofer (eds.), *Zur Logik religiöser Traditionen* (Frankfurt a. M., 1998), 227-63.

God's action – for example, in holy people, in holy places and times, and in holy writings or words, etc. However, no worldly or historical appearance of the godly is itself "God." Any absolutism in the world, when it is asserted as "God" (whether as a feature of nature, a particular human being, a human institution or relation, such as power, work, wealth, desire, etc.) represents not the worship of God, but the worship of idols.

Hence every appearance of the divine in the world must bear the character of a sign, and every revelation of the godly through signs and witnesses is simultaneously a veiling of God through sign and witness. Since no one outside the experience of faith can point to or grasp one absolute thing that irrefutably represents God over and above another, religious faith at its core stands as a free process of interpretation and witness: a free entering into the interpretation of the symbolic revelatory and hidden character of the godly in the world.

Where religious faith truly operates and thrives within this dual revelatory-concealing framework, however, claims to absoluteness and the capacity for tolerance need not be opposed. They are necessarily opposed only when they hinge on two fundamentally mistaken positions, or two opposing self-misunderstandings that overemphasize hard distinctions to one extreme or the other. On the one hand, we can see how overemphasizing the identity of worldly sign and divine content either neglects or suppresses the difference between God and the World and thereby leads to worship of images or idolatry. On the other hand, overemphasizing the difference between earthly signs and divine content neglects or suppresses the unity of God and the World, and thereby leads to iconoclasticism or the banishment of the godly from this world.

The first misapprehension is characteristic of religious fundamentalism. It implies not only a dogmatic error (the identification of one's own truth with the divine truth), but also results in and is recursively fueled by fanaticism and intolerance. This divine truth, in whose possession one believes oneself to be, is directed against all non-believers who are necessary representatives of untruth – and opposition to them can be accomplished through violent means, if necessary.

The second misapprehension is characteristic of religious liberalism. This mistaken form of religious faith also rides on a dogmatic misunderstanding: because of the historically apparent close connection between faith in God and violence, self-righteousness and discord, God's transcendence and distance is strongly emphasized in order to free God from complicity in human affairs. The further God is pushed into the distance, the less worldly he is, and the greater the limitation is on his concrete action in the world. This overemphasis on God's transcendence and distance from the world is connected to a kind of unlimited tolerance, which in the face of the indeterminateness of various religious claims to truth, limits itself to an external and formal limitation of potential conflicts. In this understanding, everyone is holy in his own way, and we should disturb each other as little as possible.

Understandably, these two types of error do not exist in isolation. They require each other for their own legitimation and justification. Fundamentalism, which insists on the presence of God in the world – since all being, life, and salvation depends upon it – finds itself affirmed in the face of a correctly identified liberal misunderstanding of religion that banishes religion to the private and subjective sphere and shows a lack of religious reverence for the worldly signs of the Holy. Fundamentalists often cite Western liberalism explicitly as a reason for their own understanding of religion and culture. Liberals likewise feel justified in their convictions in the face of bloody conflicts caused by fanatics and zealots. In the face of religious terrorism, how should religious truth claims be understood as anything other than a potential for violence? Shouldn't inner-worldly conflicts be transferred to the so near yet so distant silent mystery of the divine, where they cannot cause any trouble?

The preceding reflections lead me to the following conclusions: 1) that the fundamentalist and the liberal misunderstandings of religious faith are inseparably connected, such that neither error can be seen in isolation from the other, 2) since both religious fundamentalism and liberalism are based on constitutive structural elements of religious experience, what is viewed as "fundamentalist" and "liberal" in religious communities and churches must be regarded as a set of extremely complex and highly nuanced phenomena. Hence it is useful to understand both within a continuum, the one end of which is pure misunderstanding of faith and pure disbelief, where either the difference between God and the World or the unity of the two is not taken into account. On the other end of the continuum, authentic faith may be viewed as including within itself the positive insights of both fundamentalism and liberalism. Indeed, it is in the healthy tension between the two wherein the freedom that sustains true faith in God and true thinking about God resides. And for this reason, it is precisely this tension that warrants our critical respect.

Maureen Junker-Kenny

Ethics, the Hermeneutics of Memory, and the Concept of God

From an *ethical* perspective, the conference theme "God in Europe's global dialogue" cannot ignore the backdrop of the violent history of the twentieth century between peoples in Europe. What can the concept of God contribute to a future that must deal with memories that have marked and divided the Continent, East, Middle, and West, North and South, aggressors, victims, winners, and losers? While the abandonment of countries that had themselves been victims of aggression and conquest to the power sphere of Stalin is now being rectified with the enlargement of the European Union (which itself has been called the greatest political success story of the twentieth century), the trauma of the *Shoa* and the bitterness of two world wars continue to haunt the offspring of the victims, survivors, perpetrators, and contemporary witnesses.

I shall enter the circle of the hermeneutics of memory first by comparing two different approaches to the link between memory and ethics, those of Paul Ricoeur and Avishai Margalit. One of our abilities as "capable subjects" is to be endowed with memory. But is the faculty to remember matched by a corresponding ability to forgive? Ricoeur's counter-thesis to Hannah Arendt, who sees promising and forgiving as two properties of human agency at the same level, is that forgiveness has to be opened up from elsewhere. Second, I shall consider some of the philosophical reasons why the question of forgiveness cannot be resolved at a secular level and must be examined before the step to theology is made, and third, I shall draw conclusions from debates on memory and on forgiveness, as the "eschatology of memory,"[1] for the concept of God and for the interplay of religious convictions in debates in the public realm.

---

[1] P. Ricoeur, *La mémoire, l'histoire, l'oubli* (Paris, 2000), 595 (hereafter MHO). Translations (as of all other quotes from German and French) are my own.

Memory and Ethics

A tempting, lingering Viennese option that still held good at the end of the nineteenth century, a Johann Strauss tune played throughout the famous 1985 exhibition "Wien 1900", "*Glücklich ist, wer vergißt, was doch nicht zu ändern ist*" (Blessed be he who forgets what can never more be changed), no longer cuts any ice at this stage of European experience. In contrast to this motto, the kind of forgetting outlined by Ricoeur is not denial, escapism, or shallowness. Across the mountains of debris in a history of suffering to which he refers with Walter Benjamin's angel of history, Ricoeur offers the idea of striving towards a "happy, i.e., salved memory" and a "happy oblivion" that opens up the future by breaking the stranglehold of the past. In contrast to the "effacement" of memories, the forgetting contained in forgiveness is called an "*oubli de réserve*"(MHO, 656).

In *La mémoire, l'histoire, l'oubli*, Paul Ricoeur questions the idea of a "duty to remember" as a response to the atrocities committed. But why should this not be the least we can do, as survivors and as Europe's children born after 1945, to remember the victims and to work out peaceful ways of encountering the different other? What Ricoeur questions is not the task of remembering, which he endorses and grasps in the terms of another Viennese (and then exiled Londoner) thinker, Sigmund Freud, as "work of memory," *Erinnerungsarbeit*. It is the level of ethics designated by the deontological term "duty" that he considers too far removed from a person's primary self-understanding and that happens at the teleological level of striving for a flourishing life. After sketching the three levels of his ethical theory, I shall try to locate memory in each of the levels and compare the way in which Ricoeur links them to the approach Avishai Margalit takes in his "*Ethics of Memory.*"

The Reconciliation of Aristotle and Kant in Ricoeur's Hermeneutical Theory of the Self

If until the end of the 1980s teleological and deontological ethics counted as antitheses, we owe it to the work of philosophers like Charles Taylor, Hans Krämer, and Paul Ricoeur that a combination of the two-theory traditions now seems possible. In his theory of self, published first in 1990, *Oneself as Another*, Ricoeur seeks to link the two divorced traditions of ethics, the Aristotelian striving for a happy life of *eudaimonia*, and the Kantian ethics of obligation, as two different but indispensable steps. There is no moral identity without personal identity, i.e., without integrating a person's hopes and visions of a good life with the moral requirement to recognize the other's equal freedoms even when it hurts a person's self-interest.[2] The task of remaining true to the authority of reason present in the subject's autonomy, which Kant took for granted, must be made one's own by investing it with personal value. Ricoeur captures this move as the progression from the "self-esteem" arising from a person's ability to act, to "self-respect," which is won against the resistance to carry through the benevolence towards the other in conflict.

When – as in the typically Kantian theories of the justification of morality – the guiding interest is to reconstruct the transcendental – as opposed to the real – conditions of a freedom, freedom understood here in its highest form as the ability to bind oneself to the law of autonomy, the level that counts in the everyday, actual pursuit of freedom remains out of sight. The possible relationship between the wish for a flourishing life and morality is left unexplored. The *motivation* important for the identity of the subject, to live up to the demand of autonomy, and the *application* of the moral law to specific situations, remain outside the theory. Ricoeur fills the first gap by going back from the level of obligation to that of the "reasonable desire" for a flourishing life; the second neglected task, applying the norm to situations, is accomplished at the third level of "practical wisdom" or "wisdom in judgment," which safeguards singularity in a context-sensitive interpretation of the deon-

---

2 Up until recently, questions of the "good life," marked as "evaluative" as opposed to "normative," have been below the threshold of J. Habermas' discourse ethics as it only deals with universalizable interests, which personal strivings are not. His move in 2001 to "embed" Discourse Ethics in a "species ethic," however, changes the picture. Aware of the "weakness" of the power of reason and the danger that the whole "language game" of morality may be undermined by unilateral genetic intervention, he engages the level of values present in everyday life. While he may be far from assuming, with Ricoeur, that what people desire is "to live well with and for others in just institutions," he now recognizes the potential of the pre-normative level of people's self-understanding. It is remarkable for a defender of the "power of the better argument" to concede that arguments fail ("ins Leere laufen") in the face of silent ("lautlosen") consequences of mute habitual practices which are able to shake egalitarian universalism. "Gegen diese theorielose, aber praktisch folgenreiche Unterminierung hilft allenfalls die stabilisierende Einbettung unserer Moral in ein gattungsethisches Selbstverständnis, das uns den Wert dieser Moral zu Bewusstsein bringt, bevor wir uns an die schleichende Revision der vorerst selbstverständlichen Unterstellungen von Autonomiebewusstsein und intergenerationeller Gleichstellung gewöhnen." (J. Habermas, "Replik", in *DZPhil* 50 (2002): 283-98, 295). The English translation of this article is included in *The Future of Human Nature* (Cambridge, 2003).

tological rule.[3] What this achieves for the normative level of moral obligation is that it gets "grounded" in the teleological level of self-realization, a move that Kant intentionally skipped. It also ensures for the level of striving that it does not descend into naked self-interest, a danger which a more harmonistic conception like Charles Taylor's plays down.[4]

A Communitarian and a Phenomenological Perspective on the Ethics of Memory[5]

The first issue that poses itself for any philosophical analysis is which approach it will take. In this analysis, I shall argue that Ricoeur's phenomenological method arrives at a different determination of the relationships between memory and self, morality, and God than Avishai Margalit's communitarian approach.[6]

In his reflections on *mneme* and *anamnesis*, spontaneous and searched-for memory, Ricoeur offers a general analysis of the constitution, the abilities, and disabilities of the self, not a particular point of departure or a specific link

---

3 Cf. P. Ricoeur, *The Just*. Translated by D. Pellauer (Chicago, 2000); *Le Juste* 2 (Paris, 2001). For a discussion of the role of "practical wisdom" between rule and singularity, see my "Capabilities, Convictions, and Public Theology" in M. Junker-Kenny (ed.), *Memory, Narrativity, Self and the Challenge to Think God: The Reception within Theology of the Recent Work of Paul Ricoeur* (Münster, 2003).

4 For a comparison of the approaches of J. Habermas, A. Honneth, H. Krämer, Ch. Taylor, and P. Ricoeur to ethical and moral identity, see H. Haker, *Moralische Identität* (Tübingen, 1999) who arrives at a similar conclusion (154).

5 For an enlarged version of the following analysis, see my comment on Ricoeur's Donnellan Lecture, "The Difficulty to Forgive," in: "Two Itineraries - Memory and Forgiveness," both in M. Junker-Kenny (ed.), *Memory, Narrativity, Self*.

6 Since, for Margalit, the link between memory and ethics arises not just from the philosophical position of Communitarianism, but from its foundational role in the Jewish tradition, the philosophical debate between the two approaches also touches on questions in Jewish-Christian dialogue. In his article "Erinnerung," J.B. Metz traces the modern understanding of the concept as mediating between reason and history back to its philosophical and theological roots in Plato and in the Jewish and Christian traditions of thinking. As communities, they are constituted by the memory of God's actions in history. "Art. Erinnerung," in *Handbuch philosophischer Grundbegriffe*, ed. H.M. Baumgartner / C. Wild (Munich, 1973), 386-96. The background of Jewish thinking, which is reflected in Margalit's approach, cannot be explored here. I am grateful to Eveline Goodman-Thau for pointing out the importance of Hermann Cohen's religious hermeneutics. See her *Aufstand der Wasser: Jüdische Hermeneutik zwischen Tradition und Moderne* (Berlin / Vienna, 2002), 173-209.

to a certain aspect of being human. In contrast to Margalit, for whom memory forms part of "thick relations," i.e., of the life of natural circles of belonging, like families, religions, and nations, which constitute "ethical communities of caring," Ricoeur does not tie memory to one level of his theory of ethics. This difference has consequences for the way in which the level of universalizing morality is reached and where religion is seen to enter the picture.

In *Oneself as Another*, the different types of action that the self becomes aware of in hermeneutical reflection on its pursuits yield three levels of ethics:[7] striving, being normatively obliged, and mediating norm and situation in a "practical wisdom" that keeps trace of the singularity of each person. Ricoeur's phenomenological access allows memory to be applied to all of them. Memory plays a role at the *first level* of personal identity, since it is part of the repertory of human capabilities that generate self-esteem. More specifically, it functions in reconstructing the sense of the unity and life plan, which forms a person's vision of her life as flourishing.[8] The narrative identity of a

---

7 Cf. C. Mandry, *Ethische Identität und christlicher Glaube* (Mainz, 2002), 139. 144: "The orientation of life and moral obligation are rooted in a reflexive structure of the self-understanding of the self which essentially includes the relation to others .... The three moments – ethics, morality, practical wisdom – distinguish in a phenomenological way the modes in which the self relates to its agency and thus to itself, to the other and to social institutions."

8 The way in which individual memories are related to the totality of one's life is also the reason why the claim that memory provides immediate certainty fails. Both Ricoeur and Michael Theunissen criticise W. Dilthey for this thesis, which reformulates at a philosophical level what is no less problematic for being everyday consciousness. "Dilthey ascribes to all experiences immediate certainty, since the contents we are therein privy to are identical with inwardness itself. This does not stop him from positing a nexus between experiences and the whole of life. As they can only be mediated therein, he winds up contradicting himself. Even if grounding experiences (Erlebnisse) are conceivable without the whole of life, recollection grounded therein does indeed forge a relationship with the latter, and nowhere more so than when it is at its most creative. Such high-grade recollection in any event excludes immediacy. Generally recollection is ... highly flawed: full of gaps and ruptures, at the grip of interpretations that dictate to it the present and alter the past, if indeed they do not falsify it. It goes without saying that such a defective recollection is even more remote from being able to immediately reproduce reality." (*Scope and Limits of Recollection*, 17-18). Theunissen's critique of what he calls "Erlebniserinnerung" as the currently dominant concept of memory turns to Hegel to supply the possibility of sharing the memory of events one has not witnessed oneself by "appropriation." Margalit's distinction between "common" and "shared" memory makes the same point that memory is not only constituted by participation, but also by the communication of witnesses and testimonies. For Theunissen, refuting the claim that the seemingly immediate Erlebniserinnerung is the only form of recollection is important for the possibility of

life is constructed through the selection of significant memories that explain the present position and guide future choices. The danger of too close a link between memory and personal identity is a manipulation that obstructs memory. As Ricoeur writes, "Here one would have to go into the overlaps between memory and identity and describe the many ways in which memory is falsified through the detour of narration with its dense passages and its selected gaps, its accentuations and its moments of silence."[9] Ricoeur's demand for a "politics of just memories" as part of recognizing others can be seen to form part of the *second level* of the rule of justice. Memories also come in at the *third level* of "practical wisdom" where the gap between a norm and its application is bridged by going back to the initial orientation towards a good life "with and for others, in just institutions."[10] The latitude provided by the space of application and provoked by conflicting duties calls on one's personal moral identity to decide. The decision is made on the basis of "convictions" arising from experiences of value that have proved sustainable and defendable as norms personally appropriated over the course of one's life. It is here that religious values can come in and also have a role in public life.

Both Ricoeur and Margalit take account of both types of ethics, Aristotelian and Kantian, and ascribe separate tasks to them. By redescribing them as

---

later generations to relate to the past. If it were the only form, museums, monuments, and national days of remembrance would not be able to engage citizens. "If younger Germans have had opened for them a past beyond their experience, one inaccessible to the war generation for all its eyewitness credentials, it was due to appropriation" (54). In her review of Theunissen's Leopold Lucas-Prize lecture, Aleida Assmann underlines how a concept of memory that includes the appropriation of something other (Fremdem) is able to "prolong personal memory beyond the threshold of experience (Erlebnis). In contrast, Erlebniserinnerung does not have a binding quality for others and does not open up a way into the (political) future." ("Verkettung durch Schuld?" in *Deutsche Zeitschrift für Philosophie* 50 [2002]: 664).

9 P. Ricoeur, *Geschichtsschreibung und Repräsentation der Vergangenheit* (Münster, 2002), 19. In his Donnellan Lecture, "The Difficulty to Forgive," he highlights this selectiveness as a problem not only of truth, but also of forgiveness: "Let us add another important instance of forgetting, linked to the selective side of story telling; no understandable or acceptable narrations may be constructed without putting aside inappropriate events or episodes. It is on the basis of this ambiguous status of forgetting that our own reluctance to forgive forges its own strategy of elusion and evasion; a clever art of oblivion is patiently worked out for the sake of self-protection against the return of unbearable memories. It is against those fences that forgiveness is bound to fail." M. Junker-Kenny (ed.), *Memory, Narrativity, Self.*

10 P. Ricoeur, *Oneself as Another* (Chicago, 1992), 172.

"thick" and "thin" relations, however, Margalit construes the relationship between the ethical and the moral planes in a different way. Despite many similar presuppositions, observations, and conclusions, this becomes the source of other important differences in construction:

> Morality is greatly concerned ... with respect and humiliation ... attitudes that manifest themselves among those who have thin relations. Ethics, on the other hand, is greatly concerned with loyalty and betrayal, manifested among those who have thick relations ... Because it encompasses all humanity, morality is long on geography and short on memory. Ethics is typically short on geography and long on memory.[11]

The starting point of Margalit's enquiry into the ethics of memory is his "thick relations" to which memory is assigned. The "important point for memory," he writes, "is that, because it is enmeshed with caring, memory belongs primarily to ethics, not to morality" (38). "Neighbor," although an "ambiguous term" belonging to both camps, comes to be defined as the one with whom one has a common history or a history mediated by an imagined community (44). In contrast, the spontaneous benevolence Ricoeur assumes at the first level of striving for a flourishing life is not defined by the particular community with which one shares a history. It is a good will more general than the sympathy directed to one's circles of belonging. By opting for greater particularity at this level, Kant's project of universalization appears in a different light for Margalit.

At first sight, his statements that "symmetry is not necessary for understanding the foreign other" and that "reciprocity is not the aim of morality" seem to remain below the level of Kant's concept of morality. However, it is seen as important "to overcome our natural indifference to others" (33) for whom we do not care. The "universal core" of morality is said to consist in "overcoming a particularist attitude and to see what is human in the other."[12] While for Ricoeur, the human tendency towards violence is the reason for having to move beyond the first, "naive" level of striving to the normative level of morality, for Margalit it is indifference, especially to other people's suffering. But why is morality not credited with implying the orientation towards reciprocity and symmetry? It is not that Margalit seeks less but that he is ready to accept less from the other side. By endorsing Martin Buber's idea

[11] A. Margalit, *The Ethics of Memory* (Cambridge MA: 2002), 8. Further page numbers are in the text.

[12] "Interview," in *Information Philosophie* 31 (2003): 34-39, here 34.

of "encompassing relations" which opens up the possibility of one-sided understanding even if the other person or other culture remain self-enclosed, he goes beyond an idea of strict reciprocity that ends if and when the other side fails to respond. Buber's insistence on extending the willingness to understand the other, even if this openness is not reciprocated, is adopted as the highest guideline. With Buber, Margalit can envisage the generosity of one-sided "encompassing relations" which by most standards would be supererogatory. Yet, morality is still described as constituting only "thin" and remote relations. What he sees in Kant is "the 'Christian' project of turning morality into ethics (by making all relations thick)."[13] It is true that "the Jewish universalistic approach," exemplified for him by "rabbi Ben Azzai, Moses

---

13 Margalit, *Ethics of Memory*, 45. The following page numbers are included in the text. Margalit reminds the reader of Stalin's murder of the peasant class and then approaches his first question "from the perspective of two religious projects .... Who will remember the murdered kulaks and who should remember them? First, why cannot the kulaks be remembered by humanity at large? That is, why cannot humanity be shaped into a community of memory and why cannot it be formed into an ethical community, based on the thick relation of caring? The Christian project is an effort to establish, in historical time, an ethical community based on love. This community, ideally, should include all of humanity, and it should be based on the memory of the cross as an ultimate sacrifice for the sake of humanity ... with a little helping of grace, humanity can and should be established as an ethical community of love. The Jewish project retains the double tier of ethics and morality at least for historical times, and postpones the idea of a universal ethical community to the messianic era. Jews are obligated to establish themselves as an ethical community of caring. The force of the obligation is gratitude to God for having delivered their ancestors from the 'house of slaves' in Egypt. The crucial role of memory for the Jewish community is to serve as a constant reminder of this debt of gratitude. In distinction from ethics, morality in the Jewish view, is based on a different source. It is based on the debt of gratitude all of humanity owes God for having been created in His image."

The common feature between Judaism and Christianity is: "They both base their obligation on a debt of gratitude that should be kept in memory. The memories for which we ought to be grateful are positive memories: creation, the sacrifice on the cross, Exodus. These are memories of divine gifts to humanity, or in the case of Exodus, to the Jews."

His skepticism concerning the ability to carry through an adequate response to the second question is reinforced by the absence of such religious resources in a purely moral community confronted with memories that inspire revenge: "Should not the kulaks be remembered by humanity, even if humanity is regarded ... as a moral community? Ought not this moral community to have some minimal sense of memory .... Gulags, Majdanek, Hiroshima ... as warning signposts in human moral history?" The question concerns the resources open to a secular understanding when a humanistic concept is put into doubt by the knowledge of the deeds the human person is capable of carrying out.

Mendelssohn, and Herman Cohen," understands "neighbor" in the same way as Kant for whom "being on the same planet with other human beings is enough to make them neighbors" (41-42). But essentially, for him "the 'Jewish' project" amounts to "keeping morality and ethics apart" instead of turning one into the other. The universalizing approach of Kant is seen in its origin as the outcome of one specific religious heritage and not as an autonomous idea of practical reason that has its validity independent of its historical roots.

Ricoeur, on the other hand, treats morality as a general human feature, expressed in the Golden Rule as well as in the different formulations of the Categorical Imperative. A criticism of Kant is implied in enclosing obligation between striving and equitable judgment, but it does not put the project of normative morality into question. Kant's "Idea of Eternal Peace" is greeted as being an eschatological enterprise at heart, but the Categorical Imperative of respect for the other is taken as the valid autonomous definition of morality, not as an enthusiastic overstepping of what can be demanded at the universal as opposed to the particular level.

For Margalit, particular communities of belonging are candidates for care. Yet the author of the "Decent Society" also warns of the danger of particularism. "An exclusive identification with one's own people is in itself immoral."[14] While both agree that each level has to be taken on its own merits, while still related, Margalit is critical of inappropriate mediation. He investigates whether the attempt to view humanity in ethical or "caring" terms as a "family" is conceptually possible and in the end agrees it is. But remaining skeptical with regard to its empirical possibility, he opts for the "better" instead of the "best," a community on "thin," moral, not on "thick" terms of caring. He also thinks it wise to start with ethical communities:

> So, if conceptual contrast does not require actual contrast, then transforming humanity into an ethical community of caring and of shared memory is not a conceptual impossibility. Still, such a transformation is very difficult to achieve. This does not mean that we should give up on the regulative idea of the human commonwealth as an ethical community of caring. But it does mean that in the meantime we should aim for a second best, that is, turning humanity into a moral community.[15]

---

[14] "Interview," in *Information Philosophie* 31 (2003): 34-39, here 38.

[15] Margalit, *Ethics of Memory*, 77-78. Further page numbers in the text.

The implication is that the Kantian project to treat every human being as neighbor could be overtaxing for the moral forces available to humanity, especially in the face of the impulse to seek revenge for inflicted suffering. It is seen as safer to develop the moral outreach beyond the "brother to the other" (cf. 73) from the basis of a natural community of caring. For Ricoeur, the problem is not lack of motivation to treat the distant other as a relation, since the benevolent orientation also towards anonymous others is part of our desire to live well. The difficulty arises at a later stage, "at the bottom of the pit" of entrenched hostilities. Here, the only way forward, forgiveness, is a grace opened up by God that is not available to humans as a natural part of their agency.

His answer to this problem is theological and confirms in this respect Margalit's view of the weakness of unsupported "thin" relations of a morality that founders on the cliffs of concrete histories of guilt. Margalit's perceptive attempt at historical stocktaking suggests that it is at risk already as a religious project, but more so as a project of reason. Even on religious terms, based on "gratitude" for both creation and redemption on the cross, the extension of including all of humanity into the realm of caring has seemed to be too wide to sustain. Since for Margalit it is communities that are defined by memories, the question is "whether humanity, as a moral community, ought to have some minimal shared moral memories, or whether the business of memory should be left entirely to smaller ethical communities" (78). Affirming the moral need to remember "striking examples of radical evil and crimes against humanity, such as enslavement, deportation of civilian populations, and mass exterminations" (78), because they "undercut the root of morality" (79), he points out how "immeasurably difficult ... the politics of constructing this memory" is set to be: to sustain effective instead of "soulless and bureaucratic" institutions, to avoid the "danger of biased silence," as well as the danger of wiping out crucial specifics in monuments "erected by humanity, for humanity" (81) instead of by the "community of memory connected to the perpetrators" in repentance to their victims. For him, one of the proposals for the Holocaust memorial in Berlin with the inscription "Thou shall not kill" is an example of such studied abstraction. The decisive step of "re-establishing oneself as a moral community" through repentance (81) is skipped. Thus, Margalit gives a moral argument for his preference for those "projects of shared memory ... that go through natural communities of memory" faced with engaging "painful traumatic memories from the past." In addition to the moral imperative to admit one's guilt, it is also a question of which project is more likely to succeed: "This (going through natural communities of memory) I believe is not as utopian as the two universalistic projects I mentioned, mankind as an ethical community or mankind as a moral community of memory (82)."

Is it also in the context of a "natural community of memory" that remembering the victims holds an aspect of promise? "Even the project of remembering the gloomiest of memories is a hopeful project. It ultimately rejects the pessimist thought that all will be forgotten, as expressed by Ecclesiastes: "There is no remembrance of former things ...(1:11)." (82)

Margalit shows impressively how high, and possibly unattainable, the stakes are in the universalistic project of turning humanity into a brother- and sisterhood. Taken as a secular endeavor, it can only proceed from traumatizing memories, not from God's past deeds and future promise: The "candidates for memory in the case of humanity as a moral community are negative ones, mostly of terrible acts of cruelty. Such memories do not inspire gratitude. Instead, they inspire an appetite for revenge (73)." Unlikely to face up to historical guilt, memory escapes into abstractions insulting by their lack of truth, which must be concrete. Before investigating (in the next section) upon what element readiness to change can be based, the problem this analysis must raise is that of the willingness to remember traumatic events and actions.

Both Ricoeur and Margalit question the appropriateness of the expression "duty to remember."[16] For the German philosopher Michael Theunissen, how-

[16] For Margalit, the collective subject addressed and the nature of the obligation are not evident: "Are we obligated to remember people and events from the past? If we are, what is the nature of this obligation? Who are the 'we' who may be obligated to remember: the collective 'we,' or some distributive sense of 'we' that puts the obligation to remember on each and every member of the collective? I reach the conclusion that while there is an ethics of memory, there is very little morality of memory." (7) For Ricoeur, constitutive elements of remembering are modified beyond recognition by a general imperative: its origin as a religious practice in a family setting that reminds one of the "thick relations" in Margalit, the relationship between past and future that depends on not having manipulated anamnesis, and its orientation towards truth, to be ensured through the critical work of historiography: "Here the pace slows down. I want to say how important it is not to fall into the trap of a duty to remember. Why? Because the word "duty" claims to introduce an imperative, a command where initially there was only an exhortation (Ermahnung) in the frame of offspring, along the sequence of generations: You will tell your son ....' Then because one cannot transpose an enterprise of remembering, thus of looking back, into the future without doing violence to the practice of anamnesis as such, not without a trace of manipulation; finally and especially because the duty to remember nowadays is recommended with the intention of short-circuiting the critical work of historiography. This carries the danger of fixing the memory of one or to alienate it from the sense of law

ever, there is a "moral duty" (*sittliche Pflicht*) of the perpetrators and their offspring to remember.[17] But would this be possible without rising to the level of morality? "Thick relations" are cemented, as Margalit says, by memories, not only of grandeur but also of suffering. But what becomes of "thick relations" when they are confronted with the memory of crimes committed by their own members? Instead of facing what Ricoeur calls the "unpardonable," will this memory not be avoided at all costs, and the crimes denied or set on a par with the suffering endured in return? If the "thick relations" of one's natural circles of belonging exhausted our self-understanding, such memories would be doomed to forced oblivion or repression. Does Margalit's demand to "re-establish oneself as a moral community" through repentance (81) not imply the need to rise above natural relations? It is also true that in his analysis, the primary level of "thick relations" is not viewed as sufficient and the clue given for the task of the next level is that "morality is needed to overcome indifference." But how does one get there? Do the labels attached to this plane, "thin," "abstract," "detached," "ad hoc," "minimalist"[18] sufficiently express what it stands for? Do they not delegate morality from the ranks of an equally original mode of human agency to the status of a derived and difficult extension of caring?

Margalit's and Ricoeur's assessments are remarkably similar insofar that they identify the need to correct reductive, self-interested tendencies within reciprocity through the one-sided offer of "encompassing relations," or of "generosity" and "love."[19] But Margalit's communitarian approach, while allowing him to establish an inherent link between memory and ethics at the

---

and justice. This is why I propose to speak of work of memory and not of duty to remember." (P. Ricoeur, *Geschichtsschreibung*, 19-20).

17 The English translation of his speech (which does not distinguish between ethical and moral relations) rightly chooses "moral," not "ethical" to render "sittliche Pflicht." Cf. Theunissen, *Scope*, 69.

18 Cf. M. Walzer, *Thick and Thin: Moral Argument at Home and Abroad* (Notre Dame / London, 1994)

19 Other similarities with Ricoeur include the assessment that it is necessary to "block expansionist tendencies of moralism"(14), a high regard for the task of the historian, expressed by Margalit's idea of founding an "Institute for Contested History" and attention to the relationship between remembering and forgetting, and forgiveness: "An ethics of memory is as much an ethics of forgetting as it is an ethics of memory. The crucial question, 'Are there things we ought to remember?' has its parallel, 'Are there things that we ought to forget?' Should we, for example, forget for the sake of forgiving?" (17)

first level, endangers its connection to the second level from which recognition of guilt, other than the betrayal of loyalties to one's own, depends. The problem of moving from the ethical to the moral plane also exists when the first is identified as the teleological orientation towards the good life. Yet the gap between happiness and virtue is bridged by the sense of direction Ricoeur gives to the "self-esteem" that emerges from the experiences of self-reflected agency. In orienting it towards the "self-respect" attained at the deontological level, he seems to assume a basic continuity.[20] Despite the change of register from "striving" to "obligation," the continuity between the first and second levels is expressed to be stronger than in Margalit's move from particular community to humanity. For Ricoeur, the discontinuity, as we shall see, is more marked when it comes to the abyss that failure means for self-respect: the two incapabilities of doing good, and of being ready to forgive. The theological perspective opened up by the link between memory and ethics arises from a different basis: not already in the universalizing project, as such, which for Margalit continues to be marked by the Christian attempt to turn even the remote other into a brother and make all relations "thick;" with Ricoeur, for whom the sense of obligation is part of the original experience of the self, the religious perspective definitively comes in with the voice of forgiveness.

Forgiving as an Integral Part of Human Agency, or as Divine Gift?

Memory is one of the "capacities" of a self that, as *Oneself as Another* has explored, is also capable to speak, act, and judge. Is the self equally capable to forgive? Ricoeur's answer is no. There is a "significant asymmetry" between two types of action that deal with the temporal conditions of human agency: promising and forgiving. Agency is limited, not just because there is always the backdrop of receptivity and of suffering, but because it depends on a forgiveness that has to be offered.

A final attempt at clarification based once again on a horizontal correlation is proposed with the pairing of forgiveness and promise. In order to bind itself by promise, the subject of action should also be able to unbind itself by forgiveness. The temporal structure of action, i.e., the irreversibility and unpredictability of time, calls for the answer that the performance of action can

20 The problems I see in this assumption are treated in greater detail in my article on "Capabilities, Convictions, and Public Theology" in M. Junker-Kenny (ed.), *Memory, Narrativity, Self*.

be mastered in this twofold way. My thesis here is that a significant asymmetry exists between the power to forgive and the power to promise. The impossibility of authentic political institutions of forgiveness testifies to this. This is how at the heart of selfhood and at the forum of imputability, the paradox of forgiveness is uncovered, sharpened by the dialectic of repentance in the great Abrahamic tradition. It is about nothing less than the power of the spirit of forgiveness to untie the agent from her act" (MHO, 595).

Crucial in *La Mémoire, l'histoire, l'oubli* is thus the arrival of forgiveness from beyond human powers. There are two misconceptions about forgiveness that Ricoeur wants to refute before offering a philosophical reconstruction that respects its paradoxical nature. Its interpretation in categories of exchange is unsatisfactory; the closeness in several languages between "gift" and "forgiveness" is misleading because it may insinuate the balance of offer and counter-offer, a culture of ritualized and dependable exchange. Ricoeur insists that the offer of forgiveness between persons is free and not to be taken for granted. In the religious context of the exculpation of the human sinner by God, his critique of conceptual impasses in which "theological quarrels" have landed the subject of justification is even more pronounced. Since no one is owed forgiveness, to understand it as a symmetrical relationship misses its core.

Hannah Arendt's attempt of including forgiveness into a theory of action is different; it leaves the context of exchange and is less marked by a *do ut des* expectation, but it also locates the act of pardoning at the level of a generic human faculty. Arendt's rich biblical and linguistic references and her acute observations of the decisive departures of Christian from antique Greek culture notwithstanding, Ricoeur goes straight to the points where he differs from her interpretation: the need to link a theory of agency with a concept of self (1), and the relationship of human to divine pardon (2).

The Temporal Dimensions of Agency and the Self

In her distinction of "action" from "labor" and "work," Arendt attributes a "self-remedying" quality to action. In intersubjective agency, she holds that we can correct our actions without further residue. For her, the need for forgiveness arises from two weaknesses: the "darkness of the human heart" which seems to result in unreliability, and the human lack of sovereignty over time. Both of these limits to human agency are treated at the ontological level of species features, not as subjective insights into one's own temptability and inclination to instrumentalize the other. For her, the problem is fickleness, not the mystery of evil. She keeps this dimension out of the analysis by classifying it as incommensurate to the range of misdeeds forgiveness can cope with. The crimes against humanity that Ricoeur refers to under the category of *imprescriptibilité*, the refusal to limit persecution of the perpetrators, are declared as outside the scope of both forgiveness and adequate punishment. While the procedural decision not to start with limit questions may be justified, the danger is that the phenomenon of evil will be kept out of sight as well.

Ricoeur's analysis differs in that he speaks not of two "weaknesses," but of two "mysteries" and "inabilities." The first, committing the fault, accentuates both the action and the inability to do what is good, thus specifying what the "darkness of the human heart" encompasses. The second is the "inability to forgive oneself," which Arendt also maintains but attributes to a somewhat exterior factor: the inevitable lack of perception of oneself. The major shortcoming of her analysis in Ricoeur's view is that it neglects the link between agent and act and only pays attention to the relationship between the act and its temporal conditions. If the subject of agency were analyzed further, it would not be possible to maintain the alleged symmetry between forgiving and promising as self-contained human faculties.

Forgiveness poses a question principally different from the one about representing the past, on the level of memory and history and with the risk of forgetting. The question put now concerns another mystery (*énigme*) – it is a double one: on the one hand, it is the mystery of a fault (*faille*) that paralyzes the power to act of the "capable human being" that we are; and it is, by way of response, the mystery of the eventual lifting of this existential incapacity that is designated by the term "forgiveness" (MHO, 593).

The otherwise capable self has to face the insight into the offence it committed and of its own incapacity to help itself. The question then is how "imputability" and "forgiveness" can go together without canceling each other out.

Ricoeur takes his immanent critique further to point out a contradiction in Arendt's positioning of forgiveness in the political sphere: Its difference from promising had first been marked by aligning it with love, which, as Ricoeur specifies, is marked by its singularizing glance. Arendt stresses its apolitical, indeed, "antipolitical" character. To get from here to her new interpretation of forgiveness in terms of *philia* is clearly a "jump" and not consistent with the first, radical qualification as a love blind to qualities, intimate and close. *Philia* in the antique political sense, is, as Ricoeur points out, exactly not the world-forgetful ecstasy of Arendt's description of love. The difference from promising therefore cannot be the intensely personal nature of forgiving since this is later muted to political friendship. For Ricoeur, the difference consists in the need for forgiveness, unlike promising, to be opened up to agents from beyond their own human powers. He classifies Arendt's detailed semantic analysis and discussion of New Testament passages as "suiting her own line of argument" (MHO, 632).

The Relationship of Human to Divine Forgiveness

While theologians may be taken by Arendt's unreserved recognition of Jesus' epoch-making insight into the need for forgiveness, Ricoeur focuses on the way in which she appropriates it into a secular understanding, leaving Jesus as the historical inaugurator of an idea, the validity and effectiveness of which are independent from him. To this secularizing sweep, he opposes the "verticality" of the relationship and metaphors such as "light" and "voice." He translates these images into categories of the self, or more precisely, the *ipse* aspect of the self, which is the organizing center of action. The paradox is between the imputability of the agent who has committed unpardonable acts, and an impunity arising from forgiveness that would not do justice to his freedom as an agent. His solution is to draw a distinction between the self and his acts.

Under the sign of forgiveness, the guilty person will be held as capable of something other than his deficits and faults. He or she will be restored to the capacity to act, and action to the capacity of continuing – you are worth more than your acts (*tu vaux mieux que tes actes*) (MHO, 642).

Holding on to the notion of imputability, which takes human freedom seriously, Ricoeur goes on to draw a distinction within this freedom. If one were to use the terms of a philosophy of subjectivity, it would be the distinction between transcendental and real, formal and material, abstract and concrete freedom.[21] It is possible to restore the original possibilities of a person's freedom to him by not fixing him to what he has done. At the first level, this can

[21] For an explication of the relevance of these categories for theology, see T. Pröpper, *Erlösungsglaube und Freiheitsgeschichte: Eine Skizze zur Soteriologie*, 2nd ed. (Munich), 183-84.

only be done by the victim, leaving matters still at the intersubjective human level, as Arendt does.

Yet for Ricoeur, there are two incapacities that have to be reversed. The agent can only be delivered of the first incapacity, to have acted wrongly, by having the sources of goodness reopened and turned back into the original capability that manifests itself in the fundamental benevolence towards the other which was expressed in the wish to live well with and for others. This is what "the great religions" do.[22] Yet also the second incapacity, to be unable to forgive oneself, needs God as well as the victim to open up forgiveness. "Il y a le pardon" seems to say that forgiveness has been brought into this world, and humans can avail of it when they forgive their aggressors, and when they accept forgiveness from their victims. The acknowledgement of the need to lift both incapacities comes close to what justification by faith, not works, meant for St. Paul.

While the "there is" (*il y a*) leaves it open as to how it came into existence, Ricoeur's choice of text to highlight it roots it in the Christian experience of God. Before, he had spoken of the "Abrahamic experience." But now the compassionate monotheism he refers to is particular and not overarching: The model of the "there is" is 1 Cor 12: "But now there are faith, hope, and charity." St. Paul's assertion that they will "remain" is taken to bring an atemporal, eternal quality of time into the conditions of finiteness, a promise that forgiveness is here to stay (cf. MHO, 639). He elucidates this promise with Kierkegaard's praise of forgetting as a liberation from worry. In his "Edifying Discourses" he evoked the Gospel's comparison of human fretting with "the lilies of the field and the birds of the sky that do not work but are dressed as magnificently as Solomon in his glory" (MHO, 656).

It is this kind of forgetting that resolves human unquiet; a "reserved," "qualified, or "discretionary" forgetting (*oubli de réserve*), which Ricoeur calls the "final incognito of forgiveness." Can it prevail against the pernicious type of loss of memory, an annihilation that effaces the traces to which Ricoeur is as opposed as Margalit? It is here that Ricoeur transposes a line from the *Song of Songs* into the domain of his theme of memory and forgetting. Its assurance that "Love is as strong as death" is "echoed" in the wishful last sentence of the book, "The forgetting of reserve is as strong as the forgetting of effacement."

[22] Cf. his interview with F. Ewald, "Dossier, Paul Ricoeur: Un parcours philosophique," in *Magazine littéraire* 390 (2000): 20-26, here 25.

Against Arendt, he has shown that the nub of the problem is whether the self can be liberated, which it only can if it is regarded as more than an agent.

The Concept of God Implied in Forgiveness as the "Eschatology of Memory"

The *Epilogue*'s enquiry into the initiative to forgive and the acceptance of being forgiven concludes the analysis of memory and historiography with an "eschatology" for which the "optative" is seen as the appropriate mode (3). Returning to the question posed at the beginning of how Europe's future can be forged from divisive memories, consequences and critiques of Ricoeur's most recent reflections for philosophically mediated theological theories of action and for theologies of the public realm can now be stated.

Theories of Action, Religion, and Theology

Both Habermas and Ricoeur are sensitive to the limit questions posed by a history of suffering that have been explored by theologians in dialogue with Habermas in the past thirty years.[23] What does Ricoeur's concept of forgiveness, which insists on an irritatingly "other" dimension within historiography, contribute to this debate? Where does it leave philosophy and the human sciences if the critically reconstructive work of historians depends on a horizon that is constituted by something described as "poetry," "voice," and "hymn"?

In comparison with the Frankfurt School's transcendental pragmatic theory of action, I can see several features that recommend Ricoeur's hermeneutical approach: the development of a theory of ethical agency from a theory of the self; the inclusion into ethics of the levels of teleological striving and of practical wisdom which take up questions of motivation, application, and crosscultural validity in the sense of an "inchoative universalism"; and his insistence on an understanding of tradition that is more than "convention" and provides a "symbolic network" of meaning. The anthropological dimensions, the interest in innovative, creative, metaphorical uses of language, provide a more adequate philosophical framework. From a Christian viewpoint, his

[23] Pioneering and foundational for most subsequent theological critiques has been Helmut Peukert's *Science, Action and Fundamental Theology*, transl. J. Bohman (Cambridge MA, 1984).

interpretation of the prophetical call has a theological richness that many reconstructions in Habermas' vocabulary fail to achieve.

Yet, problematic for theological reception is Ricoeur's disregard for what seems to be more than just some of its misleading historical "quarrels", e.g., on "nature" versus "grace." The discourse level of theology seems to be too close to the philosophy of religion to be able to be true to the religious experience it reflects on. While Habermas recognizes theologies that employ the "light of reason," Ricoeur seems to be suspicious of them. Once the differences between philosophical and religious self-reflection are noted, what would be wrong with a theology that understands itself as the "argumentation of the conviction," as in C. Mandry's mediating proposal?[24] The "discourse of the hymn" (Ricoeur) could make the hymn more beautiful by understanding it as part of a cosmic symphony interpreted by historical musicians who give resonance to it through their expression.

A second observation concerns the setting of the "voice." For Ricoeur, the model of Christian existence is the prophet summoned by God out of the community. In this emphasis on an individualizing call, the concept of the religious community and the ways in which it is affected by the "economy of the gift" remain underdeveloped. Interpreting Christian identity from the experience of reading scripture does not provide a comprehensive enough framework. Due to both his suspicion of theology and his neglect of the communal dimensions of faith, the function of the community as providing a context of meaning in struggling with the cultural frameworks of the different ages remains out of sight. The question of the (unfolding, digressing, renewing) identity of Christianity cannot be posed.

The Interplay of Religious Convictions with Debates in the Public Realm

With regard to religious contributions to public debates, Ricoeur's concept of "conviction" opens up a much more interesting relationship than John Rawls' who also employs this term for the personal views which are integrated into the "overlapping consensus" on norms of justice. His exclusion of not only religious but any value convictions deviating from the "overlapping consensus" turns it into the smallest common denominator in a pluralist society with a definite tendency towards a minimal standard of ethics. Missing in Rawls are

24 Cf. C. Mandry, *Ethische Identität und christlicher Glaube* (Mainz, 2002), e.g. 263.

the possible contributions that "convictions" can make to morality, in contrast to the drive to plumb for the average of all of convictions taken together with norms. In "Love and Justice," Ricoeur has shown the mutual fruition of both the religious and the secular approach. Each is driven beyond itself by the other: the golden rule is challenged by the command to love one's enemy; this "hyperethical" demand is kept from becoming unethical by squaring it with the logic of equivalence of the "rule" of justice.[25]

Ricoeur thus manages to give religious convictions a standing that need not disguise their origins in certain, definable, particular inherited experiences. The concepts of God arising from them and their ethical consequences is what Europe's global dialogue is about. This investigation comprises the experiences mentioned at the outset, of militarism with God at the service of the Fatherland, of defeat, with God as the totally other to culture, the white man's God of the colonial acquisition of fortunes from exploitation, and the supersessionist God of constructing Christian identity by denigrating the Jews. All these are experiences that have marked Europe's God as much as the great cultural struggles and syntheses from Antiquity onwards. It is by grappling with these memories that Europe's Christianity may redeem itself and have something to offer to today's globalized struggles.

Forgiveness as the Eschatology of Memory

Ricoeur takes care to distinguish his use of "eschatology" from "metaphysical or theological projections" which have been named "chronosophies," in opposition to the "chronologies and chronographies of historical science" (MHO, 646). In contrast, he wants this theological term to be understood as the "hori-

[25] C. Mandry describes his procedure of making the Christian faith fruitful for general morality as follows: Es geht darum, "die Moralität der Moral dadurch voranzubringen, daß vor-moralische Sinnerfahrungen und Sinnpotentiale in die moralische Erschließung von konkreten Problemstellungen eingebracht warden .... Die Erzählungen, Bilder, Metaphern und Denkweisen der christlichen Religion können mit Visionen und Hoffnungen den begrifflichen Moraldiskurs anstoßen, sie kann aber auch ein Mehr an Gerechtigkeit und an Anerkennung zwischen Personen zu denken geben .... So kann das Partikuläre des christlichen Glaubens dazu beitragen, die Universalität der Moral noch universaler zu machen - d.h. sie aus dem Universalen dem Anspruch nach zur volleren geschichtlichen Universalität in Bewegung zu setzen und zu halten." (*Ethische Identität*, 289). Cf. also his analysis of the Golden Rule and the command to love one's enemy in his contribution to *Interdisziplinäre Ethik*, ed. by A. Holderegger / J. P. Wils (FS D. Mieth) (Freiburg / Fribourg, 2001).

zon of accomplishment of an historical knowledge that is conscious of its limits." Evoking the "Angel of History," Walter Benjamin's interpretation of a picture by Paul Klee, he asks what today's tempest would be that paralyzes the angel. Instead of the now much-contested idea of "progress," which for Benjamin was the force catching the widespread wings of the angel and sweeping him away from paradise over the debris of history, Ricoeur suggests history itself. In a turn from the theory of historiography to every subject's practical responsibility, he clarifies that the "presumed meaning of history" ultimately does not depend on the work of the historians he has analyzed in the first part of MHO, but on citizens. It is their task to join the bitter works of memory and mourning on which forgiveness conveys the touch of grace, *charis*, and playfulness.

It is here that forgiving joins itself to the work of memory via the work of mourning: At the end of the third study, the effect was mentioned of which the dialectic between memory and projection of the future has on the work of the historian; with its help, the lost possibilities, the unkept promises of the past, are liberated. This liberation of past possibilities entails that the past – speaking in an image: the "past that does not want to pass" – stops pursuing the present. In a word, forgiving bestows on what remains hard work in the work of memory and in the work of mourning the touch of grace.[26]

If forgiveness is the "eschatology of memory," does this mean that theology has the last word since this is not a dialectic that can be resolved by human efforts? To see the ending of Ricoeur's recent book just as a vindication of the supremacy of faith and as a goal scored by theology against its rival philosophy would mean to remain bound within the logic of enmity. Instead, it has to be understood, not as an easy victory of a believer's theoretical understanding of the world, but as an invitation to draw from the bloodstained stuff of history threads that can be worked into a tapestry of hope. The works of memory and mourning cannot be skipped, and a concept of divine promise that ignores the heritage of hatred would not be up to the level of what is needed from God: the restoration of the ability to act, the liberation of the sources of the good – including those of Europe – from their state of obstruction, and the reopening of a communal future.

---

[26] P. Ricoeur, *Das Rätsel der Vergangenheit* (Göttingen, 1998), 155-56.

Amador Vega Esquerra

Mystical and Aesthetic Experiences in Modernity

1. The erosion of representative language in the modern world, and the resulting loss of fields of meaning, shows the urgency of establishing a new relationship with the holy that allows us to master this linguistic crisis. It is nevertheless difficult to imagine a possible set of criteria that would do justice to the equivocal character which the holy has enjoyed since time immemorial, especially in an environment wherein traditional religious language scarcely seems able to unearth the holy from the profane ashes in which it is buried, since it fails to muster the strength necessary to restore to life the images of God in the historical religions that have been shattered since Nietzsche formulated his critique. Rather, we require a new perspective that allows us to grasp the entirety of the existing profane world, so as to feel in its presence the same mysterious power that allowed primitive cultures to view a stone or tree as a holy and venerable object. All this could lead us closer to the holy, although this presupposes the abolition of what was until recently considered an unquestioned and necessary connection to religious discourse.

Basically, our primary attention is not religious language; not because we have drawn a premature conclusion that this no longer preserves the numinous aspect of the holy (to use Rudolf Otto's expression). The numinous can be perceived only in its worldly presence and in virtue of its manifest appearance; hence we can call it a "hierophany," following Mircea Eliade. The present situation which began with the processes of secularization has certainly led to an increasing mistrust of traditional religious languages, influenced by the erosion of the sense of the holy, as we mentioned; at the same time, however, the search for a place of refuge in the face of the massive secularization of the trivial is becoming increasingly urgent. In modern society human beings suffer from the lack of a criterion of truth, as a consequence of the almost complete absence of a spiritual authority that would enable them to skillfully situate themselves within a system of coordinates that might break through the present-day labyrinths of language which negate the individual and keep him at a distance from reality.

If our analysis is to resist the temptation of reverting to typologies which all too often prematurely turn the object of study into an abstract entity removed from the reality about which our analysis wishes to say something, we must necessarily turn to the materials that offer the best chances for research into the holy in modernity. With the abdication of the traditional cultures, especially in the Western world, the task of religious language is no longer to mediate to us the power of the holy, since we have already lost the key to this language, as Eliade correctly notes.[1] In my opinion, the processes of creating and destroying figures in contemporary art show us most clearly those behavioral patterns are manifest which were once the exclusive province of traditional religion. The great creative power of images in modern art, independent of the commercial market for art works, is probably derived from the fact that art has taken hold of the creative and destructive power proper to myths – a power whose usual modes of expression embody the kind of attitudes one finds in the iconoclastic movements in periods of spiritual reformations.

The sacramental capacity of modern art cannot be directly connected with the effect of the work of art on the observer who approaches it with a more or less devout or cultic attitude (in the sense of Romano Guardini's distinction regarding religious representations).[2] Here we are interested neither in the simple aesthetic expression nor in the intention of the artist. The presence of the sacred in art is shown in its ability to integrate ritual processes, as well as in the specific forms of expression which those ritual processes have always chosen.

The first artistic *avant garde* movements in Europe were deeply impressed by the findings of ethnological field trips, first in Africa and later in Oceana. The first objects to be seen in greater numbers in the museums and art exhibitions of Paris, London, and Berlin formed the foundation for a new anthropological hermeneutics of culture: its greatest challenge was to make fresh discoveries on the basis of the investigation of the ritual function of images and objects of many cultures without written traditions. What were initially mere objects of study for ethnologists and anthropologists soon became the impetus for a spiritual renewal in the language of the plastic arts and still more clearly in painting. Many artists, for example Picasso, were quick to make the forms of expression of primitive cultures their own, which conse-

---

1 M. Eliade, *El vuelo mágico y otros ensayos sobre simbolismo religioso* (La permanencia de lo sagrado en el arte contemporáneo), edited by V. Cirlot und A. Vega, 3rd ed. (Madrid, 2001), 139-46.

2 R. Guardini, *Obras Completas 1* (German: Kultbild und Andachtsbild) (Madrid, 1981).

quently led to an essential change not only in the way of observing the world, but also in relation to the conception of the phenomena themselves. As scholars have noted, the emergence of the phenomenological movement in German philosophy coincides with the birth of Cubism in Europe,[3] which is why the first decades of the twentieth century are an experimental period of great interest for our investigations.

Of all the forms of expression that were successfully experimented with in these years, abstractionism is, without a doubt, the one that won the greatest acceptance. The abstract artists' interest in representatives of primitive cultures is due both to the destructive power that comes to expression in those mythical worlds and to their approach to material things. One can certainly say that both the primitive and the abstract artists have an immense solidarity with the material. Sculptors such as Brancusi, members of cultures that until recently maintained traditional forms of expression, now began to chisel stones with a reverence and technique familiar to the people of the Paleolithic age. In a certain sense, it was twentieth-century art that manifested the holy in its greatest pluriformity.

A clear example of the capacity of art to integrate ritual processes is the oeuvre of the Russian-American artist Mark Rothko.[4] A tireless reader of Greek tragedies, Rothko began in the 1940s a series of compositions strongly surrealistic in character, in which themes of classical mythology found a central place. His paintings of myths, for example, Iphigenia, would have nevertheless probably been viewed simply as pictures with a simple religious theme had not Rothko discovered in the process of shaping his works the power of sacrifice – both creative and destructive. Inspired by his reading of Friedrich Nietzsche's *The Birth of Tragedy*, the artist recognizes in the ritual offering of the body the "destruction of the *principium individuationis*" as a new life principle. His paintings in those years, corresponding to the teaching of the mystery religions in Nietzsche's sense, search for an artistic idiom to represent the fragmentation of the image of the body. A few years later, this leads him to a fundamental rejection of the human form, as an illegitimate object of

[3] H.-R. Sepp, "Annäherung an die Wirklichkeit. Phänomenologie und Malerei nach 1900," in *Edmund Husserl und die phänomenologische Bewegung* (Freiburg i. Br., 1988).

[4] A. Vega, *Zen, Mística y Abstracción: Seis estudios sobre el nihilismo religioso* (Madrid, 2002), 109-29; also "Sacrifice and Creation in the Work of Mark Rothko: The Transitional Years" in *Mark Rothko: Katalog der Ausstellung*, edited by Fundació Miró (Barcelona, 2001).

representation. Doubtless this all had consequences for representational language itself, which had already proven incapable of mediating the entire power of the mystery of life and death.

The insight into the irrelevance of human representation for the expression of fundamental emotions led Rothko to search for a new form of expression as a substitute for physical blood offering, so as to further plumb the mysteries of the human soul; his rapprochement with depth psychology led him to see himself as an explorer of these depths. In order to venture into the area of pure abstraction, Rothko distanced himself from mythological themes; in doing so he followed the example of the North European peoples, who, according to Worringer, sought a place of refuge from the arbitrariness of natural forms in geometric systems of representation.[5] Rothko follows *de facto* the tradition of Hasidism, which had already preceded him in Europe. The mystical traditions, full of the language of negativity, are clearly manifest during the last decades of his life in the so-called "black paintings" as well as the large format murals and triptychs that he worked on for various American institutions. The artist's strong desire to involve the observer in the ascetic-mystical process from purification via enlightenment to a connecting unity, in the sense of a universal mystical grammar, is particularly evident in the "Harvard Mural." Rothko understood himself as the last rabbi of western art, and he was thoroughly conscious of the fact that he was now in the possession of the spiritual authority that in earlier ages had been entrusted to the scribes.

In his contribution to the chapel of St Thomas University in Houston, Texas, this ritual process reached its apogee: via sacrifice and the ascetic path, one finally reaches a space dedicated to contemplation. A series of large triptychs in dark violet tones envelops the observer who has penetrated to this point in the temple where no god is accorded the privilege of a divine image.

For a scholar interested in the forms of manifestation of the holy, the question of the spiritual legitimacy of such artistic statements cannot, in my view, be overestimated; it is indispensable, however, to recognize the basic structure inherent in every hierophany. As we already mentioned, a relationship between the cultic object venerated by primitive cultures and the cultic object of the images in modern art cannot be denied. One must however also ask to what degree such forms of expression in modern art are able to grasp the characteristic processes of representation in the historical religions, whose

---

5 W. Worringer, *Abstraktion und Einfühlung: ein Beitrag zur Stilpsychologie* (Amsterdam, 1996).

complex theologies refuse to abandon conceptual abstraction in favor of another abstraction, whether plastic or material. As far the recognition of the sacred in art goes, the criteria may not be either more complete or better, since the works of art or the arts themselves entirely take over the object of those theologies.

In reality, times of spiritual crisis have always meant radical upheavals in historical development. One example is the longlasting conflicts about the sacral value of images in the Byzantium of the fifth to eight centuries, or in Europe too during the reform movements of the sixteenth century. Even if the strong theological element in these conflicts points to the particularity of those cultures and to the historical elements, we must not overlook the prior history of the problems we have mentioned here, which reaches back to much earlier times.

The rejection of anthropological representations of the divine in the history of religion is attested to in early Buddhism as well as in the literature of the bible; but it is also evident in Islam and other religions. The origin of what we can generally call reform movements is a strong desire for a pure form and the return to an unfalsified language, free from the accretions and commentaries that get attached to the original model in the course of tradition. Here the difficult tension between renewal and tradition is evident. Despite all their differences, the primary concern of these spiritual movements was to put an end to attempts to turn the divine into a thing.

The modern world begins its iconoclastic period with Nietzsche's formulation of the "death of God." As subsequent studies have shown, this proclamation of the death of God is not directed to the living God of religions, but rather to the conceptualized God of the Western metaphysical tradition.[6] And in fact, the intellectual movements generated by this way of looking at things, e.g., theology after the death of God, maintained the expectation of a new beginning, which was to be made possible by this radical position. Since then, the emergence of nihilism has been interpreted very variously. A simple classification of nihilism within traditional aesthetic movements was not fruitful, since this increasingly led to a refusal to undertake the necessary rethinking of the essence of the holy in a world in which the divine revelation had become obscure. On the other hand, the attentive study of the tradition of "negative theology," which is ultimately based on Christian theology, as well as the at-

[6] J.-L. Marion, *El ídolo y la distancia* (French: *L'idole et la distance*) (Salamanca, 1999), 15-38.

tempts by Japanese students of Heidegger to found a new universal philosophy, open up bold new perspectives in the endeavor to discover the holy in the modern world. In Heidegger's own intellectual development he accepted the "end of metaphysics" – i.e., of an entire way of thinking – and turned his attention to the poets of the holy, especially Hölderlin, but also Rilke, Paul Celan, and even René Char. In his last work he openly advocates listening to the poets since the power of the holy is reserved to them alone.

The immense difficulty of recognizing the holy in the voice of the poets poses one of the greatest challenges to our hermeneutic. The problem is not at all new. Why has the profane language of poetry always been a powerful vehicle for the mediation of the highest spheres of religious enthusiasm? From the *Song of Solomon*, in which nature-bound language succeeds in resisting all temptations to idolatry, to the work of St John of the Cross,[7] which is entirely dedicated to the "holy delirium" of the soul that ventures into the "dark night" (an unmistakable and appropriate symbol for the holy), the context of the profane appears, paradoxically, to be the best refuge for that which should be protected precisely from the non-holy. However, a through analysis of texts would be required to make this point.

The claim that the holy and profane are in radical opposition (e.g. Mircea Eliade) and that the holy keeps the profane at a distance because of its divine being or because it seems to be something forbidden (taboo), is simply an inadequate explanation of the unique nature of the holy. This opposition is in fact clear in traditional societies, in which the two realms are demarcated by various levels of organizational and functional separation. The holy cannot indeed be controlled or domesticated by arbitrary human action; but in traditional societies the cultic forms of its representation are carried out by a priest, who enjoys a spiritual authority power thanks to the power which is entrusted to him and publicly recognized. The situation in modern societies is entirely different; as we have mentioned, the processes of secularization have made the holy hidden or unrecognizable. The ambiguity of the holy, which reveals itself in light well as in darkness, allows us to explore new avenues for gaining clarity about its effects and persistence, even when it seems to be absent. What was lost with modernity is not so much the holy, but rather its religious representation. The crisis affects the religious environment and its language, that is, the religious image of an entire epoch, but not the element that cannot

[7] J. Baruzi, *San Juan de la Cruz y el problema de la experiencia mística* (French. *St. Jean de la Croix et le problème de l'expérience mystique*) (Valladolid, 2001), 619.

be held fast by rigid forms of representation. Accordingly, this is a crisis of models of representation. Nevertheless, we should not allow ourselves to gloss over the wretched condition of the numinous today. The holy can, however, change itself and assume any shape at all, thanks to its lack of fixed forms and to its "chaotic" nature. Here is precisely the difficulty of developing a set of criteria that does justice to the distinction between what is holy and what is not.

The religious environment, in which the holy was usually at home, bears the primary responsibility for this state of neglect. With the toppling of the gods, the holy is an exile in a world that fails to recognize it; despite its vitality it lies buried in earthy darkness, or to use an image from a biblical story, swallowed up in belly of a whale. In light of the structure of its recent history, we can assume that the holy must struggle free from the "belly" of the profane in order to reemerge with full vigor into the light in the very world which keeps it hidden, and this may mean that the world becomes a sacred totality, or that new avenues of redemption open up. In this new situation, the condition of poverty is one important element of the holiness of the holy. Detachment from its essentially religious attributes meant that the holy abandoned its holiness with reference to what we might call the *activitas ad intra,* in order to remain in the profane sphere as the holy *ad extra.*

Eliade speaks of an element of non-differentiation or absolute identity of the holy and the profane as a characteristic of our time. Certainly, the language of the holy has been usurped and used in banal contexts of representation. What finds employment in spite of everything is the mask-like quality of the holy, the idol; for it is undeniable that the inaccessibility of the holy can lead to this crude falsification. By contrast, the mystery of the holy seems to be blazing new trails in processes of representation which avoid explicitly religious language, through new worlds such as that of abstract art.

Rainer Maria Rilke is right to locate the holy or the inexpressible beyond language; nevertheless, without language we have no insight into the experience of that to which language refers. Hence every renewal of either language or its systems of representation – whether representational or not – finds its starting point in the same cultic context from which it originates; otherwise one runs the danger of losing oneself in the "jungle of symbols." When an artist such as Joseph Beuys proposes to overcome Christian iconography, his starting point is the symbolism of the cross.[8] Beuys' perspective, strongly

[8] F. Mennekes, *Beuys zu Christus* (Stuttgart, 1989).

influenced by the theosophy of Rudolf Steiner, is oriented toward a cosmic conception of Christianity, not much different from what Eliade characterizes as the "cosmic Christianity" of central European peasants. It is here that the pagan-profane element preserves the holy in the human person, and awakens it continually to new life. This is not a matter of syncretism. In my view, the strong desire to overcome Christian iconography involves the rejection of a language that was incapable of grasping the entire mystery of the divine-human nature of Christ. The earthly and the heavenly aspects are derived from that which is beyond both aspects, because both are parts of creation. Neither of these aspects in isolation helps do justice to the incomparable essence of the "holy of holies" with anything more than an incomplete representation. Rothko's final paintings, the "bodies of light," allow us to recognize to some degree an idea of redemption that strongly resembles Jewish-Christian Gnostic ideas.[9]

Our interest here is not the question of the orthodoxy of this reception of the theology of the earliest Christian centuries in modern art, but the fact that this art itself, in its own language, took up the fundamental problems of the representation of "the holy of holies." Since art is also language, we understand the degree to which its mediating character is useful for our purposes.

It is always the verbal character of language that allows the holy to be revealed, but this in no way requires a representational *Ersatz* language; this would inevitably lead to a farce, to a mockery of the sacred and of the subject with sacral authority. This does not imply that the essence of the holy is exhausted in its expression. Nevertheless, the fact that language is needed if the holy is to be experienced bestows a uniqueness on language in relation to the understanding of this experience. When Rothko judges a certain kind of paintings as useless, this is because the observer is held at a distance from the painting, instead of coming closer to it. Is it possible to avoid a representational language that has become a purely communicative phenomenon, with clear signs of violence in the communication itself, and with a tendency to idolatry? How should a new type of language endowed with the power of proclamation look, so that what it says is understood by the addressee, not with the assistance of conceptual hermeneutical keys, but rather on the basis of the hearer's preparedness to accept it? Is it conceivable to have a hermeneutic of the manifestation of the holy, i.e., the holy in the profane, what we

[9] S. Scully, *Mark Rothko: Corps de lumière* (Paris, 1999).

called the holiness of the holy? How far can such a hermeneutic of the holy arise in the context of contemporary aesthetic discourse?

2. This topic involves many questions from the perspective of the intellectual and spiritual tradition of Christianity. It has always been a challenge for scholarship to achieve a systematic description of the so-called spiritual senses. Several historical monographs exist, but until now there has been no satisfactory interpretative framework that would do justice to the paradoxes of this spiritual anthropology. The degree to which one can speak of senses, when the higher capacities of the soul move into the background through the work of the Spirit, does not only concern the use of different languages (e.g., the use of allegory, Alexandrian theology) but can also lead to a new discussion about the object which human language seeks to reach. We propose an approach to the topic which attempts to harmonize a systematic discussion of sensuous (aesthetic) understanding with a discussion of what we encounter in a manner that the phenomenology of religious knowledge calls "super-sensuous."

Even if the aesthetic path appears to have no access to the perception of the holy – for here the mystagogic treatises of the Western spiritual tradition (e.g., Dionysius the Areopagite) give priority to the ascetic path – we must not forget the fact that the experience of the most unutterable and transcendent aspect of the divine on the basis of one particular understanding of the holy becomes the source of an outburst of sensuous exuberance. All this calls into question not only the appropriateness of the traditional religious languages for expressing the holy, but also the specificity of the religious fact itself as well as the field of its specifically religious meaning. It would not be difficult to show, for example, how the literary expression, even in an extremely sensuous form, is based on a deep numinous experience, as in the case of the biblical *Song of Solomon*. But why does an author in a clearly religious context choose the profane expression in order to proclaim his profound knowledge of God and God's love? The examples offered by the Christian tradition differ greatly; but certainly the example of St John of the Cross is unique. In his writings, the reservation about sensitivity, even in spiritual matters, serves only to intensify the sensuous outburst which is clearly open to a deeper perception of the holy through its touching and unity with the divine.

As we have already seen, the body represents a basic receptive structure for the understanding of the manifestation of the holy; however, we have equally seen the dangers resulting in an exaggeratedly literal interpretation of the human body. In the work of Rothko one is confronted with the idea of a spiritual body very similar to the body of the resurrection portrayed by Matthias Grünewald under the influence of Lutheranism. Modern art reflects the tension inherent in the tradition, even if no established religious orthodoxy is responsible for it. Here the artist does not use his freedom to blaze new trails in a capricious way; it is interesting to observe the extent to which artists in a secularized context renounce originality in their individual modes of expression, in order that they may serve the truth. The conformity of life and truth (in the Scholastic sense) which we can see in the personal development of an artist such as Mark Rothko is extraordinary; his work, influenced by Nietzsche's idea of the artist, witnesses in an impressive way to a close connection with life, which demands its sacrifices. And it is evident that behind this lies the idea of the necessary *sacrificium* that leads to new life, from the perspective of the artist, to a creative life. Here, the work takes over the function of preaching in religion.

A hermeneutic that attempted to grasp the religious elements of artistic forms and languages would be meaningless, unless it simultaneously pointed out a path of redemption that was not limited to the liberating character of aesthetic experience but was anchored primarily in an absolute context of meaning, i.e., a model of universal holiness.

Let us look at another example. Anthony Caro's installation "The Last Judgment" is an invitation to a walk past the scenes of horror of the twentieth century. The way from the "The Door of Death" to "The Gate of Heaven" is a long one. Going from one half-open door to the next, life takes a path that passes by masks, torture chambers, confessionals, tonal representations of the tragic myths of Mediterranean cultures, until finally one reaches the pottery trumpets of the four angels who announce the end. The horizontal representation of human existence stands in contrast to the proclamation of the return of Christ at the end of time and the descent of power from heaven onto the Earth.

Abstract art has attempted by processes of disfigurement to create in painting a realm free from images; and thus intends to create an open space for this coming. It is necessary to have an empty temple at one's disposal, as Meister Eckhart expressed it in one of his German sermons (*Intravit Iesus in templum*), so that the Lord could enter it. The paintings of Rothko, the sculptures of Caro and the art of Matthias Grünewald create conditions in which heaven opens up vis-à-vis Earth, so as to redeem the entire creation. This upward and downward movement of the divine, as for example in the Neo-

Platonic scheme of Scotus Eriugena in *De divisione naturae,* offers a complete image of revelation in which we can see much more clearly the yearning of the revelation to remain in material things as a sign and a reminder of that light which will shine forth on the day of judgment from the abyss of horror in order to redeem this horror itself. Modern Art is probably the only form that does not shun the dark, indeed, the demonic aspect of the holy, even if it thereby endangers its own existence. Far from being a theology of *privatio boni,* modern art has confronted the mystery of what C.G. Jung has called the "shadow" of God. The symbolic art of Rothko and Caro contains aspects that allow us to describe them as prophetic art; since they contain the promise of eternal religious truths, even if the weak personality of the artists must suffer under the power bestowed on them, even to the point of the extinction of their own persons.

The following theme is one of those that are hard to understand: to what extent is the artist in a secular artistic context, i.e., an environment without cultic consciousness – with the exception "religious art" in the specific sense of that term – worthy of mediating what traditionally (e.g., in the iconography of the Christian East) is understood only as the activity of divine grace in a purified subject? The modern artist does not possess the sacramental power of the priest; nevertheless his work to some extent offers him the space for the self-sacrifice that every cultic action demands. If our intention is an investigation of language, then we can certainly conclude that the work of art, as something existing independently of the artist, witnesses to the necessity of sacrifice. Where there is a sacrifice, there can also be a new creation; this appears to me the most certain element in a list of criteria which does not wish to make religious-aesthetic distinctions on the basis of the "religious" character of art. It is not the "religious" element that leads to the manifestation of the holy, but the ability of a work of art to manifest the willingness of the person to sacrifice himself in his desire to furnish a "model of communication"; and this would be the second element of the criteria we seek here. A third element is the most important; namely, the readiness for a spiritual encounter with the mystery, since this – thanks to its renunciation of self-absorption – is the perfect model of what it means to preach. Contemplative observation, readiness for sacrifice and proclamation: these might be some of the concepts of this grammar of the holy in modern art. They are dependable since they all form the foundation of a continual creative process, whose goal is the creative empowerment of the human person.

3. The fundamental structural element of our reflections, always in view of these three possible criteria, is connected with the creative capacity of each artistic and religious expression. As we have already concluded, religious language evidently does not always embody the mystery of the holy, even when it claims to; nor does it always function as a creative power. In every process by which the holy manifests itself, there is a clear consciousness of its duality. The holy always manifests itself in its dual form as *tremendum et fascinans* (Rudolf Otto); it can reveal its terrifying aspect through the demonic, which as Paul Tillich saw, always seeks out the nearness to the divine in order to appear.[10] Perhaps indeed it is precisely the negative forces that underscore the holiness of what is being affirmed, as we often see in pictures of the Last Judgment. The question is simply to what extent the creative energy of the individual is attributable to his partisanship for the good and the beautiful or, alternately, comes from a work inspired by the demonic temptation to cross boundaries, whose main identifying mark is the lack of light, i.e., its obsession with discovering the reasons for evil and suffering. It is not a matter of requiring art to do justice to its improvable origins and not only to be beautiful and good, but also true; but rather of requiring that it devote itself to the well-being of the soul, when even the horror of existence can find comfort. The criteria for distinguishing true from false, good from evil, beautiful and ugly, cannot form the foundation of a methodology that will give us certainty about a work of art, whatever its nature. This does not mean that such criteria remain within the realm of pure abstraction; but it is clear that they have no power to make a judgment. They drive the spirit to orient itself in the drama of one's own judgment of a work of art. Using this criterion, it would be very difficult to judge the work of Jackson Pollock, for example. In his large paintings from the 1940's it is certainly possible to recognize the drama of the human soul, which seeks the light that can break out only at the cost of individual obliteration. It is a light that arises out of the darkness, a darkness so gloomy that it succeeds in swallowing up the artist in his creative process.

The creative artistic process is truly paradoxical. From a mystical-religious viewpoint, the work emerges from the destruction of the "I" as a product of sacrifice directed toward a sublime renunciation. In modern art, nevertheless, it is extremely difficult to distinguish self-sacrifice for the good of a greater project viz. the proclamatory character of the work of art from a de-

---

[10] P. Tillich, *On Art and Architecture*, ed. by J. Dillenberger (New York, 1989), 102-18.

structiveness that in Pollack's case is based on his excessive ego. But the enigmatic character of the holy occasionally requires the sacrifice of those who, as St Augustine puts it, contribute their own gloom to the darkness. The darkness was present prior to the will of the individual, and it is characteristic for the world in its fallen state, even when individual creativity has received the power to let the light shine in the darkness.

There are languages in pictorial art that are on the same level as the blood offering of primitive religion, as we see for example, in the surrealist period of Rothko. Nevertheless, he was clearly able to overcome this phase in favor of a more abstract idea of sacrifice. Some works plainly show the three elements of the reception of the holy: from the beginnings of his oeuvre, the paintings of Balthus are filled with contemplation, sacrificial offering, and proclamation; the language of the profane grasps here the full depth of the *mysterium* in its purest form, in which the fallen nature of that which is human surrenders itself over to the divine, before it is tainted anew with a divided consciousness that sometimes decides for the good and other times for evil. But neither the good nor the true are at home in a painting. A good work of art makes the observer change his way of seeing; even a work that can be wrongly perceived as a provocation (because it entails a difficult balancing act) ultimately frees the aimless and morally obsessed spirit from its chains. This implies that there is a dialogue between the work and the soul of the observer, which is why a good work, full of light and mystery, can say absolutely nothing to one observer, while for another person, who has ventured too deep into the night, the same picture will enlighten the despondent soul and open up a vista on the whole world, thanks to its proclamatory ability. It undoubtedly remains a mystery why some works of art possess this capacity for proclamation; this mystery is hidden in art and the holy, which have their roots in the same primal origin of all Being. Hence the scholar of religious phenomena in modern art does not have to look to causes or principles of origin. Rather, the scholar must investigate the condition in which modern art exists.

When art speaks of the religious kind of truth, it does so in order to distinguish it from the worldly kind of truth. In other words, what this art brings to expression is neither the things of this world nor its essence, but the light of every unveiling which makes the claim to truth.[11] Art thereby witnesses to its capacity to offer a picture of the transformed world, a preview of the fullness

[11] M. Henry, *C'est moi la verité* (Paris, 1996).

of the glory announced in revelation. Its deeply eschatological meaning cannot however, keep art from being in a continual process of transition. Its sacramental power can be based on the fact that it intuitively grasps that intermediary world (*mundus imaginalis*) about which Henry Corbin has written at length, in which that which the senses perceive becomes spiritual and the spiritual can be perceived by the senses. It must however be constantly emphasized that the condition of the world as a sacramental space is due to its intermediary position, not because the world itself as a genuine totality is perfect.

The degree to which art is a discourse about truth depends upon the directness of its capacity for expression; in other words, it is not the content, whether it be figurative or abstract, that speaks to the observer, but the desire to form a space all around, when the work of art reveals itself to be the greatest opening that completely breaks through the world. In this sense art fills a holy need, since it opens the door through which all human suffering must experience its saving meaning. Art situates itself in the world, but also outside the world: by sanctifying the eye that links the external reality with the internal reality. The resacralization of that which lies concealed in the profane makes reality fragile – thereby allowing the holy to escape the death to which it would have been condemned in the purely religious sphere – and this also points to the transitory character of the holy in the world. But we must save for a later, more detailed investigation the answer to the question: What is the world in relation to the holy?

Translated by Michael Parker

Georgios D. Martzelos

Kataphasis and Apophasis In the Greek Orthodox Patristic Tradition

Introduction

Two main interdependent features of the theology of the Church Fathers, when they refer to the meaning of God, to His relation to the world, or even to their divine experiences, are the kataphatic and apophatic ways in which they describe them. This is because the distinction between the uncreated God and the created world does not constitute merely an ontological distinction for the Fathers that they accept without realizing the deeper, direct gnoseological consequences and implications. The most imminent gnoseological consequence of this ontological distinction is that although the uncreated God is truly related to the created world through His energies and becomes known by them during their manifestation in Creation and in History, in His essence – in the nature and the way of His energies, as well as in the way of His existence as a Trinity of Persons – He remains completely transcendental and unapproachable. In this sense, God is, for the Fathers, simultaneously known and unknown, explicit and ineffable, revealed and hidden, *Deus revelatus* and *Deus absconditus*, or *Deus secretus* and *Deus publicus*, as the holy Augustine would characteristically say.[1]

These two gnoseological aspects of God form the basis upon which the Fathers have built two different and seemingly contrary theological routes. The kataphatic route, or kataphatic theology, as it is usually called, refers to the approachable, understood, and known aspect of God, while the apophatic route, or apophatic theology, refers to the unapproachable, incomprehensible, and unknown aspect of Him. The development of these two theological routes is closely connected to the thriving of patristic theology and characterizes the approach of nearly all the great Church Fathers, especially of the Cappadocian Fathers, Basil the Great, Gregory the Theologian, and Gregory of Nyssa, Dio-

[1] See In Psalmum LXXIV, 9, PL 36, 852: " (Deus) ... ubique secretus est, ubique publicus, quem nulli licet, ut est, cognoscere, et quem nemo permittitur ignorare." Cf. In Evangelium Joannis tractatus XIII, 5, PL 35, 1495: "Omnia possunt dici de Deo, et nihil digne dicitur de Deo."

nysius the Areopagite, Maximus the Confessor, John Damascene, Symeon the New Theologian, and Gregorius Palamas.

The Meaning and Gnoseological Significance of Kataphatic and Apophatic Theology

In addition to the above two distinctions, the distinction between the essence and the energies of God and the distinction between the created and the uncreated are viewed in the patristic tradition as God's revelation to the world and the foundation of knowledge of God as experience in the history of Divine Economy. In other words, the knowledge of God is not the fruit of an intellectualist meditation but rather of an existential relationship with God on a course toward the purification, enlightenment, and perfection of man, a knowledge that comes to man through personal experience founded on God's revelation.[2]

In this sense, man, based on God's revelation as a Trinity of Persons and having experience of the divine energies that are imprinted on the Creation and in History, is able to form a real and positive image of God, rendering to Him various kataphatic divine names that either merely indicate the way of His existence as three divine Persons (hypostatic idioms) or reflect the variety of His energies and thus respond to the reality of the divine nature. Accepting, in this way, the revelation of God recorded in the Holy Scriptures, man calls the Persons of the Holy Trinity "Father," "Son," "Word of God," and "Holy Spirit," in reference to the birth of the Son and the procession of the Spirit from the Father. Seeing also the kindness, wisdom, power and justice of God's energies that are manifest in the Economy, man calls God, respectively, kind, wise, almighty, just, etc. All these divine names, or even the pictorial representations that are met with in the Holy Scriptures, either simply indicate the particular manner of the three divine Persons' existence or express the diversity of God's relations to the world, thus composing the essence of kataphatic theology. Consequently, kataphatic theology or *kataphasis*, as the Fathers often call it, is "the thesis of all (beings)," the attribution of positive

---

[2] See G.D. Martello's *Essence and Energies of God according to Basil the Great: Contribution to the Historic-Dogmatic Inquiry of the Orthodox Church's Teaching About the Essence and Energies of God* (in Greek), 2nd ed. (Thessalonica, 1993), 123ff. N.A. Matsouka, *World, Man, Society according to Maximus the Confessor* (in Greek) (Athens, 1980), 187ff.

qualities to God that stem from His revelation as a Trinity of Persons and His causal relationship with the world. And this relationship is achieved, as we have said, on the basis of God's energies as manifest in the Economy.[3] Precisely in this sense, God as the only cause of the world's beings, made and unmade, is considered by St. Maximus as "the only mind of the understanding and the understood, and word of the saying and the said; and life of the living and the lived, and as everything being and made for everyone, for those which are and are made."[4] In other words, all the so-called kataphatical names that are attributed to God, if they don't signify the particular way of the three divine Persons' existence, they do, however, presuppose and express the exact causal relationship between God and the world. As St. John Damascene notes, summing up the earlier tradition of the Fathers, God is called "both being … and essence" as "the cause of all beings and of all the essence"; "He is called both word and reasonable, both wisdom and wise" as "the cause of all words and wisdom, of both reasonable and wise." In a similar way, He is also called both "mind and mental, life and alive, power and powerful." He is called by many other similar kataphatical names, as the cause of all beings and of the properties that describe them.[5]

But while God, as the cause of all beings, is and becomes everything for all "that is and that is made," He Himself, as the Church Fathers emphasize, is beyond "to be" and "to be made" of the created beings.[6] The ontological difference between the created and the uncreated does not permit a substantial relationship between God and the world. The only possible relationship between them is the one accorded to the energies. That is why all the kataphatic names rendered to God characterize, in the patristic view, only and exclusively either the particular way of the three Persons' existence or the energetic relationship of God with the world and not His being itself. None of these names is capable of describing or expressing the divine essence in a way that

3 See Dionysius Areopagite, *De mystica Theologia, ad Timotheum*, 1, 2, PG 3, 1000 B; 3, PG 3, 1033; Cf. Maximus Confessor, *Mystagogia, Prooemium*, PG 91, 664 B; Quaestiones et dubia 190, ed. J. H. Declerck, *Maximi confessoris quaestiones et dubia*, Corpus Christianorum, Series Graeca 10 (Turnhout / Brepols, 1982), 132.

4 See *Mystagogia, Prooem.*, PG 91, 664 A: "ο μόνος νους των νοούντων και νοουμένων, και λόγος των λεγόντων και λεγομένων· και ζωή των ζώντων και ζωουμένων, και πάσι πάντα και ων και γινόμενος, δι' αυτά τα όντα και γινόμενα."

5 See Expositio accurata fidei orthodoxae 1, 12, PG 94, 848 A.

6 See Maximus Confessor, *Mystagogia, Prooem*, PG 91, 664 AB. John Damascene, PG 94, 845 CD.

gives us even rudimentary knowledge of it.[7] Knowing the essence of God, as well as of the indissolubility connected with the essence is, for the Fathers, impossible for created beings and, is due to their lack of understanding. "Hence, to know the divine essence," says Basil the Great, "is to feel His incomprehensibility."[8] John Damascene, extending the incomprehensibility of the divine essence to the whole divine being, underscores this point: "Then, the Divine is infinite and incomprehensible and only this can be comprehensible, the infinity and the incomprehensibility."[9] What we know of God, according to the Fathers, we came to know through His revelation, which is realized by means of His energies, manifested in the Creation and in History. That is so because God does not communicate with the created world by means of His essence, but only through His energies. Basil the Great stresses this truth, and he is supported unanimously by the later tradition of the Fathers: "We claim to know our God through His energies, and we don't claim to approach His essence; because His energies come down on us, but His essence remains unreachable."[10] In a similar way, St. Maximus, referring to a relevant passage of St. Gregory the Theologian from his speech *In Theophania,*[11] highlights the unreachability and unintelligibility of the divine essence on behalf of all the created beings:

---

7 See Gregory of Nyssa, *Contra Eunomium* 3, PG 45, 601 B: "Ει δε τις απαιτοίη της θείας ουσίας ερμηνείαν τινά και υπογραφήν και εξήγησιν, αμαθείς είναι της τοιάυτης σοφίας ουκ αρνησόμεθα˙ τοσούτον ομολογούντες μόνον, ότι ουκ έστι το αόριστον κατά την φύσιν επινοία τινί ρημάτων διαληφθήναι."

8 See Epistola 234, 2, PG 32, 869 C: "Είδησις άρα της θείας ουσίας η αίσθησις αυτού της ακαταληψίας". See also G. D. Martzelos, "Der Verstand und seine Grenzen nach dem hl. Basilius dem Grossen," in Τόμος εόρτιος χιλιοστής εξακοσιοστής επετείου Μεγάλου Βασιλείου (379-1979) (Thessalonica, 1981), 235ff.; *idem, Essence and Energies of God*, 39ff.; 66ff.; *idem, Orthodox Dogma and Theological Reflection: Studies in Dogmatic Theology* (in Greek) (Thessalonica, 1993), 83ff.

9 See 1, 4, PG 94, 800 B: "Άπειρον ουν το θείον και ακατάληπτον, και τούτο μόνον αυτού καταληπτόν, η απειρία και ακαταληψία."

10 See Epistola 234, 1 PG 32, 869 AB: "Ημείς δε εκ μεν των ενεργειών γνωρίζειν λέγομεν τον Θεόν ημών, τη δε ουσία αυτή προσεγγίζειν ουχ υπισχνούμεθα. Αι μεν γαρ ενέργειαι αυτού προς ημάς καταβαίνουσιν, η δε ουσία αυτού μένει απρόσιτος." For more on this see G.D. Martzelos, *Essence and Energies of God*, 89ff.

11 It is about the quotation "νω μόνω σκιαγραφούμενος (ενν. ο Θεός), και τούτο λίαν αμυδρώς και μετρίως, ουκ εκ των κατ' αυτόν, αλλ' εκ των περί αυτόν, άλλης εξ άλλου φαντασίας συλλεγομένης, εις εν τι της αληθείας ίνδαλμα" (Homilia 38, in *Theophania, sive Nathalitia Salvatoris*, 7, PG 36, 317 BC).

> From what God is according to the essence, that is, from the essence itself, He can never be known to exist. Because any sense of what He is, is impenetrable and completely unapproachable for all creation, equally for the visible and the invisible one, but from what exists around the essence, God reveals Himself only as existing and only to those who regard these things with due kindness and reverence.[12]

All those who are considered to be "in proximity of the essence" of God, then, do not indicate what God is. They indicate either that He "is," meaning that He exists, or they indicate what He is by what He is not.[13] In this sense, God does not receive only the kataphatic names, which, as we have mentioned, express the particular way of the existence of His hypostases, as well as the diversity of His creative and provident relationships with the world, but He is also the recipient of the apophatic names, with which He is completely differentiated from the created reality and which constitute the essence of apophatic theology. The names that are attributed to God are distinguished in two basic categories: those that denote properties that are fit for God and those that denote properties that are not fit for His divine and uncreated nature.[14] So, in order to form a vague, yet satisfactory and real image of God, both these naming categories are essential. As Basil the Great characteristically remarks, "Hence, about the names that God is called with, the ones denote the qualities that are appropriate for God, while the others the opposite, the ones that are inappropriate for Him. From these two is God's character imprinted on us, from the denial of the inappropriate and the confession of the appropriate qualities."[15]

---

12 See De variis difficilibus locis ss. pp. Dionysii et Gregorii, ad Thomam v.s., PG 91, 1288 AB: "Εκ των κατά την ουσίαν, τουτέστι εκ της ουσίας αυτής, ο Θεός ουδέποτέ τι υπάρχων γινώσκεται. Αμήχανος γαρ και παντελώς άβατος πάση τη κτίσει, ορατή τε και αοράτω κατά το ίσον, η περί του τι καθέστηκεν έννοια, αλλ' εκ των περί την ουσίαν μόνον ότι έστι, και ταύτα καλώς τε και ευσεβώς θεωρουμένων, τοις ορώσιν ο Θεός εαυτόν υπενδίδωσι."

13 See PG 91, 1288 BC: "Πάντα δε τα περί την ουσίαν ου το τι εστιν, αλλά τι ουκ έστιν υποδηλοί, οίον το αγέννητον, το άναρχον, το άπειρον, το ασώματον, και όσα τοιαύτα περί την ουσίαν εισί, και το τι μη είναι, ουχ ότι δε το τι είναι αυτήν παριστώσιν˙ αλλά και οι της προνοίας και της κρίσεως λόγοι, καθ'ούς το παν σοφώς διεξάγεται, μεθ'ών και η εναρμόνιος της φύσεως θεωρία περί Θεού είναι λέγεται , τον δημιουργόν εαυτής ότι έστι μόνον αναλόγως δεικνύουσα."

14 See Dionysios Areopagite, *De coelesti hierarchia* 2, 2-3, PG 3, 140 BCD. John Damascene, 1, 12, PG 94, 845 C - 848 A.

15 See Adversus Eunomium 1, 10, PG 29, 533 C: "Εν τοίνυν τοις περί Θεού λεγομένοις ονόμασι, τα μεν των προσόντων τω Θεώ δηλωτικά εστι, τα δε το εναντίον, των μη

In spite of the fact that both these categories of divine names are necessary in order to formulate a real and satisfactory sense of God, more suitable for God are, for the Fathers, the apophatic names, since only these are able to indicate God's superiority to the created beings. As St. Maximus states in his work *Mystagogia,* in his characteristically laconic, yet rich-in-theological-nuances style, following Dionysius the Areopagite,[16] to God we must attribute, not the being, but "rather the non-being, because that is more appropriate to be said of Him, as He is above the being."[17] Exactly the same point is made by John Damascenus, epitomizing, here, both Dionysius and Maximus:

> It is impossible to say what God is in His essence; it is rather more suitable to speak of Him by deducting everything; as He is not one of the beings, not because He doesn't exist, but because He is above all beings and above the existence itself."[18]

Indeed, whichever kataphatic name or whichever kataphatic property we attribute to God, that name or property reflects the assumed representations that have been formed in our thinking by our relevant experiences as created beings. But there is risk here of idolizing God or of creating a purely objectified and anthropomorphic image of Him, something that takes us farther away from the real meaning of God. That is the reason why Dionysius the Areopagite, on whom the later Fathers are dependent, refuses to render God within the frames of apophatic theology, properties, and names, some of which are already attributed to Him in the Holy Scripture. It is needless, of course, to point out that such a consideration of God obviously presupposes a full detachment from the word-for-word inspiration of the Holy Scriptures. Thus God for Dionysius the Areopagite is neither mind nor word, neither essence nor power, neither light nor life, neither kingdom nor wisdom, neither one nor unity, neither divinity or kindness; nor is He a spirit, as we perceive it, neither filiality nor fatherhood, nor something else of us or of the beings that we

---

προσόντων. Εκ δύο γαρ τούτων οιονεί χαρακτήρ τις ημίν εγγίνεται του Θεού, εκ τε της των απεμφαινόντων αρνήσεως και εκ της των υπαρχόντων ομολογίας."

16 See 2, 3, PG 3, 140 D - 141 A.

17 See Mystagogia, Prooem, PG 91, 664 B: "το μη είναι μάλλον, δια το υπερείναι, ως οικειότερον επ' αυτού λεγόμενον." Cf. Dionysius Areopagite, 2, 3, PG 3, 140 D - 141 A.

18 See 1, 4, PG 94, 800 B: "Επί Θεού, τί εστιν, ειπείν αδύνατον κατ' ουσίαν˙ οικειότερον δε μάλλον εκ της πάντων αφαιρέσεως ποιείσθαι τον λόγον˙ ουδέν γαρ των όντων εστίν ουχ ως μη ων, αλλ' ως υπέρ πάντα τα όντα και υπέρ αυτό δε το είναι ων."

know of; neither is He one of the non-existent nor one of the existent ones. He is neither darkness nor light, neither deception nor truth; neither is there an affirmation in Him at all nor a deduction.[19] In other words, God is nothing of the above, in the way we have shaped these concepts as meanings in our thoughts, based on the experiences we have of the created beings. God is uncreated and therefore does not exist in the same way that created beings do. And that is exactly why St. Maximus stresses that "non-being" suits God, who is the true being more than the "being" – of course, not in the sense that His being is identified with His "non-being," that would be an extreme absurdity, but in the sense that His being belongs, as he distinctively clarifies, to the "hyper-being," as His existence and nature transcend the existence and nature of the created beings.[20] Much more emphatic on this point is St. Symeon the New Theologian, who, following in the steps of Dionysius the Areopagite and Maximus the Confessor, stresses that God is unapproachable, ineffable, invisible, unspeakable, and unintelligible, as He is considered as "being naught" and "non-being" in relation to the created beings. God, as he characteristically emphasizes, "lies beyond any called name, word and verb, and for this reason is He above and beyond the perception of any intellect, as He is naught,[21] because the being naught can never be conceived by the human intellect and be given a name."[22]

---

19 See *De mystica theologia, ad Timotheum*, 5, PG 3, 1045 D - 1048 A: "Αύθις δε ανιόντες λέγομεν, ως ...ούτε νους ... ουδέ λόγος εστίν ... ουδέ έχει δύναμιν ούτε δύνα-μίς εστιν ούτε φως· ούτε ζη ούτε ζωή εστιν· ούτε ουσία εστιν ούτε αιών ούτε χρόνος· ουδέ επαφή εστιν αυτής νοητή ούτε επιστήμη, ούτε αλήθειά εστιν ούτε βασιλεία ούτε σοφία, ούτε εν ούτε ενότης, ούτε θεότης ή αγαθότης, ουδέ πνεύμα εστιν, ως ημάς ειδέναι, ούτε υιότης, ούτε πατρότης, ουδέ τι άλλο των ημίν ή άλλω τινί των όντων συνεγνωσμένων· ουδέ τι των ουκ όντων, ουδέ τι των όντων εστίν ... ούτε σκότος εστιν ούτε φως, ούτε πλάνη ούτε αλήθεια· ούτε εστίν αυτής καθόλου θέσις ούτε αφαίρεσις."

20 See *Mystagogia, Prooem*, PG 91, 664 B. Cf. the similar aspect of holy Augustine: "Deus ineffabilis est; facilius dicimus quid non sit, quam quid sit" (in: Psalmum LXXXV, 12, PL 37, 1090).

21 See Theological Speech 3, Sources Chretiennes 122 (=J. Darrouzes, *Syméon le Nouveau Théologien: Traités théologiques et éthiques*, Introduction, Texte critique, Traduction et Notes, vol. I [Paris, 1966], 162 [108-11]): "Υπεράνω παντός ονόμα-τος ονομαζομένου και λόγου και ρήματος ών, υπέρκειται και πάσης διανοίας κατά-ληψιν υπερεκπίπτει, μηδέν ων."

22 See Theological Speech 2, Sources Chretiennes 122, 148 (256-257): "Ου γαρ δύναταί ποτε το μηδέν ον υπό ανθρωπίνης εννοίας εννοηθήναι και ενσημανθήναι ονόματι." With the above-mentioned aspect of Symeon cf. Dionysius Areopagite, De mystica

This theological denial of God through apophatic theology is for the Church Fathers, in fact, a kataphasis of God. On this account, we have a real image of God only when we refuse to attribute to Him qualities of the created beings, since when we do attribute such qualities to Him, we virtually deny Him, by classifying Him within the order of the created. According to St. Maximus, "If, of course, it is imperative for us to recognize indeed the difference between God and the created beings, the affirmation of the hyper-being must be regarded as the deduction of (the created) beings, and the affirmation of the beings as the deduction of the hyper-being."[23] Or, as he states in another context, "in God the par excellence deprivations are more true, as they wholly witness the affirmation of the divinity through the complete deduction of the beings."[24] This is, moreover, the reason why Christ during His Transfiguration revealed Himself not "as conceived kataphatically through the affirmation of the beings, but as presenting, by means of the apophatic theology, the unapproachable of the divinity to be hidden."[25] Additionally, Christ's Transfiguration itself denotes, in his opinion, allegorically yet very eloquently, the transition from kataphatic to apophatic theology. When the incarnated Word, he writes, "climbs together" with His disciples the mountain of theology, meaning Thavor, and is transfigured before them, then He is no longer regarded in a kataphatic manner, being called God, holy, king or any other kataphatic name, but in an apophatic manner is now called hyper-god, hyper-holy and the rest "in supremacy called" names. And this is so because only then is "the characteristic secrecy of His essence" revealed in all its greatness, a greatness upon which the human mind is completely unable to gaze in the same way that the human eye is unable to gaze at the brightness of

---

theologia, ad Timotheum, 3-5, PG 3, 1032 C - 1048 B; Maximus Confessor, *Mystagogia, Prooem*, PG 91, 664 BC.

23 See PG 91, 664 B: "Δει γαρ, είπερ ως αληθώς το γνώναι διαφοράν Θεού και κτισμάτων εστίν αναγκαίον ημίν, θέσιν είναι του υπερόντος την των όντων αφαίρεσιν· και την των όντων θέσιν, είναι του υπερόντος αφαίρεσιν."

24 See *Ad sanctissimum presbyterum ac praepositum Thalassium, De variis Scripturae Sacrae quaestionibus ac dubiis*, 25, PG 90, 333 D; C. Laga / C. Steel, *Maximi confessoris quaestiones ad Thalassium*, I (quaestiones I-LV), Corpus Christianorum, Series Graeca 7 (Turnhout / Brepols, 1980), 165: "Επί Θεού μάλλον αι καθ' υπεροχήν στερήσεις αληθεύουσι, ποσώς μηνύουσαι την θείαν θέσιν δια της των όντων παντελούς αφαιρέσεως."

25 See Quaestiones et dubia 190, 132: "... καταφασκόμενον εκ της των όντων θέσεως, αλλά τη κατά απόφασιν θεολογία παραδεικνύς το απρόσιτον της θεότητος κρύφιον."

the sun, in spite of its presumable great visual ability.[26] Consequently, St. Maximus concludes, developing a thesis similar to Gregory of Nyssa, he is deceived, the one who, while he longs to know God, believes that "the simple and beyond all intelligence one" resembles the created beings we know of and, as a result, forms in his thinking a mistaken and idolized image of God.[27] The only way for this man to be rescued from the danger of this deception is by regarding God apophatically.[28]

As both Dionysius the Areopagite and Maximus the Confessor stress, however, neither the kataphatic nor the apophatic regard of God can lead us to the true sense of God, because God, as uncreated and transcendental in His nature, is found beyond any kataphasis or apophasis.[29] St. Maximus characteristically notes that (God) "is simple and unknown and unreachable to all in His existence and utterly uninterpreted and beyond any kataphasis or apophasis."[30] With this standpoint, the above-mentioned Fathers, in their attempt to secure the true sense of God from the danger of idolization and anthropomorphism, expand so much the limits of apophatic theology that it negates

---

26 See Questiones et dubia 191, 134.

27 See Ad sanctissimum presbyterum ac praepositum Thalassium, 25, PG 90, 333 C; C. Laga – C. Steel, *Maximi confessoris*, 165. Cf. Gregory of Nyssa, *De vita Moysis, sive De perfectione vitae ex praescripto virtutis institutae*, PG 44, 377 B: "Απαγορεύει γαρ εν πρώτοις ο θείος λόγος, προς μηδέν των γινωσκομένων ομοιούσθαι παρά των ανθρώπων το Θείον· ως παντός νοήματος του κατά τινα περιληπτικήν φαντασίαν εν περινοία τινί και στοχασμώ της φύσεως γινομένου, είδωλον Θεού πλάσσοντος και ου Θεόν καταγγέλλοντος."

28 See PG 90, 333 D; C. Laga / C. Steel, *Maximi confessoris*.

29 See Dionysius Areopagite, *De mystica theologia, ad Timotheum*, 5, PG 3, 1048 AB: "Ουδέ εστιν αυτής (meaning the cause of all beings) καθόλου θέσις, ούτε αφαίρεσις· αλλά των μετ' αυτήν τας θέσεις και αφαιρέσεις ποιούντες αυτήν, ούτε τίθεμεν, ούτε αφαιρούμεν· επεί και υπέρ πάσαν θέσιν εστίν η παντελής και ενιαία των πάντων αιτία, και υπέρ πάσαν αφαίρεσιν η υπεροχή του πάντων απλώς απολελυμένου και επέκεινα των όλων"; Maximus Confessor, *Mystagogia, Prooem*, PG 91, 664 BC: "Δει γαρ, είπερ ως αληθώς το γνώναι διαφοράν Θεού και κτισμάτων εστίν αναγκαίον ημίν, θέσιν είναι του υπερόντος την των όντων αφαίρεσιν· και την των όντων θέσιν, είναι του υπερόντος αφαίρεσιν· και άμφω περί τον αυτόν κυρίως θεωρείσθαι τας προσηγορίας, και μηδεμίαν κυρίως δύνασθαι· το είναι φημί και το μη είναι. Άμφω μεν κυρίως, ως της μεν του είναι του Θεού κατ' αιτίαν των όντων θετικής· της δε καθ' υπεροχήν αιτίας του είναι πάσης των όντων αφαιρετικής· και μηδέ μίαν κυρίως πάλιν, ως ουδεμιάς την κατ' ουσίαν αυτήν και φύσιν του τι είναι του ζητουμένου θέσιν παριστώσης. Ω γαρ μηδέν το σύνολον φυσικώς κατ' αιτίαν συνέζευκται, ή ον ή μη ον· τούτω ουδέν των όντων και λεγομένων, ουδέ των μη όντων και μη λεγομένων, εικότως εγγύς."

30 See PG 91, 664 C.

and refutes even its own gnoseological meaning. But this is the Orthodox character of apophatic theology.[31] A core intention of the theological apophatism of the Greek Fathers is to turn against any potential objectification of God, which is a risk not only with kataphatic, but also with apophatic theology itself.

On these grounds, both Dionysius the Areopagite and Maximus the Confessor emphasize that if man truly wishes to know God, aside from the spiritual prerequisites of purification and enlightenment, he must come forward stripped of any meaning or knowledge and only then will he be able to see "without eyes" and know "without knowing" the one who exists beyond any sight or knowledge.[32] And this is so because the true vision and knowledge of God is found, according to them, in His being not seen and not known. According to Dionysius the Areopagite, in a thesis similar to that of Gregory of Nyssa, only when we enter the over-enlightened divine darkness can we "through our lack of sight and knowledge see and know the one who is beyond sight and knowledge, by means of not seeing and not knowing – because that is to truly see and know."[33] As Maximus the Confessor notes in the same contradictory way, "the complete silence declares God and the outmost absence of knowledge makes Him known."[34] As man goes up the rising road of knowing God, his speech is cut down; it becomes spare because he understands that not much needs to be said to describe the mystery of knowing

---

[31] As M. Begzos observes, "Apophatisch von Gott reden heisst, dass man alle Attribute Gottes, sowohl die positiven wie auch die negativen, übersteigt" ("Der Apophatismus in der ostkirchlichen Theologie: Die kritische Funktion einer traditionellen Theorie heute," in *Θεολογία* 26 [1986]: 180; cf. also 181).

[32] See Dionysios Areopagite, 2, PG 3, 1025 AB. Maximus Confessor, *Ad sanctissimum presbyterum ac praepositum Thalassium*, 25, PG 90, 333 CD.

[33] See PG 3, 1025 A: "Δι' αβλεψίας και αγνωσίας ιδείν και γνώναι τον υπέρ θέαν και γνώσιν αυτώ τω μη ιδείν μηδέ γνώναι – τούτο γαρ εστι το όντως ιδείν και γνώναι". Cf. Gregory of Nyssa, *De vita Moysis*, PG 44, 376 D – 377 A: "Προϊών δε ο νους, και δια μείζονος αεί και τελειοτέρας προσοχής εν περινοία γινόμενος της όντως κατανοήσεως, όσω προσεγγίζει μάλλον τη θεωρία, τοσούτω πλέον ορά το της θείας φύσεως αθεώρητον. Καταλιπών γαρ παν το φαινόμενον, ου μόνον όσα καταλαμβάνει η αίσθησις, αλλά και όσα η διάνοια δοκεί βλέπειν· αεί προς το ενδότερον ίεται, έως αν διαδυή τη πολυπραγμοσύνη της διανοίας προς το αθεατόν τε και ακατάληπτον, κακεί τον Θεόν ίδη. Εν τούτω γαρ η αληθής εστιν είδησις του ζητουμένου, το εν τούτω το ιδείν, εν τω μη ιδείν· ότι υπέρκειται πάσης ειδήσεως το ζητούμενον, οίον τινί γνόφω τη ακαταληψία πανταχόθεν διειλημμένον."

[34] See 65, PG 90, 756 C: "Η τελεία μόνη κέκραγε σιγή και η παντελής καθ' υπεροχήν αγνωσία παρίστησιν."

God. And when he does enter the "beyond the mind ... darkness," then he realizes that to describe this transcendental experience not even "brevity" is needed, but only the "complete wordlessness and senselessness" (παντελής αλογία και ανοησία).[35] The "multi-named" (πολυώνυμος) and "much talked of" (πολύλογος) God is then rendered for man "anonymous" and "wordless," according to the pointed characterizations of Dionysius the Areopagite.[36] But, in order for man to be able to penetrate, as another Moses, the darkness of not knowing, where God lies hidden behind "wordlessness" and "senselessness," he must, as Maximus stresses, give up his desire to know God through natural theory, that is, the theory of the created beings, and through theology. Only then can he, "through apophasis and not-knowing," receive true experience and knowledge of God.[37] In other words, the true experience and knowledge of God presupposes the apophatic attitude of man towards God, and that is exactly why the most appropriate way to describe this experience is through the use of apophatic terminology.

To understand this better, all we must do is reflect on the apophatic way in which Apostle Paul is forced to describe the experience he had, when "he was seized into paradise." "He heard," he says, "ineffable words that no man can utter."[38] By saying "he heard," he asserts the reality of the supernatural experience of God, while by characterizing these hearings as "ineffable words that no man can utter," he underscores how poor and impotent the human language is to describe such an experience. To put it differently, apophatism functions, in this case, as the only outlet to describe as well and as objectively as possible the experience of the uncreated.

The Unity and the Empirical Character of Kataphatic and Apophatic Theology

Despite the fact that there seems to be a dialectical antithesis between kataphatic and apophatic theology, for the Orthodox tradition of the Fathers no antithesis can be conceived between them. On the contrary, between the two

---

35 See Dionysios Areopagite, 3, PG 3, 1033 BC.

36 See *De divinis nominibus* 7, 1, PG 3, 865 BC; *De mystica theologia*, ad Timotheum, 1, 3, PG 3, 1000 C.

37 See Quaestiones et dubia 73, 56.

38 See 2 Cor. 12:4.

exists an indissoluble and functional unity and relationship.[39] And this is understandable because, as we stressed in the beginning, for the Fathers of the Church, kataphatic as much as apophatic theology are not the fruits of an intellectualist meditation; they are wholly founded on the divine revelation and on experience. The Fathers taste the experience of divine energies in the Creation and in History and produce positive names for God, thus making kataphatic theology. They compare the experience of God to respective experiences they have from the created reality and reach the conclusion that no name is capable of expressing the experience of the uncreated. So they are led to the production of negative names for God, thus making apophatic theology. They thereby express the same experience of the divine revelation either kataphatically or apophatically, aiming to respectively stress either the reality of the experience of God or His transcendence in relation to the created world. That is why both are used in referring to God, without juxtaposing the one with the other. Moreover, the emphasis that both Dionysius the Areopagite and Maximus the Confessor place on the fact that God is beyond any kataphasis or apophasis,[40] leaves no room for the creation of a dialectic between kataphatic and apophatic theology. As Dionysius the Areopagite says,

> We must render to It (i.e. the cause above all, that is, God) and affirm all positive attributes of the beings, as He is the cause of all, and mainly negate all these attributes, as It is the hyper-being above all, and we must not think that the apophaseis are juxtaposed with the kataphaseis, but rather that It, meaning the one that is beyond every deduction and affirmation, is further above all deprivations.[41]

39 See Dionysius Areopagita, *De mystica theologia*, ad Timotheum, 1, 2, PG 3, 1000 B. Maximus Confessor, *De variis difficilibus locis* ss. pp. Dionysii et Gregorii, ad Thomam v.s., PG 91, 1288 C: "Εναντίως ουν ταις καταφάσεσι κειμένων των αποφάσεων, εναλλάξ αλλήλαις περί Θεόν φιλικώς συμπλέκονται και αλλήλων αντιπαραλαμβάνονται οίον αι μέν αποφάσεις το μη τι είναι, αλλά τι μη είναι σημαίνουσαι το Θείον, περί το τι είναι το τούτο μη ον, ενούνται ταις καταφάσεσιν, αι δε καταφάσεις το μόνον ότι έστι, τίποτε δε τούτο εστι μη δηλούσαι, περί το μη είναι το τούτο ον ενούνται ταις αποφάσεσι, προς μεν αλλήλας δεικνύουσαι την εξ αντιθέσεως εναντιότητα, περί δε τον Θεόν τω εις άλληλα των άκρων κατά περίπτωσιν τρόπω την οικειότητα."

40 See Dionysius Areopagite, 5, PG 3, 1048 AB. Maximus Confessor, *Mystagogia, Prooem.*, PG 91, 664 BC.

41 See 1, 2, PG 3, 1000 B: "Δέον επ' αυτή και πάσας τας των όντων τιθέναι και καταφάσκειν θέσεις, ως πάντων αιτία, και πάσας αυτάς κυριώτερον αποφάσκειν, ως υπέρ πάντα υπερούση, και μη οίεσθαι τας αποφάσεις αντικειμένας είναι ταις καταφάσεσιν, αλλά πολύ πρότερον αυτήν υπέρ τας στερήσεις είναι την υπέρ πάσαν και αφαίρεσιν και θέσιν."

Still, except for the fact that no dialectical antithesis can be conceived between kataphatic and apophatic theology, there is, as we have mentioned, an indissoluble and functional unity between them. Not once in the Orthodox tradition is the one used autonomously and independently from the other. St. John Damascene even considers that the best possible way to attribute different names to God is not the autonomous kataphatic or apophatic regard of Him, but rather the functional linkage and simultaneous use of kataphatic and apophatic theology, which, for this reason, he characterizes as the "most sweet ... linkage of the two" (γλυκυτάτη ... εξ αμφοίν συνάφεια).[42] And this is wholly justifiable, as they both presuppose the same revelation and experience of God, which they also describe, aiming to formulate a real image of God, free from the qualities of the created beings. Their becoming autonomous involves serious dangers for the same essence and content of theology. The autonomous and excessive use of kataphatic theology might disregard the transcendence of the uncreated divine nature and lead to the objectification or idolization of God and to anthropomorphism. On the other hand, the autonomous and excessive use of apophatic theology might disregard the Divine Economy and lead to theological agnosticism. That's exactly why the one cannot be conceived as independent from the other, but are found in indissoluble and functional unity and relationship with one another. In the same way that kataphatic theology rescues the apophatic one from the danger of theological agnosticism, so apophatic theology rescues the kataphatic from the danger of objectifying God, or of idolization and anthropomorphism. The one works somehow like a brake for any potential deviations or misuses of the other, with the aim of keeping intact and unforged the true sense of God.

Therefore, owing to their in-between functional unity and their empirical character, these approaches preserved Orthodox theology from the danger of God's biblical nature being distorted, keeping at the same time His immanent presence as well as His transcendence in relation to the world unharmed. They excluded from Orthodox theology the danger of becoming a field of intellectualist quest or falling from the level of theology to the level of anthropology, something that unfortunately happened in the West with the catalytic contribution of Scholastic Theology.

As is well known, Scholastic theologians have accentuated the existence of three approaches that in some ways resemble the kataphatic and apophatic theology of the Church Fathers. Their perspective entails a positive route (via

42 See 1, 12, PG 94, 848 B.

affirmationis or *causalitatis*), with which they render to God positive quailties; a negative route (via negationis), with which they render to God negative qualities; and the route of eminence (via eminentiae), with which they render to God positive qualities in a superlative degree.[43] But these three routes are in fact an intellectual reference from the created to the uncreated and are not at all related to the experience of the uncreated, which, furthermore, the Scholastics underestimated against the superior value they attributed to the intellect in order to gain knowledge of God.[44] So, without the essential-for-theology empirical base, the Scholastics were led to the shaping of an anthropomorphic image of God, thereby converting, in effect, theology to anthropology. The dramatic consequences this had for the essence of Western theology and the course of Western spirituality became evident after the end of Scholasticism and especially during the nineteenth century with the emergence of philosophical atheism.

The fact that atheism as a philosophical stream was born and raised in the West is not at all accidental. Atheist philosophers rejected the existence of God because they had formed the opinion, cultivated for so many centuries by Scholastic Theology, that God is a being approachable to the human intellect and is more or less characterized by human properties, only that He has them in the superlative degree.[45] As Feuerbach characteristically maintained, virtually replicating the understanding of God according to Scholastic Theology, "All predicates, all definitions of the divine being are basically human,"[46] and, in this sense, "God's personality itself is nothing more than the distorted and objectified personality of man."[47] In other words, God did not create man in

43 See Chr. Androutsos, *Dogmatics of the Orthodox Eastern Church* (in Greek) (Athens, 1907), 47f. J. Hirschberger, *Geschichte der Philosophie*, Part I, 9th ed. (Basel / Freiburg / Vienna, 1974), 504. N.A. Matsouka, *Dogmatic and Symbolic Theology: Introduction to Theological Gnoseology*, (in Greek) (Thessalonica, 1985), 207.

44 See also Matsouka, *Dogmatic and Symbolic Theology*, 208.

45 See M.L. Farantos, *Dogmatics* II, 1 ("The Question of God"), (in Greek) (Athens, 1977), 518ff.

46 See L. Feuerbach, *Das Wesen des Christentums*, edited by Ph. Reclam Jun, 4th ed. (Stuttgart, 1989), 355: "Alle Prädikate, alle Bestimmungen des göttlichen Wesens sind grundmensch-liche." See also page 55: "... alle Bestimmungen des göttlichen Wesens sind darum Be-stimmungen des menschlichen Wesens"; and 67: "Das Geheimnis der unerschöpf-lichen Fülle der göttlichen Bestimmungen ist daher nichts andres als das Geheimnis des menschlichen als eines unendlich verschiedenartigen, unendlich bestimmbaren, aber eben deswegen sinnlichen Wesens."

47 See Feuerbach, *Das Wesen des Christentums*, 340: "Die Persönlichkeit Gottes ist also das Mittel, wodurch der Mensch die Bestimmungen und Vorstellungen seines eignen

His image and resemblance, but rather man created God in his own image and resemblance.[48] Indeed, in spite of this atheistic and generalized formulation, this is what, unfortunately, happened in the West with Scholastic Theology; that is, there was a perception of God created in the image and resemblance of man.

But although atheism as a philosophical stream was born and raised in the West, as we have said, the fact that it was acquired and introduced in the East is hardly fortuitous. We can fully understand this, if we take into consideration the fact that apophatic theology, cultivated by the great Fathers of the Eastern Church, did not allow the creation of favorable circumstances for the birth and development of atheism. Atheism, obviously, presupposes by necessity the existence of at least one positive and objectified image of God, so that the denier of God knows beforehand what he actually denies.[49] If he doesn't know it, he also can't deny it. In this sense, the theological denial of the sense of God within the frames of apophatic theology in the East did not allow the creation of a positive and objectified image of God that could be denied. And that is why theoretical atheism did not thrive in the traditional Orthodox countries of the East, but it constituted a foreign body within their spiritual inheritance and tradition.

Wesens zu Bestimmungen und Vorstellungen eines andern Wesens, eines Wesens außer ihm macht. Die Persönlichkeit Gottes ist selbst nichts anderes als die entäußerte, vergegenständlichte Persönlichkeit des Menschen". See also page 54: "Das göttliche Wesen ist nichts anderes als das menschliche Wesen oder besser: das Wesen des Menschen, abgesondert von den Schranken des individuellen, d.h. wirklichen, leiblichen Menschen, vergegenständlicht, d.h. angeschaut und verehrt als ein andres, von ihm unterschiednes, eignes Wesen"; page 69: "... so ist auch erwiesen, dass, wenn die göttlichen Prädikate Bestimmungen des menschlichen Wesens sind, auch das Subjekt derselben menschlichen Wesens ist"; and 75: "was der Mensch von Gott aussagt, das sagt er in Wahrheit von sich selbst au.s.

48 See A. Esser, "Ludwig Feuerbach," in L. Schneider (ed.). *Das Wesen der Religion*, 3rd ed. (Heidelberg, 1983), 26. S. Holm, *Religionsphilosophie* (Stuttgart, 1960), 117. See also B. M. G. Reardon, *Religious Thought in the Nineteenth Century* (illustrated from Writers of the Period) (Cambridge, 1996), 82ff.

49 For analysis of the phenomenon of atheism from a theological, philosophical, psychological, and sociological point of view see E. Coreth / J.B. Lotz, *Atheismus kritisch betrachtet. Beiträge zum Atheismusproblem der Gegenwart* (Munich / Freiburg / Br., 1971). See also B.T. Gioultsis, *Sociology of Atheism: Thematic Limits and Problems* (in Greek) (Thessalonica, 1984).

Conclusion

We come to the conclusion that the Fathers of the Eastern Orthodox Church, projecting the kataphatic and apophatic aspect of God and stressing the empirical base of kataphatic as much as of apophatic theology, have outlined the frame of the true knowledge of God and decisively contributed to the formulation of a sense of Him free from objectifications and anthropomorphisms. And this, as we have seen, had direct and substantial repercussions for the course of theology and for the spiritual inheritance and tradition of the Orthodox East, in general.

In our times, when the rapid development of technology has formed a new reality, called by some a "society of knowledge," contemporary man, either in his close or in his broader social environment, is literally bombarded with information and knowledge that creates the impression that there are no limits to man's ability to gain absolute knowledge of the universal reality. Thus it is not easy for man to understand and acknowledge the gnoseological importance of apophatism. Knowledge has for man an exclusively kataphatic character and that is why apophatism is perceived as denial of knowledge and agnosticism. And it is also typical that this view is unconditionally accepted, not only by the average man, but even by the great intellectuals of our time, despite the philosophical apophatism of Karl Jaspers, Martin Heidegger, Karl Popper and Ludwig Wittgenstein, especially with the axiomatic philosophical principle of Wittgenstein, according to whom "of what one cannot speak, he must keep silent" ("Wovon man nicht sprechen kann, darüber muss man schweigen").

But if such an optimistic gnoseological aspect could potentially be correct and apply to the created reality, it can have no application for the uncreated nature of God. On the contrary, for the limits of knowledge are in full effect and remain unsurpassable. And the case is so because the ontological gap between the created and the uncreated, as the Fathers stress in different ways and with special emphasis, does not allow gnoseological access to the uncreated on behalf of the created. To put it differently, created beings are characterized with specific gnoseological boundaries that are intertwined with their nature and they are unable to go beyond these boundaries without running the risk of deception. That is why the only way to keep the biblical sense of God intact, offending neither His relationship with the world nor His ontological transcendence, is by using kataphatic and apophatic theology in their indissoluble unity and relationship with each other.

The theological problems that are sometimes raised within the frames of interreligious contact, particularly with our current globalized social reality, through the interfacing of Christians with representatives and supporters of different religious traditions regarding the nature and the racial hypostasis of God, have no place in the Orthodox patristic theology, since they presuppose the projection of anthropomorphic representations and properties to the sphere of the divine, and convert thus the sense of God to a purely anthropomorphic reality. But, as we have seen, the use of apophatic theology in the Orthodox patristic tradition does not allow the formulation of a sense of God with anthropomorphic properties and features that are fitting for the created reality. When the Church Fathers deny, theologically, even the sense of existence to God or of properties through which God reveals Himself to the Creation and in History, we realize that they leave no space for the formulation of an objectified nature or a racial hypostasis that will do justice to a reasonable apprehension of God. The biblical sense of God is, for the Church Fathers, completely free from such kinds of anthropomorphic perceptions and objectifycations. Yet, this admirable theological conquest could not have been attained if the Church Fathers had not used kataphatic and apophatic theology simultaneously, in an unbreakable interdependent unity. And that constitutes the greatest contribution of the Fathers of the Orthodox East – a valid confrontation to the theological problems emerging and recurring for religious traditions in general regarding the sense of God in the context of globalized social reality.

Vincent Holzer

Phenomenology and Theology: A Contemporary Exit Strategy from Metaphysics

The Theoretical Conditions of the Theological Turn: Husserl's Reception in France and the Discovery of the Notion of "Intentionality"

On the occasion of an assignment from the International Institute of Philosophy to review the state of French philosophy over the last fifteen years, Dominique Janicaud identified a new phase in Husserl's reception in France. This phase is characterized by what the author of this "assessment" refers to as the "theological turn" of French phenomenology. Does this shift reflect the influence of a type of theology that is deprived of metaphysics and is therefore eager to claim for itself a new approach to "knowledge" that endows it with a more "scientific" status? This possibility would integrate phenomenology with the classic relation theology elaborated in order to justify its dependence upon philosophy. This is a paradigm inherited from the golden age of the Scholastic period – a structure perpetuating itself in a continual search of rational justification for its expression of faith.

Dominique Janicaud does not blame theologians and their uncontrollable need to annex knowledge; but he does censure three emblematic figures of contemporary French philosophy. Presumably, these figures are responsible for the "turn" of phenomenology to theology, which is problematic because it is unconfessed in its explicit intentions. For Janicaud, this "turn" is far from intrinsic to phenomenology, since its method forbids any return to a causative transcendence, and to a smaller extent, to any immediate assimilation to ontology, considering phenomenology is defined as a method. This is exactly what is problematic. Phenomenology, which conceptualizes method, becomes an ontology finally reaching fulfillment in theology. The theoretical conditions of the theological turn are somehow based in Husserl's *reception* in France, and his first reception especially. Here, Janicaud refers to an emblematic text, written by Sartre in January 1939: "Intentionality: a Fundamental Idea of Husserl's Phenomenology."

This is a foundational text, since, as Janicaud indicates, it acted as a manifesto for the new "ontological phenomenology" of the 1940s-50s. Through the concept of intentionality, Husserl gave, to Sartre and to philosophy, the means to go beyond the alternative that still opposed those in favor of idealism and realism, as if the truth in-between could still not be found today. In 1953 and in 1967, Paul Ricoeur[1] made the same observation regarding Husserl's concept of intentionality, which was the only viable alternative to honoring yet going beyond Kantian criticism.

Husserl's focus on intentionality entails conceptualizing a method that permits a return to a level below ontological assertions about the nature of consciousness or of the *cogito*, which in its Cartesian version, was different from *res extensa,* the extended thing. For Husserl, following a line of reason that concludes with its necessary isolation,[2] the *cogito* is not separated from its relation to the thing that is both thought and perceived. To understand this idea more clearly, we can refer to the changes wrought by Husserl on the founding categories of Kantian epistemology. For Husserl, the world is an infinite regulative idea [*eine unendliche regulative Idee*], as a perspective for possible objects. However, in using the Kantian category of the regulative idea, Husserl causes it to undergo a significant transformation. For Kant, the idea is not constituent; it results from understanding. On the contrary, for Husserl, the Idea does not consist in its ability to "organize" a world, i.e., ultimately making the essential connections between things or the synthesis of impressions. It rather consists in discovering the idea that completes knowledge by listening to the world. The idea is never what consciousness gives itself to make the world thinkable; it is what is given to consciousness. What Husserl calls "constitution" consists in giving meaning to what is self-presented. The constituent consciousness, although it is absolute, does not pro-

1 P. Ricoeur, "Sur la phénoménologie," in *Esprit* 21 (1953), 821-39; *idem*, "Husserl (1859-1938)," in E. Bréhier, *Histoire de la philosophie allemande*, 2nd ed. (Paris, 1967), 183-96; text also published in P. Ricoeur, *A l'école de la phénoménologie* (Paris, 1986).

2 We know that the rule of evidence is based on a first intuition, that of the cogito. This "renewal" suppresses any possibility to establish a knowledge of the existence of God in the field of sense perception. "For Cartesians, what is given is the simple object of the intellectual intention and not the complex objects of sensation .... To know reality, we have to close our eyes, plug our ears and refrain from touching; we have to turn to ourselves and, in our understanding, search for the ideas that are clear for it" (A. Koyré, *Entretiens sur Descartes* [Paris, 1962], 217-18). For Husserl, the opposition between an inside world of representation and an outside world of transcendental things is an unbearable situation, cf. Idées directrices pour une phénoménologie et une philosophie phénoménologique pures, I., § 49, 163 (117 in the German edition of the Husserliana).

duce objects in the world – it is the act through which an "object meaning" takes shape through experience. As Paul Ricoeur pointed out in 1967:

> Husserl first gives to the notion intentionality its whole meaning: any consciousness is *consciousness of* ... (consciousness here does not refer to the individual unity of a "flow of real life" but to each different *cogitatio* turned towards a different *cogitatum*). Therefore there will be as many kinds of intentionalities and "consciousnesses" as means for a cogito to turn towards something: reality, the unreal world, the past, what is wanted, what is loved, what is desired, what is judged, etc. From a strictly descriptive point of view, intentionality escapes from the alternative of realism and idealism.[3]

It is well known that Hegel had already given to phenomenology the task of including the different components of ethical, political, religious, and aesthetic experience by considering them as signs of the Mind's unique development. Husserl, however, never studied phenomenology through this teleological perspective on metaphysical nature. As Paul Ricoeur stresses, Hegel deals with a certain form of phenomenology from which theologians have learned a great deal, not because of the complexities of this great phenomenological endeavor, but because of its germinal assertion which has a double character: first, that self-manifestation is essential for the Mind, and second that the evolution of this manifestation in the consciousness of human beings is homologous with time and history.

The phenomenological revolution consists in the commonplace assertion according to which consciousness is beyond the individual and that it is so in several ways. Logical objectivity is just one of its forms, whereas perception is its most fundamental form. Logical objectivity, in this view, builds itself on this first foundation of presence, existence, and of the world lived in a perceptive way. The alternative to realism and idealism is then overtaken by the

---

3 P. Ricoeur, "Husserl," 189. Cf. also p. 191: "[It clearly appears that] 'constituting' is not building, and even less creating, but it actually is unfolding the designs of conscious-ness mixed up in the natural, thoughtless, and naïve capture of a thing." After all, that is the meaning of the eidetic renewal that aims at deepening the phenomenological reduction by preventing any dissipation of different types of constitution. The eidetic look gives access to the categories of the being. It is always a matter of unveiling the subjective operations that give rise to a world. That is all the meaning of epoche. The latter does not make the world disappear but reveals it in its being, relative to subjectivity, and therefore in its own being. In a certain way, one must force oneself out of the world to know it better, that is to say to go from the natural attitude to the idea of science and of its ideal unification task. Epoche is precisely conceived as a suspension of judgement where all transcendental objects exist. Only this operation can make the world appear as constituted.

fact that the object transcends consciousness, and that, correlatively, the object is *inside* the consciousness because it appears to this constituent consciousness. Outside of this correlation, nothing is known and nothing is given. The double and false exteriority of consciousness and the object gives way to a philosophy of being in the world. Its themes are also those of intersubjectivity, as found in Husserl's last work in phenomenology.

The above can be easily understood since the correlation between the subject and the world, unveiled by intentionality, necessarily extends to a new relation, that of the link among multiple consciousnesses, that junction where the objectivity of perceptions can be expressed and made explicit. This is why for Husserl, descriptive phenomenology is linked to transcendental phenomenology. Indeed, Husserl professes neither rude sensualism nor naïve realism. For him, it is all about examining the meaning of intentionality. This can only be achieved through a "deepening of the transcendental distanciation regarding experience," most certainly inherited from Kant, but avoiding the radicality of Kant's split between the phenomenon and the noema.[4] Husserl's transcendental "I" does not relinquish the truth of idealism but gets rid of its Platonicism and its metaphysical correlate. There is no such thing as a realm of essences that would tower above perceptible reality. The essence of intentionality must be sought in phenomenal immanence, which is the very meaning of this other fundamental expression: intentional transcendence.[5] Con-

4 "Basically, phenomenology was born as soon as, setting aside – temporarily or permanently – the question of the being, we treated the way things appear as an autonomous problem," (P. Ricoeur, "Sur la phenomenologie," 821).

5 D. Janicaud, *La phénoménologie éclatée* (Paris, 1998), 33. In phenomenology, the consciousness at first does not know through representation, it is always the aim of something, the intentional aim of an object. Husserlian phenomenology believes that any individual reality belongs to or pertains to an essence and that this essence is accessible by the mind, the ultimate aim of knowledge. But these essences are not existences themselves. They have to be defined as meaning (vision of essences, eidetics) or sense structures and the intelligible data of the experience has to be precisely described. The radical and initial question of phenomenology is as follows: from which layers of original meaning is the intentional meaning of nature, mind, thing, and world created? How is the eidetic meaning formed, or the meaning of these eidetic objects that are nature, the thing, the world, the mind, the horizon, the figure, etc.? It is true that for Husserl, consciousness asserts itself as transcendental, not because it appears under the conditions of a priori knowledge, but because it is an absolute fact. Also, Husserl makes a distinction between the transcendental "I" and consciousness (E. Husserl, *Méditations cartésiennes*, transl. Marc de Launay [Paris, 1994], § 11, 69). Brigitte McGuire clearly expresses this: "Through the word transcendental, Husserl refers to the same subjectivity as Descartes, however it is not a res cogitans, a thing

cerning knowledge, intentional transcendence is not reduced to an affinity between the thought and the object. To understand what the phenomenological method is, representation has to be opposed to intentionality. Consciousness is not the pure presence to the self of an interiority capable of giving a representation of the world. The constituent consciousness is not a subject's awareness of a pure activity producing thought. Of course, intentional consciousness provides meaning and the act of meaning contains the essence of intentionality. But here, the consciousness is a "center of enlightenment," and as it orientates its own clarity toward the world, it enables it to show itself and to appear as a phenomenon. In accordance with this, consciousness comes out of itself to be in proximity to objects. Intentionality of knowing does not produce unity of the world through knowledge or an act of synthesis. The unity of the world is experienced as "already done or already here" (*déjà faite ou déjà là),*[6] according to Merleau-Ponty.

How Does This "Turn" Happen?

According to Janicaud, the fundamental *dissociation* achieved by phenomenology allows this theological "turn" to happen. In fact, the word "dissociation" is a loan word from Paul Ricoeur's famous typology of phenomenology, and it refers to the dissociation between the being and the appearance. This fundamental dissociation is also the basis of the alternative between metaphysics and phenomenology. When we mention phenomena, what do we mean? It is a matter of identifying how things, values, people, and any reality appear in relation with "an eventual absolute reality."[7] The shift to theology happens through an identification of this absolute reality thanks to the *concepts* of phenomenology rather than its methods. Yet Husserl never completely articulated this and consequently he never positively asserted that there was a transcendence of God that directly depended on the transcendence of meaning. Numerous contemporary philosophers, and important ones such

---

already constituted, but a subjectivity that simply constitutes transcendent things, as meaningful entities that have their own value, and that it can keep and fulfil freely. First monadically and then intermonadically," (B. McGuire, "L'origine monadique de la logique de Husserl," in *Les Etudes philosophiques* [Paris, 1998], 163).

6 M. Merleau-Ponty, *Phénoménologie de la perception* (Paris, 1945), XII (Preface).

7 P. Ricoeur, "Sur la phenomenologie," 822.

as Lévinas, Marion, and Henry, tend to change the original meaning of Husserlian intentionality into an "intention" of meaning or an "intentionality of transcendence." They insert transcendent into the immanent field of meanings to elevate phenomenology. According to Dominique Janicaud, this operation is a "jamming" (*brouillage*). "In fact, phenomenology has been kidnapped by a theology that eclipses its name."[8] This phenomenon is simple. It consists in the use of phenomenology's concepts combined with descriptions from spiritual, religious experience. According to Lévinas, it is represented by the Bible and its Talmudic commentaries. According to Jean-Luc Marion, it is the *call-and-answer structure* that characterizes the religious experience in its dimensions of abandonment and expropriation. Its fundamental model is the Christ like nature. In other words, Janicaud points to an attempt at expropriating theological referents – referents that should be beholden to the origin they lack, but that are instead conceived on the basis of phenomenological principles. Consequently, we are confronted with two types of subversion: the first is contained within philosophy; the second affects theology from the side of philosophy. In a certain way, phenomenology becomes the *tertium quid.*

We cannot analyze in detail the works criticized. This is not our purpose. What matters is our consideration of the confusion that affects philosophers when they are faced with a literature that professed itself as strictly philosophical, but tends to avoid, or at least not to respect, the rules and limits of immanence. But only immanence makes it possible for phenomenology to consider itself a "strict science of foundation." Dominique Janicaud's critical questions were the same as Jacques Derrida's regarding *Réduction et Donation* by Jean-Luc Marion. The latter conceives a phenomenon called "pure donation," which is first linked to the phenomenological primacy of the appearance as we identified it earlier. But this phenomenon of "pure donation" does not have a specific form. Marion thinks it should be understood as a "pure form" of the "donation" and the "call." This conception of what cannot be objectivized does not require phenomenological methodology in order to be coherently expressed and thought. It can resort to the Christian tradition or revival of apophatism and it can even be initiated by it. If the sources of the phenomenological ideas of Michel Henry were reviewed and updated, we would easily prove that its model comes from the mystical thought of Eck-

8 D. Janicaud, *Le tournant théologique de la phénoménologie française* (Combas, 1981), 31.

hart. And these references are admitted and explicitly treated in his impressive work, *L'Essence de la Manifestation.*

Consequently, the fundamental question is still the same. It deals with the outcome of the phenomenologies of Lévinas, the "Other" (*l'Autre*); of Marion; "the pure donation" (*la donation pure*);of Michel Henri, "the archi-revelation" (*l'archi-révélation*);[9] and, to a smaller extent, of the last work by Merleau-Ponty, "The Openness to the Invisible" (*l'ouverture à l'Invisible*). There clearly has been a shift in phenomenology in France over the last thirty years. The question now remains: Is there a feature that distinguishes it from the first reception of Husserl and Heidegger, and is this feature the break with immanent phenomenality?"[10]

The question disappears when it comes to understanding the sources of the unconfessed intentions of Emmanuel Lévinas's ideas. Indeed, they would especially be exposed to the "disaster and the catastrophe of an abandonment of the phenomena,"[11] which would benefit from ingenuous language tricks or *petitio principii.* The absolute precedence of the Other is asserted, but without any possible understanding, any determination of concrete objects. In a very harsh indictment, Janicaud asserts that "the description is no longer heuristic. It just gently places its images into an edifying place whose conceptuality has been forever blocked on the Other .... This "phenomenology" is reduced to the edifying, clear evocation of a disembodied caress and a cold eroticism."[12] The statement is harsh, but it must be taken seriously because it objectively detects a trend of conceptual corruption. This trend is intra-philosophical since, as seen earlier, Janicaud does not accuse theologians, but philosophers. Consequently, this means that theologians can and should take a stand concerning these bypassing phenomena. The judgment given by Janicaud cannot be appealed against. "Consequently, phenomenology has impulsed a return to the origin which is discovered as an extreme extenuation of any experience."[13] The methodological processes implemented result in a restoration of essen-

---

9 What Michel Henry calls in *C'est moi la Vérité*, "the phenomenological self-affection of the absolute Life."

10 Janicaud, *Le tournant theologique*, 8.

11 Janicaud, *Le tournant theologique*, 18.

12 Janicaud, *Le tournant theologique*, 30. The French philosopher from Nice alludes to the parts of Totalité et infini in which any relation to others is radically disobjectivized.

13 Janicaud, *Le tournant theologique*, 30.

tialism, although the latter comes on top of a negative theology. "In the absolute unity of his radical immanence, the being affects and tests himself so that it feels everything in him, and every content which transcends his self-experience affects him."[14] This assertion can link the ideas of Michel Henry to the Hegelian version of phenomenology; that is, "the immanence of the absolute mind to its phenomenal manifestations."[15] As Janicaud remarks, a great difference must be underlined. The divine immanence escapes into representation and knowledge objectivization. In a surprising speculative move, M. Henry's "religious" phenomenology thus links the development of Martin Heidegger's ontological difference to a "phenomenology of the invisible" and a phenomenology of Life whose affectivity constitutes the essence.[16] Indeed, affectivity is the essence of life; it can be felt – you have to feel it and let yourself be "affected" by its passive radicality. The series of oppositions between life and the world, affectivity and exteriority, immediacy and what is external seems to constitute a "contradiction" which is part of the immanence of a self-phenomenalization of Life. The conditions of the possible places for its development are always discredited as places of untruth. They are subjected to the illusory empire of exteriority and objectivization. Nature, language, and history are all the negation of absolute life, and they are never conceived as the possible place for its eternal development. Can we say again that the phenomenology of the invisible is no more than a philosophical version of negative theology?

---

14 M. Henry, *L'essence de la manifestation* (Paris, 1963), 858. Does the reader need to be reminded of the fact that for M. Henry, the self-affection of the absolute phenomenological life is opposed to the duality created by the thought operating a scission between essence and manifestation? From a phenomenological point of view, it is the opposition between philosophy of the world and philosophy of Life. The first conceives the truth in the exteriority of the world, through language, whereas the second conceives the truth as a self-revelation only supported by itself and therefore always rejected from the world conditions. Janicaud reveals a paradox. This Life is the place of an immanent experience. But self-affection continues to be "the one of life, not historical, unfinished, but forever and mysteriously linked to the self," (Janicaud, *Le tournat théologique*, 59).

15 Janicaud, *Le tournant theologique*, 61.

16 The expression "phenomenology of the invisible" was created by Heidegger in 1973 during the Zärhingen, cf. *Questions IV* (Paris, 1976).

Dominique Janicaud, the Theologians' Best Friend

In *Ideen*, published in 1913, Husserl wrote that the world constitution, in its unity, its rationality, and "in" the pure consciousness, leads transcendental subjectivity to the idea of a transcendent foundation. Once again, Husserl differentiated himself from Kant on a decisive question of teleology and receptivity to knowledge, which is not determined by human finiteness. The argument according to which the limits of human knowledge lie in people's receptivity [sensibility] is not a proof of its unabsoluteness, because the absolute being is precisely "the being which constitutes the world [Welt-konstituierende]."[17] Consequently, the idea of God is required because of the "immanent teleology"[18] associated with facts – not because facts issue from the world's being. "It is not the fact in itself (*Faktum*), but the fact as a source of possibilities and realities whose values are set according to an increasing order to infinity, which forces us to ask the question of foundation (*Grund*) and which gives "rational reasons" (*Vernunftgründe*) to think that there is a 'divine being' external to the world."[19]

In his impressive study dedicated to the Husserlian theme of teleology, Arion L. Kelkel underlines that the *Nachwort* to *Ideen*, published in 1930 as a preface to *Ideen I*, confirms the "metaphysical ambition" of phenomenology. It could be argued that metaphysics plays no part in the field of phenomenological description, since Husserl contemplates a philosophy of history. The "great *factum* of the absolute being" is history, the field where the last questions "form a unity with the questions about the absolute direction of history."[20] The program conceived by Husserl is at the crossroads of pheno-menology and metaphysical teleology, "making the latent reason evolve into the understanding of one's possibilities, and thus discovering the possibility of metaphysics as a real possibility is the only way to begin the great work of metaphysics; that is, of a universal philosophy."[21]

---

17 A.L. Kelkel, *Le legs de la phénoménologie* (Paris, 2002), 92.

18 Kelkel, *Le legs de la phénoménologie*, 94.

19 *Ideen zu einer reinen phänomenologischen Philosophie*, Erstes Buch in Husserliana, III, § 58, 139, French translation, 191, quoted by A. L. Kelkel, *Le legs de la phénoménologie*, 94.

20 Husserliana, VIII, 506, quoted by A. L. Kelkel, *Le legs de la phénoménologie*, 97.

21 Kelkel, *Le legs de la phénoménologie*, 13.

From the perspective of "essence," Husserl's phenomenology can clearly be understood as a form of transcendental idealism, since according to it, the infinite universe of meaning is accessed through a consciousness that determines the being of phenomena. This has major consequences for the philosophy of knowledge. Truth can no longer be defined as a correspondence between the thought and the object, nor as a pure relation in thought.

Ultimate Questions

Are Husserl's ultimate findings in philosophy in any way useful to theology, or should we give up the convenient "assumption" [*Aufhebung*] that phenomenological categories apply? Moreover, in the context of French philosophy, a clear shift can be observed from classic Husserlian phenomenology [descriptive phenomenology of intentional objects] to a "phenomenology of the unapparent" from Martin Heidegger; however, this conception is exposed to the "disaster and the catastrophe of an abandonment of the phenomena."[22] The source of this assumption phenomenon is not theologians, but philosophers who come over to theology. Because of them, theology undergoes fundamental changes that could be considered illegitimate on the grounds of a tradition of faith and of theological epistemologies that have proved themselves. Thus, Michel Henry, in his book *C'est moi la Vérité*, harshly confronts a perspective whose entire tradition consists in the acknowledgement of the indomitable transcendence of a free and creative God. This book tries to bring back this so-called transcendence and even the peculiarity of the dogmas supporting it, to the immanent structure of Life, as self-affection and pure presence to the self. We clearly see that we are discussing more than a theology that eclipses its name. The questions discussed remain philosophical. They especially deal with the possibility of phenomenology substituting itself for metaphysics by going beyond metaphysics through its capacity to open itself to transcendence, the absolute and the origin. Are these theological questions of the highest importance? We have our doubts, just as we doubt the relevance of Jean-Luc Marion's invitation to today's theologians. Obviously, there is a "conflict" between epistemologies.

---

22 Janicaud, *Le tournant théologique*, 18.

Georg Essen

Ethical Monotheism and Human Freedom: Theological Convergences with the Pluralism of the Modern Age

1. From the perspective of the history of religion, monotheism has almost inevitably proven to be the highest form of religion. In contrast, polytheism seems to belong to an historically outdated epoch, and in any case to be a sign of decline. Just for once, there is no dissension on this point between faith and reason, or between theology and philosophy: The God of Abraham, Isaac, and Jacob, who is also the God of Jesus, is witnessed to and believed in as the one and only God, and the God of philosophy is the One as well, since, for reason, anything else would be a scandal.

But if one takes a closer look, things are clearly not as simple as they seem. Contrary to the way in which monotheism is taken for granted and considered to be philosophically and religiously true, a rejection of monotheism, which is in part quite fierce, confronts us time and again in the modern age. This occurs above all in the context of political theories. Monotheism is regarded as suspicious because it is said to be anti-modern. According to the accusation, monotheism, understood as political monotheism, entered into an alliance with European absolutism in the early modern age. Political monotheism is put into a position here in which it opposes the model of the modern constitutional state, a state based on the principle of the separation of powers. The achievements of the French Revolution were the subject matter of this debate. The French Revolution supported freedom, equality, and brotherhood and was thus the force behind the universal recognition of human rights. On the other hand, through the French Revolution, the idea of the sovereignty of the people, the idea that all state authority comes from the people, became the basis for modern, democratic state systems.

So-called political philosophers of the counter-revolution such as Bonald, de Maistre and Friedrich Julius Stahl tried to entrench an absolutist idea of sovereignty over against this principle of the sovereignty of the people, which they opposed.[1] Here divine sovereignty and rule became the prototype for the

[1] Cf. J. Moltmann, *Trinität und Reich Gottes. Zur Gotteslehre*, 2nd corr. ed. (Munich, 1986), 207–20; Eng. ed.: *The Trinity and the Kingdom: The Doctrine of God*, transl.

sovereignty of the state. The old theocratic idea of one God, one emperor, one empire was taken up to justify the ideal of a monarchical centralized state: The absolutist ruler who can always freely exercise supreme, complete, direct, and universal power, which is due to him alone, corresponds to God's absolute power of disposition over everything he has created and which is dependent upon him. For his part, this ruler is bound neither by the constitution nor by law and regulation.

It is true that these theories concerning a premodern understanding of the state date from the seventeenth and eighteenth centuries and are no longer advocated as such today. But the interlocking of monotheism and an absolutist understanding of the state encountered here was still prevalent in the twentieth century and is being discussed seriously again today. This is of course not happening because of a desire to establish an absolutistic monarchy, but for the following reason: Modern societies are characterized by the pluralization of forms of life and by the individualization of lifestyles. They are en route to becoming multicultural and multireligious.[2] These developments, in turn, raise the questions of how much homogeneity a society really needs and what connects the people who live in it. This whole issue becomes more critical if one looks at it in light of the modern constitutional state. The democratic state founded on the rule of law would sacrifice its character of freedom if it chose to impose unity and homogeneity in a plurally constituted society by means of legal coercion.

Against this background, it was inevitable that political science and philosophy would once again become aware of a lawyer who has developed his own understanding of the state in close contact with those I have called the "political philosophers of the counter-revolution." I am referring to the German constitutional lawyer Carl Schmitt. For a long time one steered clear of him because he had been the so-called crown lawyer of National Socialism.[3]

---

by Margaret Kohl (San Francisco, 1981), reprinted with new preface (Minneapolis, 1993).

2 Cf. J. A. Ven, "Faith in God in a Secularised Culture," in *Bulletin European Theology* 9 (1998): 21–46; J.A. Ven and A. Beauregard, "Religion in Secular Society," in *Pastoral Sciences* 17 (1998): 5-20; W. Gräb *et al.* (eds.), *Christentum und Spätmoderne* (Stuttgart, 2000).

3 Cf. C. Schmitt, *Politische Theologie: Vier Kapitel zur Lehre von der Souveränität*, 2nd edition, (Munich *et al.*, 1934). (The phrase "political philosophy of the counter-revolution" can be found here on p. 67.) Eng. ed.: *Political Theology: Four Chapters on the Concept of Sovereignty*, transl. by George Schwab (Cambridge, 1985); *idem*, *Po-*

Schmitt had already grappled with the issue that modern states were struggling for their inner homogeneity. His studies led him to the view that states depend on a homogeneity concept that aims at a "substance of equality." But this substance must be protected from what is foreign and unequal. Consequently – and at this point things get nasty – the mainstay of democracy's political power is viewed as the fact that it knows how to reject or to keep at bay whatever threatens its homogeneity. For this reason, and if necessary – and now I will quote in German – the "Ausscheidung oder Vernichtung des Heterogenen" is part of democracy. [4] That is vocabulary intolerable to German ears, but not to them alone! The peculiar topicality of this thinking can, presumably, only be explained by the heightened uncertainty that characterizes modern societies and states today. And the proposal that Carl Schmitt's thinking represents leaves no room for ambiguity. The state and society are caught in a crisis for want of unity and homogeneity. Where pluralism rules, a misfortune has occurred that must be righted – namely, by giving priority to unity over diversity.

2. The theologian Erik Peterson already pointed out in 1935 that Schmitt's pre-democratic and totalitarian concept of the state was a legacy of monotheism; namely, in the words of Peterson, of "political monotheism."[5] This concept points to the interlocking of Christian monotheism with the philosophical monotheism of Greek philosophy. Peterson claims that this Hellenization of the biblical belief in God is, in turn, the real fall or sin of humankind, which

---

litische Theologie II: Die Legende von der Erledigung jeder Politischen Theologie (Berlin, 1970). Cf. B. Wacker (ed.), *Die eigentlich katholische Verschärfung ...: Konfession, Theologie und Politik im Werk Carl Schmitts* (Munich, 1994); J. Taubes (ed.), *Der Fürst dieser Welt: Carl Schmitt und die Folgen*, Religionstheorie und Politische Theologie, vol. 1 2nd rev. ed., (Paderborn *et al.*, 1985); J. Manemann, *Carl Schmitt und die Politische Theologie: Politischer Anti-Monotheismus*, Münsterische Beiträge zur Theologie, vol. 61 (Münster, 2002), 340-44.

4 "First, homogeneity is necessarily a part of democracy, and second – if necessary – the elimination or destruction of heterogeneity... The political strength of a democracy shows itself in that it knows how to dispose of or keep away what is foreign and unequal, that which threatens homogeneity. The question of equality is, namely, not a matter of abstract, logical-arithmetic frivolities, but concerns the substance of equality...." C. Schmitt, *Die geistesgeschichtliche Lage des heutigen Parlamentarismus*, 6th ed., (Berlin, 1985), 14; Eng. ed.: *The Crisis of Parliamentary Democracy* (Cambridge, 1984).

5 Cf. E. Peterson, *Der Monotheismus als politisches Problem: Ein Beitrag zur Geschichte der politischen Theologie im Imperium Romanum* (Leipzig, 1935).

gave the West an anti-democratic political theology that smacks of totalitarianism. Why? Because Western metaphysics has been marked by the theme of "the one and the many" right from the beginning. In its definitive expressions, metaphysics presented itself as a doctrine of All-Oneness, emphasizing the priority of the one over the many and understanding the one as the source and foundation of everything.[6] As a universal theory, the claim of the metaphysical understanding of oneness also included the areas of the cosmological and the political. The universal empire, which unites cities and states, is subordinated to the regulating rule of the One in the same way that the world is. Peterson summarizes this thought as follows: "The one God, the one king in heaven and the one kingly *nomos* and *logos*, corresponds to the one king on earth."[7] According to Peterson, this monotheistic justification of political power entered into an ominous alliance with Christianity. The reshaping (indeed the alienation) of Christian belief in God through the Hellenistic way of thinking about Oneness ultimately found its political equivalent in Emperor Constantine's ideology of the state. In this ideology, the idea of Oneness or unity is said to have projected in God the idea of the universal, centralized church and the universal, centralized state: "One God – one emperor – one church – one empire."[8]

It is no wonder that monotheism understood in *this* way – as I would explicitly like to add – had to be discredited in the modern age. The great plague epidemics and the turmoil of the so-called Western Schism, during which the order of the medieval cosmos broke up, stood at the beginning of the "great upheaval" between the Middle Ages and the modern age, an upheaval which started in the middle of the fourteenth century and gained dynamic force in

---

6 This idea is actually obvious: The reality we are familiar with and which we encounter in normal experience is diverse, chaotic, and manifold. But it is part of a one's lifelong interest as a human being to orient oneself in one's world, and to do so with the goal of acquiring a foothold and security in the world in order to plan one's life in a reliable way. This search for identity is in turn articulated in a striving for knowledge that seeks to discover the ultimate unity as a foundation of all that is manifold and to name the ultimate source of everything that is present in the world. For its part, however, the source can only be conceived of as oneness, since each instance of diversity and multeity presupposes the foundation of diversity and multeity. If we also add that this oneness must be thought of as infinite and immortal, then it is only consistent to identify the one with the truly divine.

7 This quote from the so-called "Tricentenary Address" of Emperor Constantine is cited by Peterson on page 78 of *Der Monotheismus*.

8 Moltmann, *Trinität*, 212.

the fifteenth century. By the time of the Reformation at the beginning of the sixteenth century, it had become completely clear that the harmonious reconciliation of society in the one body of Christ could no longer succeed. In fact, this form of providing unity had thoroughly disgraced itself. The shock of the denominational civil wars in the seventeenth and eighteenth centuries – known in the Netherlands as the Eighty Years War or, more precisely, as the Rebellion against Spain, and in Germany as the Thirty Years War – was so great that the medieval idea of *ordo* broke into pieces. The attempt to guarantee the order of nature and society through divine institutions had become suspect. The modern age mistrusted any theory that offered to reveal the world or to make it accessible by entrusting the reconciliation of difference and diversity to a metaphysical-theological concept of Oneness that sought to embrace society, the state, and the church at one and the same time.

Here I would like to call to mind, in particular, the genesis of the modern democratic, constitutional state because this history can make us aware of three things. First, we cannot really understand the modern notion of the state and society and, in its wake, the pluralism of the modern age if we do not return to that historical-social constellation in which a particular religious-metaphysical concept of Oneness thoroughly collapsed.[9]

Second, I would like to at least suggest that this historical collapse of the concept of Oneness in the modern age has left an irritating empty space to this day. The Hungarian philosopher Agnes Heller coined the metaphor of the "empty chair" for this space.[10] It is not at all surprising that we can also understand the project of the modern age as a "game of musical chairs," if I may put it that way: as a battle to occupy this one empty chair. As we know, however, this battle was anything but a children's game; it was serious in a very bloody way. If I may add, we can probably understand the European phenomenon of rightwing populism in Austria, the Netherlands, Germany, and elsewhere if we interpret it as a reaction to the blank space just mentioned. To clarify this point, I would like to draw your attention to two examples: Whether we look at the current discussion in the Netherlands on the integration of foreigners or at the strange German debate about the concept of a

---

9 Cf. H. Verweyen, *Gottes letztes Wort: Grundriß der Fundamentaltheologie* (Düsseldorf, 1991), 204-32, especially 214-22; *idem*, *Theologie im Zeichen der schwachen Vernunft* (Regensburg, 2000), 48-53.

10 Cf. A. Heller, "Politik nach dem Tod Gottes," in *Jahrbuch Politische Theologie* 2 (1997): 67–87, quote found on page 87.

"defining or guiding culture," in both instances the dispute focuses on the balance between homogeneity and plurality in an open society. In other words, the theme of "the one and the many" which has haunted philosophy since its beginnings in Greek antiquity has once again come to a head in a dramatic way in the modern age.

Third, the mood has radically changed again since the terror attacks of September 11th, 2001; it is no longer tinted in a postmodern way. This is obvious, among other things, from the fact that the criticism of Western thinking in the category of Oneness, a criticism which calls itself modern, directly, and in part aggressively, makes biblical monotheism liable for violence, terror, hate, and discord. From the most recent remarks that criticize monotheism, I will only quote one by the philosopher Richard Dawkins, who reacted to the events of September 11th with an article in *The Guardian*. This article was meaningfully entitled "Religion's Misguided Missiles" and it concluded with the sentence "To fill a world with religions, or religions of the Abrahamic kind, is like littering the streets with loaded guns. Do not be surprised if they are used."[11] The situation, however, is one in which this escalation – other examples from different countries could easily be found – has a long past history; September 11th was only a catalyst for the more recent discussion, as it were. The theory that there is a connection between monotheism and intolerance has been under discussion for a long time, not only in Europe, but also in the entire Anglo-Saxon world. The beginnings of this discussion can be traced back to the nineteenth century. In what follows, however, I am not going to discuss this debate as a whole. Instead, I would like to limit myself to one position which, as I see it, stands out by embedding the topic of "monotheism and intolerance" in fundamental considerations concerning a hermeneutics of intercultural or interreligious dialogue.

3. The renowned Egyptologist and cultural anthropologist Jan Assmann published *Moses the Egyptian: The Memory of Egypt in Western Monotheism* in 1997.[12] The book is fascinating and stimulating as well as extremely explo-

11 R. Dawkins, "Religion's Misguided Missiles," in *The Guardian* (Saturday, September 15, 2001). I am grateful to Klaus Müller for pointing me to Dawkins: Cf. K. Müller, "Monotheismus unter Generalverdacht: Philosophisches zu einem aktuellen, aber nicht ganz neuen Phänomen," in T. Söding (ed.), *Ist der Glaube Feind der Freiheit? Die neue Debatte um den Monotheismus*, QD, vol. 196 (Freiburg *et al.*, 2003), 176-213.

12 Cf. J. Assmann, *Moses the Egyptian: The Memory of Egypt in Western Monotheism* (Cambridge, 1997). In the following presentation I refer to the German translation that Assmann prepared. Cf. *idem*, *Moses der Ägypter: Entzifferung einer Gedächtnisspur*, 3rd ed. (Frankfurt a. M., 2001). (The page numbers given in the text refer to the Ger-

sive and provocative; it unleashed controversial discussions in many places.[13] Assmann's intention was to investigate and to change the European history of ideas "from the perspective of Egypt." His programmatic claim consists in overcoming or abolishing biblical monotheism. In the process, he pursues an objective that parallels exactly the line of discussion I have already named in my lecture.

The discovery of biblical monotheism, which the Jewish-Christian tradition connects to the figure of Moses, led to consequences which, according to Assmann, are simply disastrous: The Jewish belief in God established itself as a "counter-religion" based on a principle that Assmann calls the "Mosaic distinction." This concept characterizes a type of religion that is said to be revolutionary in that it was the first to introduce the distinction between "true" and "false" into the world of religions and cultures. Assmann asserts that this distinction has not only constructed a universe full of meaning, identity, and orientation, but also one – and this is what is important – "full of conflict, intolerance, and violence" (p. 17 [Eng. ed., p. 1]). The problem linked with this monotheism is not just that "every construction of identity by the very same process generates alterity" (p. 18 [Eng. ed., p. 2]). No, the keystone of Assmann's criticism is a different one: Unlike ancient polytheism, biblical monotheism was not familiar with "techniques of translation" which would have made cultural and religious distinctions more accessible or at least more trans-

---

man edition. If the reference is from the English edition or can be found there, this is noted in square brackets with the addition "Eng. ed.").

13 Cf. among others K. Koch, "Monotheismus als Sündenbock?" in *Theologische Literaturzeitung* 124 (1999): 874-84; G. Kaiser, "War der Exodus der Sündenfall? Fragen an Jan Assmann anläßlich seiner Monographie Moses der Ägypter," in *Zeitschrift für Theologie und Kirche* 98 (2001): 1-24; R. Rendtorff, "Ägypten und die 'Mosaische Unterscheidung'," in D. Becker, ed., *Mit dem Fremden leben: Perspektiven einer Theologie der Konvivenz*, Theo Sundermeier zum 65. Geburtstag, Kunst – Hermeneutik – Ökumene, vol. 2, Missionswissenschaftliche Forschungen, new series, vol. 11/12) (Erlangen, 2000), 113-22; E. Zenger, "Was ist der Preis des Monotheismus? Die heilsame Provokation von Jan Assmann," in *Herder Korrespondenz* 55 (2001): 186-91; R. Kessler, *Die Ägyptenbilder der Hebräischen Bibel: Ein Beitrag zu neueren Monotheismusdebatte*, Stuttgarter Bibelstudien, vol. 197 (Stuttgart, 2000). Cf. J. Assmann, "Die 'Mosaische Unterscheidung' und die Frage der Intoleranz: Eine Klarstellung," in R. Kloepfer and B. Dücker (eds.), *Kritik und Geschichte der Intoleranz*, (Heidelberg, 2000): 185-94; *idem*, "Es bleibt die Unterscheidung zwischen wahrer und falscher Religion," in *Frankfurter Allgemeine Zeitung* (December 28, 2000): 54; *idem*, *Die Mosaische Unterscheidung oder der Preis des Monotheismus* (Munich / Vienna, 2003).

parent. Assmann sees the cultural achievement of ancient polytheism[14] in the circumstance of its acquaintance with cosmic deities, which were worshiped in different religions under different names respectively, yet in such a way that their cosmic aspects and functions always remained identifiable and indisputable: "The sun god of one religion is easily equated to the sun god of another religion, and so forth" [Eng. ed., p. 3]. The fact that the divine names of the different religions could be translated on the basis of this functional equivalence resulted in a "reciprocal translatability of the polytheistic deities" and represents a "great cultural achievement" (p. 19). The gods were "international because they were cosmic" [Eng. ed., p. 3]. Assmann says that this is also the reason why no one disputed the reality of foreign deities in polytheistic religions. The "concept of a false religion was completely alien to antique polytheism" (p. 19).

Assmann contends, however, that monotheism, which Judaism and Christianity connect with the name of Moses, is different. It lacks a technique of translation that makes tolerance possible because belief in Yahweh as the one and only God concomitantly declares polytheism, which is cosmically oriented, to be an excluded falsehood. But why does biblical monotheism prevail as a "counter-religion"? This has to do with its "revolutionary" character as a religion of revelation. For where the one God who transcends the world reveals himself, he also expels other deities "into the realm outside of the religion meant for him, i.e., outside the world he has created and the truth he has revealed."[15] Moreover, there is no "evolutionary" or "natural" path from error to the truth claim of monotheism.[16] "This truth can come only from the outside, by way of revelation" (p. 24 [Eng. ed., p. 7]). In turn, the exclusivity of revelation produces results in the realm of history insofar as the antagonistic constellation inherent in revelation becomes identity forming with reference to history (cf. p. 24f. [Eng. ed., p. 7]). Biblical monotheism is exclusive – it excludes all else because the one true God ("Moses as a figure of memory" represents this as well) chooses a people and binds to himself humans who

14 Cf. Assmann, *Moses*, 73–82. See below.

15 Cf. J. Assmann, "Monotheismus und Kosmotheismus: Ägyptische Formen eines 'Denkens des Einen' und ihre europäische Rezeptionsgeschichte," presented on April 24, 1993, Sitzung der Heidelberger Akademie der Wissenschaften, Philosophisch-Historische Klasse, 1993, report 2 (Heidelberg, 1993), 47.

16 With respect to the distinction between revolutionary and evolutionary monotheism, see below.

move out "from the existing world into a new world of uncompromising immediacy," in which "God's will is fulfilled in an uncompromising way."[17]

As a consequence of this, biblical monotheism also professes a "jealous" God who, according to Assmann, demands love "with all one's heart, with all one's soul and with all one's strength" (p. 268). Yahweh not only binds the individual exclusively to himself, but also chooses a people for himself and creates a new social order.

Biblical monotheism constructs cultural foreignness and champions confrontation. Whoever professes the true God rejects both the reality of foreign deities and the legitimacy of foreign forms of worship.[18] This construction of "the excluded other" finds its expression in that "Grand Narrative" which is, like no other story, foundational for the biblical tradition: the "Exodus myth,"

---

17 J. Assmann, *Herrschaft und Heil: Politische Theologie in Altägypten, Israel und Europa* (Munich *et al.*, 2000), 261f. 247-64.The counter-figure to the biblical tradition is the idea of a presence of divine rule and justice as a representation and, through representation, as an idea that is connected to the Egyptian veneration of pictures. This idea of a political order, however, in which the divine is present in a manner conveyed through pictures, is vehemently rejected by the iconoclasm of biblical monotheism.

18 Assmann attributes the "Mosaic distinction" that forms the basis of biblical monotheism to the "biblical Moses." This refers to that "figure of memory" which personifies the "confrontation and antagonism between Israel / truth and Egypt / falsehood" (J. Assmann, *Moses*, 29 [Eng. ed., p. 11]). What is important is that Assmann brackets the problem of the historical existence of Moses and asks exclusively about the function that biblical and non-biblical traditions connect to Moses. Assmann's interest in "Moses" focuses on him as a figure of memory. This in turn is important for that "mnemohistory" without which the formation of religious and cultural identities would not be conceivable. But – and this is decisive for Assmann – memory must not in any way concern only the "biblical Moses." On the contrary, the goal of reconstructing mnemohistory can also explicitly take the shape of a "counter" or "deconstructive memory." That, however, is precisely what is found in Assmann's different publications about the figure of Moses: Besides or apart from the more or less semi-official presence of the biblical Moses in the cultural memory of humankind, there are attempts to bring "Moses" home to Egypt or to understand him "from the perspective of Egypt." Here the name and concept of Moses are supposed to "cause the Mosaic distinction and the space constructed by this distinction to collapse" (J. Assmann, *Moses*, 26 [cf. Eng. ed., 8]). According to the programmatic claim of the book Moses the Egyptian, the study intends "to investigate the history of Europe's remembering Egypt, especially in the second form (sc. of deconstructive memory – G. E.) in which the remembering of Egypt is brought to bear on a ... deconstruction of the Mosaic distinction" ([Eng. ed. 8]). Cf. in addition J. Assmann, *Monotheismus*; id. *Herrschaft*, esp. 247-80; with respect to the idea of "mnemohistory" advocated by Assmann, cf. J. Assmann, *Moses*, 17-43 and *passim*; *idem*, *Religion und kulturelles Gedächtnis: Zehn Studien* (Munich, 2000); J. Assmann and T. Hölscher (eds.), *Kultur und Gedächtnis*, Suhrkamp Taschenbuch Wissenschaft, vol. 724 (Frankfurt a. M., 1988).

as Assmann calls it, in which this antagonistic constellation found its appropriate expression (cf. p. 20f. [Eng. ed., p. 3f.]). The Exodus story is a construction of cultural confrontation and exclusion because in it "Egypt" has become the basic symbol of the Mosaic distinction *per se*. Egypt has been stylized into the counter-image of Israel, into a place of darkness and of lies. "Egypt" is the "epitome of untruth" which, in the perspective of the Exodus narrative, is manifested both in its polytheism and in its practice of idolatry in the sense that it makes an idol of the world. The construction of identity distances itself quite clearly with the two core elements of Egyptian religiosity: "1. Thou shalt have no other gods before me. 2. Thou shalt not make unto thee any graven image." (p. 21 [Eng. ed., p. 4]).

In other words, since Mosaic monotheism needs a concept of the enemy for its own self-definition, it blocks all intercultural translatability and lives instead from the distinction between friend and enemy. It thus paves the way for hate and violence, a potential that explodes in the narrative of the Golden Calf, the biblical primal scene of monotheistic iconoclasm, but also of theoclasm.[19]

According to Assmann, however, all this "cannot be reduced to some historical experiences in the late Bronze Age" [Eng. ed., p. 7]. The paradigm is effective and influential to this very day. Wherever the Exodus of the chosen people out of Egypt is remembered and narrated, for example in Judaism and Christianity, there is that continual formation and reproduction of cultural identity by means of separation and rejection. Indeed, the semantic dynamism inherent in this construction of the "rejected other" continues to exist where its religious character has long since been forgotten. The space that has been "severed or cloven" by the Mosaic distinction is that mental or cultural space "that has been inhabited by Europeans for nearly two millennia" (p. 18 [Eng. ed., p. 2]).

This constitutes the fundamental assertion of Jan Assmann: The "distinction between truth and error which characterizes monotheistic religion, and only it," lies at the root of that "theology of violence" which Christianity, in addition to Islam, has also taken up.[20] The Mosaic distinction forms the

---

19 Cf. Assmann, *Moses*, 268-070; *idem*, *Herrschaft*, 257-60.

20 Stating the theory about the "Mosaic distinction" more precisely, Assmann talks about Judaism having "internalized" this distinction – thus having projected the distinction between friend and enemy onto itself, as it were – and, when seen from the perspective of social history, having chosen the "path of self-exclusion." But this was not the case in Islam nor in Christianity, both of which externalized this fundamental antagonism

semantic framework of that political theology which is based on the distinction between friend and enemy. In the end, Assmann also sees the political theology of Carl Schmitt in this dangerous "tradition of revelation-theological violence."[21] With regard to this "political problem" of monotheism, Assmann's judgment is clear and unambiguous: The distinction that forms the basis of monotheism has brought so much disaster and violence into the world that it must finally be reversed and overcome. The price paid up until now by the history of humanity is far too dear.

In the brevity required by such a lecture, I will now summarize the alternative offered to us by Assmann. Only initially does it appear as if Assmann intends to sing the postmodern "praises of polytheism." But appearances are deceptive! According to him, it is not the multitude of deities and the multitude of stories connected to them that put the potential for violence inherent in monotheism in its place through a "separation of powers in the absolute" (*Odo Marquard*).[22] The cultural technique of translation that makes tolerance possible, and which polytheism is said to have mastered, results instead from the fundamental meaning that polytheistic religions attribute to the cosmos. Since they are "religions which are at home in the world and keep the world

---

and took the "path of excluding the foreign." Cf. Assmann, "Die 'mosaische Unterscheidung," 186; *idem*, *Herrschaft*, 263f.

21 Cf. Assmann, *Herrschaft*, 15-71 and 257-64. Assmann's attitude toward the political theology of Carl Schmitt is always very critical, but – with respect to the antagonism between Egypt and Israel – inconsistent. On the one hand, Assmann interprets Schmitt in the light of Egyptian cosmotheism (see below) that stands for the "typical enforced unity of rule and salvation" in political contexts. In this respect, there is an affinity between "symbolic Egypt" and Schmitt insofar as the latter sees the foundation of political order in the unity of rule and salvation (70). On the other hand, Assmann sees the political theology of Schmitt in the tradition of that biblical mono-theism whose "inherent ... violence" Assmann wants to expose (264) – something which I have just pointed out.

22 Assmann points out instead that the affirmation of an impassable multeity in no way forms the vanishing point of ancient religious polytheism, and that, conversely, the rejection of "oneness" does not explicitly constitute the special nature of multeity (cf. Assmann, "Monotheismus," 6f.). And likewise, Assmann's criticism of the Mosaic distinction between "true" and "false" does not aim at a postmodern indifference to truth. Concerning the notion of the "Egyptian" coming closer to monotheism, Assmann says that "if this debate concerned and concerns the dissolution of the Mosaic distinction, then not at the expense of the truth, but at the expense of its excluding and exclusive definition" (Assmann, *Moses*, 280).

going" Assmann applies the term *cosmotheism* to them.[23] What is decisive is that this idea is borne by the "concept of a functionally divided and divinely animated or inspirited universe in which humankind finds and maintains its place" (p. 82 [Eng. ed., p. 54]). The polytheistic worldview interprets the "world as divine and structures the godliness of the world as a collaboration of many differentiated deities."[24] With the cosmos as a universal reference point for the diversity of divine names, the functional equivalencies of these names can, in principle, be directly translated by the various religions. Against this background, it is finally also clear that the question about whether the divine is one or many is not the decisive problem for cosmotheism because it understands how to mediate the opposition between monotheism and polytheism "inside religion."[25] This is so because "behind" the divine names there "are always common cosmic phenomena" that, for their part, are not controversial (p. 81 [Eng. ed., p. 53]). For Assmann, this "natural identity beyond all cultural differences" is important because it guarantees "the reciprocal translatability of the polytheistic deities" (p. 19). Consequently, it is thus perfectly logical to understand cultural and ethical differences as "merely superficial phenomena" that cannot affect the deep foundation of universal religious truth. This truth is based on "natural evidence, that is, on reference to experiences that [have been] accessible to all humankind" (p. 81 [Eng. ed., p. 53]).

---

23 J. Assmann, *Stein und Zeit: Mensch und Gesellschaft im alten Ägypten*, 2nd ed. (Munich, 1995), 59. Concerning the concept of cosmotheism, cf., in addition, the literature given in note 15. Here I can refer only to the comparison between Akhenaten's cosmotheistic monotheism of the sun, on the one hand, and the biblical monotheism of a strictly world-transcendent God on the other, a comparison which runs through Assmann's entire argument. Both are in agreement, and these remarks will have to suffice, that they can be interpreted as a revolutionary revelation-monotheism and that an anti-polytheistic dynamic is inherent in them. And in what sense do they differ? "Akhenaten's monotheism is cosmological, a religiously interpreted natural philosophy. Biblical monotheism is historical, political, and moral; it finds its primary expression in historical narrative, legislation, and a constitution." Assmann does not explicitly assert a causal or thematic connection between "Akhenaten" and "Moses," nor does he construct a "historically" verifiable line of tradition. That the two have been connected to each other as "figures of memory" and also occasionally identified with each other is the only thing that is mnemohistorically significant for Assmann. Assmann, *Monotheismus*, 35. Cf. *idem*, *Moses*, 47-87.

24 Assmann, *Monotheismus*, 36.

25 Cf. Assmann, *Monotheismus*, 46 (the emphasis by means of the quotation marks is mine).

What has thus far been implied must be specifically pointed out. Cosmotheism is based on an understanding of the world that is convinced of the "divinity of the world." Cosmotheism, however, attributes this "divinity of the world" to the "worldliness of the divine."[26] From my perspective, the systematically central and, in my opinion, genuinely explosive core of Assmann's thesis is this cosmotheistic identification of the world and the divine.

Why this is true suddenly becomes clear in view of Assmann's breathtaking reinterpretation of the tetragrammaton of Exodus 3:14 through the cosmotheistic tradition just mentioned.[27] Exodus 3:14 states: "I am who I am" or "I am the I-am-here." No matter how this passage might be spelled out in detail through exegesis, the interpretation that Assmann himself gives it is undisputed. A god says, "I am who I am ... *who does not and must not refer to anything beyond myself in order to be able to say of myself that I am in truth God.*" He is that reality that is, by definition, different from the world and from humans, a reality whose presence or "being here" for humans occurs in the medium of a self-proof which is irreducibly free and remains free.[28]

Assmann is able to discern that, historically, this name that Yahweh calls himself, "I am the I-am-here," underwent an "Egypto-Hellenistic" interpretation in the cosmotheistic sense. This interpretation can be traced back to Plutarch and Proclus. It attained an enormous topicality in the philosophy of the Enlightenment at the end of the eighteenth century – for instance, in the works of Gotthold Ephraim Lessing and Karl Leonhard Reinhold, but also in the esthetics of Schiller and Beethoven.[29]

---

26 Assmann, *Stein*, 59. For cosmotheism, the decisive problem is less the question about the oneness or the multeity of the divine than the question of the worldliness or non-worldliness of the divine.

27 For the following, cf. Assmann, *Moses*, 173-205, *passim* [cf. Eng. ed., 115-43]; *idem*, *Monotheismus*.

28 Cf. Assmann, *Monotheismus*, 12f. Exodus 3:14 knocks the bottom out of all cosmic identifications and is nothing short of "the denial or the negation of such cosmic immanence." (*Monotheismus*, 13); cf. *idem*, "Die 'mosaische Unterscheidung'." 191.

29 At this point, I am expressly not following Jan Assmann on the extended excursions he takes in order to trace the tradition of "cosmotheism" all the way back to the Egyptian religion, and I am also omitting his attempts to track down the usually hidden presence of cosmotheism in the history of religion. For individual examples, cf. Assmann, *Moses*, 88-242; *idem*, *Herrschaft*, 265-80.

The cosmotheistic rendering of Exodus 3:14 reads: "I am all that has been and is and shall be; and no mortal has ever lifted my mantle."[30] This saying very clearly expresses the fundamental intention of cosmotheism. It is not simply looking at the "oneness of the world or of being" which it then seeks to attribute to the "uniqueness of its source" or to the "principle that it is kept going." Rather, by asserting the "divinity of the world" together with the "worldliness of the divine," cosmotheism denies in principle what determines the fundamental difference for biblical monotheism: namely that God is by definition a different reality from humans and the world.[31] The rendering of the biblical "I am the I-am-here" as "I am all that is" asserts the identity of the divine with the cosmos.

This is also the reason why cosmotheism is not polytheism, but in principle monotheism, or, more precisely, an *all-one-monotheism* which identifies the one God with the one cosmos. He is the one God who is everything, the All-One.[32] This fundamental idea gets its more precise definition through the following thesis: For cosmotheism the question concerning the worldliness or other-worldliness of the divine is the question that decides everything else and a question which cosmotheism itself knows how to answer unequivocally – The absolute One as the One is at the same time All as if all is in one. Consequently, this all-one-monotheism leads in the end to the basic formula of *pantheism*: *Hen kai pan* – "one-and-all" or the "All-One." It is therefore consistent that Assmann's "deconstructive memory" of cosmotheism is explicitly

30 Assmann, *Moses*, 182 [Eng. ed., 118]. As Assmann has convincingly proven, this formula can be traced back to Egypt and is the epochal legacy for which the world has Egypt to thank. For individual examples that reconstruct the convoluted paths by which this version of the inscription on the Temple of Sais, which clearly comes from Plutarch, reached the philosophy of the seventeenth and eighteenth centuries, cf. Assmann, *Moses*, 118-210. As Assmann explains, the interpretation of the biblical name of "Yahweh" in the light of cosmotheism appears to have been the work of Reinhold who, however, seems to be just one link in a long chain of tradition reaching back to antiquity. Cf. Assmann, *Moses*, 173-86; *idem*, *Monotheismus*, 12f.

31 Cf. Assmann, *Monotheismus*, 11, 26f.; *idem*, *Stein*, 59.

32 A monotheism which is based on the postulate of the all-one is guided by the insight "that, in the final analysis, all gods are one, manifestations of a single, all-embracing divinity" (Assmann, *Monotheismus*, 46). Although Assmann definitely considers dropping the concept of monotheism for characterizing the specifically cosmotheistic "thinking of the one" (cf. Assmann, *Monotheismus*, 12), he uses it nonetheless to characterize the thinking of the all-one since the postulate of the all-one does not in fact contest the singleness and uniqueness of the all-embracing divinity at all (cf. Assmann, *Monotheismus*, 46f.).

looking for the connection to the Spinozism of the age of Goethe and at the same time for the connection to that renascence of the Spinoza renaissance which we can observe again today.[33]

Assmann provides the renewed connection to Spinoza's "(in)famous formula *deus sive natura*" (p. 26 [Eng. ed., p. 8]) with a systematic claim that makes the actual thrust of his "deconstructive memory" of the figure of Moses clear. As soon as the recasting of biblical monotheism as cosmotheism occurs, and the most fundamental of all distinctions – the distinction between God and the world – is abolished, the Mosaic distinction, which has split and torn the world apart, immediately disappears (cf. p. 26 [Eng. ed., p. 8]).

The "worldliness of the divine" premise summons insight that the divine is accessible to general experience in the medium of the veneration of the cosmos. Thus the disclosure of the divine is entrusted to natural evidence. Consequently "truth" becomes a matter of "knowledge" which is accessible to all; it is in no way bound to its revelation. As a result, cosmotheism circumvents the exclusivity that is constitutive of the monotheistic claim to revelation.[34] On the one hand, God, understood as the "All-One," does not bind humans or a chosen people exclusively to himself and therefore does not provoke the authorized enforcement of his "jealous" covenant obligation in the social-cultural areas of people's lives.[35] On the other hand, the distinction be-

33 "The kai of the Greek formula has the same meaning as Spinoza's sive. It does not mean 'addition,' but identification. In its most common form, the formula occurs as Hen to pan, 'All Is One,' the world is God. This is what 'cosmotheism' means" (Assmann, *Moses*, 209 [Eng. ed., 142], cf. Assmann, *Moses*, 28. 173-210). Concerning the diverse varieties of the Spinoza renaissance, cf. H. Timm, *Gott und die Freiheit: Studien zur Religionsphilosophie der Goethezeit*, vol.1: *Die Spinozarenaissance*, Studien zur Philosophie und Literatur des neunzehnten Jahrhunderts, vol. 22 (Frankfurt a. M., 1974); S. Thissen, *De Spinozisten: Wijsgerige Beweging in Nederland* (1850-1907), Nederlandse Cultuur in Europese Context, 18. IJKpunt 1900, vol. 3 (The Hague, 2000); D. Pätzold, *Spinoza – Aufklärung – Idealismus: Die Substanz der Moderne*, 2nd enlarged ed. (Assen, 2002); J.I. Israel, *Radical Enlightenment: Philosophy and the Making of Modernity 1650-1750* (Oxford, 2002).

34 See above.

35 In this context Assmann calls to mind the notion of the deus otiosus, which assigns the role of being otiosely withdrawn from the world to the Supreme Being. Such a god – this is the crux of its meaning – ignores people's concerns and does not intervene in their fates. Consequently, the notion of the deus otiosus differs in a fundamental way from the Yahweh of the biblical tradition. The latter is imagined as a historically active player who himself executes his reign directly. In contrast to Yahweh, a deus otiosus does not exhort anyone to move from the "world of what exists" into a "new world of uncompromising immediacy." Cf. Assmann, *Monotheismus*, 46f., note 114;

tween "true" and "false" disappears where truth is not revealed, but nonetheless evident. Since there is nothing divine within the horizon of cosmotheism that is in principle incompatible with what has already been revealed to general human experience, the Mosaic distinction, understood as an antagonistic constellation in which "falsehood is made the object of rejection and persecution in the severest of ways," is overcome. The friend-enemy distinction of Carl Schmitt would also be overcome. For whenever the *theological* difference between truth and falsehood, between God and idol, disappears, the bottom will be knocked out of that *political theology* for which this distinction serves as a theological basis.[36]

But why should one recommend the "Egyptian truth" of cosmotheism as a hermeneutics of intercultural or interreligious dialogue? According to Assmann, the problem accompanying modernity, the problem of "the one and the many" detailed at the beginning of my lecture, loses its bite. The question that has haunted Western philosophy from time immemorial of whether priority is due the one over the many, or the reverse, loses its explosive nature when the pantheistic credo, The one God is all that is, was, and shall be, functions as a *medium* which overcomes and dissolves all religious distinctions and cultural conflicts. On the one hand, the possibility of an intercultural and interreligious communication in the medium of the *Hen kai pan* seeks to grasp the true nature of the concept of pluralism as a superficial phenomenon: The many can be granted its space without hindrance because the concept of oneness has already been previously identified with the many. But according to this logic, the one does not expressly claim a priority over the many since – at least for us – the one is only perceivable in the diversity of its manifestations.[37] On the other hand, this conception is not supposed to endanger the oneness of the one

---

idem, *Herrschaft*, 260 (The quotations found here on page 261f. refer to biblical monotheism).

36 Cf. Assmann, *Herrschaft*, 257-64.

37 For the significance of the motif of "hiddenness," which can mediate between oneness and multeity, cf. Assmann, *Monotheismus*, 46. The argument reads as follows: Since the one as the Supreme Being is hidden and quite specifically does not appear, it gives the many space. Unlike the biblical "monotheism of revelation," the cosmo-theistic "monotheism of hiddenness" does not suppress, negate, or destroy the many, while the hidden one at the same time supports and sustains it. Concerning the Egyptian topos of "a visible and a hidden god" cf. *idem*, *Moses*, 250–268.

because the one is everything and not only lies ahead of and forms the basis of the many, but also encompasses it at the same time.[38]

Cosmotheism invites us to leave the biblical "semantics of sin" behind us (p. 281).[39] If we follow Assmann, the "consciousness of sin," which is always accompanied by a "bad conscience" and from which in turn the "yearning for redemption" arises, is "perhaps" one of the "most important motives for calling the Mosaic distinction into question" (p. 282).[40] But what should take the place of the consciousness of sin? Assmann recommends the "moral optimism" of cosmotheism because it is not based on a "bad conscience," but "on the consciousness of a reconciliation with both God and world" (p. 281).

Conclusion

In conclusion, I will limit myself to two tasks: Firstly, I intend to condense the religious-historical and philosophical-historical material concerning cosmotheism processed by Assmann into its systematic content; and secondly, from this perspective, I would like to clarify some aspects of my criticism, and along with them, some indispensable theological options.[41]

---

38 Assmann develops this fundamental idea with regard to the "evolutionary" character of all-one-monotheism: On the one hand, it grows "in a gradual way as a late and mature stage" from prior forms of religion and does not assert itself as something that has overcome them in a destructive or negating way. On the other hand, it also does not reject the multiformity of the polytheistic realm of gods. Instead, a monotheism that is based on the postulate of all-oneness is guided by the insight that in the final analysis all the gods are one, manifestations of a single, all-embracing divinity. Cf. Assmann, *Monotheismus*, 46f. See above.

39 On what follows cf. Assmann, *Moses*, 277-82. See above.

40 "Seen from the point of view of Egypt, it looks as if sin has come into the world with the Mosaic distinction. This is perhaps the most important motive for challenging the Mosaic distinction. Whoever discovers God in Egypt does away with this distinction" (Assmann, *Moses*, 282).

41 Assmann definitely presents his "deconstructive memory" with the emphatic claim that it is a "cosmopolitan opening up by means of doing away with boundaries" (Assmann, *Moses*, 26). But it is then all the more amazing that in an initial reply to critics of his theses concerning the "Mosaic distinction" he points out that his reflections are "without any systematic-theological relevance" (Assmann, "Die 'mosaische Unterscheidung'," 188). In my opinion, however, this self-restriction is contrary to the tradition of that "deconstructive memory" in which Assmann explicitly places his own studies concerning biblical monotheism. This form of memory is of course far from indifferent, since and insofar as, firstly, it is ideologically critical towards the interpretive monopoly of dominant traditions, and secondly, by exposing repressed options,

The current discussion of monotheism is a salutary provocation for Christianity. It is salutary because, motivated by ideological criticism, it uncovers the dark side of Christianity's history wherein forced conversions were unscorned, dissenters were burned, and the freedom of untold scores of people was constrained by fear. There is an affecting history of monotheism that has in fact stimulated hate and violence. And for the sake of our own credibility, we must not let this history fade away in the glare of a poorly made apologetics. Yet apologetics is altogether different from a well-reasoned discourse that goes to great lengths in making clear, unbiased distinctions. An *apologia* for monotheism, therefore, does not necessarily warrant placement on the ideological margins. On the contrary, such an *apologia* is credible to the degree that it connects the defense of monotheism with a humane interest. Is it not possible that biblical monotheism is of indispensable importance to the success of human freedom, and for the humanity of our social existence?

I would like to proffer a question: Is it really true that a cosmotheistic reinterpretation of the tetragrammaton of Exodus 3:14 humanizes monotheism, as Assmann thinks? I have my doubts, and for the following reason: The self-revelation of God in the form of the I-predication "I am the I-am-here" does indeed articulate itself initially as a self-reference, as Assmann emphasizes. And it is likewise correct that Yahweh refers to nothing beyond himself in order to be able to say of himself that he is in truth God. But must we not vehemently contradict one central point of Assmann's? Must we not deny that divinity's I-predication's not immediately and directly referencing the world necessarily prefigures the sort of Mosaic distinction he so stridently fears?

There is much that argues in favor of the opposite. Only the non-identification of God with the world makes a theology of creation possible that is capable of grasping, in any way at all, the concept of the world's *positive* lib-

---

it seeks to accentuate that which Critical Theory once called "dangerous memory." If one adds that the uncovering of the mnemonic history connected to the name "Moses" is explicitly related to questions concerning a cultural identity of the present day and age, then Assmann's attempt to relate cosmotheism to explosive subject areas like "religion and violence" would by no means be as indifferent as the remark just made seems to insinuate. Be that as it may, the following comments are to be understood primarily as an attempt to take "cosmotheism" seriously as the ideal-typical alternative, as it were, to biblical monotheism and to question it accordingly since cosmotheism is imagined to be the form of monotheism that – unlike biblical monotheism – is not supposed to be structurally violent nor constitutively antagonistic. That is in any case the thrust of Assmann's argument, which must be examined on the basis of his systematic claim.

eration into irreducible independence. Only the profession of God as the creator of the world *ex nihilo* leads in turn to a concept of secularity without which there would be no free shaping or structuring of history and the world.[42] Whoever aggressively professes "Spinoza's (in)famous formula *deus sive natura*" and expressly aims at abolishing the "distinction between God and the world" (p. 26 [Eng. ed., p. 8]), as Assmann obviously does, must at first still show how he or she intends to rescue a notion of freedom at all. Our interest in rescuing what is humane prohibits us from giving up such a notion.

But what is freedom? In order to give a theological answer to this question we must revisit the formula "I am the I-am-here." The assertion that God's self-revelation in the form of the I-predication does not immediately recognize a relationship to the world is exclusively a cosmotheistic perspective. It is correct that in the light of biblical monotheism we are not permitted to understand the cosmos as the self-manifestation of God. But Exodus 3:14 speaks explicitly of God's presence, of God's being here. The tetragrammaton refers the revelation of God back to his freely given proof of himself which – and this is decisive – is experienced by Israel as exodus, as liberation. Exodus 20:2 expressly states: "I am the Lord your God who brought you out of the land of Egypt, out of the house of slavery." The characteristic of Yahweh's relationship with the world that is defined in this way is found in Psalm 88:1 where the tetragrammaton of Exodus 3:14 is paraphrased as follows: "O Yahweh, God of my salvation."

What are the consequences of these considerations for our topic? First, a monotheism that locates the foundation of its determination in the tetragrammaton understood in this way is an *ethical* monotheism. Incidentally, this monotheism also embraces a Mosaic distinction, if you choose to call it that, the distinction between slavery or bondage and freedom, between oppression and liberation.[43] Second, ethical monotheism refers to the fact that the individuating gaze of the one God calls people to a freedom that means re-

---

42 I have tried to outline the consequences resulting from the cosmotheism in Spinoza's tradition for the concept of history in my essay "Zechen auf 'fremde Kreide'? Philosophisch-theologische Überlegungen zur Angewiesenheit der historischen Vernunft auf die Sinnvorgaben des biblischen Monotheismus – Eine Rückfrage an Jan Assmann," in J. Schröter, ed., *Konstruktion von Wirklichkeit: Geschichte als Sinnbildung und die Anfänge des Christentums* (Berlin / New York, 2004). In this essay, I try to demonstrate at the same time that the emergence of biblical monotheism has also led to an understanding of reality as history.

43 Cf. E. Zenger, *Was ist der Preis des Monotheismus?* 190f.

sponsibility for themselves and for their neighbors. Whoever chooses to call the semantics of sin so radically into question as Assmann does must, in turn, face the question of whether the rejection of the guilt context of freedom and responsibility is not a betrayal. The possibility for naming, in any way at all, the injustice done to the victims depends on this context. And another possibility depends on this association; namely, the possibility of our plea directed to God that he remain faithful to his covenantal promises: "Are your wonders known in the darkness, or your saving help in the land of forgetfulness?" (Psalm 88:12). Third, and formulated with regard to an intercultural and interreligious hermeneutics, if we interpret the relationship between the one and the many in light of an ethical monotheism, we are called upon to determine this relationship in an ethical way and to explain it within the frameworks of freedom. What follows, ethically, from a monotheism that holds central the relationship between the liberating freedom of God and the liberated freedom of humans? Must we not speak up in a resolute and reasoned way for the position that this God, the God of Jesus, is, and remains, a "universal theme, a theme of humanity"?[44] Does the monotheistic-critical suspicion of intolerance also apply to that Mosaic distinction which insists in a universal way on the difference between freedom and bondage? It is true that ethical monotheism brings this difference into play as the criterion of truth, of true existence, and that cosmological myths slip into the status of falsehoods or gaps in the face of this criterion. But those who want to reverse the biblical break with cosmological myth must know what they are doing. They are tearing the fabric of morals and conscience, of guilt and responsibility, to pieces. And finally, can we not provide the Mosaic distinction between freedom and bondage with a universal claim to validity on the grounds that universal responsibility corresponds to belief in the one and only God? I have never comprehended why moral universalism should be understood as an enemy of individualism. On the contrary: Moral universalism guarantees the equality of all people, makes their freedom possible and protects them. And I do not understand the assertion that the idea of oneness necessitates the coercive integration of the many as its consequence, or why this should be so if we sustain the idea of oneness in the consciousness of freedom.

---

44 J.B. Metz, "Die letzten Universalisten," in *idem*, *Zum Begriff der neuen politischen Theologie* (Mainz, 1997), 156-59, here 156.

Ioannis Kourembeles

Christian Monotheism: Exclusivity or Openness to Otherness?

Introduction

These days there is a need for an ecumenical movement that will not have, as its only target, the healing of past schisms through dialogue but will attempt to approach unity through today's multiplicity of religious expressions. In spite of some growing reactions against interconfessional and interreligious dialogue, Christians from all over the world recognize the benefits and importance of dialogue, yet they are still troubled about the varieties of religious expression. Thus, the view that the phenomenon of syncretism is a fact of life in global society that should be taken seriously is heard even from the mouths of Christian theologians who point to the relationship between syncretism and pacifism as an example of their good will in promoting interreligious dialogue.[1]

Christianity is now moving toward a dialogue, along with Islam and the Asian religions, that is informed by and has implications for the entire "global world."[2] It is the world in its entirety that encompasses both *the globalization of our civilizations* and the profoundly insular *variety of our civilizations*. We live in both worlds simultaneously – we live inside them and we experience

---

1 See L.M. Dolan, "Development and Spirituality: Personal Reflections of a Catholic," in P. Mische / M. Merkling (eds.), *Global Civilisation? The Contribution of Religions* (New York, 2001), 279: "We need in that congress to ask questions such as: What is syncretism today? Is syncretism a natural consequence of living in a secularized world? Should we see the adoption of different forms of Christianity by indigenous peoples, with their veneration of ancestors and their love of nature, as a form of syncretism? Who is God and who is Jesus? What does Incarnation mean for 6 billion people? What does the fundamental principle put forward at the World Day of Prayer for Peace in Assisi, 'to be together to pray but not to pray together', mean in today's stage of interreligious dialogue?"

2 Here the meaning given to a future "global ethical system" applies, something that is worth rendering in the words of Robert Muller: "The world is becoming so interdependent, it is like one body. We have a nervous system that is very advanced. We have a global brain. Now we need a global heart and a global soul», which M. Aram complements as follows: "I would add that we also need a global conscience, based on a global ethic" ("Gandhian Values, a Global Ethic, and Global Governance," in Mische / Merkling, *Global Civilisation*, 100).

them as ensconced in and interactive with a multireligious, multicultural society. Society in both of these dimensions also operates on another plane, the plane of "electronic society," since through the Internet it is possible for us to be in touch with all the corners of the Earth.[3]

It is generally accepted that the most influential social determinants of today are not ideological, political, or financial but rather cultural at a time when religion has the first word in a world that seeks unity on the basis of values.[4] The history of Europe has proved that we have been influenced by many cultures and that we are constantly in touch with new ones in the multicultural arenas where we live. Additionally, we are all aware of the fact that religion has not always been a factor in creative movement and evolution, and that the terrors of war and human alienation have often motivated religious ideology and organization.[5] This is an important point, because – without intending to invalidate the distinctions and differences between religions and their cultures – European thought and experience, especially since it has been fermented with the experience of diversity, could work as an antidote against the extreme centralized trends of globalization.[6]

---

3 Regarding common characteristics for the one world and the changes or problems of the peoples that have emerged with their encounter, see P. Mische, "Toward a Civilisation Worthy of the Human Person," in Mische / Merkling, *Global Civilisation*, 11f. In this collective volume, the Muslim S. Mahmod-Abedin, in "Islam and Global Governance," 289, expresses himself on this point with the following remarkable words: "However, the increasing heterogeneity created by burgeoning populations and greater geographic mobility, and the sharpened sensitivities toward roots and identities in an increasingly pasteurized and homogenized world at the mercy of the multimedia, make the task of addressing the spiritual and the moral even more challenging. Never in history was there greater awareness of the variety in races and nations, and never before was the vast segment of humanity exposed so graphically to man's inhumanity to man, conveyed vividly in tabloids and on television screens in living rooms across South and East."

4 See Mische / Merkling, *Global Civilisation*, 2-3. 26: "The question before us, then, is not whether a new world order will emerge in response to new global imperatives, but rather what kind of world order? Based on what worldview? What values? What ethic and ethos? What kind of leadership will guide and shape it? Without religious identity, prospects for global humane governance are without the spiritual character that can mobilize and motivate on a basis that is far more powerful than what the market, secular reason, and varieties of nationalism have to offer."

5 See also Mahmoud-Abedin, "Islam," 284.

6 See also the interesting criticism of "Dominius Iesus" that Johann Reikersdorfer makes, "Zum Orthodoxieproblem von Dominus Iesus," in M. J. Rainer (ed.), *Dominus Iesus: Anstößige Wahrheit oder anstößige Kirche? Dokumente, Hintergründe, Standpunkte und Folgerungen* (Münster, 2001), 102-11, here 110f.

There are, of course, contemporary thinkers[7] who merely accept a skeptical pluralism. They are in agreement with each other and claim that the globalization trends, which are favored by economy, standardization, exchange of views, and interests, promote, in their turn, a curiosity for local, idiosyncratic, experimental, and not so generalized expressions of life and are suspicious of every attempt toward unity (unification). It is then considered that every thought of unification, even within the Christian *ecumene*, within the dialogue among religions and the universal right of the movement of human rights, will be finally dismissed within the frame of this logic (in terms of the particular). That is, it will be dismissed as a vain or even as an authoritarian trend.[8]

It seems, however, that the diversity and complexity of the way of life in modern society also leads to *the philosophy of diversity* and of the particular, as well as to the adoration of distinction and variety. Yet if we consider the claim that diversity and pluralism belong to the real, the good, and the substantially nice, we can see that since all these evaluations take place primarily within theoretical dialogue (which favors the development of differences and distinctions), when it comes to observing these ideals in real action, we are confronted with a paradox – how do we observe others in order to evaluate our interactions with them in a manner that is free enough from our culture bound theory so that we are also able to deeply comprehend the diversity of the other in an authentic way? Yet one glance at current events reveals that ultra-conservatism and xenophobia in modern Europe stem from a decrease in and a neglect of familiar religious values, since nothing that comes from outside can harm man (or his culture), more than what comes from inside.[9]

---

7 See T. Ahrens (ed.), *Zwischen Regionalität und Globalisierung* (Hamburg, 1997), 20 and 249 (discussion of W. V. Lindner and S. Kempin on the book by T. Sundermeier, *Den Fremden verstehen: Eine Praktische Hermeneutik* (Göttingen, 1996).

8 For our consideration here see also A. Houtepen, "Ökumene und Gottesfrage (Die Bedeutung des Monotheismus in einer multikulturellen Geselschaft)," in *Ökumenische Rundschau* 50 (2001): 39-54, especially p. 39f.

9 See *Christ in der Gegenwart* 52 (2002): 425: "It is not dangerous the outside challenge through a religion that Europe keeps foreign in its core, but rather the leading neglect of religion by the spiritual interior of the majority of the population, a factual ignorance and a conscious reflection of the afterthought 'over the last things'. We are really dealing with a new enemy – an enemy not of many Gods, but rather of one God .... The fate of Europe hangs decisively, in the future as well, on the shape of spiritual attitudes. It will not be a matter of little interest for the forming of the European Union, whether the question of God will fade out as avoidable private views of the world or whether people will raise it to be the primary thing in their existence, to a fight for a better social, cultural, political life" (in German). See also the article of I.

This raises several questions: In our current, modern global context, how can and should one talk about God and religion? Is it possible for "faith in God" to enter this multireligious / multicultural arena with a competitive disposition, and is it possible that (Christian) monotheism might be found to be the most viable, the most spiritually "useful" faith perspective before all other viewpoints? Can monotheistic faith be a positive unifying factor in globalization, communication, and the eradication of differences within society in a manner that addresses all that is topical while speaking to universal notions and questions about life and death? Can we ignore the fact that Christian monotheism, in spite of its being based on Trinitarian faith, is itself a topic for debate and dialogue within Christian communities? And can we ignore that Muslim theologians, having Christian theology of the West in mind, are critical of Christianity's distinction between the sacred and the profane, the religious and the mundane, proffering instead that all spheres of life are religious?[10] So, we must ask ourselves, does Christian monotheism have the critical, theological resources within it to extend a dialogical bridge toward its contending interlocutors? Does it have the ability to assume the vanguard toward mutual understanding within interreligious and multicultural discourse in a way that goes beyond words, amounting to genuine social harmony?

We believe it does. The Trinitarian monotheism of Christianity has proved that through the distinction between *hypostasis* and *nature* it can achieve discursive unity-in-otherness as easily as it can achieve otherness-in-unity. In what follows, we will further explore this distinction.

The Comprehension of Trinitarian Monotheism

In the relationship between the faithful and Christ, the faithful's experience of the Trinitarian God can be clearly seen. For the faithful, the spirit of life is the

---

Petrou, "Multiculturality as a Social Fact and Social Demand," in *Καθ' Οδόν* 16 (2000): 5-17, where there is the question of the evolution of communication.

10 Mahmoud-Abedin, "Islam," 285, for instance, expresses himself as follows: "All matters of this world, from the most complex to the most mundane, are subject to religious concerns. In that sense, everything is sacred, and religion is part of everyday life and not a ritual confined to specific acts on specific days. Nevertheless, the French sociologist Emile Durcjheim maintained that religious phenomena emerge when a separation is made between the sphere of the profane – the realm of everyday utilitarian activity – and the sphere of the sacred: the numinous and the transcendental."

spirit of Christ and God.[11] However, this is not meant dualistically; for in Orthodox Christology, Christ is God. In Moltmann's view, however, duality and division are the distinctive features of this theological expression. In other words, he believes that "in the communion of the faithful with Christ, the God of Christ becomes the God of the faithful."[12]

Here it becomes evident that Trinitarian Theology is not properly correlated with Christology. Moltmann underscores that "the 'Father of Jesus Christ' has nothing to do with the family fathers or the homeland,"[13] intending, of course, to say that this God is not connected to the patriarchical or political God of ancient religions. Yet there is great validity to the theological truth that Christ himself, as God, reveals in His person a Trinitarian God of love (1. John 4:16). Assuredly, Christianity is the "religion" of "freedom in love." Still, we wouldn't dare to distinguish the term *Christ* from the terms *God* and *the Spirit*, on the basis of their hypostatic distinction without stressing, at the same time, the communion of the divine essence that vouches for monotheism. The expression of Moltmann gives us the impression that Trinitarian Theology and Christology are confused when the common energy of the persons doesn't appear to be based on their "in essence relationship," but rather on an external type of cooperation.[14] And it should be noted that Moltmann himself further on endorses all those elements of terminology that underscore the theological assertion that the meaning of God is connected with Christology, since Jesus, the Son of God, is of one essence with the Father.[15]

---

11 See more in J. Moltmann, *Trinität und Reich Gottes: Zur Gotteslehre* (Munich, 1980); *idem*, "Im weiteren Raum der Trinität," in: *idem*, *Erfahrungen theologischen Denkens: Wege und Formen Christlicher Theologie* (Gütersloh, 1999), 266-90.

12 Moltmann, *Monotheismus*, 117: "In der Christusgemeinschaft wird der Gott Christi zum Gott der Glaubenden. Das 'Abba'-Geheimnis Jesu öffnet sich zum 'unser Vater'. Als Jesus das Abba-Geheimnis Gottes und sich selbst darin als den ‚geliebten Sohn' enteckte, verließ er seine Familie und begann, im Kreis der Armen des Volkes (ochlos) zu leben (Mk. 3,31-35)."

13 Moltmann, *Monotheismus*, 117.

14 Moltmann, *Monotheismus*, 118: "According to the witness of the New Testament, the 'grace of Christ' and 'the love of God' and 'the communion of the Holy Spirit' act in the experience of the redeemed and reborn life together. The persons that act together within are personally different: Christ-God-Spirit, yet they are socially bound together toward the redemption of the created beings, toward the eternal community of God. The new experience of life in Christianity is as liberating as the experience of the Exodus in Israel ..." (translation mine).

15 Moltmann, *Monotheismus*, 118: "In the Christian Trinitarian dogma, the Trinitarian experience of God reaches its meaning. This takes place by means of the fact that the

We observe, thus, a confusion in the use and exploitation of common terms in Christian theology, when Christian theologians attempt to enter into dialogue with other religions, in this case, with Islam. And, in this way, Christian monotheism sets itself up for misunderstanding and weakens its eschatological premises.[16] Indeed, Moltmann is of the opinion that "for Christianity the totality and universality of God of Christ belong to eschatology" (*fur die Christenheit gehoren Universalität und Totalität des Gottes Christi in die Eschatologie*).[17] The genitive "*des Gottes Christi*" does not make clear that Christ is God, and a big question is left unanswered by Moltmann's eschatological view, which, moreover, overemphasizes the perfection of the *eschata* and doesn't stress the (soteriological) significance of the incarnated presence of the Divine Word in the world.[18] That's why the question arises for Moltmann whether Christian monotheism can indeed be characterized as monotheism. Along these lines, the example of Areios provides us a cautionary tale.

Areios considered the Word to be the first creation of God because his intention was to support the monarchy in Trinity. So he turned Christ into a mere teacher of ethics. The Church decided against Areios and in favor of Gr. Athanasios in terms of Trinitarian faith; however Areios found supporters even later: in the years of the Reformation these were the Sokinians, and in the earlier years the Humanists of Christ. In these cases it seems that being a Christian and believing in God were two different things. We emphasize this because the logic of preparing the way for an Islamic understanding of the

---

meaning of God is bound with Christology. Jesus, 'the Son of God' is with the Father and the Spirit of one essence ..." (translation mine).

16 We stress this point because the most important, we could say, chapter in the Orthodox theology is the union of the divine with the human, a union that has an eschatological dimension. And, of course, this dimension is not a mellontology, but rather a viable historical event in the very face of the Divine Word, who, in His face, turned the "eschatic" emptying, the "eschatic" philanthropy into reality.

17 See Moltmann, *Monotheismus*, 118.

18 See Moltmann, *Monotheismus*, 119: "Then will the threesome God become only one God and His magnificence will penetrate all things and shed light on them. Then, for the first time, will someone be able to say that God is 'the reality of everything defined'. (R. Bultmann, W. Pannenberg). Then, for the first time, can one speak of a limitless omnipotence, eternal presence and omniscience of God. But in history these superior qualities of God have been defined, outlined and formed by Christ" (translation mine).

Christian notion of God could in effect be preparing the way for a new type of neo-Arianism.

In keeping with the above, it has become evident that comprehension of Trinitarian monotheism is not taken for granted in Christian theology. That is, in the event that a divergent comprehension of God-Christ emerges within dialogue, Christianity may converse with Islam about Christ as one more prophet,[19] but it cannot demonstrate the evangelic truth that God Himself became human. Yet, it is regarding this truth that Christianity has a debt to the entire world, a debt to declare that the natural relationship among the Trinitarian persons is open for participation to all humans through Christ.

Indeed, one could argue that Christianity's obligation is to view the other from the evangelic prospect that teaches how God takes His stand towards man, and not just how man perceives God. We have thus, an interest in seeing that Christ (God Himself) regards His creation (humankind) as unique and does not wish for this creation to be excluded from the community that God offers. Christology doesn't simply teach that God is one, but also that all of humanity is one with God on the basis of His incarnation[20] and His passion for the sake of all men.[21]

---

19 J.B. Cobb (ed.), *Christian Faith and Religious Diversity* (Minneapolis, 2002), 31, sums up the contemporary trends as follows: "Many Christians today, however, would share Muhammad's rejection of the doctrine of the Trinity as he understood it. He thought that the doctrine of Trinity denied the unity of God, and he shared with Jews a strong commitment to that unity. In fact, however, classic explanations of the Trinity, espe-cially in the West, insist that the unity of the three persons of the Trinity is to be preserved. One may question the success of some of these formulations in adequately preserving the unity, but the intention is not at odds with Islamic concerns. Christians believe in one God, not three Gods. Muslims (like Jews) also recognize that there are many names for God, highlighting different aspects of the way God relates to the world."

20 This very important element is for Orthodox Christology one of the outstanding theological issues that can help even the culture of globalized thought and life on the basis that this thought places importance on the commonly accepted point of the oneness of the human family. See on this common point the proposals of R. Falk (in: Mische / Merkling, *Global Civilisation*, 58). It is worth mentioning the sense of unity in many religious views, as well. In Hinduism, for example, we come across the view, "The whole world is to be dwelt in by the Lord, whatever living being there is in the world. So should you eat what has been abandoned; and do not covet anyone's wealth" (P. Olivelle (transl.), *Upanisads* [Oxford, 1996], 249), which has to do with the supporting of justice for all human beings and the harmonious life among them (See K. R. Sundararajan, "Hinduism and Global Society," in Mische / Merkling, *Global Civilisation*, 96-97). Among the values of M. Gandhiji, as well, the question of unity holds good position (the truly noble know all men as one) (see M. Aram,

The Islamic view, which Christian theologians such as Moltmann try to address, finds three gods in Christian Trinitarian theology, and it definitely does not place importance on the *social dimension* of Christian monotheism[22] and on the fact that this dimension does not remove monotheism from the interrelation of the divine incarnation and the theosis of man.[23] This perspective offers a compelling invitation to Christian theologians to enter into dialogue

---

"Gandhian values, a Global Ethic and Global Governance," in Mische / Merkling, *Global Civilisation*, 102. 103) or even in Jain's values of the religious system ("we are all one, all interdependent") (see P.N. Jain, "Way of Life," in: Mische / Merkling, *Global Civilisation*, 112).

21 We come across the issue of sympathy as a means of man's deliverance from passion in other religions, too, such as Buddhism (see e.g. S. Sivaraksa, "Religion and World Order from a Buddhist Perspective," in Mische / Merkling, *Global Civilisation*, 128-51, here 128f.). However, in the Orthodox Christian teaching it is not just about a moral command but rather about the passion of God Himself, in His flesh, who suffers the same as all men, and the proving of death as being powerless before man's ontological relationship with God.

22 Therefore, Christian monotheism is philanthropic *par excellence*. Let's not forget that this prospect gives meaning to God's revelation, as it happens in the Old Testament. Otherwise, there monotheism would face the charge of being misanthropic and atheistic, as was the case with the neighbors of the Jews: "Their imageless worship and their resolute denial of the gods of their neighbors brought upon the Jews the stigma of atheoi, "atheists" or godless. As thoroughgoing monotheists, the Jews disregarded the gods of the heathen as non-existent, or denounced them as elilim, nothings, or sfedin and seirim, demons and satyrs, and as toebah, abominations" (see . S. Cohon, "The Unity of God: A Study in Hellenistic and Rabbining Theology," in: *Hebrew Union College Annual* 26 [1995]: 425-79, here 430). In the paradigm of Christ God's personal involvement, the matter of the salvation of man is factually seen.

23 The view, e.g., of Confucianism about unity-oneness of heaven and Earth (oneness between heaven and humanity) (S. Sivaraksa, "Religion and World Order from a Buddist Perspective," in Mische / Merkling, *Global Civilisation*, 129f.) would have for Christianity a pure philosophical character, since the unity between God and man that it projects has a personal and ontological character. For instance, while M.E. Tucker discusses Confucianism (*idem*, "Working Toward a Shared Global Ethic: Confucian Perspectives," in Mische / Merkling, *Global Civilisation*, 109-11) he observes the following: "Cheng Cung-ying has described the organic naturalism of Confucian cosmology as characterized by 'natural naturalization' and 'human immanentization' in contrast to the emphasis on rationality and transcendence in Western thought. This sense of naturalism and holism is distinguished by the view that there is no Creator God; rather the universe is considered to be a self-generating, organic process. Confucians are traditionally concerned less with theories of origin or concepts of a personal God than with what they perceive as the ongoing reality of this generating, interrelated universe."

with Muslim theologians who assert a central disunity in the Christian model.[24]

For a Better Understanding of Monotheism

The dilemma that Moltmann puts forward is whether monotheism should be understood exclusively (*exclusiv*) or inclusively (*inclusiv*). Many agree, from a theoretical standpoint, that monotheism is mainly exclusive and that it therefore excludes polytheism. The one God does not *permit* other gods beside Him. Moreover, social reality demonstrates that communities that consider themselves monotheistic are usually not tolerant of the gods of other religions. In the Old Testament, faith in the one God forbids the worship of other gods and such worship is considered gravely sinful. Where this exclusivity extends, however, to the level of violence, and where this violence is justified based on claims of exclusivity, this kind of exclusivity cannot be said to represent God's disposition toward man.

A Christianity that is based on violence could never stand with open eyes before Christ's martyrdom for all people. Therefore, contemporary theological problematics that intend to stand firmly on the issue of monotheism must take into consideration the Christian perspective of the one God in relation to the prospect of salvation for all men. If there is an authentic monotheism from this perspective, it is because every man is able to participate in divinity because one of the three persons of the Holy Trinity has lived incarnated in the world.[25] If inclusiveness means we must base our thinking

[24] "While, exoterically, the religions of the world are many, esoterically they are one: they arise from and return to a common source, and possess within themselves the resources for an extended epistemology by means of which the unity of existence may be discovered and the human personality transformed" (A.A. Said and N.C. Funk, "Islamic Revivalism: A Global Perspective," in Mische / Merkling, *Global Civilisation*, 308-30, here 330). See also J. Woodall, "Humanity's Coming of Age: The Bahai Faith and World Order," in Mische / Merkling, *Global Civilisation*, 342, 343-4: "What the peoples of the world have thus far denied is the reality of the oneness and wholeness of humanity as the children of one loving Creator."

[25] The discussion of the interesting view of A. Gesche, where he makes a distinction between "absolute" and "relative" monotheism in Christianity, does not belong to the limited space of this study. Instead, however, we will submit the summary of his article so that anyone interested can have a general idea and be able to compare it with our own, the above mentioned, view: "The author first of all attempts to establish that the Christian confession of God must simultaneously imply confession of mankind and that without this it simply ceases to exist. Secondly, and more difficult to handle,

on the premise of there being many religions, many Gods, as Moltmann does, then, the next logical step would be to declare Hinduism as the most genuine form of monotheism![26] Thus far, however, the trend has fallen short of this extreme, settling instead on theological pluralism, which we shall discuss further on.

Before humankind can unite, or even peacefully coexist, within global civilization,[27] Christianity must soteriologically come to terms with that unity through the person of the Divine Word, since the religious cooperation required of that unity is not abstract, but must rather be based on the resilience of faith. On this basis, what is needed is less a "Christian" monotheism than a "Christocentric" monotheism." By the term "Christocentric," we naturally presuppose soteriology. Here we do not position Christ as a rival against the great prophet of the Islamic religion, and we do not argue by means of an antithetic theology. We merely attempt to extend and broaden the theological significance that the openness of the flesh of the Word has offered throughout the created world, something that becomes a reality in Christ's incarnation. Aside from the intercultural value of this fact, its worth for the unity of humankind is significant, not because human strength is the basis and center of it, as we have seen in nationalism and communism, but rather because it offers the flesh of God as a point of unity for all diverse peoples.

That many Western theologians show great sympathy towards this prospect is not accidental. For instance, (the Catholic) Andreas Malessa says:

> Each religion wants to appease God with moral acts and beg Him with personal sacrifices. Jesus, on the contrary, points out: God shouldn't be appeased and is not exorcised; no one can bribe Him with something and make Him his instrument. Why not? Because He has already given away His power for the weakness of a

---

is the assertion that the very idea of God implies relationship with mankind. Hence the author believes that he can speak of "relative" monotheism as opposed to "absolute" monotheism. Mankind is the finiteness of God, his fortunate finiteness which allows him to be God, that is to say a "God-of" and not a Divinity" [A. Gesche, "Le christianisme comme monotheisme relativ," in: *Revue theologique de Louvain* 33 [2002]: 437-96, here 496].

26 *Monotheism*, 121-22: "Can polytheism, as it is seen in the world of the Hindu God in every hinduistic temple, be monotheistic? It is possible and it is also explained by religious teachers in India. There is, namely, also an inclusive monotheism ....What we see in the many figures of God is the one divinity .... Only in the many can the One be shown. That's why the hinduistic polytheism is the real inclusive form of monotheism."

27 See Mische / Merkling, *Global Civilisation*, 3.

defenseless child in the cavern and His dominion for the slavery of a servant who washed the feet (of others). Because He offered Himself as sacrifice instead of asking for one. Incarnation and self-sacrifice, I believe so, happened not out of necessity but out of love.[28]

Trinitarian Community and Openness of Christians to the World

We are dealing here with an issue that seems to preoccupy many contemporary theologians. Vorgrimler[29] raises the topic with regard to those who view the life of the Trinitarian God as an everlasting loving conversation. He, himself, admits the existence of a loving community of men in conversation and communion with God, and he counts (unfortunately) Christ himself among these men,[30] yet, he underscores that the main issue concerning Christ is the inter-Trinitarian loving community of persons (*"It is more about the construction of a community of God-persons")* made possible through him. The fact that Christ is considered human in this example, among men who live in communion with God, is problematic (and according to dogmatic terminology, Nestorian) and shows that the attempt to humanize Christ in this way, so that Hindus and Muslims may understand Christianity to be monotheistic, in effect belittles the identity of the person in Christ.

The use of Western psychology played no small part in the development of the idea that the inter-Trinitarian community of the persons of the Holy

28 "Jede Religion will Gott mit moralischem Wohlverhalten beschwichtigen und mit persönlichen Opfern beschwören. Jesus dagegen zeigt: Gott muß nicht beschwichtigt werden, ist nicht zu beschwören, man kann ihn mit nichts bestechen und für nichts instrumentalisieren. Warum nicht? Weil er seine Allmacht bereits gegen die Ohnmacht eines hilflosen Kindes in der Krippe und seine Herrschaft gegen die Knechtschaft eines Füße-waschenden Dieners getauscht hat. Weil er sich selbst bereits als Opfer hingegeben hat, anstatt Opfer zu fordern. Inkarnation und stellvertretendes Sterben, so glaube ich, geschahen im übrigen nicht aus Notwendichkeit, sondern aus Liebe" (see *Christ in der Gegenwart* 51 [2002]: 424. See also *Christ in der Gegenwart* 1 [2003]: 6, where the "Universality of Christianity" is stressed).

29 See "Randständiges Dasein des dreieinigen Gottes? Zur praktischen und spirituellen Dimension der Trinitätslehre," in *Stimmen der Zeit* 220 (2002): 547-52, here 550f.

30 "First of all, in order to clear up a misunderstanding, we must stress here that a loving community in God is self-evident for the faithful: Henoch, Moses, Elia, Abraham, Isaac, Jacob, the man Jesus, Stephan are according to the biblical revelation next to God; the ecclesiastical tradition has counted Mary among them all along" (Vorgrimler, "Randständiges Dasein," 550) (translation mine).

Trinity is a loving one.[31] That is why today there is an intense effort, through the use of apophatic terminology, to demonstrate that the love of God is not something that can be comprehended through the criteria of human potentials. But this does not mean that we should condemn the love that is conveyed through Western theological thought,[32] the Trinitarian community here being understood as a loving one. We simply need to make clarifications.

First of all, it must be stressed that there is currently a tendency to consider as mistaken the expression of the second Vatican Synod, which, through the Trinitarian prospect, attempted to emphasize community, something that it transferred to ecclesiological thought as well.[33] This marks the beginning of what we might call "Communio-Ecclesiology," which sees the ecclesiastical community in the Trinitarian community.[34] It is clear that the second Vatican Synod places emphasis on the Trinity as a community of persons.[35] This is evident in the way Catholic theologians of today attempt to elucidate this point so that any extremity within Triadology-Ecclesiology might not be misunderstood and dismissed. Hence, as to why this cannot apply for the Church as well, since the one divine essence exists in three persons that form a community, Ratzinger responds to an evangelical theologian as follows:

> It grieves me to oppose Mr. Jungel once more. First of all, we have to note that the Church of the West during the transfer of the Trinitarian formula in Latin did not directly adopt the eastern formulation, according to which, God is one essence in

---

31 Saint Augustine, in his effort to show the similarity of the essence of the Spirit with the Father and the Son, was inclined to characterize the Spirit with such names that have to do with the ad extra expression of the persons of the Holy Trinity, such as love and gift of God. With these names he was trying to express the beyond human time relationship of the Trinitarian persons. Thus, one had the basis for the construction of the teaching of the Filioque (see, e.g. *De Trinitate*, PL 42, 1080-1086). For more on this issue see G. Martzelos, *Orthodox Dogma and Theological Reflection*, vol. ii (Thessalonica, 2000), 113ff. (in Greek).

32 H. Vorgrimler mentions as characteristic of the new examples that of P.J. Cordes, *Communio-Utopie oder Programm* (Freiburg, 1993).

33 *Lumen Gentium* 4 quotes the words of Cyprianos of Carthage that the whole Church appears as the united people through the unity of the Father, Son and the Holy Spirit.

34 H. Vorgrimler considers important for this occasion the work of Cordes, *Communio-Utopie*; B. Forte, *La chiesa-icona della trinità* (Brescia, 1984), K. Koch, *Im Glauben an den dreieinen Gott leben* (Fribourg, 2001), 41-63.

35 H. Vorgrimler expresses to the contrary ("Dasein," 551) and says that: "From the reflections on community of the Synod is not necessarily deduced the conclusion that the 2nd Vatican Synod had perceived the Trinity of God as a community of persons" (translation mine).

> three hypostaseis (Subsistenzen), but rather the expression "hypostaseis" was translated in the expression "persons", because the term "Subsistenz" in Latin, as such, did not exist and was not fit to express the unity and the distinction among Father, Son and Holy Spirit. Above all, I am decisively against the way, which comes into fashion today, of the direct transfer of the Trinitarian mystery into ecclesiology. This can't be. And so we end up having three gods.[36]

The problem, therefore, is indeed a neo-idealism (Neoidealismus) that is well developed in contemporary Western theology (not that it doesn't happen with contemporary Orthodox theologians, as well), which overemphasizes freedom in each Trinitarian person as a characteristic element of personal composition in order to demonstrate the distinction among the three hypostaseis of the Holy Trinity. The opposition to this tendency is natural and well aimed.[37] Still, this itself is not reason to minimize the theological importance of the Trinitarian distinction of the hypostaseis. From an Orthodox point of view, we could underline the theological truth that God is not Trinitarian by virtue of being homoousian but because the common source and root origin of the one Trinitarian divinity is the hypostasis of the Father[38] who pre-eternally gives birth to the Son and pre-eternally generates the Holy Spirit. But even on this issue we risk falling into neo-Arianism. As we know, ancient Arians considered the relationship between the Father and the Son as a *relative* and not a *natural* one. Thus, the unity of the Trinitarian persons was considered as similar to the one that the members of the Church have with the Father. They stressed that "*the way of the existence of the Son in the Father can be based*

---

36 *Frankfurter Allgemeine Zeitung*, 22.9.2000, 51: "Es betrübt mich, daß ich auch hier Herrn Jüngel widersprechen muß. Zunächst einmal ist schon anzumerken, daß die Kirche des Westens bei der Übertragung der Trinitarischen Formel ins Lateinische nicht die östliche Formulierung direkt übernommen hat, wonach Gott ein Wesen in drei Hypostasen ('Subsistenzen') ist, sondern das Wort Hypostasen wurde mit dem Ausdruck 'Personen' übersetzt, weil der Begriff Subsistenz im Lateinischen als solcher nicht existierte und nicht angemessen wäre, um Einheit und Verschiedenheit von Vater, Sohn und Heiligen Geist zu formulieren. Vor allem aber bin ich ganz entschieden gegen die immer mehr in Mode kommende Art, das trinitarische Geheimnis direkt auf die Kirche zu übertragen. Das geht nicht. Da enden wir in einem Drei-Götter-Glauben."

37 For a thorough dogmatic confrontation of this tendency we refer to C. Stamoulis, *About Light: Personal or Natural Energies? Contribution to the Contemporary Discussion on Holy Trinity Problematics in the Orthodox Field*, (in Greek), (ed. Τό παλίμψηστον) (Thessalonica, 1999) (cf. my book review in *Orthodoxes Forum of the University of Munich* 2 (1999), 218-222).

38 On Christian Triadology in relation to the charges of gnostics for the existence of polytheism in the Old Testament see Cohon, "The Unity of God," 458f.

on an agapology cut off from any natural relationship."[39] Here, then, the Son and the Spirit are degraded to the level of created beings. To avoid such a line of reasoning one ought to underline the relationship of the other two Trinitarian persons with the Father, their source, a relationship that is natural and not moral. In this way, the anthropomorphic use of Ecclesiology over Triadology is avoided.

Here, Orthodox theology takes a clear stand, which, by means of a theological paradox, rejects extreme kataphatism and extreme apophatism. Man knows God through the divine actions (energies) in an empirical way and not an intellectualist one, and so he can attribute to Him different kataphatic theonymes, which refer to the diversity of His actions and render representatively God's relation to the world. One could thus say that Trinitarian Theology is developed from Soteriology,[40] since from what God does, we comprehend His identity.[41] The expression is not aimless that, since the *ad extra* expression of God is Trinitarian, therefore, God is Trinitarian, as well,[42] or, even better, that the relationships between God and human are patterned on the inter-Trinitarian relationship.[43] The names of God, such as Creator and Savior, are without effect unless they are connected to the way in which man receives and regards the actions of the Trinitarian God. In this case, the distinction between the uncreated God and the created world, which we have already

---

39 See Stamoulis, *Physis and Agape*, (in Greek), (Thessalonica, 1999), 44ff., upon which we draw our argumentation that objects to the contemporary neo-Arian agapology (the study "Physis and Agape" in English see under the title "Physis and Agape: The Application of the Trinitarian Model to the Dialogue on Ecclesiology of the Christian Churches of the Ecumene," in *The Greek Orthodox Theological Review* 44 [1999]: 451-66).

40 In this way, one could also accept the view that "we are able to address God, then, only because God first addresses us, for the same reason that our knowledge of God must follow in the wake of God's knowledge of us" (J. Andrew Fullerton, "God by any other Name?," in *Modern Theology* 18 [2002]: 171-81, here 174).

41 We could stand positively on the principle of K. Barth: "Where the actuality exists there is also the corresponding possibility." (cf. *Church Dogmatics*, II/1 [Edinburgh, 1957], 5).

42 The economic Trinity is based on the pre-eternal Trinity and is not irrelevant to it. The severe distinction between eternal (Οΐδια) and economic (οικονομικο) Trinity has become an object of criticism by Catherine Mowry Lacugna in her *God For Us: The Trinity and Christian Life* (New York, 1991).

43 What people know of God is irrelevant to God's nature, but rather has to do with His actions; that is, the relationship of God with man is an energetic one (C. Stamoulis, *Physis and Agape*, 47).

mentioned, does not constitute for the Fathers an ontological distinction irrelevant to its connection with gnoseology. That is, although God becomes known to the creation through His actions – in His essence, in nature, and in the manner of expression of His actions, still also in His way of existence as a Trinity of persons – remains transcendental and unreachable. Hence, God is, at the same time, known and unknown, explicit and ineffable, revealed and hidden.[44]

If we keep all the above in mind, then we can understand without misinterpretation the fact that Christ Himself projects the Trinity as a model of society affecting the lives of the faithful ("...*so that all become one, as we are one*").[45] This projection is also relevant to Christ's urging His disciples to teach in all nations, baptizing in the name of the Trinity. Hence, Christian monotheism is not unsociable, in the sense that God is restricted to His essence and talks only through His prophets. The distinction that Orthodox theology accentuates between the *essence* and *energies* of God denotes that God is not self-restricted. God communicates *energetically* with creation and man, but also directly (hypostatically) everyday with the Church, since the Holy Eucharist provides the possibility for the incarnated Word to be received within us. So here the mobility and sociability of God are stressed, a mobility that does not only refer to the relationship of God with the world and with man, but also to His inter-Trinitarian existence.[46]

In this way, the evangelic word, always mobile, ought to be regarded as always incarnated (in every environment where it is fostered) and coordinated with the morphological elements of cultures it wishes to touch. This was the case in the early Christian years, when the incarnated evangelic word came in contact with the nations,[47] and this is something that must not change, since

---

44 See on this matter G. Martzelos, *Kataphasis and Apophasis according to Maximus the Confessor*, (in Greek), Offprint from the records of the 22nd Theological Conference with the theme "Saint Maximus the Confessor," (Thessalonica, 2001), 159-72.

45 John 17:21. Christ himself projected the divine unity. According to Mark. 12,:29 Jesus referred to Deut. 6,:4-5 as an important element and based on it the command of Lev. 19:18 for the due love toward our fellowman. Although the other parallel excerpts Mat. 19:16ff., and 22:34ff. and Luke 18:18-30 do not include this, they insist on the reference to the unity of God that is based on the divine fatherhood (see also Mat. 5-7). See also S.S. Cohon, "The Unity of God," 451.

46 See Martzelos, *Orthodox Dogma*, 92f.

47 See Martzelos, "The Incarnation of the Word as a Fundamental Missionary Principle of the Ancient Church," (in Greek), in *Introductory Lessons of the Theological Circle in the Open University* (in Greek) (Thessalonica, 2002), 281-309, here 285-87.

Christ is not just a historical person, but rather "*yesterday and today the One and the same and for ever.*" (Hebrews 13:8). We stress this point because it seems that in the dialogue among Christianity, Judaism, and Islam, there is a tendency for a Christian inclination toward *tropical monarchianism* (*modalism*), in the effort to convince the others that they, too, are monotheists. What seems to be absent in these cases is the sense of Christ as Man-God, as the *ecclesiastical center* expressing the redeeming power of Christianity and of Christian monotheism.

Rahner, for instance, in his attempt to speak monotheistically about Islam, focuses his theological terminology on Father God. He says that Father God, in the history of God's revelation to the world, is not far from creation, and is revealed to it as the eternal life in truth and as love (in other parts he replaces these words with Word and Spirit).[48] But how can one perceive the expression that *the one and inconceivable God is close (nahe) to Christ,* when, at the same time, it is underlined that Christ is not just any prophet? If He is not just any prophet, why is it not explicitly stated that He is the second person of the Holy Trinity? It is a fact that Islamic theologians accuse Christianity of having three gods. But is it scholarly, from a Christian point of view, to turn toward *tropical monarchianism* in order to communicate with Islam[49]?

48 See H. Vorgrimler, "Dasein," 549. Here we might have an agreement with the view of those who claim that "Father, Son and Holy Spirit" are common names and not simply special names, see A.F. Kimel, "The God Who Likes His Name: Holy Trinity, Feminism, and the Language of Faith," in A.F. Kimel (ed.), *Speaking the Christian God*, Grand Rapids, 1992), 188-208.

49 Besides, on another occasion, K. Rahner supports the view that "(the) 'immanent' Trinity is the necessary condition for the possibility of God's free self-communication" (*The Trinity*, [London, 1970], 102, ftnte.1). In other parts he expresses himself as follows: "In the revelations, and the fact of the salvation, the faithful had to do with the unspoken mystery of the not tangible, unoriginated God, named Father, who does not exist and remain in a metaphysical distance, but rather the Creator, himself, wants to announce to all His non-conception and dominion and freedom as their eternal life in truth and love. This one and inconceivable God is in an impervious way historically close to man in Jesus Christ, who is not just any prophet in an open line of prophets, but rather the final and impervious self-completion of the one God in history. And this one and same God announces Himself to men as the Holy Spirit, in the very middle of the human existence for the salvation and completion that God Himself is. There are also for the Christian faith two radical and final facts, ways of existence of the one God in the world, which are the provided free from God, final salvation of the world, in history and transcendence. These two facts exist and always succumb to differentiation, when they mutually presuppose each other" (translation mine) (See K. Rahner, "Einzigkeit und Dreifaltigkeit Gottes im Gespräch mit dem Islam," in *Schriften zur Theologie* 13 (Zürich, 1978), 139f..

Allowing readers to answer the above question for themselves (directly), we attempt to provide an answer (indirectly) for ourselves, through reference to other views of contemporary theologians. At this point, let us refer to the importance that is placed on Christian Trinitarian Theology in relation to modern society. According to Boff, who depicts man in modern society as yearning to belong to a social whole, Trinitarian Theology is a solution, since the Trinitarian communion provides a model for a society that promotes participation as well as individual distinction.[50] Indeed, it is commonly accepted that the first Christian community attempted to live according the model of the Trinitarian community, while subsequent generations of Christians tended to get carried away by political structures, instead of focusing on the biblical relationship between God and men. What we are talking about here is a relationship that is characterized by "emptying" (κένωση) and "inclusion" (συμπεριχώρηση). "Emptying" in this regard means our giving of ourselves for others for the sake of a common good, as in the emptying of the Word (Philip. 2, 5-11), where the salvation of all men is achieved. The term "inclusion" (συμπεριχώρηση) refers to the acceptance of others, to the simultaneous acceptance of unity and distinction. A model of unity is found in the Trinitarian communion of the essence, while distinctions are rendered with hypostatic particularity. This entire synthesis of unity and distinction could be rendered with the patristic term "inter-inclusion" (συμπεριχώρηση). The ecclesiological Basis for this inclusion is the body of Christ.

As we know, for the heresiarch Areios, the Father is a divine essence, which is distinct from that of the Son; Areios said that only the Father is eternal and uncreated; the Son is a creation, superior to other creations. Arius was really far from the liturgical expression of the Church, which wanted to demonstrate the pre-eternal relationship of the Trinitarian hypostaseis and experienced the ecclesiastical way of life through the (saving) manifestation of the Trinitarian unity in the world. Today, in perspectives such as that held by Boff, we can detect an intense anti-Arian climate, in which there is no underestimation of the Word. Boff stresses that each divine person is asserted from the other divine persons and points out the significance of unity in combination with the otherness of the persons. He considers that community is achieved by means of participation and mutual emptying.[51] In this case, we have the projection of the Trinity as the perfect community, with an under-

[50] See *Holy Trinity, Perfect Community* (Maryknoll, 2000), XIII.

[51] Boff, *Trinity*, 3.

scoring of the fact that the Trinitarian heresies failed because they did not grasp the importance of the three hypostaseis in unity and the unity of God in the three hypostaseis. Tropical Monarchianism maintained that the One God had three different ways of expression. Three-theism (Tritheismus) spoke of a faith in three different gods and denied a relationship of unity in divinity. Both heresies offered rational simplifications that tried to downgrade the perception of the mystery of the Trinity as a perfect community.[52] To avoid such pitfalls of reasoning, as we mentioned above, one must honor the relationship of the other two Trinitarian persons with the Father, their source, as natural and not moral. Accordingly then, the trend of contemporary theologians to favor simple expressions of the dogma is very important.

Finally, we must address the theological claim that God is love (1. John. 4, 8). This simple expression is fundamental for Trinitarian teaching. Man knows God as love and as self-given, something that is a challenge for and an invitation to every man (*love each other, as I have loved you* {John. 3, 34}). Yet this has been explicated by modern theologians to mean "*God is the lover, the beloved, and the love between them*," in reference to the three divine persons. From an Orthodox point of view this rendering cannot be considered scholarly, because it is based on the teaching of *Filioque,* [53] and strains of neo-idealism are apparent here as well. Yet emphasizing the understanding of God as love is not something that should be extended to the particularity of the person, but rather to the manifestation of God for people through their common energies.

We can see in the thought of the majority of modern theologians that while some are inclined toward Tropical Monarchianism, others favor the hypostatic distinction and acknowledge the Trinitarian unity as an essential element for the development of social relations in the world, according to the model of the Trinitarian relationship and the ecclesiastical community.[54] But

52 Boff, *Trinity*, 56-57; J. Neuner / J. Dupuis, *The Christian Faith* (Staten Island, 1996), 136.

53 See T.J. Scirghi, "The Trinity: A Model for Belonging in Contemporary Society," in *The Ecumenical Review* 54 (2002): 333-42, here 336: "The Spirit, proceeding from both, is the bond of the love between them: "God is the lover, the beloved, and the love between them".

54 See Scirghi, "Trinity," 337-38: "The communitarian theory resembles a Trinitarian model in that the individual and the community are viewed as co-existent: there is no being apart from belonging. Furthermore, we are made in the image of God and the image of God is Triune, with the Three existing in an eternal communion of agape, a relation-ship of mutual giving and receiving .... The sacrament of baptism in the name

when we speak of Christian openness to the world, we must mean the loving unity that Christianity offers to modern society as a model of social life, a model based on the Trinitarian example of Christ's self-giving to the world, a paradigm of unity that is inclined against contemporary social individualism.[55]

Hence, we wouldn't disagree with the view that the divine community is a mystery of "inclusion," since it is of the nature of the Trinity to open up (*ad extra*) and thus become empirically understood by man. Indeed, the incarnation of the Word introduced the Trinity to human history, with its demonstration that the distinction between *created* (man) and *uncreated* (God) is not a partitioning of these two realities. It is very likely that this Trinitarian model of community was the basic premise for relations in the first Christian communities, among themselves and with the broader world (Prax. 4, 32, 34-35).[56]

Exclusiveness and Pluralism

Among Christians there seem to be two responses to religious differentiation: that of exclusiveness and that of pluralism. The crucial point for the exclusivist perspective is that only the Christian faith is salvific, and that whatever virtues another religion may present, it cannot offer access to the highest truth that is identified with Christ. Christianity maintains that denial of Christ as the one Lord and Savior of all men is denial of the truest of all truths.

From the pluralist perspective, Christ provides a valid route to salvation, but not the only one. Pluralists maintain that one comes to discover other routes to salvation through dialogue and experience with other religious traditions. The criterion for judging a religion here is the degree to which salvation is made accessible to its individual members. What constitutes "salvation,"

---

of the Triune God is a sign of belonging: the anointed members of the church no longer belong solely to themselves, but to Christ .... Celebration allows us to enter into a more profound communion with the social groups that define us."

55 See Scirghi, "Trinity," 341: "The claim that the Trinity is the basis for human belonging makes a strong political statement, for it insists not only that human beings are social but that the ground of all beings lies in belonging to one another. Moreover, the Trinity provides the deepest foundation possible within the Christian tradition for the rejection of the bias towards individualism ...."

56 See also Scirghi, "Trinity," 336.

however, is a point upon which the pluralists disagree. What they do agree upon is the assertion that all religious traditions share a common goal, and they claim that by holding this understanding, theologians are in a position to view religious traditions outside their own with greater objectivity and impartiality. Upon these grounds, they invite the exclusivists to overcome their introversion.

Although the pluralists' respectful disposition toward other traditions is admirable, it nonetheless lacks critical depth by avoiding a thorough enough analysis of what makes religions and salvific perspectives differ from one another. If pluralism views all perspectives as equal, then the term "pluralism" loses its real meaning. At the outset, it is important to refute the claim that the pluralist approach is primarily triumphalist; that is, that its true agenda is to project universalism with a one-upmanship agenda over and above the universalist claims of rival perspectives. What the pluralists do have to offer us is their willingness to acknowledge common values, and their openness to interreligious dialogue for the sake of the common good. In this way, Christians must admit to at least this degree of pluralism if indeed they affirm their faith in God's universal love for all His creatures – and this is key – for all His creatures *including those* who do not believe in Him or are His enemies. If Christian monotheism represents this soteriological message of universal love authentically, then it cannot embrace a *fully* exclusivist approach to religious differences.

Exclusiveness of Christianity?

In the social life of our times, we are all aware of the revival of different cultural and religious traditions under the influence of crucial factors, one of which we consider especially noteworthy.[57] This is the fact that modern man can no longer dispute the truth that there are no superior and inferior civilizations, but must acknowledge rather the various and permissible forms of human expression.[58] Clearly, Christian theology shares a debt with all other religions to give this issue its fair attention. This acknowledgement not only informs comparisons between Christian and non-Christian religions but even juxtaposes between Eastern and Western Christianity, and of especial sig-

[57] See on these points Petrou, *Orthodox Theology*, 214-5.

[58] Petrou, *Orthodox Theology*, 215.

nificance, self-inquiry on the part of Christians searching for spiritual and theological solutions in the ecumenical tradition of the Church, not as a cultural and historical commodity, but rather as a factor of redemption for all men, without exception.[59] Theology is not completely dependent on conditions of social reality, but it synthesizes these conditions within dialogue as a support to and vehicle of communication, and within that synthesis theology attempts to further its own soteriological message.[60] And no matter how much a religion modifies its language as an aid to dialogue, it is nonetheless true that each religion generally regards itself as the only possessor of the one truest truth.

What then, could a possible Orthodox stance be regarding this matter? We would dare say that *the flesh of Christ has enough room not only for every man, but for every religion, as well.* In this way, Christianity does not act as a constraint on social development, but rather affects those developments soteriologically. Hence, the moment that man tries to shake off any religious authority, Christianity does not impose one more, but rather suggests the compliance of that authority with the contemporary social demands of religious pluralism. Along these lines, there is another daring assertion regarding terminology as well as essence: We could say that *religious pluralism can assume hypostasis in the hypostasis of the Word* who was incarnated for all His creations, that is, for every man (of every tradition). It seems, herein, that *monotheism does not claim exclusiveness*, but rather lovingly opens up to Christ's sameness of essence with all His creatures. In this way, the evangelical message can be elevated in the modern world, something that represents the sincerest aims of Orthodox theologian-sociologists.

Of course, one could claim that the above expression has the Word as its center of gravity and, consequently, that it declares and underscores the exclusiveness of Christianity. Yet to refute that claim, one must simply acknowledge the importance of the opening up of Christian monotheism to oth-

---

59 We truly believe that for Orthodox theology, speaking to the modern world must not rest on the historical models of the past, but rather on the theological prospect that the theological tradition of the past opens up for its spreading to the modern world, when it is not considered that theology is served by other sciences, but when it serves them to show them off in relation to God. It is a contemporary phenomenon for someone to think that he speaks theologically and like a Christian, when, in the development of the (anthropological) word, Christ and the Redemption offered by God are absent. One thinks today that by talking specifically about man and in the abstract about God, he has grasped the theological word.

60 See regarding our thoughts here also Petrou, *Orthodox Theology*, 213.

ers – and this is the key point – the significance of the evangelic exhortation to love even one's enemy. Let us not forget the key passage of the New Testament regarding the criterion upon which God judges men, Matthew 25: 31-46. Here it is clearly stressed that living in accordance with God's will involves helping the hungry, the thirsty, the naked, the sick, the imprisoned. Besides, if someone reads Paul (Rom. 2:9), he will realize that the apostle stresses God's grace and not mankind's ability to judge. The apostle maintains, of course, that the ones who don't believe lead a sinful life, which denotes a failure to recognize God, yet he does not speak of them in a punishing way.[61] Of course, the evangelic excerpt, upon which one stands with great caution regarding the issue of the exclusiveness of Christianity, is the passage declaring that *nobody approaches the Father without me* (meaning Christ). Surely the subject here is the Divine Word, of whom John speaks in his prologue. In this case, we want to emphasize this fact as a self-obligation on the part of Christians toward openness to others. That is, if the sameness of Christ's essence with that of all men is the bridge here, then that understanding in itself raises all men towards the Father, and therefore we must not interpret the evangelic expression exclusively, but rather pluralistically[62] or, even better, ecumenically.[63]

The exclusiveness of Christianity (*Die Absolutheit des Christentums*) is a problem fervently debated by modern scientific theology and one producing a rich bibliography on the subject.[64] As we know, in the multireligious reality of contemporary multicultural societies, men and women are confident that they can define their own self-hood, yet to claim that multiculturality is a kind of universal religion and to condemn it on those grounds is common in funda-

---

61 Very interesting questions about ecclesiological exclusiveness and openness are found in the article of G. George Florofsky, "The Doctrine of the Church and the Ecumenical Problem," in *The Ecumenical Review* 2 (1950), 152-61.

62 Furthermore, since nothing in the world came into existence without the creative intervention of the Word and since the Word is the image of the Father, the expression that through the Word man knows the Father can be understood from this aspect, as well.

63 Here we discern the basic difference of today's ecumenism from the ecumenical spirit of the undivided ancient church. The Orthodox Church underlines the Christological truth, since Christology is the base for the genuine anthropology (see G. Mantzaridis, *Christian Ethics*, (in Greek), vol. I. [Thessalonica, 2002], 277).

64 We refer here to the highly remarkable study of Reinhold Bernhard, *Der Absolutheitsanspruch des Christentums. Von der Aufklärung bis zur pluralistischen Theologie der Religionen* (Gütersloh, 1991).

mentalist circles and is easy to do. What is most evident in multicultural movements, even where multireligiosity plays a role, is the aim to elevate the status of those formerly relegated to disadvantageous positions of otherness within society, and to resist being defined and ruled by self-appointed authorities. And Christianity, here, since it has as its core the spirit of *diakonia*, is naturally in favor of these multicultural-multireligious aims. Christianity does not regard itself as culturally superior to the religious cultures of others, but it testifies to its soteriological power with a spirit of *diakonia*, a spirit it draws from the Cross and the Resurrection of Christ for the sake of mankind. With this theological approach, Christianity has an "exclusive" goal in response to contemporary "ecumenism" whenever and wherever that leads to religious syncretism, even where this syncretism is understood fundamentally as an attempt at pacifism.[65] In its theological testimony, Christianity must be "absolute" because "human beings, like the whole of creation, acquire their full dignity within the fellowship or communion of the Holy Spirit in the body of Christ, where sin and death are abolished."[66]

Conclusion

Within multicultural society, God can be found in many places and in many forms, and the question of God is alive and well in its broad reception as a process of learning and seeking with others. As Christians, we are called to take into consideration the syncretism of our times and the seasonal transformations of our ideas, but also our weakness to fully conceive of God's reality. This means that the exclusion of others, a tendency that increases in direct proportion to the stress we place on social difference, is not in agreement with the Christian spirit. However, in order for us to fully and authentically respond to this call, an understanding of Christian monotheism must be clarified first among Christians themselves, so that their debates with other religions might be based securely on dogmatic theology.

Skepticism has shown itself to be an ineffective stance in interreligious dialogue. Indeed, skepticism can prove dangerous – an attitude provoking conflict rather than understanding. In all cases, the concomitant social and

[65] See also G. Mantzaridis, *Ethics*, (in Greek), 279-80.

[66] See N. Matsoukas, "The Economy of the Holy Spirit (the Standpoint of Orthodox Theology)," in *The Ecumenical Review* 41 (1989): 398-405, here 403.

possible political affiliations and crosscurrents that emerge in the self-representations of any religious group within a multicultural society must be taken into serious consideration, particularly where restoration of "original" values and practices becomes a primary concern, as we have seen with some "fundamentalist" groups within Judaism, Islam, and Christianity. All too often, the push for this type of "restoration" takes place at the expense of critical thought and open dialogue, as Alain Finkielkraut[67] has noted, nearly guaranteeing the kind of violence that has already left its bloody traces in European history.

Exclusion and anathema, exile and violence, do not belong to the kingdom of God, because God is, energetically, love. God does not wish for the death of the sinner, but for his repentance and his God-inspired life. Ecumenical and interreligious dialogues are a natural expression of such a hermeneutic viewpoint, and, instead of being disregarded or obstructed, their contribution to theological and dialogical training must be acknowledged, most especially for their power of suasion in civil confrontation with agnostic culture. If, therefore, contemporary, global, multicultural society is in need of a moral religious authority,[68] then Christianity has a great theological and social responsibility to stress the soteriological power of the Christian message for all of humankind, not only for Christians.

The Christian world faces a crucial question: whether it will successfully respond to the call to spread the evangelical message of salvation within contemporary society. The question may be simplified: Exclusiveness or Inclusiveness? The answer is not irrelevant to Christological soteriology, and looking backward, toward "restoration" in reversion to the Scholastic past, is no alternative, because it is incomprehensible in today's multicultural world.

---

67 A. Finkielkraut, *La défaite de la pensée* (Paris, 1987).

68 Mahmoud-Abedin, "Islam," 305.

Georges De Schrijver

Christian Faith in the Postmodern Context: The Case of Gianni Vattimo

Vattimo and The Question of Religious Pluralism

Postmodernity allows for religious pluralism and continually reveals that there are as many options for religious belief and practice as there are persons and communities. Of course, none of these parties can be said to be in possession of the whole and full truth – each lives by his or her perspective life-option, whereby no perspective can be proven more plausible than another. This is what the pluralistic condition in late modernity is all about, and Gianni Vattimo is well aware of it.

Yet, for Vattimo, because he is an expert in cultural studies, this free-wheeling "relativism" cannot be the right answer to the crisis of metaphysics. Time and again, he warns against those versions of hermeneutics that simply wind up in relativism, "versions which take hermeneutics purely as a philosophy of the irreducible multiplicity of perspectives."[1] For Vattimo, the pure celebration of irreducible multiplicity is suspect, because it brackets the question of one's anchorage in a place or within tradition. He discovers, in other words, the importance of a tradition (and of traditions in plural), and he links this to Heidegger's analysis of *Dasein* (our "being there"). It is only, he says, when one becomes aware of one's unavoidable mortality and *thrownness* into existence, that one will be able to also appreciate our thrownness in the contingent fabric of a language and a tradition. Willy-nilly, one finds oneself in the continuation of a tradition – a tradition among many other traditions – tradition "understood as the active inheritance of the past as an open possibility, not as a rigidly determined and determining schema."[2]

We can better understanding now why Vattimo could speak of his "coming home to religion" after so many years of "nihilistic" existence. Indeed, he is convinced that cultural traditions, with their particular schemas of interpreting reality, are at bottom rooted in particular religions. It therefore comes

---

1 G. Vattimo, *Beyond Interpretation: The Meaning of Hermeneutics for Philosophy* (Cambridge, 1997), 91.

2 Vattimo, *Beyond Interpretation*, 90.

as no surprise to see how, in recounting his life story (a "nihilist" who became again a Catholic, or at least a neo-Catholic), Vattimo ventures to make a decisive link between the philosophical "weakening of Being" (of strong structures) that took place in the European tradition, *and* the "weakening of God" as testified to in the Christian message of God's self-emptying in Christ.

Vattimo makes it clear that the awareness of the "weakening of Being" does not simply prepare us for welcoming religion again. What matters, he says, is that "the incarnation, that is, God's abasement to the level of humanity … will be interpreted as the sign that the non-violent[3] and non-absolute God of the post-metaphysical epoch has as its distinctive trait the very vocation for weakening of which Heideggerian philosophy speaks."[4] Indeed, "nihilism is too much 'like' *kenosis* for one to see this likeness as simply a coincidence, an association of ideas."[5] Between both exists a structural resemblance. Post-metaphysical "weakening" is the "unfolding" of the history of God's self-abasement as this history reaches us through interpretive processes that took place behind our back – including the "secularizing" interpretation of the Gospel message.[6]

Listening, thus, to the call that reaches him from the "unfolding" or "history of its effects" (*Wirkungsgeschichte*) of the Christian tradition, Vattimo is struck by the relevance-for-today of the Gospel's message: charity *(caritas)*, love, and self-giving. To put these directives into practice – in new circumstances and with new tools of organization – not only makes us Christians, as we should be Christians today, but also links us back, through the long chain of the "unfolding" of Christian tradition, to the "founding myth" of God's *kenosis* in Christ (as we shortly will see, the word "myth" has no negative connotations for Vattimo). Incidentally, some years ago, Vattimo became a member of the European parliament. In this function, he is committed to programs of peacekeeping and non-violence.

At this juncture, we meet with serious difficulty. Vattimo advocates the recognition of a plurality of traditions. He invites each one to recover his or her cultural roots in order to gain the inspiration necessary for redescribing

---

3 Vattimo mentions, various times, the influence René Girard had on his basic insights.

4 G. Vattimo, *Belief* (Cambridge, 1999), 39.

5 Vattimo, *Beyond Interpretation*, 52.

6 Vattimo speaks up for a "positive" meaning of secularization. "Namely the idea that lay modernity (in Europe) is constituted above all as a continuation and desacralizing interpretation of the biblical message." (Vattimo, *Belief*, 41).

the meaning of one's life in a "nihilistic" fragmented context. Additionally, Vattimo has himself returned to his cultural roots: God's self-abasement in Jesus Christ, which he links with "weak thought," hereby suggesting that this way of thinking can also be appropriated by those living outside the Christian or post-Christian Occident. One might ask, however, whether such an approach boils down to an excessive exaltation of Christianity at the expense of the very dignity of other religions. This is the decisive, but also the most troublesome, question we must address.

God Revealed in Many Symbolic Manifestations

At the outset, I must say something about Vattimo's respect for the typical message of myths (recall that he terms the incarnation a "myth"). For Vattimo, myths and symbolic language are the proper tools of religion – of all religions. However, he observes, when Western philosophers – Hegel, for example – appropriated religious myths, they tended to transpose those myths into schemas of purely rational thought. So the proper message of the myth that is suprarational was neglected by Western philosophers and viewed with condescension – as part of a culture that had not yet attained the higher stage of rational understanding. The East – the whole of Asia as the cradle of the world religions – was seen as "irrational," whereas the West, particularly since the rise of modern philosophy, was regarded as the locus of rational thinking. To go beyond Hegel, Vattimo has recourse to Schelling, who developed a much more appreciative view of mythologies. What remains to be done, Vattimo says, is to honor the proper contents of religious myths, instead of mutilating them by interpreting their narratives for purposes other than those for which they are intended. In this, he follows his master Luigi Pareyson, from whom he learned the following insight:

The mythic character of the encounter with the divine does not arise from the roughness of human faculties yet to be educated in rational thought. It arises from the essence of the transcendent itself, which is revealed only in speaking to the whole of man as a natural being, imposing itself in forms that cannot be appropriated, as is the case with myth, poetry, and languages charged with images and emotions.[7]

---

7 Vattimo, *Beyond Interpretation*, 55.

Vattimo welcomes Pareyson's stress on the power of myths to evoke the symbolic manifestation[8] of the divine in concrete facts and events. He further appreciates that for Pareyson this openness to symbolic manifestations is not at all a sign of immaturity. On the contrary, symbolic manifestations are the very essence of religiousness – a fact that has been brought to our attention by God's incarnation in Christ. He boldly declares:

> Christ is not just a special case of a "generic" sensible revelation of God: it is He that makes possible, through his incarnation, every symbolic manifestation of the divine. Christ does not undermine the myths and stories "of false and lying Gods": he makes their signification of the divine possible for the first time.[9]

Here we are far removed from interpreters who have a propensity for distinguishing the Christian "myth" of the God incarnate from "mythical understandings" in other religions. For them, God has fully revealed himself only in Jesus Christ. Christ renders present, through words and gestures charged with images and emotions, the Godhead's inner life. And because of its ability to *disclose* the inner life of God, this revelation must be termed "substantial." Indeed, they emphasize, here we see how the "universal" (the divine) reveals itself in this "particular" figure. Therefore this revelation is unique and cannot be compared to the approach of non-Christian religions. For non-Christian religions always start from the "particular," viewed as a pointer to the "universal" (the divine). In Hinduism, e.g., the many Gods – Brahma, Vishnu, Shiva – all direct our attention to the one Absolute. The many Gods, thus, are particular characters pointing beyond themselves to the "universal" (the supreme Being); but this view is not on the same footing as Christian revelation where one confesses that the "universal" (the Absolute) has singled out the concrete figure of Jesus Christ to make him the "symbolic manifestation" of its inner life. In short, in this view, non-Christian religions are viewed as so many forms of "reaching out" for the Holy; whereas, in Christianity, the Holy God is seen as drawing near to make Himself visible in a tangible form, and this purely on his own initiative.

For Vattimo, this way of thinking smacks of foundationalism and logocentrism, and he rejects it. He refuses to engage in a pyramidal way of thinking because of its tendency to regard the lower echelons as inferior or, at best, just preparatory, ways for the real thing to come. If one thinks through what

8 Allegory and symbolic manifestation are two categories used by Schelling.

9 Vattimo, *Beyond Interpretation*, 55.

the incarnation of Christ really means, he says, one will stop "taking Christ as opening the way to a recognition of ancient myths as partially and provisionally true, yet rendered obsolete by his coming."[10] He thus affirms that all the world religions have, in and through their worship, access to the "full presence of the symbolized in its sensible manifestation."[11] And, he adds, this is so thanks to the self-abasement and weakening of God in Jesus' human existence. Has Vattimo, one wonders, lost himself so much in religious fervor that he begins to speak "in tongues," when evoking the marvel of the so many, and so varied, sensible manifestations of the divine in the world's holy places, temples, and rituals? And what is still more amazing: why does he underline so much the centrality of Christ in this event? How are we to understand that this one Christ, through his incarnation, makes possible the emergence of a plurality of religions, giving evidence of their true religiousness, in their diversity and difference?

Kenotic versus Philosophical Plurality

I must confess that this is a main crux of Vattimo's work – his *Arcanum*,[12] or arcane site, that one can only get at through serious initiation. Indeed, it took me some time to see through the veil spread over this secret place, and to begin to see the detour Vattimo had to make to reach his insight. This "detour" consists in clarifying the difference between an Aristotelian type of plurality and a Pauline type of plurality. He proceeds by juxtaposing the two following quotes: "Being is said in many ways" (Aristotle),[13] and "in multifarious and many ways God has spoken to our fathers through the prophets until he recently spoke to us through his son" (*Letter to the Hebrews*).[14] This juxtaposition underscores the distinctive approaches underlying the two types of plurality: the philosophical approach and the kenotic approach. What is the difference between the two, and why does it matter? Aristotle's notion of the

---

[10] Vattimo, *Beyond Interpretation*, 55.

[11] Vattimo, *Beyond Interpretation*, 55.

[12] I take this term form Dietrich Bonhoeffer.

[13] Aristotle, Metaphysics IV,2. 1003 a 33: "to on legethai pollachoos."

[14] Letter to the Hebrews, 1: 1-2): "multifariam, multisque modis olim Deus locutus patribus in Prophetis, novissime ... locutus est nobis in Filio quem constituit heredem universorum" (Vattimo just gives the Latin text, without translation).

plurality of Being says that truth can be expressed and experienced in various ways (through poetry, theater, rhetorical discourse, dialectical thinking, etc.). Yet, he objects, this theoretical pluralism is of little help to those (from whichever cultural setting they come) who want to interpret their lives in response to a call that reaches them from *their* "unfolding" tradition.

Theoretical pluralism is an objectivistic construct that lacks the ability to guide one's existential practice of hermeneutics. It only offers a theory about the refraction of the oneness that "*is*" into its many forms which share in this "*is*": it is a doctrine of "plurivocity" launched from a value-free metaphysical background. Indeed, underneath the affirmation of multiplicity, there is always the tendency to think in terms of substance (giving priority to a "proper meaning" which reduces all the rest to analogies). As a consequence, only lip service is paid to the irreducible plurality of the many voices (those of religions included). If one says, for example, that besides *logos* (logical reasoning) there is also *mythos* (mythical evocation), this statement is made from the standpoint of *logos,* thus affirming the superiority of the latter. A thinking that starts with substance cannot avoid introducing hierarchies. But even when one would try to remove "substance" from the argument, one is still left with an objectivistic construct in which persons are not passionately involved. Vattimo says:

> For Aristotelian ontological pluralism, even denuded of its reference to substance, remains an objectivistic-metaphysical thesis: the Being is said in many ways because, and only because, it *is* in many ways – irreducible to be sure, yet nonetheless articulated *as one* (in the sole descriptive presupposition that "reflects" them in their plurality).[15]

Aristotle's plurivocity, then, is still worlds apart from the type of hermeneutics Vattimo wants to promote: the personal or collectively shared redescription of meaning in the midst of a fragmented world, carried out by people belonging to different cultural horizons, and from the background of these horizons.

This brings us to the citation from the Letter to the Hebrews. What is it that captures Vattimo's attention in this text? And from which angle does he look at it? Answer: from the history of hermeneutics. Vattimo makes it clear that he locates himself within the history of hermeneutics, which started with the interpretation of the bible. Yet, he says, from this tradition, modern hermeneutic schools only kept alive the need to interpret our lives, without both-

---

[15] Vattimo, *Beyond Interpretation*, 47.

ering any more about the content of the bible. Dilthey (1833-1911), developed hermeneutics as "general philosophy," emancipating it from "the dogmatism in which it was bound as a technique in the service of biblical exegesis."[16] This allowed him to pay attention to human historicity, which, however, he still approached too much in terms of historiography (models to live by were heroes and geniuses of the past). It was only when Heidegger drew attention to "the relation between temporality and the historicity of existence" that hermeneutics really began to be seen as a search for meaning. This step was decisive because a place could now be given again to religion. Yet, Vattimo observes, the rediscovery of religion in general (the re-appreciation of its mythico-poetical language) did as yet not lead to a recovery of the core message of Christianity. And it is to this recovery that Vattimo himself will turn. For him, it is not enough to acknowledge that the Christian tradition has given rise in Western culture to a continuous practice of interpretation; one must also regard Christianity's message as constitutive of the West. He says:

> Modern hermeneutic philosophy is born in Europe not only because here there is a religion of the book that focuses our attention on the phenomenon of interpretation, but also because this religion has at its base the idea of the incarnation of God, which it conceives as *kenosis*, as abasement and, in our translation, as weakening.[17]

Behind this bifurcation, there are two schools of approach to the phenomenon of secularization – a school that regards secularization as "emancipation from the Christian tradition" and a school that sees "secularization as the authentic destiny of Christianity (and not as its abandonment and negation)."[18] The first holds that hermeneutics will lead to the elimination of the content of the Christian dogma, whereas the second uses hermeneutics to interpret this content in such a way that it may again speak to contemporary people in their secularized contexts. Vattimo belongs to the second school. He is convinced that secularization is not something accidental in Christianity but "rather a 'drift' inscribed positively in the destiny of *kenosis*."[19] He does not tire of pointing to the organic link existing between God's *kenosis* in Christ, secularization, and the nihilistic "weakening of Being." Hermeneutics (which causes

16 Vattimo, *Beyond Interpretation*, 47.

17 Vattimo, *Beyond Interpretation*, 48.

18 Vattimo, *Beyond Interpretation*, 51.

19 Vattimo, *Beyond Interpretation*, 50.

secularization) "drifts away" from the fixed meanings of Christian tradition in order to rediscover a Christianity moved by the Spirit (Joachim de Fiore) – by a Spirit who makes one discover "charity as the single most decisive factor of the evangelical message."[20] It is through charity (losing oneself) that Christ's legacy comes to live again within our contemporary civilization:

> The nihilistic "drift" that hermeneutics reads in the "myth" of incarnation and crucifixion does not cease with the conclusion of Jesus' time on earth, but continues with the descent of the Holy Spirit and with the interpretation of this revelation by the community of believers.[21]

It is from this background of the liberty of the Spirit that Vattimo rereads the core message of the saying "in multifarious and various ways God had spoken to our fathers through the prophets until he recently spoke to us through his son." He regards it through the lens of the contemporary weakening of Being – the dissipation of a unifying center – which, in turn, he connects to the key event of God's self-abasement in Christ.

For Vattimo, this saying proclaims that God's self-abasement in Christ is the "key event conferring meaning on the many preceding and succeeding events (of revelation)."[22] This is the only possible meaning for him, for a reading which would hold that the revelation culminating in Christ renders all the previous revelations obsolete would implicitly declare that the Christian interpretation process has come to an end, an assertion which, from a point of view of hermeneutics, is sheer nonsense. If there is a "superiority" within the revelation in Christ, this can only mean that this event was truly capable of setting free the manifold manifestations of God, while at the same time "linking" this release to the self-giving of God in Christ – a self-giving that is also a plunge into temporality, and hence into a pluralization that can no longer be led back to a unitary center. When the various ways in which God speaks to humankind are *de facto* already forming a plurality, then this plurality is "liberated" now to itself, precisely because it has been brought into relation to a center that "gives itself up." The various religions are, thus, each in their own way, injected with the fluidity of self-giving, charity, commiseration, etc., and it is up to them to make these virtues prosper from the background of their respective religious and cultural traditions. That is the underlying "logic" of Vattimo's exposé, which he summarizes as follows:

20 Vattimo, *Beyond Interpretation*, 51.

21 Vattimo, *Beyond Interpretation*, 49-50.

22 Vattimo, *Beyond Interpretation*, 48.

> It is not a matter of using the Gospel paradoxically to re-evaluate ancient mythologies, but rather of rethinking more concretely the secularization of Christianity as a liberation of the plurality of myths, not only the ancient myths, but also and above all those of religions with which Christian ecumenism deals today: a liberation made possible by the incarnation of Jesus, that is, by the *kenosis* of God.[23]

Until the end, Vattimo continues to wrestle with the way in which an existential "return" to religion differs from a philosophical appropriation of religious verities. Engaging Hegel, he tries to make this point clear. Hegel, he says, has the tendency to build a system of growth and deployment. So when Hegel looks at the relationship between non-Christian religions and Christianity, he tends to regard the former as "under way" to something higher that is to be found in Christianity. Christian revelation is superior to, and "overcomes," all previous revelations. Yet, Vattimo asks, what if Christianity (looked at from the *kenosis* of God) consists precisely in a downward movement? Can, in this case, the schema of "overcoming" still be upheld? In fact, the only way out of this dilemma would be to put Hegel "on his head," that is, to preserve his interest in "systematic thinking" (by calling attention to logical connections) and at the same time to take seriously the core element of God's self-abasement in Christ.

This core meaning cannot be captured by philosophical reason; one can only get at it "in accordance with a 'law' of religion."[24] It is only by responding to a call – which reaches one from the past – that one can become part of this "downward movement," emotionally and intellectually. Yet, if one looks at the logic that rules this process, then the outcome is the opposite of Hegel's centripetal synthesis. For a blessing is now given to centrifugal dispersal. This logic makes it clear that the world's multifarious religions are also caught up in this release. Each of them is called upon to "incarnate," in its own way and with the means of its particular culture, the (divine) kenotic virtues made manifest in Christ as the sensible form of God's dwelling among us.

---

23 Vattimo, *Beyond Interpretation*, 55.

24 Vattimo, *Beyond Interpretation*, 53: "at least in the sense that it is not by its own decision that the subject is committed to a process of ruin, for one finds oneself called to such a commitment by the 'thing itself'."

Concluding Remarks

I conclude this analysis by raising two questions. First, Vattimo has reached a vision in which the many religions are seen as having a family relationship with each other because of their link with the *kenosis* of the most Holy. He has tried to grasp this family relationship from the inner side of spirituality and religiousness, thus avoiding the pitfall of an external approach which would only be able to establish a classification of analogous truth forms within the climate of a plurivocity of Being (Aristotle). The avoidance of this pitfall (which ultimately leads to cultural relativism in matters of religions) is, undoubtedly, a serious step forward. Yet, for getting at this inner side of spirituality – an inner side Vattimo confesses also exists in other religions – Vattimo had to pay a price. In order to familiarize himself with the realm of spirituality (as this exists worldwide), he deemed it necessary to plunge into his own tradition (what else could he do to avoid an external approach?). And, of course, this has influenced the way in which he tries to get at the inner side of non-Christian religions. Naturally, these attempts will be colored by what Vattimo, as a Christian, has learned from God's self-abasement in Christ.

God's *kenosis* in Christ is, in other words, the lens through which Vattimo looks at the mystical core of other religions. Is he to be blamed for this approach that one could still call "Christocentric" (although this "center" is paradoxically defined in terms of self-release and self-abasement)? I would not blame him, for one must seriously ask the question as to whether an inter-religious encounter will be possible at all, at the level of spirituality, to be sure, except by going back to the roots of personal spiritual tradition. For only then, after having reached these roots, can one start having real contact with the ways in which other religions render thematic their respective ideals of self-giving. I am convinced that a deep understanding of one's own tradition of *kenosis* is indispensable for awakening to a sensitivity that spontaneously appreciates other religions' approaches to emptiness and "letting go." In this appreciation one can even engage in non-Christian mysticism.[25]

The second question: Can one also blame Vattimo for wishing that all the world-religions may, in their own way, and according to their own rhythm, enter a process of secularization? Here, too, I would hesitate to blame him,

---

[25] Anthony de Mello, for example, has increasingly integrated elements of Buddhist mysticism. Yet, underneath all this one will always recognize his profound assimilation of the *Spiritual Exercises* of Ignatius of Loyola. See C. Valdes, *Unencumbered by Baggage: Anthony de Mello. A Prophet for Our Times* (Anand, 1987).

since this concern of his is also to be found among Indian thinkers, who – like Raimundo Panikkar – seek to differentiate between a secularization that claims to simply replace religion, and a secularization that sees itself as part of the further "unfolding" of one's religious tradition.[26] Secularization, in its positive dimension, suggests that religious traditions should move beyond their "familiar settings," in order to "incarnate" their basic values and virtues in the every day life of today's complex world. In India, this would mean engaging in a practice of spirituality outside the compound of temples and ashrams, while never forgetting the wisdom gained in these sacred places. Yet, precisely here, a serious objection could be raised against Vattimo's thesis that secularization is the logical outcome of a kenotic religion (Christianity in this case). For him, it is clear that the gospel message of God's self-abasement, in combination with (nihilistic) hermeneutics, must necessarily lead to a self-emptying that has no other anchorage than "reading the signs of the times" in the secular milieu. Is Vattimo correct in imposing this schema of Christian tradition on non-Christian religions? And is he not ruling out other (Asian?) lines of development that may reshuffle the classical relation between the sacred and the profane? In this case, he would still be influenced by Hegel who sought to decipher the logic of history from a Western standpoint.[27] I leave the answer to this question to the readers. At any rate, Vattimo is fully aware of our epoch as an epoch of ecumenism. In this light, he advocates a Christianity that recognizes the fact that it is not the sole possessor of truth. He does this by asking the following pointed question about Christianity's relationship to other religions:

The question of ecumenism might be put as follows: What can be the relation between Christianity and other religions with which it has come into ever more intense contact in modernity and that, in modernity, it can no longer treat as errors – precisely because the experience of encountering them has left it unable to think of itself as the sole objective and exhaustive metaphysical truth (missions can no longer follow in the footsteps of colonists)?[28]

---

[26] See R. Panikkar, *Worship and Secular Man*, Secularization: Philosophical Reflections (London, 1973), 24-55.

[27] Vattimo has "inverted" Hegel's system, yet even then some traces of Hegel's logic remain.

[28] Vattimo, *Beyond Interpretation*, 55.

Armin Kreiner

Models of Divine Action in the World

John Cobb has asserted that if God were not understood as "some kind of a cause of events" in the world, then there would be no reason to speak of God at all.[1] To speak of God as a cause of events means to speak of God's power. There is deep disagreement, however, on how to adequately understand divine causal agency.[2] Even the question of whether the concept of "action" or "effect" is more adequate is disputed. To speak of God's action presupposes personal categories, since only a being with particular beliefs and intentions can "act" in the proper sense of the word. A non-intentional causation by contrast can be described as "effect." In the following, it is presupposed that the concept of "action" is preferable when referring to God's agency, so that divine action can be understood by analogy to human or personal action.

In the history of Christianity, different models have been developed to conceptualize God's action in the world. Some of these models will be presented and discussed here. These models can be arranged along a continuum: on the one end of the continuum is the maximalist thesis of God's sole and universal efficacy. This thesis holds that everything is caused by God alone. On the other end of the continuum is the minimalist thesis that God, after having created the world, does not act in the world at all. This position is often denoted as "deistic."[3] Both positions are burdened with numerous problems, so it is not surprising that alternatives to them have been developed. The key to understanding divine action is the concept of divine power as omnipotence. All models can be seen as interpretations of this attribute.

The Maximalistic Model

The maximalistic position maintains that God is the direct and immediate cause of everything that happens in the world. In this strong sense, God is un-

1 Cf. J.B. Cobb, "Natural Causality and Divine Action," in O.C. Thomas (ed.), *God's Activity in the World: The Contemporary Problem* (Chicago, 1983), 101.

2 For an instructive overview cf. R. Bernhardt, *Was heißt "Handeln Gottes"? Eine Rekonstruktion der Lehre von der Vorsehung* (Gütersloh, 1999).

3 For the various meanings of this concept cf. Bernhardt, *Handeln Gottes*, 180-86.

derstood as the sole determining cause of reality.[4] According to this model, every actual state obtains because God has willed or caused it.[5] Hence there is a complete and asymmetrical causal dependence of the world on God, but no causal dependency of God on the world.

Some Christian thinkers argue that this model of divine action yields the only coherent interpretation of divine omnipotence, i.e., an omnipotent being by definition has to be understood as the sole cause of everything.[6] This argument is scarcely plausible, however. Omnipotence can be defined as the power to actualize all states describable in a logically consistent way. If God were indeed the only cause of everything, this would mean that God actualizes all past, present, and future states. The assumption that an omnipotent being uses its power in the sense of being the only cause of all events seems to be logically consistent. By contrast, the assumption that an omnipotent being can exercise its power *only* in terms of sole efficacy is obviously inconsistent. It rather contradicts the assertion of divine omnipotence, since it implies that God cannot do something that is logically possible, namely create beings who are able within certain limits to act or affect things independent of the divine will. The existence of freely acting beings is at least logically consistent. If the concept of omnipotence were to exclude their existence, there would be a logically consistent state that God could not actualize. Consequently, God would not be omnipotent. So it follows that the assumption that an omnipotent being must, for logical or other reasons, be the sole cause of everything that happens, is inconsistent. It would not contradict God's omnipotence if God did not cause all events but only permitted some, or at least did not prevent them.[7] It follows then that omnipotence does not necessarily

---

4 In his polemic against Erasmus, Luther emphasized that as a result of God's omnipotence, omniscience, and immutability it follows "irrefutably, that all human action and all earthly events occur necessarily and unchangeably even when things do not appear unchangeable and necessary. That is because of the will of God. This will always reach its goal. It cannot be hindered .... It must come to pass, and indeed at the place, at the time, in the manner and to the extent that God intends and wills." Cf. M. Luther, *Vom unfreien Willen*, 33f.

5 Concerning Luther and Calvin, Eleonore Stump speaks of "God's complete determination of everything." On this point, see E. Stump, "Petitionary Prayer," in: R. Swinburne (ed.), *Miracles* (New York, 1989), 168f.

6 Cf. M. Luther: "By omnipotence I understand not the power that can do anything, but refrains from doing many things, but a power that is actually effective and powerfully effects all in all." (*Vom unfreien Willen*, 147).

7 Cf. S.T. Davis, *Logic and the Nature of God* (London, 1983), 69: "... God's omnipotence entails that he can control every event in world's history if he wishes ... but

mean "being the only cause of everything."[8] The thesis that God is the sole cause of everything is therefore only *one* possible interpretation, but not the only consistent interpretation, of omnipotence.

There are a number of good reasons that speak against interpreting omnipotence in the maximalistic sense: (1) First, such an interpretation of divine omnipotence would exclude free will and consequently moral responsibility. (2) Moreover, if God were the sole cause of everything, s/he would also be the immediate cause of all evil in the world. (3) Finally, the doctrine of creation would not be shown to be more consistent, but rather to be entangled in absurdities, since the idea of a world thoroughly and completely controlled by God does not make either metaphysical or theological sense. Such a world could scarcely be distinguished as a reality distinct from God, since being real presupposes a certain ontological independence as well as the power to causally influence oneself and others: "If we are totally devoid of power, we are not actualities."[9]

These objections make it nearly impossible to interpret God's action in the world as an indication that God is the only cause of everything.

The Minimalistic Model

The radical alternative to the idea that *only* God acts in the world is the position that God does not directly act in the world at all. According to the minimalistic or deistic model, divine action is primarily limited to the original act of creation. By this act, God somehow installed the world as a stage upon which everything happens according to the immanent laws of nature. Once God has created the universe s/he no longer intervenes in the world, but leaves it more or less to its own devices. All events are either caused by the natural laws established by God or through the free actions of creatures. The

---

not necessarily that he does control every event." Cf. also Stump, "Petitionary Prayer," 170: "There is, of course, a sense in which, according to Christian doctrine, God's will is always done on earth. But that is the sense in which God allows things to happen as they do (God's so-called permissive will)."

8 Cf. K. Ward, *Religion and Creation* (Oxford: Clarendon, 1996), 170: "It is coherent to hold that God is capable of determining all beings, though God may not wish to do so."

9 D.R. Griffin, *God, Power, and Evil* (Philadelphia, 1976), 268.

attractiveness of the deistic understanding of God increased with the success of scientific explanations of inner-worldly events. This success made an appeal to divine intervention more and more superfluous. Despite this, deism has remained an extreme minority position within the theistic traditions.

The Model of Secondary Causality

The traditional alternative to the two extreme positions is the thesis that God acts primarily through the mediation of created or secondary causes. The modern version of this traditional view is the thesis that God acts *exclusively* through secondary causes.[10] This model will be presented and discussed here. The traditional version, according to which God acts both directly and through secondary causes, seems to be more or less trivial. The thesis that God acts exclusively through secondary causes can be interpreted in at least two different ways. It is questionable whether this model actually constitutes a viable alternative to the models of universal divine causality or deism.

One possible interpretation is to understand secondary causality in the context of a hierarchically structured ordering or web of causal relations. In this case, God might completely determine events through her/his effects on the highest level of the hierarchy thereby causing subsequent effects on the lower levels.[11] According to this interpretation, God acts both through individ-

---

[10] Thomas Aquinas does not assert that God works exclusively through secondary causes, cf. *Compendium theologiae*, c.136: "manifestum est quod praeter ordinem causarum secundarum agere potest." Cf. also *Summa contra gentiles*, III, c. 102: "Therefore it belongs to God alone to work miracles. For He is above the order that contains all things, as one from whose providence the whole of this order is derived. Moreover His power, being absolutely infinite, is not confined to any special effect, nor to the producing of its effect in any particular way or order." What R. Bernhardt calls the "classical form of secondary causality" with respect to Aquinas; that is, the view that God does not intervene but only acts through secondary causes reflects a rather modern interpretation. Cf. R. Bernhardt, *Was heißt "Handeln Gottes"?*, 384f.

[11] Cf. Thomas Aquinas, *Summa contra gentiles*, III, c. 78: "Since it belongs to divine providence that order be preserved in the world; and suitable order consists in a proportionate descent from the highest to the lowest, it is meet that divine providence should reach the most distant things according to a certain proportion. This proportion consists in this, that just as the highest creatures are subject to God and governed by Him, so the lower creatures are subject to and governed by the higher. Now of all creatures the highest is the intellectual, as was proved above. Therefore the very nature of divine providence demands that the remaining creatures be ruled by rational creatures."

ual acts (at the highest level of the causal hierarchy) and also through the mediation of secondary causes. Secondary causes are seen as the instruments God uses to act in the world.

This understanding of secondary causality is certainly not deistic, because in this view God acts in the world in the proper sense, even if not directly or unmediated. It is questionable, however, whether this instrumental interpretation of secondary causality really differs from the idea that God is the sole cause of everything that happens in the world. In both cases, God seems to be the cause of all inner-worldly events. The decisive difference is that in the one case God is the direct cause and in the other the indirect cause. There is no substantial difference between saying that God actualizes a certain state by causing it immediately or by initiating a chain of causes that achieves its desired end. In both cases, the result corresponds to God's will, and in both cases, it is caused unilaterally by God.[12] The decisive difference consists in the fact that the kinds of events that are to be expected differ drastically if God acts only by secondary causes. If, for whatever reasons, God does not act outside the order of secondary causes, then all events outside their range are ruled out. With such an interpretation, the doctrine of secondary causes turns out to be the "light" version of the maximalist thesis that God is the universal cause of everything. The only difference is that those events traditionally described as miracles have now been excluded.

God's action through secondary causes can be interpreted in still another way. The second interpretation presupposes that secondary causality is nothing other than the working out of natural laws created and sustained by God. As the creator and sustainer of nature, God guarantees the preservation of the natural structures and processes s/he originally installed.[13] These structures were established by God in order to enable the actualization of the effects God intended. But this is not done by pulling triggers on the highest level of the causal hierarchy. The secondary causes act as they do by virtue of the power originally invested in them; that is, without any additional divine interventions. In this case, it would still make sense to claim that God acts in a manner mediated by secondary causes. But the meaning of this statement has strongly shifted compared to the instrumental interpretation. The secondary

12 Cf. also Thomas Aquinas, *Summa contra gentiles*, III, c. 24.

13 Maurice Wiles reduces divine action to a single "master act" and rejects the idea of discrete divine actions. This "master act" is the act of creation. The "sub acts" are realized by creatures. Cf. M. Wiles, *God's Action in the World*, London, 1986), 96f.

causes no longer form the context within which God acts by instrumentalizing these natural laws. The action of God is, rather, limited to keeping them in existence. In the last analysis, this interpretation results in reducing divine action to the actions of creation and preservation. This seems to be precisely the characteristic feature of the minimalistic understanding of divine action. The fact that God's preservation of secondary causality can be understood in the sense of *creatio continua* does not really change anything. It indeed allows one to speak of a respective action of God in the present, insofar as God guarantees the validity of natural laws at any point in time.[14] It even allows one to speak in a strongly modified sense of God's "universal efficacy."[15] As long as this ever-present activity of God is limited to the mere preservation of the natural laws, the difference from a deistic understanding is finally only a terminological difference. If God's action were actually limited to creating and preserving the natural laws, then all talk of God's acting in the world could be dispensed with. – Depending on how one interprets it, the theory of secondary causes tends either toward a covert form of deism, or turns out to be just a restricted version of the thesis of God's universal causality.

The Interventionalist Model

A further model for conceptualizing divine action assumes that the course of events usually follows inner-worldly regularity or secondary causes. This regularity was created by God and is sustained as long as God does not intercede or intervene. The specific difference of this model consists in the assertion that God occasionally intervenes directly in world events.[16] In such singu-

14 Cf. on this point K. Rahner, "Die Hominisation als theologische Frage," in P. Overhage / K. Rahner, *Das Problem der Hominisation: Über den biologischen Ursprung des Menschen* (Freiburg, 1961), 80: "For metaphysics, God is ... the transcendent, supporting ground for everything, not however a Demiurge who acts within the world. He is the ground of the world, not a cause alongside others in the world."

15 See on this point, for example, Rahner, "Die Hominisation," 80f.: "Methodologically it appears to be the case that whenever an effect is observed in the world, an inner-worldly cause is postulated and such a cause should and must be sought, because God ... effects things through secondary causality and the postulate or discovery of such an inner-worldly cause of an inner-worldly effect does not diminish the universal divine efficacy, but is precisely necessary, in order to distinguish the uniqueness of God's effects from all inner-worldly causation."

16 David Basinger designates this position as "classical Christian." See his *Divine Power in Process Theism* (Albany, 1988), 85f.: "... proponents of classical thought believe

lar interventions, God acts in the world in the true sense. These interventions can only be understood in distinction from the natural course of events; that is, in contrast to what would have happened if God had not acted or intervened. According to the interventionalist model, an event is a result of divine intervention if it would not have happened without a divine action, i.e., if God had left the world to itself. Traditionally, such events were designated as miracles; that is, as events through which divine influence occurs outside the order we usually observe in nature.[17] A miracle in this interventionalist sense can be related to the natural course of events in different ways: it can accelerate the natural course of events, it can surpass it, or can it contradict it.[18] Traditionally, a miracle is said to be the greater according to the degree by which it exceeds the immanent possibilities of nature.[19] A divine intervention does not always need to be discernible as such. A portion of divine interventions might remain hidden because they are indistinguishable from the natural course of events.

The interventionalist view of divine action appears to reflect the basic worldview of the biblical authors,[20] and for many religious believers[21] this

---

that God initially created the world ex nihilo. Moreover, they believe that although God at that time established certain natural laws (...) which are responsible for much of what we now experience, God has retained the power to intervene unilaterally in earthly affairs at any time. That is, God has retained the power to modify or circumvent the natural order."

17 Cf. Thomas Aquinas, *Summa contra gentiles*, III, c. 101.

18 Thomas Aquinas undertakes a different division. Cf. *Summa contra gentiles*, III, c. 101. Aquinas challenges the view that there are miracles *contra naturam*, but this only means that it belongs to nature to be subject to God. As a result, by definition no event can be contrary to nature. On this point see *Compendium theologiae*, c. 136.

19 Cf. Thomas Aquinas, *Summa contra gentiles*, III, c. 101.

20 This has been emphasized by so-called "Biblical theology." The center of Biblical tradition is the proclamation of salvation historical "mighty acts of God." See, for example, G.E. Wright, "God Who Acts," in: Thomas, *God's Activity*, 15-27. For a criticism, see among others L.B. Gilkey, "Cosmology, Ontology, and the Travail of Biblical Language," in Thomas, *God's Activity*, 42. Gilkey distinguishes between two theological tasks; the first is to find out what the biblical authors actually wanted to say; this is the task of Biblical theology. The second task is to find out what this can mean for us today. This is the task of systematic theology.

21 Cf. on this point the apt remark of F.B. Dilley, "Does the 'God Who Acts' Really Act?," in Thomas, *God's Activity*, 53: "Such a God is the sort which the man on the street worships, although it is not the God of the theologians and philosophers .... A finite God of this sort is not the biblical God as presented by theologians, although a

view is as significant as it ever was.[22] In any case, most theological attempts to explain the concept of divine action assume that the interventionalist model is hopelessly outdated.[23] Correspondingly, they concentrate on finding alternatives to this model. Most alternatives return to one of the various versions of the doctrine of secondary causes.

A first objection against the interventionalist model maintains that it results in turning God into a finite or mundane being. In this vein, Béla Weissmahr has asserted: if God were taken as the cause of an event in the "natural scientific sense" s/he would be a "natural power alongside other natural powers" and hence no longer the transcendent creator. In other words, an intervening God would her/himself become a secondary cause in the world.[24] In order to defend his thesis, Weissmahr adds that unmediated interventions would make God into an idol because they would negate her/his transcendence.[25] Weissmahr goes so far as to call the concept of an unmediated effect of God self-contradictory because God would become a secondary cause, and this would contradict her/his transcendence as the *causa prima*.[26] This thesis presupposes a certain metaphysical context within which the contradiction can first be construed.

Both objections are unconvincing. First, it is unclear why God would her-himself become a "natural power" by acting in the world, and hence a finite being in space and time. Weissmahr's formulation of a cause taken "in the natural scientific sense," is ambivalent: an act of divine intervention naturally implies an effect on the natural world and *eo ipso* on the physical causal nexus. Without such an effect, the concept of "intervention" makes no sense.

---

good case can be made that it is the biblical God presented by the Biblical writers themselves."

22 Above all, the practice of petitionary prayer only makes sense if one assumes an interventionalist understanding. On this point, see T. Penelhum, "Petitionary Prayer," in: Swinburne, *Miracles*, 153: "Christians are enjoined to pray, and at least some of the prayers they offer are prayers for things to happen. Unless such procedures are thought to be efficacious, it is hypocritical to engage in them. But surely if they are efficacious, it must be possible that God intervenes in nature from time to time in such a way that something happens that would not have happened unless the prayer had been addressed to him."

23 Cf. e.g. Bernhardt, *Was heißt "Handeln Gottes?"*, 372.

24 Cf. B. Weissmahr, *Gottes Wirken in der Welt* (Frankfurt, 1973), 68.

25 Cf. Weissmahr, *Gottes Wirken*, 69.

26 Cf. Weissmahr, *Gottes Wirken*, 71.

In a certain way, God would thereby act at the level of physical causes. Why such an act makes God into a "natural power" is, however, unclear. A person who intervenes in a purely mechanical causal nexus does not for that reason become a "mechanical" being. The underlying metaphysics of this position is implausible and at a decisive point also somehow unimaginative. But however one finally judges this later criticism, the assertion of God's omnipotence appears in any case to be inconsistent with it. A God whose power is limited by the natural laws created by him/herself would certainly not be omnipotent, because there would be a number of consistently describable conditions that s/he could not actualize.

A second objection stems not from the concept of God, but rather from the alleged fact that the inner-worldly causal nexus is a closed system. This means that all events in nature and in history can be explained through immanent causes. There would be no place any longer for an act of God. To explain events through a singular divine intervention is often not only seen as naive, but even ridiculous. Above all, it is said to contradict the methodological principle of modern science according to which "the modern pursuit of knowledge presupposes the interrelation and interconnection of all events in an unbroken web."[27] Without a doubt there is in fact a contradiction between this methodological principle and the interventionalist model. However, this still does not represent an objection against the interventionalist model, but simply affirms its falsity.[28] It remains unclear (among other things) why one

27 Cf. K. Kaufman, "On the Meaning of 'Act of God'," in Thomas, *God's Activity*, 146.

28 See e.g. R. Bultmann, *Jesus Christus und die Mythologie* (Hamburg, 1964), 13. "Modern man depends on the fact that the course of nature and history, like his inner and practical life, can not be interrupted by supernatural powers." Bultmann apparently shares this view without qualification. His attempt to make sense of the language of God's action is instructive, if not convincing. Then somehow the world is nevertheless "the realm of God's action" (101). That not only sounds paradoxical, but as Bultmann emphasizes, it is paradoxical, because while an event is "fully understandable" in the context of the course of natural and historical events, faith is "nevertheless" to be understood as "God's action here and now" (76). Naturally, this action of God does not appear in the causal gaps of worldly events or as a transcendent interruption or breakthrough. God acts in natural events, and in such a manner that remains hidden to every eye "except for the eye of faith" (71). In faith one can, for example, understand the healing of a child's threatening illness in "paradoxical identity" as a naturally caused event and at the same time as an act of God. Bultmann insists that such an understanding of God's action is not objectifiable or subject to proof. But that is precisely not the point. The point is that the causal difference of God's action disappears. If the healing can be explained completely naturally, then the talk of a causally effective action of God becomes meaningless (except in the sense of secondary causality, which is

should accept this postulate as an indubitable ontological or methodological starting point. Without giving additional reasons, just one dogma seems to be replaced by another.

A third objection is that divine interventions would somehow destroy inner-worldly causal relations. This objection has gained its force primarily from a deterministic worldview or ontology. If on the basis of deterministic natural laws one state necessarily followed from an earlier state, an external intervention would disrupt the order of the entire system. In the worst case, it would lead to a complete breakdown of the system of natural causes. Occasionally, it is maintained that a divine intervention is only meaningful in a non-deterministic worldview. Therefore the indeterminism of quantum mechanics has allegedly opened up possibilities for divine action, which had been excluded by a deterministic view.[29] Correspondingly, God's influence is restricted to the area of subatomic particles or more recently, to chaotic systems.[30] In the context of the discussion of omnipotence, however, such considerations do not play a significant role: the decisive question here is whether the concept of divine intervention is self-contradictory, and not the question whether it contradicts a physical hypothesis or a methodological principle. The former appears not to be the case, the latter, by contrast, seems to apply. That the concept of divine intervention is non-self-contradictory has nothing to do with whether one assumes a deterministic or an indeterministic worldview.[31] The capability of an omnipotent being to intervene does not depend on

---

not what Bultmann means). If the healing cannot be fully explained, the talk of God's action is meaningful, but in Bultmann's sense mythological, because it would entail an intervention of God. It is not that only the eye of faith can see what is hidden, it is that Bultmann fails to tell us what should be seen here at all.

29 Cf. W.G. Pollard, *Zufall und Vorsehung* (Munich, 1960), 25-90; also P. Jordan, *Schöpfung und Geheimnis* (Oldenburg, 1970), 153-82. On this topic compare the overview by Bernhard, *Was heißt "Handeln Gottes"?* 278-84.

30 Cf. the survey by Bernhardt, *Was heißt "Handeln Gottes"?* 290-301.

31 John L. Mackie has emphasized that the concept of a "violation" of the laws of nature is fully clear assuming a deterministic interpretation of natural laws; but given a statistical probabilistic interpretation this is no longer the case, because in this case certain events are no longer physically impossible but rather physically very improbable. From this it does not follow that the concept of miracle is no longer coherent. It still makes sense to understand miracles as a "supernatural intervention in a normally closed system." However, one cannot with complete certainty maintain that such an effect would not happen in the natural course of things. It would be more or less im-

whether there are indeterminate gaps somewhere in the causal nexus. An omnipotent being cannot be limited by the laws of physics whatever these laws may be, because they were created by her/him.[32] The thesis that any intervention would necessarily lead to chaos in the world ascribes to God a degree of power and intelligence so modest as to hardly exceed that of the average human being.

The decisive objection against the interventionalist model is therefore based neither on the supposed way it makes God finite nor on the "dogma" that the world is a closed system of causal relations. Finally, all these objections are based on another development, namely the modern critique of miracles. Though divine interventions need not be limited to events that cannot be naturally explained, such spectacular events would certainly yield overwhelming evidence that God in fact intervenes in the course of mundane events. And if the evidence for such events were undeniable, the thesis of a closed system of inner-worldly causal connections would surely have to be given up. The modern critique of miracles developed a series of arguments that were supposed to ban belief in miracles to the realm of superstition once and for all. Once this criticism is considered sound, the basis for the interventionist model breaks down. It appears to be an expression of unenlightened naivety and ignorance. The conviction that no presumed case of divine intervention can survive critical scrutiny is the unspoken principle behind all criticisms of the interventionalist model. This conviction, however, is not as immune to criticism as the proponents and heirs of Spinoza's and Hume's critique often assume.[33]

However one judges the evidence for divine interventions, it appears clear that divine omnipotence at least implies the possibility of such actions. However, in this context another burdensome problem arises, the problem of theodicy. If omnipotence includes the power to intervene in the course of events to help and heal, the question naturally arises as to why God in countless cases evidently fails to act. The number of cases in which God may intervene in hidden and completely unspectacular ways on behalf of her/his creatures may

---

probable. See on this point J.L. Mackie, *Das Wunder des Theismus* (Stuttgart, 1985), 39-41.

[32] Cf. Thomas Aquinas, *Compendium theologiae*, c. 136: "Sic autem praeter ordinem causarum secundarum operari solius Dei est, qui est huius ordinis institutor, et huic ordini non obligatur."

[33] Cf. R. Swinburne, *The Concept of Miracle* (London, 1970).

be vast in number. The lesser and greater catastrophes in which s/he fails to act are, however, equally numerous. No discernible logic underlying such interventions becomes apparent. If God actually intervenes, there are evidently no specific conditions that would lead us to expect an intervention; there are no indications that there are natural catastrophes so great or crimes so horrid that God would not allow them to happen. When s/he intervenes, we must assume that it occurs for the good of those involved. This does not mean that this is also the case where s/he does not intervene.

In the context of the problem of theodicy, the interventionalist model finally appears to be entangled in irresolvable problems. In the end, the consoling function of faith in an omnipotent intervening God is confronted with the sheer mystery of a being whose actions appear fully incomprehensible and arbitrary, who in some cases intervenes to help and save, and in other cases simply stands by while her/his creatures suffer terribly and perish.

The Model of Process Theology

This deficit is the starting point for the model of divine action developed by process theology. The process model starts with a massive critique of all traditional interpretations of divine creation and omnipotence.[34] From the process perspective, all these conceptions labor under one and the same misconception: they presuppose that God acts in the world by "coercion" or could do so if s/he wanted. Acting by coercion means that God has the power to exclusively and completely actualize any non-contradictory state of affairs. The thesis of the universal efficacy of God maintains that all states are directly caused by God in this way. The theory of secondary causes fundamentally holds to this position, even if it confines God's influence to the mediation of secondary causes.[35] Finally, the interventionalist model assumes that God has the power to determine things directly, even if s/he only occasionally or perhaps even seldom makes use of his/her power. By contrast, process theology

34 Lewis Ford, *Transforming Process Theism* (Albany, 2000), 7, maintains that Whitehead was able to overcome his agnostic or atheistic position when he found a way to think of God not as the omnipotent creator in the traditional sense.

35 On the process critique of the theory of secondary causes, cf. D.R. Griffin, "Relativism, Divine Causation, and Biblical Theology," in Thomas, *God's Activity* , 117-24.

excludes the idea that God acts by coercion.[36] In contrast to the interventionalist understanding, God does not freely refrain from exercising his/her power. God does not grant creatures a revocable degree of autonomy, self-determination, or freedom at any time. Process theology stresses that God does not have the power to affect events by coercion even if s/he wanted to. Nevertheless, process theology is committed to the Anselmian maxim according to which God is to be conceived as the most perfect being.[37] In order to substantiate this critique of omnipotence it has to be shown why an absolutely perfect being need not possess the degree of power that traditionally has been attributed to him/her.

This reasoning follows from the central assumptions of process theology. A key role is played by the rejection of the doctrine of *creatio ex nihilo*. From the rejection of this doctrine, it follows that the duality of God and the world is without a beginning and that God is not conceivable without some kind of world. In a second step, it follows that there is a certain metaphysical nature of the world, which was neither created by God nor can be arbitrarily changed by him/her.[38] The extent of God's power in the world is not limited by logical reasons only, but also by the basic metaphysical structure of the world. The power of worldly entities to determine themselves and to causally influence each other is part of this basic structure that God cannot arbitrarily suspend or disregard. Hence no event is caused by God alone. "Nothing ever happens just because God wants it to."[39] Every event is a result of the cooperation between God and creature, not by virtue of a divine "voluntary self-limitation," but rather as a result of the metaphysical nature the world.[40]

A further important role is played by the conviction that the central attribute of God is not power, but love. For Whitehead, the essence of Christianity

---

36 Miracles understood as a supernatural interruption of the usual relation of cause and effect remain therefore excluded. By contrast, some events are not necessarily excluded that are traditionally designated as "miracles." For more on this point, see D.R. Griffin, *Parapsychology, Philosophy, and Spirituality* (Albany, 1997).

37 See especially C. Hartshorne, *The Logic of Perfection* (La Salle,1962).

38 For more details, see D.R. Griffin, "Creation Out of Chaos and the Problem of Evil," in S.T. Davis (ed.), *Encountering Evil. Live Options in Theodicy* (Atlanta, 1981), 104.

39 For a fitting description cf. R. Rice, "Process Theism and the Open View of God," in J.B. Cobb / C.H. Pinnock (eds.), *Searching for an Adequate God* (Grand Rapids, 2000), 187.

40 Cf. D.R. Griffin, "Process Theology and the Christian Good News," in Cobb / Pinnock, *Searching for an Adequate God*, 13.

consists in the appeal to the life of Jesus as the revelation of the nature of God and his/her action in the world.[41] In Jesus Christ, the nature of God as love is revealed. The characteristic of love consists in acting not through coercion, but rather through persuasion.[42] An alternative conception of divine action in the world follows from this; God's creative love is a characteristic of his/her nature, and not the result of voluntary self-limitation. God does not intervene at particular points in space and time, but rather acts permanently in the world.[43] The divine influence is never a supernatural interruption of inner-worldly processes, but rather a "completely natural part" of that process.[44] God's influence consists in "persuading" or "luring" creatures to behave according to his / her will, i.e., to exhaust their own possibilities in an optimal way, so that they make more valuable and beneficial choices.[45] The power of God is the power of his/her vision of truth, beauty, and goodness that s/he offers his/her creatures.[46] Whether and to what degree creatures follow the divine call is their own decision. In this way, God persuaded matter to form increasingly complex structures, so that living beings came into existence. God worked in the same way in the evolution of living beings. From the process

---

41 Cf. A.N. Whitehead, *Adventures of Ideas* (New York, 1967), 167.

42 See on this point C. Hartshorne, *Omnipotence and Other Theological Mistakes* (Albany, 1984), 11. Hartshorne distinguishes between the power to determine every detail of what happens in the world, and the power to influence events in significant ways.

43 Cf. D. R. Griffin, "Relativism, Divine Causation, and Biblical Theology," in Thomas, *God's Activity*, 125: "God is in the environment of every nondivine event. As such, each event receives data from God as well as from non-divine causes. Accordingly, to give a sufficient explanation of any event, reference must be made to God as well as to the influence of previous nondivine events and to the self-determination of the event in question."

44 Cf. D.R. Griffin, "Process Theology," 5f. Process theism understands itself in this sense as a "naturalistic" theism. For more on this point, see D.R. Griffin, *Religion and Scientific Naturalism* (Albany, 2000), as well as *Reenchantment Without Supernaturalism* (Ithaca, 2001).

45 Cf. D.R. Griffin, "Relativism, Divine Causation," 126: "... God is the source of the lure towards novelty."

46 Cf. N.R. Howell, "Openness and Process Theism," in Cobb / Pinnock, *Searching for an Adequate God*, 62. See also C.R. Mesle, *Process Theology* (St. Louis, 1993), 86: "God is revealed to every creature in every moment in every place in the universe. God does not single out a select few prophets to talk to while excluding the billions of others. God's self-revelation is the ground of every person's freedom. God's self-revelation of love comes to all people in every moment of their lives, calling every person toward a vision of truth, beauty, and goodness."

perspective, God remains the most powerful being, but s/he is not omnipotent in the traditional sense.

By restraining the traditional predicate of omnipotence, process theism intends, among other things, to resolve the problem of theodicy. In the context of a more traditional understanding of divine omnipotence, this problem is said to be intractable, because every traditional position leads to the view that an almighty God is either the immediate cause of evil and suffering or at least that s/he allows it, although s/he had the power to prevent it.[47] This assumption, however, is said to be completely unacceptable. In response to Clark Williamson's demand not to assert any theological claim that could not be made in the presence of burning children,[48] David Griffin asks:

> Could we, in the presence of burning children, proclaim that God "remains gloriously free" to intervene in history? Do we want to say that, just as a parent can snatch its child from the path of a speeding vehicle, God could have snatched the Jews from the trains to Auschwitz – but failed to do so? ... Could we say this in the presence of burning children while maintaining with a straight face that love is "the primary perfection of God"?[49]

In Search of a Compromise

The conceptualization of divine action in process theology enjoys considerable sympathy beyond the limits of process thinking. An attractive idea for many is that God, as a being whose primary attribute is love, does not act through coercion but persuasion.[50] This idea fits much better with the general experience of the world, which does not give the impression that God intervenes permanently or even very often in a miraculous way in the course of worldly events. Despite the advantage of process theology on this point, its departure from the traditional understanding of omnipotence encounters con-

---

47 From the process perspective, this is the price one pays for a traditional understanding of omnipotence. See, for example, M.H. Suchocki, *In God's Presence* (St. Louis, 1996), 23.

48 Cf. C.M. Williamson, *A Guest in the House of Israel: Post-Holocaust Church Theology* (Louisville, 1993), 13.

49 D.R. Griffin, "Process Theology," 16.

50 Cf. among others, W. Pannenberg, *Systematische Theologie*, vol. 2 (Göttingen, 1991), 30f.; K. Ward, *Religion and Creation*, 307f.; I. Barbour, "Ways of Relating Science and Theology," in R.J. Russell / W.R. Stoeger / G.V. Coyne (eds.), *Physics, Philosophy, and Theology. A common Quest for Understanding* (Vatican City, 1988), 43f.

siderable reservations from those outside its ranks. Different attempts have thus been made to find a compromise that satisfies some of the major concerns of process theology while at the same time holding to the more traditional concept of omnipotence.

In the last decade, the fronts have shifted in a peculiar way, especially for a group of evangelically oriented theologians who favor a concept of God and a corresponding model of divine action that is called the "Open View of God."[51] This position is situated somewhere in the middle between the traditional and process approach. Its proponents depart from classical theism represented by Aquinas, Luther, and Calvin, which is associated with the idea of universal efficacy, and cautiously align with process theology without adopting its more radical contentions. Classical theism is said to be unable to do justice in a coherent way to the autonomy and freedom of created reality. The direction of causal influence runs exclusively from God to the world, and a reverse influence is either explicitly excluded or cannot plausibly or coherently be integrated into this view. This position is thought to be unbiblical and to lead, among other things, to insurmountable difficulties in coping with the problem of theodicy. These failures have been recognized by process theism and justly criticized.

However, for the proponents of the Open View process, theology's critique of the classical position goes too far at a decisive point, especially in its critique of omnipotence. While, in classical theism, independence of the world is given short shrift, process theism fails to give due justice to the sovereignty and independence of God. God and world are not pantheistically identified in process theism, but they are still too closely related to each other in a "panentheistic" fashion. The central weakness of process theism starts with the doctrine of creation and extends to eschatology. A world that is equally primordial with God can no longer be interpreted as the result of a free and sovereign creative act by God. Instead, the world becomes a metaphysically necessary entity restricting God's power. The decisive point of criticism is that a God who is dependent on persuasion can no longer guarantee that creation attains its God-intended goal: "process thought excludes

---

51 Cf. C. Pinnock / R. Rice *et al.* (eds.), *The Opennes of God: A Biblical Challenge to the Traditional Understanding of God* (Downers Grove / Carlisle, 1994).

guaranteed outcomes, either for individuals or for the cosmos."[52] How history finally ends thus remains open.[53]

The alternative both to classical and process theism holds to a more traditional understanding of divine omnipotence. According to this view, the world is not metaphysically necessary but is created out of nothing by God in freedom. Divine power includes the possibility of intervening in the course of world events or of unilaterally causing them. However, God is said to generally give priority to "persuasion" even if an act of "coercion" always remains possible for him/her and sometimes might also be employed. The traditional concept of omnipotence is therefore not considered inconsistent.[54]

From these premises, the following compromise emerges: on the one hand the idea of a "power through persuasion" is found to be convincing, on the other, the denial of God's omnipotence is rejected. God indeed acts in the world generally through "persuasion," although s/he could also act through "coercion." Hence God freely gives preference to "persuasion," even though s/he must thereby risk evil.[55] This compromise preserves the omnipotence of God. God grants creatures the power of self-determination. In principle, s/he could, however, revoke this power at any time, if s/he wanted. But in doing so, s/he would have to deny the autonomy and freedom of the creature. If God wills this autonomy of the creature, then it is obvious that s/he will generally act through "persuasion," not through "coercion."[56]

This compromise suggests itself especially if one assumes that God, in the course of history up until now, has acted in an interventionist way and that the world was created for a particular eschatological purpose. Both points form an integral part of the biblical tradition. This goal is related to human salvation and perhaps to that of other creatures as well. Under the premise that the re-

---

52 D.L. Wheeler, "Confessional Communities and Public Worldviews," in Cobb / Pinnock, *Searching for an Adequate God*, 124.

53 Cf. J.B. Cobb, *Process Theology as Political Theology* (Manchester, 1982), 77: "Indeed, history is really open." See also M.H. Suchocki's interpretation of Whitehead, *The End of Evil* (Albany,1988), 81f.

54 Cf. W. Hasker, "An Adequate God," in Cobb / Pinnock (eds.), *Searching for an Adequate God*, 233. Compare on this point, D.R. Griffin, "In Response to William Hasker," 257. Griffin emphasizes that it makes no sense to set the limits of what is logically possible independent of metaphysical premises. See also D. R. Griffin, *Evil Revisited* (Albany, 1991), 137-40.

55 Cf. from the perspective of the open view J. Sanders, *The God Who Risks: A Theology of Providence* (Downers Grove, 1998).

56 Cf. also G. Jantzen, *God's World, God's Body* (London / Philadelphia, 1984), 152.

alization of this goal implies a life after death, one must assume a power that can overcome the forces of transitoriness and death.[57] For the existential dimension of faith, the hope of life after death is decisive. In view of this hope, the notion of omnipotence plays a central role because only an omnipotent God can finally guarantee that the eschatological goal will be attained. Only an omnipotent God can guarantee that creation attains the end that God intends. Only an omnipotent God can exclude the risk of final failure.[58] If God were not omnipotent, then there would be no eschatological guarantees. The end of the history of the universe would remain completely open and uncertain. The ultimate fate of the world would depend on the decisions made by creatures who eventually might defy the divine lure. For many, this would be a price too high to be paid for consistency.

Translated by Michael Parker

57 The question of objective immortality is disputed among process theologians. While Whitehead denies it, some of his followers assume that it can be affirmed. However, God's effects here are not substantially different from his other actions. Cf. on this point D.R. Griffin, Process Theology and the Christian Good News, 36f. The same *modus operandi* through which God originally caused life and human life, could also bring about a life after death. The possibility of a soul existing without a body is endowed by God. Hence no additional intervention is required. The same goes for the resurrection of Jesus. It does not represent a supernatural miracle. Cf. on this D.R. Griffin, "In Response to William Hasker," 254f. On the body-soul problem from the process perspective see D.R. Griffin, *Unsnarling the World-Knot: Consciousness, Freedom, and the Mind-Body Problem* (Berkeley, 1998).

58 Cf. Wiles, *God's Action in the World*, 51.

Tomasz Węcławski

Thinking God in a Paschal Perspective

What Gives Us a Feeling of Discomfort in This World?

Our point of departure for this discussion is an experience, or rather, a feeling, that our expectations and the ideas nourished by them are out of keeping with the world as it is. This impression can also be described in reverse: as a feeling that the world, as it is, is out of line with what we would like and with what we would expect. This misalignment confronts us because there are things in this world that defy our neat categorization, our full comprehension. And in a sense, the world as a whole is itself such a thing. What I mean here is not an aspect of mystery that accompanies our reflection upon the world; nor is it an obscurity due to lack of information about things or events. Neither does the situation involve difficulties that have simply not yet been overcome – this is not a matter of probing and striving hard enough toward solutions. What I am referring to here are matters we are well familiar with, matters obvious and accessible, yet ones that persist in leaving us puzzled.

Consider the magnitude of this world, and the immense quantity of creatures that form it. It is not simply the sheer number of created individuals and species that is difficult to grasp. Consider also the vast amount of images and descriptions of every single thing – the abundance of possible points of view, modes of experiencing and expressing the vistas that open before us, the richness of planes, perspectives, and frameworks within which we can locate and recognize what exists. Usually, we are scarcely aware of the multitude of reference points at work within a given culture, not to mention within ourselves.

Our everyday experience – and to a great extent our education as well – constantly filters and simplifies our view of the world. We operate within our simplified outlooks on a daily basis, where it proves sufficient, and otherwise we would indeed find ourselves at a loss. Still, we cannot help asking what hides behind such useful measures, so we stop to reflect upon the virtually ungraspable scales of magnitude in our world – dimensions within and beyond conventional space and time that are almost imperceptible, or utterly exceed the capacity of our imagination – the unthinkably great and the inconceivably small. We wonder at the circumstances under which things happen: the never ending movements, the macro and micro fluctuations, hidden and open changes, appearances and disappearances, absorptions and secretions, bangs and flashes, waves and vibrations, thrills and shocks, sighs and gentle touches, the mingling of sound and voice, and the stillness of silence. Obviously, we can know all these things in some way, yet in truth we are at a loss as to how to think of them as a whole. We cannot refrain from asking how and why all this exists – and moreover, how and why all this is good.

When we hear, therefore, that "the various perfections of creatures (their truth, goodness, and beauty) reflect the infinite perfection of God," we can hardly avoid raising a question that stems from our experience. Namely, what *do* "the various imperfections of creatures" reflect; or to put it differently: how are we to distinguish between that which is the image and likeness of God in creatures, and that which is not. In this context, a further inevitable question is whether it is possible to consider the actual order of the world from God's point of view, so that God's intention, which makes the world what it is, would be disclosed to us. We seek through this questioning to understand God's intention by whose power human life in its concrete individuality appears in this world. Thus, the question is fundamentally about the divine (and at the same time also human) measure of the created world.

The answer, deeply rooted in the Christian tradition, but not always taken as seriously as it deserves, is this: Yes, we can see what this world is, and why it exists as it does, if we are willing to radically convert our concepts. I will now try to summarize the key components of this conversion with the help of a radical thesis.

Radical Thesis

I hereby suggest the following radical thesis: The paschal event of Jesus' death and resurrection is not only a fulcrum enabling us to see and understand the work of God, which is our world in its entirety; rather, everything that we experience as our world, ourselves included, happens (in the ontologically strongest sense) through that very nexus, in such a way that we simultaneously discover the word "God" as full of meaning. Both the world and God are given whence Jesus dies and rises from the dead. It is therein that Love for death and life speaks. This Love speaks a human language. In brief, God gets a word in.[1]

---

[1] Cf. E. Jüngel, *Gott als Geheimnis der Welt: Zur Begründung der Theologie des Gekreuzigten im Streit zwischen Theismus und Atheismus* (Tübingen, 1982), 408.

In what follows, I will consider this thesis in three consecutive steps. First, I will examine the question of Love for death and life (calling this step: *sensus*), then the crisis of freedom given to us by this Love (calling this step: *crisis*), and finally the idea of God that corresponds to such love and such freedom (calling this step: *deus*).[2]

Sensus: The Word of Love for Death and Life

It seems obvious, when speaking about Love, that we are dealing with a fundamental concept of Christian theology. We should be careful, however, not to accept this point too readily. "Love" is a fundamental concept of Christian theology not because of its overriding role within a specifically Christian idiom and practice. On the contrary: all the concreteness of Christian Love is there already, even without coinage or usage (yet) of the word "Love," and this Love would still persist, even if spoken about no longer, and indeed even if there were no speakers left to consider it.

Thus, when we ask about Love, we concern ourselves with a fundamental theo-ontological concept, one directly linked to the paschal event of Jesus as the ultimate deed of God, even if it is not immediately evident as such. The complexity of this concept is of a different order than of Jesus' death and resurrection. As opposed to the singularity of the resurrection event, the theological challenge in speaking of Love arises from a superabundance of facts, experiences, and impressions denoted by this word "love," and this diversity can obscure our way to the source and foundation of Love in the paschal event of Jesus.

We can overcome this difficulty only by seeing in the question of Love an *alteram imaginem* of the question of Jesus' death and resurrection, since we can then ask about Love with a view to its very origin, and not in connection with its various manifestations. This is by no means an abstract way of talking about Love, i.e., love in general or love "as such." Starting from the paschal event of Jesus, we ask about Love as an incomparable *concretum*, unparalleled by any other moment in history, and then as a *concretum universale*, which is related to every other moment in history. We ask about Love as an

2 The considerations that follow are a revised version of a paper of mine published in a slightly different context in: A. Wierciński (ed.), *Between the Human and the Divine: Philosophical and Theological Hermeneutics* (Toronto, 2002), 231-41.

"event of unity of life and death to the advantage of life" and in precisely this sense, about "Love for death and life."

The latter phrase can be read with a double "logical stress." The first way of reading consists in taking the expression "for death and life" as a complete description of "Love"; the second is a counterpoint reading, where "Love for death" and "life" are juxtaposed. This is not merely a linguistic triviality, since both possibilities are vital to our question.

Let us consider the following aphorism about Love: "The one who loves believes that he is already past death."[3] What is the essence of such a belief? Is it justified on its own merits? Is it to be credited on grounds of personal conviction? Or is it some kind of ecstatic, surreal experience, an elation above the ordinary course of things? Is it, perhaps, more than a relation to the reality of death, originating and experienced only in the lover himself? If so, it should then be a relation between the Love and the lover, a Love surpassing every possibility in the lover's life (including death as the last possibility). In this case, is it then the lover who confesses that he is past death, or is it the Love – which really surpasses death – speaking?

These questions are not to be answered by resorting to a general and abstract principle. Although it seems that they can be condensed into the following purely theoretical question: In what way (on what ontological level) is the lover defined by the Love with which he loves? In truth, this is a very serious question for the lover. It would be absurd to claim that the Love by which he loves arises from the powers of his own agency. It would be much more absurd to claim that the Love by which he is loved is something self-generated in this way. Where Love comes into play, reality attests that the lover alone cannot suffice unto himself. Moreover, he cannot even *be* alone. Now that the lover is (becomes) a deed of the Love by which he loves and by which he is loved, then in fact, *"between no-love and "being in love" ... he feels nothing less than just death.*" [4]

Let us ask our question again: When a lover believes that he is already past death, is this belief a metaphor for his relation to himself, or does the metaphor reflect a possible state of being wherein Love places him such that he cannot be alone (without the Love), i.e., past death? This is a rhetorical question, settled in favor of the second solution, but under one condition: that we mean no less than "Love for death and life" in the literal sense of the word

[3] Jüngel, *Gott als Geheimnis der Welt*, 446.

[4] Jüngel, *Gott als Geheimnis der Welt*, 446.

(not just any love, and certainly not a "love affair"). It is not any love, but Love for death and life, which carries the lover past death. After that, death does not detain him, but delivers him "back" into a state of all-encompassing life.

The issue regarding "the lover being sent back by death" arises here not only with regard to its paschal source and Christological meaning. It also represents the analogical character and metaphorical sense of the phrase "carries the lover past death." Just as death "no longer detains, but sends back," so also Love "carries the lover past death." However, this is where the analogy ends and discloses its surprising sense. If we can say in virtue of the presence of the risen Jesus (who was sent by death back to God and to us): there is *no* such reality as "death itself," then by the same virtue we can say: there *is* such a reality as "Love itself." The way Love itself exists is analogical to the way death exists, and at the same time, it is radically different. The way Love exists is *analogical* to death in that both states are originally relations that – with the aid of subsequent metaphors – are constituted as a hypostasis, capable of acting or abstaining from action for the subject's benefit. The way Love exists is *radically different* from death, because death (as an actually "personified" hypostasis) gives absolutely nothing to the dying one, whereas Love brings everything to the lover. It is so because death is a relation of the dying one to himself (in a literal sense: only to his own end), but Love is a relation that exceeds the self.

That is why it is possible to apply the above-mentioned twofold logical stress in the word of "love for death and life" to mean: "love for death" and "life." Thus, it is to be understood, that life (which, seen from the concrete perspective of a living person, means: everything) is possible only where "Love [ready] for death" is primary.

Can we, however, know how to access such a Love? We can evade the question by answering: Such a Love is all there, where human life is possible – but this is really only an evasion, not an answer, because we actually never know when and how life is still possible. Moreover, we know well, that life in its every shape irrevocably leads to death as a moment where it will no longer be possible. Thus, when we ask about Love, which makes human life possible, we do not expect to be given a general principle, but a concrete and confident answer. We cannot know in general whence such a Love exists and we cannot recognize it by means of a previously established universal criterion that would tell us when we have actually come across "Love for death and life."

At this point, it becomes necessary to return to an immediate and concrete reference to Jesus as dead and risen. The question of the identification of Love must arise here as it arose in the hour of Jesus' death – as an absolute "either-or." Either all that Jesus did and said is a declaration of Love for death and life, or it is a swindle and a blasphemy (or at best a tragic mistake). From the perspective of contemporary faith in Jesus, the question might seem purely rhetorical. Nevertheless, as far as it concerns the very foundation of Christian faith, even today it should be answered seriously.

Jesus alone – Jesus as a dying and dead man – cannot answer this question. On the contrary, he dies in full awareness of this question. Later, when the question receives an answer in Christ's resurrection, and when this answer ultimately proves the justice of what Jesus had said and done, we recognize with ultimate certainty that the dead Jesus *is not alone*.

The latter affirmation must primarily be taken in a literal sense. Jesus is not alone, because he really died and so he alone (by himself) certainly cannot continue to be. Then, he *"is"* not by virtue of his human nature, which is dead, but by virtue of Love for death and life, which had spoken through Jesus' human life and now allows him to be as only this Love can allow one to be. It is a Love fully concerned with Jesus' life, not his death, and thus concerned as well with all that belongs to his life and with all that his life is connected to. It is, consequently, a Love that desires the life of each and every one of us, but does not yet have it, and will never have it in a way that would satisfy that desire. However, the Love desires our lives, not in compliance with a self-centered desire, but – what is essential – in accordance with the profound desire of the desired one. Whoever understands what is meant here will not be astonished by the unambiguity of the New Testament identification of God with the Love that speaks through the life, death, and resurrection of Jesus (1 Jn 4).

Here, a fundamental theo-ontological sense of the message about Love for death and life is disclosed. Only in this context can one see what we actually do by asking what appears to be a purely theoretical question about the ontological level of love, the level upon which the lover becomes an act of the Love by which he loves and is loved. Another angle on the inquiry is this: What is the ontological level wherein the union of Love and death, expressed by subsequent metaphors, occurs? A question that follows from the previous two is fundamental for Christian theology, and reads: From whence does Christian theology derive its own concept of man and God? Or putting it even more emphatically: Does Christian theology really have its own concept of man and God? The answer is obvious: yes, but both Christian concepts are to be found in the unique moment of the ultimate self-gift of God. This answer not only points to the mode of existence of specifically Christian concepts, but also brings in the very principle of Christian faith and its theological expression: Both (the concept of man, and the concept of God) are given wherein Jesus dies and rises. It is from there that Love for death and life speaks. This Love speaks a human language. There, God gets a word in. [5]

Crisis: The Call (Name), Refusal (Sin) and Freedom (Grace)

If this were a systematic theology lecture, our task would be to examine and explain each of the concepts of this formula separately, as they are mutually connected, yet different. What we shall do instead, however, is explore another option, and view this formula as a reference to a unique theo-ontological concept of human freedom in the presence of God.

In essence, this is a question about human existence as such, but as with any broad formula, we face the danger of fatal overgeneralization – as if we could know something about "human existence" in general and consider it concretely through its abstractions. In reality, the situation is exactly the opposite – we do not know human existence as such, all we do know are men and women, each of them in his/her own place and time, and under his/her own name. This does not mean of course that we can only build a common history by recounting and recording individual human stories one after the other. Still, the concept of history makes sense (at least for Christian theology), only because it concerns the individual and concrete, i.e., named, responsibility of every man and woman to God.

Therefore, we ask about human existence through inquiry about a non-nameless freedom of every human being before God, and this requires us to consider the real context of human freedom in actual history. It comprises on the one hand the not-indifference of God in his relation to every human life (his love of every human life as a call to them, i.e., grace) and on the other hand the disbelief of (every) human being in his/her relation to God (a lack of love, a refusal to give oneself, i.e., sin).

We speak here about the constituents of the context of human freedom (grace and sin) in terms of the Jewish and Christian faith, but the experience

---

5 Cf. Jüngel, *Gott als Geheimnis der Welt*, 408.

is truly universal, and not restricted to any specific religious or cultural context. No doubt, it is the task of theology as a reflection on Christian faith to seek the source of this experience – so that its original, fundamental, and universal sense can be revealed. For the sake of this discussion, let us allow that the not-indifference of God to any human life and the disbelief of human beings in relation to God are universally accessible experiences, as intimately familiar to each human life as a person's strong bond with his or her own name, and indeed one that follows upon the very act of being named, of being declared and christened a full human member of the world.

This freedom of humanity in relation to God is recognized as a fundamental theo-ontological concept. The fundamental character of this concept becomes all the more visible when we see how essentially it is bound to our concepts about the order of this world, concepts forged decisively in the death and resurrection of Jesus. The essence of this decision (seen historically and at the same time theologically) is God's approval of the words and deeds of Jesus. This approval, however, is not restricted to Jesus as an individual, as relative to other human beings as the righteous one, that he was a "son of God" in a filial sense. This approval extends to the universal and absolute order: only in the life and death of this man, Jesus, do we find God as the source of his and our own life that surpasses death; Jesus is the Son of God. [6]

If we can say that the message of love for death and life reveals the divine dimension of God's decision (at least insofar as it shows our helplessness in the face of the end of our life), the fundamental concept of freedom reveals the human shape of this decision. If it is true that we encounter here the ultimate decision concerning the order of this world, we can know about it only from the shape it assumes in the life, death, and resurrection of Jesus. That is why the question about the shape of the paschal event is of primary significance.

If we look at the paschal event in terms of what happened historically, the core of the controversy was whether Jesus' relation to God was usurpation and blasphemy or not. In the perspective of Jesus' accusers, the contention had to do with just this one single case. They knew perfectly well (and with them we know it very well too), that Jesus was neither the first nor the last man to commit such usurpation. Since the beginning of humankind, the desire to *"be as gods, knowing good and evil"* (Gen 3:5) or to *"be equal with God"* (Phil 2,6) has been the object of usurpation. Placing these two passages to-

---

[6] Cf. Mark 1:1 and 15:39.

gether, side-by-side, might imply a faulty comparison. In fact, however, their basic similarity and simultaneous incompatibility is crucial to the understanding of Jesus in light of the question of usurpation. The disobedience of the first man, who knows good and evil, in the false hope of being like God, finds its counterpart in the obedience of Jesus, as manifested in his not availing himself of the opportunity to be equal with God , i.e., in his humility even unto death. Yet, we feel that this juxtaposition of the two attitudes, although revealing, does not explain fully God's decision in favor of Jesus. Let us note that Jesus rejects the usurpation to be equal with God, not in his divine preexistence, in some realm outside world and time, but in his earthly (i.e. human) life. That brings us to a restatement of our original question about Jesus' relation to God: Why can and must we say that Jesus *"did not cling to his equality with God,"* although that is precisely what he was (not without reason) accused of? *"You are only a man and you claim to be God"* (J 10:33). If we do not want to see the situation as an incomprehensible contradiction, we should assume that the New Testament knows two ways of "being as God," and let us add immediately – one of them represents truth, while the other, a tragic self-deception. Therefore, the core of the problem lies in what the word "to be as God" means in both cases.

The temptation to "be as God" or "to be equal with God" can concern only the kind of usurpation of God's existence that is possible for man, i.e., the attempt to appropriate divine knowledge, or divine will, or divine acts. Is this desire to "be as God" an attitude of *hubris* on the part of the person who wants to be something that he or she with all certainty cannot be? Perhaps so, but thinking along these lines implies that one is aware of usurping for oneself what can only belong to God, because where there is no awareness of a difference between seeking oneself and seeking God, there can be no actual *hubris*. However, is any human being capable of truly discerning this difference? Is it not the case rather that no man knows or can know the difference between human existence and being equal with God? Is it not so that the problem essentially consists in a false concept of God, which (deceptively) makes Him appear as a real object of human desire? Such a desire then becomes actual *hubris* in a double sense: as an unmet desire for God, and as a tragic deception as to the object of the desire.

It is precisely to such a false concept of God that biblical stories about temptation and sin can be said to refer (Gen 3 and the following chapters), particularly if we understand them, not as accounts of isolated events, but as an indication of a fundamental dimension of human existence experienced by every person in his or her own way. These stories are not a description, but an overall indication of the state of consciousness of "the first sinners," and of the consequences of their sin. It would be more adequate to say that in light of this indication, every person is a sinner, and every sinner is the first sinner.

The very first possibility open to a human being is the potential for each person to have a human future. Each person's human future is given to him or her before everything else – it always and absolutely precedes the existence of the one who is endowed with it, and so as a potentiality, it lies outside the scope of any human power. This is true not only regarding the beginning of (every) one's existence, but even more conspicuously, regarding life's end in the only form known to us, i.e., as one's moment of life before death. It is in the actual face of death where the fact emerges most starkly that no one can "be" his or her own future. However, what the fact of death at the end of one's life reveals most obviously is actually true of one's entire life: only God can be one's future. What we are talking about here is the human life and future of this very person and no one else. Human future, meaning human life, is not given to any one as something that issues from personal selfhood or agency, but on the contrary – *sit venia verbo* – it is given as that from which he/she issues. In other words, one's future is given to a person as God's call, and everyone is in a position to receive that call as one's own human name, the speech act that makes human existence decisive.

All that we have said so far about the call, name, and future of every human life corresponds to what we said earlier about sin as a false concept of God. Nobody can be the future for oneself and nobody receives one's own name from oneself. The moment one has a future, there is God consecrating it unto him/her, and it is not just any future that ensues from this, but the future of this specific individual. Similarly, when we speak about a name, it is not just any name, but each person's proper name. Nobody can receive my name for me, just as I cannot receive it for anyone else. Obvious as it may seem, this assertion has at least one consequence, which is not at all evident, i.e., the emergence of a bond of the original relation of each person to oneself and to the true or false concept of God. My "proper name" does not necessarily mean my "true name." One can receive one's own true name only from God. Where there is a false understanding of who God is, no one can know one's proper name. Only where God reveals his own name, can human life recognize its own true name.

The convergence of God's self-revelation and man's true recognition of himself occurs in the life, death, and resurrection of Jesus. Jesus who has risen, is not a usurper or blasphemer. On the contrary, He knows and reveals God's name. In light of this contention, the profession of faith in Philippians 2:9-10 fully bears out the relationship between a true understanding of God and a person's real name. We are told therein about God who *"raised him high, and gave him the name which is above all other name, so that all beings in the heavens, on earth and in the underground, should bend the knee at the name of Jesus"* – and let us note that this is not a divine name, but simply *"the name of Jesus."* This consequence does not pertain to Jesus alone. It is extended to us in God's call to us to be enlivened by the same intention as Jesus. No one can accomplish this feat in any other way than by knowing God through Jesus dead and risen.

Deus: God in Jesus Dead and Risen

In what follows, we will examine what may be considered the ultimate goal of all theological endeavor, and what must be stressed is that we are not concerned here with the concept of God as the goal or result of theological reflection. On the contrary, we consider it as a source of all possibilities for theological reflection.

Thus far, we have considered a concept of God that potentiates all human opportunities, and we have examined this concept in connection with the question about Love for death and life, and about freedom and sin. Clearly, two key points are involved here. The first point is about Love, which desires the life of each one of us, but not in a way that demands satisfaction of this desire. The second point is about the concept of God as a true or false idea of God and oneself inherent in one's original relation to oneself. Both points require an explanation revealing how and why one's original relationship to oneself could be related to a false concept of God. To gain insight into this interdependence between our idea of ourselves and a fundamental concept of God, the explanation would first and foremost play a negative role – its main (though not only) purpose being to show what it is that diverts our thought and speech away from the God we encounter in Jesus dead and risen. This does not mean, that in articulating the initial concept of God we cannot say anything positively. Our focus, however, is on the ontological structure of the statement, and not the character of its content.

Before proceeding, we should return to the issue of the task of theology. This task does not consist in thinking God as a separate entity, a "God-self" related to a salvation-expecting creature. The task of theology is to think of God as Love. And this love can only be the Love that God *is* (and not the love in which he could make himself manifest).

How can theology fulfill the task thus formulated? In light of what has been said so far the answer seems clear: theology fulfils its task when in thought and speech it delivers an account of what happened to Jesus dead and risen. The whole issue then depends on whether and how we are able to give such an account. The task cannot be carried out through reconstruction of what happened to Jesus crucified and buried, or by interpreting the evidence of his resurrection in light of what we already know (or rather think we know) about God, man, and the world.

What then must we do to fulfill this task? On a theoretical level – both ontological and linguistic – we can, or perhaps must, see things in such a way that *no* being (and, all the more, *no* person) can exist or be comprehended in itself on its own terms without its relations to another (this relation both creating the other, and at the same time, oneself). The word "no" (as in "*no* being,") here is crucial. This principle shall be applied to every knowable being – even to God, as he is knowable to us. Since he is knowable to us in Jesus dead and risen, the principle applies to the events surrounding Jesus. This is how we can arrive at the most primary and the most definitive fundamental theo-ontological concept.

The talk about God that emerges from this principle can only be a no-object-oriented speech, which means that when speaking about God we consequently avoid imagining him (thinking he must be something like this or like that), or making conjectures, that something would be the "property" of God. Although our mental habits rebel against such a mode of inference, it may be useful to suppress the instinctive reaction of disagreement and try to follow the possibilities opening before us.

We can describe the essence of this intuition as follows: God is not first a self-possessing subject that subsequently enters into a relation (and becomes something for someone). God is not even self-possessing in the ordinary sense of the word, but he is "giving-itself" and "receiving-itself." Both the words "giving" and "receiving" describe a unique reality. God can be an act of giving because he is an act of receiving; he can be an act of receiving because he is an act of giving. He is not "one who gives," but "giving-itself." He is not "one who receives," but "receiving-itself." This means consequently, that God does not have "properties" – something that pertains to him alone and to no other being. His presence must not be seen as a presence of something or someone that would exist in the same way (as self) even when not with, for, or in any other being. That is why the only property of God we can perceive is the life of each human being, to which He is giving himself and which he is receiving, and along with that, the whole of creation.[7]

Nonetheless, it would be a grave error to treat the above claims (God is not self-possessing, God has no property) as an alternative to the classical metaphysical assertions about God (that he is an absolute and necessary being, pure act, and absolute self-possessing). The mistake lies in ascribing the same ontological status to both types of utterances, whereas the above-expounded statements are to be understood as not metaphysical and not object oriented. Consistently understood, they do not allow expressions of the type: "God is (something such as) ..." or "he is not (something such as) ...." They do not contain a "teaching" or "doctrine" about God, but they express a multiform experience and belief that God is not even a "self"; that he is not a God without His relation to (every) human life and to the (entire) world. Thus, these assertions do not describe God apart from the entire creation, but express our own situation in the presence of God: the conditions and circumstances in which we can perceive his presence. They describe our own human lives, and in doing so, they speak about God who is making his own the life of each one of us.

At this point, it is worthwhile to again raise the question of how a false concept of God could affect one's original relation to oneself. If this formula actually enables us to formulate a description of the original relationship between human freedom and sin, then in the ordinary course of things, the description should first be possible in objective terms, without any reference to the events surrounding Jesus, and then linked with him *ex post facto*. However, this is not the case. Without a reference to the life, death, and resurrection of Jesus, the description is virtually impossible. The crux of the relation consists in the fact that acceptance of God's presence in Jesus dead and risen reveals the deficiencies of every other concept of God.

If this is the case, then everyone's history (name) is linked with the history (name) of Jesus, not only when the person believes that Jesus has risen, or when the person passively accepts the sign of such a belief (baptism). The bond with Jesus occurs already when one is yet nothing more than a possibil-

7 Cf. *Concilium Lateranense* IV: "inter creatorem et creaturam non potest tanta similitudo notari, quin inter eos maior sit dissimilitudo notanda," and "... licet aliquo modo concedatur quod creatura sit similis Deo, nullo tamen modo concedendum est quod Deus sit similis creaturae" (S.Th. I, q. 4, a.3 ad 4).

ity of being this very one and only human person that only he or she can be. In terms of the confession of faith in the resurrection of the crucified Jesus, this relationship is possible only because the same spirit that was and is present in Jesus is also present and acts in each human being (either accepted in the person's freedom or not). The controversy over whether or not this spirit is synonymous with God himself, or whether this spirit denotes a broadly understood spiritual bond and community between Jesus and us, is groundless in this perspective. With the proposed ontology, everyone's life is not only made possible, but also simultaneously judged by the same giving and receiving (God's), by the same Love that is manifest in Jesus dead and risen. That we can speak of God not as the one who gives and receives, but as giving itself and receiving itself (i.e. Love) is radically, fully, and ultimately visible and accessible in the life, death, and resurrection of Jesus.

When I look at the life of Jesus, I do not see God *as God*, but as a living human being. When I look at Jesus' death, I do not see God *as God*, but as a dead man. When I look at Jesus' resurrection, I do not see God *as God*, but as a victory of life over death. The phrase "I see" can of course be substituted by "I say." Thus, I only see what is human and limited – the life and death of the man Jesus and so many people similar to him. And I speak only about this. But when I speak about the victory of *this* life over death, I transcend what is human and limited without crossing the boundaries of those limits.

That is why, speaking about God on such grounds, we can use the image of an empty place where roads coming from various directions converge. All the roads lead to one place, which is known and unknown, one for all, but seen differently by each one, depending on how and where each person comes from. Before we arrive at this place, it is completely empty; nothing is there that would be ready, awaiting all of us before we had started on our way. So nothing is there that would be the same for everyone. This place fills up with what people bring on their way there. When they arrive, they find themselves and one another: one's own and the others' poverty and richness, joys and pains, disappointments and hopes, but they find them anew, like never before. This is the place where Jesus died, where we are now and at the hour of our death.

A Provisional Epilogue

Finally, a question must be raised that has not been explicitly asked thus far: What warrants our belief that the crucified Jesus rose from the dead? There is no scope for a thorough discussion of the issue here, but I feel obliged to at least say where I look for supporting evidence, and I do so in accordance with the intrinsic principle of the theo-ontology outlined in this paper. In the perspective adopted here, the foundation of our faith is to be found only in the consequences of the resurrection of crucified Jesus, wherever and in whatever form these consequences are made manifest. The reference to these consequences is possible both on a strictly theoretical plane, and on a practical one. On the strictly theoretical plane, we rely on the history of the Bible testimony on the resurrection of Jesus, and to the faith in his resurrection inherent in this testimony (in a normative and absolutely binding sense), which has developed in the history of the community founded on this faith. On a practical plane we look toward that faith community's ability to create, accept, understand, and transmit concrete signs and metaphors whose sense consists in representing what the faith of the community and its historical testimony are based in. What these signs ultimately refer to remains inaccessible in itself. However, the presence, viability, and value of what undergirds the signs and metaphors are starkly evident in the simple fact that ever-new and commonly accessible consequences *are generated by them* on the spiritual, social, and personal level. This efficacy itself warrants "belief" in the crucifixion. And the consequences are compelling when and where they manifest on the world stage, in their power to align, socially, personally, humanistically, and spiritually, even where they are not linked directly to the name of Jesus.

Leonhard Hell

Communio: A Problematic Keyword of Contemporary God-Talk

1. At the beginning of the epoch that – with a somewhat naive euphoria – we have become used to calling the "modern age," scarcely anyone would have been willing to bet that the doctrine of the Trinity could look forward to another period of importance. On the contrary, in the sixteenth and seventeenth centuries and after, for the first time since the debates of ancient Christianity, thinkers appeared who certainly saw themselves as Christian theologians, but who were nevertheless more sympathetic to the "heresiarch" Arius than, for example, his opponent Athanasius, the leading light of orthodoxy.[1]

Indeed, in modern thought, there have been occasional energetic revivals of interest in the doctrine of the Trinity – in the first half of the nineteenth century in the sphere of the so-called German Idealists and, a full century later, in the thought of such otherwise different theologians as Karl Barth and Karl Rahner.[2] Yet even these key attempts to develop the theology of the Trinity, for all their fidelity to the Church's Trinitarian confession, were primarily concerned to lessen its offense to a strictly monotheistic conception of God. It is no accident that they reject an unreflective use of the concept of "person" in the doctrine of God. When the ancient church developed its confession of faith it did not use *hypostasis* or *persona* to mean what we mean by "person" today, and a tritheistic aberration from the Church's faith could not be avoided if, without further explanation and without the use of alternative terminology (Karl Barth's *Seinsweise,* "mode of being"; Karl Rahner's *distinkte Subsistenzweise,* "distinct mode of subsisting"), we continue to speak straightforwardly of "God in three persons." Nevertheless, theologians like Barth and Rahner did indeed insist that the doctrine of the Trinity should be moved to the center of Christian faith, and therefore (for Barth at least) to the starting point of a well-ordered systematic theology. In this, they wanted not only to make clear that the doctrine of the Trinity was not merely a purely speculative attachment to Christian doctrine – their decisive intent was to se-

[1] Cf. M. Wiles, *Archetypal Heresy: Arianism through the Centuries* (Oxford, 1996).

[2] Cf. S.M. Powell, *The Trinity in German Thought* (Cambridge, 2001).

cure its place in the consciousness of believers, if not indeed to establish such a place for the first time.[3]

2. More recent Trinitarian theology does indeed share these intentions, but it often pursues them more in contradiction to the presuppositions of these earlier models than in corroboration of them. Occasionally, theologians during the past few decades have even leveled charges of heresy against the authors mentioned: "Modalism, of a masked or unconscious kind" – so reads the label that some want to stick on them. The implication here is that they are not true Trinitarian thinkers; that they have hidden what is basically a purely monotheistic concept of God behind an apparently Trinitarian mode of speech; that those who think of God as a single and thus essentially lonely subject are merely dealing with a concept of God that has its roots in the tradition of philosophical theism rather than in the saving drama of the relationship of Father, Son, and Spirit first introduced into the religious history of humanity by the proclamation of early Christianity. Accusations by, for example, the Tübingen Reformed theologian Jürgen Moltmann, made since the 1970's, are of this kind.[4] But such criticism is by no means restricted to Protestant or even to German theology: it has also been made from a quite different perspective by the Orthodox theologian (now Bishop) Ioannis Zizioulas – in his case it is linked with the familiar Orthodox accusation against Latin theology as a whole, that it has always been inclined to see the Trinity as a secondary divine attribute, thus sacrificing it to divine unity.[5] In order to complete the classical triad of denominations, a third example could be mentioned: Gisbert Greshake, a Catholic theologian of similar views, for a long time a member of the Vienna Catholic theological faculty, subsequently based at Freiburg. His comprehensive work *Der dreieine Gott* (*The Triune God*)[6] has become something of a basic text of the new Trinitarian theology, taking up and developing the critical deliberations of Moltmann, Zizioulas, and many others. Yet this is not just the special theory of a few theologians, but an

[3] For K. Barth, cf. especially the first volume of his magnum opus, *Church Dogmatics* Vol. I/1 (Edinburgh, 1936); for Karl Rahner, the collection of his principal writings on the Trinity in *The Trinity* (London, 1970).

[4] Cf. J. Moltmann, *The Trinity and the Kingdom of God* (London, 1981); on Moltmann's theology of the Trinity, see D. Coffey, *Deus Trinitas: The Doctrine of the Triune God* (New York / Oxford, 1999), 105-30.

[5] Cf. J.D. Zizioulas, *Being as Communion. Studies in Personhood and the Church* (Crestwood, 1985).

[6] (Freiburg 1997; 4th ed., 2001).

enterprise of truly European, even global scope – in this context, there are a number of important examples, to name a few: the (deceased) English theologian Colin Gunton,[7] the Yale-based Croatian Miroslav Volf,[8] the U.S. theologian Catherine Mowry LaCugna,[9] and the Brazilian Leonardo Boff.[10]

3. But what is it that unites all these (and countless other) theologians – what do they have in common in a positive sense, apart from their thoroughgoing critique of certain aspects of the Western doctrine of God? To approach an answer, let us begin at the point where they each distance themselves from what seems (to them) to be a crucial flaw of previous Trinitarian doctrine with the claim that the unity and oneness of God may not indeed be given up, but it must be broken open, and opened out to community. To give formal expression to this thought, we could speak of an original unity at the core of unity and difference. In the language of Christian confession: God lives from eternity as the community of Father, Son, and Spirit. God is a three-personed being-in-relationship, as it were, a social entity, that exists in the play of the manifold. This is called the social doctrine of the Trinity (Moltmann), divine *koinonia* (Zizioulas) or Trinitarian *communio* (Greshake). For all the differences in detail, it seems to me that the primal character of this intra-divine community is its essential point. Plurality does not have a secondary, merely derived character in the being and life of God. Rather, God is from all eternity one in the differentiation of three persons. Further, this differentiation is conceived as a relational reciprocity, as a pattern of relationships, as the play of mutuality. Thus this theology is not afraid to call Father, Son, and Spirit three subjects of the one divinity and their relationship to each other as a form of intersubjectivity. This is because true reciprocity, real relationship, is only possible between self-sufficient entities, even though they are of course self-sufficient only in a strictly relative sense. This Trinitarian emphasis – and this is the evident advantage of such concepts – not only provides the defining principle of any Christian doctrine of God, but can also allow the relationship of God to the world and God's creation itself to be marked by God's commu-

---

7 Cf. his last, summative work: C. E. Gunton, *The Christian Faith: An Introduction to Christian Doctrine* (Oxford, 2002), 175-91.

8 M. Volf, *After Our Likeness: The Church as the Image of the Trinity* (Grand Rapids, 1998).

9 C. Mowry LaCugna, *God for Us: The Trinity and Christian Life* (San Francisco, 1991).

10 L. Boff, *Trinity and Society* (Maryknoll, 1988).

nal nature. The world in its character as creation, including its universal, regional, and individual dimensions can and must be understood as realities characterized equally and originally by plurality and unity. None of these dimensions can or should be weakened in favor of the other: this is as true for the cosmos as for humanity, for society as for the Church, for man and woman, and so on. In this way, the formulation of a fundamental principle for all theology is made possible, which leaves all previous dichotomous definitions of theology's object behind (God and world, Christ as head and as body, God and his Kingdom etc.) and embraces unity and plurality, the individual and its "other," subjectivity and intersubjectivity in the intradivine *communio*.

4. Having sketched its critical intent, its representatives, the basic alternative concept, and its prospects in the doctrine of God and in Christian theology as a whole, my task now is to develop a modest set of criteria by which one might examine the legitimacy and usefulness of this approach to the theology of the Trinity, as well as to judge its inner capacity for development. First of all, we cannot avoid bringing those normative traditions into play that are not only relevant for any Christian theology, but that are expressly brought into prominence by the theologians noted above. These are (how could it be otherwise?), in the first place, sacred scripture, especially the New Testament, which gives original witness to that event constraining us to speak of God in a way other than merely as unity and simplicity. Then we cannot neglect those formulations, of both a confessional and a theological character, that shaped this original witness into what we know today as the ancient Christian doctrine of the Trinity. To be sure, we need to take note of the fact that the authors we are concerned with draw on the testimony of these texts in order – at least partially – to go beyond them. A third complex of ideas that warrants mention is that set of modern theories that has provided some terminology for the communal doctrines of the Trinity, as well as some of their thought parameters. Finally, we will need to bring a formal criterion into play; that is, the selectivity, or power to differentiate, that these concepts bring to the handling and answering of particular questions in systematic theology.

5. There is no doubt that the New Testament proclaims both unity and relationship in its depiction of God as the Father, his Son, Jesus Christ, and the Spirit. It is evident that it speaks of distinguishable realities that can only be conceived of in their essentially and mutually relational character. Moreover, passages can be located – although not in great number and not in all sections of the New Testament – where the words chosen in the context of this unity and difference are in line with the viewpoint of the authors we are considering. Let us briefly consider two truly classical texts: 2 Corinthians 13:13 and 1 John 1:3-7. Firstly, the conclusion to 2 Corinthians, with its blessing-like character: "The grace of the Lord Jesus Christ and the love of God and the fellowship of the Holy Spirit be with you all." The word in the original Greek text that is normally translated as "fellowship" is *koinonia*. Undeniably Christ, God, and Spirit are being spoken of here, and it is said of them, in a way that bespeaks equality, that salvation in its different aspects (grace, love, community) comes from them. It should, however, be noted that this text is concerned with saving relationships between human beings and Christ, God, and the Spirit, not with specific relationships between the divine persons themselves. The use of the term *koinonia* in the first letter of John seems to have the same function: the text noted speaks of the "fellowship with the Father and with his son Jesus Christ." It is human beings who have fellowship with and participation in God, Christ, or the Spirit. This is their salvation and also the ground of their community with each other, which – once again for Paul as well as for John – can be described with the same word. This is not to say, however, that here *koinonia* always has the same meaning. The translation practice of the ancient Latin church gives us warning: it does not invariably translate this word in the same way, and certainly not preponderantly as *communio*. *Societas, unio, communicatio* are the alternatives. Further, there is no explicit indication within the New Testament that specific words are chosen for what they connote about relationship to God, Christ, and Spirit. This was the task only of later exegetes, whose task it became to reflect on intra-divine relationships, the so-called immanent Trinity.

6. At this point it is principally the Eastern Christian variant of the doctrine of the Trinity that is brought into play, particularly in the form given it by the so-called Cappadocian fathers (Basil the Great, Gregory Nazianzus, Gregory of Nyssa) in the second half of the fourth century. Often a conception is attributed to them, which – in contrast with the Western, Latin mode of thought, especially Augustine's influential theology – proceeds from the biblical testimony to the threefold reality of Father, Son, and Spirit, as it is revealed in salvation history. The unity here has been described with the term *koinonia* or something similar. In this understanding, God's essentially threefold nature is said to be conceived of as an intersubjective process of relationships, as reciprocal participation and bestowal, as the play of mutuality and as community.[11] Yet recent patristic research has taken away the founda-

[11] Cf. e.g. Gunton, *The Christian Faith*, 186.

tions of this interpretation. Not only has it recently been shown that the fundamental contrast of a Western and Eastern type of Trinitarian doctrine rests on nineteenth-century interpretations, rather than on texts of the fourth and fifth centuries; above all it has been made clear that the *koinonia* – a term the Cappadocians do in fact use – is not at all intended to express an interpersonal play of mutuality, but rather the essential participation of Son and Spirit in that divine being which the Father is by his very nature. Thus there are no grounds here for asserting an opposition between a Western essentialism and an Eastern personalism: rather, the central reference to one divine being is equally important for both traditions, and, following the Latin *persona,* the term we render as "person" can just as little be identified with what modern thought associates with that word.[12]

7. For this reason, one is inclined here to suspect that modern content is being dressed in traditional terminology. One could refer, for instance – without claiming to be exhaustive – to the fundamental distinction between "community" and "society," which is made in a particular style of sociology, as well as to the philosophy of so-called dialogical personalism. According to Ferdinand Tönnies' famous work *Gemeinschaft und Gesellschaft*[13] community, as "real and organic life," corresponding to the "essential will," is distinguished from society, which owes its life to the "electoral will." In this perspective, community is the "unity of difference," and in it "fatherhood" is realized as "rule in the sense of community ... communication from the fullness of its own life." The theological undertones (even if they are secularized) cannot, I think, be missed here. The same applies in dialogical thought, which sees each "I" as constituted through a "Thou," each being as constituted through relationships, and each spirituality constituted through the mediating space of dialogue.[14] One cannot make the immediate claim that these theoretical constructions have theological intent or that they have been generally influential on the theological projects that we have mentioned. This would be difficult to prove in detail; occasionally any such dependence is even ex-

12 Already in a work first published in 1986 André de Halleux was able to forcefully demonstrate this: cf. his *Patrologie et Ecuménisme: Recueil d'études* (Leuven, 1990), 215-68; Sarah Coakley has also pointed out the impossibility of this interpretation in her *Powers and Submissions: Spirituality, Philosophy and Gender* (Oxford, 2002), without, however, referring to de Halleux.

13 F. Tönnies, *Gemeinschaft und Gesellschaft: Grundbegiffe der reinen Soziologie*, 2nd ed. (Berlin, 1912).

14 Cf. e.g. M. Buber, *I and Thou* (New York, 1970).

pressly denied.[15] What is at issue here is the fact that broad areas of contemporary Trinitarian theology have the tendency to seek to understand elements of Christian tradition in an unmediated way in the context of such thinking. The fact that neither dialogical personalism's (psychologically formed) concept of "person" has anything to do with the (ontologically defined) *hypostasis/persona*-terminology of the ancient church, nor modern concepts of community have anything to do with the New Testament or patristic concept of *koinonia*, is often unreflectively or deliberately passed over – not to speak of the internal problems of the theories in question, which in general do not suggest that borrowings of this kind are advisable.

8. In terms of its suitability for deciding particular questions of Trinitarian theology (and beyond), it does not seem that the concept of *communio* allows sufficient selectivity. While authors educated in the tradition of the Eastern church see the clear preponderance of the Fatherhood of God as grounded in it (and correspondingly, the leading role of the episcopal office in the life of the church, reflecting the Trinitarian communion, or that of the father in a family context), others, employing the same terminology, see, in turn, precisely an egalitarian community, marked by strict reciprocity (whether in the divine life or in that of God's people or in gender relations).[16] The terminology of *communio* threatens to become a catchall: unsupported by this term itself, each puts into it what he brings from other considerations.

9. Up to now I have spoken of some strengths, and of different weaknesses, in the Christian discourse regarding the communal life of God. But finally I should not – on professional grounds, so to speak – fail to mention a dogmatic deficit of these theories. Granted, the foundational concept of *communio* as the equally originating unity of different persons should extend to all levels of cosmic, human, Christian and church life; not least in the union of God and a human being in the person of Jesus Christ.[17] Accordingly, it is also necessary to conceive of the divine Trinity itself in this way. Every form of subordination, priority, or precedence of one over the other must be excluded. The oneness and eternity of the divine Trinity demands equality in origin

15 Cf. Greshake, *Der dreieine Gott*, 152-63, 478f.

16 The clearest examples of this are probably the analyses and critique that Volf, *After Our Likeness*, makes of Zizioulas.

17 This transition from the theology of the Trinity in the strict sense to a Trinitarian theology of all these areas is most clearly and comprehensively achieved in Greshake, *Der dreieine Gott*, 217-537.

and a reciprocity of persons that expresses this originating equality. Yet this interpretation fails to recognize an essential truth, something not always emphasized in the theology of the Trinity. The familiar identity of the economic Trinity and immanent Trinity, of the three-personed God in his historical revelation and in his eternal being, does not manifest as a one-to-one correspondence. We do not believe in an eternal Son of God *because* we have encountered Jesus; but rather, because God himself has approached us in Jesus of Nazareth, we are constrained to recognize in this Jesus the eternal Son of God the Father. Further, we do not believe in the Holy Spirit of God *because* we have had spiritual experiences; it is rather because, in spiritual experience, we encounter the Son and through him the Father that we are constrained to conceive of the basis of this experience as the divine Spirit. It is not the eternal Son that is present in Jesus of Nazareth; rather, he is the eternal Son because God, the Father, is present in him. Thus it is not mere Christological caprice on the part of the author of John's Gospel, when in the famous scene the previously unbelieving Thomas addresses the risen Christ as "my Lord and my God" (John 20:28), even though we know that in this Gospel, too, God as Father and Jesus as Son are otherwise clearly distinguished. Here, in the form of a confession, the same is said as what Jesus proclaims at another point: "Whoever has seen me, has seen the Father" (John 14:9). This should not surprise us at all: rather, it is simply a necessity of salvation. Only God can redeem; he alone can forgive sin; he alone is the salvation of the world. Only whatever, or, better, *whoever* comes from God can bring this salvation and in this way be God himself: God in the event of his self-communication, the Son or the Word, God in the event of his enduring presence, God the Spirit.

But the Father is not manifest: he is the ineffable, silent mystery, the withdrawn, hidden God. Thus the Son and Spirit are indeed "God from God" as the creed says; but in this they are not at all equally originating as is the Father. God the Father, too, is "God from God," but precisely as origin of himself without origin. The Son and Spirit, in whom the Father is manifest to his creation and near and present to it, receive, in contrast, their being as "God from God" from the Father. God, the Father, is from his own self the eternal and holy one. The Son and Spirit are eternal and holy not from themselves but rather from the eternity and holiness of their divine origin in the Father. Thus the transposition or structure of reference that we have already portrayed is reflected or reproduced here: just as on the plane of the economic Trinity the Father is manifest in the Son and the Spirit, so, correspondingly, on the plane of the immanent Trinity, it is the Father who begets the eternal Word and the eternal Spirit. The presence of the unoriginated origin in salvation history is not this origin itself: and yet it is truly God himself who is visible and can be experienced in it. It was this dialectic which first challenged and impelled Christian faith toward the development and formulation of a doctrine of the Trinity. Yet the nature of this foundational question and source of any theology of the Trinity is mistaken, if, from the impetus of personalism, social philosophy, or some other set of ideas, we misunderstand the Trinity as an interpersonal *communio* of three equally originating subjects.

Translated by Robert Gascoigne

PART IV

EUROPE'S GOD IN GLOBAL DIALOGUE

Keith Ward

The Idea of "God" in Global Theology

What Is Global Theology?

The idea of global theology originated in the late nineteenth and early twentieth centuries in Europe and the U.S. It can be found adumbrated in the work of Max Muller, sometimes called the Father of Comparative Religion in Oxford, and in the writings of A. E. Hocking in America. It became an established term in Wilfred Cantwell Smith, one time Director of the Harvard Center for the Study of World Religions, and it is now quite widespread. A number of similar terms, like "comparative theology," and "intercultural theology," express the same sort of approach to theology, and that approach is perhaps more important than the precise term used for it.

The approach can best be defined by contrasting it with a traditional view in Christian theology, which can be called a confessional approach. The term "theology" was first used by the medieval writer Peter Abelard, and in medieval Europe it was conceived as a scientific – that is, systematic – development of ideas accepted as truths revealed from God in Scripture and the teaching of the Church. Thomas Aquinas held that *sacra doctrina* was the most certain of all disciplines, since it was founded simply on the exposition of truths infallibly received from God.

Few people would feel quite so certain about exactly what truths have been revealed by God in modern times. But there is still a widespread view of theology as the exposition of Christian doctrines, either from the Bible or from a study of the life and practice of specific Christian communities. This form of confessional theology is an intellectual discipline concerned primarily with the inner coherence of the beliefs of a specific Christian community. It is often undertaken on behalf of that community, and speaks primarily to it. Thus those who are licensed as teachers of Catholic theology are enjoined not to contradict the teachings of the Catholic Church in public, and they are expected to expound and defend those teachings to the best of their ability. Confessional theologians are servants of a particular Church, responsible to it for what they teach.

Global theology has a different approach. It is not conceived as a Christian discipline, carried out on behalf of some Christian church. While it is true that the word "theology" was first used by Christians and first applied only to Christian beliefs, it is quite common now for Muslims, Jews, and Hindus to speak of theology, and there is no reason at all why there should not be a Muslim or Hindu theology. This usage would refer to a systematic intellectual exposition of beliefs in communities that think they have received revealed truths from God. Obviously, Muslim and Christian theologies will differ in several respects, although there will also be many matters on which they agree – for instance, that there is one good creator of the universe.

Yet global theology goes further than this. It asks whether there is any reason why theology should be confined to a particular religious tradition in principle. Could it not take as its object of study the whole range of human religious traditions, and hence become truly global in its range? One objection to such a proposal is that etymologically "theology" suggests a study of God (*theos*) or of ideas about God, whereas some religious traditions, like Buddhism, do not use the term "God" in a significant way. A response to this could be simply to omit non-theistic religions from a considered global theology, but that would eliminate spiritual traditions of enormous depth and complexity. Another response could be to extend the meaning of the term *theos* so that it refers to a reality that is taken to be other and greater than human, or of any part of this spatio-temporal cosmos, and that is often taken to be of supreme and unsurpassable value. In fact, this is in some ways nearer to the early Greek use of the term *theos*, which by no means always referred to a personal God. In any case, we should not be limited by etymology, and we are free to extend the meaning of the word "theology" in any way that is useful.

With this in mind, I suggest that we regard global theology as the study of ideas of supernatural and ultimate realities and values, as well as the study of ways of relating to those realities and values as they have persisted throughout the history of various world cultures. Since such ideas differ widely, this discipline could not be viewed as an exposition and defense of any particular set of religious beliefs. But it could be seen as a sympathetic exposition of such beliefs and as an attempt to see how they have been defended, how they form part of the life of specific cultural communities, and how they have developed and interacted over time.

There is no apparent reason why those who teach or study such a theology should be required to have any particular set of religious or anti-religious beliefs. Of course each person will likely have personal beliefs about such important matters. Each is entitled to expound those beliefs and to explain why they are held. But it is very important that scholars, at the outset, give a fair and accurate exposition of beliefs that differ from their own, and that they show special concern in rebutting the caricatures and misunderstandings that are so common in the area of religious belief.

Is such a comparative theology in competition with Catholic or Lutheran theology? Not at all. Catholics and Lutherans are entitled to their own advocates and defenders. Global theology is a different discipline, although it shares many scholarly methods in common with Christian theology. A genuinely global theology will seek to expound the whole range of human beliefs about the objects of religious faith as far as is possible, and its various teachers may advocate a range of diverse positions without presenting their own beliefs as unjustly privileged.

How does the discipline of global theology differ from that of the anthropology of religion, or of the philosophy of religion? There is no reason why these disciplines should not overlap and reinforce one another, but the main difference from anthropology is that theology is concerned with intellectual beliefs and the reasons given for them, whereas anthropology is largely concerned with practices and behavior. Global theology's main difference from a properly comparative philosophy of religion is its particular concern with claims to revelation and transcendent experience and with the study of cumulative traditions of belief as they develop over time and in different cultures, through methodologies unconsidered by philosophers of religion.

So the discipline of global theology is possible, and it exists, whether it is called comparative or global. It takes the whole religious heritage of humanity as its object of study, and it seeks to give some account of how such a rich and diverse heritage gives rise to new problems, challenges, and developments in a world that is consciously interconnected in new and apparently irreversible ways.

I, myself, am an Anglican priest and a practitioner of a specific Christian tradition. That means that when I teach global theology I am bound to describe, analyze, and criticize things in a particular confessional way (though that confession may not be quite what people expect). For that very reason, I welcome opportunities to co-teach global theology with others whose practices and commitments differ from mine. The more such conversation is developed, the more chance there is for increased understanding. Will engagement of this kind affect my commitments and those of people who study global theology? I hope so, for, surely, I have much to learn of spiritual realities and the rich range of human responses to them. Especially significant is the way I foresee such interaction increasing my understanding of my own tradition – as I see it in the light of others – and deepening my commitment to my tradition as a valid path of spiritual growth, thereby helping me to distinguish, within my faith, the important from the superficial. Global theology can and should be an enrichment to spiritual understanding.

Four Models of the Supreme Spiritual Reality in Global Theology

Within global theology, the idea of "God" is just one idea of ultimate reality and value among many. What is most distinctive about the idea of "God" is revealed by the Oxford English Dictionary definition of "God" as a "supernatural person." I believe that definition to be a great oversimplification, as I will show in a moment. Nevertheless, the purpose in speaking of God is largely to assert that the ultimate basis of reality, and the highest possible value, is in some sense personal. It is one self-existent reality possessing something analogous to personal consciousness and will.

Religious traditions that center on the idea of "God" contrast with traditions that lack such an idea of one supreme personal reality, or that do not place such a high value on the idea. In the global history of religions, there are four main models of the way a supreme spiritual reality relates to the physical cosmos in which we exist. These models exhaust the basic set of logically possible ways in which spiritual reality can relate to the cosmos, and so they cover the whole variety of religions that accept one supreme spiritual reality as their most fundamental feature.

In many traditions, the one supreme spiritual reality may include the physical cosmos as part of itself. The cosmos may be seen as an illusory manifestation of the spiritual real (as in Advaita Vedanta), or as the "body" or physical expression of spirit (in Visistadvaita), or as the appearance of Supreme Spirit (in European Absolute Idealism). Such Idealist views see the spiritual reality as including, but as greater than, the cosmos, and tend to speak of humans, and indeed of all things, as divine, or at least as parts of the divine. They may, and usually do, use the concept of "God" to characterize supreme spiritual reality. But often, or even usually, these perspectives assert that the idea of "God" is a picture that may be useful for devotion, but must finally be transcended by the idea of an infinite and ineffable unity of which the cosmos is part. According to the great Indian philosopher-saint Sankara, beyond *saguna* Brahman, the Absolute with qualities of intelligence and will, lies *nirguna* Brahman, the Absolute without qualities, which is the true supreme reality. Brahman can be spoken of as *sat-cit-ananda*, being, consciousness, and bliss, and to that extent we may speak of a supreme Lord who is personal, but who is also much more than personal in ways we cannot imagine.

A second way to speak of the relation of spiritual reality to the cosmos is to say that spirit is quite distinct from all material reality, different from it in nature and excluding it altogether. This is the way of Dualism, which is found in clear form in Jainism, Buddhism, and some other forms of Indian religion. From this perspective, engagement with the physical world entails suffering and attachment, and the religious path is to renounce attachment, to escape suffering, and to enter into the purely spiritual realm, beyond the cosmos altogether. Thus the Tirthankaras, the ford-crossers of Jainism, are souls that have been liberated from matter, existing freely as conscious, wise, and all-knowing beings, as models for other souls to follow in their journey toward liberation from rebirth in the material world. There is no God, no supreme personal creator, in such a view. But there are many liberated souls, or perhaps one unlimited reality of wisdom, knowledge, and bliss – *nirvana* – into which all liberated souls are merged. In dualistic viewpoints, persons are not of supreme value, for they are mixtures of spirit and matter, and liberation consists in the disentanglement from matter into a supreme reality which is no longer personal in form (though it is conceived as blissful and aware, in some sense).

A third model is that of Monism, which denies all duality and asserts that spirit is identical to the material cosmos. Spirit and matter are two aspects of the same indivisible reality, and spiritual enlightenment consists in realizing the unity of all being. Many forms of Buddhism and of Chinese religion are monistic, seeing the spiritual as the order, balance, or inner essence of the physical, so that, as the Buddhist sage Buddhaghosa put it, "*nirvana* is *samsara*," the realm of liberation is the same as the realm of suffering, but perceived differently by the non-attached and liberated soul. The idea of "God" is not historically central in such traditions, but it is possible to view the spiritual essence of undivided reality as synonymous with "God," insofar as it manifests justice, order, balance, wisdom, and bliss. Some Buddhist practitioners of the monistic way are not averse to using the idea of "God." But they would insist upon a totally non-anthropomorphic idea, and they deny that God is a distinct personal being who creates the universe as an act of free will.

The fourth model is that of Theism, the view that matter and spirit are distinct, but that matter depends wholly for its existence upon an act of will by a personal Spirit (creation). This is the way classically stated by the Hebrew prophets and developed in Judaism, Christianity, and Islam. In most statements of Theism, God is a personal reality who can exist without the cosmos, but who creates the cosmos so that finite persons can come to exist and find their fulfillment in a relationship of knowledge and love with God. God is not just a model for an ineffable Absolute Spirit, or merely a way of speaking of the inner spiritual laws of the cosmos; God is a distinct and fully self-existent personal being who relates to the cosmos as a distinct personal reality.

These four models are all widely affirmed by diverse religious traditions. They are not, of course, nearly as distinct and clear-cut as I have made them here. They are combined, mixed, and related in many different ways in different part of many religious traditions. But they do present a logically possible set of relations of spiritual reality to the material cosmos, and it can be readily seen that they do express fundamental differences. They demonstrate that all religions cannot be reduced to a fundamental sameness and that any global theology must accept and explain their deep differences as well as it can.

Nevertheless, underlying the clear diversity is the fact that all religions are concerned with a supreme spiritual reality. Indeed, the basic nature of that reality, and of the way in which it is proper for humans to relate to it, is pretty widely agreed upon among most major religious traditions. Since the supreme spiritual reality is taken to be unsurpassable in value, there is wide agreement that whatever is supreme in value must at least be conscious, intelligent, blissful, wise, and compassionate. Such qualities, or qualities at least as valuable as them, must belong to any being that can be thought of as supreme.

Idealists conceive of those qualities as possessed by an Absolute Spirit that includes all other realities within itself. The supreme is not a person who relates to us as one person to others. The supreme is a spiritual reality of which we are part. However, its basic nature is that of intelligence and bliss, so if not as a person, it can be thought of as personal. The spiritual path is one of overcoming egoism and of coming to realize that individuals are part of supreme Spirit, individuals who take on the role of consciously becoming vehicles of divine expression in the world.

Dualists conceive of the fundamental value-making qualities as "belonging" to a distinct spiritual reality, a reality other than the physical cosmos, whether it is one or many (a supreme state or a set of liberated souls). Again, while such a reality may not be thought of as "a person," the state or set of souls is endowed with personal qualities of intelligence and bliss. The spiritual goal here is to overcome egoism and attachment, and to cultivate spiritual qualities so that one comes to apprehend ones own true nature as pure spirit – wise, compassionate, and blissful.

Monists ascribe the value-making qualities to this worldly reality ontologically, as seen in its spiritual aspect. They tend to deny ideas of a creator God, largely because of the great amount of evil and suffering in the world. But they do not deny the idea of one spiritual reality, a state that is wise and compassionate, and of which we can all become part when we overcome attachment to the egoistic self.

Theists ascribe supreme wisdom, compassion, and bliss to a personal self-subsistent reality, which they call "God." For them, the spiritual goal is to come to know and love God, to adore those qualities in their supreme instantiation and to share in them and express them in their own lives, insofar as they relate rightly to God.

Thus despite the differences among major religions, there is a common underlying notion of a supreme reality of wisdom, compassion, and bliss, and an agreement that the spiritual goal is one of overcoming egoism and of coming to know or to enter into or to realize unity with that supreme reality. The differences between religions spring from different ways of spelling out more precisely what the supreme values are, and from exactly how we are to come to know them. The idea of "God" is partly the result of placing personal relationship and a sense of "divine otherness" at the heart of an idea of supreme value.

Five Christian Ideas of "God"

I have attempted to identify the idea of "God" as the focal concept of one set of traditions within the greater global history of religious traditions. But of course there is not just one idea of "God." I have already suggested that Idealists and Monists both place the idea of "God" in service to expressing their own beliefs about supreme spiritual reality. But Theists, too, reveal a range of differences among themselves that the common use of the word "God" can conceal. Even in the Christian world of today, there are at least five notably different ideas of "God" that are held widely. I will now expound briefly on those ideas, so that we can firmly hold in mind the internal plurality that exists within even one set of religious traditions.

What may be called the "classical" Christian idea of "God" is one that will likely surprise many Christians. It is the idea that dominated the first thousand years of Church history and was definitively formulated in the thirteenth century by Thomas Aquinas. This idea conceives of God as a simple, timeless, impassible, and immutable spiritual reality, as the source of everything else that exists and that remains unchanged by relationship to anything it creates. God is simple by not being complex in any respect, by not having any parts or differing aspects of being, and by not being extended in space or time (which would introduce parts into the divine being). This means that God does not do anything sequentially. So creation is an eternal and timeless act of God, the whole of time, from the first moment to the last, being created in one and the same non-temporal divine act.

This idea requires us to take most Biblical statements about God metaphorically, and it forbids us from thinking that what we do changes God in any way, or that God can actually respond to us in new ways because of what we say or do. God is the changeless source of all being, and causes everything to be exactly as it is. What is future to us is present to God already. The whole of created time exists, and God's eternal decrees cannot be altered by our will. In fact, what we will is part of what is eternally decreed by God.

This idea of "God" may seem to be very impersonal, and indeed it would be quite wrong to think that the classical Christian idea of "God" is of a supernatural person. It is rather of a changeless intelligence and will that does not enter into real relationship with created reality.

It is worth remarking that the classical idea of "God" is not so far removed from the Buddhist idea of a perfect state of intelligence and bliss. The main difference is that the classical God causes the cosmos to be by an intentional act, so that it arises from the desire of a perfect being and is therefore intrinsically good. Buddhists would not agree that finite being is intrinsically good, and so their state of intelligence and bliss does not contain an analogy of "will" or "desire." Nevertheless, the idea of one changeless state of perfect bliss and knowledge is shared by many Buddhists and Christians, whether they call it "God" or not. This should caution us against making broad, over-simple distinctions between "theistic" and "non-theistic" religions. There are valid distinctions to be made, but they do not always emerge from the obvious places.

Many Christians, especially in Protestant traditions, are uneasy about the classical idea of a God who is unchanged by anything that occurs in the universe. There is no Protestant equivalent of the Catholic philosopher Thomas

Aquinas; however, it is fair to say that most Protestant theologians, especially in Germany, have been influenced by the philosopher Hegel. Hegel offered the paradigm of European Idealism, which made the whole cosmos an expression and part of the being of Absolute Spirit (Geist). For Hegel, God includes the universe, and God's nature is what it is because the universe is what it is. We, the manifest, make a difference to God. Our happiness and suffering are part of the experience of God, so this God is one changed by what happens in the universe (even though that change, for Hegel, is itself caused by God). Thus Protestant thinkers influenced by Hegel tend to stress God's suffering, meaning that the divine nature itself includes the suffering of Jesus (and indeed of every sentient being), and they think of humans as having a more dynamic relation to God, because finite human actions are also the temporal actions of God. In this view, which is held by Karl Barth, God is temporal and changing, while God also transcends temporality and change.

A variant of the Hegelian view is Process Theology, which stresses, even more, the way in which the acts of finite creatures determine the future. For Process theologians, God does not unilaterally determine the future. It is finite creatures (ultimately, what Process thinkers sometimes call "actual occasions" or "events" who freely and creatively determine what is to happen. God has to wait and see, even though God puts forth all the possible futures from among which creatures will choose. The Process God is to some extent at the mercy of creatures, and Process theologians stress that the love of God is not all-determining power, but a persuasive influence that endures risk and suffering in order to lead creatures to greater good. Among theistic viewpoints, this one holds creaturely freedom at its maximum. God contains all possibilities for the future and perhaps exerts an influence on how things go. But creatures are responsible for what happens, and the future world must accept the consequences for the present actions of its members. Some theologians find that this idea of "God" best represents a Christian idea of a suffering, patient, loving God who is responsive to human acts but does not completely determine what they shall be.

We can see that Christian ideas of "God" span a wide range, from thinking that God determines everything (the classical view) to thinking that God determines hardly anything (the Process view), and from thinking that God does not change at all to thinking that God is in a continual and unending process of change. Many contemporary theologians, however, regard all of these views as outdated and unacceptable – they are all examples of metaphysical thinking, of abstract theorizing, of determining the nature of reality from an armchair. There are those who claim that this sort of philosophy is no longer viable in a scientific age. Consequently, a number of theologians, especially in Europe, have tried to construct non-metaphysical ideas of God. D.Z. Phillips and Don Cupitt (though they are very different from each other) are good examples of thinkers who have made this attempt.

In this theological approach, all factual knowledge is provided by the sciences. What God-talk achieves is the positing of an objective ideal of Goodness, in the light of which human lives are judged and by which they are challenged. The Good has no causal input into the universe, but it stands as an eternal lure of Love, which, as Aristotle put it, causes simply by being loved. This may seem very different from the Biblical idea of an active, responsive God. Still, it is not so different from the classical view, which also posits a timeless perfection as its supreme ideal and interprets most Biblical talk of God as metaphorical.

The fifth widespread contemporary Christian idea of "God" is perhaps the most popular, and it is the idea of "God" as the supreme Person: omnipotent, omniscient, and perfectly good. Strange as it may seem, this is a very recent view among theologians, as the idea of a divine personality has, historically, been thought to limit God unacceptably. But Christian personalism was strengthened by the writings of Martin Buber, whose notion of an "I-Thou" relation at the heart of reality has reinstated the idea of personal relationship and community as a supreme value. Some modern theologians find that the idea of "God" as Trinity enables them to think of God as a sort of community of persons. Most personalists, however, view God as a supreme Person who creates other persons in order to fulfill the divine perfection by relating to those persons in shared experience and action, both for good and ill.

I point to these five Christian ideas of "God" in order to show that, even in one religious tradition, there is not just one agreed upon idea of "God." When we explore these ideas more fully, we find that they arise through a variety of complicated interactions within specific cultural and philosophical contexts. Seeing the idea of "God" in light of global theology expands consideration of this variety of interactions to the whole world, and in doing so makes possible an even greater range of understandings.

Some Implications for Believing in God.

What implications do these findings have for belief in God in modern Europe and in the modern world? The first implication is that they provide a bridge to understanding: different religions are not simply closed by nature to one another, such that no tradition can really make sense of another tradition. On the contrary, a global theology reveals that many religions share a common idea of the divine as supreme reality and value, and a common idea of the spiritual journey as the overcoming of egoism in quest of a fulfilled relationship with such a reality. Moreover, some basic features of the supreme reality are shared, albeit at a general level. We can also see that religions are concerned with similar spheres of thought and activity, and that with all of this in common, they are capable of understanding one another perfectly well.

A second implication of our findings is that the many differences between religious views largely reflect the different models for relating the spiritual to the material, to different sets of originative experiences that give access to the spiritual, and to different historical traditions which have adopted fundamental worldviews that then influence how experiences are described and extended. Witnessing the great myriad of human cultures, psychologies, and histories, it is not at all surprising that such diversity exists. It would be much more surprising if it did not. Religious diversity can be seen as the natural condition of humanity, and not as degeneration from some imagined primordial unanimity of belief. As such, diversity can be celebrated as a manifestation of human creative imagination in the interpretation of religious experience, and not as a regrettable fall into heresy.

This suggests a third implication – that many religious traditions are epistemically on par with one another; that is, no tradition is clearly better justified or warranted in its thinking than any other. Of course, we must make informed and well-considered choices about rationality and moral acceptability. But we must recognize that human beings differ conscientiously about such choices, and that a number of traditions rely on experiences and arguments that do not compel, and seem unlikely ever to achieve, universal assent. This gives rise to what John Hick has called Epistemic Pluralism. We live in a world wherein the justifications given for various different beliefs, both religious and non-religious, are not universally compelling. The consequence is that no reasonable person can any longer say that their own tradition is certainly true, and that others are certainly false, or at least not worth consideration. This does not warrant the assertion, however, that all viewpoints in a range of incompatible views are equally true. The implication is that they are more or less equally justified, as far as we can see. The truth, while it must exist, may forever elude us, and cannot be grasped by any one of us with absolute certainty.

This entails a fourth implication: that epistemic humility is warranted in global theology. Religious believers who are aware of the global diversity of faiths must renounce claims to absolute certainty and resolve to test and extend their own insights against the claims of others.

Finally, a fifth implication is that religious believers must learn to respect difference as an integral part of the search for truth. If religion is serious about truth, we must test our claims to truth ruthlessly against our competitors'. If we are to see the limitations of our own viewpoints, we must have the courage to contrast them with the viewpoints of others. If we are to understand ourselves, we must see how and why others understand us.

To this extent, global theology becomes an obligation of faith, at least for those with the time and ability to undertake it. The requirement here is not the impossible one that we should spend all our time learning about the huge number of faiths in the world, which would be confusing and unprofitable. The requirement is that we should cultivate the ability to see the history and logical placing of our own belief in God, in its global context as far as is possible for us. We should be open to learn from others, and be prepared to respect and honor others' views. While sustaining commitment to our own beliefs with all the moral seriousness that requires, we must be ready to deepen and expand our beliefs with a willingness to understand the spiritual beliefs and practices of others, insofar as they impinge upon us.

I hope I have demonstrated that the idea of "God" is not one, but many ideas, with diverse histories and cultural influences, existing within a range of views of the spiritual and the material. I hope I have shown that restricting attention to one's own religious tradition may have an undesirably narrowing and obscuring effect. I hope, too, that I have shown the value of locating our own ideas of "God" within the context of global diversity, and of treating diversity in a sophisticated and nuanced way, instead of in an oversimplifying way that replicates stereotypes. To do this is to advance human understanding in one of the most basic and influential spheres of human life. That is good both for its own sake and for the sake of the increased tolerance and respect that it will almost certainly engender.

Josef Wohlmuth

Twentieth-Century Jewish Thought as a Challenge to Christian Theology

"Jewish thought" is a broad concept. In order to limit my exposition in this paper, I will concentrate on only a few questions by a select group of authors, keeping to the area of my own professional competence, viz. European Jewish thought as this bears on the *philosophical* debates of the twentieth century and the way its themes present a challenge to Christian theology. One can readily imagine that this challenge is so great because it touches on questions about which the similarities to Christian theology are greater than the differences. Issues that were once a source of polemics can today – after the experiences of the twentieth century – become the starting point of a dialogue in which both sides participate as equals, and from which each side can learn. The three authors I wish to treat are Franz Rosenzweig, Emmanuel Levinas, and Jacques Derrida. In different ways, each of the three situates his philosophical thinking in relation to the Jewish tradition. Nevertheless, all three understand themselves as philosophical thinkers in the European context, precisely in those contexts where they do not conceal their indebtedness to Judaism. Here I shall concentrate on the problem of transcendence, the related question of the God-world-man relation, and the resulting problems for religious language. I want to proceed by briefly presenting each position and the respective challenge to Christian theology, summarizing my conclusions at the end of this paper.

Franz Rosenzweig's Rediscovery of Judaism and His Doubts About the Strict Monotheism of Christianity

In his book *The Star of Redemption*, published in the years immediately after the First World War, Franz Rosenzweig, perhaps the most theological of the three authors treated here, made one of the most sweeping proposals concerning the mutual relatedness of Judaism and Christianity.[1] He identified Judaism

1 Cf. F. Rosenzweig, *Der Mensch und sein Werk, Gesammelte Schriften*, Part II: *Der Stern der Erlösung*. 4th ed. (The Hague, 1976; first edition, 1921 with printed marginal title from the second edition). The numbers in brackets refer to this edition.

as the religion of eternal life, with immediate access to God, and identified Christianity (as mediated by Jesus Christ) as the eternal way, emphasizing that despite the similarities between the two, there was a difference which represented a genuine challenge to Christian theology. Both religions have an intensive relation to the world and emphasize the human role in the work of redemption.[2] Rosenzweig defends the thesis, following Hermann Cohen, that one who speaks of a correlation between God and the world is speaking of two different realities which preserve their own respective "facticity" through their relation to each other.[3] Characteristic of Rosenzweig's work, especially in *The Star of Redemption*, is his understanding the whole of reality as a network of relationships, which one can represent by means of the figure of the star of David.[4] God, human beings, and the world are correlated on the one hand, as are creation, revelation, and redemption on the other. Bernhard Casper correctly emphasizes that despite his similarity to Schelling, Rosenzwieg nevertheless does not identify the becoming of the world with that of God. "In contrast to a theogonist, one will speak here of an *incarnated* thinking."[5] Stéphane Mosès writes: "The knowledge of the world in its existence, i.e., of the creation, and the relation to other human beings and the projection into the future, i.e., the redemption, form together with revelation itself the complete landscape of human experience."[6] In this landscape, Judaism stands for the absolute quality of divine eternity, located outside every system and all history. This means that it represents for Christianity too "the only indubitable proof of the truth of its faith." According to Rosenzweig, if Christianity were to distance itself from Judaism through a gnosticizing spirit-

2 In *Das dialogische Denken*, B. Casper cites a passage from Franz Rosenzweig he believes "is reminiscent of the Christological paradox of Chalcedon." Rosenzweig had written, in the introduction to an edition of the Jewish writings of Hermann Cohen, "... correlation, in which God and man come together exactly because they remain essentially separate." (B. Casper, *Das dialogische Denken: Franz Rosenzweig, Ferdinand Ebner und Martin Buber*, 2nd ed. [Freiburg / Munich 2002], 172).

3 Casper, *Das dialogische Denken*, 171.

4 It is above all the relation of God, world, and human person. None of these entities can be spoken of in isolation from the others, even if this did not reduce their respective differences. Rosenzweig's second triad (creation, revelation, and redemption) underscores the idea that God can be spoken of only in relation to these entities, and so in the context of the world.

5 Casper, *Das dialogische Denken*. Casper included this excursus on Schelling in the second edition.

6 Cf. S. Mosès, *System und Offenbarung* (Munich, 1985), 208.

ualization, it would endanger its own foundations.[7] Since we still await the redemption, this is the "most unreal" of all unreal situations. The Jewish liturgy is the only place where eternity can already be experienced in the mode of an anticipation in the temporal dimension.[8]

This systematic view leads Rosenzweig to see Judaism and Christianity as "two faces of the one truth" (p. 147). The consequences he draws for his description of Christianity are serious, and turn the traditional view on its head. The religion of eternal life is a strict monotheism and Judaism, as a people, is already with the Father. Christianity, the religion of the eternal way, has not yet come to the Father. Christianity is the religion of individuals and is permeated by dualities (such as church and state) and it is at risk of losing the strict Jewish monotheism en route. This change of perspective suffices to reverse Hegel's philosophy of religion, where Christianity stands at the end of a process of development as the absolute religion, and this reversal proves a clear provocation for traditional Christian thought. This departure from Hegel's system was one of Rosenzweig's main philosophical concerns from the time of his dissertation onward.[9]

Rosenzweig's new understanding of Judaism from the perspective of its liturgy was a key experience in his own life, as he faced the question whether to convert to Christianity or remain a Jew. The Jewish liturgy seemed to him the "burning glass of eternity in the cycle of the year" (p. 152). In the liturgical celebration, historical time and eternity meet, and here he describes eternity as follows: "Eternity is not a very long time, but a tomorrow that could just as well be today. Eternity is a future, which without ceasing to be future, nevertheless is present. Eternity is a today, that is however conscious of being more than today" (p. 250). Cultic time is a time in which the past remains perpetually present. For Rosenzweig the "forms of liturgy" are a "silent anticipation of a world that is radiant in the silence of the future" (p. 327). The keyword "silence" points to a central dimension of Rosenzweig's understanding of the liturgy. Silence is important not only because the kneeling of the community in silence on Yom Kippur is a key moment in the liturgy, but also because eternity is a world that lies beyond all language and

---

7 Mosès, *System*, 220.

8 Mosès, *System*, 134. Mosès considers the concept of anticipation one of the most central concepts in *The Star of Redemption*.

9 Cf. F. Rosenzweig, *Hegel und der Staat*, 2 vols. (Munich / Berlin, 1920) (reprint in one vol.: Aalen, 1962).

passes beyond all language to flow into silence. Hence Rosenzweig attributes a genuinely sacramental significance to silent "gestures." Since, according to Rosenzweig, Christianity lacks a feast of reconciliation, it lacks the immediacy provided in Judaism by the gestures of kneeling and keeping silence.[9]

Redemption, whose final goal is God himself, is unimaginable without the human person. Rosenzweig can go so far as to write: "God redeems himself in the redemption of the world through the human person, and in the redemption of the human person by means of the world. Human being and world vanish in redemption, but God brings himself to fulfillment." A little further on in the same text, Rosenzweig specifies the concept of eternity with relation to the becoming of God: "Eternity makes even the moment something everlasting; it is a perennialization. The phrase 'God is eternal' means that for him, eternity brings him to fulfillment" (p. 288). God brings himself to fulfillment, as he writes in another place, in the judgment. "The final judgment, which has a proleptic character in all eternity, annuls the separation after confirming and indeed by confirming it, and extinguishes the fires of hell." In the final judgment, which God himself carries out in his own name, all that is enters into God's "all-ness", and every name into his nameless "one" (p. 265). The final result, summed up in the briefest fashion, is: "all and one" (p. 266). When Rosenzweig speaks of the vanishing of the human person in redemption, this means that the eternal dimension in the human person transcends all time in those moments in which he is loved and himself loves (since love of God and love of neighbor form a unity: cf. pp. 288f.); and just as the human person began in the silence of the original quality that existed before all time began, so too he will end in silence. "In eternity is silence" (p. 290). Nevertheless, Rosenzweig notes that the concept of eternity is different when applied to the religion of eternal life (Judaism) and that of the eternal way (Christianity). "Eternal life and eternal way – these are as different as the infinity of a point and of a line." (p. 379). Christianity is on the way "which leads from the Christ who has come to the Christ who will come again" (p. 379). "The way ceases when the homeland is reached" (p. 422). This is reached at the end of history, when there emerges "a kingdom freed from strife and contradictions, in which God will be all in all" (p. 446). Rosenzweig writes, no doubt alluding to 1 Cor. 15:28, that Christianity does not take seriously enough the idea that God will be "all in all," because as the religion of the eternal way, it

9 Eternity is when God himself speaks the final word, which itself can no longer be a word. "He does it. He is the Redeemer" (265)

concentrates on the Son. Christianity regards the "God all in all" only as a theologumenon, as an idea which does nothing to alter the fact "that he [the Son of Man] was turned into a God in the course of time"(p. 458). Only Judaism adheres to the "God all in all" and gives it the place which is its due. But it thereby stands opposed to Christianity. The deepest reason for Christian hatred of the Jews is that Judaism forces Christianity to acknowledge the idea that it is a "way" of mission to the Gentiles, which implies a continuous process of translation – and this means that Christianity itself does not attain to the truth, but is never more than en route towards it (p. 459). Nevertheless, Christianity shares in the work of preserving the truth, which is confident that God's promises for humanity as a whole will be fulfilled, and takes as its banner the "primal Jewish affirmation" that God is faithful.[10]

By demonstrating the great closeness of Judaism and Christianity, Franz Rosenzweig shows that they are both concerned with eternity, but he also points out their greatest divergence, which is based on different understandings of eternity and finds its expression in the deification of the Son. Although Christianity conquered paganism, it at once fell back into paganism by failing to persist in strict monotheism. Judaism, as the religion of an eternity consisting in a single point, has already arrived at the destination which Christianity, as the religion of the eternal way, has still to reach. Judaism thus remains a thorn in the flesh of Christianity.

One important element in Rosenzweig's work is clearly a critique of language. The last word is no longer a word, but rather eternal silence. This appears to be the essence of mysticism, in his eyes (p. 458). But Christianity too, for all its emphasis on the incarnation, knows a critique of language, which generates a Trinitarian mysticism. At any rate, it is striking in this connection to see how wide an echo some words of Karl Rahner have found in twentieth-century Christian theology – words probably formulated without any knowledge of Rosenzweig's work – viz., the affirmation that God is the last Word before silence falls.[11] Despite this reservation about words, however, Rahner found it important to show that both modes of God's self-communication (in truth and in love) have a "modal," temporal and provisionary character, yet do not destroy monotheism. I believe that the challenge posed by Rosenzweig's strict monotheism of silence consists in asking whether the interpretation of

10 Cf. Casper, *Das dialogische Denken*, 185.

11 Cf. K. Rahner, "Meditation über das Wort Gott," in K. Rahner, *Grundkurs des Glaubens. Sämtliche Werke* 26 (1999), 48-55, here 50.

Jesus must necessarily lead to a Christology which endangers the unity of the idea of God, or pulls absolute transcendence down into the vortex of finitude. The declaration *Dabru emet* maintains that Jews and Christians worship the same God,[12] and Jewish dialogue partners no longer assert that an incarnational Christology makes this in principle impossible.[13] At the same time, as Franz Rosenzweig sees it, Judaism must be aware of its vocation to take scrupulous care to avoid any form of the deification of the human person, since this could obscure or even destroy the "God all in all."

The Jewish Critique of Christian Theology

The Jewish tradition does not use the word theology and considers its Christian use to be a Greek coinage which stands or falls with one's appraisal of the Greek form of rationality. This raises once again the language problem, particularly with regard to the extent to which propositional statements in Christian theology may claim validity.

In his essay "God and Philosophy" (1975), Emmanuel Levinas observes in almost apologetic tones that Western philosophy means "a destruction of transcendence."[14] Philosophers are quick to accuse the Bible of thinking about God in a way that fails to reach the heights of the philosophical debate. Yet according to Levinas, philosophy is nothing other than "immanence itself" (p.92). Philosophy could perhaps admit that the word "God" originates out of a religious tradition, but it understands God language as "propositional speech on a topic, i.e., as if it had a meaning related to a disclosure, to the manifestation of a presence" (p. 94). Is then God language possible only as affirmation

---

12 This refers to Nr. 1 of the Jewish response to Christians and to Christianity from September 11, 2000 entitled *Dabru emet* (Speak Truth). Cf. text in T. Frymer-Kensky *et al.* (eds), *Christianity in Jewish Terms* (Boulder, 2000), XV-XVIII.

13 H. Cohen is also the one who drew attention to the fact that medieval Jewish thought credited Christianity and Islam with the merit of "spreading monotheism among the peoples." Even the rabbis did not accuse Christianity of rejecting monotheism, and understood the Trinity as an "association" (shituf). It is in this context that Cohen locates the correlation between Christianity as a religion for the whole of humanity, and the Christian conviction that Jesus is the one Messiah. Cf. H. Cohen, *Religion der Vernunft aus den Quellen des Judentums: Eine jüdische Religionsphilosophie*, 3rd ed. (Wiesbaden, 1995), 280.

14 E. Levinas, "Gott und die Philosophie," in B. Casper (ed.), *Gott nennen* (Freiburg / Munich, 1981), 81-123, here 83.

about a topic? Appealing to Descartes, though also parting company with him, on the question of a possible proof of God's existence, Levinas arrives at the conclusion that the idea of God, as an idea of the infinite, differs from all other concepts and ideas. "The idea of God shatters thinking …" (p. 96). The concept of God is antecedent to the idea of my own self; it is an idea posited in us, not an idea we ourselves posit. The idea of God is related to createdness. (p.98) Like my own beginning, it lies beyond my own disposal, it is an-archic; it is too old to be reached by thinking, and at the same time it determines thinking. No longer do Being and appearing coincide. The subject is constituted by its very incapacity to comprehend the infinite. The subject is not that which intentionally posits itself. The infinite calls all thinking into question; it is the trauma of waking up. The infinite generates a longing in the subject which cannot be stilled by the satisfaction of wants and needs. It is an infinite longing directed towards that which lies beyond Being, viz. towards the Good.

But if this is so, as Levinas himself objects, can one be certain of transcendence? (p.103) Might not the longing derive from one's intention? Might we not perhaps discover that the subject is simply following its own interests in the quest for transcendence? How can one be certain that the desire for the Good, for that which is beyond Being, actually signifies transcendence? In section fourteen of this essay, he presents what I see as the central points of the argument. In conversation with Plato, Levinas develops a short phenomenology of Eros and Agape. When love in enjoyment loses the measurelessness of longing, it becomes concupiscence (in Pascal's sense). Love reverts to self-interest, and so to immanence. Is there a transcendence that exists beyond the erotic and beyond self-interest? Insofar as longing is fixed on the infinite, it (unlike Eros) can not stop short at an attainable goal. Instead of satisfying its hunger, the longing makes hunger truly grow! The ego could consume the other in its own self, but instead, the self actually separates the other from the ego by means of the longing! This is how transcendence happens; this is how longing actually generates detachment. But what does this mean more precisely? The longing must transcend Being and immanence. This in turn presupposes that "that which is deserves my longing, or God, must remain separate in the act of longing … close, but distinct – holy" (p. 105). "This is possible only if that which deserves my longing directs me toward that which is unworthy of desire, toward that which is utterly unworthy of desire, namely the other." This occurs in an awakening to nearness, that reaches to the point of vicarious substitution. In this way, the transcendental self is deprived of its core, which is the *conatus essendi.* The transcendence of goodness takes its place: love without eros, and so the selfness of the subject. (p. 106). This opens up the possibility of a further dimension which is not limited to Being and unlocks the sphere of holiness, in which human ethics becomes a reality. Levinas concludes section fourteen with the remark that God is antecedent to every neighbor and distinct from every neighbor. There is a "transcendence to the point of absence" which reminds us that this is a "divine comedy" whereby the word "comedy" can refer either to temple or theater, and in any case points to a "plot" in which the laughter sticks in my crawl as I draw near to my neighbor and see his helplessness (p.108). "The nearness of the neighbor remains a diachronic break, a resistance put up by time against the synthesis of contemporaneity" (p. 110). Levinas can thus speak of the "birth of the religion in the Other"; this is different from the understanding of revelation in Heidegger, for example, who speaks of "revelation in the conceptuality of the disclosure of Being" (p. 112).

This responsibility cannot be derived only from the freedom of the subject, nor thought of as a kind of contract; otherwise one remains at the level of the "coldness of Cain" (p.110) who asked whether he was his brother's keeper. In reality the subject is summoned, antecedently to every decision, and nobody can take its place. One must hear the other's inability to escape as the cry "which has already been cried out to God" (p. 112). Therefore, in concluding his paper, Levinas can write: "The moment in the intellectual history of the West at which suspicion is cast on philosophy is not arbitrary. To recognize with the – or a – philosophy that that which is real is rational and that only the rational is real, and to refuse to smother and keep secret the cry of those who want to reshape the world the day after they have attained this understanding, is already to operate with a claim to meaning which cannot be understood by the act of intellectual comprehension" (p.121). The almighty Logos and the system of contemporaneity hand over language to a system of signs that has subjected itself to an ontology in which there is no place for transcendence. And this means that subjectivity is destroyed in the traumatic division of the self. *E contra,* however, the transcendence which indicates its presence in the subject exists only in a questionable certainty. The diachronic character of this puzzle shatters the unity of the transcendental apperception, in which immanence always triumphs over transcendence (p. 123) Subjectivity is the temple and theater of transcendence (p. 119) and hence continues to play the comic role of ambiguity (p. 108).

This approach too poses provocative questions to Christian theology. For example, could it ever be satisfied with this kind of ambiguity? If not, does it necessarily revert to arguments in the field of onto-theology? Does the Greek word *logos,* which plays such an important role in the Johannine interpretation of Jesus and which involved the early church in controversies that threatened to tear it apart, merit the suspicion of importing into the divine dimension of Jesus a propositional quality which reduces its transcendence to the immanent sphere, instead of radicalizing it? And is not precisely this the mechanism by which Christology's claim to truth has been a dangerous claim to power? A more basic question is whether the ontological type of language about God as *ipsum esse* is necessarily subject to the critique Levinas raises so that even the emphasis in the aftermath of the Fourth Lateran Council on the principle that analogy entails a greater difference than similarity would still be inadequate. Would it remain inadequate even if we quoted one of the key statements of the New Testament, "God is love" (1 John 4:16), since even these words are still speaking of that Being which (we suspect) must be interpreted as *contatus essendi*?

The work of Jacques Derrida has been of decisive importance in the second half of the twentieth century and will probably continue to be influential. Derrida criticized Emmanuel Levinas, but never cast any doubts on his closeness to him.[15] In his critique of a theology carried out by means of propositions, Derrida's position is not much different from that of Levinas. Derrida's plea for a trans-rational mysticism located beyond religions bears his own unmistakable imprint, and calls into question Christian theology with its reference to substantial contents. I wish here to briefly draw attention only to two aspects of his thinking.

In his extensive article "Giving Death,"[16] Derrida engages in conversation with the Czech philosopher Jan Patočka[17] and with Søren Kierkegaard[18] about

---

15 Cf. J. Derrida, *Adieu. Nachruf auf Emmanuel Lévinas* (Munich / Vienna, 1999).

16 In the following I cite the German version, under the title "Den Tod geben" in A. Haverkamp (ed.), *Gewalt und Gerechtigkeit: Derrida-Benjamin* (Frankfurt / M., 1994), 331-445. Cf. also J. Hoff, *Spiritualität und Sprachverlust: Theologie nach Foucault und Derrida* (Paderborn *et al.*, 1999), esp. 132-41; T. Beyrich, *Ist Glauben wieder-holbar? Derrida liest Kierkegaard* (Berlin / New York, 2001), esp. 129-228.

17 Especially with reference to his paper, "Ist die technische Zivilisation zum Verfall bestimmt?" in J. Patočka, *Ketzerische Essays zur Philosophie der Geschichte* (Stuttgart, 1988), 121-45. "Religion is responsibility, or else it does exist." This is Derrida's summary, in the form of a proposition (332). For Patočka, history can not become a reality subject to total control, because it is very fundamentally "bound to responsi-

the biblical text of Abraham's sacrifice (Gen 22), which he sees as involving basic questions of human existence and history that go beyond the kind of historical-critical reconstruction of the text attempted by modern biblical scholarship. Abraham comes before a mysterious, frightening God, to whom he dares only answer: "Here I am." Everything else remains in silence. Abraham's silence becomes the keeper of the mystery.[19] The literary figure of Abraham is confronted with an dilemma: "If I offer to him what I hate, namely death, it is not a sacrifice. I must offer that which I love. I must come to the point of hating what I love, in the very moment, in the second, where I give him death" (p. 391). The "moment" in which Abraham draws his knife and hears God's voice, becomes a paradox: the duty and responsibility of faith come into conflict. Abraham takes absolute responsibility for the sacrifice of his son, by sacrificing the universal ethical duty not to kill. Abraham can be true to God only "in breaking his oath, becoming a traitor to his own people and to the uniqueness of each one of them …" (p. 395).[20] The intervention of God follows "in the moment where there is no longer any time, where time no longer exists, i.e., it is as if Abraham had already killed Isaac." (p. 399). The utmost test is complete. In the public eye, Abraham is already a murderer. God's intervention comes only where this "utmost" dimension is present, and this makes Abraham a witness to "the absolute

---

bility, faith and gift" to the point of the gift of death, "which puts me in relation to the transcendence of the Other, with God as self-forgetting goodness – and gives me what it gives me in a new experience of death" (335). This involves a mysterium tremendum, "the fear and trembling of the Christian in the experience of the sacrificial gift" (336).

18 In Kierkegaard's *Fear and Trembling* the relationship between ethics and language is central, since the first task of language is "to rob me of my individuality" (387).

19 This means that the human person does not stand in an "absolute duty" immediately before God, as in the Kantian categorical imperative. One is confronted with the terrifying transcendence only where gift and death are brought together: "the gift that I receive through God, insofar as God holds me in his gaze and takes me into his hand, while remaining inaccessible to me; the terrifyingly asymmetrical gift of this mysterium tremendum requires an answer of me, awakes me to accept the responsibility it gives me only by giving me death, the mystery of death, a new experience of death." (362)

20 "I can answer the one, or the One, i.e. the Other, only in sacrificing the other" (397). Naturally, we note that Derrida's exposition nevertheless ascribes great importance to the Kantian imperative. He does not discuss the completely separate question that is posed by God's apparent self-contradiction when he gives the command to kill the child of the promise.

faith, which neither can nor may bear witness in the presence of human beings" (p. 400). Thus Abraham remains in the absolute mystery. "God decides to *give back,* to give back life, to give back the beloved son, from that moment where it seems certain that a gift bereft of all economic barter, the gift of death – and the death of that for which no price can be paid – has been made, without any hope of exchange, reward, circulation, or communication" (p. 422).

We almost have the impression that in the exposition of this biblical text, Derrida abandons all the reticence he usually practices with regard to the use of the divine name, when he writes at a subsequent point in his analysis:

> For me, God is the name of the possibility of preserving something hidden and secret, something that is visible internally, but not externally. As soon as there exists this structure of a consciousness, of being with itself, of a speaking, that is, a bringing forth of invisible meaning, as soon as I have a witness in me, *thanks to the invisible speaking as such*, which the others do not see, and consequently is *both different from me and closer to me within than I am to myself,* as soon as I preserve a hidden relationship with my own self and cannot put everything into words, as soon as there is a mystery and a hidden witness within me, there exists that which I call God, (there is) that which I call God in me. Now I can call myself God – an affirmation difficult to distinguish from "God calls me by name, God calls me," for under these conditions I call, or am called, in secret. God is in me, he is the absolute "I," he is this structure of invisible interiority, that one calls "subjectivity" in Kierkegaard's sense of the word. (p. 434)

What happens to the concept of God in Derrida's argumentation here? On the one hand, it seems that the theory of the moment banishes the concept of God into an uttermost transcendence; on the other hand, even though we may be reminded of Augustine's *interior intimo meo,* the concept of God risks becoming insufficiently distinguishable from the interiority of the subject. At any rate, the return from the moment of absolute gift (cf. p. 422) into economic barter does not allow us to forget the abyss from which this return takes place. And it is probably this aspect that both presents a challenge to Christian theology and at the same time makes it an offer worth considering. Derrida's critique of theology is not a shallow, "liberal" sort of critique; it is related to the inscrutable notion of God and has an effect on the way every language (not just that of theology) is to be understood. This will be briefly discussed in the next section on the problem of negative theology.

Mysticism and Negative Theology

In *Except for the Name*, Derrida continues the discussion of negative theology which he began in *Like Not Speaking*.[21] In addition to the classical mystical dialogue partners, Dionysius the Areopagite and Master Eckhart, Derrida engages in dialogue with the *Angelic Wanderer* of Angelus Silesius.

According to Derrida, so-called "negative theology," as traditionally understood, is in danger of a formalization that abstains from "every content and every idiomatic signification, all presentation of representation, images and even, for example, the name of God" (p. 81). There is even the "possibility of a monumentalism which establishes the canon."[22] The outcome is a language that, as it were, creaks. According to Derrida, the negations are therefore not the true starting point of this language, since one is confronted with the astounding *fact* that negative theology attempts to eradicate all predicates, and "strives to live in the desert" (p. 83). This last word leads to the question: "Is not the desert a paradoxical metaphor for *aporia*?" (p. 84).[23] Like Angelus

---

21 First published in English in the conference volume, *Derrida and Negative Theology*, ed. by H. Coward and T. Foshay (Albany, 1992); quoted from the German edition, J. Derrida, "Außer dem Namen (Post-Scriptum)," in *idem*, *Über den Namen* (Vienna, 2000), 63-121.

22 Angelus Silesius was part of the Scholastic tradition, like Dionysius. But an abiding characteristic of their language is the way in which they speak of the "unknown God," "cancelling the antitheses of negative and positive, Being and nothing, something and nothing, and simultaneously transcending every theological attribute." (82)

23 The image of the desert suggests unmarked ways and tracks. Derrida emphasizes that negative theology exists (*consiste*) beyond its attempts "to dispense with every consistency." (84) At the same time this language remains readable and audible; negative theology as language is not simply nothing. Rather, the singular event of speech imprints something as "excess or surplus" on the body of a language and leaves behind "the relic of an inner onto-logical semantic self-destruction," which is symbolized by the desert. "Certainly, the 'unknown God' (*Der unerkante Gott*, IV, 21) who is misjudged or unknown ... does not say anything, and nothing is said about him which could endure ..." (85f.). The other voice adds: "Except for his name ...." And immediately a further expansion follows: "Except for the name which does not name anything that could endure, not even a deity .... God is the name for this bottomless collapse, which turns language into an infinite desert" (85f.). The next passage must be quoted in full: "The trace of this negative operation is inscribed in and on it as an event. There is (*il y a*) this event, which remains, even if what remains is no more substantial or essential than this God, nor ontologically more definable than this name of God, of which we are told that it does not bestow names on that which is – neither 'this' nor 'that'. Indeed, we are told that it is not something that exists in the sense of the term 'it exists': he is not that which exists, but lies beyond all gifts (*Gott über alle Gaben*, IV, 30)" (86). Derrida draws attention to the fact that this is expressed in

Silesius, Derrida points out that that which lies beyond God is not a place, but a "transcendental movement" which ultimately goes beyond even the divinity of God. Silesius says: "I still have to pass through GOD into a desert" (I:7, cited p. 95). This movement radically sunders Being from knowledge, existence from recognition. The rupture applies to the "I" as well as to God. Derrida speaks here of two powers: the power of a "hypercriticism for which nothing seems certain any longer, neither philosophy, theology, science, common sense, nor the slightest *doxa*"; and the power of the "authority of this didactic voice," which nothing and no one can contradict. It is a question of "passion" (in both senses of that word: pp. 96f.). The contradiction is accepted; one must lay claim to the paradox. Within itself, therefore, "This theology bears negativity as a principle of self-destruction" and holds every thesis, every belief, every *doxa* "in a state of oscillation" (p. 97).[24] Yet even if one negates all Being (God is not, God is neither this nor that) the main concern is

> to utter Being as it is, how it is, in its truth, even if that truth is metaphysical, meta-ontological. It is a matter of keeping a promise, speaking the truth whatever the cost, bearing witness, surrendering to the truth of the name, confronting the thing itself as it must be called by name, *i.e. beyond the name.*" (p. 98)

To this extent, the *Angelic Wanderer* is not a negative theology. It speaks of God beyond images and idols and beyond Being.[25]

Silesius too in the form of a prayer in which he asks for nothing, i.e. not for some particular "thing," but rather for God himself as gift. The Name of God is related to the local character of the Word: "The place is the Word." "Der Ort is das Wort," (I, 205, quoted 87). This place is not geographical: "The place itself is in you. It is not you who are in the place: / The place is in you! / If you cast it out / eternity is already here" (I, 185, quote p. 87). Here the critique of language is once again taken to extremes. It is striking that the expression "negative theology" appears only within the sphere of Greek philo-sophy and onto-theology and is present in the New Testament or Christian mysticism, but not in the intellectual constructions of Jewish, Islamic or Buddhist culture. In Christian philosophy the apophasis represents "a kind of paradoxical hyperbole." (93).

24 Derrida notes here that the epoché of negative theology shows certain similarities with the scepticism of the skeptics and with phenomenological reductionism. On the one hand the epoché has a destructive effect, in that it brackets off every thesis and even all ontological and theological propositions. It commits patricide and uproots. On the other hand, it is a kind of second movement of uprooting, as if it would be contradicted for some important reason, as if it could be "counter demonstrated." (97f.)

25 When mystics speak of an absolute transcendence which reveals itself within, this corresponds to a Neo-Platonic mentality, according to Derrida. But precisely the self-

Thus it is Derrida's thesis that the logic of affirmation and denial is insufficient to discover that ground – or as Plato says: "to discover that ground beyond language where the foundations are laid of the possibility of keeping a promise or speaking the truth." This ground itself, like a desert, does not represent pure negativity; nor is it however the simple antithesis of negativity, in the sense that it would be the positive character of propositional language. In a sense, it is an open space, and I leave it to the experts to clarify whether this is closer to Heidegger's *es* or to the Platonic ideal as interpreted by Emmanuel Levinas.

Un Dieu Homme?: The Question Emmaūel Levinas Puts to Christology

If we want to see where Jewish thinking in the twentieth century came astonishingly close to Christianity – and how it became a great challenge to Christian theology precisely in this closeness – I believe that we shall find an instructive example in *Un Dieu Homme?,* written by Emmanuel Levinas in 1968. The question he considers here takes up and radicalizes the motif of the correlation between God and the human person in Franz Rosenzweig. Levinas draws on two fundamental ideas from Christian language about the God-man for his philosophy: 1) the idea of the lowering or humbling of the Creator, who descends to the level of creatures,[26] and 2) the idea of vicarious substitution which at the same time means the unsubstitutability or uniqueness of the subject.[27] Taken together, both aspects establish a very close relationship between "God" and "the human person." To speak of one or of the other

---

interiority in traditions from metaphysics to onto-theology and phenomenology to revelation, are fundamentally contested. Hence negative theology is "one of the most remarkable manifestations" of a "self-differentiation" (101).

26 Levinas explains the first question of the idea of the condescendence of God or the humility of the Creator: this idea allows one to grasp a relationship to transcendence differently than the naive or pantheisitic thinking has always sought to do. The emergence of "human gods" was frequent in paganism. But if the gods became visible, they would lose their divinity. Hence it is not by chance that philosophy (until Hegel) either conceived of God as not having a relation to the world, or saw the world as being absorbed in the Absolute. "As the world, according to the poets, absorbed the gods into itself, so for the philosophers, the world disappeared into the absolute." (74). The entire problem of a traditional philosophy, which gives the Absolute a place among other categories in ist system, is that it makes the Absolute a possible contemporary.

27 "Substitution" literally means: placing under, taking someone's place.

in isolation would fail to do justice to the question in the title *Un Dieu Homme?* According to Levinas, God cannot directly show himself unless he humbles himself and enters into the creation. God is fundamentally an entity from the immemorial past. God's humility consists in the fact that when he appears, he appears only as "absence." God's lowering leaves behind an echo or a trace of his unapproachable transcendence. This is, as he summarizes it, the trace as "the nearness of God in the face of my neighbor" (p. 73, 78). Levinas writes: "The relationship to the infinite is not knowledge, but a nearness which does not however abolish the incomparability of what which cannot be completely grasped" (p. 79).

The second aspect is the idea of vicarious substitution. Levinas describes the lowering of God as the "transubstantiation of the creator in [or: into] a creature" (*dans cette transubstantiation du Créateur en créature*) and holds that in this transubstantiation, "the concept of the God-man" confirms "the idea of substitution" (p. 79 slightly modified). In this connection, Levinas also uses the word "incarnation" in a non-metaphorical, i.e., bodily sense.[28] This leads to the important theorem of the "incarnate subject," which however is not a biological concept, but denotes uttermost passivity.[29] Incarnation means a "recurrence" to the uttermost limit of creatureliness, antecedent even to the "*materia prima*"[30] and hence to all spoken language, where the subject is given an infinite responsibility as a gift of creation. So Levinas can write: "The 'I' is already chosen, antecedently to every decision, to bear the entire responsibility of the world" (p. 82).[31] According to Levinas, the second aspect

28 According to Levinas the body is "the contraction in itself of selfhood and its bursting apart": E. Levinas, *Jenseits des Seins oder anders als Sein geschieht* (Freiburg / Munich, 1992, 242).

29 "Selfhood in its passivity, without the arché of identity means: [being a] hostage" (Levinas, *Jenseits*, 253). The subject, which in the recurrence comes in a sense back in the time before its constitution, is directed to accept a vocation which is not identical with the egoistic destiny. This subject cannot keep itself aloof from the guilt and damnation that effect everyone. As Being, the subject exists for its own self, a self-consciousness; as a self it exists for everyone, and bears responsibility for the universe, for "bearing the universe" (257).

30 Cf. Levinas, *Jenseits*, 242 ff. The "recurrence" goes back behind even the *materia prima* and points to the absolute passivity which was foreign to Greek philosophy (cf. 243f.). Recurrence is "a movement which goes back even behind the identity" (252). The subject shows itself in its uttermost passivity, "like an echo of a tone, which is heard even before the tone sounds" (245).

31 In my view, one must interprete Levinas as radically in categories of the subject as he has been interpreted in the categories of otherness.

of the idea of a "God-man" implies that the individual human being cannot be understood as an example of the genus humanity. He likewise derives from this idea the notion that the human person is the substitute for the messianic human being, who bears within himself the idea of the infinite as a longing for the good.[32] It follows that where God's truth appears in the world, it appears as a persecuted, humiliated truth.[33]

To recapitulate this line of thought in brief outline, one can say that because Levinas does not attribute substitution to one particular human being, but to *every* human person, his position diverges widely from the Christian interpretation of Jesus, despite all the similarities. On the Christian view, Jesus can take substitution upon himself as the God-man, who is the "Word" or Son, born of the Father, and is absolutely unique by virtue of his origin. *E contra, Un Dieu Homme* would actually open the door to a radicalization of the Christian interpretation of Jesus. In his perfect being as God and man, Jesus would be no longer the highest instance of the relationship between God and the human person (as in Rahner), but an absolutely unique and incomeparable event, so unique that Jesus is not subject to categories of comparison at all. It is a question of such a fundamental "uniqueness," which affects every human subject that it cannot be grasped in words – this is the trajectory of a Christological mysticism that we shall discuss below.[34]

Christian Mysticism as a Response to Jewish Thought

How much critique of language can Christian theology bear? According to Derrida, negative theology makes the heart of Christianity (as Angelus Silesius understands this) "independent of every literal language of the New Testament events: the coming of Christ, the passion, the dogma of the Trinity and so forth" (p.101). At its outermost edge, mysticism frees itself "from all

---

32 The final sentence in the brief essay in *Un Dieu Homme?* is: "Messianism is this apogee in Being, the reversal of Being 'persevering in its Being' – which begins in me" (82).

33 Cf. S. Sandherr, *Die heimliche Geburt des Subjekts: Das Subjekt und sein Werden im Denken Emmanuel Lévinas'* (Stuttgart / Berlin / /Cologne, 1998), esp. 198-212.

34 One can ask whether the uniqueness of Jesus is adequately accounted for if we simply value him more than all other persons in his Messianic character. Formulations of comparison ("more, more than, different to") entangle Christology in a superficial apologetics.

definable faith." It implies dissidence, a breaking away from the authority of the church, a rupture with the social contract for the sake of universalization. On the other hand, this dissidence can claim to fulfill the promise of Christianity, "in that it responds in this way to the call and the gift of Christ, as it echoes from all eternity to eternity" and bears witness to it (pp. 101f.) Here the critique of Christian theology as *speech* is more radical than in Levinas. In Franz Rosenzweig, language tends imperiously toward silence; in Derrida, it tends imperiously toward a trans-logical mysticism. In Levinas, language finds its goal as it were in a mysticism of the incarnate subject. Babel as the place of the confusion of tongues; the desert as a wide space which transcends even the Being of God; the yearning for God, and radical atheism – these are key phrases Derrida uses in his attempt to indicate what "negative theology" could be. This negative theology is caught in the unresolved tension between a universal language and its mechanisms on the one hand, and the inviolable mysteries on the other which cannot be translated "except as untranslatable seals." For Emmanuel Levinas too, the problem of translation is a fundamental problem of language, and of language's logical and trans-logical possibilities.[35]

Reviewing Derrida's analysis, is it possible to summarize what he means in his circuitous attempts to describe what "negative theology" can mean? Jean-Luc Marion, who spoke very critically of Derrida on many specific points at Villanova in 1997, also appeals to a mysticism which is aware of the necessary critique of language, and attempts to arrive at a concept of God that goes beyond the Scholastic *ipsum esse* and beyond onto-theology.[36] The critique of a concept of God as "name" which must distinguish itself radically from all other concepts, because it cannot be reduced to the logic of affirmation and denial, is also familiar to the Christian tradition. Theology itself has repeatedly expressed great reservations vis-à-vis any closed rational system that threatened to be limited to the logic of that which can be expressed in propositions; but this critique never raised its objections in the form of an assault on thinking, but rather derived them from the experience that revela-

35 Cf. J. Wohlmuth, *Die Tora spricht die Sprache der Menschen* (Paderborn *et al.*, 2002), esp. 32-35.

36 Cf. J.-L. Marion, "Au nom ou comment le taire," in *idem*, *De surcroît* (Paris, 2001), 155-95. Cf. the clarifying remarks on Marion's position in T. Specker, *Einen anderen Gott denken?* (Frankfurt a. M., 2002), esp. 237-60.

tion provokes thinking. If Christianity were not to understand itself today as a mysticism based in the mystery of the name, it would be defenseless, in the context of European culture, against the critique of religion in the nineteenth and twentieth centuries, as well as against the critique of philosophers inspired by Judaism, such as Rosenzweig, Levinas and Derrida. Derrida's critique of the dogmatic forms of the idea of God is to be taken seriously in as much as the Christian doctrine of God, in using terms such as "Father," "Son," and "Spirit," gives the impression of being a language about objects, a language that seems to offer resistance to the reductionism of phenomenology. Against all attempts to absolutize the world or to disempower transcendence, Jewish-inspired thought in the twentieth century has moved in the direction of mysticism, which at first sight is a counter-movement to the development in Christian theology, for the latter must be called a return to the phenomenological starting points, which teach with almost *one* single voice that the Trinitarian form of the idea of God does not depend upon mysterious knowledge of the situation within the Godhead, but rather on events or "appearances" in which transcendence has made itself known in the world.[37] Although the mystery of silence which Rosenzweig advocates may prompt Christian objections, it nevertheless points the way ahead, by indicating that the language of faith and of Christian theology must be kept open for the *name*.

---

[37] As participants in the Jewish-Christian dialogue have recognized, this applies to a number of systematic proposals in the field of Trinitarian doctrine. Karl Barth, Karl Rahner and Urs von Balthasar have become the most important proponents of a new salvation-historical doctrine of the Trinity, which has generated a debate among Christians that is still in progress. Cf. P. Ochs, "The God of Jesus and Christians," in T. Frymer-Kensky *et al.* (eds.), *Christianity in Jewish Terms* (Boulder, 2000), 49-69. Peter Ochs refers primarily to the American Lutheran theologian Robert Jenson, who defends a salvation-historical doctrine of the Trinity where God is identified as the one who freed Israel in the desert, and raised Jesus from the dead. (62) Where Jenson prefers to speak of the incarnation of the Word, he can not only appeal to early Christian tradition but also creates bridges to the Jewish tradition, according to which God is the author of the Word of revelation. (65) Cf. also D. Tracy's "God as Trinitarian" with its emphasis on the salvation-historical understanding of the Trinity, 77-84. Cf. J. Wohlmuth, "Zum Verhältnis von ökonomischer und immanenter Trinität und der Rezeption: Eine These," in *idem*, *Im Geheimnis einander nahe* (Paderborn, 1996), 115-38. Gisbert Greshake's monumental work on the Trinity is somewhat reserved with respect to a throughgoing salvation-historical approach to Trinitarian theology. This raises important epistemological questions which cannot be treated here. Cf. G. Greshake, *Der dreieine Gott* (Freiburg / Basel / Vienna, 1997), esp. 127-50.

A Christological Mysticism?

It appears to me that Christology and Emmauel Levinas agree on important points and that perhaps Levinas can help Christology rediscover its mystical dimension. As a Christian one can also say that God's self-lowering, which already begins with creation, is the only form of God's revelation in the world and that this revelation is not reduced to the logic of affirmation and denial, but at most puts constraints on this logic. Classic Christology employs the term "Greek"("unmixed"), coined by the council of Chalcedon in 451, to ensure that God and the human person in Jesus may not be confused with one another – and this is a fundamental concern of Jewish thinking in general. It would certainly be valuable to analyze the closeness of Levinas' reflections to classical Christology, especially if one employs Karl Rahner's exposition to bring this up to date.[38] Rahner emphasized above all the humanity of Jesus and reflected on the *relationship between Creator and creature* in order to reach an understanding of God and human person in Jesus. If two *created* entities were brought into a relation of mutual proximity, they would necessarily suppress one another. This is not so in the relationship between God and creature, where one should note that "only a divine Person can possess as its own a freedom which is really distinct from its own self, in such a way that this freedom does not cease to be truly free, even with respect to the divine Person who possesses it; yet it is this freedom which qualifies this Person itself as its ontological subject" (p. 182). Precisely under the assumption that Jesus is a perfect human being, Rahner writes, "The relation of the Logos-Person to its human nature must be thought of precisely in such a way that autonomy and radical proximity attain in the same way their unique apex, which is qualitatively incommensurable with all other instances – yet precisely this is the unique apogee of a relationship between Creator and creature" (p. 183). For Rahner, this has soteriological consequences too. Jesus becomes the mediator of salvation. Perhaps much of what Rahner elaborates here under the key term "logos" seems to be a matter of strict logical deduction; but this is not how he describes the mysterious unity of God and the human being.

In addition to Rahner's interpretation, one could draw here on Wolfhart Pannenberg's Christology, explicitly a Christology of *kenosis*, and therefore a

---

[38] Cf. K. Rahner, "Probleme der Christologie von heute," in *Schriften I* (1954), 169-222. Cf. K. Rahner, "Chalkedon – Ende oder Anfang?," in: A. Grillmeier / H. Bacht (eds.), *Das Konzil von Chalkedon*, vol. 3. 5th ed. (Würzburg, 1979 [1954]), 3-49.

suitable dialogue partner for Emmanuel Levinas.[39] Pannenberg holds that Jesus did not attempt to prove his divinity through an elevated claim to authority. Rather, Jesus kept his own person wholly in the background while he proclaimed the kingdom of God, and showed in his humanity that he was concerned only with God and his kingdom. Here too, propositions are not the starting point for Christology. "In the controversy about the figure of Jesus, it is of decisive importance that he did not place his own person at the center of attention, but rather God, the nearness of God's reign, and God's fatherly love" (pp. 375f.) Jesus accepted that his own person (as savior) required an expressly divine confirmation (p. 377). Pannenberg writes: "The renunciation of any position of dignity in the presence of God that would go beyond the measure of creatureliness reveals itself to be a condition of his sonship, which is mediated through self-lowering (Phil 2:8). This constitutes the indirectness of Jesus' identity with the Son of God" (p. 416).

To summarize, both Franz Rosenzweig and Emmanuel Levinas posit a close-meshed network of relationships between God and the world (God, world, and the human person), so that one can speak of an incarnational dimension of Judaism in both thinkers. The incarnational, which has a certain significance in the context of Jewish-Christian dialogue, is of great importance in the formation of a Christian mysticism.[40] Such a mysticism can certainly find inspiration in each of the three authors we have considered. For example, Christian mysticism speaks of the indwelling of the Holy Spirit in the innermost depths of the person, and does so in a trans-logical sense. In the theory of uncreated grace, the indwelling of God in the human being is con-

39 Cf.. W. Pannenberg, *Systematische Theologie*, vol. 2 (Göttingen, 1991), 365-440.

40 While *Dabru emet* says little about Christology and especially the relationship between Christology and theology, the commentary volume Christianity in Jewish Terms deals extensively with these points. It is appropriate, for instance, that Peter Ochs in his essay "The God of Jesus and Christians" explains that the Jewish and Christian doctrines of God are largely the same, but with differences which become very clear in the doctrine of the incarnation, which Jews cannot accept – although they certainly may ask what this doctrine could signify for non-Jews. Elliot R. Wolfson's work on incarnational themes in Rabbinic literature largely involves Jewish traditions that were familiar to patristic theology, inasmuch as they depend on foundations in the Jewish Bible. Cf. E. R. Wolfson, "Judaism and Incarnation: The Imaginal Body of God," in *Christianity in Jewish Terms*, 239-54. Cf. also Randi Rashkover, "The Christian Doctrine of Incarnation," in *Dbru emet*, 254-61; Susan A. Ross, "Embodiment and Incarnation: A Response to Elliot Wolfson," in *Dabru emet*, 262-68. Other essays in the volume have implications for the doctrine of the incarnation, whether with regard to the question of God or soteriology. But we cannot discuss this in detail here.

ceived perhaps even more intensively than Derrida dares to suggest in general terms when he discusses transcendence in the subject. Since the Holy Spirit is at the same time the Spirit of Jesus Christ, interpreting Jesus is not only the work of historical criticism, but also involves pneumatological insight into the mysteries of the life of Jesus and of his incomprehensible person through in the celebration of the liturgy. Like Rosenzweig, Christianity too understands liturgy as a source of mysticism. The idea of God in the narrower sense of the word as the absolute origin ("Father") already inspired the mysticism of the early Church, and can take on new meaning if it is linked with the Jewish mysticism of the name. Naturally, the Jewish side can ask Christianity whether its understanding of incarnation preserves the absolute *mysterium tremendum* of the mysticism of the name, or whether it confines the idea of God to the immanence of our thought. If the latter were to occur, the idea of God would be subject to the suspicion of remythologization, a suspicion already expressed by Max Horkheimer and Theodor W. Adorno.[41] But if an affirmation like Col 1:15, where Jesus is described as "the image of the invisible God," were taken as decisive, then Christology could justifiably be expounded step by step as an initiation into the mysticism of the name. This would also lend greater plausibility to the claim that mysticism need not yield place to dogmatics, as Derrida believes. Accordingly, Christological mysticism would not in the least mean the abandonment of strict Jewish monotheism. If the conversation with contemporary Jewish-inspired thinkers resulted in a Christian theology that did not blur the distinction between transcendence and immanence as a result of the intimate bond of God and human person in Jesus Christ, then the first thesis from *Dabru emet*, according to which Jews and Christians worship the same God, would have a chance of being accepted by both sides, and could also be taken seriously by philosophy. And with regard to the differences which would still remain between Judaism and Christianity, Franz Rosenzweig's thesis of their complementarity would be a helpful basis for a peaceful coexistence.

Translated by Michael Parker

---

41 M. Horkheimer / T.W. Adorno, *Dialektik der Aufklärung* (Frankfurt ,1969 [New York, 1944]), 186.

Ghasem Kakaie

Ibn 'Arabī's God, Eckhart's God: Philosophers' God or Religion's God?

Prelude

It is difficult to provide a definition of God in which all plausible views are included and upon which all schools can agree. The dominant view is that God is the Origin of the universe and enjoys a kind of transcendence and sacredness; I call this the God of the religious believer or Religion's God. In philosophy, however, there are various conceptions of deity: The gods of ancient Greece, the unmoved mover of Aristotle, the necessary Being of Avicenna, the God of Aquinas's theism, the God of Spinoza's pantheism, the panentheistic God of some mystical philosophies, the One of Neoplatonism, the God of process philosophy, the God of existential philosophies, the ultimate concern of Tillich, God as the impersonal ground of Being, and arguably, Heidegger's *Dasein*.[1] The God of philosophy is often an object not a person; something not someone, unchangeable, absolute and unlimited. But the God that is worshiped in ordinary religion "is a person and to be a person, an entity must think, feel, and will. In spite of being called unchangeable, he is angry with us today, pleased with us tomorrow".[2]

God, of course, is understood differently in the different religions and even between Abrahamic religions. The God who has no son according to Islam, for example, may differ from the God who has a son, as in Christianity. However, theistic religions in general and Abrahamic religions in particular, share many beliefs about God. I take these shared claims to be the attributes of Religion's God, and consider certain philosophical theologies to be closer to Religion's God than others; other philosophical theologies – pantheism, for example – differ a great deal from the God of the ordinary religious believer.

In this article I will provide a brief account of the traditional God of theism or Religion's God, a brief account of the God of pantheism and panentheism, and then a more extensive discussion of God in Meister Eckhart and Ibn 'Arabī's theory of Unity of Being (*Waḥdat al-Wujūd*). Both Eckhart and

---

1 M. Levine, *Pantheism* (London, 1994), 12.

2 W.T. Stace, *Mysticism and Philosophy* (London, 1961), 179.

Ibn 'Arabī have been depicted as pantheists. But there are great gaps between the doctrine of the Unity of Being and pantheism. Indeed, if one were to compare these thinkers' understanding of God and contemporary Western philosophical views, their views would be closer to panentheism rather than pantheism. The important point is that Ibn 'Arabī, and to some extent Eckhart, managed to think from the point view of the unity of Being, while maintaining important aspects of the God of ordinary religious believers.

The God of Theism

The God introduced by Revelation is more consistent with theism's God than with the other philosophical gods. Theism's God is a sacred power that is dominant throughout the universe and actively exercises this power. God, according to such theism, is mysteriously present in our very being, and is present through special effects such as revelation or miracles at particular times in specific historical events.[3]

The God of theism is personal; "He" is Aware and Willing. Certain personal qualities such as knowing, believing, and willing may be attributed to Him, although he is free from other kinds of personal qualities, such as sentiments and wishes.[4] He is a person who is eternally free, Omnipotent, Omniscient. He is a spirit which is present everywhere. He is absolute good and the source of moral obligations.[5] He possesses qualities that make human prayer possible and meaningful. Finally, while He undertakes the conservation of the Universe, he is independent from it and does not need it;[6] He is necessarily free and at the same time unchangeable and impassive.[7]

According to Macquarrie, among all the qualities of creatures, personality is the most plausible attribute that could apply to God; a thing which is impersonal does not deserve to be called God. Thus traditional theism sometimes suffers from anthropomorphism. In fact, however, it is closer to the truth for traditional theists to think of God as "Supra Personal."[8] In this way, His tran-

3 Levine, *Pantheism*, 107f.

4 Levine, *Pantheism*, 159.

5 Levine, *Pantheism*, 53.

6 Levine, *Pantheism*, 158.

7 H.P. Owen, *Concepts of Deity* (London, 1971), 142f.

8 Levine, *Pantheism*, 150.

scendence also may be maintained. For in this view, God is beyond the world of creatures and is not similar to anything. Thus, theism is able to hold on to the main attributes of the Religion's God, which are as follows: unity, personality, transcendence, creativity, holiness and the source of moral value.[9]

Because theism accepts these religious elements on the one hand, and commitment to rational justification on the other, it must confront problems and difficulties and attempt to offer solutions. For example: Is the concept of the eternal and timeless God coherent and can one conceive of a "timeless" being? Did time begin when the universe did? Where was God before creation? How can something be created out of nothing? Why did creation take place when it did and not before – and what was God doing in the meantime? Why did God create this world and not some other better world? Should God have created anything at all? How can an immutable being create? Are immutability, impassibility and simplicity compatible with the efficacy of prayer and God's responsiveness to human action? Is God's timelessness compatible with biblical theology?[10]

Pantheism's God

Pantheism is regarded as a philosophical approach to the problem of God. Though its origin may be mystical, it can also be considered a philosophical view. A great variety of thinkers have been considered to be pantheists. To gather all of them under the same title is extremely difficult. To be brief, it can be said that "[w]hat all pantheists do have in common (by the very definition of pantheism) is that the totality of all that is does not divide into two great components, a creator God, and a created world."[11] In other words, while theism's God is transcendent and personal, pantheism accepts neither the existential transcendence of God nor the claim that God has a personality.
If theism's God is transcendent and that of pantheism is immanent in all things, one cannot say that the two views differ in the number and quality of God's attributes; the debate between the two concerns whether theism's God exists or not.[12] According to theism, a God which is immanent in all things is

9 Owen, *Concepts of Deity*, 150.

10 Levine, *Pantheism*, 177.

11 T.L.S. Sprigge, "Pantheism," in *The Monist* 80 (1997).

12 Levine, *Pantheism*, 94.

not God. With respect to personality, however, the debate between the two *is* over God's attributes. Most versions of pantheism deny that God is a person. Pre-Socratic philosophers, Plotinus, Bruno, Spinoza, and even Lao Tzu do not regard God as a person. According to Michael Levine, "I know of no prominent versions of pantheism that conceive of God as a person."[13]

Pantheism, therefore, involves the following two characteristics: i) it rejects God's transcendence beyond the world and the possible distinction between the Creating God and the created world, and ii) it does not regard God as personal.[14] Pantheism is able to solve some problems faced by theism. By reinterpreting creation as the disclosure of the absolute, for example, it avoids some of the difficulties related to the theory of creation from nothingness. However, by denying the personality of God and God's transcendence, it distances itself from the God of the religions. This is the case because firstly pantheism does not know God as the creator of the world, and secondly it is unable to justify the anthropomorphic characters attributed to God in sacred scriptures. In particular, it cannot acknowledge the kind of consciousness that God possesses in all religions, and it certainly cannot make sense of God's Incarnation in Christianity.[15]

On the other hand, since pantheism's God is close to the absolute God of the philosophers, some advantages of theism become problems for pantheism. If God is not personal and no change is admitted in Him, for example, He cannot be loved. Thus, the love felt by the believers in praying cannot make sense to pantheists. In the pantheistic school, there is no trace of the interaction that thinkers such as Ibn 'Arabī have with their God. In general, the God worshipped by them is other than the God about Whom Ibn 'Arabī writes:

> Because of piety *(taqwā)*, we are given Divine intuition, and God through theophany undertakes to teach us, and we understand what reason is not able to understand through thinking. I mean the things that are introduced in the sacred texts through transmitted evidence that reason regards as impossible. Thus, the believer's reason goes on to interpret them, and the pure believer accepts them ... [the mystic, however, intuits them]. Then the people of unveiling see God's right hand, His hand, both of His hands, God's eye, God's eyes which have been attributed [in the sacred texts] to Him. They see His step and His face as well. They see attributes such as God's delight, His surprise, and His transformation from one form to another ... all and all. Thus, the God worshipped by the

13 Levine, *Pantheism*, 11.

14 Whether one should speak of consciousness as opposed to personality is an interesting question that I will not pursue here. However, see Levine, *Pantheism*, 148.

15 Levine, *Pantheism*, 147.

> believers and the people of intuition is not the same as the God that is worshipped by the people of thinking.[16]

Ibn 'Arabī, Eckhart, and Pantheism

Eckhart and Ibn 'Arabī have both been labeled pantheists by many an interpreter. Charles Adams, for example, has claimed that Ibn 'Arabī taught a sort of pantheism according to which only one reality exists that is God, meaning that God is nothing other than the "sum of all things."[17] Presumably, the sum of all things is not more than the sum of its members. On my interpretation, however, the God that Ibn 'Arabī and Eckhart wrote about is quite distinct from pantheism. Both thinkers believed that beyond the apparent world there is an essence that is free from any relation and correlation and completely independent of the universe. Thus, there is a deep gap between those who believe in the absolute hidden world and those who see nothing other than the seen world and regard God as the sum of the parts of this very world. R.W.J. Austin is, I think correct when he advises that to attempt to categorize Ibn 'Arabī's teachings in different ways such as pantheism or monism impedes rather than assists in understanding his vision of Reality. His doctrine of the Oneness of Being means that God is far more than the sum of its parts or aspects.[18]

Of course, this paper would not be necessary if one could not find occasional phrases in the work of Ibn 'Arabī and Eckhart that suggest a kind of pantheism. Ibn 'Arabī almost sounds like Spinoza on God as the single substance who receives various attributes, when he writes:

> Verily God is All-Subtle. It is because of His Subtlety and Mercy, that in everything, which is called with some name or limited to some limitations, He is the same as that object .... Though concerning the beings of the world it is said that this is the sky, this is the earth, this is rock, tree, animal, angel, sustenance or food; in every object there is the same essence. As Ash'aris say, the entire world is one concreted substance. That is, it is a single substance. This is the same as what we say that [in all objects], the essence is the same. Ash'aris also said that the substance comes into difference because of accidents. This is also the same as what we say that the essence comes into difference and plurality because of forms and relations so that making a distinction may be possible. Thus, it can be said

16 *Al-Futuḥāt al-makkīya* (Meccan Openings), vol. 2 (Beirut, n.d.), 38.

17 M. Sells, *Mystical Languages of Unsaying* (Chicago, 1994), 261, ftnte 40.

18 Cf. R.W.J. Austin, *Ibn al-'Arabī, The Bezels of Wisdom*, Lahore, 1988).

> that this object differs in terms of form or accident or temperament – or whatever other name you like –, and it is the same in terms of existence.[19]

Such paragraphs suggest that careful attention must be given to theological details. Ibn 'Arabī regards God as existence non-conditioned as the source of a division (*lā bi sharṭ maqsami*). The pantheists' God is conditioned by something (*wujūd bi sharṭ-i shay'*) at the level of existents or is at most, existence non-conditioned as a division (*lā bi sharṭ-i qismi*). These descriptions clarify the issue; these two Gods are quietly different. To elucidate the issue further, existence can be classified, as terms of the levels of theophany, as follows:

The nonconditioned existence as a source of division	1- negatively conditioned existence = oneness 2- existence conditioned by names and attributes = unity	= hidden world
	3- existence non-conditioned as a division = Divine breath (Truth by which the world is created) 4- existence conditioned by creaturely determination = world	= seen world

For many philosophers, God is the same as existence negatively-conditioned, that is, He is free from all conditions and independent from all things. The pantheists' God is the same as the existence conditioned by creaturely individuation. This existence, according to Ibn 'Arabī and Eckhart, is not God but the universe. Neither mystic would associate God with the fourth level. (There have been some Sufis, of course, who have believed that God is immanent in the world.) The noble verse "And He is Who in the heaven is God, and in the earth God" (the Holy Quran; 43:84) suggests that God is restricted to no level. He is in the heaven God, and in the earth God. Pantheists seem to suggest that He is in the heaven, heaven; and in the earth, earth.

According to Ibn 'Arabī, "divine breath" can be described as the essence of the world and the same as all things. This is existence conditioned as a division, and is what has been manifested through the Holy Emanation. According to the eternal rule "He/ not He", one can say that the universe is, at the same time, Him and not Him:

---

19 *Fuṣūṣ al-ḥikam*, ed. by Abu'l 'Alā''Afīfī, al-zahra Publications, 1366 A.H. solar/ 1987 A.D., vol. 1, 88f.

> As regards the universe, say whatever you like. You are free to believe that it is creature or to maintain that it is God, and if you like you can say that it is God and the creature. And if you like, say that it is in all aspects neither God nor creature. And if you like, believe in bewilderment."[20]

Some pantheists may regard God to be associated with all existents, not in a conditioned way, but absolutely. Ibn 'Arabī's and Eckhart's God, however, is free even from this absoluteness; it is "non-conditioned as a source of division" which is present in all four mentioned levels. Thus, Ibn 'Arabī and Eckhart's belief in the station of Oneness and station of unity makes them distinct from pantheists and brings them closer to another view which is called panentheism.

Panentheism's God

Unlike pantheism, panentheism attributes a kind of transcendence over the universe to God. Panentheists believe in the hidden beyond the seen. Those who believe in the Unity of Being speak sometimes of union "with" God and at other times they speak of union "within" God. The first is indicative of some kind of becoming and suggests that the two essences of God and the creature "come into" union. The second phrase implies some kind of being, that is, it suggests that the two objects "are" in unity. According to Ibn 'Arabī and Eckhart, the becoming and being that we have set forth are, in fact, the same;[21] the second, however, is closer to what is called panentheism.

Panentheism which has been coined by combining four words "pan" (= all), "en" (=in), "theo" (=God) and "ism" (=believe in), means belief in "all things in God." Ibn 'Arabī and Eckhart have been associated with panentheism because they believed in a transcendental existence for the objects in the Divine world. As Ibn 'Arabī says: "No one of the beings of the world and no object is outside God. But, every quality which is manifest in the world, has an essence in the presentation of the Truth .... It is God's dignity that existence of nothing be outside Him. Since if the existence of something is outside Him, then He has no command of that thing."[22]

---

20 *Fuṣūṣ al-ḥikam*, 112.

21 Sells, *Mystical Languages of Unsaying*, 169.

22 *Al-Futuḥāt al-makkīya*, vol. 2, 484.

According to Ibn 'Arabī's line of reasoning, one who grants something cannot lack that thing. God's encompassing of all things means that he contains all things. Eckhart believes that the objects have come out from God but have remained inward. He means that they are in God, in a manner reminiscent of Jesus Christ, who says: "I yet remained in the father." Matthew Fox claims that such a view is a sort of panentheism: "It means that all is in God and God is in all. Such a doctrine differs from heterodox pantheism, which means literally all is God and God is all."[23] The following may confirm the claim that Eckhart believes in some sort of panentheism:

> He created all things in such a way that they are not outside himself, as "ignorant people falsely imagine. Everything that God creates or does he does or creates in himself, sees or knows in himself, loves in himself. Outside himself he does nothing, knows or loves nothing; and this is peculiar to God himself."[24]

Ibn 'Arabī's God and Eckhart's God

In defining the nature of mysticism, it is common to affirm that mystical experience is experience of the immanence of the divine and of unification and unity in essence with it, in contrast to the experience of the divine as transcendent. The religious, however, tend to emphasize the transcendence of God.[25] So when a religious mystic speaks about union with God, the union becomes one of contemplation, similarity, love ... anything short of absorption. By contrast, those mystics that talk seriously of absorption and avoid the language of self and real union with God should be considered non-religious mystics.[26]

Regardless of how much the argument alluded to above is correct, it is certain that Ibn 'Arabī's and Eckhart's God is the same as the God of the two Abrahamic religions, i.e. Islam and Christianity. Ibn 'Arabī's God is the same as the God who manifests with all his names and attributes the beauty and glory that came down in the Holy Qur'an. The God of Eckhart, who was a Christian preacher and a disciple of Aquinas, is the God of The Bible and very close to theism's God. The most important aspects of theism's God,

23 M. Fox, *Breakthrough* (New York, 1991), 72.

24 Fox, *Breakthrough*, 73.

25 R. Otto, *Mysticism East and West* (New York, 1976), 158.

26 Levine, *Pantheism*, 135, ftnte. 14.

which make it distinct from pantheism's God, are, as we have already indicated, first, His transcendence and second, His personality. While preserving these two aspects of God, Ibn 'Arabī and Eckhart try to establish their systems based on the unity of existence and seat the religion's God at the top of this unity.

In this regard, Muslim thinkers inspired by the Holy Quran and verses such as the verses of the *Ikhlāṣ Sūra* (Q 112) have placed more emphasis on God's transcendence "over" creatures and His Glory, and less emphasis on His personality. In contrast, in Christian theology, since God has been personified and manifested as Christ Jesus, emphasis on God's personality is unavoidable and more emphasis is often put on His beauty than His glory to the extent that this God is either Himself a man and lives among us or at least, He is man's father. That is why in such a theology, love is emphasized more than fear. According to Eckhart this is why many prayers begin with "Our Father" and not "Our Lord;" the former title shows more kindness and love.[27]

In light of these two different kinds of traditional emphasis in Christian and Islamic theology, it is surprising that Ibn 'Arabī and Eckhart go in the opposite direction. Indeed, Ibn 'Arabī puts more emphasis on God's personality and Eckhart pays more attention to God's transcendence. To explain, it should be noted that most philosophers regard God not as a person but as an object and mention Him as "that." Ibn 'Arabī, however, holds that true mystics regard God as a person and not as an object and their approach to God is of three sorts, which is manifest in three kinds of remembrance (*dikr*). The highest remembrance of some mystics is "He" (*huwa*), that of others is "Thou" (*anta*), and that of still others, such as Abū Yazīd, is "I" (*anā*).[28] Ibn Arabi himself tended to use "He" or "Thou" in his remembrance of the divine. Eckhart, however, sometimes speaks of "He" which is the same as the station of the essence of One and the absolute hidden, and sometimes speaks about "I" which is the station of annihilation. Eckhart speaks less of "Thou".

The conclusions that I draw from these observations include the following. Ibn 'Arabī puts more emphasis on the creature's servitude and on God's personality. Eckhart, by contrast, puts more emphasis on the Lordship on the creature's side and the absolute transcendence on God's side. Both mystics, however, may be regarded as modifying the ideas of theologians and the cultures of their own times. And this modification brings emphasis to an aspect

[27] Fox, *Breakthrough*, 495.

[28] *Al-Futuḥāt al-makkīya*, vol. 2, 297.

of God that had been ignored in that culture and at that time. Neither theologian, however, is unbalanced in their modifications; both discuss both God's transcendence and His personality.

Conclusions

The God of the "unity of Being", as introduced by Ibn 'Arabī and Eckhart, differs from the philosophers' God and the pantheists' God. Their God is the God of the Holy Quran and the God of The Bible. For both the philosophers and the pantheists, God is not a person. For the former, God is existence negatively-conditioned and for the latter, God is existence nonconditioned as a division. Neither of these two Gods are transformable. Attributes such as knowledge and will and freedom cannot be attributed to Him, much less attributes such as mercy, kindness, delight, disgust, doubt, and the like.

In his *Incoherence of Philosophers*, while criticizing philosophers who have regarded God in His creation to be caused and not free, al-Ghazālī says: The agent must be willing, choosing, and knowing what he wills to be the agent of what he wills. Averroes criticizes al-Ghazālī, stating that:

> This is not self-evident .... He who chooses and wills, lacks the things he wills, and God cannot lack anything he wills. And he who chooses makes a choice for himself of the better of two things, but God is in no need of a better condition. Further when the willer has reached his object, his will ceases and generally speaking, will is a passive quality and a change, but God is exempt from passivity and change.[29]

As has been argued, if one regards God as entirely transcendent, there will be a deep gap between such a God and the God of the religious. How can we worship a God of whom we have no knowledge? How can such a God become angry toward us? How can we satisfy Him when angry? How can one repent in His presence? How can a God who is not passive accept one's repentance? And above all, how can one love such a transcendent God? The history of paganism shows that mankind always avoids a God who is perfectly transcendent and cannot love Him. Humankind seeks a God with whom they can find some similarity. Paganism is an exaggeration of this insight.

---

[29] M. Sells, *Mystical Union in Judaism, Christianity, and Islam* (New York,996), 222, ftnte 21 (on "Bewildered Tongue").

At any rate, philosophers who believe in pure transcendence can never call people toward God. As Ibn 'Arabī puts it:

> If there was no trace of religion which has brought Divine news, no one would know God; and if we were contented with the intellectual evidence which rationalists think that lead one to Godhead, and if we stopped in that He is not such and such, then no creature would love God. When divine news came down through the language of religion suggesting that God is so and so- news that is inconsistent with the appearance of rational evidence- we love God because of these affirmative attributes .... God has introduced himself only through the news about Himself such as He is kind toward us, His mercy applies on us, He has kindness, mercy and love, and He comes down in limitations and conditions ... [this is because] we symbolize Him and imagine Him in our heart, in our *Qibla*, and in our imagination as if we see Him. Nay, but we see Him in ourselves, for we know Him through His own definition and not through our thought and idea.[30]

Ibn 'Arabī claims that Noah's tribe did not accept his call since he called them toward pure transcendence. His call was discriminatory (*farq*). If, however, Noah combined transcendence with analogy, and if his call like that of the Holy Prophet (Muhammad) was Quranic (a combination of transcendence and analogy), he would be followed.[31]

Ibn 'Arabī's theology is a theology that can serve the religious. He knew that what was needed was the knowledge of the names of God, not the knowledge of God's essence; for religion calls people toward the names of God and not his essence (Godhead). Although, Ibn 'Arabī's God has a single essence, he has many names and manifestations. He is One God and at the same time He is various. Every day, every moment, and for every one, He manifests Himself anew, in different ways. He is not the same manifestation for two persons in the same moment or for one person in two various moments. Not only in various religious creeds, but also for Muslims who follow the same Imam in congregation prayer and pray towards the same *Qibla*, God is different, though there is no more than One God:

> In Congregation, everyone who prays in his privacy converses with his God and God encompass him ... for the people of congregation, God is manifest in the totality of oneness and not in the oneness of totality. For, every person in the congregation converses with his Lord according to his intention and knowledge, as is required by His presence. That is why He becomes manifest for them in the totality of oneness. That is, they are preceded by totality. Then He relates that to oneness so that, despite their various aims, ideas, qualities, temperaments and

30 *Al-Futuḥāt al-makkīya*, vol. 2, 326.

31 *Fuṣūṣ al-ḥikam*, vol. 1, 70.

> relations, they may not regard, in their worships, something to be associated with God. That is why their questions and demands may be various. But if God became manifest for them in the oneness of totality, because of the precedence of oneness, no one would be able to look at the totality. And if this was the case, their aims would become the same aim, their requests would become the same request, their quality of presence would become the same quality and their knowledge of God – the exalted – become the same knowledge. But this is not the case.[32]

According to Ibn 'Arabī, every one has her/his own Lord who is other than the Lord of others; if one knows her / his own self, she/he knows her / his Lord. This can be true because God is not manifest as the oneness of essence (Godhead), but only becomes manifest in the station of names and attributes, and according to the demands of fixed entities. There is a manifestation for every name, and that name is the Lord of that manifestation. And since names are numerous, their manifestations as well will be numerous, and accordingly, lords will be numerous; and every one in every condition has a lord devoted to her/him and to that condition. The lord of everyone in every condition, is the manifestation of God as a name which fulfils one's need in that moment and one has to call Him through that name; the sick call Him the Healer, the sinner calls Him the Forgiver, and the poor calls him the Giver. God is One and is not conditioned, but every one has his own lord in every moment:

> Every being is satisfied by its Lord. If some being is satisfied by its lord it is not necessary to be satisfied by the lord of the others. Since every being has received a particular form of Lordship [from among the various forms of Lordship], and it is not the case that all beings receive from a single form. Thus, for every bondman, only what is suitable for him is determined, which is the same as his lord. No one receives from Him because of His oneness. That is why people of Allāh deny manifestation in oneness.[33]

Unlike the philosophers' God, Ibn 'Arabī's God is not only an agent but a receptacle as well. Some materialist philosophers have conceived the universe as only matter. Others have said: "Give me matter and direction, and I will build the universe," while still others thought that, in addition to matter and direction, motion (and time) is (are) necessary as well. Theistic philosophers regard the matter that materialists speak of as receptacle. Further, they hold that there is an agent and mover who is necessary to make changes in matter. In Ibn Arabi's intellectual system, which is based on the unity of Being, it is God who plays all of these roles. In other words, the substance of the universe

---

32 *Al-Futuḥāt al-makkīya*, vol. 3, 193f.

33 *Fuṣūṣ al-ḥikam*, vol. 1, 91.

is the Divine breath; the forms of the world are His manifestations; and the changes in the world are changes in His manifestations:

> All the world is contained in three mysteries: its substance, its form, and transformation. There is not a fourth thing. If you ask from where transformation was found in the world, we will respond that God has described Himself as "Every day He exerciseth (universal) power" (the Holy Quran; 55:29). There are various attributions. God has described Himself to be cheerful because of the bondman's repentance. The Holy Prophet also has said: "God will not become tired unless you may become tired". Those who know Him, i.e. prophets, have said that in the Resurrection Day, he will become angry towards us so that he has never been so angry and he will never be, as His glory requires. Thus, they attribute to Him the state before this anger, when He has not been described with this anger. It has been reported in reliable traditions that in the Resurrection Day God will change into various forms. And change is the same as transformation .... God accepts to become manifest in various forms for His bondmen. Also, He has not created the world at the pre-eternal time, but after that. At the pre-eternal time, He had been described to be able to create the world and to become manifest in the form of the creation of the world or not.[34]

Thus, Ibn 'Arabī's God, receiving all forms, is continuously changing. He is both the Giver and the receptacle, He both makes loans to His bondmen and takes loans from them. He becomes hungry, thirsty, and ill with his bondmen; and at the same time, He Himself is the Feeder, Satisfier, and the Healer:

> Only he who does not believe denies Divine attributes. God says: "And lend unto Allah a goodly loan" (the Holy Quran; 73: 20). And He says I was hungry and you did not feed me, I was thirsty and you did not satisfy me. All of these, He has stated. Thus, God – the Exalted – does not avoid from attributing such things to Himself. In this way, He warns us that He will become manifest in the manifestations in accordance to their potentiality .... There is no relation, unless it has a relation with the God and a relation with the creation.[35]

Ibn 'Arabī's God is continuously interacting with His bondman. He loves us so that He receives every attribution which is related to us:

> The truthful lover is he who will be attributed with the beloved's attributions, and not he who brings the beloved to the level of his own attribution. Don't you see that God – the Glorified –, when he loves us, comes down towards us through His hidden graces; and in a form which is suitable for us and far from His own greatness and majesty? When we come to His home to pray Him, He will become cheerful. When after returning from Him, we again repent He will become cheerful. When He sees a young who should be under commands of youth desires, free

---

[34] *Al-Futuḥāt al-makkīya*, vol. 2, 254.

[35] *Al-Futuḥāt al-makkīya*, vol. 1, 587.

from these commands, He surprises … He degrades on behalf of us, and reveals Himself in our hunger, thirst, and illness.[36]

Eckhart's God suffers together with mankind. In The Bible it has been written:

> Then shall he say also unto them on the left hand, Depart from me, ye cursed, into everlasting fire, prepared for the devil and his angels: For I was hungry, and ye gave me no meat: I was thirsty, and ye gave me no drink. I was a stranger, and ye took me not in: naked, and ye clothed me not: sick, and in prison, and ye visited me not. Then shall they also answer him, saying, Lord, when saw we thee hungry, or thirsty, or a stranger, or naked, or sick, or in prison, and did not minister unto thee? ...Verily I say unto you, Inasmuch as ye did it to one of the least of these, ye did it to me.

Inspired by these verses Eckhart says: "God suffers with man … God suffers with me, and suffers for my sake through the love which he has for me."[37] He teaches that the perfect detachment of the mystic forces God to act.[38]

In line with Christian culture, Eckhart believes that there is more love in the word "father" than the word "Lord." In other words, because of His love, God has become manifest as man's father; thus, many supplications begin instead of "Oh, our Lord" with "Oh, our heavenly father." God, because of His love and kindness, came in the form of man and received human essence. "Now you must know that lovable humility brought God to the point in which he lowered himself into human nature."[39] So it is said that Eckhart's God is a caring, passionate God and it distinguishes his God from many philosophical conceptions of God.[40]

Based on evidence such as that cited above, the God of Eckhart as a Christian is the familiar God of all Christians. However when the mystic begins to theologize about the unity of Being, he no longer seeks such a God.

---

36 *Al-Futuḥāt al-makkīya*, vol. 2, 256. This is a *hadith* cited from the prophet Mohammad. When one of God's servants is hungry, He says to the others, "I was hungry, but you did not feed me." He says to another of his servants "I was ill but you did not visit me." When the servants ask him about this, he replies to them, "Verily so and so was ill, if you had visited him, you would have found me with him. So and so was hungry, if you had fed him, you would have found me with him."

37 Fox, *Breakthrough*, 157.

38 B. McGinn, in M. Sells, *Mystical Union*, 188.

39 C. Smith, "Meister Eckhart on the Union of Man with God," in *Mystics of the Books* (New York, 1993), 244.

40 Fox, *Breakthrough*, 157.

He distinguishes Godhead and God in the station of divinity. For Christians, there are three Persons are in the station of divinity. Eckhart, however, seeks annihilation in the Godhead and achievement of that station. That is why he says: "We pray that God may release us from God."[41]

As we saw, Ibn 'Arabī's God is in the station of Divinity and not in the station of the essence. He is a God who becomes manifest through various names and not a God which is placed in the darkness of the essence. Thus, Ibn 'Arabī seeks to know the names and not the essence. This is the point at which Ibn Arabi's God becomes distinguished from Eckhart's God. Eckhart loves the Godhead and not the names: "Thou shalt love God as he is, a non-God, a non spirit, a non-person, a non-form. He is absolute bare unity."[42]

He who seeks to arrive at the Godhead does not tolerate even the plurality of names. That is why, Eckhart's God, unlike Ibn 'Arabī's God who is various and plural, is a God in whom no variety and plurality is admitted:

> A person who truly loves God as the one and for the sake of the one and union no longer cares about or values God's omnipotence or wisdom because these are multiple and refer to multiplicity. Nor do they care about goodness in general, both because it refers to what is outside and in things and because it consists in attachment.[43]

Thus, Eckhart loves a God who has no name and definition. "He is nameless; He is the negation of all names. He has never been given a name."[44] Every one, whatever desire and potential he has, should ignore these things and seek only a God who is beyond his desires and potentials. The sick should not call him the Healer, for in this way, the Healer which is in the station of divinity will become more beloved than the Godhead: "If you are ill and you ask for health, then health is dearer to you than God. Then he is not your God."[45]

Thus, it can be said that Ibn 'Arabī and Eckhart each seeks a different aspect of God. For, according to one scholar, God in the station of God and God in the station of Godhead, are two aspects of the same God, and approaching these two aspects is approaching two kinds of God. Some mystics seek unity and union with God, among them is included Ibn 'Arabī, and others seek for

41 Sells, *Mystical Languages*, 188.

42 W. R. Inge, *Christian Mysticism* (New York, 1956), 160, ftntc. 1.

43 *Teacher and Preacher* (New York, 1981), 224.

44 Fox, *Breakthrough*, 175.

45 O. Davis, *God Within* (New York, 1988), 63.

the God without modes (*Deus sine mids*).[46] Eckhart belongs to this second group.

It is worth asking how one can relate to a God without modes and know him; for, it seems that such a God is inaccessible to reason and is beyond our knowledge. Indeed, according to Eckhart a God of whom we can have knowledge is not God: "If I had a god whom I was able to know, I would never be able to regard him as God."[47]

Thus, the way to arrive at God for Eckhart is knowing nothing, seeking nothing and having nothing, i.e. annihilation. If I become colorless, I will arrive at the colorless one: "Since it is God's nature that he is unlike anyone, we must of necessity reach the point that we are nothing, in that we can be removed into the same essence he himself is."[48] According to Eckhart, in that unity of essence (Godhead), all dualities and distinctions will go away and we come from being something to being nothing.[49]

Eckhart's views concerning God remind one of the views of certain branches of Hinduism and Buddhism where man's end is to arrive at "annihilation" and "*nirvana*." This kind of mysticism, which puts more emphasis on negation, is quite different from Ibn 'Arabī's mysticism, which rests upon the affirmative aspect of the Divine names. According to some scholars of mysticism, Eckhart is similar to those Asian mystics who wish to sink in the bottomless sea of the Infinite.[50] It is difficult to resist the comparison when reading statements such as the following: "People must … be quite divested of all similarity and no longer resemble anyone. Then they are truly like God. For, it is God's peculiarity and nature to be without any equal and to be similar to no one. May God help us to be thus one in the unity that is God himself?"[51]

At the stage of nothingness described by Eckhart, there is not variety within God; the God of all will be the same. All varieties, pluralities, and debates will vanish away. This is a marked contrast with Ibn 'Arabī's God. Ibn 'Arabī's God will become manifest for mankind through the totality of oneness and Eckhart's God through the oneness of totality. In the oneness of to-

46 Otto, *Mysticism*, 158.

47 Fox, *Breakthrough*, 183.

48 Fox, *Breakthrough*, 328.

49 B. McGinn, "The God Beyond God," in *Journal of Religion* 61 (1981): 11.

50 Inge, *Christian Mysticism*, 160, ftnte 1.

51 *Teacher and Preacher*, 358.

tality, there is no motion, no movement, and no sound. All is silence, stillness, and the darkness of Godhead. As Eckhart says: "Everything in the Godhead is one, and of that there is nothing to be said. God works, the Godhead does no work, there is nothing to do; in it is no activity, God and Godhead are as different as active and inactive."[52] Furthermore, God in itself is motionless unity and balanced stillness.[53] As Mileman puts the matter: "Eckhart's God in that darkness of essence is empty even of knowledge and will."[54]

Ibn 'Arabī and Eckhart call our attention to two Gods. Ibn 'Arabī seeks to worship God even if He is in this world of corporal forms, whereas Eckhart wants to go even beyond the Divine world and arrive to Godhead – there, even worship makes no sense, for that is the station of liberty and not of servitude. Like Eckhart, Ibn 'Arabī sees "other than Allāh" as "Not He" in which "He" is manifest. Thus, he seeks to achieve a station where he is able to see "He" and "Not He" together, and thus to come to affirmation of "He / not He". Eckhart, however, seeks only for "He", i.e. that hidden identity.

According to Eckhart, all causes will vanish or at least will be invisible for the mystic. For Ibn 'Arabī, however, the perfection of man's perception requires that all things be seen as they are. That is, both incomparable with God and similar to Him. And this is to give every thing what it deserves. That is why Ibn Arabi, though he believes that "There is nothing other than Allāh", criticizes those who claim to see only God.[55]

One of the reasons behind the difference between the two mystics, is perhaps that Eckhart, in addition to being a Christian, is a great philosopher. That is why one scholar says:

> Although he speaks of a laughing and suffering God, when he put on his philosopher's cap, he was apt to lose touch with the biblical God and mistake the stillness of love for the unmoved Mover. In his view, the Incarnation and Passion of the eternal word affected the immovable detachment of God as little as if He had never become man. God having no motives acts without them.[56]

Eckhart's Neo-Platonist attitude in regarding God beyond existence helped his view and caused him to depart from belief in a God like Ibn 'Arabī's God.

---

52 F.C. Happold, *Mysticism. A Study and Anthology* (New York, 1963), 273.

53 Cf. E. Gilson, *History of Christian Philosophy* (New York, 1955).

54 B. Mileman, "Suffering God," in *Mystical Quarterly* 22 (1996): 77.

55 W.C. Chittick, *The Self Disclosure of God* (New York, 1998), 194f.

56 D. Steindle Rast, *Meister Eckhart from whom God Hid Nothing* (Boston / London, 1996), xiv-xvi.

For, there is a great distance between Ibn 'Arabī's God and that of Philosophy, even Neo-Platonism. According to Lossky:

> God revealed to us in the Judeo–Christian revelation is a Personal God, concrete and alive, rather than some cold, impersonal abstract Essence. A transcendent Essence is really just a philosophical notion, so Eckhart's mysticism which is concentrated on perception of the Divine Essence is not truly Christian but a form of Gnosticism.[57]

To defend Eckhart and justify his difference from Ibn 'Arabī, the issue can be seen from another angle, however. I believe that these two great mystics responded to the theological exaggerations which were dominant in their times and cultures. Their dual emphasis on the personified God and transcendent Godhead stemmed from the exaggerations made by the thinkers of their times. Muslim philosophers and theologians had made God so transcendent they even regarded him as an unconceivable essence of whom no knowledge can be obtained and with whom no relation may be made. In facing them, Ibn Arabi places emphasis on God's personal attributes which have been abundantly mentioned in the Holy Quran and traditions even if the theoreticians denied them on the basis of their reason. On the other hand, in Christianity, God is not only personal but, in some respect, identified with man. Jesus is God who has been incarnated in man's form. Thus, this God is not transcendent at all and has human attributes such as body, blood, and meat. In facing this, perhaps, Eckhart was encouraged to place emphasis on a Godhead which is beyond Father, Son, and Holy Spirit.

---

57 Smith, "Meister Eckhart," 243.

Bettina Bäumer

Can the Hindu Experience of God Enrich the European Concept of God?

Glory be to you, O Essence of Consciousness / Appearing in many forms as Agni, The Moon, the Sun, Brahmā, Viṣṇu / The mobile and the immobile beings.
Utpaladeva, *Śivastotrāvali* 2.1[1]

European Christianity can no longer live in isolation and remain closed to the God experience of other religions. The encounter of religions takes place in a variety of ways – positive in dialogue, negative in confrontation, and in a syncretistic mixture, in all kinds of esoteric movements. The meeting of European Christianity with Hinduism is less developed than its meeting with, for instance, Buddhism, but it is an essential convening, both for an intercultural and an interreligious understanding, as well as for a revival of Christianity.

It has become apparent that the European concept of God has been largely drained of living content and of a corresponding spiritual experience – no longer does it incite reactions of atheism, an indication of its provocative influence, as it used to about fifty years ago; even worse, it has become boring and ineffective for the majority, especially for the young generation. The concept of God can only be filled with meaning if it is accompanied and informed by spiritual experience. What we find within Hinduism is testimony to a still-living experience of God in a variety of ways, as handed down by unbroken traditions of spirituality. Meeting with religions and spiritualities of this type, instead of being a threat to the Christian faith, as suspected and asserted by official Church representatives, is, on the contrary, a unique chance to revive the European experience of God.

Many European Christians, and post-Christians, are no longer satisfied with a monolithic and absolutistic monotheistic concept of God – a concept that is, in fact, not even in accord with the Trinitarian concept and experience.[2] There are many reasons for a critique of monotheism,[3] which has led to

---

1 Cf. C.R. Bailly, *Shaiva Devotional Songs of Kashmir. A Translation and Study of Utpaladeva's Shivastotravali* (Albany, 1987).

2 Cf. R. Panikkar, *The Trinity and the Religious Experience of Man* (New York, 1973), and later developments of the same theme.

innumerable misuses and misinterpretations, absolutisms and imperialisms, but it is not my task to go into these here.[4] What is important is that a meeting of the Western critique of monotheism with Hinduism and its multiplicity of divine manifestations can be an occasion to discover common ground and to share mutual concerns and insights. Pluralism is not just a necessary evil, as many Christians and theologians tend to think; pluralism arises through insight into the manifoldness of both the Divine and the human.[5] In order to illustrate this statement, I want to focus on three aspects of the experience of God in Hinduism, and on the possible inspiration and enrichment that could be derived from these aspects by Christianity.

The Manifold Nature of the Divine

The first aspect I want to consider is the so-called Hindu polytheism, which for centuries has been decried as heretic by theologians and missionaries without proper understanding.

A Hindu would simply ask, before going into the intricacies of (any particular) theology, How can the fullness of the Divine be limited to a single concept, image, or experience? Is the Divine (to use a neutral term) not free to express it/him/herself in many ways to fulfill the ultimate longings of human beings? This perspective does not require in any way a relativistic multiplication of a singular deity called "God." On the side of Divinity, it means precisely the freedom of the Ultimate Reality to assume any name or form; on the human side it means that every believer has a personal, intimate relation with a particular aspect of the Divine Reality, called *iṣṭadevatā*, "the chosen Divinity," without excluding the validity of other forms of the same Divine Reality for other people.

The idea and practice of *iṣṭadevatā* could be viewed in incarnational terms: for a particular devotee, God takes a particular form with which the devotee is familiar. The two maintain a personal relationship: the *iṣṭadevatā* is one whom the devotee worships and from whom the devotee expects protection. This God-form is sometimes independent and may differ from the cen-

[3] Cf. by way of example: A. Halbmayr, *Lob der Vielheit: Zur Kritik Odo Marquards am Monotheismus* (Innsbruck / Vienna, 2000).

[4] Cf. some of the papers contained in this volume.

[5] Cf. the works by Jacques Dupuis, Perry Schmidt-Leukel and others.

tral tradition to which the believer belongs (mostly by family association): e.g., one may be a Shaivite while personally worshipping a form of the Goddess. There is no contradiction involved here, and this practice can even be explained in theologically satisfactory terms. The way the devotee gets his or her *iṣṭadevatā* may be through a direct personal experience, such as through grace received in a particular temple or place of pilgrimage, or it may be given to the devotee by a *guru* in initiation, with the appropriate *mantra*.

Confronted with a multitude of Gods, Divine and semi-Divine beings, the Hindu theologian has a variety of options, some of them hierarchical, assigning different functions to different manifestations of the Divine, while maintaining the ultimate oneness of the Divine Reality. Here different philosophies and theologies come into play, none of which ever deny the existence or the role of "other" Gods.

In many traditions, not only within Hinduism, God or the Divine is compared with the Sun, with its innumerable rays illumining everything. In the Kaśmir Śaiva tradition, this simile illustrates the relation between the unity of God and his manifold forms and energies. If we were to limit the Divine to a single concept, this would amount to confining the Sun to its reflection in a water pot. Thus, Abhinavagupta states: "How could the thousand-rayed Sun shine in a pot of water?"[6] The Hindu therefore, without losing sight of the one Divine source, will not set limits on that source's manifestation.

Among the many ways of expressing the manifoldness of the Divine are the recitations of the "thousand names" of a God or Goddess and the myriad hymns to different Gods, starting with the *Ṛgveda* itself, the most ancient sacred text of Hinduism. It has been rightly observed that the "thousand names" litanies (the number one thousand standing for "innumerable" in the Indian tradition, according to *Ṛgveda* 10.90) with the multiplication of epithets of the Divine and their identification with diverse concepts and realities, are precisely an expression of the inexpressible and unnameable nature of the Divine, for the Divine's omnipresence, not for its multiplicity. At the same time, these epithets and identifications open possibilities for meditating on the Divine from any possible focal point, positive by identification or negative by negation.

Corresponding to the divine names are the symbolic and iconographic forms of Gods and Goddesses as they are found in temples. In the entire sym-

6 *Tantrasara* 2, concluding verse. Cf. B. Baumer, *Abhinavagupta. Wege ins Licht* (Zürich, 1992), 86f.

bolism of the Hindu temple, it is clear that the outer representations are secondary manifestations of the central godhead in the sanctum. There is a hierarchy that corresponds also to the various functions of the minor deities in relation to the central God. What appears as a confusing multiplicity of gods to an outsider is therefore not confusing to the Hindu worshiper who knows the functions of the various manifestations of the – ultimately – one Divinity. In many sacred Hindu theological texts and commentaries, we find expressions such as this one from the *kāmikāgama:* God assumes all forms, though he is formless, just like water or a mirror, for he pervades everything, living and inert.[7] And the same *āgama* affirms:

> The God of gods is beyond any argumentative proof, he depends on nothing else, rather the others depend on him. Hence he is free, independent. Lord beyond the sequence of space and time. He is all-pervading, eternal, omniform, gracious (Shiva). Being omnipresent, he fills everything; being eternal, he has neither beginning nor end; being of universal form, he is revealed in conscious and unconscious beings, because of his wonderful manifoldness (*vaicitrya*).
>
> *Tantrāloka* 1.58-62[8]

The theological reason for this manifoldness is the absolute freedom of the Lord, and the metaphor used is that of play. He can take any forms in a playful way, without any binding necessity, and thus he reveals his autonomy.

Regarding the relation between the one God and the many, or more specifically the nature of the relationship between devotees and the different Gods they follow, certain verses of the *Bhagavadgītā* are frequently quoted, and their interpretation is relevant to our discussion. Here Kṛṣṇa speaks to his devotee, Arjuna:

> To those who worship Me, meditating on Me alone, to them who are permanently established in yoga (spiritual practice), I bring attainment of the highest reality and the security that they cannot fall down from that state. (23)
> Even those who are devotees of other gods and sacrifice to them with faith, they also sacrifice to Me alone, although they use different methods. (24)
> (For) I am the enjoyer and the Lord of all the sacrifices ....
>
> *Bhagavadgītā* 9.23-25

---

7 Quoted by Abhinavagupta in his *Tantrāloka* 1.66.

8 Abhinavagupta, *Tantrāloka with Commentary by Rajanaka Jayaratha*, 12 vols. (Srinagar ,1918-1938). Cf. the French translation of the first five chapters: Abhinavagupta, *La lumiere sur les Tantras*, transl. by Lilian Silburn and Andre Padoux (Paris, 1998).

What is important is that the "Me" of Kṛṣṇa is not interpreted in any restricted sectarian sense, but his "I" is the Supreme Lord. Abhinavagupta explains this theological perspective:

> In all acts of sacrifice, which are prescribed by various injunctions aiming to please Indra (and other gods), that God – who is the Self (*atman*) of one's own, whose essence is the creation of the universe, who continuously manifests himself as the multitude of gods, and who connects all this universe like the thread in a garland of flowers – is in reality the object of all sacrifices. This is because he is behind the manifestation of all the gods such as Indra, etc. Therefore, the fact that the Lord is the aim of all sacrifices stands logically justified.
>
> Abhinavagupta, *Gītārthasaṃgraha* on 9.23-27[9]

Concluding a discussion on many ways and forms of the Lord, Abhinavagupta exclaims in his *Tantrāloka* (1.92), "Indeed, in what form does the Supreme Lord not appear by virtue of the fullness of his freedom? He in truth accomplishes the hardest of things!"

The Feminine Aspect of the Divine

The second aspect of the Hindu concept and experience of God that could (and, to my understanding, should) enrich a one-sided Christian concept of God is the feminine aspect of the Divine: the Goddess in her manifold forms. While remaining conscious that God – the transcendent-*cum*-immanent Reality – is beyond gender, nevertheless, every representation of the Divine, in language, in iconic imagination, in myth, etc., is necessarily expressed in one of the three genders of human language: masculine, feminine, or neuter.

The feminist theologians are right to stress the one-sidedness of a masculine monotheistic God, with all its attending theological, sociological, and psychological consequences in Western Christianity. But instead of subsisting on a thin portion of feminine aspects in the Jewish-Christian tradition, this one-sidedness could truly be balanced – spiritually, psychologically, and theologically – by a real encounter with the Indian Goddess.

But what does "femininity" mean when applied to the Divine? This is not only a question of gender, but also of culture, and the Divine feminine in the Indian – Hindu – culture probably means something quite different from what an American feminist understands of the same. The complementarity and mu-

---

9 Cf. Abhinavagupta's Commentary on the Bhagavad Gita, *Gitarthasamgraha*,transl. by Boris Marjanovic (Varanasi, 2002).

tual enrichment to be gained from such an encounter are therefore not only religious, but also cultural, psychological, and, ultimately, spiritual.

The Indian Goddess assumes a multitude of expressions – from the most primitive and gross to the most subtle and spiritual. She may be the partner of a male god, as an expression of the complementarity of opposites; she may be the indispensable and inseparable power or Energy of the Divine (*śakti*), or she may be completely independent from any male god and even more powerful than all the male gods put together, as in the myth of Durgā. She may be the virgin, the wife, or the mother. Hindus here always remain conscious that all the forms of the Goddess are aspects of the *śakti*, the Divine Energy.[10]

There is a dynamic and yet non-dual relationship between Śiva, the great Lord (Parameśvara), and his Energy, *śakti,* which is often compared to the relationship between fire and its power to burn. In fact, Śiva would be totally inactive without his *śakti* or *śaktis*, and it is they who are responsible for the creation, maintenance, and reabsorption of the world, as well as for the liberation of souls. She is the mediatrix and the souls can only be united with the Lord through Her.[11]

Without going into greater detail about the religiosity and theology of the Goddess, what is important is that Śakti is a power to be experienced (in fact, the Supreme Lord is beyond experience), and spiritual practice is directed at awakening the same Divine Energy in one's own body – which even has its correlate in Christian terms, where it is called the "temple of the Holy Spirit"!

The Apophatism of Advaita

The third aspect of a Hindu experience of God comes close to the apophatism of the Greek Fathers and of the medieval mystics. It is not only the negation of all attributes in the Divine, the *nirguṇa brahman* of the Upaniṣads and Vedānta, but the insight which is so forcefully expressed in the Upaniṣads, that God can never become an object of knowing or sense experience:

---

10 Cf. "Śakti: die gottliche Energie," in B. Baumer, *Trika: Grundthemen des kaschmirischen Sivaismus* (Innsbruck / Vienna, 2003), 127-39.

11 Cf. *Vijñana Bhairava* 20-21. *Vijñana Bhairava: The Practice of Centring Awareness.* Commentary by Swami Lakshman Joo (Varanasi, 2002), 18f. German translation: B. Baumer, *Vijñana Bhairava: Das gottliche Bewusstsein* (Grafing, 2003).

He is other than the known / And also beyond the unknown ....
That which cannot be expressed by words / By which words are spoken
Know that to be Brahman / Not what people worship here
That which cannot be thought by the mind / By which the mind thinks
Know that to be Brahman / Not what people worship here.
That which cannot be seen by the eye / By which the eye sees.
Kena Upaniṣad 1.4-7[12]

What is intended here is not a simple negation, but the assertion that the Divine cannot be known because he is the Knower, the ultimate subject, the real "I." But if God cannot be objectified in any way, it does not mean that he cannot be experienced. This insight can be ratified in spiritual practice and experience, in meditation, which leads to a personal spiritual transformation. The common phrase of the Upanishads is: Who knows Him becomes Him (*ya evaṃ veda sa eva bhavati).* To know God, one has to become him, and in Tantra it is said that one cannot worship God unless one becomes Him. Both imply a complete process of transformation, whether in knowing or in ritual. This is described as a blissful and liberating experience, as one of the frequently quoted verses of the *Taittirīya Upaniṣad* says:

Whence words recoil, together with the mind,
Unable to reach It – whoever knows
That bliss of Brahman has no fear.
Taittirīya Upaniṣad 2.9

Certainly, the Upanishads also contain positive meditations on the Ultimate Reality (Brahman or Ātman), but they are constantly aware of the danger of stopping at any level of identification, and of the need to go beyond any thought, idea, or concept of the Divine.

The very title of our conference could be challenged on the basis of the Upanishads: "Thinking God ..." – because the thought "God" is not God, and the concept of God is not the thinker's experience of him. To quote again from the *Kena Upaniṣad*:

If you think that you know it well / You know very little – just a form of Brahman
The form that is in you or in the gods / [illegible]
I do not think that I know it well / Nor do I think that I know it not
The one of us who knows it, knows / He knows not that he does not know
He by whom it is not known, by him it is known /

12 Cf. R. Panikkar, *The Vedic Experience* (Delhi, 1985ff.), 684. Cf. also P. Olivelle, *The Early Upanishads* (Delhi, 1998).

> He by whom it is known, he does not know
> It is not understood by those who understand /
> It is understood by those who do not understand
> *(yasyāmatam tasya matam, mataṃ yasya na veda saḥ,*
> *avijñataṃ vijanatām, vijñatam avijanatām)*
> *Kena Upaniṣad* 2.1-3

It is not sufficient to state the paradox that God can only be known by not-knowing, etc., unless this is accompanied by a spiritual experience that goes beyond all words and thoughts (*vikalpa* in all the Indian spiritual traditions).

I do not mean to say that this apophatic approach is absent in Christianity, nor that there is no corresponding mystical experience. But within current Christian practice and theology, these aspects are very much neglected and marginalized. Is this not the reason why many Christians longing for such an apophatic experience turn so readily to Buddhism for practical guidance?

Conclusion

The implications of the three points I have made concerning the Hindu experience of God and Goddess are farreaching, both at the theological and the spiritual level. Historically, the concept of God in "Western" theology, past and present, has been molded by, and bears traces of, Jewish, Greek, Roman, Slavonic, Germanic, British, and American cultural perspectives and contexts. This synergy characterizes the incarnation process of thinking about God and of God language in general (all this is not to be taken in the singular, but in the plural). Yet the prevailing Western idea of God has been so closely associated with a Western (historical and cultural) superiority complex, that every affirmation of the superiority of the Christian God over all the other Gods was not so much an assertion of spiritual superiority but of cultural-historical superiority.

If we dissociate this concept of God from all kinds of Western imperialisms (the last one being "globalization"), then there may be a place for Hindu concepts of God in Western Christianity – as an accepted challenge with the potential to deepen and enrich Christian thinking, as an opportunity to overcome our conceptual and experiential limitations. Instead of superiority, it is time to adopt an attitude of humility, of openness to the spiritual riches of other cultures, such as Hinduism.

The French Benedictine Henri Le Saux (Svāmi Abhiśiktānanda was his Indian name) was a pioneer in the field of Hindu-Christian experience who brought farreaching theological consequences. After a years-long crisis of conscience, with the fear of losing his Christian faith if he immersed himself in the Hindu experience of God, he overcame and was able to integrate the "two" experiences. Toward the end of his life, he wrote in his spiritual Diary "Christ loses nothing of his true greatness when he is freed from the false forms of greatness with which myths and theological reflection have decked him out. Jesus is the marvelous epiphany of the mystery of Man, of the Purusha, the mystery of every human being, as were the Buddha and Ramana (Maharshi) and so many others."[13]

Fear can be overcome in spiritual awakening, and Abhiśiktānanda is a luminous example of such liberation, with all its consequences. And once we overcome the fear of losing our own concepts of God, we can discover other God-experiences: at the level of simple religiosity, at the level of high theological reflection, and most important, at the level of spiritual experience. This requires fearlessness, a sign recognized across cultures as a mark of authentic spirituality.

In this light, the three aspects of the Hindu experience of God mentioned in this paper could be viewed as an enrichment: pluralism, then, is not a theoretical construct, nor a necessary evil, but an insight into the manifold nature of the Divine. Feminist theology, then, is not an (often aggressive) revenge and reaction to a one-sided masculine concept of God, but an encounter with the Divine Feminine at all levels of experience. And *apophatism* or *advaita* (non-dualism) does not remain a negative theological statement, but leads to a stripping of all concepts in a blissful, mystical experience.

It is only the mystic who can exclaim, like Utpaladeva, the great Shaiva philosopher of tenth century Kaśmir:

> Glory to you, O God / Who can be worshiped in any manner
> In any place / In whatever form at all
> *Śivastotrāvali* 2.20

This approach does not invite relativism. It invites European Christianity toward a much needed opening to a more universal understanding of Divine nature.

[13] Abhiśiktānanda, *Ascent to the Depth of the Heart: The Spiritual Diary (1948-1973) of Swami Abhishiktananda (H. Le Saux)*, ed. by R. Panikkar (Delhi, 1998), 367.

Marcus Schmücker

Thinking God in South India: The Theistic Vedānta of the Viśiṣṭādvaita School

The theistic tradition of Viśiṣṭādvaita Vedānta is still flourishing. It originated and developed in, and has been passed down through, the South Indian religious centers of Kāñcipuram and Śrīrāṅga. Many scholars and practitioners have contributed to the tradition's formulation,[1] but Rāmānuja[2] and Veṅkaṭanātha[3] are by far the most important.

Rāmānuja redacted the teachings of this tradition for the first time and created a body of work upon which a formal school was later founded. Three generations later, Veṅkaṭanātha explicitly drew on the teachings of Rāmānuja. His numerous works are characterized by further developments, as, for example, by the influence of the Pāñcarātra tradition. Veṅkaṭanātha's works display a very precise rendering of the teachings of Rāmānuja and a systematization of the teachings of many other authors[4] who either lived before Rāmānuja, like Nāthamuni and Yamunācārya, were contemporaries of him, or lived after him. These treatises mainly extrapolate Rāmānuja's teachings or defend them against philosophical and theological objections of other traditions, especially the tradition of the Śaṅkara school, and also the logicians of the Nyāya-Vaiśeṣika school. Veṅkaṭanātha's work, however, is not merely characterized by its system-

---

1 For a first overview see S. Padmanabhan, "Immediate Successors of Rāmānuja," in *Theistic Vedānta*, ed. by R. Balasubrahmanian, in *History of Science, Philosophy and Culture in Indian Civilization*, vol. II, Part 3, ed. by Chattopadhyaya (Delhi, 2003), 108-32.

2 Traditionally dated 1017-1137.

3 Traditionally dated 1268-1369.

4 See Padmanabhan, "Immediate Successors," 109-127. The stated lifetimes of the successors of Rāmānuja are, in the order given by Padmanabhan: Kūreśa (1010-1116), Parāśarabhaṭṭa (1074-1138), Varadaviṣṇumiśra (10th-11th century), Nañjīyar (11th-12th century), Varadanārāyaṇabhaṭṭāraka (12th century), Śrīviṣṇucitta (1106-1206), Vātsya Varadācārya (1165-1275), Periyavāccān Piḷḷai (1159-1240), Seneśvarācārya (13th century), Meghanādārisūri (12th-13th century), Sudarśanasūri (13-14th century), Nārāyaṇārya (12th-13th century), Piḷḷai Lokācārya (1205-1326), Ātreya Rāmānuja (1220-1310).

atization of Rāmānuja's teachings and his followers. Veṅkaṭanātha not only uses Sanskrit, as Rāmānuja did – he also writes in the languages of South India, such as Tamil, Maṇipravāḷa, and Prākrit.[5] His work, therefore, addresses not only members of the highest class of society, i.e., those schooled in the orthodox brahmanical tradition of the *Vedas*, but it speaks to persons with no training outside of their regional vernacular.

Thus, it is clear that in Veṅkaṭanātha's works, different religious traditions are reflected and integrated under a common system. Veṅkaṭanātha refers to the teachings of the Upaniṣads, especially the theistic teachings, in which Viṣṇu-Nārāyaṇa is named as the highest God; he resumes the tradition of writing in Maṇipravāḷa style,[6] and in his works in Maṇipravāḷa, he deals among other things with the theological concepts of the twelve Āḷvār's, the so-called saintly lords.[7] Moreover, his work is influenced by the themes of the Nyāya-Vaiśeṣika school, although these topics are rendered through Veṅkaṭanātha's own interpretative lens.

Additionally, Veṅkaṭanātha addresses the sources of the Pāñcarātra tradition, defends their doctrine, and overtakes important teachings and theologoumena in his own writings. Also noteworthy is that Veṅkaṭanātha expands both the literature of praise songs (*stotra*) and the corpus of polemical debate with other philosophical traditions of the Vedānta, such as that of Yādava, Bhāskara, and the Advaita Vedānta school of Śaṅkara.[8]

5 For Veṅkaṭanātha's works in Prākṛt as for example the *Acyutaśataka*, see, Steven Paul Hopkins, *Singing the Body of God: The Hymns of Vedāntadeśika in Their South Indian Tradition* (Oxford, 2002), 215ff.

6 This tradition begins with a voluminous commentary, called *Ārāyirappaṭi to Nammāḻvār's Tiruvāymoḻi,* written by a disciple of Rāmānuja, Tirukkurukkai Pirā- Piḷḷai. For a special reference to this work see K.K.A. Venkatachari, *The Maṇipravāḷa Literature of the Srīvaiṣṇava Ācāryas, 12th to 15th Century A.D.* (Bombay, 1978), 61ff. For the composition of Nammāḻvār's Tiruvāymoḻi, see Hardy, *Viraha-Bhakti*: *The Early History of Kṛṣṇa Devotion in South India* (Oxford, 1983), 325.

7 Their songs on the God Viṣṇu are handed down in the *Nālāyirativiyappirapantam,* which is divided in twenty-three sections, and split into four books. See Hardy, *Vira ha-Bhakti*, 247ff. For the translation of Āḷvār as "saintly lords," see Hardy, *Viraha-Bhakti*, 250-51.

8 Veṅkaṭanātha's most important works dealing with polemical debates are the *Śatadūṣaṇī* (ed. by Annangarāchārya [Conjeevaram, 1940]), a work consisting of sixty-six disputes and refutations of important advaitic doctrines, and the *Paramatabhaṅga* (ed. by Vīrarāghavācarya, Madras 1978), which is not as well known, consisting of twenty-four chapters each of which is devoted to the refutation or defense of a different philosophical school or system.

Theological Questions

Before I outline some of Veṅkaṭanātha's main philosophical views regarding the nature of the ultimate Being, I should mention the context through which I will approach his theology. If one considers different concepts of God in other religions from the viewpoint of the philosophy of religion, one may ask in which way God, as a transcendent, absolute, and most high Being, is reflected in His relation to worldly and finite beings. Under which aspects is God experienced or described, so that God can manifest for the believer, can be contemplated, reflected upon, approached, or worshiped? Another question is how can God remain in His absoluteness or transcendence without being affected by the finiteness of every worldly being? In other words, how is the difference between the highest Being and finite beings reflected? By reason of this difference, how does one explain that the highest Being is knowable or can be thought to exist in relation to the world? How can a mutual relation between the Absolute and the world be possible without the Absolute losing its absoluteness while nonetheless being present in the world? And how does one solve the contradiction that God is eternal yet would become insignificant for the believer if He had no relation to the non-eternal world? What is the optimal context through which to consider these questions, and in what way are these questions relevant for Veṅkaṭanātha's theological system, a system wherein the God Viṣṇu-Nārāyaṇa plays the central role?

I will start with one of Veṅkaṭanātha's manifold descriptions of God's absoluteness given in the beginning of his chapter about God (*īśvarapariccheda*) in the Nyāyasiddhāñjana.[9] Here he enumerates all the distinguishing marks[10] of God through which it becomes clear how everything that exists relies on God as its central reference point. But nevertheless

---

9 For my following quotations and translations I refer to the third chapter (*īśvara-pariccheda*, "Chapter about God") in Veṅkaṭanātha's *Nyāyasiddhāñjana* (ed. by Aṇṇaṅgarācārya [Madras, 1940]), hereafter abbreviated as NySiddh. For an approach to this chapter of the *Nyāyasiddhāñjana* from the perspective of comparative theology, see Francis X. Clooney, "Vedānta Deśika's Īśvarapariccheda (Definition of the Lord) and the Hindu Argument about Ultimate Reality," in *Ultimate Realities*, ed. by Robert Cummings Neville, The Comperative Religious Project (New York, 2001), 95-123.

10 NySiddh 225:1-3: *sarveśvaratvam, vyāpakatve sati cetanatvam, sarvaśeṣitvam, sarvakarmasamā-rādhyatvam, sarvaphalapradatvam, sarvādhāratvam, sarvakāryotpādakat-vam, sarvajñānasvetarasamastadravyaśarīrakatvam.*

He is at same time a completely transcendent and absolute Being: God is the Lord of all and everything; His consciousness is all-pervasive (*vibhu*) in contrast to the consciousness of the individual soul (*jīva*), which is comparatively atomic in size (*aṇu*) and comprehension. Thus God can know everything; He is to be worshiped through all activities; He bestows all results of any action by individual souls; He is the support of everything; He is the cause of all effects; every substance other than His own knowledge belongs to his body,[11] and He possesses, as part of His own nature, the quality that whatever He wishes becomes true. Further, in his teachings about God, Veṅkaṭanātha elaborates that He is on the one hand "fully present" (*pūrṇa*)[12] in every entity, but on the other hand, He is not limited by time, by any place, or by any other being.[13] On the contrary, He is nevertheless the support (*adhāra*) for everything that can be known as different from Him.[14] He is described by every word in the *Veda;* every word therein denotes Him. Thus, even though His existence cannot be inferred, His superiority and His characteristic marks are said to be revealed by the authoritative sources (*śruti*), i.e., the *Veda*.

Allowing, then, that God is an absolute and transcendent Being, in which way is He reflected in His relation to worldly and finite beings or other entities different from Him? Every entity different from God must not only be supported (*ādheya*) by Him, but must also be directed (*niyāmya*) by Him, and be in service (*śeṣa*)[15] to Him. Rāmānuja already presents this idea in his exegesis of the relevant Upaniṣads. In his understanding of passages of the *Bṛhadāraṇyaka-Upaniṣad* (3.1.7), he connects the *theo-*

---

11 For a discussion of the idea that God has a body and His relation to it, see below. Veṅkaṭanātha explains NySiddh 208:15-16, the concept of an intelligent / conscious being, by arguing that intelligence (*caitanya*) is different from the body.

12 See Nysiddh 225:26-226,15.

13 For the development of the teaching of the so-called *triparicchedarāhitya*, Brahman's "being free from time, place and being" see Gerhard Oberhammer, *Materialien zur Geschichte der Rāmānuja-Schule II: Vātsya Varadagurus Traktat des Brahma in der kontroverstheologischen Tradition der Schule*, Veröffentlichungen zu den Sprachen und Kulturen Südasiens 28 (Vienna, 1996), 11-49.

14 See Nysiddh 229:18-29.

15 For the meaning of the term *śeṣa* for Veṅkaṭanātha in his discussion with his companion Maṇavāḷamāmuni, see Patricia Mumme, *The Śrīvaiṣṇava Theological Dispute: Maṇavāḷamāmuni and Vedānta Deśika* (Madras, 1988), 81. For the meaning of *śeṣa* for Rāmānuja, see John Braisted Carman, *The Theology of Rāmānuja: An Essay in Interreligious Understanding* (Bombay 1981), 147-57.

legoumenon of the Inner-Ruler (*antaryāmin*), identified in these passages of the *Bṛhadāraṇyaka-Upaniṣad* as the supreme Brahman, which is taught in the *Subālopaniṣad* as Viṣṇu-Nārāyaṇa.[16] Rāmānuja attempts to prove that only this highest Being is able to support the world and to direct it, because to Him belong all conscious and non-conscious beings *as* constituent of His body (*śarīra*).

It is through this "self"-referential relation that the body of God is carried by, directed by, and in service to Him,[17] depending fully upon Him for its existence. Even though God is in this way related to every worldly being, each entity retains its own distinctive nature. And even though each entity forms the body of God, He Himself is not affected by the pleasure or pain of individual souls (*jīva*) caused by their own *karman*, or with the defects of unconscious beings (*acit*).

The different views about the relationship between God and His own body, starting with Rāmānuja's definition[18] – specifically, the relation

---

16 The personal Viṣṇu-Nārāyaṇa and the impersonal Brahman are identified explicitly by Veṅkaṭanātha in the beginning passage of the section about God in his *Nyāyasiddhāñjana* (NySiddh 225,6): "He is the single one, because the Śruti state that He has no second [and that] He is devoid of the equal and of the better. Only He is Brahman." (*advitīyasamābhyadikadaridratvaśravaṇād asāv ekaḥ. sa eva brahma*).

17 In his *Vedārthasaṃgraha* Rāmānuja expresses the body-soul relationship in the following words (quoted translation of J.A.B. van Buitenen, Rāmānuja's *Vedārthasaṃgraha: Introduction, Critical Edition and Annotated Translation*, Deccan College Monograph Series 16, 114. 235): "The relation between soul and body mean the relation between substratum and dependent entity incapable of functioning separately, between transcendent controller and thing controlled, between principal and accessory. In this relation the one term is called *ātman* or 'soul', because this is the one who obtains an object since he is in all respects the substratum, the controller and the principal; the other term is called body, i.e,. form, because it is a modification (*prakārabhūtam*) that is inseparably connected since it is in all respects a dependent entity, thing controlled, and accessory. For such is the relation between the individual soul and its body. Consequently, inasmuch as all things constitute the body of the Supreme Spirit, He can be denoted by all terms." (*ayam eva cātmaśarīrabhāvaḥ pṛthaksiddhyanarhādhārādheyabhāvo niyantṛniyāmyabhāvaḥ śeṣaśeṣibhāvaś ca. sarvātmanā-dhāratayā niyantṛtayā śeṣitayā ca – āpnotīty ātmā sarvātmanādheyatayā niyāmyatayā śeṣatayā ca – apṛthaksiddhaṃ prakārabhūtam ity ākāraḥ śarīram iti cocyate. evam eva hi jīvātmanaḥ svaśarīrasaṃbandhaḥ. evam eva paramātmanaḥ sarvaśarīratvena sarvaśabdavācyatvam.*)

18 In his commentary to Brahmasūtra 2.1.9, Rāmānuja defines the body as follows: "Any substance [dravya] that an intelligent being [cetana] is able compeletely to control [niyantum] and support [dhārayitum] for his own purposes, and the essential nature of which is entirely subservient [śeṣatā] to that intelligent self, is his body." Quoted

between a conscious being and that which is always controlled, supported, and used by the conscious being for its own fulfillment – became after Rāmānuja more and more nuanced in the discussions by his followers. This is evidenced by Veṅkaṭanātha's dealing with more or less four[19] definitions of God's body and of its relation to Him. God's body is not only formed by the plurality of conscious Beings; that is, every individual soul or every unconscious being, it also consists, for Veṅkaṭanātha, in the eternal manifestation (*nityavibhūti*) that is different from the three attributes (*sattva, rajas, tamas*) of primary matter (*prakṛti*) and in its essential nature consisting of the so-called "mere *sattva*" (*śuddhasattva*).[20]

Veṅkaṭanātha divides God's body into two types: one body is eternal (*nityaśarīra*); one is not (*anityaśarīra*). Time (*kāla*), primary matter (*prakṛti*), the individual soul (*jīva*), the eternal manifestation (*nityavibhūti*) and the bodies of eternal (*nitya*) and liberated (*mukta*) souls belong to the eternal body of God.

The non-eternal body of God is further divided into two types: one is formed by *karman;* the other is not. For example, the twenty three entities (*tattva*) produced from primary matter (*prakṛti*), beginning from "the great principle" (*mahat*) to Earth or the embodiments (*mūrti*) like Keśava, Mādhava, etc., or the innumerable incarnations like Rāma, Kṛṣṇa, etc., are all impermanent bodies worn by God but belonging to His non-eternal body. In the same way, the bodies taken occasionally by the liberated or eternal souls on Earth belong to God's impermanent body. All these are not formed by *karman*. In contrast to these, the bodies of human beings, or of animals, belong to the class of bodies made by *karman*.[21] However, all the elements supported by and in service to God are never thought to be in complete identity with Him – they are permanently different from

---

according to Carman, *Theology of Rāmānuja*, 127. For further discussions of the body-soul relationship in Rāmānuja, see Carman, *Theology of Rāmānuja*, 124-33.

19 For the discussion of the different definitions of God's body and their relation to each other, see NySiddh 208,7ff.

20 For a more detailed explanation of the historical development of the concept of the *nityavibhūti*, see Gerhard Oberhammer, *Materialien zur Geschichte der Rāmānuja-Schule V: Zur Lehre von der ewigen* vibhūti *Gottes*, Veröffentlichungen zu den Sprachen und Kulturen Südasiens 34 (Vienna, 2000), 57ff.

21 For Veṅkaṭanātha's extensive division of bodies made by karma see, for example, NySiddh 210: 7ff.

Him, but belong to Him inseparably. In the chapter about God (*īśvara-pariccheda*) in his *Nyāyasiddhāñjana*, Veṅkaṭanātha summarizes the crux of his view regarding God's relationship to everything different from Him in the following words:

> And therefore, [it is accepted], in accordance with the means of valid knowledge, that everything, that is different from Him is in relations (*saṃbandhāḥ*) [with] Him such as being a supporter and being supported, being a ruler and being ruled, being a body and possessing a body, being subordinate and being the Principal, being cause and being effect, etc.[22]

The Basic Concept

What then is the basic idea by which Veṅkaṭanātha conceives of the relation between God and His body? Within what kind of framework can we say that God's relationship to all the other beings is reflected by him, so that the difference between both does not imply any a contradiction?

Veṅkaṭanātha characterizes God's connection to other beings by the relation between the qualifier (*viśeṣaṇa*) and the qualified (*viśiṣṭa*). In Veṅkaṭanātha's view, God is the qualified (*viśiṣṭa*), or something that must be qualified (*viśeṣya*). As we will see, one example of the qualifier is the world itself. The logical implication of the qualifier-qualified relationship is that neither of these binaries can exist without the other. The qualifier and the qualified can only exist together; they are never known or proved as separate states of being (*apṛthaksiddha*). That each is incapable of an independent existence does not mean that each is identical with the other. On the contrary, to qualify something, the qualifier (*viśeṣaṇa*) must be absolutely different (*atyantabhinna*) from the qualified. Yet it is clear that both are not mutually exclusive; for example, when we say that a part of the body, like an arm, is different from the body itself, we also say that the arm inseparably belongs to the body, at least conceptually. If,

22 NySiddh 233.16: *tena ca tadvyatiriktasya nikhilasya ādhārādheyabhāveśvareśitavyatvaśeṣaśeṣitvaśarīraśarīribhāvakāryakāraṇabhāvādayo yathāgrahaṇaṃ saṃbandhāḥ* .... The next sentence is of immense importance for Veṅkaṭanātha's theology of the Goddess Śrī and Her relation to God, but its theological implications regarding the concept of God's absoluteness cannot be considered here, because it requires its own full discussion. The sentence runs in connection with the forgoing sentence quoted: *śriyā saha tu. dāmpatyaṃ śāśvataṃ* .... "And [these relations] are together with Śrī [as well]. The partnership of the Two [i.e. Viṣṇu and Lakṣmī] is permanent ...."

therefore, something is called different and at the same time inseparable, this does not necessarily imply contradiction; rather it can underscore a form of unity where things (a body and its parts) reveal this sort of interdependence.

The Position of Advaita Vedānta

Before I go on to explain Veṅkaṭanātha's descriptions of the kinds of relationship between God and the entities different from Him, I would like to contrast the basic idea of the relationship between the qualifier and the qualified with a fundamentally different understanding of the highest Being, i.e., Brahman as taught in the Śaṅkara school of Advaita Vedānta, one of the most important traditions to challenge the Rāmānuja school. The Śaṅkara school of Advaita argues for a Brahman without any qualifycation; that is, without a body that consists of conscious and non-conscious beings.

Veṅkaṭanātha's refutation of the teachings of this school consists precisely in the argument that one cannot speak of a single reality, i.e., Brahman without any qualification, without accepting a difference of some sort, and thus without any relationship to the world. If something were different from the highest Being, it must be interpreted as a qualification of God himself. Whatever the qualifier might be for Veṅkaṭanātha, it is not lower in level or degree than God. Both the qualified God and what is qualifying Him are in the same manner *real*, whereas, according to the tradition of the Śaṅkara school, everything different from the highest Being is not understood as a real qualification, but as the result of non-real ignorance (*avidyā*) and thus in itself, as thoroughly non-real. Consequently, according to this school of thinking, Brahman does not possess "being" or "consciousness" by way of qualification, but is considered identical with "pure consciousness." Only Brahman that *is* "pure consciousness" is declared as the only true reality and therefore as the ultimate being "without second" (*advaita*). For the tradition of the Śaṅkara school, the central term "having no second" (*advaita*) therefore carries a meaning exactly opposite to its interpretation in the Rāmānuja school: Everything different from the highest Being is not viewed as God's qualification, but as a cognitive/spiritual misapprehension caused by the non-real ignorance (*avidyā*). But as we have seen, the concept of God's unique being as qualified by something different from Him is characteristic for Veṅkaṭanātha's thinking and of the Rāmānuja school in general, and it provides the meaning for the tradition's name: the compound *viśiṣṭādvaita* here must be understood as *viśiṣṭasya advaita*, i.e., as the qualified Brahman, Viṣṇu-Nārāyaṇa, the one having no second.

How was it possible for Veṅkaṭanātha to reject this Advaitic concept of pure Brahman? The pivotal point in the Advaita school arguments consists in missing what for Veṅkaṭanātha is an important supposition: what is denied from the Advaitic point of view (e.g., any entity existing as real in difference from Brahman) must be presupposed according to Veṅkaṭanātha's reasoning and asserted as undeniable in every regard. If the Advaitin denies the reality of the world in his argumentation, because for him only Brahman is held to be real, and if the world is said to be caused by non-real ignorance (*avidyā*), then the Advaitin, according to Veṅkaṭanātha's counterargument, has already accepted a difference between the only real Brahman and the non-real ignorance. If something "exists" apart from Brahman and is known to be different from him, then the Advaitic meaning of the word *advaita* would be contradictory. For Veṅkaṭanātha, in his own theological system, such an error would not be possible. If something is said to be different from Brahman, it can be interpreted as a qualification of God himself. One cannot say that the highest Being is without qualifications and is therefore not possible to objectify through language precisely because by speaking the sentence "Brahman is without any qualification" one necessarily accepts Brahman as an object of speaking and necessarily gives Brahman the qualification that "it has no qualification." Otherwise, one could not have said: "Brahman has no qualify-cation." The following short quotation makes Veṅkaṭanātha's refutation of a contradictory Advaitic statement more explicit:

> If you (i.e. the Advaitin) object that [the sentence] "Brahman is without any qualification" is only idle talk (*abhilāpamātram*), then what was [already] said by us would be proved, because in reality you are not refuting a qualification, and you are finally affirming [with these words] that Brahman is an object of your idle talk. If you respond that this is not possible for a pure entity (*vastumātrasya*), then it is not true [by the following reason]: If an entity is said with the words: "It is expressible" or "it is not expressible", then the

object would in fact be expressible, because it is connected with the words "expressible" and "not expressible."[23]

Veṅkaṭanātha's polemical debates with the Advaitic Śaṅkara school reveal the difficulty in constructing an argument for a highest Being without relating that Being to something else. Even if it is accepted that such a being exists as the only real Being, the demand persists within this logic that such a being should be unthinkable, inexpressible, and unframeable as a concrete point of reference. Yet under such conditions, any articulation at all is at risk for the charge of reductionism, even ultimately the claims of the Advaitins themselves. Perhaps finding the most reasonable approach, after all, is best left to the mystics.

Examples of God's Relatedness

Let us return to the question of how the relation between the highest Being and the finite is understood by Veṅkaṭanātha. We have seen that, for him, the concept of God and His relation to everything that can be called different from Him is based on the concept of the relation between the qualified and the qualifier. According to him, God's qualifiers have various forms: His own essential qualities (*svarūpanirūpakadharma*); the plurality of souls (*cit*), who are destined to become liberated or are so already;[24] insentient entities (*acit*), such as material matter (*prakṛti*); the eternal appearance of God (*nityavibhūti*), in which all eternal liberated beings reside[25]; time (*kāla*); and the knowledge (*jñāna*) that is known as a

---

23 NySiddh 227:14-16: *brahma nirviśeṣam ity abhilāpamātram iti cet, tarhi siddhaṃ naḥ samīhitam vastuto viśeṣapratikṣepābhāvāt, antataś cābhilāpagocaratvasya vidhānāt. vastumātrasya tad api nāstīti cen, na, avācya vācyam iti vā vastuni pratipādite. Vācyam eva bhaved vastu vācyāvācyavaco 'nvayāt.*

24 For Veṅkaṭanātha's division of individual souls (*jīvavibhāga*) into souls in the state of *saṃsāra* (*saṃsārin*) and souls not in *saṃsāra* (*asaṃsārin*), see NySiddh 215,19-216,10. The former group of *saṃsārin*s is split again into souls remaining eternally in the state of *saṃsāra* and souls to be liberated at a future time. The second group is divided into souls who never were in the state of *saṃsāra* (*nityamukta*) and souls who attained liberation from the state of *saṃsāra* (*mukta*).

25 The eternal manifestation (*nityavibhūti*) is, as said above, also understood as a kind of material (*śuddhasattva*) by which for Veṅkaṭanātha God's embodiments (*mūrti*) or His appearances on earth (*avatāra*) are made of.

qualification (*dharmabhūtajñāna*) of God by whose all-pervasiveness (*vibhu*) He can know everything.

On one hand, one can never conceive of God without qualifications. On the other hand, God is not identical with them; He has qualifications; He is specified by them, but He is not relativized or diminished by them. God can remain in His absoluteness without being affected by the change of every worldly being, while at the same time He can be connected with the world through His own will, by ruling, directing, and supporting the world. Thus the concept of qualification establishes exactly God's absoluteness: Veṅkaṭanātha explains God as the only being that cannot be relativized by another being, precisely because there is no other second being; that is, no other god that can be characterized by all things that are different from Him. For example, other gods like Śiva or Brahmā in relation to Viṣṇu are interpreted by Veṅkaṭanātha only as individual souls (*jīva*). Thus he says in his chapter about God:

> Neither Brahmā, nor Rudra (i.e. Śiva) [can be the highest Brahman]. For they are proved to be individual souls, because of the authoritative scripture's (*śruti*) teaching that they are created, that they are dissolved, that they are subject to *karman* etc.[26]

The following passage in the opening section of Veṅkaṭanātha's Nyāyasiddhāñjana which describes Brahman's, i.e. God's relation to every conscious and non-conscious being, makes his view more explicit:

> Brahman is the one (or single) reality that has every conscious and non-conscious being as its mode. Even though there is an complete difference between a mode and what is characterized by a mode as well as among (*mithas*) the modes the designation of the oneness (*ekatva*) and the negation of something different due to an intention of the oneness, etc., of the qualified is in respect to this [i.e. Brahman].[27]

"Complete difference" (*atyantabheda*) here means that Brahman, i.e., the highest God Viṣṇu-Nārāyaṇa, remains eternally different from everything that could qualify Him, yet it is this difference that enables Brahman to be qualified – it establishes a relationship between the qualifier and the

---

[26] NySiddh 225:11-12: *nāpi brahmarudrādeḥ, teṣāṃ sṛjyatvasaṃhāryatvakarmavaśyatvādiśravaṇena jīvatvasiddheḥ*).

[27] NySiddh 187: 5: *aśeṣacidacitprakāraṃ brahmaikam eva tattvam. tatra prakāraprakāriṇoḥ prakārāṇāṃ ca mitho 'tyantabhede 'pi viśiṣṭaikyādivivakṣayaikatvavyapadeśas taditaraniṣedhaś ca.*

qualified (what in the quotation above is called the relation between a mode (*prakāra*) and the supporter of the modes [*prakārin*]). And, because this "complete difference" enables Brahman to be qualified, Brahman can exist in oneness (*ekatva*) with His qualifiers (*viśeṣaṇa/prakāra*) and can thus be understood as *advaita*, "having no second." Again we can see that in Veṅkaṭanātha's view, God/Brahman is to be qualified by everything that can be known as different. Therefore He has no equal, no second that can be characterized in the same way by all qualifiers.

Another concept fundamental to the theology of Veṅkaṭanātha, based on the relation between the qualifier and the qualified, is his classification of all the objects of knowledge (*prameya*) as substance (*dravya*) or non-substance (*adravya*). For him there are six fundamental substances (*dravya*) as mentioned above: God, i.e., the highest self; the individual self; primary matter (*prakṛti*); the eternal appearance (*nityavibhūti*), time (*kāla*); as well as the knowledge that is defined as being a qualifier of the self (*dharmabhūtajñāna*). These substances never exist without a non-substance (*adravya*) acting as their qualifier.[28]

For Veṅkaṭanātha, everything that is different from God is explained in the same way as a non-substance is described in its relation to the underlying substance: Just as a substance is characterized by different states, so is God. For the manifestation of the world belonging to His body (*śarīra*), this means the following: If the world is defined as "being in the subtle state" (*sūkṣmāvasthā*), then God, as the underlying substance, is said to be in the state of the cause. If His body is said to be in the unsubtle state, i.e., the gross state (*sthūlāvasthā*), then He is defined as being in the state (*avasthā*) of effectivity. And as a substance itself remains unaffected, because only its state exists within the sphere of change, in the same way, for God, every change lies in the realm of His body, which is absolutely different from, but belongs inseparably to Him. Therefore Veṅkaṭanātha can say that God

> is accepted very well (*eva*) as the basis of modifications, because [of His] garment qualified [by conscious and non-conscious beings], as is the case for [the qualifications of] childhood, youth, age, bulkiness etc. in reference to the

[28] They are called inseparable (*apṛthaksiddha*) from the underlying substance. See for example NySiddh 233:4: *āgantuko 'pṛthaksiddho dharmo 'vasthā.* "The state is a qualification that is added and that cannot be separately established."

> soul that is without modifications [but which] in its essence is qualified by a human body, etc.[29]

Although the differing states of the body during the aging process imply a series of actual modifications (*vikāra*), the soul remains unchanged and unaffected.

To summarize, we can say that for Veṅkaṭanātha everything that can be thought as different from God is related to Him in such a way that no single thing can be said to exist separate. And on the same time He can remain in His absoluteness without being affected by anything different from Him. Thus, Veṅkaṭanātha says that on the basis of authoritative scripture, there is no equivalent or more highly valued second other than God (*īśvara*) because everything different from God qualifies only Him. The statement of no equivalence is founded on God's relatedness to everything that is different from Him. This paradigm is described by Veṅkaṭanātha (see NySiddh 233,14-17) as the relation of the supporter to the supported, of the ruler to the ruled, of the Principal (*śeṣin*) to the subordinate (*śeṣa*), of that which is characterized by a body (*śarīrin*) to the body itself, and as the relation of cause (*kāraṇa*) and effect (*kārya*). God is not limited by all that stands in necessary relation to Him, i.e., by the supported (*ādheya*), the ruled (*niyāmya*), the servant (*śeṣa*), etc., because everything different belongs only to Him.

---

[29] NySiddh 230,3: *viśiṣṭaveṣeṇa vikārāśrayatvaṃ tv iṣṭam eva, manuṣādiśarīraviśiṣṭe svarūpato nirvikāre puṃsi bālyayuvasthaviratvasthūlatvādivat.*

Aasulv Lande

Thinking and Naming the Ultimate in Buddhist Theology

During the last two millennia, different types of Buddhism have emerged within a variety of cultural contexts. At first glance, the sheer range and degree of diversity presented by Buddhism's various forms makes their classification under one rubric seem spurious at best. Nonetheless, it is useful and rewarding to look for the common features of worldwide Buddhism. For example, it is reasonable to generalize by stating that within Buddhism there is a trend toward going "beyond." In what follows, I will explore ways of naming and thinking this "beyond" – particularly as it manifests within contemporary expressions of Buddhism regarding ultimate and immanent reality or nature.

Buddhist Terms for Ultimate Reality

Worship in all Buddhist traditions consists in taking refuge in the "three treasures," which represent a threefold ultimate reality: the Buddha, Dharma, and Saṅgha. When Japanese Nichiren Buddhists takes their refuge in The Lotus of the Good Law, and the Pure Land Buddhists in Amida Buddha – these singular entities should be seen as interpretations of the threefold Buddhist reality. The term "Buddha" means "the enlightened one," ultimate reality personified. Some buddhas and *bodhisattvas* (prospective buddhas) take on special, eschatological roles. Mitraya (*Miroku bosatsu*), a *bodhisattva* who is to appear at the end of this age, is one such example.

"Dharma" means "universal law," and this term relates to ultimate reality by pointing to its structure. The concept of "dependent origination," within structures and as ultimate structure, is a key element in Buddhism, by which notions such as personal unity, soul, personality, and identity are radically questioned. This conceptual framework points to the continually radically changing character of any essentiality.

The third of the treasures, the Saṅgha (the Buddhist community) cannot directly be called an ultimate reality in the same way the Buddha or Dharma can. Saṅgha is neither a structure nor a metaphysical reality; *saṅgha* expresses the link between human beings and the "reality beyond," and it promises a real path extending toward Buddha status from the world of sentient beings. The term connects ultimate Buddhist existence to conditions and life in the immanent world. From different angles and with varying emphases, these three key terms and their derivations mark the sphere of Buddhist ultimacy.

Starting with this threefold Buddhist mode of ultimate, salvational existence as a point of departure, one might start reflecting upon how Buddhist ultimate reality should be understood, if it can be an "object" of understanding.

Problems

In what follows, I will focus on what I call the problem of Buddhist incarnation. The concept itself is implied in Buddhism by the interaction and co-existence of (a) immanent reality, including aspects of *saṅgha*, and (b) the ultimate reality as illustrated by terms such as Buddha, dharma, and indirectly by *saṅgha*. The interplay of immanence and ultimacy within Buddhism raises important questions: How does Buddhism actually handle the question of these two realities? How are the two realities integrated? Do the two realities work in complementary relationship or in dualist opposition to one another? To borrow a Christian term, how is the process of "incarnation" within Buddhism – that is, the question of relating ultimate reality to immanent reality – really undertaken?[1]

---

1 Among three relevant ways of addressing ultimacy and immanence in the Western perspective, one might first imagine the neglect of both concepts. This does not mean that one simply says that there is neither – it means that one is not concerned with such ideas and tries to translate them into manageable terms. This is especially obvious in positivist approaches inspired by the emerging Natural Sciences. In philosophies with this function, one looks for meaningful queries; that is to say, questions that in principle are verifiable and falsifiable in accordance with accepted criteria. It implies for instance that one in empirical theologies would hesitate to speak of, e.g., "God in Global Dialogue" – but would readily engage "The Concept of God in Global Dialogue"; any admittance of the existence of "God" would be unacceptable according to the presuppositions of such a theology or philosophy.

The standpoint of "conditional thinking" opens up a second way of approaching ultimacy and immanence. By this, I mean thinking in so called transcendental categories, originating in Kantian thought, according to which one explores our human capacities for understanding, a capacity that is based on forms of cognition such as time and space – which are then not seen as objectively existing, but are recognized as conditional for understanding existence. Ultimacy and immanence are not here neglected – but one looks at the conditions mobilized in human cognition, thought, or language when either is named and described.

In approaching these questions, I will begin by looking at some terms derived from the three standard concepts of Buddhist ultimacy. The first is "Buddha nature" (*bussho*). The concept is intimately connected with Japanese Buddhist thinking and teaching. It also relates to a number of other terms such as "original Buddhism" (*hongaku shiso*), a term which might be substituted by "Buddha nature" in most places. As there has been a century long concern with the understanding of Buddhist reality in the Kyoto school of philosophy, I will also look at terms used by the protagonists of this school of thought, terms such as "absolute nothingness" (*zettaimu*).

There are some Buddhist theologies that oppose ideas of "Buddha nature" or even the term "nothingness." I refer here to the ongoing debate on "critical Buddhism" and also on a new Buddhist trend named "engaged Buddhism."

Is "Buddha Nature" Adequate for Expressing Buddhist Ultimacy?

For some[2] it is clear that the concept of a Buddha nature can be traced back to the founder of the Japanese Tendai sect, Saicho (Dengyo Daishi 767-822), who had been dispatched to China in the early ninth century by the Japanese emperor and developed upon return one of the great branches of Buddhism in Japan based on a classification of spirituality by degree of supreme enlightenment. Saicho also connected these classified types of enlightenment to different Buddhist sūtras. The Lotus Sūtra came to signify the supreme enlightenment and thus came to represent the crown of Buddhist insight.

Supported by the imperial house, the Tendai sect ascended to a high position in the hierarchy of Japanese political power and soon achieved the right to legitimize the ordination of monks. Thus it actually controlled the official, religious world. This high position, however, also implied a close connection to the state and endowed the religious organization with a chief responsibility for national unity. In this context, Saicho formulated the *hongaku shiso*,

---

The third type of approach might be termed transcendent thought. The ultimate and/or the immanent completion or fulfills: God is considered a *summum bonum* – an extension of immanent reality, or by means of a negative theology, as a reality outside immanence, but which is incapable of being expressed in immanent terms. Also in the case of "negative" theology or philosophy, the ultimate appears as fulfillment of immanent qualities.

2 J. Hubbard and P.L. Swanson, *Pruning the Bodhi Tree: The Storm over Critical Buddhism*, Honolulu: University of Hawai'i Press 1997, 4ff

which, in subsequent Japanese religious history, crystallized into a general Buddhist dogma. It declared that all beings partake in "Buddhahood," which we might see as a capacity for, or even a degree of, enlightenment. Trees, rocks, and rivers, together with sentient beings, all have Buddha nature, according to this doctrine. Saicho became, however, involved in a dispute with a representative from the earlier introduced Japanese sect Hosso-shu (Yogācāra Buddhism). In 817, in a pamphlet entitled "On Buddha Nature" (*Busshosho*), a monk from Hosso-shu, Tokuitsu, questioned the universalist ideas of Buddhahood and propagated a critical view: one could not claim that all beings – sentient as well as non-sentient – qualified for an inclusive and all embracing Buddhahood, he argued. Saicho responded with the treatise entitled "Vanquishing Misunderstandings" (*Hokke kowaku*), wherein he argued for an inclusive, universal understanding of Buddhahood. At least in the contest for power and general acceptance, Saicho is considered to be the winner of the contest.

This early debate between Saicho and Tokuitsu engaged with questions that are still salient today in discussions about the nature of the ultimate in Buddhism. Saicho and Tokuitso queried whether the ultimate could be considered a core factor in national or possibly even universal world harmony. Alternatively, they asked whether the ultimate could be located within personal attitude – by constant seeking and preparation on the part of the practitioner. And they questioned whether the ultimate could found in essentialist or in relational terms.

It can be argued that the idea of a universal Buddha nature has permeated the Japanese history of religious ideas since the reign of Prince Shotoku in the early seventh century. Prince Shotoku's concept of harmony (*wa*) was decisive in permitting the harmonious coexistence of different religious and social forces in the country. Within Japanese society, this mood of interpretation has been maintained in different forms and in different degrees of sophistication.

One of Saicho's contemporaries, Kukai (Kobo Daishi 744-835) founded Shingon-shu at Mount Koya and developed the idea of an inherent Buddha nature. The doctrine might be said to have attained an especially prominent position through Kukai. He taught that it was possible to attain enlightenment within a person's lifetime. Legends about Kukai narrate how the great founder was transformed during meditation into a shining figure radiating the light of a Buddha as proof of his attainment.

Later Buddhists, such as the Tendai monk Dogen (1200-1253), the founder of Soto-zen, criticized the idea of an inherent Buddha nature (*hongaku shiso*). Pure Land Buddhism and Nichiren Buddhism, both formed around the time of Dogen, displayed a critical attitude to such an idea at various stages based on the tenets of the Lotus Sūtra and the general Buddhist belief in the age of *mappo*, an eschatological time period when ethical, moral, and spiritual laws were said to be in decay. Resistance to the idea of a Buddha nature by these sects was connected to their faith in the appearance of Maitraya, a bodhisattva coming to usher in a new age of justice and truth. Mainstream Buddhism was, however, less critical, and it related well to the politically inspired concerns of Kukai and Saicho.[3] Herein, one does actually see a type of ultimacy expressed by the connection between ideas of Buddhist reality and concerns regarding concrete, human conditions in the world.

Buddhist Ultimacy in the Kyoto school

The Kyoto school comprises the work of a number of philosophers – mainly Nishida Kitaro (1870-1945) and his successor Tanabe Hajime (1885-1962), and later, Shinichi Takeuchi, Keiji Nishitani, Shizuteru Ueda, among others. The question arises as to what kind of ultimacy representatives of this school would propagate. The founder of the Kyoto school, Nishida Kitaro, provided a philosophical breakthrough with his book *A Study of Good* (*Zen no kenkyū*),[4] wherein he introduced the term "pure experience." At first glance, one might expect the concept to represent a transcendent notion. But, this is not the case. The pure experience expresses, rather, a qualitative content that is strongly informed by Zen experience. The concept has an empirical, psychological focus inspired by William James. There is also a connection between the thought of Nishida and the Yogacara philosophy, according to which consciousness is the only reality.[5] One must keep in mind, however, that for

3 This kind of Buddhist thought might be compared to ideas of transcendence also found in certain Christian approaches where one finds the concept of the ultimate as *summum bonum*, or in a more dialectical sense, as fulfillment by negative terms, where the ultimate transcends the capacity of human language and cognition.

4 Nishida Kitaro, *Zen no kenkyū* (A Study of Good) 1911/87, Iwanami Shoten Tokyo (A recent English translation by Abe Masao and Christopher Ives, *An Inquiry into the Good*, 1990).

5 Cf. F. Buri, *The Buddha – Christ as the Lord of the True Self: The Religious Philosophy of the Kyoto School and Christianity*, Translated by Harold H. Oliver, Mercer University Press, Macon, Georgia 1997 (Original German *Der Buddha-Christus als der Herr des wahren Selbst*, 1982 by Verlag Paul Haupt), 37-64.

Nishida subject and object merge into one. Objects observed and experienced merge with the experiencing self – an insight that naturally corresponds to Zen experience. Later, in *The Fundamental Problems of Philosophy,*[6] when Nishida moved on to a broader and more universal grasp of philosophy, he introduced the concept of "nothingness," where he attempts to develop a dialectical dynamics of nothingness, breaking the intuitive identity between the subject and the object. Nishida coined the phrase "logic of the identity of absolute contradictories,"[7] with which he tried to counteract the spontaneous identity of self and object. It remains a question whether he managed to achieve this. His metaphysics consists of pairs of concepts such as "individual" and "universal," "I" and "Thou," "God" and "humanity." His dialectic is radicalized with his metaphor of "living by dying," which he uses repeatedly. It reveals that he is concerned with a philosophy of existence oriented from the standpoint of Zen experience. The question remains as to whether he was successful in progressing beyond the dominating concept of intuition that softens his dialectic and provides a mystical oneness between his experiencing subjectivity and experience itself.

The latter point is leveled as criticism against Nishida by his successor at Kyoto University, Tanabe Hajime.[8] Let it first be said that these two thinkers use similar terms such as "nothingness," "absolute nothingness," and the "self identity of absolute contraries." But beyond the similarities of expression, there lurks a difference. This difference is largely seen in light of the two respective Buddhist trends with which they identify themselves: Zen Buddhism and True Pure Land Buddhism. Whereas Zen can be said to be a religion of self identity with meditative experience, True Pure Land, inspired by Shinran, is based on faith: the sinner is saved by taking refuge in Amida Buddha, the Other Power. Any self-salvational potential within the believer is rejected by this "Protestant" Buddhism. For Tanabe Hajime, the latter view is strengthened by three additional factors. The first is his acceptance of the Protestant Christian emphasis on the radical faith of the sinner. A second influence stems from Kierkegaard, the well-known protagonist of radically dialectical philosophy. Third, is the enhancement of Tanabe Hajime's sharp dia-

---

6 Nishida Kitaro, *Fundamental Problems of Philosophy*, Sophia University, Tokyo 1990 (Original Japanese publication 1933/34).

7 Cf. F. Buri, *The Buddha*, 55.

8 Tanabe Hajime, *Zangedo to shite no tetsugaku* (Philosophy as Metanoetics), Vol 9 Complete Works, Chikuma Shobo, Tokyo 1963.

lectic by his personal war experience. His postwar publication, *Philosophy of Repentance,* also called "Philosophy of Metanoetics,"[9] has a strong and energetic tune of repentance coined in philosophical terms. Here he stands in strong polemic against his predecessor Nishida. Earlier, he promoted a nationalist philosophy that underlined the concept of "middle" (*chu*) as a national entity mediating between the individual and the universal; postwar he turned to a more radical and humble position. His emphasis now was on loosening the ego by immersion in absolute nothingness, arising from the Other power into New life. Expressions carrying this implication appear frequently in his treatise on repentance: "Absolute Nothingness which grants me a new life of resurrection, is experienced by me as Nothingness qua Love." In this experience, he attests that "the Great Nay is in itself the Great Compassion."[10]

The philosophical conflict between Nishida and Tanabe is considered exaggerated by many observers, who look for unity in the Kyoto school and interpret apparent contradiction in light of personal difference and scholarly envy. One must keep in mind, however, the specific characters of two Buddhist streams, which in spite of related religious and historical roots (Kamakura Buddhism), foster different dynamics of salvation.

As to the "ultimate" in Buddhism, these two thinkers ascribe to the terminology of "nothingness" and related concepts.[11] If concepts such as "absolute nothingness" are generally embraced by transcendentalist thinkers – does their use by the Kyoto school necessarily indicate as espousal of transcendental, conditional thinking about the ultimate? Although Nishida eventually worked himself into a Kantian transcendental philosophical framework and embraced Fichte's "*tathandlung*" as a keystone of his philosophical approach, it is my impression that transcendental thought never became a central concern of his or of the Kyoto school. Nishida, the founder of the Kyoto school, maintained throughout his philosophical career, a concern for "existence itself," rather than for the conditions of existence.[12] Approaching "nothingness" with dialectical sophistication, Nishida holds to a type of transcendent thought with strong essentialist ideas.

---

9 In Japanese *Zangedo to shite no tetsugaku..*

10 Translation by F. Buri, *The Buddha*, 71f

11 The Japanese Buddhist scholar Hanaoka Eiko develops an integrated perspective on these two thinkers: *Zettaimu no tetsugaku.Nishida tetsugaku kenkyū nyumon* (The Philosophy of Absolute Nothingness. Introduction to the Study of Nishida Philosophy) Sekai Shisosha, Tokyo 2002.

12 Cf. F. Buri, *The Buddha*, 48ff.

Tanabe, in his early, nationalist philosophy of "*chu*," seems to take a similar stand. Apparently, however, he breaks through the shell of essentialist ultimacy in his late work, *Zangedo to shite no tetsugaku (*Philosophy of Metanoetics). His interpretation here approaches a radically relational position. Although I consider both thinkers to reflect an incarnational type of ultimate thinking in their prewar works, I do find development toward radically relational thought in the works of the postwar Tanabe.

Ultimacy According to Critical Buddhism

The current discussion regarding *hongaku shiso* (implying the idea of a Buddha nature) has become a strong controversy within Japanese Buddhist circles. The two persons who have taken the lead in this debate are the Komazawa University scholars Matsumoto Shiro and Hakamaya Noriaki. One must keep in mind the longstanding debate between scholarly Buddhism and organizational Buddhism in Japan. One stimulus to the argument is the fact that over the centuries Japanese Buddhism has continually been transformed by the shifting Japanese context and cultural milieu. An example is the controversy between proponents of historical criticism of Buddhism and apologists for Japanese Buddhist realities. Parallel to similar Christian polemics, the book by Watanabe Shoko *Japanese Buddhism* clearly illustrated the discrepancy between the widespread Japanese "funeral Buddhism" and an original Buddhism of enlightenment and liberation. One might view the efforts of Matsumoto and Hakamaya as a comparable, scholarly attack on mainstream, popular Japanese Buddhism.

In 1989, Matsumoto released a collection of essays, *Dependent Origination and Emptiness.*[13] In the first essay, he claimed that the doctrine of *nyoraiso* (*tathāgata-garbha*), which might be translated "Buddha-womb" is not Buddhism. Matsumoto is actually against the idea of an inherent universal Buddhahood and avers that Buddhism is the teaching of non-self (*muga*) and causality (*engi; pratītyasamutpāda*). He refers to what he claims is the original teaching of Buddha, who discovered the twelvefold chain of dependent arising during his enlightenment under the Bodhi tree, and writes, "The crucial point is the denial of any eternal, substantial, underlying basis or locus

[13] Matsumoto Shiro, *Engi to ku, Nyoraiso shiso hihan* (Dependent origination and Emptiness), Tokyo: Daiso publishers 1989.

on which everything else depends upon or arises from."[14] To Matsumoto, the existence of this "locus" is contrary to what Buddha had in mind. The idea of a "*nyoraiso*" (*tathāgata-garbha)*, a seed or womb of Buddhahood inherent in all sentient beings, is thus a deviation from true Buddhist thought. He also relates his criticism to the contemporary ethical situation and claims that the idea of *nyoraiso* actually leads to discrimination; as all differences between good and bad, strong and weak, poor and rich according to the principle of *nyoraiso* are eliminated and everything attains the same validity. The misunderstood and frequently held doctrine of Buddhahood, he argues, thus supports discrimination and injustice. The doctrine of dependent arising is not an arising from and a return to an all-encompassing One. The doctrine does not signify a "thing" but points at a sequence of nonessential properties.

In his third chapter,[15] Matsumoto confronts the modern Japanese ideas held by critics such as Umehara Takeshi, who adheres to "proto-shinto" ideology – that is, the view that Japanese society is permeated by fundamental Shinto conceptions. Umehara supports an understanding of Japanese Buddhism in accordance with Prince Shotoku's ideas of harmony (*wa*) from the seventh century. He supports the view of universal Buddhahood, also held by personalities such as Shinto ideologist Motoori Norinaga and postwar writers Kawabata Yasunari and Mishima Yukio. The proto-shinto view is traditionally marketed in the West as "Japanese Buddhism." As a Buddhist himself, Matsumoto rejects such ideas. He concludes his chapter by stating that we are inclined by nature to love ourselves and our country; however, the "Japanese Buddhist" establishment doctrine implies rejecting self and loving only the "other" (God or Buddha). He concludes with the following strong sentence: Buddhists should not love Japan. [16]

The other famous critique of establishment Buddhism is Hakamaya Noriaki, also of Komazawa University. Hakamaya maintains that to be a Buddhist is to be critical – and puts forward his understanding of Buddhism as criticism. In his book *Critical Buddhism*[17] he censures the Kyoto school for its basic philosophical premises, which he sees as a form of *hongaku shiso* – the

---

14 Hubbard / Swanson, *Pruning the Bodhi Tree*, 9.

15 The chapter is called "Bukkyō to Shinji " (Buddhism and Shinto Rituals. Considerations contra Japanism), cf. Matsumoto Shiro, *Engi to ku, Nyoraiso shiso hihan*, 99ff

16 Matsumoto Shiro, *Engi to ku, Nyoraiso shiso hihan*, 99ff

17 Hakamaya Noriaki, *Hihan Bukkyo* (Critical Buddhism), Tokoyo: Daiso Publishers 1990.

idea of an inherent enlightenment in all sentient beings, and he does not consider the differences between Tanabe and Nishida to be large enough for alternative evaluations. Like his colleague Matsumoto, Hakamaya discounts the affiliation between Buddhism and socioreligious harmony (*wa*), which he views as a practical excuse for uncritical syncretism and as a theoretical fulcrum for political elites in coercing uniformity from above. In place of the essentialist dimensions of enlightenment doctrine, Hakamaya recommends the practice of faith. Referring to the Lotus Sūtra, he interprets faith as believing in the words of Buddha and then distinguishing rationally between what is right and what is wrong. The idea of the ultimate is here given an eschatological tinge and contrasted with essentialist ideas. Despite its analytic sophistication, however, Critical Buddhism fails to reconcile the philosophical disjuncture between immanent reality and Buddhist ultimacy. While the attempt is to refute what is perceived as a veiled essentialist doctrine in favor of a non-essentialist view, the polemics of Critical Buddhism merely swing in opposition to their opponents and thereby end in replicating the kind of dualism they seek to avoid.

Ultimacy in Engaged Buddhism

The premises of Engaged Buddhism can be traced back to the Thai Buddhist monk Buddhadasa. His interpretation of Buddhism has a marked emphasis on relevance to daily life, whereby "ultimate" conceptions such as *nirvāṇa* are interpreted in social terms. This Buddhism has maintained its social emphasis and relevancy and counts as one of its remarkable achievements the nonviolent struggle with the American intervention in Vietnam in the 1960s. Prominent among its adherents was the Vietnamese Buddhist Thich Nhat Hanh, who later on moved to Europe and currently continues his socioreligious activities at a center in France, Plum Village. The Siamese lay Buddhist Sulak Sivaraksa has also actively supported Engaged Buddhism, with a strong emphasis on social justice and liberation from suppression. Ecological awareness has become a chief concern of the movement– not least, the struggle to preserve forests in Thailand. The movement sees itself as a counterforce to social oppression and consumerism on a world scale. Currently based in Sulak Sivaraksa's Bangkok, Engaged Buddhism operates through a global network.

Participants come from diverse religious backgrounds, illustrating its wide, ecumenical character. [18]

In spite of a radical character reminiscent of Critical Buddhism, this movement is based on a social transformation. Nirvāṇa is not a concept "beyond," it is a social reality. Enlightenment implies social understanding. I am tempted, therefore, to conclude that this Buddhist stream conceives ultimacy as an incarnational reality, one that avoids the dualist conundrum with its stress on truth in praxis.

What Kind of Ultimacy?

In the wake of this brief survey of main Buddhist tenets, the question remains: How are the relationships between immanent reality and ultimate reality in Buddhism reconciled and combined? It is clear that there is a strong *tradition* within Japanese Buddhism that adheres to a universal concept of Buddha nature. A "Buddha nature" originating in a synthesis of political and religious concerns dominates the image of the ultimate in mainstream Japanese Buddhism, under girded by the "harmony" principle of Prince Shotoku in the sixth, and Saicho and Kukai in the ninth, century, that is maintained more or less to this very day. Ideas of a primordial Buddha nature stemming from an original Buddhism are enforced by the continued interaction between people in the private sector and those in officiating Buddhist institutions. The ultimate appears in the immanent world by means of a dynamic which might be termed "uncritical incarnation." It actually means that the horizon of Buddhist ultimate reality in terms of enlightenment, non-self, and dependent origination is determined by its integration into a category formed by the needs of the people and of the political authorities.

---

18 A number of publications have come out of this strand of concern. Cf. Sulak Sivaraksa, *Seeds of Peace: A Buddhist Vision for Renewing Society* (Prefaced by Dalai Lama and Thich Nhat Hanh), International Network of Engaged Buddhism, Bangkok 1992; Johnathan Watts, *Entering the Realm of Reality: Towards Dhammic Societies*, Suksitg Siam, Bangkok 1997.

Against "uncritical incarnation" there are frequent instances of marked protest. Already during the early stages of Buddhist history, there were attempts to foster a pure religiosity aloof from state influence or popular religious practice. The Lotus scripture, formed by a critical, revivalist, and egalitarian ethos, has played an important role in this process. This scripture has often inspired what we might term "prophetic" Buddhism. The Buddhist thought of Buddhadasa and his successor Sulak Sivaraksa stems from a Thai context and might be termed similarly. In addition to these "critical incarnationists" a new critical scholarly tradition has emerged, particularly in Japan. One might point to the more radical dialectics of Tanabe Hajime in his postwar philosophy of repentance. Here he breaks with the uncritical incarnational thought of his predecessor Nishida and promotes a radical ultimacy based on his philosophical interpretation of the Buddha. This type of ultimacy – a radical *metanoia* – I prefer to term "critical incarnation."

In the final analysis, however, it must be said that the clearest formulation to date of Buddhist ultimacy can be observed in the academic tradition of Komazawa University, presently represented by the two Zen academics Matsumoto and Hakamaya, both with a strong Buddhist and scholarly commitment. Following a Western inspired tradition of historical criticism, represented earlier by Watanabe Shoko, these scholars resort to original Buddhist texts that imply strong and broad social criticism. They speak for a Buddhism from a time before relationships to the state were established: a Buddhism of a *saṅgha* with pure religious concerns. I would argue that another factor has influenced this trend in thinking: Western democracy and global communication have brought forth the "postmodern," which resonates with Buddhist insight and thus gives contextual incentive and reinforcement to the development of Buddhist thought on the topic of ultimacy. Yet the sharp criticism of "Buddha nature" by Matsumoto and Hakamaya seems to imply a view of Buddhist ultimacy that stands in a dualist relation to immanent reality. Is "critical dualism" then an appropriate term? However it is labeled, it seems clear that a purely critical standpoint unmotivated by the social is not possible as a means to reconcile questions of ultimacy and immanence. As we have seen, the Buddhist "beyond" shapes up differently across the board – ranging from a synthesis of ultimacy and social concerns on one hand to a dualist tension between ultimate Buddha and social reality on the other.

Norbert Hintersteiner

Intercultural and Interreligious (Un)Translatibility and the Comparative Theology Project

Comparative Theology, Old and New

It is reported that on September 11, 1893, marking the commencement of the first World's Parliament of Religions, the Liberty Bell at the Columbian Exposition in Chicago was sounded ten times in honour of "what were [then] considered the world's ten great religions: Hinduism, Buddhism, Jainism, Zoroastiranism, Taoism, Confucianism, Shintoism, Judaism, Chrisitianity, and Islam."[1] Those ten religions did send delegates to the Parliament, where each religious group was asked to "make the best and most comprehensive statement of the faith it holds and the service it claims to have rendered to mankind."[2]

Among the European scholars invited was one of the greatest sons of Holland, the pioneering Dutch Calvinist scholar of religion Cornelius Petrus Tiele (1830-1902), who had been teaching the history of religions at Leiden since 1873 and became professor there in 1877. Interestingly enough, while Tiele, in the ensuing years, evolved to become one of the principal founders of the Scientific Study of Religion, the public address he wrote in 1893 for the first World's Parliament of Religion was titled "On the Study of Comparative Theology."[3] With this topic he could be sure to address issues that were at once proper to his individual scholarly expertise, appreciated by open-minded Protestant circles and at the same time relevant to the ecumenical concerns of the Parliament.

Today, we hardly remember that in the latter half of the nineteenth century, Comparative Theology was a very popular, highly regarded, and respect-

---

1 R.H. Seager, *The Dawn of Religious Pluralism: Voices from the World Parliament of Religions, 1893* (La Salle, 1993), 15.

2 J.M. Kitagawa, "The History of Religions in America," in *The History of Religions* (1987): 5.

3 Cornelius P. Tiele, "On the Study of Comparative Theology," in John Henry Barrows (ed.), *The World's Parliament of Religions: An Illustrated and Popular Story of the World's First Parliament of Religions, Held in Chicago in connection with the Columbian Exposition of 1893*, vol. 1 (Chicago, 1893), 583-90.

able intellectual-spiritual pursuit.[4] To be sure, different from what Comparative Religion and the Scientific Study of Religion became later on, comparative theology in its study of world religions then drew the self-same conclusion as Christian theology, that Christianity was fundamentally different from all other religions, and thus, in the last analysis, beyond compare. This singularity of Christianity was often expressed in a vaguely oxymoronic phrase: "uniquely universal."

In the opinion of these first theological comparativists, Christianity alone was truly transhistorical and transnational in its import, hence universally valid and viable at any place, anytime; whereas all other religions were particular, bound and shaped by geographical, ethnic, and other local contingencies. The "uniquely universal" religion of Christ was seen as the religion of the world. The argument appears to have been that one must first be fully convinced of the unique and universal truth of Christianity before one can even begin to view other religions with equanimity. Sharing this perspective, comparative religionists were dedicated in the later half of the 19th century to intensive study of the various religions in all their branches, with the goal of facilitating comparisons between Christianity as the absolute religion with other religions, for the ultimate purpose of proving that Christianity alone is the perfect religion that includes the best features of all religions and surpasses them in fulfilment.

The value-laden panoramic survey of "old," "inferior," and "false" religions, which these comparative religious studies provided, with its evangelizing and missionizing agenda so unequivocally pronounced, would likely not only embarrass contemporary scholars of religion but also offend the pluralist doctrine of today's world religions discourse more generally. Today, it has become a prevailing ethic and custom to edit out from both academic and public discourses on religion any sign of hierarchical valuation, any overt expression of self-serving and self-elevating motives lurking behind the work of comparison – that is, motives other than those in the interest of science or of the ecumenical harmony of the world. Nowadays, we generally discredit such claims as naive at best, disingenuous at worst. However, the difference between them then and us today might seem less a matter of greater or lesser scientific sophistication or divergent analytic principles; rather, it may have to

4 Comparable with the contemporary world religions discourse; cf. T. Masuzawa, *The Invention of World Religions* (Chicago, 2005), ch. 2, "The Legacy of Comparative Theology," 72-104.

do more with whether one feels *entitled* to hold a certain stance – such as regarding the compatibility between Christian universalism and comparative religion – and to announce it in public. And since we find ourselves incapable of taking these pronouncements seriously, there is little incentive today to reexamine the nineteenth-century reasoning that might have made it feasible for these authors to advance such an argument in earnest.

Finally, on a side note, history has it that the first Dutch scholarly comparative theology record, Tiele's address prepared for the World's Parliament of Religions in 1893, in the end struggled less with the argument of a religiously unique stance of a comparative theologian vis a vis a more or less biased comparative religion scholar, but more with what might otherwise be conceived as the Dutch problem of international visibility: The aging savant of the old world – Tiele was 63 years old by then – chose namely to participate at the World's Parliament of Religions from afar, sending his essay to be read, rather than appearing in person at the "jubilee of civilization."

However, while Comparative Theology was a vital discourse at some places in Europe in Tiele's times – a discourse which, due to the intellectually biased stances taken, became critiqued and rejected by the evolving disciplines of Comparative Religion and Religious Studies in the 20th century – today, some of the more compelling influences in the field come from the United States.

And indeed, during the last two decades, in the Anglo-American world, comparative theology as the theologically conscious study of religions other than one's own has become – once again and most assuredly under a different paradigm – an exciting and quickly developing field. Scholars have produced an increasing number of studies that either the authors or others have identified explicitly as "comparative theology," new groups and academic affiliations have been formed under this name, and professorships for this field are getting established at high and low ranking universities. To be sure, as we find with the related discourse of intercultural theology, comparative theology is a constructive and reflective theological discipline that is mature in neither its theoretical nor its practical dimensions. As indicated earlier, important historical lessons from its prehistory and its 19th century legacy still need to be learned in its new contemporary usage and unfolding.

Given the new beginnings of comparative theology, it shall be interesting and beneficial to at least assess, in a preliminary fashion, some of the questions and theses put forward in the newly evolving discipline. I would like to do this in four steps: First, I will locate comparative theology at the crossroads of crosscultural and interreligious translation processes, accompanied by a claim that theology always was and is an inherently comparative discipline. Second, I will then give an understanding of the practice of comparative theology through some of its contemporary definitions. Third, this is followed by an analysis ad exemplum of the comparative work of one of the pioneers of contemporary comparative theology, Francis Clooney, including some systematic points which become visible as essential in the contemporary fabric of a new comparative theology. Finally, I will conclude with a heuristic lense as epistemologically instructive entry point to the discourse and practice of comparative theology; namely, the matter of translatibility or untranslatability of concepts and traditions.

I. Locating Comparative Theology

Before we approach the contemporary practice of comparative theology, let us be reminded that reflection on "other religious traditions," though articulated in various ways, has occurred in the Christian tradition from its beginnings. Other religious traditions around the world too have had to shape their self-understanding in light of their religious others, before comparative theology as an academic discipline pathed its way.

Theology, in this sense, argues John Renard – an early advocate for comparative theology in its new appearance –, has always been an inherently comparative discipline:[5] He claims that major developments within the theological systems of communities of faith frequently grow out of at least implicit comparisons among systems of thought or doctrinal options presented by those communities as they define themselves. Such implicit comparison is part of the larger process of "development of doctrine." He further suggests that the history of religious thought also offers examples of explicitly comparative thinking of several kinds. Many have been in response to the adversarial impulse we find in polemical and apologetical writings. In addition, he mentions the theological genre known as "heresiography": While it often arises from apologetical motives and ultimately serves polemical purposes, sometimes it hints at the beginnings of a more dispassionate and "objective" account of how theological schools develop and disappear. Along these lines,

[5] John Renard, "Comparative Theology: Definition and Method," in *Religious Studies and Theology* 17 (1998): 3-18, here 3-4.

he thinks that one also finds examples of explicitly comparative thinking that take serious account of other systems, acknowledging the best they have to offer and even appropriating and incorporating congenial elements. Thomas Aquinas' evaluation of important features in the thought of major Jewish and Muslim thinkers, is a prominent example, even when Thomas ends up passing a negative judgment. Other examples, Renard names, are the processes and results of Christianity's encounters with, and efforts to accommodate new cultural matrices, the comparative theological practices expressed and exemplified in the various missionary translation efforts.

Francis Clooney, the most outspoken of the new American comparative theologians, too, claims,

> that keeping with its history as a primarily Christian enterprise rooted in particular crosscultural and interreligious encounters, comparative theology lies in closest continuity, not with the theology of religions as a discipline dedicated to thinking about religions, but with the concrete crosscultural and interreligious encounters of Christians with other cultures and traditions as well as with missionary scholarship, wherein theorizing about one's religious others occurs in particular places and frequently in close conversation with those others.[6]

At the Crossroads of Crosscultural Translations

Given comparative theology's crosscultural location, a more recent set of reflection in the related academic discipline of crosscultural (or intercultural) theology with its roots in missiology is important to recall here; namely, when it theorizes and studies the practice of missionary translation and crosscultural theological development.

On a scholarly basis Lamin Sanneh's *Translating the Message: The Missionary Impact on Culture* (1989) has been recognized in this regard as one of the most illuminating treatises on the signifance of missionary translation.[7] In contrast to the Muslims' "nontranslatability" of the sacred Arabic, according to Sanneh, the Christian expansion has been rooted on "the principle of translatability."[8] The translatability of Christianity made the missionary translators

---

6 Cf. F.X. Clooney, "Comparative Theology," in *The Oxford Handbook of Systematic Theology*, ed. by J. Webster, K. Tanner, and I. Torrance (Oxford, 2007) (forthcoming).

7 L. Sanneh, *Translating the Message: The Missionary Impact on Culture* (Maryknoll, 1989).

8 Sanneh, *Translating the Message*, 197.

"the agent of such cultural incubation of Christianity by exposing the message to new climates, believing that cultural differences, however deep and ancient, could not constitute an impenetrable barrier against crosscultural exchange."[9]

Andrew Walls, former missiologist in Edinburough, adds somewhat more theological moments to reflection on crosscultural missionary translation. He views the history of salvation as beginning with God's divine activity of translation from which the missionary retranslation of Christian faith into vernacular languages has been required and legitimated in Christian history. He claims:

> Divinity is translated into humanity, but into specific humanity, at home in specific segments of social reality. If the Incarnation of the Son represents a divine act of translation, it is a prelude to repeated acts of re-translation as Christ fills the Pleroma again – other aspects of social reality.[10]

The missionary encounters with other religions in Christian history and the subsequent translations of the Christian message into the vernacular languages have transformed the confessional continuity of Christian faith, as the traditional authenticity of Christian faith of the Western world has been challenged by the vernacular operation of the non-European languages. Through the missionaries' crosscultural translation, says Walls, the Christian faith

> is effectively expanded, put to new use; but the translated element from the source language has also, in a sense, been expanded by translation; the receptor language has a dynamic of its own and takes the new material to realms it never touched in the source language.[11]

Walls further argues that the vernacular operation of translation is "not about substitution, the replacement of something old by something new, but about *transformation*, the turning of the already existing to new account."[12]

As indicated already above, Francis Clooney too acknowledges the connection of crosscultural theology and comparative theology. He claims that comparative theology is linked to the study of Christianity's crosscultural processes and therefore heir to a long and rich tradition of exchange – being a

---

9 Sanneh, *Translating the Message*, 198.

10 A. Walls, *The Missionary Movement in Christian History: Studies in Transmission of Faith* (Maryknoll, 1996), xvii and 26-27.

11 Walls, *The Missionary Movement*, 29.

12 Walls, *The Missionary Movement*, 29.

positive phenomenon, despite the dark side of colonialist missions – and shares with missionary writings a deep practical concern for the particularities of other religious traditions and for the specific ways in which the Christian faith interacts with different faiths. Clooney thinks that despite numerous misunderstandings and tragic and shameful moments of hostility and violence, we can affirm that throughout history the Christian relationship with various religious cultures has nonetheless often proceeded with subtlety, sophistication, and boldness. Therefore, one needs to acknowledge that constructive interreligious exchange has been occurring for a very long time, and comparative theology is not an entirely new beginning.[13]

An Example: "The Church in the Shadow of the Mosque"

To introduce an historical example of comparative theology being rooted in crosscultural and interreligious translational practice and discourse, I want to hint us to the seldom told story of the Christians from the 8th and 9th century onwards in the Middle East, who at home in the world of Islam, came to express their very denominational identities in the idiom of Islamic religious culture and in translational encounter with the evolving patterns of Islamic religious thought: As those Christians of the now called Oriental Churches found themselves as having to live more permanently as "Church in the Shadow of the Mosque," as Sidney Griffith in his pioneering research on this unique history so aptly puts it,[14] those Oriental Christians then adopted the Arabic language. Here we can picture two Arabic-speaking, religious communities (Christians and Muslims) influencing one another through language and practice in daily social, economic and intellectual intercourse. We can certainly imagine the opportunities provided to them for what might nowadays be called a translational comparative theological process that inevitably gave way to the development of Christian theology in a new register.

As Griffith elaborates, the translational process and comparative theological enterprise are visible to us now in the ways their writers articulated their Christian doctrines in parallel to, and almost in tandem with, the evol-

[13] Cf. Clooney, "Comparative Theology."

[14] In the following I rely on S. Griffith, *The Church in the Shadow of the Mosque* (Princeton, 2007 [forthcoming]). Griffith's pioneering work in this field shows how the earliest Christian treatises in Arabic are carried from both, crosscultural translations (theological and philosophical) and comparative theological processes.

ving patterns of Islamic religious thought during the same historical period: Christians sought to defend the reasonableness of their distinctive doctrines in terms of religious idiom they shared with their Muslim interlocutors and counterparts, who, in accord with the teachings of the Qur'ān, often rejected the central Christian doctrines. In contrast with the previously standard modes of Christian discourse in Greek or Syriac, the Arabic-speaking Christian writers, Griffith elaborates, often constructed their arguments on ways of thinking which the Muslims had initially elaborated in view of commending their own faith in the Qur'ān and in the traditions of the prophet Muhammad. More often than not, these Christian texts appear to be exercises in a Christian version of *kalām*, the characteristically Islamic style of religious discourse in Arabic. The apologetic agenda for the Christian *mutakallimūn* (theological controversialists, systematic theologians) in the Islamic world was largely set then via a translational act in response to the challenges to Christian faith voiced by Muslims in the early Islamic period.

Griffith illuminates that the outcome of such a crosscultural as well as interreligious translational encounter and comparative theological process is that the discourse of the Christian *kalām* acquires a unique conceptual profile. For example, the approach here to the doctrines of the Trinity and the Incarnation reveal an effort to express the former in terms of the contemporary Islamic discussion of the ontological status of the divine attributes, the Qur'ān's "beautiful names of God," and the latter in terms of the Islamic discussion of the signs of authentic prophecy and true religion. The intention of the Christian discourse composed in the Arabic language was certainly both to sustain the faith of Christians living in that world and to commend the reasonableness and credibility of Christianity to their Muslim neighbors in their own religious idiom. Griffith tells us, however, that most of the Arabic Christian writers strove to translate and to clarify the doctrines and distinctive confessional formulae of their several denominations in their Arabic treatises and tracts, rather than to rethink in the Islamic milieu how best to articulate the Christian message anew.

To close this window into a particular historical example of comparative theology rooted in crosscultural and interreligious translation and to link it with a notion of comparative theology which shows an openness for a rereading of the religious past towards future learning, Jack Renard's definition shall be quoted here. He writes in his article from 1998:

> [Comparative theology, or theology in comparative context,] is the study of how theological change has taken place historically in the context of interreligious relations, and of the implications of serious interchange between and among religious traditions for the future of Christian theology.[15]

Regarding Renards definition of comparative theology asking for implications of historical research on interreligious encounter and theological change for contemporary and future theology, one could at least say two things building on the above example: First, the claim of Oriental Churches's history to be the imperative ground for interreligious dialogue between Christians and Muslims seems to be unimpeachable especially since it is true that even through the long centuries of mutual hostilities the fortunes of the two communities have become, more than ever, inextricably intertwined. Second, one would hope that contemporary intercultural and comparative theology, intent as it is upon establishing friendly relations with Islam in many parts of Europe today, could acknowledge these Christians' long experience of living – with all consequences – in the "Shadow of the Mosque," and thus give them a more prominent voice in contemporary theological discourse, thereby translating their contextual theological struggles and acchievements toward the goal of effective intercultural exchange with Muslims today.

II. Comparative Theology in Its Modern Definitions

As one surveys today's practice of comparative theology, one discerns that it has various motivations. For some it is focused on the fact of religious pluralism and the diversity that surrounds us today; for others, it begins with a sense of religious mission towards people of other religions; for still others, it is simply

> *fides quaerens intellectum, faith seeking understanding,* in a world of many religions, when the world's complex religious diversity and its richly diverse religious traditions have become a topic of explicit consideration, and when the theologian is willing to understand better his or her faith in light of that pluralism in its particular forms, perhaps impelled too by a sense of responsibility to aid one's own community to live better in the pluralistic context; and still others may under-

[15] Renard, "Comparative Theology," 6.

> take comparative theology primarily on intellectual grounds, because comparative study is interesting and challenging for theologians as it is for religionists.[16]

Given the historical perspective on comparative theology we gained thus far, let us now turn to a few explicit definitions of comparative theology. Besides the one of Jack Renard given above, I limit myself here to only three authors: David Tracy, Keith Ward, and Francis Clooney, giving extra weight to present Clooney's contributions, due to his pioneering work in the field.[17]

For a view into the formal beginnings of the dominant contemporary understandings of comparative theology, I refer us to David Tracy's essay in the Macmillan *Encyclopedia of Religion* (First edition, 1987).[18] Tracy, a systematic theologian at the Divinity School at the University of Chicago, argued already in 1987 that the fact that

> theology itself is now widely considered one discipline within the multidisciplinary field of religious studies impels contemporary theology, in whatever tradition, to become a comparative theology ... on strictly theological grounds; the fact of religious pluralism should enter all theological assessment and self-analysis in any tradition at the very beginning of its task.[19]

Tracy underscores two important features of comparative theology. First, it is a discipline within the history of religions, in which theologies from different traditions are compared; second, it is "a more strictly theological enterprise ... which ordinarily studies not one tradition alone but two or more, compared on theological grounds"[20] – apparently for the purposes of the Christian theologian. For Tracy, comparative theology indicates either a straightforward comparison of theologies by an observer who may or may not be a theologian, or an evaluative comparison of doctrines by a theologian from one of the compared traditions.

---

16 Cf. F. X. Clooney, "The Emerging Field of Comparative Theology: A Bibliographical Review (1989-95)," in *Theological Studies* 56.3 (1995), 521-550, here 521.

17 At the same rank, one also would need to explore the work of David Burrell, James Fredericks, John Renard, and Robert C. Neville for their profound contributions in contemporary comparative theology and towards reshaping it as a viable discipline. For the latter cf. his essay in this volume, 513-29.

18 David Tracy, "Comparative Theology," in: *Encyclopedia of Religion* 14 (1987), 446-55.

19 Tracy, "Comparative Theology," 446.

20 Tracy, "Comparative Theology," 446.

Keith Ward, an Anglican, formerly Regius Professor Emeritus of Divinity at Oxford University, in his four volumes in comparative Christian systematic theology, has also stressed the necessarily interreligious nature of theologizing as it is reconceived today, indicating in 1994

> that theology is the discipline of reflection upon ideas of the ultimate reality and goal of human life, of God, and of revelation. It can be undertaken by people of many diverse beliefs. It is better undertaken in knowledge of and in conversation with those of beliefs other than one's own.[21]

Consequently, people who theologize according to this awareness explore given theological topics – such as creation or revelation – in several traditions and then articulate positions in light of common features that have been discovered. Such scholars deserve to be recognized as "full and proper theologians." Ward also proposes to distinguish between confessional theology and comparative theology. By confessional he means "the exploration of a given revelation by one who wholly accepts the revelation and lives by it," and by comparative theology, "an intellectual discipline which enquires into ideas of the ultimate value and goal of human life, as they have been perceived and expressed in a variety of religious traditions."[22] The former is focused on specific revelation, the latter on God's wider work in the world. Ward locates his work in systematic theology in the latter category as primarily comparative and not confessional in nature, even if they quite evidently shed light on the doctrines and values considered in confessional theology. Ward, in his project, investigates broad themes across a range of world religious traditions, but lacks the close engagement with the particulars of other faith traditions and remains unspecific to what extent his confessional theology actually changes, while broadly studying and comparing traditions on certain themes.

Francis Clooney, Professor for Comparative Theology at Harvard Divinity School in Boston / Cambridge, has been developing his method of comparative theology for quite some time and can be considered as the most prolific of schoolars in contemporary comparative theology. Clooney, both a trained Indologist and a Jesuit theologian, has specialized in Sanskritic and Tamil theological literature. From there, he has pursued his Christian theology in dialogue with many of the theologies of Hindu traditions, well aware that the

---

21 K. Ward, "Towards a Comparative Theology," in *idem*, *Revelation and Religion: A Theology of Revelation in the World's Religions* (Oxford, 1994), 3-49, here 46. Cf. T.W. Bartel, *Comparative Theology: Essays for Keith Ward* (London, 2003).

22 Ward, "Towards a Comparative Theology," 46ff.

great theological differences that separate Vedic religions from Biblical religions are unlikely to collapse any time soon.

Clooney has been developing his method of comparative theology for quite some time. In his 1990 essay "Reading the World in Christ" he offers a succinct view of his methods and their benefits:

> I will describe the practice of comparative theology as the dialectical activity of reading and rereading the Bible and other Christian texts in a new context formed by non-Christian texts; I will argue that this activity brings about a significant change in one's Christian theology, even before an explicit theological assessment of the phenomenon takes place.[23]

And in a 1995 survey article on developments in comparative theology, Clooney suggests that one can understand comparative theology as "constructive theology"

> distinguished by its sources and ways of proceeding, by its foundation in more than one tradition (although the comparativist remains rooted in one tradition), and by reflection which builds on that foundation, rather than simply on themes or methods already articulated prior to the comparative practice. Comparative theology in this third sense is a theology deeply changed by its attention to the details of multiple religious and theological traditions; it is a theology that occurs only after comparison."[24]

Clooney has maintained these basic positions, though he has refined them over the years.

III. Clooney's Comparative Theology

In order to understand contemporary comparative theology beyond some of its definitions, it is useful to take a closer look to the actual comparative theological work being done by its contemporary pioneers and outstanding figures. In the following, I shall do this ad exemplum by studying Clooney's comparative theological work more closely. First, I will look at his process and practice of comparative theology as visible in his monographs, and second I will present some of the more systematic points on the discipline of comparative theology which he himself finds evolving from the actual work

[23] F. X. Clooney, "Reading the World in Christ," in G. D'Costa, *Christian Uniqueness Reconsidered: The Myth of a Pluralistic Theology of Religions* (Maryknoll, 1990), 64.

[24] Clooney, "The Emerging Field of Comparative Theology," 522.

being done in the field, formulating core issues of the emerging new discipline.

Projects and Process

Clooney to date has authored eight monographs. Four of them contain his most sustained analysis of the process of comparative theology: *Theology After Vedanta: An Experiment in Comparative Theology* (1993), *Seeing through Texts: Doing Theology Among the Srivaisnavas of South India* (1996), *Hindu God, Christian God: How Reason Helps Break Down the Boundaries between Religions* (2001), and *Divine Mother, Blessed Mother: Hindu Goddesses and the Virgin Mary* (2005). In these books, he describes himself as "a comparative theologian" who prefers to allow juxtaposed texts of diverse religious traditions to inform one another and transform those who read them.

Clooney's probing of *how* this happens is less pronounced, and secondary to his primary objective to learn from Hindu texts and allow that knowledge to transform his understanding of Christian texts. A certain amount of development in Clooney's work over the twelve years of inquiry presented by these four books, and the progression is pronounced, with each book building upon the others towards a more complex understanding of comparative theology, while breaking ground in some areas to expand the field's conceptual territory.

Each of Clooney's books contains a greater or lesser amount of commentary on the process of comparative theology itself, though the bulk of this writing involves the explication of a particular Hindu text or texts along with their formal commentaries. This is all undertaken against the backdrop of religious practice, which Clooney illustrates so that a Christian reader, unfamiliar with a tradition, can fruitfully engage with its texts. Clooney then proposes some comparative readings in Christian literature, sometimes leaving it at that, while at other times conducting a back and forth reading of the juxtaposed material.

In the following, I bring forth some of Clooney's main points regarding the process of comparative theology as found in four books.

Clooney's *Theology After Vedanta: An Experiment in Comparative Theology* builds on his earlier indological study, *Thinking Ritually: Rediscovering the Purva Mimamsa of Jaimini*, and is, as the title indicates, an extended exercise in comparative theology, guiding the reader through Christian texts in light of Advaita Vedanta texts.[25] Clooney opens with some guiding principles of the practice of Advaita Vedanta and demonstrates how they offer Christian theologians a basic framework for comparative theology. The middle three chapters contain an analysis of an Advaita Vedanta text, the Uttara Mimamsa Sutras. In the final chapter, Clooney undertakes a comparative reading of the Uttara Mimamsa Sutras and Thomas Aquinas' *Summa Theologiae*, suggesting two specific similarities in the texts. This last chapter also contains further analysis of the process of comparative theology and a list of strategies for pursuing it. The insights into the process of comparative theology developed by Clooney in *Theology after Vedanta* center on three themes, 1) the claim that religious texts are rooted in a tradition, and so are their readers; 2) the suggestion that engaging with religious texts can transform the reader; and 3) the assertion that the results can be useful and justifiable but not definitive.

As distinct from comparative religion, comparative theology does not ask readers to bracket their own beliefs when engaging the beliefs of another tradition. Their own beliefs and belief in the importance of knowledge compel readers to seek out the ideas of others who believe differently and to evaluate those beliefs. The religious ideas encountered in a particular text can only be understood when seen in their original context. Clooney therefore advocates reading religious texts along with their formal traditional commentaries, their related scriptures, and in light of normative religious practice. Together these become "the Text" which becomes the source of the definitive meaning of any particular passage. To understand and evaluate a religious text of another tradition requires a reader to become deeply and holistically engaged in that tradition.

To practice comparative theology well, comparativists must, says Clooney, "renounce comfortable presuppositions and convenient shortcuts to truth."[26] "If comparison really does enrich our knowledge of God, this increase will only occur gradually .... We cannot tell at a glance what the other tradition will teach us."[27] If comparative theology is committed to writing

---

25 F.X. Clooney, *Theology After Vedanta: An Experiment in Comparative Theology* (Albany, 1993); *idem*, *Thinking Ritually: Rediscovering the Pūrva Mīmāmsā of Jaimini* (Vienna, 1990).

26 Clooney, *Theology After Vedanta*, 167.

27 Clooney, *Theology After Vedanta*, 197.

from this widened Text framework, the available lexicon for research and reflection will continually be enriched, and the challenge to comparative theologians to rethink their own tradition's theology after serious engagement with another tradition will become self-evident. The final determination of truth, of evaluating the theology of another tradition and ones own, will have to be deferred until after comparison is complete, "not merely as the restatement of an earlier position after a brief detour into comparison."[28]

Perhaps the most important result of this sea change in comparative theology is that the kind of engagement it entails begins to transform readers as they move from the stance of passive observers of a text to participants in the Text. As comparativists rethink their home tradition, they are not likely to make or refute truth claims about another tradition based on any perceived degree of correspondence to their own tradition. For instance, Christians are not likely to replace "Jesus Saves" with "knowledge of Brahman saves," or even to place these concepts on par with one another. Moreover, Clooney suggests that the Christian comparativist may loose the ability to make the claim that knowledge of Brahman does not save.

On a practical level, in *Theology After Vedanta*, Clooney puts forward five strategies for reading texts from different traditions comparatively.[29] The first is "coordination," which takes into account similar terms, themes, and parallel modes of operation in the compared texts. Second is "superimposition," which temporarily imposes one reality onto another for the sake of reflection and heuristic change in perspective. Third, Clooney suggests that we place the texts in conversation with each other. Fourth is attentiveness to metaphoric, diaphoric, and epiphoric tensions brought into relief by the juxtaposition of texts. These tensions – interpreting them, synthesizing them, or extending their meanings through comparison – powerfully compel the reader to engage with the material. The fifth strategy is to arrange texts in collage, thereby unsettling previous understandings of any given text by removing it from its "legitimate" context. Clooney concludes that these strategies are not meant to be definitive, because comparative theology cannot produce definitive results.

---

[28] Clooney, *Theology After Vedanta*, 187.

[29] Clooney, *Theology After Vedanta*, 168-75.

Clooney's *Seeing Through Texts: Doing Theology among the Srivaisnavas of South India*[30] focuses on the Tiruvāymoli, a ninth century song about a young woman whose life figuratively came to an abrupt halt when she went to visit a temple in Tirutolaivillimankalam and there, with a glance, fell in love with the Lord Nārāyaňa For the rest of her life, she could not forget what she had seen. In a format similar to *Theology After Vedanta*, the first chapter of this book gives background information and suggests how we as modern Christians might read and understand the Tiruvāymoli. The next three chapters offer a more detailed analysis of the text, and the final chapter presents some readings of the Tiruvāymoli as compared with various Christian texts. The comparative endeavors in *Seeing Through Texts* are presented with the collage strategy detailed in *Theology After Vedanta*, with sections of the Tiruvāymoli juxtaposed with at least fifteen other texts from five Christian and one other Hindu source. Clooney does not analyze the significance of these specific comparative readings or follow any of them through. Rather, he challenges readers to draw their own conclusions about their meaning and to develop their own comparisons.

The most important new insight of this book on the process of comparative theology is within its title, "seeing through texts." Clooney discerns that religious texts have a way of making the realities of which they speak "real" as well as the potential to influence readers in dangerously effective ways. As he explains, words are windows. "Words make proximate what they obscure; understanding them, (re)voicing them, one begins to see through them: they are limited, and they are windows."[31] Seeing another tradition through its texts, "there is at least a possibility, perhaps a probability, that one is going to be drawn into what one studies and changed by it."[32] As the young woman at Tirutolaivillimankalam learned, glances are not always casual.

This potential danger is also the primary new benefit that the comparative method offers theology – its ability to transform theologians "who take seriously traditions other than their own while yet remembering where they are coming from."[33] To accomplish this, the contemporary theologian must read texts of other traditions along with the believers of other traditions, and in

---

30 F.X. Clooney, *Seeing Through Texts: Doing Theology among the Srivaisnavas of South India* (Albany, 1996).

31 Clooney, *Seeing Through Texts*, 9.

32 Clooney, *Seeing Through Texts*, 305.

33 Clooney, *Seeing Through Texts*, 251, cf. also 36.

ways that allow contemporary audiences to somehow establish familiarity while retaining point of view, "whereby we borrow their explanations without respecting their interpretations."[34] Their explanations draw us into the world-view of the text, a dangerous place to be, but our own prior commitments govern our understanding and appropriations of the material. In the end, we make up our own minds about the meanings of the texts we read.

Seeing Through Texts signals two additional important contributions by Clooney, his call for a move towards an incipient Hindu-Christian community and for a move away from the encompassing narratives of theologies of religion. Both of these movements are an outgrowth of Clooney's deferral of any comprehensive systematic interpretation of the comparative readings between Hindu and Christian texts. Such deferral is required, he argues, because of the currently limited amount of comparative understanding between these two religious groups, but there is no reason to demand that this deferral be indefinite. "It is surely reasonable to insist that at some point, after doing many comparisons and on that basis, comparative study put forward not simply a series of practical examples, but also a comprehensive and systematic explanation."[35] Such systematization must wait for the right conditions before it can proceed. One important condition is the growth of an integral community that shares these dual loyalties and thus needs a single, comprehensive perspective. Such a community has yet to form.[36] For the same reason, any encompassing narrative of a theology of religion should remain open and incomplete in order to leave room for new alignments and the drawing of new religious boundaries regarding who is inside and who is outside the community.[37]

In *Hindu God, Christian God: How Reason Helps Break Down the Boundaries between Religions*,[38] instead of focusing on one single Hindu text, each chapter pursues a particular topical question in systematic theology on the doctrine of God and gives the responses from a number of Christian and Hindu theologians. The overall effect is to show that there is already a great amount of overlap in systematic theological arguments between Hindu and Christian scholars.

---

34 Clooney, *Seeing Through Texts*, 35.

35 Clooney, *Seeing Through Texts*, 298.

36 Clooney, *Seeing Through Texts*, 299.

37 Cf. Clooney, *Seeing Through Texts*, 300-01.

38 F.X. Clooney, *Hindu God, Christian God: How Reason Helps Break Down the Boundaries between Religions* (Oxford, 2001).

Clooney situates his entire project in *Hindu God, Christian God* within the broader realm of Christian theology and within the broader category of a theology that crosses the boundaries of divers religions. In doing so, he offers his own views on the purpose of theology, details some of its important distinguishing features, and shares insights into his own methodology. *Hindu God, Christian God* also includes commentary on what sort of theology is appropriate for today and where Clooney hopes to see theology in the future. He adopts Anselm's view of theology as "faith seeking understanding," and in line with the rational character of the book, he stresses the noetic component of this, that the goal of theology is knowing God "more completely and intelligently."[39]

Clooney lists four aspects of theological discourse meant to foster this knowledge in today's world; to wit, theology should be interreligious, comparative, dialogical, and confessional. Clooney argues that theology can and frequently does operate across Hindu and Christian traditions based on a common logic that draws on disparate scriptural and traditional sources, but, he says, this common discourse does not demand common conclusions between Hindu and Christian theologians. Differences coexist with similarities, and Clooney offers no overarching theory that sees Hinduism or Christianity subsuming the other to become one religion. For Clooney, theology can be thought of as one thing, even though different religions cannot. Theological comparison works best when it opens into dialogical conversation between theologies, where theologians are accountable to one another in their willingness to speak, in their commitment to listen, and in their courage to argue with theologians from other traditions about what is plausible and theologically true. Clooney believes this kind of fruitful dialogue is possible because Christians and Hindus share something fundamental in common: human reason.

While Clooney argues that theology is one interrelated thing across religions and cultures, he argues in the opposite direction regarding religion itself, refusing to concede the unification of different religions. While advocating an inter-theology, Clooney does not necessarily advocate an inter-religion. Instead, Clooney tries to find "bridges of learning and reason to cross otherwise broad gaps between religious people possessed of their own dearly held beliefs."[40] It is unclear whether he would prefer the creation of a new

39 Clooney, *Hindu God, Christian God*, 7, cf. also 13 and 173.

40 Clooney, *Hindu God, Christian God*, 7.

inter-theology existing somewhere between established religious boundaries, or simply that the particular theology of each religion might benefit from a meaningful encounter with the theology of other traditions. He has argued on both sides of this issue, noting that the sides are not mutually exclusive. For example, Clooney suggests that a comparative theologian, in order to gain a deep reading of another religion's theology, might seek answers to questions about the convergence of religions in the following way:

> Is God "the God of our Lord Jesus Christ" or "Narayana, whose spouse is Laksmi" or "Siva, Lord of the Pasupata"? Is it a fact that God has become embodied in Jesus Christ but not in Rama and Krsna? Is the Word of God expressed in the words of the Veda and the Saiva Traditional Texts but not in the Bible? Does it matter whether I gaze upon a *linga* or a Sacred Heart image in my home? ... Though rhetorically impressive and in some ways logically urgent, such disjunctions, baldly stated, are not likely to be fruitful in an interreligious, comparative, and dialogical context. Again, even if such dichotomies and the choices they compel upon us originate in confessional theology, persuasive responses today still have to wait upon the hard work of a fully interreligious, comparative, dialogical, and (then) confessional theology. Resolving this dichotomy by proffering a firm choice is a fruitful though only initial step in this richer theology, which is Hindu, Christian, and more. Once it is made, one must still talk about it with fellow theologians who are members of other religious traditions.[41]

An important thing to note about this comparative approach is that it is necessarily oriented to the examination of details rather than entire religious systems. Throughout Hindu God, Christian God, Clooney demonstrates that when we look at the real details of specific theological positions and the polemical styles through which they are proffered in disparate religious systems, we find broad similaritities among specific differences. Even the way that different religions argue for their own uniqueness is often similar.[42] But such similarities and differences do not in themselves justify larger judgments about the absolute unity or plurality of different traditions. In this, Clooney contrasts his approach with the work of Jacques Dupuis, Mark Heim, and others in the recent theology of religions. Throughout his work, Clooney avoids offering any robust theology of religions, while he puts forward ideas that are requisite to developing such a theology. Clooney views his own approach as an alternative to varieties of interreligious dialogue and the theology-of-religions discourse that either rests on claims of a universal truth belonging to

---

[41] Clooney, *Hindu God, Christian God*, 179f.

[42] Cf. F.X. Clooney, "Hindu Views of Religious Others," in: *Theological Studies* 64 (2003): 332.

all religions or on Christianity's unique stance towards universalism. His ideas still lean towards inclusivism, but he is open to accepting other possible Christian theologies of religion as Christianity itself is transformed through the process of dialogue. For this reason, Clooney does not want to separate comparative and confessional theologies. They need to be distinguished, he concedes, but the most productive theological approach is a dynamic one that moves among and between them. The transformation that comes with this approach is Clooney's immediate comparative theological goal. Indeed, through each small transformation, entire religious systems could eventually be transformed, perhaps leading to a convergence of once separated traditions, perhaps not.

Clooney's *Divine Mother, Blessed Mother: Hindu Goddesses and the Virgin Mary* is in many respects a sequel to Hindu God, Christian God.[43] Here we see, not an encounter with rational brahmanical theologies, but an exploration of the potential for poetic imagery of worship and devotion to help break down the boundaries between religions. Clooney compares Hindu Goddess hymns to Christian Marian hymns by examining their literary metaphors and symbolic imagery in a manner that refuses to privilege any one text over the other. Clooney's method dwells in between the texts, "where the ideas and practices of Hindu and Marian devotional traditions are problematized and intensified by close proximity."[44] Clooney conducts a back and forth reading of the texts, and encourages the reader to do the same, with the firm conviction that as the hymns are read, they will lead the reader the devotional core of which they speak. This can be devotion to Mary or devotion to Sri, or devotion to one of the other goddesses studied, depending on the hymn. Each act of comparison bears its own internal logic and reveals intriguing insights into Christian theology. Further insight is then stimulated when different but related comparisons are examined as a group: for any particular comparison, Clooney resists offering a definitive analysis or interpretation.

The comparative readings undertaken in *Divine Mother, Blessed Mother* reveal intriguing similarities among the differences between various Hindu and Christian theologies, while resolutely maintaining that comparisons yielding different insights could be equally valid and useful, provided they are conducted with the same methodological care. It is not that doing comparative

43 F.X. Clooney, *Divine Mother, Blessed Mother: Hindu Goddesses and the Virgin Mary* (Oxford, 2005).

44 Clooney, *Divine Mother, Blessed Mother*, 24.

theology in general leads to any grand and resolute theory. Rather, particular comparisons yield particular insights, insights that might be revised in the future under the influence of other particular comparisons. Thus nothing is proven in a hard sense about Christian texts in light of Hindu texts, but Clooney calls upon us to pay closer attention where we might be guided by such endeavor.

In sum, while remaining open to possibilities of conversion and to the potential for different religious traditions to converge in the future, Clooney seems to believe that for now the greatest benefit comparative theology affords us is its power to change comparative theologians through their voluntary engagement with other traditions' scriptures and commentaries, so that when theologians subsequently read the texts of their own traditions they will see them differently. The fruits of comparative theology are not available for picking by casual passersby, Clooney would insist. One must become involved in the process. Clooney's readers are constantly being challenged to enter into the process, to read the texts of other traditions, and to let them speak for themselves. Clooney does not simply want to be an interpreter of Hindu texts; he wants to make them available to a new audience. Hence his stress on the process of comparative theology, more than on the conclusions of any particular comparison.

Elements of a Systematic Profile

While the authors and insights become more, as more comparative theological projects get carried out, it shall, however, be possible to state some major systematic points informing the self-understanding of the contemporary comparative theology discourse. Let me conclude this section, by focusing again on Clooney and reiterating some of his more systematic claims for comparative theology as stated by him in his essay "Comparative Theology" in the *Oxford Handbook of Systematic Theology*:[45]

A first point which Clooney makes is that if theology is to be comparative, we must first of all admit the interreligious nature of theology itself; theologizing, defined as *faith seeking understanding* or in some analogous way, is a religious thinking practiced by people in different religious tradi-

[45] Cf. for the following the sections "The Multiple Dimensions of a Comparative Theology" and "Some Concerns" of his essay "Comparative Theology."

tions. While "theology" has a specific history in the Christian West with specific meanings, it is not necessary to be restricted to a Christian context only. Thus, for example, it seems evident that we can refer also to Hindu theology. We can notice that Hindu traditions are not oblivious to differences which support reference to the "theological," as shall have become evident in a complex fashion in Clooney's own studies (as we have seen above). Similarly, one can argue for "Islamic" and "Jewish" theologies, with specific differences noted, but also, in light of greater differences, for "Buddhist theology," "Shinto theology," or "Taoist theology." etc.

Second, Clooney goes on to argue that if theology is an intellectual religious activity practiced in various cultural settings, and if theologians can profitably notice similarities and differences in method and content across religious boundaries, this comparative and interreligious theology must be conceived and practiced as a properly dialogical activity. As such, the theologian owes it to members of the other tradition to understand and appreciate, even when one disagrees. Theologians in this way become at least doubly accountable.

Third, though inevitably dialogical, Clooney claims, comparative theology can remain confessional, even apologetic. The dialogue essential to an interreligious theology must be vital enough that it can become an argument in which differences are highlighted, accentuated, and debated. Even after comparison, during the give and take required by dialogical exchange, and after certain necessary *defamiliarizations* from one's own tradition, theologians should be able to affirm the content of their faith as true, deepening a sense of its intelligibility for those who believe it already, and proposing persuasive arguments in order to demonstrate the truth of their faith.

Fourth, in the Christian theological context, one often begins reflection on religious pluralism with questions about the uniqueness of differing religious paths, the value of religious conversion, the narrower or broader resources within one's tradition for taking other religions seriously. In the theology of religions discipline, one can think of oneself, and more often of others, as exclusivist or inclusivist or pluralist theologians, depending on how one balances Christian claims with respect to other traditions. However, so Clooney claims, usually this theology of religions approach requires no particular knowledge of any other tradition, since it is justified on internal Christian grounds. While he does not wish to dispute the importance and even necessity of a theology of religions, he argues with others like James Fredericks,

Stephen Duffy, Hugh Nicholson, and Klaus von Stosch,[46] that this theology is properly subsequent to the practice of comparative theology; it illumines the meaning of comparative work rather than judging whether comparative work is possible. For him it has to remain an open question though, if comparative theology can be charged with concealing an implied theology of religions, wherein alone comparative work has its significance.

Fifth, another important point made by Clooney is that comparative theology seems to imply and even call into existence a new religious community with a new "interreligious faith" explored in "comparative theology," and no longer viably traced back to a particular faith community and its theological discourse.[47] Clooney throughout his work keeps saying that comparative theological engagement unsettles the certainties and boundaries of theologizing and redefines the de facto community of theologians. He claims, if comparative study proceeds honestly and fruitfully, the comparative theologian begins to live continually within a wider theological horizon; a new theological community begins to extend itself across settled religious boundaries and through the conversations one's loyalties and one's life of faith become more complexified. At times, thinks Clooney, a comparative theologian may find himself or herself taking the other theologies very seriously, even preferring them on some key issues. The positive edge about this extended conversations, he keeps repeating, is that such attentive theologians will be more complex figures whose learning may make sense in multiple contexts, yet without perhaps being entirely at home in any of them.

Having reviewed ad exemplum one author's concrete comparative theological work together with some systematic contours evolving from it for the new discipline, I return now to my earlier prosposal, namely to locate comparative theology at the crossroads of crosscultural and interreligious translation processes (cf. section I above). In the final section, therefore, I would like to abstract to this matter again and suggest that comparative theology can indeed seek to explore its theoretical foundations in conversation with other

46 J. Fredericks, "A Universal Religious Experience? Comparative Theology as Alternative to a Theology of Religions," in *Horizons* 22 (1995): 67 87; S.A. Duffy, "A Theology of the Religions and / or a Comparative Theology," in *Horizons* 26 (1999): 105-15; Hugh Nicholson, "A Correlational Model of Comparative Theology", in *The Journal of Religion* 85 (2005): 191-213; K. von Stosch, "Komparative Theologie – ein Ausweg aus dem Grunddilemma jeder Theologie der Religionen," in *Zeitschrift für Katholische Theologie* 124 (2002): 294-311.

47 Cf. Clooney, *Divine Mother, Blessed Mother*, 24.

disciplines also concerned with issues of crosscultural and conceptual translation.

IV. Seeking Ground: The (Un)Translatibility of Concepts and Traditions

While the discussion around intercultural translation or untranslatibility is of course a large one across disciplines, two related, more recently developed, and in some way contrasting fields of enquiry – Comparative Religion and Philosophy – can perhaps help us bracket our concluding reflection.

What can be characterized as "downfall" at large of the general comparative studies in religion in the mid-20th century onwards can be attributed to the increasing refutation of various philosophical and epistemological foundations – the phenomenology of religion included. If a "New Comparativism" in the study of religion is to become viable, then it – and this pertains to theology as well – must be founded on other epistemological premises than those employed hitherto.

Scholars ruminating on theoretical and philosophical soundings for a new "science of comparative religion," such as Jeppe Sinding Jensen from Aarhus University, are convinced

> that the comparative and general study of religion after the linguistic turn must be construed epistemically as an intersubjective semantic construction which produces in its mappings, modelling, framings of theoretical objects and phenomena, etc. a [new] stock of sharable and expandable public knowledge.[48]

Borrowing from philosophy of science, semiotics, and cognitive sciences, he proposes a "translational turn" for a new comparative religion.

Learning the relevant lessons from relativism and postmodernism, he seeks to employ a holist semantics as foundation that, on the one hand, shall recognize an epistemic stance of (more or less) incompatible and incommensurable religious "frameworks," and additionally allow to extend the "principle of charity" to, what he calls, the "translations of religions."[49] Without going into further details on holist semantics and the set of theories he employs to reestablish the possibility of a new comparativism, central to his

---

48 Jeppe Sinding Jensen, *The Study of Religion in a New Key: Theoretical and Philosophical Soundings in the Comparative and General Study of Religion* (Aarhus, 2003), 433.

49 Jensen, *The Study of Religion*, 369.

theoretical argument is the translatability of concepts across religions and cultures. "It is precisely," Jensen claims, "because of the translatability of concepts both *in religions* and in the *study of religion(s)* that it is possible to discuss across religions in comparative studies and across theories in a general study."[50]

However complex and nuanced theoretical groundwork for establishing a new comparative study of religions needs to be, inquiry into the *translatibility* of concepts, or their *untranslatibility*, in and across religions is definitely a crucial one. And, needless to say, the epistemological and philosophical soundings in such recent scientific study of religion striving for a new comparativism, are important ones for a theory of comparative theology as well.

To complement the translational turn in the theory of comparative religion from a philosophical angle, it is helpful to consider Alasdair MacIntyre's argument for what he terms tradition-constituted enquiry. This position is one of the more intrigueing heuristic philosophical models elaborating on the issue of translation and untranslatability of traditions I have encountered in recent years. MacIntyre's concept of tradition-constituted enquiry is linked with a claim for traditions' incommensurable uniqueness, on the one hand, with a proposal for a kind of epistemological bilingualism, on the other. I consider his approach a useful heuristic lense to describe the process of comparative theology theoretically.

MacIntyre's reasoning goes as follows: When two historical traditions interact, it is possible that participants within each respective tradition are able to recognize that the participants of the other tradition are reflecting on the same issue, as they are reflecting upon, defining "same" here, not by external, universal standards, but by standards internal to the traditions in which each participant already stands, i.e. only within a tradition-constituted enquiry. Interaction between traditions occurs by a specific process of understanding the untranslatable and incommensurable of another tradition; a process MacIntyre describes as learning "a second first language."[51]

One might object that texts and traditions they embody do get translated successfully across traditions nonetheless. MacIntyre would say, however, that such translations are produced by people who inhabit both languages as

[50] Jensen, *The Study of Religion*, 343.

[51] For a detailed analysis of MacIntyre's model and of the related questions of translation and incommensurability see N. Hintersteiner, *Traditionen überschreiten: Angloamerikanische Beiträge zur interkulturellen Traditionshermeneutik* (Vienna, 2001).

first languages. When such individuals first come to speak two incommensurable languages, they become aware that they are unable to translate from one to the other, that any attempt to do so merely falsifies the thought of the original language.[52] But they may subsequently acquire the ability to translate adequately. For this to happen, the language into which they are translating needs to have been enriched (or find itself enriched by the translation itself) in a complex comparative process.

For MacIntyre there is an additional reason why coming to know a tradition from within like a second first language benefits our first language. For it is only in this way that we can experience an incommensurability, a truth or uniqueness that only the inhabitants of a single tradition – any tradition – are able to perceive. Learning other traditions like "a second first language," through a kind of bilingualism, reveals the truth that there are incommensurable traditions.

One of the illusions from which religious generalists or comparative religionists may suffer is the belief that any system of beliefs can be adequately represented in their compendium of knowledge. MacIntyre calls this "a blindness to the possibility of genuine alternative conceptual schemes."[53] The only cure for this blindness is to learn a new language from the inside, so as to come to be at home in it. For it is only when we are able so to inhabit a second tradition and language that "we learn that we are unable to translate what we are now able to say in our second first language."[54] Thus, incommensurability "cannot be recognized, let alone characterized adequately, by those who inhabit only one of the two conflicting conceptual schemes," but only "by someone who inhabits both alternative conceptual schemes."[55]

In short, MacIntyre hopes to demonstate how different, intractable or competing traditions can be comparatively evaluated against one another. The task requires, as his model suggests, a complex "empathetic conceptual imagination" that allows one to understand and evaluatively argue with those from other traditions.[56] In the end, it allows the determination of whether one might possibly have a more illuminating account of one's own tradition,

---

52 A. MacIntyre, *Whose Justice? Which Rationality?* (Notre Dame, 1988), 387.

53 A. MacIntyre, *Three Rival Versions of Moral Enquiry: Encyclopedia, Genealogy, and Tradition* (Notre Dame, 1990), 44.

54 MacIntyre, *Whose Justice? Which Rationality?* 387.

55 MacIntyre, *Three Rival Versions*, 113f.

56 MacIntyre, *Whose Justice? Which Rationality?395*

which one might then be able to incorporate, or to which one converts due to a more rational viability. This model, I propose, can serve as heuristic and epistemological lense most useful for a theory of comparative theology built around untranslatibility and translation of vastly different religious traditions.

Against such translational philosophical and epistemological stance, comparative theology concedes that close attention to another tradition's theology might indeed lead to scepticism about the viability and translatability of concepts and words across theological boundaries, in different languages or in translations that may present us with seeming similarities and innumerable distinctions and subtle differences. However, and quoting again Clooney, comparative theology in that context best aims at the following trajectory:

> The meaning of other religions to an insider in one tradition shifts from a simple question about "the religions" to a whole series of complex choices and smaller questions about particular theological topics. Progress on the largest questions – which religion is the truest or best, what is God and how does God save the world? – slows down, while swifter progress is made in refining the analysis of many smaller theological topics. While different traditions do not mean the same things, the differences will not be so great as to destroy the possibility of comparative theological consideration, either in terms of the materials compared or the substantive project of learning how to make theological sense in a multi-tradition context.[57]

To conclude, by presenting various heuristic epistemological lenses and material fields on translation or untranslatability across disciplines related to comparative theology, I have not been aiming at developing an integrated approach towards a theory of comparative theology. However, the theoretical and material angles provided can be suggestive for such. I am convinced that inquiry into the proposed material and epistemological fields of crosscultural and interreligious translation will prove an helpful entry point as comparative theology seeks to advance in exploring its theoretical foundations, parallel with many more concrete projects and studies.

57 F.X. Clooney, "Comparative Theology."

Perry Schmidt-Leukel

Limits and Prospects of Comparative Theology

In 1995, Francis Clooney published his impressive survey on "Comparative Theology" in which he summarily reviewed more than forty books – all taken as more or less examples of "comparative theology." In his opening sentence, Clooney introduced "comparative theology" as a new development, as "an exciting and quickly developing field, and a relatively uncharted one."[1] In the same year, the American journal *Horizons* published an article by James Fredericks in which he presented "comparative theology as an alternative to a theology of religions."[2]

It is well known that American trends and fashions make their way to Continental Europe without much delay. Thus it was in 2001 that Norbert Hintersteiner recommended "comparative theology" as the most suitable theological approach to the plurality of religions and reiterated Fredericks' claim of comparative theology as an alternative to an exclusivist, inclusivist, and pluralist theology of religions.[3] In 2002, another young German and Roman Catholic theologian, Klaus von Stosch, joined Hintersteiner and demanded – in the face of an alleged insoluble *grunddilemma* of every theology of religions – a transition to "comparative theology."[4] Meanwhile, in 1999, James Fredericks published his monograph "Faith among Faiths," where he sharpened his earlier attacks on theology of religions and at the same time increased his praise of comparative theology as the effective rescue. "Currently," says Fredericks, "the quest for an adequate theology of religions is at an impasse,"[5] which, he feels, is primarily an "impasse over the pluralistic

---

1 F.X. Clooney, "Comparative Theology: A Review of Recent Books (1989-1995)," in *Theological Studies* 56 (1995), 521-550, here 521.

2 Thus the subtitle of J.L. Fredericks, "A Universal Religious Experience? Comparative Theology as an Alternative to a Theology of Religions," in *Horizons* 22 (1995): 67-87.

3 N. Hintersteiner, *Traditionen überschreiten: Angloamerikanische Beiträge zur interkulturellen Traditionshermeneutik* (Vienna, 2001), 318-20.

4 K. von Stosch, "Komparative Theologie - ein Ausweg aus dem Grunddilemma jeder Theologie der Religionen?" in *Zeitschrift für Katholische Theologie* 124 (2002): 294-311, here 294.

5 J.L. Fredericks, *Faith among Faiths. Christian Theology and Non-Christian Religions* (New York, 1999), 8.

model."[6] But, proclaims Fredericks, "In comparative theology, Christians will find a way beyond the current impasse in the theology of religions."[7]

Given these steep assertions, my subsequent remarks amount to something like *bad news* and *good news*. To deliver the bad news first, I'm going to demonstrate that there is neither a way out of the theology of religions nor any theological alternative to the three basic options of an exclusivist, inclusivist, or pluralist approach. The only escape from this would be in avoiding the types of questions that a theology of religions must address. But, as I will try to show, if "comparative theology" is really taken as genuine *theology* while it at the same time remains seriously *comparative*, it cannot avoid these questions. On the contrary, their urgency will become even more strident. Consequently, my bad news for Fredericks and his German followers is that "comparative theology" will not lead out of the impasse of theology of religions but straight ahead into it. The liberating good news, however, is that the theology of religions is not at an impasse at all. Quite contrary to what Fredericks holds, the pluralist option in particular may be seen as a promising path into the theological future, a way ahead to which comparative theology can and should make an essential contribution.

First, I will explain briefly how I understand the theology of religions and its three basic options. Second, I will show why comparative religion cannot function as an alternative to the theology of religions. And in my third and final point, I will indicate in what sense comparative theology can contribute to the theology of religions in general and to a pluralist version of it in particular.

Theology of Religions

The term "theology of religions" usually refers to the Christian theological reflection on the relationship between Christianity and other religions. In a broader sense, however, it could designate an analogous reflective activity in each of the religions. Basically, a theology of religions – Christian or non-Christian – must answer two questions: firstly, how to interpret the claims / beliefs of other religions vis-à-vis one's own claims/beliefs, and secondly, how to interpret one's own claims / beliefs vis-à-vis the claims / beliefs of

6 Fredericks, *Faith among Faiths*, 10.

7 Fredericks, *Faith among Faiths*, 10.

others. When I say, "interpret," I mean interpretation in the broad sense that encompasses understanding *and* assessment, so that this kind of interpretation asks not only for the correct meaning but also for the potential truth of respective claims or beliefs.

These two basic questions of the theology of religions belong intrinsically together because they are mutually conditioning. To answer one of them has decisive effects on answering the other. Thus there are not really two questions, but a double question – much like an ellipse with two equally important foci. I am not saying that the "theology of religions" is nothing more than the effort to answer this double question. Certainly there are many more related questions and sub-questions. But nonetheless, the answer to this double question is of central and basic significance. That is, in dealing with any of the related questions, one will have to face this crucial double question.[8]

In order to address the double question, it is necessary to consider the meaning of the category "religion." Whatever "religions" might be or do, one certainty is that they entertain some beliefs, usually expressed through propositional claims, but also deeply embedded beliefs in ritual, morality, the arts, etc. Among these beliefs we find factual claims, i.e., assertions about what exists or what does not exist, value judgments, and practical instructions. One central religious belief, as William Christian framed it, is that there is "something more important than anything else in the universe."[9] While this may be true even for the so-called secular religions (the great ideologies of the nineteenth and twentieth century), the traditional religions assume that this "something," which is more important than anything else in the world, is a transcendent reality; that is, it is not one of the finite realities of this world. In one way or another religions claim to have some form of knowledge or revelation of this transcendent reality. And they not only make the value judgment that this reality is the highest good, but they also instruct people to live their lives in such a way that it properly reflects the utmost importance of ultimate reality. Let us call such a proper orientation of life, and the further eschatological hopes connected with such a life, "salvation." Then we can say that religions, at least the traditional ones, claim – each in its own way – to mediate a salvific knowledge or revelation of transcendent reality.

---

8 For a broader analysis of various tasks of a Christian theology of religions see P. Schmidt-Leukel, *Theologie der Religionen: Probleme, Optionen, Argumente* (Neuried, 1997), 11-64.

9 W.A. Christian, *Meaning and Truth in Religion* (Princeton, 1964), 60.

Let us now call this claimed property "P", so that P = mediation of a salvific knowledge of ultimate / transcendent reality. Thus "P" is a property of a religious community or tradition if this tradition not only claims such a mediation but claims so rightly, that is, if this claim is true.

In so far as the basic double question of the theology of religions is focused on the issue of religious truth claims, it can be reformulated as the question: Is "P" a property of religions?

Then what follows are these logical alternatives: Either P is not a property of any religion (because there is no such thing as a transcendent reality, so that all the respective claims are false) or P can be found among the religions. If P is a property of religions, we can ask further whether P is realized only once or more than once. And if P is realized in more than one religion, we can ask whether there is something like a singular maximum of this realization or not. This leads us to a fully disjunctive classification with four different options: (0) *Atheism/Naturalism*: Salvific knowledge of a transcendent reality is mediated by none of the religions (because a transcendent reality does not exist). (1) *Exclusivism*: Salvific knowledge of a transcendent reality is mediated by only one religion (which will be naturally one's own). (2) *Inclusivism*: Salvific knowledge of a transcendent reality is mediated by more than one religion (not necessarily by all of them), but only one religion among them mediates it in a uniquely superior way (which again will be naturally one's own). (3) *Pluralism*: Salvific knowledge of a transcendent reality is mediated by more than one religion (not necessarily by all of them), and there is none among them whose mediation of that knowledge is superior to the rest.

Let me now add some clarifications: **(1)** As I said previously, if the four options are so defined, we have a classification that is fully disjunctive and therefore *logically comprehensive*. That is, every option within the theology of religions (in so far as it entails an answer to the opening question) can be subsumed under one of the four definitions and there is no further option left. Therefore one must decide in favor of one of them. **(2)** The first option – that is, the *atheist/naturalist* one – can be excluded as a religious or theological option. It is a logical possibility, and, no doubt, a realistic one. But because it rests on the denial of a transcendent reality, it cannot be a theological option. Therefore a theology of religions has to decide between the three remaining options. **(3)** Every religion can theoretically define its relationship to the other religions by one of the three remaining options; that is, the suggested taxonomy is not exclusively confined to a Christian theology of religions.

However, as a classification of *Christian theological options*, it would take something like the following shape:

Christian *exlusivism* would mean that saving revelation can be found only within Christianity and not within any other religion. This does not necessarily entail that all non-Christians are lost. Soft or moderate exclusivists could hold that there are ways by which God can save non-Christians as individuals (for example, through a post-mortem encounter with the gospel). But, according to my definition, Christian exclusivism would deny any positive salvific role to the non-Christian religions.

In contrast to this, Christian *inclusivism* would hold that non-Christian religions sometimes entail elements of revelation and grace that are capable of supporting a salvific life. But since, according to Christian inclusivism, all salvation is finally rendered through Christ, the revelation to which Christianity testifies is, in a unique sense, superior to any other forms of knowledge of God, which, when compared to the Christian revelation, remain necessarily deficient, fragmentary, incomplete, implicit, and obscure.

Christian *pluralism* would hold that some other religions – usually at least the major world religions – are in a theological sense on par with Christianity: According to Christian pluralism, they testify to the same ultimate transcendent reality, despite the different forms this testimony takes, and they do so with the same genuine authenticity and equal salvific potential.

In my subsequent reflections I will use the terms *exclusivism*, *inclusivism* and *pluralism* in the sense of these definitions only. Let me clarify: By *exclusivism* I do not mean *any type* of exclusive claim. Every truth claim is in some sense exclusive, for it excludes the truth of its logical opposite. To criticize such an exclusivism would be intellectual suicide, because a proposition that would not exclude anything would no longer have any specific meaning and would therefore become unintelligible. In this sense, therefore, each of the four defined options would be exclusivist.

Further, by *inclusivism* I do not refer to cases wherein statements about or assessments of another religion are expressed with recourse to the ideas, values, and terminology stemming from the religious tradition of the person who makes these statements. It is true that the serious study of another religion may lead to a significant widening and change of one's own religious horizon and eventually also to a transformed terminology. But it also seems to be a hermeneutical law that every process of understanding and interpreting something new has to start from one's own existing conceptual framework. In this *hermeneutical* sense, each of the defined positions would be inclusivist.

Finally, by *pluralism* I do not mean the relativistic feeling that all religions or even all worldviews or value systems are somehow equally good (or equally bad), because from this premise there would be no way of making any universal judgment at all. According to such a loose and indeed undisciplined understanding of "pluralism," none of the four defined positions would be pluralistic. In contrast, I understand the pluralist option precisely as a value judgment of other religions – a judgment that acknowledges theologically their equal validity as means to salvation. Moreover, *pluralism* as a distinctive option within a theology of religion is different from theories of political or social pluralism. Within a pluralistic society there will always be a wide plurality of all kinds of worldviews and religious ideas and systems. And among all these various views there will always be some that from a "theology of religions" perspective are considered to be false, others being regarded as insufficient, and again some others that could be seen as different but equally valid. The ethos of a pluralist society does therefore not require a pluralistic theology of religions but the virtue of tolerance; that is, the willingness to tolerate, as far as possible, those worldviews or religions one disapproves of. A pluralistic theology of religions is therefore not an expression of toleration but of appreciation. And, as such, it cannot and may not replace the important social virtue of tolerance.[10]

The Limits of Comparative Theology

The theological approaches labeled "comparative theology" by no means share the same understanding of what they are doing. What they have in common is marked by two features: firstly, the pursuit of interreligious comparison – usually embedded into interfaith dialogue – and secondly, the conviction that this is an adequate and fruitful form of doing theology in a multireligious context. I think Clooney hits the mark when he presents comparative theology as "the doing of constructive theology from and after comparison."[11]

The *theological* nature of the comparative activity is what distinguishes comparative theology from the purely phenomenological approach of "comparative religion" and from its more recent sociologically oriented versions

---

10 Cf. P. Schmidt-Leukel, "Beyond Tolerance: Towards a New Step in Interreligious Relationships," in *Scottish Journal of Theology* 55 (2002): 379-91.

11 Clooney, "Comparative Theology," 522; *idem*, *Theology after Vedanta: An Experiment in Comparative Theology* (Albany, 1993), 4-7.

running frequently under the name "religious studies." According to Keith Ward, comparative theology "enquires into ideas of the ultimate value and goal of human life, as they have been perceived and expressed in a variety of religious traditions." And it "differs from what is often called "religious studies," in being primarily concerned with the meaning, truth, and rationality of religious beliefs, rather than with the psychological, sociological, or historical elements of religious life and institutions."[12]

Quite similarly, Francis Clooney states that "as theology, comparative theology consists most basically in faith seeking understanding; its ultimate horizon can be nothing less than knowledge of the divine, the transcendent," while it "is marked by its commitment to the detailed consideration of religious traditions other than one's own."[13] James Fredericks chimes in with Ward and Clooney by affirming that "doing theology comparatively means that Christians look upon the truths of non-Christian traditions as resources for understanding their own faith."[14]

Thus the broad theological nature of comparative theology consists primarily in its explicit interest in the question of truth. However, there are some noteworthy differences among the comparativists when it comes to the issue of confessional theology. According to Ward, comparative theology does not require a "tradition-neutral investigator,"[15] and will always be undertaken "from a particular perspective."[16] But, says Ward, comparative theology should be "prepared to revise beliefs if and when it comes to seem necessary."[17] In this regard, Clooney and Fredericks are far more reluctant. On the one hand, Clooney does affirm that comparative theology "is a theology deeply changed by its attention to the details of multiple religions," but on the other hand, he says, "the comparativist remains rooted in one tradition."[18] And as Clooney makes clear, this sets strong and narrow limits to any possi-

---

12 K. Ward, *Religion and Revelation. A Theology of Revelation in the World's Religions* (Oxford, 1994), 40.

13 Clooney, "Comparative Theology," 521.

14 Fredericks, *Faith among Faiths*, 140.

15 Ward, *Religion and Revelation*, 47.

16 Ward, *Religion and Revelation*, 49; see also K. Ward, *Religion and Community* (Oxford, 2000), 339.

17 Ward, *Religion and Revelation*, 48.

18 Clooney, "Comparative Theology," 522. See also his slightly cautious remarks on Ward's approach in *idem*, *Hindu God, Christian God: How Reason Helps Break Down the Boundaries between Religions* (Oxford, 2002), 25-27.

ble transformation or revision of that tradition.[19] Similarly, Fredericks speaks about the "demanding and transforming truths of other religions"[20] and "the power of non-Christian religions to inspire new insights within us."[21] But he warns against the danger of "losing our commitment to the Christian tradition" and recommends like Clooney that we "remain rooted" in it.[22] Fredericks' advice is to live with the "tension between commitment to Christianity and openness to other religious truth" and to "resist the temptation to overcome this tension."[23] Thus comparativists agree that the comparative reflection is undertaken from within a particular perspective and starts from a specific religious or confessional background. But they disagree on the question of how much that perspective – and thereby one's own religious background – may legitimately be transformed or revised through and as a result of the comparative reflection.

The importance of this observation will become clear when we ask about the relation between comparative theology and the theology of religions. I do not want to deny that both are different. But I strongly dispute Fredericks', von Stosch's, and perhaps Hintersteiner's claim that comparative theology provides a real alternative to the theology of religions that could effectively avoid any of their three basic options. A clear difference between the theology of religions and comparative theology is that comparative theology is dedicated to specific religious traditions and the comparison of particular texts, thinkers, ideas, rituals, etc., while theology of religions deals more with the various theological interpretations of religious diversity in general. So Fredericks has a point in stating that:

> Unlike theologies of religions, comparative theology does not start with a grand theory of religion in general that claims to account for all relegions .... Instead of theories about religion in general, comparative theologians are interested in study-

19 See particularly F.X. Clooney, "Reading the World in Christ: From Comparison to Inclusivism," in D'Costa, Gavin (ed.): *Christian Uniqueness Reconsidered: The Myth of a Pluralistic Theology of Religions* (Maryknoll, 1990), 63-80.

20 Fredericks, *Faith among Faiths*, 170.

21 Fredericks, *Faith among Faiths*, 170.

22 Fredericks, *Faith among Faiths*, 170.

23 Fredericks, *Faith among Faiths*, 170.

ing other religions on their own terms and then exploring their own Christian faith using what they have learned about the other religions."[24]

This concreteness, i.e., the specific interest in particular religions and topics, is indeed what distinguishes comparative theology from the theology of religions. And this difference marks its strength as well as its limits. The comparative theologian may start her work without any elaborated general theory of religion or without any explicit option of a theology of religions (but she might very well harbor something of that sort as an undeveloped, implicit background assumption). However, the systematic and consequent pursuit of the comparison – if it is carried out theologically; that is, with a prior interest in the truth and value of the investigated religious ideas or beliefs – will sooner or later lead to a point where the question of the relationship between the non-Christian and respective Christian beliefs becomes unavoidable. And then there will emerge, quite naturally, the four options that either both beliefs are wrong, or that one is true and the other wrong, or that one is more adequate or comprehensive and therefore more true than the other, or that both are different but equally true. However, these four options are nothing more than the basic options within a theology of religions. And since, for logical reasons, there is no further option left, the comparative theologian will then have to make her choice and so enter the field of the theology of religions.[25]

As Clooney has admitted from his own experience, there is a point when the comparison of, for example, certain Vedânta and Christian texts will unavoidably lead to the confrontation between the Vedântist claim that all salvation comes through knowledge of Brahman and the Christian claim that all salvation is brought about through Christ.[26] Certainly, it is not at all immediately evident whether these two claims are compatible or incompatible – and if so how. But when the comparativist starts to discuss this question, she is practicing the theology of religions. If she attempts to avoid the kinds of

---

24 Fredericks, *Faith among Faiths*, 167f. See also von Stosch, "Komparative Theologie," 307: "Komparative Theologie bemüht sich nicht um eine religionstheologische Vogelperspektive, sondern wendet sich dem konkreten Einzelfall und damit spezifischen Feldern der Auseinandersetzung zu. Es geht ihr nicht um Allgemeinaussagen über die Wahrheit einer oder mehrerer Religionen, sondern um das Hin- und Hergehen zwischen konkreten religiösen Traditionen angesichts bestimmter Problemfelder, um Verbindendes und Trennendes zwischen den Religionen neu zu entdecken."

25 For an extensive discussion of the three option within a Christian theology of religions see my *Theologie der Religionen*.

26 Clooney, *Theology after Vedanta*, 189ff.

questions that arise in the theology of religions (because "comparative theology" is claimed to be the viable alternative), she must regard her work as complete whenever conflicting, or apparently conflicting, claims are laid bare. If that is the case, then she has not proceeded beyond the classical aim of "comparative religion", i.e., a purely phenomenological comparison without pursuing the issue of truth. Therefore, I hold that there is no way for comparative theology to remain comparative and genuinely theological and at the same time to avoid the type of questions discussed in the theology of religions. Avoiding them would mean that either comparative theology loses its theological character and falls back into comparative religion, or, from a certain point onwards, it ceases to continue its comparative reflection and reverts to the reiteration of confessional standpoints. In neither way would comparative theology achieve its envisioned goal. Consequently, it is not the theology of religions that leads to an impasse. On the contrary, this is precisely the fate of any form of comparative theology that would deliberately close itself off from the type of discussion carried out in the theology of religions by presenting its approach as an alternative. And I cannot avoid the conclusion that Fredericks' suggestion that we live with unresolved tension between confessional commitment and interreligious openness is nothing more than advice to nestle in and make oneself complacent at the very dead end of this impasse. There is, however, absolutely no need for comparative theology to refrain from collaborating with the theology of religions.

The Prospects of Comparative Theology

Not all comparativists share Fredericks' views of comparative theology as an alternative to the theology of religions. In Ward's numerous and extremely valuable contributions to comparative theology,[27] both forms of theological reflection go hand in hand, and his own standpoint oscillates slightly between an open form of inclusivism and – as he himself once called it – a "convergent pluralism."[28] With a few reservations, something similar could be said

[27] Cf. K. Ward, *Images of Eternity: Concepts of God in Five Religious Traditions* (London, 1987); *A Vision to Pursue: Beyond the Crisis in Christianity* (London, 1991); *Religion and Revelation*; *Religion and Creation* (Oxford, 1996); *Religion and Human Nature* (Oxford, 1998); *Religion and Community*.

[28] Ward, *A Vision to Pursue*, 175.

about the pioneering efforts of Ninian Smart and Steven Konstantine.[29] Francis Clooney, too, maintains that there is "a path from *comparative theology* to the *theology of religions,*"[30] and in his aforementioned review article on "comparative theology,"[31] he points to all the major publications on the theology of religions that were published in the period covered by his review as examples. Clooney even holds that comparative theology "best eventuates in the inclusivist position."[32] This is indicative of what I regard as one of the distinguishing prospects of comparative theology: by way of theologically comparing specific Christian and non-Christian beliefs; that is, by carefully investigating the hermeneutical range of their possible meaning and the epistemological range of their possible truth, the comparativist can and should attempt to argue in favor of one of the three basic options of the theology of religions. Through contributing concrete and specific case studies, comparative theology can help to increase or decrease the overall plausibility of an exclusivist, inclusivist, or pluralist view.[33]

Concerning the relationship between comparative theology and theology of religions, Clooney has emphasized "that the sequence is important, and that ... the theology of religions comes only *later* ...."[34] That is, "after comparative reading, a transition from textual / comparative theology to a theology of religions is made."[35] I agree that this is broadly a correct description. However, the compared Christian and non-Christian texts or beliefs might already entail certain explicit or implicit assumptions about other religions. And if the comparativist starts his work from a specific religious or confessional tradition, it is doubtless the case that he, as part of his own religious background, will already be influenced by those religious convictions that have their own implications on the truth claims entailed in the beliefs of oth-

---

29 N. Smart / S. Konstantine, *Christian Systematic Theology in a World Context* (London, 1991).

30 Clooney, "Reading the World in Christ," 72

31 Clooney, "Comparative Theology."

32 Clooney, "Reading the World in Christ," 66; similarly pp. 64, 67, 72ff; also Clooney, *Theology after Vedanta*, 195f.

33 Thus I agree with Clooney's remark on the three options of a theology of religions that in order to "be taken seriously in a comparative context, each will have to be rewritten with a far great (sic) commitment to detail and examples." (Clooney, *Theology after Vedanta*, 194).

34 Clooney, "Reading the World in Christ," 66.

35 See also Clooney, *Theology after Vedanta*, 193f.

ers. To bracket or exclude the implications of one's own religious presuppositions would once again mean to fall back into the business of a purely phenomenological comparison – and apart from that, there are good reasons to doubt whether such a bracketing is possible at all.[36]

In any case, if comparative theology wants to be more than comparative religion, then the comparative reflection may very well lead to a point where some of one's own religious presuppositions are seriously drawn into question, so that revision and change of those presuppositions might seem unavoidable, and the only way one could remain rooted in one's own tradition would be to suggest a significant transformation of that tradition. This is exactly what has happened to a number of Christian pluralists, particularly those who arrived at a pluralist position after long, intensive, and utterly serious dialogues with non-Christian religions.[37] Addressing Clooney and Fredericks, Paul Knitter has therefore rightly remarked, "While we have to be aware that we bring our theological baggage to the journey of dialogue, that doesn't mean that during the journey we may not have to rearrange, or even dispose of, some of that baggage."[38] If proponents of comparative religion exclude, at the outset, the possibility of revision and significant transformation as a potential result of their comparative work,[39] or if they denounce such transformation as distortion,[40] then the seriousness of their endeavors is questionable. But if comparative theology is open to revision and significant transformation, it can then make significant contributions to the type of future theology that pioneers of religious pluralism have designated "World Theology"[41] or "Global Theology"[42] – that is, as Wilfred Cantwell Smith has de-

---

36 Cf. R. Panikkar, *The Intrareligious Dialogue* (New York, 1978), 39-52; P. Heelas, "Some Problems with Religious Studies," in *Religion* 8 (1978): 1-14; D. Wiebe, *Religion and Truth: Towards an Alternative Paradigm for the Study of Religion* (The Hague, 1981); P. Schmidt-Leukel, *"Den Löwen brüllen hören": Zur Hermeneutik eines christlichen Verständnisses der buddhistischen Heilsbotschaft* (Paderborn, 1992), 106-41.

37 See my review article "Pluralistische Religionstheologie: Warum und wozu?" in *Ökumenische Rundschau* 49 (2002): 259-72.

38 P. Knitter, *Theologies of Religions* (Maryknoll, 2002), 236.

39 See, for example, von Stosch, "Komparative Theologie," 297f, for whom the revisionist elements of a pluralist approach are sufficient to rule it out as a Christian theological option.

40 Cf. Fredericks, *Faith among Faiths*, 169.

41 W.C. Smith, *Towards a World Theology: Faith and the Comparative History of Religion* (first published 1981) (Maryknoll, 1989).

scribed it, "a theology that will interpret the history of our race in a way that will give intellectual expression to our faith, the faith of all of us, and to our modern perception of the world."[43]

If comparative theology holds to this vision, it must keep in mind that the wider context of every particular comparison is nowadays a global context. Comparison should thus be carried out with the awareness that the whole picture must not only be a multireligious one, but one that also takes into account the important insights resulting from modern scientific worldviews. Once more, I think, Keith Ward has got the agenda for comparative theology right. Allow me, then, to conclude my remarks with his programmatic words:

> The religious situation of our world requires an attempt, at least on the part of those committed to reflection, to interpret traditional beliefs in the light of our ever-growing knowledge of the material cosmos, and in awareness of the many differing traditions of belief that exist about the nature of human existence in the world. One needs to ask how far traditional formulations of belief in any tradition may need to be revised because of new scientific knowledge, and how much they may reflect an ignorance of other traditions of belief that may either be complementary to or be highly critical of them.[44]

---

42 J. Hick, *Death and Eternal Life* (first published 1976) (Houndmills ,1990), 29-34.

43 Hick, *Death and Eternal Life*, 125.

44 Ward, *Religion and Community*, 339.

Klaus von Stosch

Comparative Theology As an Alternative to the Theology of Religions

The Dilemma of a Theology of Religions

In what follows, I offer a critical response to Perry Schmidt-Leukel's paper "Limits and Prospects of Comparative Theology," in which he attempts to reveal the mistaken efforts in the pretension of comparative theology to find a "way beyond the current impasse in the theology of religions."[1] Schmidt-Leukel's "bad news" for comparative theologians is that "comparative theology" will not lead out of the impasse of theology of religions but straight ahead into it. Schmidt-Leukel tries to console comparative theologians with the "good news" that the theology of religions (and especially his pluralist option) "is not at all an impasse," but "a promising path into the theological future."[2]

My bad news for adherents to the theology of religions, as it is understood by Schmidt-Leukel, is that no theoretical solution of this dilemma is possible within their current philosophical framework. My good news is, *pace* Schmidt-Leukel, that comparative theology is a "way beyond the current impasse in the theology of religions."

Before elaborating on this second point, let's look for a moment at Schmidt-Leukel's "promising path into the theological future." I do not think that religious believers can accept a pluralist answer to the problems of a theology of religions. One simply cannot insist on the truth of one's beliefs while accepting that the opposite of one's beliefs is equally true. One must hold that one's own beliefs are at least closer to the truth than the beliefs of those who disagree with those beliefs – otherwise one should change one's beliefs. In Keith Ward's words: "It may sound arrogant to say that a particular view that I happen to hold is more adequate than another; but it is an inescapable claim for anyone who reflects on what truth claims logically require."[3]

---

1 J.L. Fredericks, *Faith among Faiths: Christian Theology and Non-Christian Religions* (New York, 1999), 10.

2 Cf. P. Schmidt-Leukel, "Limits and Prospects of Comparative Theology," in this volume, 493-505.

3 K. Ward, *Divine Action* (London, 1990), 201.

Within the philosophical framework of traditional realism, there is no coherent possibility for claiming that contradicting religious beliefs have equal value. Hick's and Schmidt-Leukel's claim of a *Real an sich* is not a convincing solution, because, after Kant, it is nonsense to investigate the nature of a *Ding an sich* or to compare and evaluate different manifestations of it. As Armin Kreiner relates:

> Das Postulat eines ‚Real *an sich*' erscheint wie eine (im schlechten Sinn) metaphysische Adhoc-Hypothese, die das pluralistische Grundanliegen angesichts der Tatsache divergierender Wahrheitsansprüche retten soll, aber kaum überzeugend retten kann. Denn es bleibt letztlich unbegreiflich, wie ein transzendentes Wesen a authentisch als ϕ erfahren werden kann, obwohl a an sich nicht ϕ ist. Darüber hinaus bleibt ebenso unbegreiflich, wie die Beschreibung von a als ϕ eine adäquate Handlungsdisposition gegenüber a evozieren soll, obwohl doch a an sich gar nicht ϕ ist[4].

Thus pluralism is no coherent solution to the problems of the theology of religions. Moreover, inclusivism provides no acceptable answers to the questions of the theology of religions either, because it fails to appreciate difference without transforming it into identity.[5] The command of charity requires that I not devaluate the beliefs of my neighbor. For, as Radhakrishnan states, "to despise the gods of other people means to despise these people themselves, for they and their gods belong together."[6]

To summarize, there is no solution for the dilemma of a theology of religions that upholds religious believers' contradicting truth claims while it attempts to appreciate difference and diversity in the field of religions.

I would now like to turn to Schmidt-Leukel's "bad news" for comparative theologians that "'comparative theology' will not lead out of the impasse of theology of religions but straight ahead into it." I do not agree with this statement for the simple reason that comparative theology, as I would like to inter-

---

4 A. Kreiner, "Philosophische Probleme der pluralistischen Religionstheologie," in R. Schwager (ed.), *Christus allein? Der Streit um die Pluralistische Religionstheologie*, QD 160 (Freiburg / Basel / Vienna, 1996), 118-31; here 129; cf. Ward, *Divine Action*, 198: "How, then, since my view is known to be false, can I be sure mine is an authentic way to salvation? I conceive salvation as knowledge of the Real (of God); but the Real is unknowable; so I must be mistaken. If I am wrong about what salvation is, how can I coherently claim to achieve it by the path I follow?"

5 Cf. K. von Stosch, *Glaubensverantwortung in doppelter Kontingenz: Untersuchungen zur Verortung fundamentaler Theologie nach Wittgenstein*, Ratio Fidei 7 (Regensburg, 2001), 327-34.

6 S. Radhakrishnan, *Weltanschauung der Hindu* (Baden-Baden, 1961), 42.

pret it, has a philosophical framework that excludes the possibility of a theoretical comparison of religions.[7]

The Philosophical Framework of Comparative Theology

The philosophical framework I would like to propose for comparative theology is the philosophy of the later Wittgenstein in the interpretation of internal realism. For our context, the central point of Wittgenstein's investigations is the insight that the meaning of religious beliefs is not accessible without reference to practice. And practice is not accessible separate from our "language-games." In this view, we can only understand the meaning of the religious elements of our world pictures by referring to their embeddedness in our language-games, which are the instances in Wittgenstein's later philosophy wherein our ways of acting and the understanding of them are originally connected.[8] This is why religious beliefs cannot be understood without reference to concrete "language-game-practice." And it also explains how people who use the same terms sometimes cannot contradict each other when these terms take on different roles within their language games, especially when these terms are embedded in specific (often tacit) levels of grammatical propositions (regarding our world-pictures).

Moreover, concerning religious beliefs, insight into the language-game-praxeological foundation of their meaning reveals a further problem. At least in the tradition of Western philosophy, "God" must be defined as a "being than no greater can be conceived," or at least as something "unconditional." But humans, as conditional beings, can only express their faith in an unconditional being in a conditional way. It is therefore not possible to express the belief in such a being in a conditional way without leaving room for doubt and misunderstanding. Humans can doubt (from an internal or external perspective), for grammatical reasons, whether a conditional way of expressing belief is really an expression of the belief in an unconditional being. And they can doubt whether a contradiction, on the cognitive-propositional level, as regards such an unconditional being, remains a contradiction when considering its praxeological roots

[7] Cf. K. von Stosch, "Komparative Theologie - ein Ausweg aus dem Grunddilemma jeder Theologie der Religionen?" in *Zeitschrift für Katholische Theologie* 124 (2002): 294-311.

[8] Cf. J. Schulte, *Erlebnis und Ausdruck: Wittgensteins Philosophie der Psychologie* (Munich / Vienna, 1987), 26. 31.

They can always ask whether their form of life is really regulated by their belief in God because there is (for internal reasons) no intrinsic correlation between their actions and the corresponding regulative/grammatical propositions.[9] The claim, then, to the universal validity of a regulative proposition expressing the belief in God cannot, as a "hinge proposition," be realized in all one's actions. That is why one cannot eliminate the contingency of the regulative status of religious belief, and that is why one must furnish reasons for it. And – in our context – that is why one cannot compare the truth claims of different religions in general.

Different believers within one religion and in different religions are not merely playing different language games. The meaning of their grammatical propositions, which are the basis of all possible argumentation, may differ among them. Or, at least, they can differ to such an extent that persons unwittingly speak of different things while using the same terms. The lack of sensibility for the regulative role of religious belief can lead to complete darkness in the theological or philosophical inquiry. According to the later Wittgenstein, ignoring the difference between grammatical or regulative propositions on the one hand, and encyclopedic or empirical propositions on the other, is not only the "congenital defect" of metaphysics,[10] but it is also and especially the main cause of error in the philosophy of religion and – I would like to add – in the theology of religions.

Comparative Theology as Way Out of the Impasse of Theology of Religions

The attempt of the theology of religions to provide a pluralist or inclusivist interpretation to the differing truth claims of different religions is mistaken because one cannot construct a general interpretation of these truth claims at all. One must investigate truth claims within their language-game-practice. Attention must be turned to specifics, and one must search for the meaning of religious beliefs by turning to their concrete embedding. Theological investigations must be developed as a collection of examples that consider individual meanings

9 Cf. K. von Stosch, "Was sind religiöse Überzeugungen?," in H. Joas (ed.), *Was sind religiöse Überzeugungen?* (Göttingen, 2003), 96-139.

10 Cf. L. Wittgenstein, "Bemerkungen über die Philosophie der Psychologie," in L. Wittgenstein, *Werkausgabe* VII, 6th ed. (Frankfurt a.M., 1994), I, no. 949; L. Wittgenstein, "Zettel," in L. Wittgenstein, *Werkausgabe* VIII, 5th ed. (Frankfurt a.M., 1992), 259-443, here no. 458.

in representative language games according to differing types of religious belief. And it makes no sense at all to establish a theory evaluating the amount of "mediation of a salvific knowledge of ultimate / transcendent reality in different religions."[11]

The impossibility of such a theory is the reason why Schmidt-Leukel's claim that comparative theology is no alternative for the theology of religions is wrong. *Pace* Schmidt-Leukel, the systematic and consistent pursuit of comparative theology does not lead to a general theory of religion and to an exclusive option of a theology of religions. Nevertheless, it may be true that comparative theology will sooner or later lead to a juncture where the question of the relationship between non-Christian and the respective Christian beliefs becomes unavoidable. But this question only arises concerning those concrete beliefs investigated by comparative theology. It does not arise concerning Christian or non-Christian beliefs in general.

Thus Schmidt-Leukel is right in asserting that only "comparative religion" can avoid the question of truth concerning the diversity of religious beliefs. Although comparative theology has to deal with the question of truth, it – in contrast to a theology of religions – does not assay to compare religions in general. Such a general comparison would lead to complete darkness. Comparative theology focuses on particularities, and at this micro level, it evaluates believers' truth claims while considering their pragmatic and regulative role. This restriction of theological attention to the individual case allows the appreciation of diversity without the need for relinquishing one's own religious perspective.

Nevertheless, there is no guarantee for the comparative theologian that her engagement with another religion will not lead her to conversion to that other religion. As she continues to discover the richness of another religious tradition, she may find herself attracted by the other way of believing, by the new language-game-practice laid open to her through the enterprise of comparative theology. Equally possible, she could learn something new about the tacit level of her own beliefs. Revisions of the comparative theologian's world-picture could become necessary. Or, as Schmidt-Leukel puts it, "comparative reflection may very well lead to a point where some of one's own religious presuppositions are seriously drawn into question, so that revision and change of these presuppositions may seem to be unavoidable."[12] I do admit that the comparative approach may predispose one toward revising one's own cognitive frameworks

11 Cf. P. Schmidt-Leukel, "Limits and Prospects."

12 Schmidt-Leukel, "Limits and Prospects."

for religious belief. I even admit the possibility of conversion. But, for grammatical reasons, I cannot admit that a revision of the constitutive basis of a religious tradition is possible without admitting that, by this revision, one thereby leaves the tradition. One simply cannot contradict the central claim of a religious tradition and at the same time remain a religious believer within it.

Concerning the Christian tradition, the crucial question is whether or not the belief in Jesus Christ is compatible with a pluralist account. On the micro level, it is possible to ascertain whether the rejection of, or relativizing of, belief in Christ is rooted in a language-game-practice equal in value to my own. I may discover that a Muslim must renounce this claim because he cannot secure an adequate grammatical role for it within his world-picture. And a Christian may disavow his own belief in Christ on the same language-game-praxeological level (just think of the new crusades in our days). Comparative theology thus permits the traditional claim of uniqueness in Christology without devaluating any rejection of this claim. However, this possibility does not intend to give up the Christian claim of uniqueness, as it is proposed by the pluralist option in the theology of religions. As far as I can see, such a pluralist revision is not possible without leaving the framework of Christianity. Surely this evaluation is fallible and reversible. But I do not see any good reason for such a revision.

Nonetheless, in the perspective of comparative theology, one can try to renounce claims to absolute certainty and to learn to respect difference. One can also try to deepen the understanding of one's own beliefs by paying attention to other traditions, and by reformulating one's own principles in light of the criticisms other traditions may make. Francis Clooney gives an interesting demonstration of such a possibility by showing, impressively, how comparative practice can lead to a widening of theological vision. Such attempts provide an alternative to the theology of religions in the same measure as they renounce any attempt to adopt God's point of view. As perspectival beings, we cannot compare world-pictures as comprehensive; we can only compare specific elements of our world-pictures without ever being able to finalize our evaluations of their relationship to the question of truth. What we can do is widen our horizons through interreligious dialogue and comparative practice. Yet we will never establish a rationally based theory that is capable of evaluating different religions or the diversity of religions in general. This is my bad news for any theology of religion. My good news is that such a theory is not necessary for an appreciation of diversity. In the attention we give to particulars, we can learn to appreciate difference as difference by becoming aware of the regulative dimensions of the meaning of difference.

Robert Cummings Neville

The Role of Concepts of God in Crosscultural Comparative Theology

Concepts of God in Comparison

The obivious problem with concepts of God as crosscultural comparative categories is that some religions do not have them, or conceive gods in relatively trivial ways. To appreciate why this is a problem, however, it is important to see why concepts of God are so attractive for comparative purposes. The main reason is that, at least for the monotheistic religions, the categories spelling out divinity refer to what is religiously most important. God is the center around which all other religious elements move. Whether conceived in metaphysical ways as creator or in existential ways as judge, savior, lover, goal or eschatological finisher, God is conceived in the monotheistic religions to be the most important reality for human life, concepts of which determine more of all the other religious notions than any of them directly affects the concepts of God. So naturally comparative theology ought to be able to recognize what at least some religions take to be the most important reality and compare religions in respect of it. If a religion cannot be compared to others with respect to what it takes to be most important, the comparisons that are left seem trivial. Religions can be compared on their respective attitudes toward eating popcorn, but so what? Religions can be compared with respect to their moral codes, but, without connection to the concepts of God, moral codes fail to be religious for the monotheistic traditions. The same is true regarding many other things in respect of which religions can be compared: without connection to God, the comparisons seem to distort the heart of religion, for the montheisms.[1]

---

[1] Although some of the comparative points to be made in this essay are in need of much justification, the expository points about individual religious or theological traditions are commonplaces. Encyclopedias or introductory text books can be consulted if necessary. The comparisons themselves come from a richer ground than can be explained with particular citations, however. I had the privilege to direct the Crosscultural Comparative Religious Ideas Project at Boston University which engaged a collaborative team of scholars in a self-corrective process that ran from 1995 to 1999, the public results of which were published in three volumes: *The Human Condition*, with a foreword by Peter Berger, *Ultimate Realities*, with a foreword by Tu Weiming, and *Religious Truth*, with a foreword by Jonathan Z. Smith, all edited by myslef (Albany, 2001). Many of the comparative points made in the present essay arose from that collaboration, and some are to

Monotheisms do not have a monopoly on God. Most forms of Hinduism have important conceptions of God. Many recognize a pantheon of gods, but usually with a hierarchical order; their theological traditions usually affirm a sophisticated monotheistic reality underlying a variety of apparent manifestations. Advaita Vendanta is even more intensely "mono" than most forms of West Asian monotheism that suppose some duality between God and the world. In East Asian religion, concepts of the Dao, the Great Ultimate, Heaven and Earth, Principle, and the like play roles similar to concepts of God, similar enough that comparison is fruitful (if also seductively treacherous) to lay out similarities and differences.

Of course it has long been recognized that God is conceived differently in different religions. More recently we have become conscious of the fact that radically different conceptions exist within the same religion, marking out different and perhaps conflicitng roles. Perennial philosophers, for instance, have pointed out Neo-Platonic-like similarities of strains within Judaism, Christianity, Islam, Advaita Vedanta, and other religions, while noting that each of those religions has other strains that reject the perennial philosophy.[2] Most theistic religions have very personal conceptions of God as well as highly impersonal concepttions, often in conflict for use in interpreting sacred rituals and texts.[3] Sorting these different concepts and their various roles within religious practice is the very stuff of theological comparison.

The attractiveness of concepts of God to the great Western comparative projects of the 19th and 20th centuries is understandable. In fact, comparing pantheons was of interest in the ancient Western world as well as in India. Part of the Axial Age phenomenon analyzed by Jaspers was a consciousness of the culturally transcendent character of otherwise conventional notions.

Nevertheless, important forms of Buddhism, such as the Theravada, do not have concepts of God or gods. Popular forms of Buddhism have thousands of gods that are religiously trivial. Although some forms of Mahayana Buddhism treat Emptiness as something like a theistic category of the absolute, other Ma-

---

be found in the publications. The experience of the collaboration goes beyond any particular comparison.

2 Huston Smith is the most influential historian of religions to employ the Perennial Philosophy. See his *The World's Religions: Our Great Wisdom Traditions* (San Francisco, 1991); revised edition of *Religions of Man* (1958).

3 On personification of the ultimate in religious symbols, see my *Religion in Late Modernity* (Albany, 2002), ch. 4.

hayan forms such as the Madhyamaka deny ontological reference to ultimate or absolute realities. For Buddhism, the main point of the religious practice is to find release from suffering, according to the Four Noble Truths, and any realities that might aid that are religious only as expedient means to release. High-powered concepts of divinity are usually thought to be inexpedient.[4] If concepts of God are important comparative categories for religions, then Buddhism turns out to be not a religion, or only a deficient one. This is a disastrous result for the intended objectivity of scholarly theological comparison.

The case of Buddhism has highlighted the bias of comparative work that originates in the Western world. To put the point simply, with minimal oversimplification, Western comparativists' enthusiasm for concepts of God was revealed to be a strong prejudice that the monotheist, mainly Christian, conceptions of God define religion itself. When dealing with non-monotheistic religions, this Western comparative project has treated their basic notions as "analogous" with conceptions of God, as illustrated above. As mere analogues with God, Brahman and the Dao are poor versions of the prime analogate of their referent. Hegel made the best case for this way of thinking when he analyzed a wide range of conceptions of religious' objects according to their roles in a large dialectic culminating in his version of Absolute Christianity. For all his insights into the intricate structures and relations among religious ideas, however, his project is now rightly recognized as arbitrary apologetics for his own religious heritage: Buddhist, Vendanta, and Confucian dialectics would have the gradings of other religions turn out to be quite different.

The reaction in many quarters against the dominance of concepts of God in Western crosscultural theological comparison has been to demonize the very project of theological comparison. That project seems to illustrate the folly of logocentrism and fuel the oppressive distortions of orientalism. The better part of scholarship, according to this reaction, is to eschew theological comparison and work on microstudies of particular religious texts and circumstances. The absurdity of this reaction is that one cannot say that a comparative apporach distorts unless one has some more basic comparative perspective within which to stand. To say that a comparative project imposes alien categories, such as those of God on non-theistic religions, presupposes a comparison between what the categories say about the religion and some other more priviledged information about the religion. So the more honest strategy for correcting bias in comparison

[4] See "Cooking the Last Fruit of Nihilism: Buddhist Approaches to Ultimate Reality" by Malcolm David Eckel with John J. Thatamanil in *Ultimate Realities*, ch. 6.

is to find ways of comparison that are vulnerable to correction for bias. This requires taking a deeper look at comparison.

Theoretical Issues in Comparison

The deeper comparative question to ask about concepts of God is, in what respects do they interpret reality?[5] Comparison is always in some respect or other. The cliched joke about comparing apples and oranges turns on the supposition that one should compare items with respect to being different kinds of apples, or different kinds of oranges; the joke does not work if the intent is to compare apples and oranges with respect to being different kinds of fruit. The "respect" in which things are compared is the "comparative category" being used. Confusion about the respects in which things are compared, usually occasioned by misleading relations of language, lies behind many theological confusions.

Respects or categories of comparison are not mere conceptual tools whose instrumental worth lies within the comparative project or scheme. Rather, comparative categories aim to pick out the respect in which the items compared themselves interpret reality. Thus, the interpretive context and purpose of comparison rests on a more basic interpretive relation that in turn illustrates a more general notion of interpretation.

The more general notion, I propose, is best understood in terms of Charles Peirce's theory of semiotics.[6] In Peirce's theory, an interpretation takes a sign to stand for an object in certain respect. An interpretation is an existential act, a way of engaging the object by means of the sign that represents it in a certain respect. If the object is a river, for instance, "brown" represents it in respect of color, "southward" in respect of direction of flow, "in the Mid-West of America" in respect of place, and "Mississippi" in respect of name. The context and purpose of interpretation determines the relevant respect in which to interpret the river. To say that a sugar cube is both white and sweet is not a contradiction because those attributes interpret it in different respects. To say that God is both love and light is not a contradiction because, presumably, those attributes stand for God in different respects. Is the uneasy compatibility of God's alleged justice and

5 On this general theory of comparison, see chapter 1 of *The Human Condition* and chapter 8 of *Ultimate Realities*, both by Wesley J. Wildman and myself.

6 I have analyzed Peirce and developed his ideas in my own ways, reflected in the current essay, in *The Highland around Modernism* (Albany, 1992), ch. 1; *Recovery of the Measure* (Albany, 1989), divisions 1 and 4; *Normative Cultures* (Albany, 2002), ch. 3.

mercy also to be adjucated this way?[7] To answer the question requires becoming more precise about the respects in which they stand for God in given interpretations.

Since the "linguistic turn," we are accustomed to think of all signs as mental or linguistic entities.[8] From this we tend to think of the objects and further interpretants of signs also as mental or linguistic entities, and before long people are saying that everything is a "text" because we cannot talk about anything at all that is not itself a sign or referred to as a sign. Peirce, however argued rightly that things in this world are really and extramentally related to one another according to semiotic patterns. A brute action according to a physical law he regarded as the effect standing for the cause in respect of the physical law, with the interpretation being the new situation. I let slip the cup that falls to the floor and breaks: the breaking cup stands for my slip in respect of the law of gravity and the whole event is the interpretation. To continue with that example, my wife's glare interprets the slip in respect of my inattentive manners, and the host's rush to mop the coffee, muttering that he'll fetch another of his great aunt's antique cups, interprets the slip in a complex, double-meaning respect that both levies and lightens blame in a social situation. In matters of religious thought, we can ask about the respects in which the concept "God" interprets reality and we can alternatively ask how God, so conceived, interprets reality. The latter means to ask what God means in respect of what and for what or whom. For instance, God means Creator in respect to the existence of the world for the monotheistic religions; God also means Judge in respect of the ultimate worth of nations and individual people, for those religions, etc. In monotheistic categories, God belongs to the categories that mark out the respects in which God is significant for, that is interprets, one thing or another. God is interpreted by those categories, and we should understand that those categories are the respects in which God is interpreted for certain interpreters.

Peirce's is a realistic view of truth in interpretation. Not all theistic religions interpret God in the same respects. Moreover, the conceptual categories are at best wise stabs at getting the real categories or respects of interpretive relation right. Nevertheless, in respect of the world's existence, either God is its creator

7 See "Religious Dimensions of the Human Condition in Judaism: Wrestling with God in an Imperfect World," in *The Human Condition* and "Ultimate Realities: Judaism: God as a Many-sided Ultimate Reality in Traditional Judaism," in *Ultimate Realities,* both by Anthony J. Saldarini with Joseph Kanofsky.

8 See Richard Rorty's edited book, *The Linguistic Turn: Recent Essays in Philosophical Method* (Chicago, 1967), including his introduction.

or not, and this does not depend on how theistic theologies think about it. The philosophic problem for theology at this point, of course, is that even asking the question to be answered realistically depends on our historically contingent concepts to frame the question. To ask about the world's contingency supposes some conceptual metaphysics or other, and there are many among which to choose that give different versions of contingency.

So interpretive theology, necessary to produce theological concepts to compare, needs to control for three dimensions of its context. First, it has to ask the realistic questions: is God or is God not the creator of the contingent world? Second, it has to ask the hermeneutical questions: does the theology at hand have adequate categories to interpret the realistic situation, for instance understanding contingency? Third, how do the cultural values and purposes of the theological interpretive project at hand select and control for the respects in which it aims to interpret reality and can these be justified as the best?

To summarize this section, a general Peircean notion of interpretation has been laid out that points up how a theological interpretation aims to interpret its object, e.g. God, in certain respects, e.g. the contingency of the world. Two different religions or theologies can be compared only where they are found to have concepts interpreting the same object in the same respect.

Observations about Ultimacy

We are now almost ready to ask in what respects concepts of God interpret their objects so that we can compare their concepts. A linguistic confusion needs to be dealt with first. "God" is both a common noun and a proper noun. When we speak of monotheisms, "God" as a common noun is common to all. The Jewish conception of Yahweh, the Christian Trinity, and Muslim Allah are overlapping but somewhat different proper names for the common noun with different theological conceptions and symbol systems. "Brahman," "Dao," "Emptiness," "Buddha Nature," and "Heavenly Principle" are also common nouns in a sense, with different conceptions within each family of religions that use those titles as proper names, and they all are somewhat like. To minimize confusions, in what follows, "ultimacy" or "the ultimate" will be used as the common noun of which various concepts of God, Brahman, Dao, Buddha Nature, etc., are versions to be compared. The restated topic of this essay, then, is the role of concepts of *ultimacy* in cross cultural comparative theology.[9]

In what respects do concepts of ultimacy interpret their object? To answer that question with the formulation of a proper hypothesis, three observations are in order: an historical one, a point about two senses of ultimacy, and a metaphysical observation.

The historical point is that in all or nearly all the great religious traditions with a traceable history the earliest representation of the ultimate were highly personalistic or personified. That is, the ultimate was represented as a super human being with an intensification of human powers beyond the ordinary, and the world was conceived as the product of superhuman making. Usually, the ultimate was one super being among others, though superior, as Zeus to Apollo, Yahweh to the other gods who should not be put before him by the Israelites, Shangdi the Chinese sky god, Indra, Vishnu, Dyaus or some other top god in Indian pantheons. These ultimates were conceived as intensely personal, like human persons only more so. They were thought to have places within the cosmos and to interact with human and other personal beings as well as natural forces.

As the great religions developed, the highly anthropormorphic images of the ultimate were supplemented if not supplanted by less anthropomorphic concepts. Within the history of Israel, the Yahweh of the Ten Commandments was to be put first among all the gods by the Hebrews because he was their own god (not necessarily because he was better than the gods of the Egyptians and Canaanites – that had to be proved in battle); the God of the creation narratives is absolutely supreme; the God of Second Isaiah was Lord of all nations, not only Israel; the God of Job was to be conceived expressly beyond human categories; and the God of St. John was both love and light, not loving and illuminating only, but love and light itself. Within the first centuries of Christianity God the Father was conceived on the model of the Neo-Platonic One beyond being and distinction; for Thomas Aquinas God is the Pure Act of Esse. In Indian religions Buddhism was, among other things, an anti-anthropomorphic reaction against the personifications of divinity in the Vedic traditions. In Chinese religions both Daoism and Confucianism took form by explicitly denying the anthropomorphism of the early Shangdi worship, which they took to be superstitious. To use the rhetoric of the Western monotheisms, the danger with the anthropomorphic concepts is that they become idolatrous, mistaking something non-ultimate for the ultimate.

9 On the proper vagueness of the notion of *ultimacy*, see the "Introduction" to *Ultimate Realities* by Wesley J. Wildman and myself.

In all these traditions, after the Axial Age when the cosmos came to be considered as as whole, the ultimate as unitary, and human beings as individuals defined before the ultimate rather than in terms of their land and kin, a spectrum of rhetoric was maintained with extremes of anthropomorphic personification of the ultimate and of abstraction of the ultimate to principles or something "beyond" definition.[10] But the religions took their classic rhetorical forms by fixing on some portion of that spectrum. The Western monotheisms fixed on the rather anthropomorphic rhetoric of God as a player in an historical narrative. Liturgies, songs, and stories emphasize the personal aspects of God. In Judaism, that narrative strongly defines the people Israel. In Christianity the salvation-history theme has always been strong, especially since the rise of Biblical reformation through that suppressed metaphysical medieval theology; strong anti-anthropomorphic elements also exist within Christianity. In Islam, because of the very great importance of combating idolatry, the anti-anthropomorphic elements predominate, although the rhetoric of Allah as a person remains.[11] In India, the reconstitution of the Vedic and Upanisadic traditions as Hinduism over against Buddhism included extremes of the non-anthropomorphic "principle" concepts, as in Advaita Vedanta, although it also kept highly sophisticated personalistic conceptions, as in Ramanuja's Visisthadvaita Vedanta. Buddhism, for all its anti-anthropomorphism in concepts of the ultimate (to the extreme of denying ontological reference entirely in Madhyamaka), returned to personalistic notions in devotion to bodhisattvas such as Avaloketishvara or Guanyin. For whatever reason, the Indian religions occupy a broad expanse across the middle of the spectrum. In China, the triumph of anti-anthropomorphic and anti-supernatural Confucianism and Daoism in the early Han dynasty was a major cultural / political transformation. The center of rhetoric of those traditions is highly abstracted or devoted to principles rather than personification. Nevertheless, even Confucianism with its rejection of Shangdi insisted on waiting for the mandate, i.e. will of Heaven, and Daoism developed into elaborate cosmologies with pantheons in its medieval period. The religions usually called theistic are those whose center of rhetoric comes from the anthropomorphic end of the spectrum, whereas the religions that are not theistic take their center of rhetoric from the other end.

---

[10] On the spectrum of personification and abstraction, see "Comparative Conclusions about Ultimate Realities" by Wesley J. Wildman and myself in *Ultimate Realities*, ch. 7. On the Axial Age, see Karl Jaspers' *The Way to Wisdom*, translated by Ralph Mannheim (New Haven, 1954).

[11] See S. Nomanul Haq's "Ultimate Reality: Islam," in *Ultimate Realities,* ch. 4.

The observation about two senses of ultimacy is this: whereas the bias of thinkers from monotheistic traditions is to give an ontological interpretation of ultimacy – an ultimate being or ultimate ground or principle, the bias of thinkers from some other traditions is to give an anthropological interpretation of ultimacy – religion as an ultimate quest for release from suffering, from ignorance, or perhaps from disharmony. Where the ontological ultimate is construed to be a reality or characteristic of reality, or something really transcending all that (bearing in mind the mystics), the anthropological ultimate is a characteristic of a life process, a drive, a quest, or something like that. Usually the two are connected and religions have only predominant biases. The ultimacy of the ontological God in the monotheistic traditions determines an ultimacy to human life and its obligations, guilts, and redemption. The ultimacy of self-realization, attunement, and religious virtuosity in the East Asian religions of India, the ontological characters include ultimate realities. The ultimacy of the quest for enlightenment, release from suffering and rebirth, and the achievement of non-attachment, as well as the ecstasies of worship in the various religions of India are all related to the ontological characters of things. For most of the religions of India are all related to the ontologocial characters of things. For the forms of Buddhism that deny ontological ultimates, that denial still is based on a reading of the ontological characters of things, e.g. Emptiness, pratitya samutpada.

Paul Tillich has been explicit in tying ultimate ontological reality to ultimate concern, his phrase for the anthropological ultimate. In one of his most important essays he distinguishes

> two ways of approaching God: the way of overcoming estrangement and the way of meeting a stranger. In the first way man discovers *himself* when he discovers God; he discovers something that is identical with himself although it transcends him infinitely, something from which he is estranged, but from which he never has been and never can be separated. In the second way man meets a *stranger* when he meets God. The meeting is accidental.[12]

Tillich calls the former way "ontological" and the latter "cosmological," which differs from the usage here. Here the way of overcoming estrangement is the anthropological ultimate and the meeting with God as a different being is one version of the ontological ultimate. Tillich's point is that the latter is flawed. The way of overcoming estrangement, however anthropological on our account, is the way of connecting with ontological ultimacy, on his view. In comparative

[12] See his "The Two Types of Philosophy of Religion," in *Theology of Culture*, ed. by Robert C. Kimbell (New York, 1959), 10.

perspective, it must remain an open empirical question whether the anthropological and ontological ultimates are to be so happily connected. A properly vague hypothesis to connect them will be presented shortly.

The metaphysical observation is the hypothesis that ontological ultimacy partly, though not exclusively, has to do with the problem of the one and the many. The problem of the one and the many has several versions. One version is to start with a recognized plurality and ask how these are ultimately unified so as to be possible together. This version is well expressed in Neo-Platonism and the Perennial Philosophy. Another is to start with fundamental unity and ask how the plurality of things there seems to be is possible or actual. Non-dualist theologies treating plurality as illusion and the origins-from-non-being philosophies of East Asia express this version. The more general statement of the problem is to account for how the world can be both many and also have the unity it does. The existence of a somewhat unified manifold is a puzzle at the heart of reality. Ultimate reality is what makes possible both plurality and unity together.

One consequence of this for theology is that candidates for the ontological ultimate need to constitute the ground of one and many together and not merely be one of the many, or the one apart from the many.[13] If the alleged ultimate were one of the many, for instance God as a being among others, or a one apart from the many, for instance a Neo-Platonic One apart from its emanations, then that which contains the alleged ultimate plus the rest, or makes possible their togetherness, would be "more ultimate."

The different religious traditions have various ways of formulating the problem of the one and the many. The hypothesis here is that many of those ways are attempts to recognize and articulate the real one-many structure of things. So most traditions contain pressures to criticize inadequate formulations of the one/many character of ultimacy. The Yahweh among other gods in the Ten Commandments is too small; so is the Yahweh whose justice and mercy treat only Israel. In fact the monotheistic interpretation of creation came quickly to be that anything that could be distinguished from anything else, hence both parts of the many, cannot be the ultimate. The medieval principle that God must be simple, common to many Muslim, Christian, and Jewish theologians, was perhaps not so much derived from love of Aristotelian notions of perfection as from the fact that complexities and hence only one of a larger many. The Indian appreciation of fundamental unity exerted constant pressure to treat the many

---

13 This analysis of the one and the many is dealt with at length in my *God the Creator*, rev. ed. (Albany, 1992); original edition Chicago, 1968, part 1.

gods as manifestations of deeper underlying realities, however diverse their functions. This Buddhist emphasis on pratitya samutprada, variously interpreted, resisted attempts both to reduce the perceived many to substantial unitary realities and to reduce the unity of phenomenal experience to separate integral units with their individual own-being. The East Asian intellectual environment resisted any attempt to identify a single determinate ontological cause for things, often saying that things arise from non-being, or indeterminate nothingness. The ontological pluralism of the Confucian tradition, accounting for nature as the result of Heaven and Earth combined, was unsteady in respect of the unity of the two ultimate principles, with Zhuxi claiming half-heartedly that Heaven (Principle) produces Earth (Material Force) and Wang Yangming, his rival, saying that all is Principle. The struggles between those two schools of Neo-Confucian philosophy should be read as grappling with how not to be idolatrous with the problem of the one and the many.

An Hypothesis About the Respect in Which Concepts of Ultimacy Interpret Reality

An hypothesis can now be formulated about the respect in which concepts of God or versions of the ultimate interpret reality. *Concepts of ultimate reality, within the semiotic systems of their culture, stand for that in reality in respect of which human life is to be considered as having ultimate significance. "Ultimate significance" means whatever value or meaning a person or group has in a context that is not qualified by any larger or alternative context, though the value in question might be made up of the contributions of many subcontexts internal to the ultimate one.* This hypothesis can only be proved or substantiated by a thorough review of religious notions of the ultimate, a task of a lifetime. The following portions of this essay shall just gloss the hypothesis.

A tension always exists between recognizing the culture-bound or historical character of all conceptual constructs and recognizing that these are aimed to be really correct by those who use them and that they evolve through complicated corrective processes of engaging reality in their terms. All concepts, of course, are indeed culture-bound and historically developed. The hypothesis reflects this in the extreme vagueness of the phrase, *that in reality in respect of which human life is to be considered as having ultimate significance.* In pre-axial age religions, for instance, concepts standing for reality in that respect might be a system of totemic animals that gives one's tribe identity and preeminence relative to the tribe over the hill. Genuine pagan pantheons, in which different natural functions are governed by different gods with no supreme god, define ultimate human significance as responsive to the many gods in their functions. Axial age religions of the sort mentioned earlier have both subsidiary conceptions of the cosmos as a whole that bound the context of significance, and subsidiary conceptions of the individual as given significance relative to that cosmic context as well as to more local contexts such as family and territory. Different Axial Age cultures bond the cosmos differently. Ancient China conceived it as a great blob of *qi* structured according to macrocosmic and microcosmic yin-yang patterns.[14] The ancient Near East conceived it as a hierarchy of planes with somewhat different causal structures and different kinds of agents (angels of various orders, demons, etc.). Similarly different conceptions of individuality exist, related differently to the respective conceptions of the cosmos. As a rough generalization, virtuosi in East Asian religions aim at attunement to or harmony with the ultimate context of the cosmos, and virtuosi in South Asian religions aim at righteousness or justice, although all models are present in each of the cultures with some configuration or other. Comparative ethnography can trace the various configurations.

The other side of the tension is that religions cope with the realities of their situation. Religious conceptions guide people in the most pervasive aspects of their lives, shaping their behavior by the contours of the conceived ultimate context and the priorities of ultimate significance (about which more shortly). Reality is a hard teacher. If a society's conception of the cosmos does not countenance the existence of the barbarians, and they suddenly appear over the hill, the conception has to shift; if the conception says the higher celestial planes are filled with angels and better science finds hot rocks in the void, the conception is cor\rected, albeit often with difficulty. Sometimes not facts per se but considerations of intellectual elegance correct conceptions of the ultimate. The argument above to the effect that a God conceived as alongside the many is not as ultimate as whatever includes both God and the many is an example of the reality of the structure of intellectual possiblility correcting conceptions inadequately though through (an example at least for those for whom deep thinking is important). However different religions might be in their conceptual structures, their adherents intend the conceptual structures to be true to reality and not merely what their group happens to think. Only recently have people argued that being faith-

[14] See the fine discussion in Livia Kohn's "Chinese Religion," in *The Human Condition*.

ful to an ethnographic conceptual / behavioral scheme can be substituted for making a case for the non-arbitrariness of a group's views.[15]

Human value or significance is conceived in many different ways within and among the world religions. The focus of the hypothesis is on *ultimacy* in value. People are valuable in many obvious ways: for what they contribute and do, for the roles they play in society and history (often defined by family roles), for how they are regarded within their society and the influence they have, for their achievements of personal character, integrity, intellectual or artistic accomplishment, and so forth. Cultures define these forms of human value variously, though with many overlaps that support conditions for universal morality. All of these values are relative to time and circumstance. Is there not some context in which a person, or group, simply is the sum total of values (or disvalues) achieved and significances for others and the world? This is a reformation of the question of the anthropological ultimate: what is it that defines a human being ultimately?[16]

Confucianism and Daoism, and in part Chinese forms of Buddhism, say that all of one's values (and disvalues) are ultimately contextualized by the ways one harmonizes with the processes of reality. They disagree about the relevant process, Confucianism emphasizing social ones, Daoism natural ones, and Buddhism mental ones. They agree, each in its own ways, that the ultimate meaning of one's life is how, where, and to what degree one's harmonizing with the procesșes gives one the power and identity of the cosmos (appropriately defined).[17] Indian and other kinds of Buddhism take release from suffering to be the immediate goal of human life, with practiced detachment as the means. What makes release from suffering itself results from a vast ontological mistake of misidentifying what is real; enlightenment in Buddhism is not so much about an ontological object but about enlightened ones being ultimately right ontologically.[18] West Asian religions focus more on the processes of living justly than

15 The position of George Lindbeck, for instance, in his *The Nature of Doctrine* (Philadelphia, 1984).

16 On the question of ultimacy and human nature, see my "Human Nature" in *Religion in Late Modernity*.

17 On the idea of the sage or perfected one, see "Ultimate Reality: Chinese Religion" by Livia Kohn with James Miller in *Ultimate Realities*, ch. 1, and "Truth in Chinese Religion" by Livia Kohn and James Miller in *Religious Truth*, ch. 1.

18 See "Beginningless Ignorance: A Buddhist View of the Human Condition" by Malcolm David Eckel with John J. Thatamanil and "To be Heard and Done, But Never Quite Seen: The Human Condition According to the *Vivekacudamani*" by Francis X. Clooney, SJ, with Hugh Nicholson, in *The Human Condition*, chs. 3 and 4 respectively.

those of harmony or enlightenment, though all are present. Ultimate matters in justice are often symbolized by persons and communities being judged by God as by a king. Even when the anthropomorphic symbols are dismissed for more abstract transcedent ones, the ultimate concern of Jews, Christians, and Muslims is to be justified before the ultimate as a means of praising God. The Christian logic is to say that God in Christ presents people as justified before God, even when they do not deserve that.

The hypothesis about the respect in which conceptions of the ultimate represent their objects can relate the spectrum of conceptions of the ontological ultimate from highly personified forms to abstract ones to the distinction between the ontological and anthropological ultimates. The hypothesis refers to *that in reality in respect of which human life is to be considered as having ultimate significance.* "That in reality" is the ontological ultimate. The anthropological ultimate determines the respect in which "that" is taken to be ultimate. This point is easy to make in the case of those conceptions of the ontological ultimate that fall toward the personifying end of the spectrum. The human interest to attain ultimate harmony, enlightenment, or salvation with respect to righteousness easily personifies the conditions in reality that determine how that is possible. Confucians wait upon the mandate of heaven, Buddhists appeal to Guanyin or think about understanding Emptiness as approaching Buddha nature, and monotheists pray to God for deliverance and salvation. Petitionary prayers in all religions suppose a cry from the bottom of the heart for what is ultimately most needed and important, and such a cry is addressed as to an interpretive listener.[19]

Conceptions of the ultimate focused more toward the abstract or transcendent end of the specturm are just as much interpretive in terms of the anthropological respect, though they might not seem so at first. For those theological traditions that have sensed or articulated the logic of the one / many formal criterion of ultimacy, the character of the anthropological ultimate has been keyed to the ontological conception. One's ultimate quest has to do with relating to the ground of the one-and-many configuration of the cosmos, conceived as best one's culture can. The conception of that which answers to the anthropological quest for ultimacy is that which defines the ultimate context in which one's ultimate value or significance is to be found.

19 On this interpretation of prayer, see James P. Carse's brilliant *The Silence of God: Meditations on Prayer* (New York, 1985).

The extremes of the ontological / anthropological distinction would seem to lie outside the generalization just made. The extreme ontological side is characteristic of those traditions with detailed and explicit discussions of the one and many problem, such as Buddhism, several forms of Hinduism, and Christianity and Islam. In these traditions, hypotheses about how the one/many character of the world is grounded can be formulated without any reference to human life. They can be phrased in modern evolutionary terms as compatible with the possibility that no human life would have arisen at all. They can be purely metaphysical theories or hypotheses that would affirm what they do irrespective of any human significance. Nevertheless, they would not be taken to be religiously interesting as referring to the ultimate unless they shaped the anthropological quest for what is ultimately important; that shaping comes in the presentation of the grounding of the one and many in life. The metaphysical hypothesis shapes the sacred canopy, as Peter Berger puts it, in terms of which life has ultimate meaning (or no ultimate meaning on some conceptions).[20]

The extreme of the anthropological ultimate might be in some Theravada and Madhyamika Buddhist theologies that concentrate exclusively on human mental transformations and positively reject the value of any ontological hypotheses. This would seem to be a successful abandonment of all ontological ultimates. Nevertheless, those forms of Buddhism do have ontological hypotheses, namely, that nothing in reality has its own-being and that all phenomena reduce to the relativities of pratitya samutpada. The Buddhist ontological hypotheses deny that there is any ontologiclly ultimate object such as a God, Brahman, the Dao, or any transcedent creative source or principle. Yet it is precisely that total absence of any ontologically ultimate object that is the ontological reality in respect of which human significance is to be found: the lack of own-being is what makes non-attachment the ultimately important way of dealing with suffering. The ontological conception that nothing has ontological own-being needs to find its place on the spectrum from personifying to abstract conceptions.

We come finally to say how concepts of God or the ultimate legitimately can function in crosscultural comparative theology. Concepts of God and other names for the ultimate articulate what exists in reality that gives human life ultimate significance. Some kinds of secularism and atheism say that life indeed has no ultimate significance, and when developed with articulate sophistication these views say why reality does not sustain any ultimate signifcance for human

[20] Peter Berger, *The Sacred Canopy: Elements of a Sociological Theory of Religion*, Garden City, 1967).

life. Comparison needs to be able to point out cultures whose ontological views preclude anything that might give ultimate significance. As noted already, some forms of Buddhism conceive of ultimate reality as lacking ultimate objects, gods, or principles, yet as having a truth condition that defines the ultimate path of detachment; ultimate peaceful detachment, released from the bondage of suffering, is possible for these Buddhist views because nothing ontological is absolute enough to be worth attaching to. Some interpretations of ultimate significance might not seem very ultimate at first glance. To have a God-given purpose seems more instrumental than ultimate. To achieve a certain standing in a community might not seem ultimate. Yet for some cultures, things like that are significant because of how they relate individuals and communities to God or some other version of the ontological ultimate.

Comparative projects can ask religious (or anti-religious) cultures what they conceive in ontological reality that orients ultimate human significance. Some will answer with gods that govern the real, others with a creator God or Principle or Dao that orients ultimate human significance. The comparative process can say how each of these theologies specifies the vague category of the respect in which the respective ontological reality conveys human significance. Then those various specifications can be compared, saying which ones are in agreement or disagreement, how they overlap or fail to connect, and how some theologies are positive about the ultimate and others deny it.

Of course, at the same time that such comparisons of concepts of the ultimate is being carried on, attention must be paid to different conceptions of ultimate human significance. That is as broad a topic as that of comparative gods, and not to be addressed here.

The thesis defended here about the respect in which concepts of God or the ultimate represent their objects is an hypothesis. It has been proposed as a way of integrating an otherwise confusing and politically hot discussion, and have indicated some of its power to bring religions into comparative perspective without bias or saying that they have to be alike to be compared. This proposal about comparison works well with differences as with similarities. Nevertheless, the defense of the hypothesis here has been only suggestive. Honesty requires listing some potential difficulties for it.

Given the structure of the hypothesis, comparativists need a steady sense of what ultimate human significance is. There is not such a thing now, and therefore the investigation is struggling with two variables that define one another. Nevertheless, we have come to know that all of our comparative categories can be called into question, and that of ultimate human significance is no exception. It should have its turn as the topic.

Monotheists might argue that only highly personified conceptions, those customarily called God, are important enough to be candidates for comparison, and that the more abstract conceptions such as Dao or Principle fail to articulate the intensity and seriousness of the ultimate category. The hypothesis can be defended against this complaint by showing how those more abstract notions in their turn define ultimate human significance.

Because worship is the primary way of relating to the ultimate in many religions, the reference in the hypothesis to ultimate human significance is misplaced. Conceptions of God, it might be argued, represent ontological reality in respect of what is worthy of worship. The hypothesis, so the criticism goes, focuses too much on the human subject to define the ultimate and too little on the glory of the ultimate itself. The defense against this objection would have to show that ultimate human significance derives not from some finite human need but from the character of the defining ultimate ontological reality. The advantage to the reference to ultimate human significance is that it explains why the respect of interpretation of reality by means of concepts of the ultimate is ultimately important, reflecting the anthropological ultimate.

These and other objections need to be thought through before much confidence can be put in the hypothesis sketched here. The hypothesis is vulnerable to correction as that probation is made.

List of Authors

Bettina BÄUMER (Austria) (1940) has lived and worked in India since 1967. Habilitation and Visiting Professor of Religious Studies at the University of Vienna; senior researcher at Indian Institute of Advanced Study, Shimla (India); publications include volumes on Kalatattvakosa, Silparatnakosa, Silpa Prakasa, etc.; German translation of and commentary on the Upanisads, Yoga Sutra, Vijnana Bhairava, Abhinavagupta; *Trika: Grundthemen des kaschmirischen Sivaismus* (2004).

Peter BEYER (Canada) is Professor of Religious Studies, University of Ottawa, Canada; publications include *Religion and Globalization* (Sage, 1994), *Religion in the Process of Globalization* (Ergon, 2001) and *Religions in Global Society* (2006).

François BOUSQUET (France) (1947) is Professor of Fundamental Theology at the Institut Catholique de Paris (1999-); studies in philosophy and history of religions at the Sorbonne, theology at the Intitut Catholique de Paris (1973-1978) and Sciences et Histoire des Religions at Sorbonne-Paris IV; D. Theol. (1996, Institut Catholique de Paris); Visting Professor in Beirut; publications in philosophy, fundamental theology, and theology of religions; author of *L'esprit de Plotin* (1976), *Camus le méditerranéen - Camus l'Ancien* (1977), *Le scandale du mal* (1987), *Croire* (1991), *Le Christ de Kierkegaard* (1999), *La Trinité tout simplement* (2000).

Georg ESSEN (Germany) (1961) is Professor of Dogmatic Theology at the Faculties of Theology and Religious Studies, University of Nijmegen (2001-); Habilitation in 2000 and D. Theol. in 1994, Münster; publications include: *Historische Vernunft und Auferweckung Jesu: Theologie und Historik im Streit um den Begriff geschichtlicher Wirklichkeit* (1995), *Die Freiheit Jesu: Der neuchalkedonische Enhypostasiebegriff im Horizont neuzeitlicher Subjekt- und Personphilosophie* (2001), *Kant und die Theologie* (2005).

Jacques HAERS (Belgium) (1956) studied mathematics and philosophy and wrote a doctoral dissertation in philosophy (Oxford) on Origen's understanding of creation. He is a Jesuit and a professor at the Faculty of Theology at the Catholic University of Leuven and also teaches at the Centre Sèvres, Paris; director of the Master's Program in Conflict and Sustainable Peace as well as of the Centre for Liberation Theologies. His main interests include theologies of encounter, globalization, and peace studies. Publications include *Theology and Conversation: Towards a Relational Theology* (2003), *The Myriad Christ: Plurality and the Quest for Unity in Contemporary Christology* (2000).

Leonhard HELL (Germany) (1958) is Professor for Dogmatic and Ecumenical Theology, Johannes Gutenberg-Universität Mainz (2001-); D. Theol. (1991, Tübingen); author of *Entstehung und Entfaltung der theologischen Enzyklopädie* (1999), *Reich Gottes als Systemidee der Theologie: Historisch-systematische Untersuchungen zum theologischen Werk B. Galuras und F. Brenners* (1993).

Norbert HINTERSTEINER (Austria) (1963) is Assistant Professor for Foundational and Comparative Theology at The Catholic University of America, Washington D.C. (2004-); Professor of Intercultural and Comparative Theology at Utrecht University (2005-07); 2000, Doctorate in Systematic Theology at St.Georgen, Frankfurt. Monograph: *Traditionen überschreiten: Anglo-amerikanische Beiträge zur interkulturellen Traditionshermeneutik* (2001).

László HOLLÓ (Romania) (1966) is Associate Professor of Moral Theology and Social Ethics, Faculty of Roman Catholic Theology, Babes-Bolyai University of Cluj-Napoca and of Alba Iulia (1997-); D. Theol. at the University of Innsbruck; publications in moral theology and social ethics; author of *Mindenheitenrechte in Europa im Hinblick auf Südtirol und Siebenbürgen: Der Öffentlich-keitsauftrag der Kirche und die Minderheiten* (2004).

Vincent HOLZER (France) is Professor of Fundamental and Doctmatic Theology at Institut Catholique de Paris (1994-); D. Theol. (1994, Rome); author of *Le Dieu Trinité dans l'histoire: Le différend théologique Balthasar-Rahner* (1995).

Maureen JUNKER-KENNY (Germany) is Associate Professor of Theology at Trinity College, Dublin; teaches Christian Ethics / Practical Theology; 1989, Ph.D. from the University of Münster; 1996, Habilitation at the University of Tübingen; publications include: *Memory, Narrativity, Self and the Challenge to Think God: The Reception within Theology of the Recent Work of Paul Ricoeur* (2004; co-edited with P. Kenny), *Faith in Society of Instant Gratification* (1999), *Argumentationsethik und christliches Handeln. Eine praktisch-theologische Auseinandersetzung mit Jürgen Habermas* (1998), *Das Urbild des Gottesbewußtseins: Zur Entwicklung der Religionstheorie und Christologie Schleiermachers von der ersten zur zweiten Auflage der Glaubenslehre* (1990).

Armin KREINER (Germany) (1954) is Professor of Fundamental Theology at the Faculty of Catholic Theology, University of Munich (2003-); Habilitation in 1991 and D. Theol. in 1985, Munich. Publications include *Ende der Wahrheit?* (1992), *Gott im Leid* (1997), *Das wahre Antlitz Gottes* (2006).

Anne KULL (Estonia) (1959) is Professor of Systematic Theology at the University of Tartu (2005-); Ph.D. 2000 from the Lutheran School of Theology at Chicago on *Theology of Technonature Based on Donna Haraway and Paul Tillich*; articles on science and religion; nature, technology and theology.

Ghasem KAKAIE (Iran) (1957) is Assistant Professor of Philosophy and Theology at Shiraz University (1994-); studied philosophy and mysticism at Qum University and Transcendental Philosophy at Tarbiat Mudarres University in Tehran. Publications in comparative theology and mysticism; monograph: *Waḥdat al-Wujūd from the Viewpoints of Ibn 'Arabī and Meister Eckhart* (2003).

Ioannis KOUREMBELES (Greece) (1963) is Assistant Professor of Dogmatic Theology, University of Thessaloniki; studied theology in Thesaloniki (D. Theol.), Erlangen and Heidelberg (Germany); publications in dogmatic theology and comparative theology; publications include *Ecumenical Examples in the History of the Church* (2003) *Neochalcrdonianism: A Dogmatical Point of Division?* (2003), *The Homily of Patriarch Proclus "On the Most Holy Theotokos" and the Answer of Nestorius* (2004).

Aasulv LANDE (Norway) (1937) is Professor Emeritus of Missiology and Ecumenical Theology at Lund University (since 1994); interreligious dialogue in Japan 1965-1980; doctoral studies in Uppsala, 1981-88; Ecumenical Lecturer at Bir-mingham University, Selly Oak Colleges 1990-94; publications in missiology and history of religion, particularly in the area of interreligious dialogue and contextualization.

Georgios D. MARTZELOS (Greece) is Professor of Orthodox Theology and Dogmatics at the Aristotle University of Thessaloniki (1983-); studies in Thessalonica, Athens and Heidelberg; publications include: *Substance and Energies of God according to St. Basil the Great* (^{2}1993), *Genesis and Sources of the Definition of Chalcedon*, (1986), *The Christology of Basil of Seleucia and its Ecumenical Importance*, (1990), *Orthodox Doctrine and Theological Reflection: Studies on Dogmatic Theology* (1993 and 2000).

András MÁTÉ-TÓTH (Hungary) (1957) is Professor of Religious Studies at the University of Szeged. D. Theol. and Habilitation (1991 and 1996, Vienna); research and monitoring of project *Aufbruch* on religious changes in Central Eastern Europe after 1989 (with M. Tomka and P.M. Zulehner), 1996-2001; publications: *Theologie in Ost(Mittel)Europa. Ansätze und Traditionen* (2002), *Kirche im Aufbruch. Zur pastoralen Entwicklung in Ost(Mittel)Europa: Eine Qualitative Studie* (2001), *Nicht wie Milch und Honig: Unterwegs zu einer Pastoraltheologie Ost (Mittel) Europas* (2000).

John D'ARCY MAY (Australia) (1942) is Associate Professor of Interfaith Dialogue, ISE, Trinity College (1987-); STL Gregoriana, Rome, 1969; D. Theol. (Ecumenics) Münster; D. Phil. (History of Religions) Frankfurt, 1983; Ecumenical Research Officer with Melanesian Council of Churches, Port Moresby, and Research Associate at the Melanesian Institute, Goroka, Papua New Guinea, 1983-87; Publications include: *Christus Initiator. Theologie im Pazifik* (1990), *After Pluralism: Towards an Interreligious Ethic* (2000); *Transcendence and Violence: The Encounter of Buddhist, Christian and Primal Traditions* (2003)

Robert Cummings NEVILLE (USA) is Professor of Philosophy, Religion, and Theology at Boston University. He has taught at Yale University, Fordham University, SUNY College at Purchase, and SUNY Stony Brook, and holds honorary doctorates from Lehigh University and The Russian Academy of Sciences. He is past president of the American Academy of Religion, the American Theological Society, the Metaphysical Society of America, and the International Society for Chinese Philosophy. He has published many articles and twenty books, the last of which is *On the Scope and Truth of Theology* (2006).

Hans-Joachim SANDER (Germany) (1959) is Professor of Dogmatic Theology at the University of Salzburg; D. Theol. and Habilitation, Würzburg; visiting scholar at the Center for Process Studies in Claremont, CA (1987-1988); dissertation on Whitehead's process philosophy; Habilitation on Peirce and the signs of the times at Vatican II; publications in systematic theology and philosophy of religion.

Perry SCHMIDT-LEUKEL (Germany) (1954) is Professor of Systematic Theology and Religious Studies and Founding Director of the "Centre for Inter-Faith Studies" at the University of Glasgow. Among his most recent publications are: *War and Peace in World Religions* (2004), *Buddhism and Christianity in Dialogue* (2005), *Gott ohne Grenzen* (2005), *Buddhism, Christianity and the Question of Creation: Karmic or Divine?* (2006), *Understanding Buddhism* (2006).

Marcus SCHMÜCKER (Germany) (1965) is a research fellow at the Institute for Cultural and Intellectual History of Asia of the Austrian Academy of Science (1996); D.Phil. (Indology, 1997); publications include: *Weder als seiend noch als nichtseiend bestimmbar. Vimuktātmans Lehre von der Realität der Welt* (2001); *Raumzeitliche Vermittlung der Transzendenz. Zur sakramentalen Dimension religiöser Tradition* (1999, coedited with G. Oberhammer), *Mythisierung der Transzendenz als Entwurf ihrer Erfahrung* (2003, coedited with G. Oberhammer).

Georges DE SCHRIJVER (Belgium) (1935) is Professor Emeritus of Foundational Theology and occupant of Chair of the Centre for Liberation Theology at the Catholic University, Leuven (1987-2000); Visiting Professor in Asia and Africa; publications in philosophical theology, political theology and theology of cultures; author of *Recent Theological Debates in Europe: Their Impact on Interreligious Dialogue* (2004).

Karel SKALICKÝ (Czech Republic) (1934) is Professor of Fundamental Theology at the Lateran University (1982-1994) and of the University of South Bohemia in České Budějovice (1994-). Licentiate and D.Theol. at the Lateran University in Rome. 1967-1990; editor-in-chief of the Czech exile magazine *Studie* (published in Rome); Visiting Professor in Zambia, Equador, Guatemala, and Puerto Rico; administrative posts in České Budějovice since 1999; author of *Čeští svědkové promýšlené víry: filosofie a teologie v interakci u současných česk* (2005).

Peter STILWELL (Portugal) (1946) is Professor of Fundamental Theology and Religious Studies at the Catholic University of Lisboa. D. Theol. (1994, Rome); doctorate in Fundamental Theology at the Gregorian University, Rome, in 1994, with a thesis on a Portuguese poet: *A Condição Humana em Ruy Cinatti.*

Klaus VON STOSCH (Germany) (1971) is scientific collaborator in Systematic Theology at the Philosophical Faculty, University of Cologne (1998-2007); Habilitation in 2005, Münster, and D.Theol. in 2001, Bonn; publications include: *Glaubensverantwortung in doppelter Kontingenz: Untersuchungen zur Verortung fundamentaler Theologie nach Wittgenstein (2001); Gott – Macht – Geschichte: Versuch einer theodizeesensiblen Rede von Gottes Handeln in der Welt (2006), Einführung in die Systematische Theologie (2006).*

Amador VEGA ESQUERRA (Spain) (1958) is Professor of Aesthetics at the University of Pompeu Fabra, Barcelona; Ph.D. from the Albert Ludwigs Universität of Freiburg i.B., Germany; publications include: *Zen, mística y abstracción* (2002), *Ramon Llull and the Secret of Lyfe* (2002), *Arte y Santidad. Cuatro lecciones de estética apofática* (2005), *Tratado de los cuatro modos del espíritu* (2005).

Keith WARD (England) (1938) was Lecturer in Philosophy at the Universities of Glasgow, St. Andrews, London and Cambridge, Professor of Moral Theology and later Professor of the History and Philosophy of Religion, London University, Regius Professor of Divinity, University of Oxford; is now Professor of Divinity, Gresham College, London; Fellow of the British Academy; publications include: *Comparative Theology* (1994 - 2000; 4 vols.) and *Pascal's Fire* (Oxford: Oneworld) on issues in science and religion.

Tomasz WĘCŁAWSKI (Poland) (1952) is Professor of Fundamental and Dogmatic Theology in Poznan (Pontifical Theological Faculty and Mickiewicz University) (1990-); theological studies at the Gregorian University in Rome (1980-1993); publications include: *Wielkie kryzysy tradycji chrzescijanskiej* (1999), *W teologii chodzi o Ciebie: przewodnik po zródlach i skutkach teologicznej wyobrazn* (1995), *Zwischen Sprache und Schweigen: Eine Erörterung der theologischen Apophase im Gespräch mit Vladimir N. Lossky und Martin Heidegger* (1983).

Siegfried WIEDENHOFER (Austria) (1941) is Professor of Systematic Theology, J.W. Goethe University, Frankfurt a.M. (1981-); studied Catholic theology in Graz, Bonn, Münster, Tübingen, Regensburg (D.Theol., Habilitation); publications in systematic theology include: *Das katholische Kirchenverständnis* (1992), *Kulturelle und religiöse Traditionen* (2005), *Tradition and Theories of Tradition* (2006).

Josef WOHLMUTH (Germany) (1938) is Professor Emeritus, Chair of Dogmatics at the University of Bonn 1986-2003; D.Theol. (1975, Regensburg); dean of the Theological Study Year at the Dormition Abbey in Jerusalem 2003/04; publications include: *Die Tora spricht die Sprache der Menschen: Theologische Aufsätze und Meditationen zur Beziehung von Judentum und Christentum* (2002), *Emmanuel Levinas. Eine Herausforderung für die christliche Theologie* (1998), *Verständigung in der Kirche.Untersucht an der Sprache des Konzils von Basel* (1983).

Lightning Source UK Ltd.
Milton Keynes UK
21 May 2010

154472UK00001B/86/P